SAGE
Premium
Video

BOOST COMPREHENSION. BOLSTER ANALYSIS.

- SAGE Premium Video **EXCLUSIVELY CURATED FOR THIS TEXT**
- **BRIDGES BOOK CONTENT** with application & critical thinking
- Includes short, auto-graded quizzes that **DIRECTLY FEED TO YOUR LMS GRADEBOOK**
- Premium content is **ADA COMPLIANT WITH TRANSCRIPTS**
- Comprehensive media guide to help you **QUICKLY SELECT MEANINGFUL VIDEO** tied to your course objectives

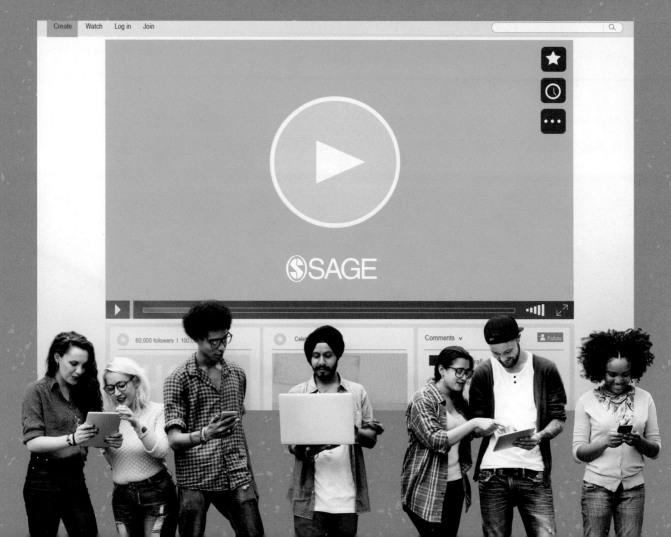

" Praise for

Introduction to **Teaching**

Making a Difference in Student Learning

3

Gene E. Hall · Linda F. Quinn · Donna M. Gollnick

"

"The Hall textbook takes a holistic approach to introducing the teaching profession to students. The textbook is progressive and current. It is much more than a traditional textbook in its ability to challenge students to think about topics from multiple perspectives and truly facilitates learning."

—Dana Hilbert
Cameron University

"Comprehensive, useful, informative, well-organized."

—James T. Jackson
Howard University

"This textbook provides students with a very comprehensive understanding of teaching and learning across the PK–12 educational system."

—Brandolyn Jones
Lone Star College–Kingwood

"All-inclusive with so many resources."

—James Kenyon
University of Nevada, Las Vegas

"A step in the right direction."

—Harold London
DePaul University

Introduction to
Teaching

EDITION 3

*This dedication provides a unique opportunity for the authors to express their appreciation for a few of the many
people who have made a significant difference in the learning opportunities for children and adults. We dedicated the first edition to
"all the great teachers we have known." In the second edition, we again acknowledged the great teachers we have known and got specific.
We named some who had significantly impacted us professionally, and in some cases personally.*

*We are dedicating this edition to the thousands of teachers who are retiring after many years in the classroom.
Think about the large number of students each of them has taught over the years. They have made a difference for so many.
They have strived to help all of their students learn. They have attended many meetings, prepared many lessons, and graded many student
assignments. They also have the satisfaction of being greeted by many of their past students who are now successful adults. Many of them
now are teachers and administrators.*

*These retiring teachers can tell you about the funny things that happened over the years and the special moments of joy.
Their efforts centered on learning, helping their students learn, and consistently working to become even better teachers.*

*Be sure to say "thank you" when you meet these experienced teachers. After all, without them,
you would not now be on your way to becoming a great teacher.*

Introduction to Teaching

Making a Difference in Student Learning

EDITION 3

Gene E. Hall
Professor Emeritus, University of Nevada, Las Vegas
President, Concerns Based Systems, Inc.

Linda F. Quinn
University of Nevada, Las Vegas

Donna M. Gollnick
Education Consultant

Los Angeles | London | New Delhi
Singapore | Washington DC | Melbourne

FOR INFORMATION:

SAGE Publications, Inc.
2455 Teller Road
Thousand Oaks, California 91320
E-mail: order@sagepub.com

SAGE Publications Ltd.
1 Oliver's Yard
55 City Road
London EC1Y 1SP
United Kingdom

SAGE Publications India Pvt. Ltd.
B 1/I 1 Mohan Cooperative Industrial Area
Mathura Road, New Delhi 110 044
India

SAGE Publications Asia-Pacific Pte. Ltd.
18 Cross Street #10-10/11/12
China Square Central
Singapore 048423

Acquisitions Editor: Steve Scoble
Editorial Assistant: Elizabeth You
Content Development Editor: Jennifer Jovin
Production Editor: Laureen Gleason
Copy Editor: Melinda Masson
Typesetter: C&M Digitals (P) Ltd.
Proofreaders: Liann Lech, Scott Oney, Alison Syring
Indexer: Karen Wiley
Cover Designer: Janet Kiesel
Marketing Manager: Jillian Ragusa

Printed in Canada

Library of Congress Cataloging-in-Publication Data

Names: Hall, Gene E., author. | Quinn, Linda F., author. | Gollnick, Donna M., author.

Title: Introduction to teaching : making a difference in student learning / Gene E. Hall, Professor Emeritus, University of Nevada, Las Vegas, President, Concerns Based Systems, Inc., Linda F. Quinn, University of Nevada, Las Vegas, Donna M. Gollnick, TEACH-NOW Graduate School of Education.

Description: Third Edition. | Los Angeles, California : SAGE, [2019] | Includes bibliographical references and index.

Identifiers: LCCN 2018038492 | ISBN 9781506393896 (Paperback : acid-free paper)

Subjects: LCSH: Teaching—United States—Textbooks.

Classification: LCC LB1025.3 .H34 2019 | DDC 371.102—dc23
LC record available at https://lccn.loc.gov/2018038492

This book is printed on acid-free paper.

19 20 21 22 23 10 9 8 7 6 5 4 3 2 1

BRIEF CONTENTS

DETAILED CONTENTS

PREFACE

Welcome to *Introduction to Teaching: Making a Difference in Student Learning* (3rd edition). We are pleased and honored to have had the opportunity to develop this new edition. Instructor and student feedback from the first two editions has been overwhelmingly positive. This feedback and our continuing professional experiences have been combined to make this edition even better. Our colleagues at SAGE also have been significant contributors to this book being so good.

The three-author team has wide-ranging experiences and deep knowledge about today's schools and teacher education. We continue to be very active in teacher education, accreditation, and research. Each of us spends extensive time in schools and learning about the latest teacher education initiatives. We are fully engaged in today's schools, always experimenting with new approaches to teacher education, and frequently collaborating with colleagues across the United States and in other countries. The members of our author team have a strong commitment to improving teacher education, and we have each worked on that goal in a variety of ways.

Over the past few years, as we would meet and talk about what is happening in today's schools, we came to the conclusion that most of the textbooks for introductory teacher education courses do not accurately represent how schools and instruction are changing. Similarly, in many teacher education programs, the increased emphasis on state-mandated testing, standards, and the importance of assessing versus testing is not receiving as much attention as needed. We strongly believe that future teachers need an introduction-to-teaching textbook that is heavily grounded in the new paradigm for schools, which is focused on student learning.

We decided to write an introduction-to-teaching textbook that is grounded in today's schools, places a heavy emphasis on understanding student learning, and acknowledges the challenges of teaching while also emphasizing the joy to be found in this profession. That such a book is needed and desired is now reflected in our developing the third edition.

Also, the emerging pressures from many sources—including policy makers, parents, and society in general—have led to schools and teachers responding in a number of new ways. Given all that is happening, this was the right time to prepare this new edition. We have updated each chapter's basic content and inserted new examples of the many neat ways that teachers and schools are responding to today's pressures and needs.

A quick look through most introduction-to-teaching textbooks can leave the impression that they all are the same. However, a closer look reveals there can be significant differences between these texts. The differences go beyond how the books are organized and their design. The overall philosophy of textbooks for the introduction-to-teaching course can vary dramatically. In this book, we have worked to ensure that the view of teaching we reflect is grounded in what schools are really like today and where they are headed in the near future. The examples, discussion questions, and field activities throughout promote deep understanding of what it takes to become a teacher who improves student learning.

Our goal in writing this introduction-to-teaching textbook is to help future teachers prepare for one of the most important, challenging, and worthwhile professions there is. We all know from our own experience when we were students what it means to have an exceptional teacher. We also know what it means to have a teacher who is not exceptional. We have combined our expertise to write a textbook that will help you become one of those exceptional teachers.

THEMES

In the first edition, we established a set of key themes. These were identified through our work in schools and teacher education and in our research agenda. Each theme is carried across each of the chapters in this text. Each of these themes is foundational to your becoming a great teacher. Continue to reflect on what each of these themes means and how you as a teacher shall bring them to life in your teaching.

Focus on Learning.   The most important theme of this book, as is reflected in the subtitle, is *making a difference in student learning*. In the past, including when each of us went through our teacher education program, the major focus was on describing what *teachers* do. It was "teacher-centered." We were taught about lesson plans, classroom management (which was called "discipline" in those days), and developing units. Today, the focus has shifted to being *learning-centered*. The most important purpose of teaching and schools is to have all students learning. This focus on learning extends to the adults in the school, too. High-quality teachers (and principals) are always thinking about how what they are doing is affecting student learning, and what they can learn now to have even greater effectiveness.

Understanding and Using Data.   Most of today's schools have more data available than can be used effectively. The importance of data should not be underestimated. However, learning how to use data and making decisions based on data are new skills for most teachers. One important resource for using data efficiently and well is technology. Each chapter has a box feature that provides examples of the ways teacher candidates, teachers, and principals can use data.

Real Educators, Real Schools, and Real Students.   Given that each of us has been a teacher and teacher educator for a long time, we know that it is important to include the words of teachers and other education professionals. Therefore, every chapter begins with an interview of a real educator who is working in schools and school districts at this time. Some chapters begin with an interview of a first- or second-year teacher, while others introduce a more experienced educator. Each interviewee has solid recommendations for beginning teachers today. Because schools cannot succeed without good leaders, other chapters begin with an interview of a school or district administrator, and the opening interview for one of the chapters features school law experts. There is no escaping the importance of legal aspects of education, so we thought it would be important for you to read firsthand about the legal perspective and how it affects the responsibilities of teachers and the opportunities for all students to learn.

Using Technology for Learning.   We all see how the many types of technology are being used by students. Integrating technology into instruction can be powerful, so uses of technology are referenced throughout this book. In addition, with this text, SAGE provides users with access to several useful and innovative technology-based resources, one of which is a set of videos of real classrooms. We asked expert teachers with interesting classrooms to share what they are doing, and then produced these videos specifically for this book. We have just added some interviews with principals in which we ask them what they look for in hiring teachers.

Facing Challenges.   Now is not only a very important time to become a teacher; it is also a time during which schools are facing many very difficult problems. Today's students are more diverse than ever before. For the first time in the history of the United States, there are governors and legislators who are questioning the importance of public schools and reducing their support of teachers. In a textbook designed to introduce aspiring teachers to real schools, we must address these serious challenges and explore ways to deal with them.

Joy in Teaching.   We would be remiss if we did not also address the important theme of *joy* in teaching. There is much joy in teaching, but it is easy to overlook when you're confronted with all the work and challenges. So, throughout this text, we have made reference to joy in teaching. There are cartoons throughout, as well as a special feature called **Teachers' Lounge**. For this feature, we asked teachers and colleagues to share humorous, touching, and insightful stories from their experiences. As you become a teacher, we will welcome your contributions to this feature in future editions.

FEATURES

As you read this text, you will find interesting and useful features.

Educator Interviews open each chapter and offer an authentic look at what it means to be a teacher today. Each chapter-opening interview is paired with Questions to Consider that are designed to stimulate critical thinking about the chapter topic and prepare you to engage more deeply with the material that follows.

Learning Outcomes at the beginning of each chapter guide the readers to think about what they should take away from their reading.

Summaries close each chapter and are designed to help teacher candidates focus on key chapter content.

Class Discussion Questions challenge students to think critically and apply what they have read in discussions with others.

Self-Assessments allow you to examine your current level of understanding of the chapter content. There is an *Assessing Your Learning* rubric that you can apply. With it, you can identify areas of weakness that may require additional study or attention. The rubric stays the same for each chapter, while the indicators of your level of learning are specific to each chapter's content.

A **Field Guide for Learning** concludes each chapter and provides students with opportunities to extend their learning beyond the pages of this book. Each field guide represents a critical resource to help students develop the knowledge and skills that we find in expert educators by providing suggestions for classroom observation activities, reflection questions to promote journaling, portfolio builders, and suggested books and websites for further study.

Stories and Examples are important ways to learn about teaching (and improving student learning), so each chapter includes plenty of these to illustrate the basic ideas.

Thinking Differently is a new feature. Given all the rules, procedures, and structures, in many ways today's educators are boxed in. We believe that an important part of being a great teacher is being able to think outside the box, or at least push the walls of conventional thinking. So, in this feature, we introduce novel approaches that some teachers and schools are trying out. These are introduced to illustrate some of the ways that today's educators are thinking outside the box.

We also have a number of engaging boxed features:

Understanding and Using Data boxes present a set of research findings or data for you to form an understanding of the information and attempt your own analysis. Using data is now a very important skill for teachers. Follow-up information and sample answers are provided on the ancillary website.

Challenging Assumptions boxes engage future teachers in confronting "common sense" conclusions they may hold about education practices that are, in fact, not supported by research. We have provided examples of surprising research information that we hope will encourage candidates to question the obvious, and to be rigorous when investigating and implementing teaching strategies.

Teachers' Lounge boxes feature inspirational, humorous, and unexpected classroom moments shared by educators from across the country. These boxes offer the reader a behind-the-scenes glimpse at the stories teachers share with one another in the teachers' lounge that define the day-to-day experience of what it means to be a teacher.

Video Cases feature video clips that bring the reality of the modern classroom into focus. Each box features two or three questions that prime students to think critically about the accompanying video (online).

Connecting to the Classroom boxes offer a convenient summary of suggestions for teaching best practices presented in the chapter.

WHAT'S NEW?

Preparing the next edition of a book always is a challenge for the authors. We see much of the previous edition being useful and important to retain. There are the necessary changes such as updating sources and references. Readers and instructors will have provided reviews and suggestions based on using the previous edition. The authors and their editors will have ideas about how to make this next edition even better. At the same time, making too many changes can lead to instructors not seeing our textbook as being the same as the previous edition that had worked so successfully.

In other words, there is a need to balance making changes and continuing to preserve the core content and elements. The feedback about the first and second editions from instructors and teacher education candidates has been positive and encouraging. We authors have been pleased with the reception that our textbook has received. There has been no glaring fault or demand for making a major change.

Therefore, our efforts have been to preserve, update, refine, and enrich. This does not mean that this edition is not new: It most certainly is. In addition to the usual updating of sources and refining of the wording, we have made the following changes in major elements to make this textbook even better.

- *Thinking Differently:* As discussed above, this new feature showcases creative ideas that teachers and administrators are bringing into their schools to solve needs not met by conventional methodologies, or to simply explore other ways to achieve the goals they have for the school community.

- *New Exceptional Educator Interviews:* The third edition includes 16 new interviews with teachers and administrators.

- *Updating Content:* Changing views of public education and implementation of the current ESEA (aka ESSA) are important to update. There are completely new topics emerging that now need to be addressed such as the teacher walkouts in several states and trauma-sensitive approaches to teaching. The latest research is represented as well as introducing current issues and topics within the discussions and the features.

- *Updating Tables, Figures, and Sources:* Recent information about funding, court cases, and new federal and state statutes, as well as new approaches to curriculum and instruction, has been included.

- *Identifying Additional Student Differences:* Native Hawaiians and Other Pacific Islanders are now reported separately whenever possible from Asians. Another difference is the importance of recognizing the need for providing safety for lesbian, gay, bisexual, transgender, and queer or questioning (LGBTQ) students.

- *Emerging Teacher Economic Concerns and Changing Politics* came to the forefront just as we were intently drafting the manuscript. In the spring of 2018, teachers initiated state-wide boycotts in several states. During the same period, the U.S. Supreme Court ruled against public teachers as employees being required to pay union dues. The *New York Times* and *Time* magazine produced major publications that described the economic and classroom challenges teachers are facing. It is amazing the challenges teachers are facing at a time when what children need are excellent teachers.

Taken together, we have a new edition that builds on the strengths and successes of the first and second editions. The interviews and stories, as well as the content updates, make this edition the best yet for instructors and our readers—in other words, for teacher education candidates.

DIGITAL RESOURCES

$SAGE coursepacks

Instructor Resources

SAGE coursepacks and SAGE edge online resources are included FREE with this text. For a brief demo, contact your sales representative today.

SAGE coursepacks for instructors makes it easy to import our quality content into your school's learning management system (LMS).* Intuitive and simple to use, it allows you to

Say NO to . . .

- Required access codes
- Learning a new system

Say YES to . . .

- Using only the content you want and need
- High-quality assessment and multimedia exercises

***For use in:** Blackboard, Canvas, Brightspace by Desire2Learn (D2L), and Moodle.

Don't use an LMS platform? No problem, you can still access many of the online resources for your text via SAGE edge.

With SAGE coursepacks, you get

- Quality textbook content delivered **directly into your LMS**
- An **intuitive, simple format** that makes it easy to integrate the material into your course with minimal effort
- **Assessment tools** that foster review, practice, and critical thinking, including
  - Diagnostic chapter **pre-tests and post-tests** that identify opportunities for improvement, track student progress, and ensure mastery of key learning objectives
  - **Test banks** built on Bloom's Taxonomy that provide a diverse range of test items with ExamView test generation
  - **Activity and quiz options** that allow you to choose only the assignments and tests you want
  - **Instructions** on how to use and integrate the comprehensive assessments and resources provided
- **Assignable SAGE Premium Video** (available via the interactive eBook version, linked through SAGE coursepacks) that is tied to learning objectives, and produced exclusively for this text to bring concepts to life, featuring
  - **Footage from real classrooms** showing what a typical day is like in an elementary or a secondary school; you will see lead teachers and paraprofessionals working together in small groups with their students, as well as students learning together as a class and in smaller, differentiated groups
  - **Engaging interviews with teachers and principals** sharing the biggest joys and challenges of being an educator, as well as their passion and enthusiasm for their students
  - **Corresponding multimedia assessment options** that automatically feed to your gradebook
  - Comprehensive, downloadable, easy-to-use *Media Guide in the Coursepack* **for every video resource**, listing the chapter to which the video content is tied, matching learning objectives, a helpful description of the video content, and assessment questions
- **Chapter-specific discussion questions** to help launch engaging classroom interaction while reinforcing important content

- Exclusive **SAGE journal articles** built into course materials and assessment tools, which tie influential research and scholarship to chapter concepts

- Editable, chapter-specific **PowerPoint**® **slides** that offer flexibility when creating multimedia lectures so that you don't have to start from scratch

- **Sample course syllabi** with suggested models for structuring your course that give you options to customize your course to your exact needs

- **Lecture notes** that summarize key concepts on a chapter-by-chapter basis to help you with preparation for lectures and class discussions

- **Integrated links to the interactive eBook** that make it easy for students to maximize their study time with this "anywhere, anytime" mobile-friendly version of the text; it also offers access to more digital tools and resources, including SAGE Premium Video

- **Select tables and figures** from the textbook

$SAGE edgeselect™

Student Resources

edge.sagepub.com/hall3e

SAGE edge for students enhances learning. It's easy to use, and it offers

- An **open-access site** that makes it easy for students to maximize their study time, anywhere, anytime

- **eFlashcards** that strengthen understanding of key terms and concepts

- **eQuizzes** that allow students to practice and assess how much they've learned and where they need to focus their attention

- **Exclusive access to influential SAGE journal articles** that tie important research and scholarship to chapter concepts to strengthen learning

- **Video resources and multimedia links** that appeal to students with different learning styles

Interactive eBook

Introduction to Teaching, Third Edition, is also available as an **Interactive eBook** that can be packaged with the text for just $5 or purchased separately. The Interactive eBook offers hyperlinks to original videos, including **video cases** that feature **real classroom footage** showing what a typical day is like in an elementary or secondary school, as well as engaging **interviews with teachers** sharing the biggest joys and challenges of being an educator. Users will also have immediate access to study tools such as highlighting, bookmarking, note-taking/sharing, and more!

A FINAL IMPORTANT NOTE

Teaching is hard work; in fact, becoming an exceptional teacher is very hard work. Although we have years of experience in schools and thinking about teaching and learning, we still have times when we wonder about our own effectiveness and what we could be doing differently that would help our students learn more. All the thinking, doing, and reflecting that is necessary to be an exceptional teacher can be exhausting. It is important that teacher candidates and teachers have a life outside of teaching. To paraphrase an old saying, if you only teach, you will indeed become a dull teacher. You will see in several of the interviews that our interviewees have made reference to what they do outside of teaching.

To be an exceptional teacher requires having a balance. Teachers can't be "on" 24 hours a day, seven days a week. Teachers need time to power down and regenerate. This is one of the reasons the photos we have inserted below are of ourselves in nonprofessional educator settings. Teaching is hard work, and you rarely stop thinking about it, so it is important to have a life outside of school.

As competitive as we are, it still is important to be able to say to others, and to yourself: **Have fun!**

Gene E. Hall, professor, husband, father, and grandfather, with son Greg and grandson Malcolm (Glenwood Canyon, CO)

Linda F. Quinn, professor, wife, mother, grandmother, and dog mistress

Donna Gollnick, administrator, mother, scholar, avid reader, and baseball fan

ACKNOWLEDGMENTS

The authors want to express their appreciation for the many talented colleagues and professionals who have contributed to the creation of this book. The thoughtful and insightful contributions of our "real educators," the constructive feedback from reviewers, and the Teachers' Lounge authors who shared their experiences all have made this book better, more informative, and grounded in the best of teaching and schooling. We also express our appreciation for our teacher educator colleagues and their candidates who adopted the first and/or second editions. Their compliments and feedback have reassured us that developing a fresh approach has indeed been worth doing.

Based on all our experiences in producing this book, we see ourselves as being fortunate to be members of the SAGE author family. It has been a positive, professional, and successful experience. Without the early insight and leadership of Diane McDaniel, then executive editor, we would not have had this opportunity. For the third edition, we had the pleasure of working with Karen Omer and Steve Scoble, acquisitions editors, who continued the vision set by Terri Accomazzo for the second edition.

Jennifer Jovin, content development editor, has been our day-to-day pace setter. She has worked with us to set the calendar and then monitored our progress. She has provided gentle reminders when needed, and never a discouraging word. Many others at SAGE have contributed their expertise, including Elizabeth You, editorial assistant; Laureen Gleason, production editor; Melinda Masson, copy editor; and Nathan Davidson, photo researcher. Throughout, the SAGE editorial and production teams have been highly professional and good at what they do. This has truly been a team effort where each of us has shared and learned. To all, we say thank you.

Another important set of contributors comprised the teacher educators who took time from their busy days to review early drafts of our manuscripts. The reviews were substantive and constructive. Also, the reviews arrived in time so that we authors were able to refer to them in clarifying (what we thought were perfect) explanations, making changes (by emphasizing and adding important points), and being reminded of why this book is based not only in what schools are like today, but in how important it is to keep pointing out the joy in teaching and learning.

Reviewers of the third edition:

Dana Hilbert
Cameron University

Harold N. London
DePaul University

James T. Jackson
Howard University

Naomi Jeffery Petersen
Central Washington University

Brandolyn E. Jones
Lone Star College–Kingwood

Josephine Tabet Sarvis
Dominican University

James Kenyon
University of Nevada, Las Vegas

Reviewers of the second edition:

Lauri Pepe Bousquet
Le Moyne College

Tracey Garrett
Rider University

Beth A. Childress
Armstrong Atlantic State University

Katie Lewis
Texas A&M International University

Suzanne Cordier D'Annolfo
University of Hartford

Joanne Newcombe
Nichols College

Thomas Sheeran
Niagara University

Karen A. Vuurnes
South Texas College

Laura B. Turchi
University of Houston

Reviewers of the first edition:

Pamela W. Aerni
Longwood University

Claudia Green
Corban University

Angie Jones Bales
Bossier Parish Community College

Pam Green
Southwestern College

Tanisha Billingslea
Cameron University

Steven R. Greenberg
Bridgewater State University

Lauri Pepe Bousquet
Le Moyne College

Janice A. Grskovic
Indiana University Northwest

Jesse Chenven
Central New Mexico Community College

Sam Guerriero
Butler University

Pamela Chibucos
Owens Community College

Felecia A. B. Hanesworth
Medaille College

Garnet Chrisman
University of the Cumberlands

Dana Lewis Haraway
James Madison University

H. Jurgen Combs
Shenandoah University

Dana Hilbert
Cameron University

Diane G. Corrigan
Cleveland State University

Bethany Hill-Anderson
McKendree University

Elaine Bacharach Coughlin
Pacific University

Jennifer Holloway
Cameron University at Rogers State University

Charles Edward Craig Jr.
Tennessee Technical University

Johnnie Humphrey
John Tyler Community College

Camy Weber Davis
Oakland City University

MeHee Hyun
Antioch University Los Angeles

Darryl M. De Marzio
University of Scranton

Rebekah D. Kelleher
Wingate University

Thomas S. Dickinson
DePauw University

Leonard Larsen
Des Moines Area Community College

Rebecca Fredrickson
Texas Woman's University

Nina Mazloff
Becker College

Jill E. Gelormino
St. Joseph's College

Reney McAtee
Tennessee State University

Carol Gilles
University of Missouri

Jane McCarthy
University of Nevada, Las Vegas

Amanda Lee Glaze
Jacksonville State University

Kathy J. McKee
Multnomah University

Deena McKinney
East Georgia College

Sarah K. McMahan
Texas Woman's University

Linda A. Mitchell
Jacksonville State University

Madonna Murphy
University of St. Francis

George Noblit
University of North Carolina at Chapel Hill

Denise Patmon
University of Massachusetts, Boston

Nina Gunther Phillips
Bryn Athyn College

Rebecca Pitkin
Dickinson State University

Thomas A. Raunig
University of Great Falls

Donna Redman
University of La Verne

Suzanne Roberts
Florida College

Phillip Russell
University of Arkansas, Fort Smith

Marjorie Schiller
Central Arizona College

Brian Schultz
Northeastern Illinois University

Eric-Gene J. Shrewsbury
Patrick Henry Community College

Richard K. Simmons
College of DuPage

Darlene Smith
Walters State Community College

Janet Stramel
Fort Hayes State University

Douglas Sturgeon
Shawnee State University

Lucia Torchia-Thompson
Reading Area Community College

Curtis Visca
Saddleback College

David Vocke
Towson University

Harold Waters
Southern Wesleyan University

Gail Watson
County College of Morris

Colleen M. Wilson
Jacksonville University

We would also like to extend a special thanks to the teachers and administrators of the Dedham Public Schools in Dedham, Massachusetts, who graciously allowed us to film their schools and classrooms: Superintendent Michael Welch, who gave us permission to film in his district, coordinated with us for months on the filming logistics, and put us in touch with some of his enthusiastic and dedicated teachers, and Amy Hicks, executive assistant to the superintendent, who also assisted with these efforts; Principal Edward Paris and teachers Alexandra Zahka and Lisa Stanton Walsh of Riverdale Elementary School; Principal Jim Forrest and teachers Meghan Armstrong, Liz Amato, and Ariel Katz of Dedham High School; and Principal Paul Sullivan and teachers Emily Hutton and Amy Laboissonniere of the Early Childhood Education Center. We loved visiting your classrooms and witnessing firsthand the joy and dedication you put into your teaching.

Gene E. Hall, PhD, became professor emeritus at the University of Nevada, Las Vegas, in 2017. He continues to be involved in projects in the United States, and elsewhere, that are engaged in implementing change. He has had a career-long involvement with the development of programs and national accreditation of teacher education. He began his career as the science methods instructor and faculty team member for the experimental Personalized Teacher Education Program (PTEP) at the national R&D Center for Teacher Education, The University of Texas at Austin. Subsequently, he was a faculty member at the University of Florida and the University of Northern Colorado. He has twice been the dean of a college of education. He also has had career-long involvement with studies of the change process and development of tools and applications of the Concerns-Based Adoption Model (CBAM). He is coauthor of *Implementing Change: Patterns, Principles and Potholes* (5th edition) and *The Foundations of Education* (17th edition).

Linda F. Quinn is a professor in the College of Education at the University of Nevada, Las Vegas (UNLV). She was a member of the UNLV faculty from 1991 to 1995, and rejoined the faculty in 1999 after four years as a visiting professor and associate dean at the University of Northern Iowa. Before coming to UNLV, she had a rich and varied career in public and private schools in the United States, and in Iran and Japan. She has taught upper-division courses in curriculum development, classroom management, and instructional strategies. Her research interests focus on all aspects of teacher professional development, distance education, and global education. She is an annual contributor to national meetings of the Association of Teacher Educators and the Northern Rocky Mountain Educational Research Association. Reports of her research have been published in journals and as book chapters. She currently lives in Henderson, Nevada, with her poet husband and two lovable labs.

Donna M. Gollnick is an author and education consultant. Until August 2018, she was the vice president for quality assurance at TEACH-NOW Graduate School of Education, an online teacher education program in Washington, DC, that prepares teachers around the world. Previously, Dr. Gollnick was senior vice president for accreditation at the National Council for Accreditation of Teacher Education (NCATE) and director of professional development at the American Association of Colleges of Teacher Education (AACTE). She is coauthor with Philip Chinn of *Multicultural Education in a Pluralistic Society*, which is in its 10th edition, and is coauthor of the textbook *Introduction to the Foundations of American Education*, in its 17th edition. Dr. Gollnick is a past president of the National Association for Multicultural Education (NAME). She has been recognized as a Distinguished Alumna by the School of Family and Consumer Sciences at Purdue University and the Rossier School of Education at the University of Southern California. The AACTE honored her as an "Advocate for Justice" in 1998.

TODAY'S TEACHERS, STUDENTS, AND SCHOOLS

1 BECOMING A TEACHER

TEACHER INTERVIEW

Mr. Luis Zaldaña

Luis Zaldaña

Meet Mr. Luis Zaldaña, an English teacher at Sunrise Mountain High School. Mr. Zaldaña teaches English 10, English 10 Pre-AP, and Advanced Placement English Language and Composition for 11th- and 12th-grade students. His class sizes range from 30 to 40 students, and he has been teaching for 10 years; he taught in private schools for the first five years and has been teaching in the public school context over the last five years. Prior to this, he was a teacher's assistant for six years in various special education middle school programs. He decided to invest in teaching because he believes the aim of education is enabling humans to flourish. He tries his best to do his part to make the world a little better.

The School Community

Sunrise Mountain High School (SMHS) is located in East Las Vegas, Nevada. The school community is a highly transient one (over 35% transiency rate in 2015–2016), with almost all of the students eligible for Free or Reduced-Price Lunch services. There are over 2,500 students enrolled, mostly from minority communities. SMHS also has the highest population of English Language Learners in the Clark County School District. Yet, for all its challenges, SMHS boasts of an award-winning robotics program, the top student newspaper in the district, and a graduation rate of over 90% for the class of 2017. When we consider that not very long ago (2012) only 36% of the students were graduating, there is much to be proud of at SMHS.

Q: What brings you joy in teaching?

A: With a vision for education as a means of human flourishing, I find the greatest joy when students discover that education is a powerful tool they themselves are responsible for wielding, and what they do with it can change their lives and the lives of others. My experience has been that the more students are challenged to cultivate a habit of excellence, with a safe and positive classroom culture, the more likely they are to see the value in what school can offer as it applies to their particular contexts. All students, at heart, want to live in the fun of learning new things, and it's our job to give them that without losing the rigor and authenticity of gaining knowledge that causes us—students and teachers—to grow into better people.

LEARNING OUTCOMES

After reading this chapter, you should be able to do the following:

1. Identify the range of variables that influence teachers and teaching.

2. Know the steps one can take to earn a teaching license.

3. List reasons educators consider teaching a profession similar to law and medicine.

4. Look at the ways to find a job and assess which one will work best for you.

5. Develop patterns of behavior that will contribute to a successful career as a teacher.

6. Track your personal and professional growth as a teacher and the directions that growth can lead.

Q: How do you know that each student is learning?

A: There are certainly a variety of ways to measure learning as it happens in a day's lesson. Yet I have found one of the most effective ways to know how students are progressing is to lead them to establish their own goals for learning and guide them in metacognitive practices to continually refine and reflect on their efforts toward attaining these goals. This avoids the danger of having students simply repeat information, equipping students, rather, to demonstrate their knowledge in more meaningful ways. Creating this kind of learning community paves the way for students to assert themselves and object, as one of my students recently did, "Mr. Zaldaña, no one wants to take a multiple-choice quiz! Can we have a Socratic Seminar about this?" As I see it, this approach more closely reflects the dynamic and complex nature of teaching and learning, which, after all, is a process, not an event. There is a self-evident quality about students who are really "getting it." They want to keep learning. They want to show you what they know. There's a hunger in their eyes.

Q: How do you as a teacher learn? What are you learning at this time?

A: My learning begins with realizing that knowing or not knowing certain things shapes me as a person. So, what I'm learning, if it's not incidental, has to really matter; it must make a difference. I also need to know that what I seek to learn is realistic for me to accomplish. If I were to summarize it, I would say that my learning begins with a vision for the end goal, a genuine desire to reach it, and the means by which I may do so. Presently, my focus on learning to be more effective as a teacher than I have been in the past has led me to engage with current research on the topic more regularly. I've asked my colleagues if I can observe them as they teach to glean what I can. I've invited others to observe me in the classroom and provide feedback to spur me on. I ask my students to take my pulse so I can see what needs to change throughout the year. I reflect, I plan, I experiment. Teaching is an art; it is deliberate; it is recursive; and there is always the gnawing awareness that there's so much more to learn up ahead.

Q: What advice do you have for those who are studying to become teachers?

A: Determine, as you step into this profession, what kind of teacher you will be! Teach the way you would love to learn and be the kind of teacher you would love to learn from. There are certainly difficulties on the horizon, and it will be easy to get lost in them, but I believe the great responsibility of teachers is to shape human lives for the good. That outweighs it all, and we have to recognize that it does not happen accidentally. There will surely be students for whom you wish you could have done more. But, with perseverance, with a transparency about your craft, with an intentionality to continue to excel, with a teachable spirit, you can find yourself free to reap the reward of a student who returns and says, "Thank you. You changed my life." And you'll know if you have done your job well when you can say to that student with sincerity, "Thank you. You changed mine."

Questions to Consider

1. Mr. Zaldaña's experience tutoring students and a desire to make the world a better place led him to teaching. What other experiences or beliefs that people have or hold might lead them toward choosing teaching as a career?

2. What are some of the joyful images that come to mind when you think about being a teacher?

3. Would teaching in a rural area be much different from teaching in a large urban area like the one where Sunrise Mountain High School is located? Why? Why not?

4. Do high school teachers usually get hired to teach the content in which they are experts? Why? Why not?

INTRODUCTION

Starting out on any journey requires a certain amount of anticipation, hope for a successful outcome, and a sense of adventure. James H. Duke Jr. (1982) relates the journeys in life to climbing mountains ever upwards toward self-discovery and realization of attained wisdom and maturity. The journey you are about to embark upon is of unknown length and often characterized by uncharted territory, so your earliest decisions regarding this journey should be thoughtfully considered.

There are probably as many reasons to become a teacher as there are teachers. Every teacher has a personal story that served as the beginning of the journey toward a professional career as a teacher. The major steps you will take on this journey are varied, rigorous, and amazing. Since your journey will be both personal and professional, it will be shaped by your personality, by your life experiences (present and past), and by the professional learning and growth of your knowledge (pedagogical and content), the skills you have acquired, and your attitudes. In most ways, who you become as a teacher is up to you. And you are not alone. According to the Bureau of Labor Statistics (2011, as cited in Ingersoll, Merrill, & Stuckey, 2014, p. 6), PreK–12 teachers form one of largest occupational groups in the nation.

Teaching is a noble **profession**. It is a joyful profession. Teaching is also hard work. Teaching is a demanding profession that requires making hundreds of decisions during a school day, managing 20 to 40 students or more hour after hour, analyzing data about learning, and interacting with parents and colleagues. Teaching has never been easy even in earlier times when the classroom was a one-room schoolhouse. In addition to making sure all of their students were learning, teachers in former times had to build the fire to keep the school warm and sweep up after the students went home. Teaching requires high levels of sustained energy, effort, and motivation. Since you are reading this text, you are no doubt thinking about teaching as a career.

Is teaching the right choice for you? Some candidates in teaching have started along this career path because they enjoyed going to school. Some follow in the footsteps of parents, aunts, or uncles. Others want to be part of kids' lives, to advocate for children, and to give children exciting, meaningful experiences to help them become educated adults. Many remember a favorite teacher and want to have the same influence on others that that teacher had on them. Teaching seems familiar because we have all spent so much of our lives in classrooms. It is possible to think that teaching can't be too difficult because many of our teachers made it seem easy. We saw teaching through the eyes of the students, not the teachers. Teachers have a very different view of classrooms. This text will help you explore the profession of teaching and help you decide if it is the right profession for you.

WHY TEACH?

Mr. Zaldaña probably always had a desire to learn and to help others learn. His experiences as a tutor helping special education students achieve success brought him a sense of worth and a conviction that he should complete his journey to becoming a teacher. What brought you to consider a career in teaching? Most teachers say they want to teach because they believe they can make a difference in the lives of their students. Many secondary teachers report they chose teaching because they love the subject they are teaching. Some chose teaching because they love to learn. Some chose teaching because of the personal interactions teaching affords. Teachers are generally happy with their work, and teachers in the United States rate their lives better than all other occupation groups, trailing only physicians (S. Lopez & Sidhu, 2013). Most of us are happy to be doing something we love, that allows us time to be with and support our families, to be a part of something larger than ourselves, and that gives us a sense of personal worth. We can find all of this through teaching.

The Joy of Teaching

In a Gallup-Healthways Well-Being Index (Rich, 2013), teachers ranked above all other professions in answers to questions as to whether they had "smiled or laughed yesterday." Teachers have to be able to

Teachers get to work with people of all sizes, and every day brings something to be happy about.

laugh, to get their students to laugh, and to laugh with their students. Learning should be fun. Smiles and laughter can brighten up any situation, relieve stress, and possibly make whatever difficult task is at hand less daunting. The joy that bubbles up when a group of students are pleasantly surprised or excited should never be squelched. New teachers may be admonished, "Don't smile until Christmas," but hopefully you'll never find yourself in such dire circumstances. A bit of silliness now and then does not exclude the serious aspects of teaching.

A favorite science methods professor of one of your authors (Linda) made every class a delight. He would laugh, joke, and tease us into learning complex concepts. He often reminded us that he was serious but not somber about science education, and then he would smile. It is the playfulness and spirit of teachers that endears them to students. And it is what students remember of their teachers. There is funny stuff about what happens between students and their teachers on the Internet. One of our favorite websites for silliness about teaching is www.rd.com/funny-stuff/funny-teacher-stories. It's easy to laugh along with the students and the teachers when you read what the students said and what they did. As you read through this book, check out the Teachers' Lounge features for more humorous and heartwarming stories teachers have to tell.

It is through the sharing of stories that teachers become aware of the strong ties they have to their professional community. Sharing stories also provides a venue for understanding the mysteries of teaching and why it is so rare and marvelous to be a teacher. Ask teachers you know to tell you a story about something funny that happened to them while they were teaching. As their stories unfold, watch their faces, and you will see the joy in teaching.

The joy and rewards of teaching vary from teacher to teacher. The best teachers truly enjoy working with children and youth. They find a challenge in ensuring that underserved students learn at high levels and take joy in the academic success of all students. Former teacher and author Jonathan Kozol shares ideas about how to put the fun back into learning in his latest book, *Letters to a Young Teacher*. Francesca, the first-grade teacher Kozol shares teaching stories with, finds joy amid her struggles to reach the most recalcitrant of students. Kozol tells Francesca, "I think teaching is a beautiful profession and that teachers of young children do one of the best things that there is to do in life; bring joy and beauty, mystery and mischievous delight into the hearts of little people in their years of greatest curiosity" (Kozol, 2007, p. 8). Every teacher has a story about the joy he or she finds in teaching. Teachers treasure these moments and are always willing to share them.

One of most joyful parts of teaching is to see students achieve at high levels. This achievement could be physical, social, or creative as well as intellectual. All are important in the development of the whole person. During your teacher education program, you will learn how to develop **lesson plans** and deliver instruction to meet the needs of all students. You will be expected to be creative in developing rigorous and engaging lessons that draw on the cultural background and prior experiences of all of your students. Your joy and success as a teacher will be expressed when students learn the concepts you are trying to teach.

Intrinsic and Extrinsic Rewards

Mr. Zaldaña finds joy in teaching when his students discover that education can be a powerful tool for improving their own lives. The joy in teaching can be found in a variety of ways. Most teachers experience **intrinsic rewards** when students grasp the concept or task they have been teaching. Students are as different as night and day. Some students are successful in everything they pursue. Some are not. Some students are involved. Others are not. Some students actually resist learning. When teachers can engage students, they are rewarded for their efforts. The more teachers are able to bring students together in a learning community, the more they are rewarded. It is a positive cycle that excellent teachers strive to perpetuate. It is challenging to try to meet the needs of each individual student, and it is genuinely exciting when teachers can accomplish this. Teaching is never boring. It is different from minute to minute, and there is no single formula that works for everyone.

Intrinsic rewards can also result in what teachers do for themselves. When Mr. Zaldaña reads current research on his practice or invites colleagues to exchange classroom visits with him, he is helping himself learn. When he asks his students to "take my pulse," he is constantly aware of what he might change in his approach to teaching and what is going well. Mr. Zaldaña definitely reflects on his teaching and how his students are learning.

Extrinsic rewards for teachers come in the form of acknowledgments from students, from other teachers, from parents, and from prestigious awards such as Teacher of the Year. It is interesting to learn how the extrinsic reward of becoming a Teacher of the Year also provides intrinsic rewards through reflection on professional growth. Search for Sydney Chaffee, 2017 National Teacher of the Year, on YouTube and watch her express her compassion for teaching and her courage for taking risks.

Teachers enjoy seeing their students be successful.

The rewards of teaching can come from a variety of sources.

iStock/monkeybusinessimages

iStock/Steve Debenport

Teachers receive visits and letters from former students thanking them for inspiration, comfort, and happiness. Sometimes teachers are surprised at the influence they have had on certain students. When that mischievous student who made them want to tear their hair out, day after day, shows up in later years with a smile and a thank-you, the reward is clear. Parents write thank-you notes, volunteer to be a teacher's aide, and bake treats for special occasions. Other teachers ask for help with a specific problem, or ask to use a lesson that you have developed. Their appreciation of your skill as a teacher is rewarding. Teachers of the Year receive public accolades and have the opportunity to share their expertise with others through speeches and demonstrations. Some awards are even accompanied by money. Receiving payment for going an extra distance is rewarding, but most teachers will tell you it is not the money that brings them joy in teaching.

Making a Difference

Can you think of a teacher who made a difference in your life? It may be one who really cared about you, persuaded you to apply for college, challenged you to learn, or helped you develop self-esteem.

Professional athletes, presidents of companies, and national leaders often attribute their success to a teacher. Teachers may not know until years after a student has left their classrooms that they had such an impact.

Parents believe that teachers make a difference in their children's lives, especially when it comes to learning. Many parents know who the good teachers are in their schools and do everything they can to ensure their children are in those teachers' classrooms. According to an August 2017 Gallup Poll of the public's attitudes toward the public schools, 79% of Americans were completely or somewhat satisfied with the state of their own child's education. However, only 47% were completely or somewhat satisfied with K–12 education in the United States. It is clear that when parents know the teachers at their children's schools and see the direct impact the teachers have on their children's lives, they are more likely to view the education their children are receiving as positive.

Research validates parents' beliefs that effective teachers do make a difference in student learning. In fact, teachers have been shown to have the greatest influence over student academic growth (Nye, Konstantopoulos, & Hedges, 2004). In 1996, Sanders and Rivers, along with their colleagues at the University of Tennessee, compiled achievement data from standardized tests for students in Tennessee schools and followed the data through successive years of school. They found that two students who performed at the same level in the second grade could be separated by as many as 50 percentile points by the fifth grade if one of them had an effective teacher and the other an ineffective teacher for the next three years. Gladwell (2009) estimated that the difference between a very good teacher and a very bad one is "a year's worth of learning in a single year" (p. 318). Effective teachers do make a substantial difference in student achievement (Marzano, Pickering, & Pollack, 2001), and teacher effectiveness also increases across the first several years (Henry, Bastian, & Fortner, 2011). Other researchers have found that the influence of teachers on student achievement is greater than any other observable factor such as small class sizes (Darling-Hammond, 1999; Rivkin, Hanushek, & Kain, 1998). These are very good reasons for you to strive to be an effective teacher. Excellent teachers hardly ever stop thinking about the subjects they teach. When you discover a subject that you love, the best way to enjoy it for the rest of your life is to teach it to others.

Teaching as Practice and Research

When you become a teacher, you will spend every day of the school year, and some days when you are not actually teaching, using the knowledge and practicing the skills that you gained during your teacher education program. You will also be researching the practice of other teachers and reading research studies to improve your knowledge and skills just as Mr. Zaldaña is doing. What you may not be aware of is that you will also be conducting research on a regular basis. Teachers are considered to be practitioners while others, usually academics, conduct research on what teachers do, think, and practice. Teachers are actually research practitioners. Every lesson, every encounter with students, every paper corrected becomes a source of data for teacher reflection and decision making. Teachers naturally compile data over time to judge the effectiveness of a lesson or student growth in learning. Learning is a process, and keeping track of how it occurs and evolves is a part of teaching. Change is intrinsic to schooling. Understanding how any of us learn and how teachers think, learn, and develop skill in practice is becoming of greater interest to policy makers and academic researchers. In 2017, the James S. McDonnell Foundation announced a new program to fund educational research on the science of teaching and expand the understanding of teachers as learners and as agents of change in education. Teachers will definitely play a huge part in research in this area. For you as a future teacher, it will be important to document your growth and to track changes that may have meaningful results for you and for your students.

How will you know that students are learning at the expected levels? One of the most superficial measures will be performance on standardized tests, which are required annually in most schools. Of course, you will want students to perform well on those tests, but they measure only a narrow slice of the knowledge that students should be acquiring. And they don't measure student development in areas other than knowledge and comprehension. Teachers are also helping students develop skills to use the knowledge they have learned in real-life situations. Teachers provide opportunities for students

THINKING DIFFERENTLY
THE POWER OF REFLECTION

Most teacher education programs encourage the teacher candidates to spend some time reflecting on teaching practices—to contemplate the success of lessons that have been planned and taught. Reflection is a powerful tool and necessary if teachers wish to grow professionally. Reflecting on the fun times you've had with students is probably not something you've been asked to do on a regular basis, but it can certainly remind you of why you teach. In a discussion thread in one of Linda's courses, a teacher working on her master's degree commented that the things she loved about teaching she never ended up writing about. She talked about a magical fall day with her students being engulfed in a windstorm of fall leaves, stopping to make piles of the leaves, and then throwing them in the air and running through them. Another teacher in the class responded to this story with the following:

The more classes I take, the more I overreflect and the more complicated everything becomes. I start to see the words, algorithms, data, research, numbers, statistics, and strategies and get so overwhelmed. But it is when I strip away all of these things and enjoy a simple moment sitting on the carpet with three students using play spatulas to pick up letter-shaped cookies or when I hang up the "I miss you" notes from previous students or taking last-day-of-school selfies with my first-year class that I am reminded why I am here and what keeps us all coming back each day and each year. Thanks for sharing your leaf story! It made me smile and think of my own stories like that I have had with my students!

---

to analyze and think critically about the subject. They help students develop **dispositions**, or attitudes and behaviors, that will show they value learning. Joy is seeing examples of student learning in multiple forms that convince you that a student is ready for the next grade.

The Teaching Profession

Most teachers consider themselves professionals. However, all too often teaching is identified by many as a semiprofession as compared with the professions of law, medicine, architecture, engineering, and accountancy. One reason is that teaching does not provide the same monetary advantages or prestige as the traditional professional fields. Another reason is that teachers appear to have relatively little control over the policies defining their work. Other professionals or policy makers select

iStock/fstop123

Teachers collect data on student growth to make decisions about instruction.

the curricula, set rules, and develop learning standards. Most teachers have limited access to an office, telephone, and secretary. The structure of a teacher's day leaves little time to interact with colleagues to plan or challenge each other intellectually.

Merriam-Webster defines *profession* as "a calling requiring specialized knowledge and often long and intensive academic preparation." All states require at least a bachelor's degree to be eligible for an initial license to teach. Traditionally, states have required some specialized preparation in education that includes student teaching or an internship. A growing number of universities are requiring teacher candidates to have a bachelor's degree in a content area before they begin graduate work in education. Thus, over time, teachers can receive their specialized preparation for teaching at the graduate level. Many teachers today have a master's degree and continue to participate in Professional Development activities throughout their careers.

Being a Professional

A profession sets standards for entry into the profession. In addition, its members apply standards and codes of ethics to themselves and others, disciplining one another when necessary by removing licenses from offenders. Professionals provide services to clients. Their work is intellectual, requiring specialized knowledge and skills. They are bound by an ethical code that guides their relationships with clients and colleagues. They also have an obligation to practice their profession in ways the public would find acceptable. In professions other than teaching, standards and rules are set by the professionals themselves. These standards often include codes of ethics as well as standards for practice. However, in teaching, standards and rules for teachers are usually established by school administrators, members of the school board, and state legislators.

Teachers as Leaders

To be a teacher leader, teachers must become involved in the teaching profession beyond their own classrooms. Teacher unions provide an opportunity for teachers to negotiate contracts that outline salary and working conditions. Teacher organizations in most states conduct annual or semiannual statewide meetings for their members. These meetings provide Professional Development opportunities, a chance to network with other teachers, and a mechanism for becoming involved at the state level. You can stay engaged with your subject area and other educational interests by joining national organizations such as the National Council of Teachers of Mathematics (NCTM) or the National Council of Teachers of English (NCTE). Many of the national organizations have state affiliates of which you could become a member or even a leader. Through teacher organizations, teachers can serve on accreditation teams that evaluate schools and universities in their state or across the country. One sign of a true professional is active and continued involvement in professional organizations at local, state, and national levels.

Two of the InTASC Model Core Teaching Standards and Learning Progressions for Teachers 1.0 (Council of Chief State School Officers, 2013) include professional learning and leadership and collaboration components. Standard 9 states that "the teacher engages in ongoing professional learning," and Standard 10 states that "the teacher seeks appropriate leadership roles . . . and to advance the profession." You will read more about these InTASC standards later in the chapter.

Experienced teachers are being asked to become leaders in their school communities and to help novice teachers become expert practitioners. They are often considered the onsite teacher educators to support university and college programs that require field experience for the candidates. They serve as mentors and coaches disseminating best practices for colleagues. They demonstrate credibility and accountability in their actions and are willing to take on the additional responsibility leadership requires.

Setting and Upholding Standards

Teachers work with professors, parents, and the general public to set standards for students and teachers in their school districts, states, and national organizations. In some states, teachers have the majority control of professional standards boards that have the responsibility for developing licensure standards for teachers and other school professionals. When necessary, these boards withdraw licenses from teachers whose behaviors have led to malpractice. In states without professional standards boards, these functions are usually provided by a state board of education, whose members have been elected or appointed by the governor.

Accreditation

Colleges and schools of education and specific teacher education programs are held to professional standards. Most other professions require their members to graduate from an accredited program before they can take the state licensure examination. In the past, some states required teacher education programs to be nationally accredited by the National Council for Accreditation of Teacher Education (NCATE) or the Teacher Education Accreditation Council (TEAC). Now these two accrediting agencies have merged into one accrediting body with the new name Council for the Accreditation of Educator Preparation (CAEP). Once you begin teaching, you are likely to be involved every few years in an accreditation visit by the state and/or regional accrediting agency such as the Northwest Accreditation Commission (now part of AdvancED).

When a college of education hosts an accreditation visit by a Board of Examiners (BOE), team members will want to talk to the teacher education candidates and ask questions about specific programs and field experiences. The team may ask you about your portfolio and what you have learned about working with students from diverse populations. They may ask how you know that the students you teach are learning. They are also likely to ask you about the quality of teaching at the university, particularly by education faculty members. Accreditation teams want to make certain that the teacher candidates are prepared to meet the challenges of the profession and to meet the needs of all students.

A visiting accreditation team expects the educator preparation program to have a system in place that provides assessment data on what teacher candidates are learning and how well they are demonstrating this knowledge. Teacher preparation programs can create an assessment system tied to the mission and goals of the institution, or they can implement educational programs designed to assess teacher candidate learning. Taskstream, Tk20, and edTPA are all such assessment systems, and in fact you may be asked to use one of these systems as you begin your teacher education program. Teaching is a profession where the first-year teacher is expected to be capable of the same job as someone who already has some experience as a teacher. Software programs and assessment systems can help you catch up to your more experienced peers even before having a classroom of your own.

Licensure

To teach in a public school, teachers must be licensed by a state agency to teach a specific subject (e.g., mathematics or social studies) at the middle or high school levels. Early childhood, elementary, special education, physical education, music, and art teachers are licensed to teach children in specific grades such as preschool, primary, K–6, or K–12. If you graduate from a state-approved program, which is connected to national accreditation, you have usually met the requirements for a state license. You also will be required to pass a state licensure test in most states. Some states will grant a provisional license that allows you to teach for three to five years before meeting all of the requirements for licensure. Several years of successful practice and possibly completion of a master's degree is normally required to attain a professional license to continue teaching. Requirements are different when you apply for a license in a state other than the one in which you graduated. The second state may have additional requirements that you must meet and may have higher cutoff, or qualifying, scores on the required licensure tests such as the *Praxis*® Core exam or content exams. If you plan to move to a different state to teach, check the requirements for a license so that you can take the appropriate courses during your program.

National Board Certification

Teachers with three years of experience are eligible to apply for national certification by the **National Board for Professional Teaching Standards (NBPTS)**. Applicants provide evidence in the collection of documents that are compiled in a portfolio to demonstrate meeting standards for their subject area at a specific age level. Each portfolio must include a videotape of the teacher teaching a lesson, **reflections** on teaching, and an analysis of student work. In addition, the teacher must complete assessment exercises at a testing center. Teaching performance is judged by experienced teachers using **rubrics** aligned with standards. Many states and school districts cover the costs for teachers to participate in this process.

What are the advantages of seeking national board certification? Most applicants report that the process helped improve their teaching and the performance of their students. They learned to reflect on their practice and make changes to improve student learning. A 2004 research study (Goldhaber & Anthony, 2004) of student test scores in North Carolina supports the perceptions of these teachers. The study found that the students of national-board-certified teachers are far more likely to improve their scores on state tests than students of non-national-board-certified teachers. In addition, many national-board-certified teachers receive annual bonuses or pay raises.

Specialized Knowledge

Teachers must know the subjects they will be teaching. The knowledge and related skills for teaching the subject are described in the standards of the national organizations that represent teachers in that field. You will be expected to understand the subject well enough to help young people know it and apply it to the world in which they live. If students are not learning a concept or skills, teachers must be able to relate the content to the experiences of students to provide meaning and purpose.

The professional and pedagogical knowledge needed by teachers is outlined in the widely accepted standards of the InTASC, established by the Council of Chief State School Officers (CCSSO). In 2010, an updated version of the standards was vetted to educational organizations for public comment, and in April 2011, the new standards were adopted. The InTASC standards are used by most states as a framework for individual state standards. The InTASC Model Core Teaching Standards and Learning Progressions for Teachers 1.0 (CCSSO, 2013) are available online at https://ccsso.org. The effort behind the development and adoption of the new InTASC standards makes clear that teaching requires a great deal of specialized knowledge and skill. Teachers have to be some of the brightest people on the planet. Teaching may not be rocket science, but it is close.

Code of Ethics

Like members of other professions, teachers as a group have developed a code of ethics to guide their work and relationships with students and colleagues. Professional standards boards and other state bodies investigate teachers for infractions against the code of ethics adopted by the state. Ethics statements address issues such as discrimination against students, restraint of students, protecting students from harm, personal relationships with students, and misrepresenting one's credentials.

Being a member of a profession is more than showing up for work by 7:30 and not leaving before 4:00. The parents of students in your classroom expect that you will help their children learn. They expect their children to score at acceptable or better levels on achievement tests. They are counting on you to contribute to their children's literacy and to push them beyond minimal standards. Good teachers manage their classrooms so that students can focus on learning. The public and parents become very concerned when classrooms and schools appear out of control. As a teacher, you will have an obligation to model acceptable behavior based on the norms of the profession.

WHAT DO TEACHERS NEED TO KNOW?

When you watch teachers at work, you may wonder why they do things in a certain way, or what motivates them to address one student's behavior differently from the way they might address another student's behavior. Since you can't get inside teachers' heads and they can't stop what they are doing to explain to you the reasons behind their actions, you have to accept the fact that they do know what they are doing and why they are doing it. Understanding and being able to articulate teaching practices is something that you will learn to do in your teacher education program. Becoming familiar with the teaching standards developed by InTASC will also help you understand the specialized knowledge, skills, and dispositions specific to the teaching profession.

Teacher Education Programs

Since teachers have to be well educated, the first step in getting into a teacher education program is to demonstrate your brightness by completing university core requirements with a Grade Point Average (GPA) of at least 2.5 or higher. The advising centers at most colleges of education have complete information on what is required before anyone can be admitted to a traditional teacher education program. Visit the website of your local institution of higher education and check out the steps you must take to be admitted to one of its licensure programs for teachers.

The college of education website (www.csulb.edu/college-of-education) at California State University, Long Beach, presents a range of links to different programs and different levels of professional work, and provides numerous links to career services and advising. It is easy to find out what you must do to earn a teaching degree. All the information you need to have a successful beginning is right at your fingertips.

Ways Programs Are Organized and Why

Teacher education programs are traditionally designed to move candidates along a path of acquiring knowledge of human development and behaviors, learning about laws affecting practice in schools, gaining understanding of counseling practices as well as the impact of cultural diversity on schools and classrooms, and gathering an understanding of working with children with disabilities in regular school classrooms. Candidates who are seeking a secondary license to teach in middle schools or high schools must, in addition to the general university core, complete a specified number of courses in their elected field.

There is a great deal of debate in political and educational groups regarding the type of training necessary for teachers to receive a license. Some believe it is only necessary that a teacher know the content to be taught. Others believe knowing how to teach is as important as, and perhaps more important than, content during the early grades (Shulman, 1986). It is quite possible that future programs in teacher education will be entirely school based and candidates will learn as apprentices alongside an expert mentor. The path to becoming a teacher will offer many opportunities and novel approaches. Some will fit you to a T. Find the right path, stay the course, and you will discover a very rewarding future.

The Importance of Clinical Practice

Many teacher education programs include early clinical experience to provide the candidates with opportunities to begin to learn what teaching involves (Darling-Hammond, Hammerness, Grossman, Rust, & Shulman, 2005). A policy brief on the clinical preparation of teachers by the American Association of Colleges for Teacher Education (2010) stresses the importance of clinical experiences as a key factor in candidates' success. Lortie (1975) made it clear that observing teaching wasn't the ideal way to learn how to teach—that teacher education candidates had to be actively involved in the daily work of teachers. Now, more than 40 years after Lortie's conclusions, university teacher education programs work to align university course work with practice in the field. Field-based teacher education programs place cohorts of candidates in partnership or Professional Development schools, assign them site-based mentors and supervisors, and require evidence of reflection on practice to help the candidates develop cognitive frameworks for teaching. One such field-based program is the 21st Century Schools partnership between the University of Nevada, Las Vegas (UNLV), College of Education and the Clark County School District in Nevada.

Different Pathways to Licensure

The majority of teachers have completed bachelor's programs that prepared them for a license to teach. Most often, they began their preparation soon after high school. Although some education courses may be taken in the first two years of college, candidates are usually not admitted to education programs until they are juniors. Many education courses require candidates to complete field experiences in schools as a component of the course. Some programs require candidates to observe and work in schools several days a week. Candidates in traditional programs may student-teach under the supervision of a teacher and college supervisor during the final year of their bachelor's program.

You can study to become a teacher through many routes. Programs are delivered in college classrooms and schools. Some programs can be completed via distance learning without stepping on campus. A growing number of candidates begin exploring teaching as a career in community colleges, initially developing portfolios and working with children and youth in schools and community projects.

Most colleges and universities offer a number of pathways for becoming a teacher. Not all teacher education programs are traditional four-year undergraduate programs. Many colleges of education offer postbaccalaureate courses to meet state licensure requirements. School districts may negotiate Professional Development course work with state licensing agencies to provide on-the-job credit for individuals who have the expertise to fill high-need positions but do not have a degree in teaching or a state license to teach. A national debate regarding the credibility of differing routes to licensure is hotly contested in educational journals and the popular media.

The U.S. Department of Education provides funding incentives to colleges of education and local school districts for creating specialized routes to licensure for high-need areas of teaching. In 2011, the DOE awarded approximately $90 million to 30 grant applicants from across the United States. Many of these applications were to provide an Alternative Route to Licensure and increase the number of teachers in specialized areas.

The Five-Year Teaching Degree

Some teacher education programs are five-year programs that begin at the undergraduate level and end with a master's degree or eligibility for a license after completing a sequence of graduate courses. These programs allow more time for candidates to study the art and science of teaching and learning. They sometimes require a yearlong internship in schools, allowing candidates to practice under the guidance of professionals who provide feedback and support throughout the internship.

Many colleges of education offer teacher education course work once a student has completed an undergraduate program in a specific content area. The final or fifth year of a teacher education program generally places the candidate in a school as a teacher or co-teacher under the supervision of college faculty and school personnel. The fifth-year student gains practical experience during the day and attends classes in the evening. Once students finish their fifth year, they are eligible for licensure and are also awarded a master's degree.

Master of Arts in Teaching (MAT) or Certificate Programs

College graduates who decide that they want to become teachers after they have completed a bachelor's degree in another area have several options for pursuing a teaching career. They could choose a Master of Arts in Teaching (MAT) program that offers courses in **pedagogy**, human growth and development, assessment practices, and some form of internship. Schools in Georgia, Oregon, and Hawaii, to mention just a few, offer MAT programs to qualified candidates. You might also be interested in checking out some of the MAT programs offered in other countries, such as Canada and Australia. Many colleges and universities have certificate or licensure programs in which candidates can complete the courses and field experience required for a state license. Some of these programs are offered entirely online. Most MAT or certificate programs require observation time and supervised student teaching, giving credit to the belief that before candidates are eligible to be teachers of record, they should have some practical experience in classrooms under the tutelage of an experienced teacher.

A web search of fifth-year and MAT programs will provide you will a robust list of colleges and universities where you can enroll in a program that will lead to a teaching license and a master's degree. There is some criticism that MAT and certificate licensure programs may not offer the value that should be expected of a master's degree (Robinson, 2011). As a professional and a technology native, you will be able to search the Internet to find the program that best suits your intent.

Alternative Licensure Programs

A number of new teachers are entering the profession through alternative routes that allow them to begin teaching without any specialized preparation in teaching and learning course work or field experiences in schools. This is something that other professions such as medicine and engineering would find unacceptable. Opening the entry to teaching to anyone with a bachelor's degree challenges the status of a profession because doing so requires no specialized training. However, most states require these alternative-route teachers to take education courses and to be mentored by experienced teachers while they are teaching and completing the course work required for licensure.

Many of these alternative routes to licensure (ARL) programs are designed for adults beyond the traditional college age of 18 to 24. They build on the experience and background of candidates who often have worked for a number of years in a nonteaching field. These programs may be similar to traditional undergraduate and graduate programs, but they offer greater flexibility in scheduling courses through distance education and prompting candidates to schedule their own field observations. Many candidates in these programs are working full-time in schools or other jobs. Not all teachers complete programs at colleges and universities. School districts, state departments of education, and other organizations are also preparing teachers. The Utah Department of Education welcomes individuals who have a disposition toward teaching who don't want to go back to college, and Michigan and South Carolina allow teachers to start working while gaining certification online (Zalaznick, 2017).

Military personnel may participate in Troops to Teachers, a program to assist men and women who have completed their military service in becoming teachers. When the U.S. military organizations are downsized, many well-trained individuals must seek employment in other fields. According to Martin

(2014), "Troops to Teachers is a U.S. Department of Defense program that helps eligible military personnel begin a new career as teachers in public schools where their skills, knowledge and experience are most needed." Military personnel who sign on to this program can receive financial assistance in tuition costs and in some cases are reimbursed for the expenses of moving to a new location. Purdue University Global offers a MAT degree that is completely online and accommodates individuals who are transitioning out of the military.

Teach For America (TFA), founded in 1990, recruits outstanding students from some of the nation's most prestigious universities to teach for two or more years in low-income communities throughout the United States. The TFA candidates spend a month in intensive preparation for their initial placement. During their years of teaching, they attend monthly Professional Development meetings conducted by TFA mentors and may also attend courses at a local college of education that will lead to a master's degree. In 2016, TFA reported 53,000 alumni, 19,000 classroom teachers, and 1,000 principals in 280 school systems and 53 regions of the United States. The TFA organization receives financial support from the federal government, state departments of education, and private donors.

Graduate Licensure

Graduate licensure programs are generally limited to persons holding an undergraduate and/or graduate degree in a field other than education. Licensure programs lead to an elementary or secondary teaching license and a master of education degree. Candidates in this type of program are required to complete courses that mirror the undergraduate teacher education courses and must complete all of the clinical practice required of undergraduates.

Trends in the Teaching Force

A projected 58 million students will be enrolled in U.S. public PreK–12 schools by the year 2022 (U.S. Department of Education, 2014), and a projected 367,000 new teachers will be hired by 2022 (Hussar & Bailey, 2014, p. 13). It would appear that in the near future there will be a need for your talent. Teaching jobs become available as current teachers retire, move to other schools, or leave the profession. Over the next decade, around 700,000 teachers—almost one of four current teachers—are projected to retire. Teachers leave the profession and move from school to school for a variety of reasons. The primary reasons for moving are layoffs, school closings, and other organizational changes in a school or district. Personal reasons include family responsibilities, moving to a new location, and health problems. Perda (2013) reported that more than 41% of new teachers leave teaching in the first five years.

The teacher turnover rate in urban high-priority schools is almost one-third higher than in other schools (National Commission on Teaching and America's Future, 2003), but the largest turnover rate is in small private schools. While the rate of teachers leaving large private schools is fairly low, small private schools suffer from an annual turnover that is often one-fourth of the staff. Although teachers in private schools report greater satisfaction and that their environments are more positive than public schools, they are much more likely to transfer to a public school than their public school counterparts are to transfer to a private school (Ingersoll, 2003).

Not all new hires in a school district are recent graduates. About half of them are teachers returning to the classroom or moving from another district. A growing number of new teachers are not recent college graduates. They are military retirees or people switching from business or other careers. They often complete alternative pathways into teaching in school-based graduate programs that build on their prior experiences.

You may not be able to find a teaching job in the community in which you grew up or near the university you are attending because the schools have few openings. However, jobs do exist if you are willing to move to a part of the country where there are shortages because of high turnover, a growing student population, or a move to reduce the teacher-to-student ratio in classes. For instance, Nevada recently mandated a class size reduction for all kindergarten classrooms. This mandate has resulted in the need for nearly double the number of existing kindergarten teachers.

Opportunities to get a teaching job are greater in urban high-poverty areas where high turnover exists. Generally, urban and rural areas have more openings than suburban areas, although acute shortages exist in high-poverty suburban areas as well. If you are willing to move to another state, your job opportunities will grow. Alaska, western states, and southern states are actively recruiting new teachers to staff the schools for a growing school-age population (National Commission on Teaching and America's Future, 2003). West Virginia has reported a shortage of teachers in all areas of learning, and six additional states reported shortages in 11 areas of learning: Washington, DC; Nevada; Oklahoma; Rhode Island; California; and American Samoa (Shepherd University, 2016). All states except Louisiana, New Mexico, and New York reported a shortage in special education, and math and science were noted as shortage areas in more than 45 states. Striking out on a journey to unknown territory at the same time you are beginning a new career can certainly be daunting. Both take courage, something all teachers have, and you will be welcomed wherever you decide to go. Use technology to find your new job through a geographic information system, and locate the place that most needs you.

Where you decide to teach might be determined by the salary that you can receive. However, buyer beware: Some states offer higher salaries because the cost of living is also higher in that state. Figure 1.1 presents a list of the average starting salary for beginning teachers from school districts around the nation, as reported by the National Education Association (NEA). There is variation in beginning salaries within states due to dense population areas and need. For example, in Georgia, beginning teachers in Atlanta are likely to be paid more than beginning teachers in Savannah. Most states also offer incremental increases for longevity and course work and degrees earned. The average public school teacher salary for 2015–2016 was $58,353. Salaries in the high range were in New York, California, and Massachusetts, with South Dakota and Mississippi in the low range. For 2017–2018, starting salaries in New York range from $54,000 (bachelor's degree, no prior teaching experience) to $81,694 (master's degree, eight years of teaching experience, plus additional course work). New teachers with a master's degree but no prior teaching experience earn $60,704. Strangely enough, over the decade leading up

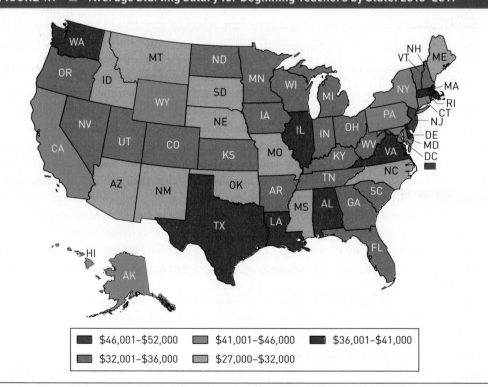

FIGURE 1.1 ■ Average Starting Salary for Beginning Teachers by State: 2016–2017

■ $46,001–$52,000	■ $41,001–$46,000	■ $36,001–$41,000
■ $32,001–$36,000	■ $27,000–$32,000	

Source: NEA Collective Bargaining/Member Advocacy's Teacher Salary Database, based on affiliate reporting as of December 2017. Adapted from http://www.nea.org/home/2016-2017-average-starting-teacher-salary.html.

Note: National Average Starting Teacher Salary = $38,617.

to 2015–2016, the average classroom teacher salary increased by 15.2%, but after inflation adjustment, the average salary actually decreased by 3%.

Most teacher contracts are for less than 12 months, but teachers can earn additional income within the school year or during the summer by having second jobs outside the school. Teachers can also supplement their base salaries when they engage in the following activities related to schools or their education:

- Serving as a mentor or staff developer

- Achieving additional teaching licenses or certifications

- Becoming national board certified

- Teaching in a subject area where there is a teacher shortage

- Working in a school more challenging to staff than other schools in the district

Teachers also may receive supplemental income for chairing departments, being team leaders, sponsoring extracurricular activities, and coaching.

Teaching Fields

The first time the idea of teaching crosses our minds, we hold an image of teaching a certain age group of children or a certain subject. One person will imagine a kindergarten room full of brightly colored centers, another will visualize herself at a board working equations with a group of serious high school seniors, another will imagine helping a group of students construct a model of the planets in Earth's solar system, and yet others might see themselves using technology to deliver distance education. Teaching is an endless array of possibilities, and for each aspiring teacher, its attraction is to a different reality.

Have you decided what subjects you would like to teach? Math? Art? History? Writing? Technology? Or all of the above? Urban and rural schools are likely to have openings for all subjects, from elementary through high school. However, not enough teachers are being prepared or retained in schools to teach mathematics and science classes, **English Language Learners (ELLs)**, and students with disabilities. Your chances of finding a job improve if you qualify for one of these high-need areas. The U.S. Department of Labor, Bureau of Labor Statistics (2015) projects above-average national growth in demand for professionals in key disciplines currently served by or aligned with programs in colleges or schools of education. A few of these programs are listed in Figure 1.2.

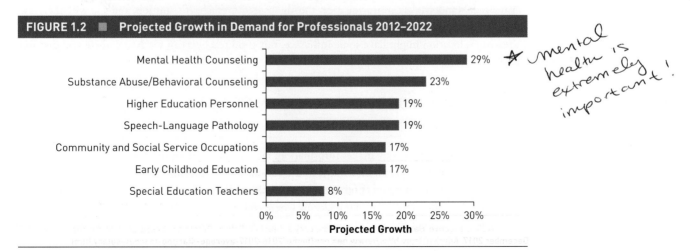

FIGURE 1.2 ■ Projected Growth in Demand for Professionals 2012–2022

✱ mental health is extremely important!

Source: U.S. Department of Labor, Bureau of Labor Statistics, 2015.

Science, Technology, Engineering, and Mathematics (STEM)

The increase in federal funding for Science, Technology, Engineering, and Mathematics (STEM) programs is the result of data showing that fewer than 50% of U.S. high school students are ready to take college-level math and fewer than 40% are ready for college-level science. Since it is anticipated that many of the job opportunities in the twenty-first century will require math skills and scientific knowledge, the federal government has made it a priority to fund educational programs that focus on STEM. There is also a concern that Latino and black U.S. students have not had equal opportunities for instruction in STEM-content learning during high school.

Many secondary schools report they have had to hire teachers who did not major in mathematics or science to teach their courses. These **out-of-field teachers** sometimes have not even minored in these fields and lack the knowledge and skills to help students learn these core subjects. The lack of qualified mathematics and science teachers in urban high schools has contributed to not offering Advanced Placement classes in these subjects and to the poor test performance of students in these schools. Many large urban school districts have an immediate need for qualified STEM teachers.

Special Education

Another major shortage area is special education teachers for all grades, from preschool through high school. These teachers may work with a classroom of special education students, but often work as resource teachers with regular teachers in inclusive classrooms. They teach students with mental, behavioral, sensory, physical, and learning disabilities. These jobs are usually very demanding, sometimes physically so, but they can lead to a great deal of joy as students become academically successful or learn to be independent. Many large urban school districts desperately need highly qualified special education teachers.

English Language Learners (ELLs)/Bilingual Students

School districts report a shortage of culturally and linguistically diverse educators, especially in areas of the country with large numbers of Latino and immigrant students. Over the past decade, the schools with these needs have expanded to smaller cities and communities in the Midwest and South where immigrants are employed and migrant workers have settled. Knowledge and skills in English as a Second Language (ESL) and bilingual education will give a new teacher an advantage in many urban and rural areas today. Large urban school districts have an immediate need for ELL/bilingual teachers. This is certainly true for Clark County School District in Nevada, where the Latino school population is now over 50% of the total school population.

As mentioned earlier, beginning teachers often want to teach in the same community where they grew up and went to school. However, the types of communities that most beginning teachers have grown up in are not always the places that need the most teachers. If you want to be sure of beginning your teaching career when you graduate, you must go where the jobs are. Highly qualified teachers are always in demand. Make certain you meet the highest requirements for any job, and you will likely end up where you want to be. In real estate, the three major areas of concern are location, location, location. In teaching, location might have some influence, but good teachers can teach anywhere and discover the joy of helping students learn.

WHAT ROLE DOES TECHNOLOGY PLAY IN THE LIVES OF TEACHERS?

In this digital age, technology makes information, fact or not, myth or marketing, as close as a finger tap or voice command. You all know how to use various forms of technology for personal purposes—to discover that new restaurant, find out what time the movie starts, pay a bill, be a fan, check up on friends, and let your circle of loved ones know where you've been and what you've been up to. It's hard to imagine life without the ease of connecting to the world that technology affords us today. As you develop your teaching persona, you will have to think about how to use technology in a professional manner and of course how to use it to help your students learn.

Technology has always provided tools for teaching and has been part of education in America since the first student in Massachusetts etched a numeral or letter on a slate. From stones for etching softer rocks, to styluses for making marks in soft clay, to shaved brushes for painting icons, teachers have used tools to enhance their practice. Chalk and blackboards made it possible for teachers to invent their own text in classrooms. Imagine where Albert Einstein would have been without a chalkboard. The science of photographic reproduction in the 19th century made it possible for teachers to show students photographs of famous art objects and historical sites in faraway places. The first Kodak slide projector, produced in 1937, offered another piece of technology for teachers to enhance instruction. Teachers also learned to use movie projectors to show select 8-millimeter and 16-millimeter films to their students. Nearly anyone graduating from a teacher education program in the 1950s had to take a course on audiovisual aids, and today's teacher candidates are often required to complete a course in technology for teachers.

Teachers can use the ever-growing varieties of technology to teach online courses.

When television was introduced in schools, there was a consensus among educators that the small screens installed in many classrooms would revolutionize teaching and learning. Televisions did not revolutionize teaching and learning. Unfortunately, typical television programming puts the viewer in passive mode, except maybe for programs like *Dora the Explorer*. (Three-year-olds are known to stand up during one of Dora's silences and yell, "Backpack!") Technology available to teachers today is fantastically improved, and interactive modes of programming are readily available.

Much of what happens when you begin teaching is a mystery. In many ways, what happens from day to day in any classroom can be surprising. You might be prepared for the worst and find the best. You might discover something wonderful that you weren't quite prepared for that stretches your knowledge and skills in ways that are new and occasionally frightening. Teaching with the technology available to teachers today adds a dimension of magic to the art and science of teaching. It poses challenges that can leave your head spinning and surprises that make you and your students go, "Wow!" Teachers today must consider technology as a tool for student learning that can foster critical thinking, and must learn to use the virtual interactive tools that their students use in their personal lives (McGrail, Sachs, Many, Myrick, & Sackor, 2011).

Educational Technology Standards for Teachers

The International Society for Technology in Education (ISTE) has developed a set of standards for teachers. These standards define the fundamental concepts, knowledge, skills, and attitudes that teachers should exhibit. Candidates seeking certification or endorsements in teacher licensure should meet these standards. The instructors at your institution are responsible for making sure that you have knowledge of the standards and that you have had the opportunity to meet some of the performance indicators. Table 1.1 lists ISTE's five standards areas with the main objective for the performance indicators. The standards are specific enough to define the broad goals of using technology in educational settings, yet general enough to allow for a comfortable fit with local circumstances. Visit www.iste.org/standards to learn more about the performance indicators for teachers. These performance indicators will give you a better understanding of what will be expected of you once you begin teaching.

WHAT DO TEACHER EDUCATION CANDIDATES NEED TO DO?

The previous section of this chapter provided information regarding jobs, salaries, and expectations for being part of the teaching profession. This section will help clarify the purpose of teacher education

TABLE 1.1 ■ International Society for Technology in Education Standards for Teachers

Standard	Example
1. Facilitate and inspire student learning and creativity	Teachers use technology to advance student learning, creativity, and innovation in both face-to-face and virtual environments.
2. Design and develop digital age learning experiences and assessments	Teachers design, develop, and evaluate authentic learning experiences and assessments to maximize learning.
3. Model digital age work and learning	Teachers exhibit knowledge, skills, and work processes representative of an innovative professional in a global and digital society.
4. Promote and model digital citizenship and responsibility	Teachers understand local and global societal issues and responsibilities in an evolving digital culture.
5. Engage in professional growth and leadership	Teachers improve professional practice, and become lifelong learners and leaders in their schools and professional community through use of digital tools and resources.

Source: Adapted from the International Society for Technology in Education (ISTE) website, http://www.iste.org/standards/for-educators © 2008, ISTE (International Society for Technology in Education), 800.336.5191 (U.S. & Canada) or 541.302.3777 (International), iste@iste.org, www.iste.org. All rights reserved.

programs and what you can do when you are enrolled. Knowing what is expected of you is one of the best ways to feel confident and to ensure you get the most out of your classes and the clinical experiences you will have to complete. Learning to teach in an actual classroom is called a "practicum." It is practice. Practice is just as valuable for a teacher as it is for a pianist learning a new piece of music. In your teacher education program, you will have to practice, test yourself, practice again, test yourself again, and most important of all reflect on your practice and how well it went. Nothing will help you quite as much as learning to reflect on your practice. All expert teachers have learned to be reflective practitioners.

How to Get Off to a Good Start in Your Teacher Education Program

Usually, people spend some time planning and charting a path before they embark on a long journey. There are maps to read and places of interest to check out to see if a side trip is warranted. Some folks even develop strategies for getting the most out of every mile. Not much planning is required for a trip to the supermarket, though a list is always helpful. But when committing to something that might be a benchmark in your life goal of becoming a teacher, planning is certainly essential.

Test of Basic Skills

Teacher candidates are usually required to pass a basic skills test before they are admitted to a teacher education program. Every teacher should be competent in the basic skills of reading, writing, and mathematics. These tests are designed to determine that future teachers have the basic knowledge and skills in these areas. In order to be admitted to the professional course work in a teacher education program, most states require that you demonstrate aptitude by achieving passing scores on basic skills tests. The Educational Testing Service (ETS) website at www.ets.org/praxis offers detailed information about taking a basic skills test. The ETS website also contains a drop-down menu for individual state testing requirements for licensure. The Pearson National Evaluation Series website provides detailed information about its test services and how you can take exams at its test centers. Some states have developed their own tests of basic skills and other tests required for teacher licensure. The California Basic Educational Skills Test (CBEST) is a standardized test administered throughout the state of

California and Oregon for individuals who want to teach at public schools. Individual state test requirements and passing scores can also be found at state departments of education websites.

Learn About Assessment Practices

Teacher candidates are not expected to be passive learners during the course work in a teacher education program to be eligible for a license to teach. You will be required to show evidence that you meet professional and state standards through a number of **performance assessments** throughout your program that demonstrate that you know your subject matter and can teach. These assessments are usually administered at three major transition points within a program: (1) before admission to the program, (2) before you can student-teach, and (3) at completion of student teaching and the program. The assessments can include standardized paper-and-pencil tests, portfolios, case studies, evaluations of your student teaching or internship, comprehensive examinations at the end of the program, and projects. You will also be expected to show that you can help all students learn. Earlier in this chapter, you read about companies that provide software and guidelines for candidates to keep track of their progress. However, even without professional software support, you will be able to track your professional growth toward becoming a teacher.

Your professors and **field-based supervisors** will evaluate your performance in the classroom on assessment rubrics that describe the areas you must reach to show you are proficient in the skills and knowledge to help all students learn. When you receive the feedback from the supervisors and professors, you will know where you need to improve your practice to meet the standards.

iStock/kali9

Teachers must demonstrate their knowledge of basic skills and their readiness to teach. Standardized tests provide states with evidence of a teacher's qualifications.

Pass Licensure Tests

Potential teachers in most states must pass one or more tests to be eligible for a license to teach. States either develop their own licensure tests or contract with a major test company such as the ETS or Pearson National Evaluation Series. A state board of education or standards board determines the **cut score** that test takers must achieve to pass the test. The score required to pass the same or similar tests varies from state to state. Your score could be high enough to be licensed in one state, but not in another. Ohio, Virginia, and Connecticut have set higher cut scores than other states as part of their effort to raise the quality of teachers in the state. Check with the state in which you plan to work to determine the tests you will be required to pass before you receive a license.

Content Tests. Content tests assess candidates' knowledge of the subject or subjects they will be teaching or the field in which they will be working (e.g., ESL, algebra, or special education). These tests generally assess the knowledge outlined in the state and professional standards for the field, which is another reason to be familiar with the standards. You should develop the knowledge bases for your field in the courses you have taken in the sciences, humanities, arts, psychology, and social sciences. Secondary and middle-level teacher candidates often major in the academic discipline they plan to teach. Some states require elementary teacher candidates to major or have a concentration in one or more academic fields such as social sciences, mathematics, science, a foreign language, or English. Are you required to have an academic, rather than education, major to be licensed in your state? Check out the state department of education website for this information.

Most states require new teachers to pass content tests before they receive the first license to teach. Many institutions require candidates to pass this test before they are eligible to student-teach. Knowledge of the subject you teach and how you teach it may seem like different sides of the same coin, but they are truly quite different. It is possible to be an expert in a field and not be able to explain one bit of it to a group of students in a classroom. Because of this, many states require that teachers pass tests in pedagogy.

Knowledge, Skills, Dispositions, and Student Learning. Knowledge is one of the easier areas to assess. The most popular assessment of knowledge is a standardized, pencil-and-paper test, which now is often completed on a computer. Teacher-developed quizzes and tests provide information on what is known or understood. Grades and your performance on papers, projects, presentations, and case studies contribute to the overall evaluation of the knowledge needed to teach.

Skills or performances are usually demonstrated as you collaborate with your peers, interact with your professors, and work with teachers and students in schools. Your skills can be observed and measured by how successful you are in helping students achieve on tests and other assessments. Field experiences and student teaching provide opportunities for you to apply your knowledge about a subject and pedagogy. You and others will assess your effectiveness in these settings. Although standardized assessments exist, they are relatively expensive to implement.

A few states require beginning teachers to complete Praxis III, in which trained assessors evaluate their performance as a first-year teacher against standards using a scoring rubric. Teacher education programs in those states emphasize the development of the skills assessed by Praxis III. Other states, including Connecticut, require their new teachers to submit a portfolio after their first year of teaching as evidence they are meeting state standards. At UNLV, at the end of student teaching education, candidates present a digital portfolio to an audience of their peers and professors. Artifacts collected for the portfolio are tied to the InTASC standards.

Many teacher education programs have identified the dispositions that you should demonstrate before you become a teacher. They might include **proficiencies** such as these:

- Believing that all children can learn at high levels, which requires persistence in helping all children be successful

- Appreciating and valuing human diversity, showing respect for students' varied talents and perspectives, and commitment to the pursuit of individually configured excellence

- Respecting students as individuals with differing personal and family backgrounds and various skills, talents, and interests

These proficiencies cannot be easily measured on a test. They come across in the papers you write, the presentations you make, the lessons you teach, and the interactions you have with students and parents in schools. Over time and in multiple ways, your dispositions are demonstrated and assessed.

In most teacher education programs, you are expected to learn how to assess student learning and how to respond when a student is not learning. During your field-based practica, you most likely will be required to collect data on student learning, analyze those data, and determine next steps if one or more students are not learning. Figure 1.3 provides an example of an assessment exercise you may be asked to complete during student teaching. See Figure 1.4 for an example of a rubric that accompanies the student learning assessment.

You might be asked to design an assessment that will help you know whether students are learning. You might be given a sample of student work and asked to analyze it and describe any concerns raised by the student's work. By the time you finish your program, you should be familiar with a number of assessments besides a test. You should also know that students learn in different ways, requiring that you teach using strategies that build on their prior experiences and cultures.

[handwritten margin note: How do you make sure students learn + how do you make sure learning takes place?]

FIGURE 1.3 ■	Assessment for the Analysis of Student Learning in a Teacher Work Sample

Teacher Work Sample Standard: The teacher candidate uses assessment data to profile student learning and communicate information about student progress and achievement.

Task: Analyze your assessment data, including pre-/postassessments and formative assessments to determine students' progress related to the unit learning goals. Use visual representations and narrative to communicate the performance of the whole class, subgroups, and two individual students. Conclusions drawn from this analysis should be provided in the "Reflection and Self-Evaluation" section.

Prompt: In this section you will analyze data to explain progress and achievement toward learning goals demonstrated by your whole class, subgroups of students, and individual students.

Whole class. To analyze the progress of your whole class, create a table that shows pre- and postassessment data on every student on every learning goal. Then, create a graphic summary that shows the extent to which your students made progress (from pre- to postassessment) toward the learning criterion that you identified for each learning goal (identified in your Assessment Plan section). Summarize what the graph tells you about your students' learning in this unit (i.e., the number of students who met the criterion).	**Subgroups.** Select a group characteristic (e.g., gender, performance level, socioeconomic status, language proficiency) to analyze in terms of one learning goal. Provide a rationale for your selection of this characteristic to form subgroups (e.g., girls vs. boys, high vs. middle vs. low performers). Create a graphic representation that compares pre- and postassessment results for the subgroups on this learning goal. Summarize what these data show about student learning.	**Individuals.** Select two students who demonstrated different levels of performance. Explain why it is important to understand the learning of these particular students. Use preformative and postassessment data with examples of the students' work to draw conclusions about the extent to which these students attained the two learning goals. Graphic representations are not necessary for this subsection.

Suggested Page Length: 4 + charts and student work examples

Source: Hussar, W. J., & Bailey, T. M. (2011). *Projections of Education Statistics to 2020* (NCES 2011–026). Washington, DC: U.S. Department of Education, National Center for Education Statistics.

FIGURE 1.4 ■	A Scoring Guide to Assess Student Learning

Teacher Work Sample Standard: The teacher candidate uses assessment data to profile student learning and communicate information about student progress and achievement.

Rating → Indicator ↓	1 Indicator Not Met	2 Indicator Partially Met	3 Indicator Met	Score
Clarity and Accuracy of Presentation	Presentation is not clear and accurate; it does not accurately reflect the data.	Presentation is understandable and contains few errors.	Presentation is easy to understand and contains no errors of representation.	
Evidence of Impact on Student Learning	Analysis of student learning fails to include evidence of impact on student learning in terms of numbers of students who achieved and made progress toward learning goals.	Analysis of student learning includes incomplete evidence of the impact on student learning in terms of numbers of students who achieved and made progress toward learning goals.	Analysis of student learning includes evidence of the impact on student learning in terms of numbers of students who achieved and made progress toward each learning goal.	

Source: Elliott, E. (2003). *Assessing education candidate performance: A look at changing practices.* Washington, DC: National Council for Accreditation of Teacher Education. Reprinted with permission of the National Council for Accreditation of Teacher Education.

Pedagogical and Professional Knowledge Tests. Some states also require new teachers to pass a test that assesses general pedagogical and professional knowledge that teachers should have to manage instruction and students. This information is taught in courses such as educational foundations, educational psychology, multicultural education, tests and measurement, teaching methods, and the course that requires you to read this book. Your specialized knowledge about teaching and learning is assessed in this group of tests. They require you to know theories in education, the critical research that guides how to teach your subject, instructional strategies, the impact of diversity on learning, and the use of technology in teaching.

Spend Time in Schools

Most teacher education programs require candidates to observe and work in schools, often beginning with the first education course. You want to make sure you really like working with young children if you are planning to teach at the primary level or older adolescents if you are planning to teach high school. You can also learn whether you have the temperament to work with 30 students at a time or to maintain a schedule that requires you to be in a classroom with students for hours at a time without talking on your cell phone, texting, or having a snack. Field experiences confirm for most candidates that they really do want to teach. Others discover that teaching is not the job for them.

Learn to Be Comfortable in Schools. Most of us found the time we spent as students in school enjoyable, and we liked going to school. That was probably one reason we were drawn to teaching. Most times, we got along well with our classmates and with our teachers. Teachers must be at school most days of the school year. The teachers we remember fondly are the ones that appeared to enjoy being at school. They were the ones who greeted everyone with a smile and shared a kind word or two with everyone they came in contact with. They appeared generally happy and happy to be sharing their days with others in a school.

The people who work in schools alongside teachers also appreciate friendly greetings and encouraging words. It is important to know the people who support your role as a teacher because they are often the ones you call for help when something nonacademic goes amiss. When you are comfortable in the schools you are assigned to, when you know the people who work at the school and what their jobs are, when you show a positive regard for each member of the school team and exude a happy character, you will be comfortable in schools and help the people who work with you feel comfortable too.

Professional Development Schools

You may be assigned to a Professional Development School (PDS) for your field experiences and clinical practice. Teachers, teacher candidates, and college professors in a PDS collaborate to support student learning. They may team-teach and take turns teaching, planning together, and supporting each other. After a few weeks of working together, students and parents often are not able to distinguish between the teacher, professor, and teacher candidate. One or more professors may spend most of their time in a PDS, working with the teacher and candidate in the classroom and providing Professional Development for faculty as needed.

School District/University Partnership Schools

These partnerships may appear similar to Professional Development Schools, given the collaboration that takes place between personnel in both institutions. The aim of a partnership between a university and a school district is to seek reform at all levels. This means that both members

iStock/Steve Debenport

Schools are busy places full of happy people helping one another. New teachers should make a point of knowing and respecting all the support staff at their school.

of the partnership have to learn to work in new ways. Institutional cultures may have to change, and while change is inevitable, it is not always welcomed. Forming a partnership is labor-intensive and not always perceived in the same way by all members of the partnership. The university teacher education curriculum may have to be revised to meet the specific needs of schools and students in a district. School structures may have to be redesigned to meet the goals of the partnership and the inclusion of teacher education candidates into the daily functions of the school. The achievement of K–12 students remains at the center of any reform effort of partnership schools, as does the Professional Development of teachers and teacher candidates.

Shadow a Student or a Teacher for a Day

Before you receive your first clinical assignment, make a concerted effort to spend a day in a school shadowing a student or a teacher. Shadowing students will help you see the school day through their perspective. Observe what work they are engaged in and how they negotiate the physical, mental, and social demands of being members of a class group. Take note of the kinds of interactions they have with other students and with the teacher. Learn how they keep track of all that is expected of them.

Shadowing a teacher will help you begin to understand what will be expected of you during a typical school day. Make an effort to keep track of the number of decisions teachers make, and what those decisions entail. Note the special routines and management strategies they have in place to keep track of the students, student work, and class and school schedules. Listen to the conversations they have with the students and with other teachers. Watch their work with an eye toward the roles you will perform when you begin teaching. It could be an eye-opening experience. If you hear students, parents, other teachers, and administrators refer to effective teachers, ask if you can visit their class to observe their interactions with the subject matter and with students.

Volunteer as a Teacher's Aide or as a Tutor

To learn more about the work of teachers, volunteer to help out in a classroom or school. Teachers have scores of duties to address, before, during, and after class, and an offer of help from a well-meaning individual is always welcomed. Visit a school near your home, meet with the principal, and explain that you are studying to be a teacher and would like to have some experience working in a school as a volunteer. Your offer of help will certainly be met with enthusiasm.

There are many ways that you can develop skills when working with students. When starting out in your teacher education program, it is good to have experience working closely with one or two children. Tutoring is a great way to become familiar with students' learning styles and to understand the difficulties some students have learning specific content. Tutoring programs at reading centers in colleges of education or in public libraries seek tutors for a variety of programs. Working as a tutor can help build your confidence and competence as a teacher.

Become a Member of a Teaching and Learning Team

You will have ample opportunity to discuss educational issues in your teacher education courses. You will learn of the theories underlying practice and discuss ways theories are demonstrated through teachers' actions. While you are involved in your clinical practice, make an effort to join a teacher group and listen when teachers discuss teaching and learning issues and develop strategies for serving students. Take advantage of the expertise that can be gained from experienced teachers. Ask questions. When you visit schools as part of your field experience requirements, note effective teaching practices that you could incorporate into your own repertoire as you student-teach and later when you have your own classroom.

To become effective teachers, we learn as we observe and practice. We test theories and strategies, expanding our repertoire of ways to help students learn. With time, we become more familiar with the subjects we teach and the students with whom we work. We become more comfortable in the classroom as we understand the bureaucratic requirements of a school and become better managers of the classroom and learning.

TEACHERS' LOUNGE
IS IT MR. OR MRS.?

Lloyd J. Goldberg

Having already completed my master's degree in elementary education, and not finding a permanent position in the previous summer, I turned my attention to working as much as possible in the schools of Johnson City as a substitute. In an attempt to meet and be known by as many people as possible, I accepted a several-day position as a kindergarten teacher. My teaching license covered Grades 1–6, but I thought my experience and general training could be easily adapted to kindergarten. In addition, I thought that the small class sizes and presence of a teacher assistant could alleviate any potential problems that might arise.

For context, Johnson City had recently constructed one building to house its K–8 classes, eliminating the middle school and several aging neighborhood elementary schools. Within the school there were no male teachers in the 30+ sections of K–3, nor were there any male administrators or office staff. Additionally, Johnson City sits on the confluence of the Susquehanna and Chenango rivers in central New York. During the winter, temperatures can easily dip below zero, and wind chills can cause dangerous situations if anyone is outside too long. As a self-preservation technique, I used to grow a full, black beard each winter.

On my first day, I was immediately ushered into the world of the little ones. Having a substitute immediately gets them into hyper-mode, and having a male teacher creates some form of irreconcilable conflict in their minds. As the day progressed, we were having a productive experience, but one little boy kept referring to me as Mrs. G, instead of Mr. G. Normally, this isn't a big deal, but he was a smart kid and was the only student to seem to have difficulty with the concept of his teacher being a man. The fact I was wearing a tie and had a full beard was of little consequence to him.

Finally, I pulled him aside and gently said, "Buddy, I don't know about your family, but in mine it is the men who have beards and we call them mister." After a few seconds of intense thought, he motioned for me to come closer to him and responded with "But my grandma has a mustache." Out of sheer respect, I let him call me Mrs. G for the rest of the time I was in the class.

—Mr. Lloyd J. Goldberg, Teacher
Third Grade, Schorr Elementary
Las Vegas, Nevada

CHALLENGING ASSUMPTIONS

Do the kinds and amounts of preservice education and preparation that teacher candidates receive before they begin teaching have any impact on whether they leave the profession after their first year on the job?

The Assumption

Some policy makers believe that teachers who enter the teaching force through an Alternative Route to Licensure with little or no supervised field experience in a school setting are just as likely to stay in teaching as those candidates who have course work related to teaching and learning and have had practice teaching experiences.

The Research

Ingersoll, Merrill, and May (2014) examined measures of teachers' subject-matter education and pedagogical preparation from data provided by two National Center for Education Statistics surveys. Their analyses demonstrated that "the type of college, degree, entry route or certificate mattered little. What did matter was the substance and content of new teachers' pedagogical preparation. Those with more training in teaching methods and pedagogy—especially practice teaching, observation of other classroom teaching and feedback on their own teaching—were far less likely to leave teaching after their first year on the job" (p. 29).

These study results suggest that what keeps teachers in the classroom beyond the first year has much to do with their pedagogical preparation apart from their other qualifications and experiences.

1. Do you know what the legislators in your state think about teacher preparation?

2. What experiences do you think are most important in learning to teach?

3. Can you cite any evidence for either of the perspectives on teacher preparation mentioned above?

Source: Ingersoll, R., Merrill, L., & May, H. (2014). *What are the effects of teacher education and preparation on beginning teacher attrition?* CPRE Research Report (#RR-82). Philadelphia: Consortium for Policy Research in Education, University of Pennsylvania.

UNDERSTANDING AND USING DATA
LICENSURE TEST SCORES

Each state sets the qualifying or cut score that test takers must achieve before they can receive a license to teach in the state. These scores differ across states as shown below:

Test	AR	CT	LA	MS	NV	OH	PA	VA
Biology: Content Knowledge	—	152	150	135	154	148	147	155
Elementary Education: Curriculum, Instruction, & Assessment	—	163	—	135	158	—	168	—
Elementary Education: Content Knowledge	—	—	150	—	—	—	—	143
English Language, Literature, & Composition: Content Knowledge	159	172	160	157	150	167	160	172
Mathematics: Content Knowledge	116	137	125	123	144	139	136	147
Social Studies: Content Knowledge	155	162	149	143	152	157	157	161

Your Task

Respond to the following questions:

1. What does this table tell you about becoming qualified in these eight states?

2. Why are scores not indicated for some states?

3. Why do some states require higher scores than others?

One way to analyze test scores across states is to look for patterns. In the table below, the red highlights indicate the state(s) with the highest qualifying score, and the blue highlights indicate the state with the lowest qualifying score. In some cases, states have qualifying scores that are close, but the range between high and low scores can be as much as 33 for elementary education for the states shown below.

Test	AR	CT	LA	MS	NV	OH	PA	VA
Biology: Content Knowledge	—	152	150	135	154	148	147	155
Elementary Education: Curriculum, Instruction, & Assessment	—	163	—	135	158	—	168	—
Elementary Education: Content Knowledge	—	—	150	—	—	—	—	143
English Language, Literature, & Composition: Content Knowledge	159	172	160	157	150	167	160	172
Mathematics: Content Knowledge	116	137	125	123	144	139	136	147
Social Studies: Content Knowledge	155	162	149	143	152	157	157	161

The Power of a Support Group During Clinical Practice.   Even though teaching involves being with groups of students every day, it can be a lonely profession if teachers don't make time to interact with one another in professional and personal settings. Sharing what works with colleagues and having them react and provide advice should be part of the culture of being a teacher. Other professions such as medicine and architecture require new graduates to practice as interns under the tutelage of experienced doctors or architects during their first years of practice. In many regards, field experiences and student teaching are intended to serve this purpose. Teachers who welcome teacher education candidates into their classrooms as co-teachers represent a special group who are not only experts in their profession but also eager to give back to their profession by helping others succeed. These teachers will guide you through the myriad dimensions of teaching. They will give you feedback on your teaching assignments and actively listen to your concerns. They become your colleagues in learning to laugh when the unexpected happens and to cheer you onward when your steps may not be so sure. They are also responsible for making sure that you meet standards for clinical experience, so they will expect your best effort and may admonish you when your performance is not acceptable. Be ready to accept constructive criticism as well as the praise that will certainly be yours to enjoy.

Understand the Role of Your Mentor or Cooperating Teacher

Many years ago, the *Harvard Business Review* let the business community know that "Everyone Who Makes It Has a Mentor." The article went on to advise new members of business that if they didn't have a mentor, they should go find one (Collins & Scott, 1978). Soon after this pronouncement, the teaching profession began to look at what support mentors to new teachers could provide, and a formal construct for mentoring in teaching was developed. Of course, experienced teachers who serve as mentors to beginning teachers have always been around even without being called mentors. Your cooperating teacher is one of the mentors you will encounter on your journey to becoming a teacher. Other mentors may come in the form of professors, relatives, colleagues, and friends. If you don't seem to have a mentor, ask questions, and one will magically appear.

How to Set the Stage for Success in Your First Teaching Job.   There is so much you need to know before you enter the classroom that first day. It has been said that if you desire a perfect ending, then the beginning must also be perfect. Your teacher education course work and clinical experience will program you for success in your first teaching job, but the guarantee that you will be more than ready rests solely on your shoulders. To paraphrase Eleanor Duckworth, an emeritus professor of education at Harvard, to truly understand a thing you have to learn it for yourself. All the lectures, all the assignments, and all the visits to schools will not have prepared you at all if you have merely gone through your program with your eyes on the degree at the end of the line. The best way to be prepared for that first teaching job is to develop the habit of asking questions, reflecting on each new step you take, collaborating with others, and always trying to broaden the horizon ahead by looking at it through perspectives different from your own.

HOW DO YOU KEEP TRACK OF YOUR GROWTH AS A TEACHER?

As humans, we are strangely programmed to keep track of changes in our environment and in ourselves. We track the weather, our weight, the stock market, and the standing of our favorite football team. We even use almanacs to help us track events that will happen in the future. Teachers use **benchmarks** such as "surviving the first year," "successfully completing a round of parent–teacher conferences," and "having students make Adequate Yearly Progress on standardized exams" to track their progress and to set personal standards for their continuous Professional Development. Teaching is replete with standards of all types. In addition to setting personal standards, it is a teacher's responsibility to be familiar with school district, state, and national standards at all levels.

Know the Standards

You may feel overwhelmed with standards, but if you can't talk about standards during your job interview, you will not be the top candidate for the job. Most schools have adopted a standards-based curriculum and provide their teachers with power standards and Common Core State Standards (you'll find more about the Common Core in Chapter 10). It is not only the standards for the students you will be teaching that affect your work: The teacher education program in which you are enrolled should be standards based. Your program should be preparing you to meet the InTASC standards mentioned earlier in this chapter. You are also expected to know the professional standards for your field (e.g., mathematics or early childhood education). Are you familiar with any of these standards?

Student Standards

New teachers should know the student standards for the subject they will be teaching. All states have developed student standards that indicate what students at different grade levels should know and be able to do in a subject area. The tests that students are required to take annually in mathematics, reading, writing, science, and social studies are based on the state standards. Many state standards are based on national standards developed by national organizations such as the International Literacy Association (ILA), National Council for the Social Studies (NCSS), and American Association for the Advancement of Science (AAAS). These standards provide a guide for what you should be teaching in those core curriculum areas. They can be used to develop your own performance assessments to determine what students are learning. The state tests also provide feedback, although limited, on what students have learned. State standards can be accessed on the website of your state department of education.

Teacher Standards

National professional associations have also developed standards that describe what teachers should know and be able to do to teach a specific group of students (e.g., ELLs or students with disabilities) or a specific subject such as physical education. If teachers meet these standards, they should be able to help students meet the student standards.

After you have taught for three or more years, you may decide to apply for national board certification. The NBPTS standards expect accomplished teachers to do the following:

- Be committed to students and their learning.

- Know the subjects they teach and how to teach those subjects to students.

- Be responsible for managing and monitoring student learning.

- Think systematically about their practice, and learn from experience.

- Be members of learning communities.

In addition to these general expectations, the NBPTS has standards for teaching each subject area for specific age levels such as early childhood, middle childhood, early adolescence, and young adulthood. Your teacher education program will help you develop the foundation to meet these standards later in your career. A number of colleges and universities have redesigned their master's degrees to reflect these standards and help teachers become nationally certified.

There is no time like the present to start down the path toward successful teaching. Take advantage of the assignments and experiences you are required to complete, always thinking about how they relate to the subject or students you will be teaching next week or in a few years. In the activities at the end of each chapter in this book, you are provided opportunities to apply your knowledge to the realities of classrooms and schools. These activities can be incorporated into a portfolio of your work that will show your growth as you learn how to teach over the next year or two, and can be used later during your interview for a job.

Begin a Portfolio

A **portfolio** is a collection of your work, including papers, projects, lesson plans, and assessments. It serves many purposes. During your program, the artifacts (i.e., the documents and presentations) in your portfolio show your growth as a teacher from the first education course you take to completion of the program. Your written papers may have been submitted as part of your course work, or they may be written reflections of your experiences working with students. They show that you understand a particular topic in your field as well as your writing skills, and demonstrate your ability to analyze issues and classroom situations.

Lesson plans, which you will develop later in the program as a detailed guide for your instruction of a topic, show that you understand the subject that you are teaching and that you can select appropriate instructional strategies for helping students learn. Evaluations of your field experiences and student teaching by your school and university supervisors provide evidence of your effectiveness in the classroom. Samples of student work related to the lessons you teach, along with your analysis of the student work, and reflections on how effective your teaching was and what you would do differently the next time, provide evidence that you have the knowledge, skills, and dispositions critical to a teacher's work. The artifacts in your portfolio can serve as evidence that you meet state and professional standards that were discussed earlier in this chapter.

Like architects and artists, new teachers select examples of their best work for portfolios to be presented at job interviews. These portfolios should also include demographic information that presents your credentials: a résumé, transcripts, child abuse clearance, criminal background clearance, and teaching license. Any awards or honors that you have received should be added to this portfolio. Letters of recommendation from faculty and/or your supervising teachers should be included along with any letters of appreciation or commendations from parents or students.

You may not be asked to present a portfolio until you are further along in your program. However, the task of compiling a portfolio will be much easier if you begin now to collect and organize your papers, projects, evaluations, and student work. You may be surprised to see your own growth over time. Technological advances have made the creation of digital portfolios commonplace. One advantage to the electronic portfolio is that it provides you the opportunity to highlight your technology skills—one of the requirements of many standards. To assist you in beginning your portfolio, each chapter in this book suggests one or two tasks for that purpose.

iStock/lisafx

Maintaining a digital record of professional growth and achievements is one way teachers can document their careers and share information with others.

Reflect on Your Observations and Practice in Schools

Reflection, a valued skill in teaching, allows you to think about the effects of your choices and actions on students, parents, and other professionals in the learning community. According to Kottler, Zehm, and Kottler (2005), reflection is among the most important missions of a teacher. It is an extremely complex and demanding process that requires a lifetime of dedication. Others have found that reflection improves the professional knowledge of teachers and serves as a powerful tool for individual learning (Oner & Adadan, 2011). Teachers can achieve Professional Development through continuous reflection (Ayan & Seferoglu, 2011), and reflection can be promoted through documentation of actions. Creating a portfolio is one way you can keep track of what you do and record how well it seems to play out. Once you have the documentation, you can revisit specific events or actions over time and reflect on what might be improved. Reflective teachers are able to articulate why they chose one instructional method over another, analyze the effectiveness of the approach when they use it, and choose another approach for a student who did not learn.

Early in your program, you will be observing teachers and working with small groups of students rather than teaching. However, you can begin to develop your reflection skills in both these school settings and activities in your college classroom. One popular process is the maintenance of **journals** in which you summarize your thoughts about and reactions to the major things you observed or experienced in a class or school. Journal entries should be brief, candid, and personal. You should record how you were affected by the events and why. You may be surprised, angry, puzzled, delighted, or apathetic. You may not believe what you are reading or seeing. You may want to step in and change something. You may have learned a new strategy for accommodating the needs of a student with disabilities. The journal allows you to regularly record (usually daily or weekly) your reflections on what you are learning. As you read your journal later, you will see how your thoughtful reflections helped you define your own teaching.

Begin Collaborating With Peers and Professors

One way to help you determine whether you want to teach is to talk and work with teachers and other school professionals. You will begin to get a better sense of what it is like to be a teacher rather than a student. Ask them why they chose a particular lesson, responded to one student in one way and in a different way to all of the others, and used a particular assessment. Be helpful to the teachers you are observing when they ask for assistance and sometimes even when they don't seem to need your help.

You should begin to develop your collaborative skills as you work with other candidates and professors on campus. You are likely to be assigned to work with your peers on group activities. These activities provide you the opportunity to be a leader in planning and delivering papers and presentations. To be successful, you will have to work with people with whom you have many common experiences and others with whom you have little in common. You may have to assist others, and sometimes do some of their work for the good of the team. When you are in the classroom, you will find similar dilemmas as you work with other teachers. You may also have a better understanding of the group dynamics of students when you assign them to group work in the classroom. It is wise to begin now to learn to collaborate with professional colleagues. In a year or two or three, you will be amazed at where your journey to become a teacher has taken you.

CONNECTING TO THE CLASSROOM

This chapter has provided you with some basic information about the need for qualified teachers, where the jobs are, how to become licensed, and some of the circumstances you might encounter during your first few years of teaching. Below are some key principles for applying the information in this chapter to the classroom.

1. Effective teachers make a difference in student learning.

2. Professional teachers are responsible for the well-being of their clients (students).

3. New teachers have a better chance of success at the start of their careers if they receive support from teachers with more experience.

4. A school's curricula will be guided by the state or school district's standards for students.

5. Teacher standards identify the key knowledge, skills, and dispositions that teachers should demonstrate in the classroom.

6. The collection of your work in a portfolio should provide evidence that you have met standards and that you can help students in your classroom learn.

SUMMARY

Five major points were discussed in this chapter.

- Teaching is a challenging profession that requires its members to be very knowledgeable, skillful, and in possession of the necessary disposition for working with students.

- The rewards of teaching can be both intrinsic and extrinsic, as teachers help students acquire knowledge and develop skills.

- Teacher education candidates need to become familiar with standards for PreK–12 students and standards for

teachers, and to demonstrate competency in content areas through performance on standardized tests.

- Teacher education candidates need to spend time in schools observing experienced teachers and working with students.

- Activities that contribute to a teacher's development include the initiation of a portfolio, reflection on one's practice, and collaboration with colleagues.

KEY TERMS

accreditation 10

benchmarks 28

cut score 21

dispositions 9

English Language Learner (ELL) 17

extrinsic rewards 7

field-based supervisors 21

intrinsic rewards 7

journals 31

lesson plans 6

mentors 10

National Board for Professional Teaching Standards (NBPTS) 11

out-of-field teachers 18

pedagogy 14

performance assessments 21

portfolio 30

profession 5

proficiencies 22

reflections 11

rubrics 11

standards-based curriculum 29

CLASS DISCUSSION QUESTIONS

1. Some teachers believe that the accountability measures imposed by policy makers stifle their creative abilities as teachers. In what ways do you think teacher creativity might be hampered by having to administer Norm-Referenced Tests of student achievement under district or state mandates?

2. What are some of the ways you learned about the teaching profession even before beginning your teacher education program?

3. This chapter suggests that teacher education candidates should be able to show evidence that they meet the InTASC

standards. Why is it necessary for teachers to possess the knowledge, skills, and dispositions identified in these standards? Which of the InTASC standards do you personally find most important? Why?

4. Do you consider teaching a profession similar to law and medicine? Why? Why not?

5. Why is it important to track your professional growth during your teacher education program? How can tracking your growth as a professional help you in the future?

SELF-ASSESSMENT

What Is Your Current Level of Understanding and Thinking About Becoming a Teacher?

One of the indicators of understanding is to examine how complex your thinking is when asked questions that require you to use the concepts and facts introduced in this chapter.

Answer the following questions as fully as you can. Then use the Assessing Your Learning rubric below to self-assess the degree to which you understand the complexities of becoming a teacher.

1. How would you explain to someone who was not an educator why teaching is a profession?

2. Why is it important for teachers to possess specific knowledge and skills?

3. How can a teacher's competency in a content area be assessed?

4. When should someone who is a teacher candidate begin collecting artifacts about his or her professional growth? Why?

Assessing Your Learning Rubric

	Parts & Pieces	Unidimensional	Organized	Integrated	Extensions
Indicators	Elements/concepts are talked about as isolated and independent entities. Some important names are provided in isolation.	One or a few concepts are addressed, while others are underdeveloped, or not mentioned.	Deliberate and structured consideration of all key concepts/elements.	All key concepts/elements are included in a view that addresses interconnections.	Integration of all elements and dimensions, with extrapolation to new situations.
Becoming a teacher	Some reasons and necessary skills are provided with little or no connection between or among them.	Teaching is described in relation to knowledge of content and classroom instruction.	Multiple roles that teachers perform are described.	A holistic view of the many facets of becoming a teacher is provided.	Teaching and becoming a teacher is described as professional growth.

FIELD GUIDE
FOR LEARNING MORE ABOUT . . .

Becoming a Teacher

A field guide is a book or pamphlet people can bring along when exploring their surroundings. The term *field guide* is generally used to help people identify wildlife or other objects in nature. In biology, field guides are designed to help the reader identify specific birds, plants, or fish by studying their features and characteristics. Field guides can help people distinguish one object from another that might look similar but is not.

In this text, the term *field guide* is a metaphor. The activities described at the end of each chapter will help guide you through your investigations of the foundations and purposes of schooling in America. In a sense, you will be creating your own field guide of evidence of teaching and student learning. As a field biologist would do, you should take field notes as you complete the activities outlined for you at the end of each chapter. These notes should include facts and descriptions of your observations. Your field notes should also include date, time of day, the grade or group you are observing, and your reflections and "Aha!" moments. Keeping such detailed data is a form of journaling.

Persons engaged in field work also collect artifacts such as pictures and samples of what they are studying. John James Audubon (1785–1851), an American naturalist, completed more than 400 life-size paintings of birds in his expeditions into the field. You will not be expected to collect a specific number of items or even attempt paintings of the classrooms you visit, but you should have evidence of teaching behavior, student responses, and school organization and culture.

Once you have become comfortable in schools and in the classroom, you should begin to compile your field notes into a portfolio—a collection of evidence of your growth toward becoming a teacher. Each chapter in this text will introduce field guide activities such as observation of the school and classroom environments, specific portfolio tasks, and the practice of journaling. When you complete each of the suggested activities, you will have ample evidence that you have a thorough understanding of schooling in America.

Ask a Teacher or Principal	Ask one new and one experienced teacher to recall their first year of teaching. If they could start over, what would they do differently? What had they been well prepared to handle when they first entered the classroom? What were their greatest challenges? What recommendations do they have for making your first year successful? What amusing stories do they have to tell?
Make Your Own Observations	Both teachers and students are expected to meet standards in today's schools. The NBPTS states that teachers should be (1) "committed to students and their learning," (2) "know the subjects they teach and how to teach those subjects to students," (3) be "responsible for managing and monitoring student learning," (4) "think systematically about their practice and learn from experience," and (5) be "members of learning communities" (NBPTS, 2002). For one of your next visits to a school, select one of these five expectations and record evidence that you see of teachers in the school demonstrating it.

(Continued)

(Continued)

Reflect Through Journaling	Begin an entry in your journal about why you want to teach. Why do you want to teach a specific subject? Why do you want to teach at the preschool, elementary, middle, or high school level? Where would you like to teach when you complete your program? Why do you want to teach in a specific location? What adult, if any, had an influence on your decision to teach? As you observe and work in schools over the next few years, you may want to revisit your reasons for teaching and update them based on your new experiences.
Build Your Portfolio	Many people report that a teacher has made a great difference in their lives. Write a short paper on the influence one or more teachers have made on your life. Describe what the teacher did in the classroom that impressed you. Begin to develop a list of characteristics of teachers who are making a difference. Later you can return to this paper and list to determine if you are developing the same characteristics in yourself as you saw in the teachers you admired.
	Learn the standards for teaching in your state. Make a list of the proficiencies related to knowledge, skills, and dispositions that you are expected to demonstrate in the classroom. During your field experiences, when you achieve one of these standards, place a checkmark by the standard and indicate how you know that you have achieved the proficiency (e.g., the assessment used and your score). As you progress through your teacher education program, continue to add checkmarks until you have met all the standards. This exercise will help you become very familiar with the standards and will also be tangible proof of how much you have learned.
Read a Book	In *Those Who Can*, by Neil Bright (2013), you will read about master teachers and what they do to encourage, inspire, and promote student learning. You will also read about ways teachers express their professionalism both in and out of the classroom. This book is one that you should talk about with other teachers. Bright's comments should be discussed and implemented whenever possible. The book can serve as a guide and a comfort zone when your first forays into teaching do not turn out as you would like.
	In a fresh look at what teachers and administrators can do to make schools places where teacher and students want to be, Nancy Atwell's *Systems to Transform Your Classroom and School* (2013) provides a detailed look at what engaging teachers do to establish environments in which all students can learn. As you read this book, talk and think about ways you will implement some of the practices in your own future classroom.
Search the Web	National Teachers of the Year: Visit www.ccsso.org/national-teacher-of-the-year to see examples of National Teachers of the Year.
	State Licensure Requirements: State licensure requirements can be accessed from the state agency in which you are interested or from the National Association of State Directors of Teacher Education and Certification (www.nasdtec.org), where you can access information on licensure requirements and state agencies responsible for teacher licensing.
	National Education Association: See the website of the NEA (www.nea.org/home/30442.htm) for an example of a code of ethics. You should become familiar with the code of ethics in your state and school district.
	Licensure Tests and Study Guides: For additional information on the licensure tests and study guides, visit the websites of the two major testing companies (www.ets.org and http:// home.pearsonvue.com/Test-Owner/Deliver-your-exam/Pearson-VUE-test-center-network.aspx). You will need to check with your state to determine which tests you will be required to pass.
Additional Web Resources	*Education Week*: The website of *Education Week* at www.edweek.org includes statistics on education and the latest news on educational practices and issues in schools and universities.

STUDENT STUDY SITE

$SAGE edge™

Get the tools you need to sharpen your study skills. **SAGE edge** offers a robust online environment featuring an impressive array of free tools and resources.

Access practice quizzes, eFlashcards, video, and multimedia at **edge.sagepub.com/hall3e**.

2 TODAY'S STUDENTS

TEACHER INTERVIEW

Ms. Kelly Maschari

Kelly Maschari

Ms. Kelly Maschari teaches one of three third-grade classes at Brent Elementary School in Washington, DC, a few blocks from the U.S. Capitol—the house of Congress. Raised in rural Ohio, Ms. Maschari has since expanded her knowledge and experience with cultural diversity after teaching in Hong Kong, Houston, and now the District of Columbia. With a bachelor's degree in business administration and marketing, she began her teaching career as an ESOL (English for Speakers of Other Languages) teacher in Hong Kong where she worked with students from the ages of five months to 13 years at a language center. In Houston, she taught at Ortiz Middle School, a charter school with a majority of Hispanic students. Since arriving in Washington, she has taught at both a charter school and traditional public schools.

Q: **What have you found are successful strategies in working with students from diverse groups?**

A: When students see themselves as a collective team, they become members of a community and active participants in helping each other regardless of their race, economic background, or gender. They learn to ask how they can help each other and their partners. Building a sense of empathy is crucial. Both Brent Elementary School and my previous school use a responsive classroom approach that focuses on social and emotional teaching strategies. We help students develop traits of empathy and caring for each other. The approach works well for most students, but other students need more concrete experiences that aren't part of the responsive classroom.

Involving parents is another critical factor in diverse classrooms. The principal at my school is very successful at engaging parents. I have now set up a consistent routine for communicating with parents and guardians through a newsletter and website that open the door for parents to contact me directly. It is a lot of work, but leads to a great payoff in which parents become more engaged in their children's learning activities. For example,

LEARNING OUTCOMES

After reading this chapter, you should be able to do the following:

1. Illustrate how the race and ethnicity of all students can be respected and valued in classroom activities so that all students have optimal opportunities to learn at a high level.

2. Evaluate the importance of holding high expectations for all students regardless of the socioeconomic status (SES) of their families.

3. Describe at least three instructional programs that are used with English Language Learners (ELLs) and explain some of the advantages and disadvantages of each of them.

4. Explain how you can build on gender differences to provide equitable instruction for both girls and boys.

5. List actions you could take to be supportive of Lesbian, Gay, Bisexual, Transgender, and Queer or Questioning (LGBTQ) students in classrooms and schools.

6. Analyze the impact of the religious beliefs of students and their families on classroom and school practices in your community.

all of the parents of my students were involved in one or more of the nine field trips that the class took last year. Finding an outlet to talk with families about differences that leads to a better understanding of one another's point of view is important.

Q: **What do you enjoy most about teaching students from diverse groups?**

A: Teaching brings me the greatest joy when I'm a part of a moment when a child feels successful in a particular skill, project, or performance.

Questions to Consider

1. What is similar and different about Ms. Maschari's class and the schools with which you are most familiar?

2. How prepared do you think you are to work in the diverse settings in which Ms. Maschari has taught?

3. What do you want to make sure you learn before you begin to work in a school with students from a number of diverse groups with which you have no or limited experience?

INTRODUCTION

The students you will be teaching may be very similar to you, coming from the same racial and ethnic group and from families with the same **socioeconomic status (SES)** as your own family. However, many new teachers find their first jobs in schools with students from groups and **cultures** with which they have little or no firsthand experience. You may have very different experiences than the students in your classroom as a result of your racial or ethnic group membership, native language, SES, and/or religion. Very few schools are segregated by **gender**, so it is likely that not all of your students will be the same **sex** as you, but some of them may have a different **sexual orientation** than you or identify their gender differently than you would expect. You are also likely to have one or more students with a **disability** in the classroom.

Both students and teachers are multicultural. We are all members of different groups in society. Our identities are influenced by our race, ethnicity, gender, SES, native language, religion, sexual orientation, and mental and physical abilities. Being a member of one of these groups impacts how we see ourselves and how we see members of another group. Religion, for instance, may have a great influence on how we think girls and boys should behave. In our society, race and economics define power relationships. Our identities are also determined by others who define us based on their observations of who we are and their experiences or lack of experiences with members of our cultural groups.

One of the keys to being a successful teacher is to care about the students in your classroom. A part of caring is to know the students, their families, and the realities of their everyday lives. This task is much easier in a close-knit community in which most families know one another because they attend the same church, synagogue, temple, or mosque. It is more challenging in large urban and suburban areas in which the histories and experiences of families differ greatly. At the same time, we are more alike than different. Because we are lifelong learners, we should continue to explore our similarities and differences as we learn about each other.

The growing diversity of the student population offers us the opportunity to learn new cultures and expand our cultural competencies. To help all students learn, we should learn as much as possible about groups other than our own before we begin teaching. Learning about the cultures of our students and communities can be one of the joyful outcomes of teaching. This chapter will introduce you to the student diversity you may encounter in your future classrooms.

HOW RACIALLY AND ETHNICALLY DIVERSE ARE OUR SCHOOLS?

We are often asked to identify our race or ethnicity on applications and surveys. Our **ethnicity** is generally determined by the country or countries from which our families or ancestors have come. **Race,** on the other hand, is a sociohistorical concept based on society's perception that differences among people based on the color of their skin exist and that these differences are important. The U.S. Census Bureau places the population into six pan-ethnic and racial groups: black or African American, American Indian or Alaska Native, Asian American, Latino or Hispanic, Native Hawaiian or Other Pacific Islander, and white. We now can choose the category "Two or More Races" to acknowledge our parents or ancestors are from different races. Still, a number of students find it difficult to classify themselves into one of these groups because they do not see themselves as a member of any of them. This section provides a brief introduction to the ethnic and racial diversity of students in schools today. Historical facts of the education experiences of these groups are discussed in Chapter 6, but you are strongly encouraged to engage in further study of these groups.

Race and Ethnicity of the Population

American Indians and Alaska Natives are the indigenous or original people who inhabited the United States. Today, 6.7 million U.S. citizens, or 2% of the population, identify as Native American, American Indian, or Alaska Native, with 2.7 million or 40% identifying as biracial or multiracial (U.S. Census Bureau, 2017b). The federal government recognizes 573 tribal governments (Bureau of Indian Affairs, n.d.), with the largest number of members being Cherokee, Navajo, Choctaw, Mexican American Indian, Chippewa, Sioux (i.e., Dakota, Lakota, and Nakota peoples), Apache, and Blackfeet. The five largest Alaska Native tribes are Yup'ik, Iñupiat, Tlingit and Haida, Alaskan Athabascan, and Aleut. One in five American Indians and Alaska Natives lives on a reservation, on trust lands, or in an Alaska native village. Over two in five American Indians and Alaska Natives live in the western United States, but nearly one in three live in the South (Norris, Vines, & Hoeffel, 2012). States with the largest percentages of American Indians and Alaska Natives are Alaska, Oklahoma, New Mexico, and South Dakota (U.S. Census Bureau, 2017b).

Native Hawaiians and other South Pacific Islanders are also indigenous to their native lands. Although they live in all U.S. states, more than half of them live in Hawaii and California (U.S. Census Bureau, 2018a). Just over 1.5 million residents identify as Native Hawaiians or South Pacific Islanders, with half of them identifying as biracial or multiracial (U.S. Census Bureau, 2017b). This group includes people who identify as Native Hawaiian, Guamanian, Chamorro, Samoan, Tahitian, Tongan, Tokelauan, Marshallese, Palauan, Chuukese, Fijian, Guinean, Solomon Islander, and other Pacific Islander groups (Hixson, Hepler, & Kim, 2012).

The ancestors of most African Americans, who made up 13.4% of the population in 2017 (U.S. Census Bureau, 2017e), involuntarily arrived in this country as slaves beginning in the early 1500s (Guasco, 2017). Over the intervening 500 years, African Americans have developed their own culture out of their African, European, and Native American heritages and their unique experiences in this country. Today, new immigrants from African and Caribbean countries continue to join this pan-ethnic group. Most African American students are greatly influenced by their group membership because of a common history of slavery and discrimination, which continues today. By middle school, most African

First (or Native) Americans live in communities across the United States but continue to celebrate and preserve their heritage in powwows, which are social gatherings that usually include competitive dancing and honor American Indian veterans.

iStock/CatLane

American students have experienced **racism** firsthand or know families or friends who have been negatively affected by racial discrimination.

Asian Americans have immigrated to the United States from numerous countries across the world's largest continent and are currently one of the fastest-growing groups in the country. Chinese Americans are the largest Asian ethnic group in the United States, with 4.9 million residents, followed by Asian Indians (4.1 million), Filipinos (3.9 million), Vietnamese (2.1 million), Korean (1.8 million), and Japanese (1.5 million) (U.S. Census Bureau, 2018a). Nearly half of Asian Americans live in three states: California, New York, and Texas (U.S. Census Bureau, 2017b). They account for over 40% of Hawaii's population and 5.8% of the U.S. population (U.S. Census Bureau, 2017e).

Latinos and Hispanics, who comprised 18.1% of the U.S. population in 2017 (U.S. Census Bureau, 2017e), have ethnic roots in many nations. Mexican Americans are the largest of this pan-ethnic group; other families come from or have ancestors from Mexico, Central America, Cuba, Puerto Rico, the Dominican Republic, South America, and Europe. The Spanish were among the early European explorers in the North and South Americas. When the United States annexed the southwestern part of the country in 1848, Mexicans were the majority population of that region. Over half of the Hispanic population lives in California, Florida, and Texas.

European Americans, who are predominantly white, comprise the largest proportion of the U.S. population. The U.S. Census Bureau reports that non-Hispanic whites were 60.7% of the population in 2017 (U.S. Census Bureau, 2017e) and are projected to be 55.8% in 2030 and 44.3% by 2060. Another 15.6% of the population are Hispanics who report their race as white (Vespa, Armstrong, & Medina, 2018). European Americans have been the dominant, most powerful racial and ethnic group in the United States for centuries. Before the civil rights movement of the 1960s and 1970s, U.S. presidents, governors, Congress, and state legislatures had almost always been comprised of white men.

The Impact of Immigration

Immigration was a major topic in the 2016 election of President Donald Trump and continues to divide Congress and the public. A national survey by the Pew Research Center in 2016 found that 6 in 10 respondents thought that immigrants strengthened the country "'because of their hard work and talents,' while just over a quarter say immigrants burden the country by taking jobs, housing and health care" (G. López & Bialik, 2017, para. 34). These perspectives will continue to be debated as Congress considers new legislation on immigration. In this section, we will look at current immigration statistics and the impact of immigration on education.

The number of immigrants obtaining permanent resident status during the past decade has been approximately 1 million persons per year (U.S. Department of Homeland Security, 2017). Nearly 7 in 10 immigrants live in the West and South, with almost half of them living in California, Texas, and New York (López & Bialik, 2017). Large cities attract immigrants with the largest concentrations found in the metropolitan areas of New York City, Los Angeles, and Miami (U.S. Department of Homeland Security, 2017). Nonmetropolitan areas increasingly are also becoming home to immigrants. As a result, rural, urban, and suburban schools across the country include students from different cultures and with many native languages other than English.

The nations from which immigrants come have changed over time, primarily because of immigration laws set by Congress. When the Johnson–Reed Act was abolished in 1965, immigration from the Eastern Hemisphere increased dramatically. The largest number of authorized immigrants in the 1960s came from Mexico (14%), Germany (7%), Canada and Newfoundland (13%), the United Kingdom (7%), Italy (6%), and Cuba

Before 1965, the majority of immigrants to the United States were from Europe. Since Congress passed the immigration bill of 1965, the number of immigrants from Mexico and Asia has increased dramatically, changing the nation's diversity.

(6%). In 2016, the largest number of authorized immigrants came from Mexico (15%), China (7%), India (5%), Cuba (6%), the Dominican Republic (5%), the Philippines (4%), and Vietnam (3%) (U.S. Department of Homeland Security, 2017). Forty-five percent of the foreign-born population was born in Mexico and other Latin American countries, 27% in Asia, and 18% in Europe (Vespa et al., 2018).

Another group of immigrants is **refugees** who have been recognized by the federal government as being persecuted or legitimately bearing persecution in their home country because of race, religion, nationality, or membership in a specific social or political group. The number of refugees differs from year to year, with a high of over 207,000 in 1980 to a low of 26,785 in 2002, to 84,995 in 2016, and a drop to 53,716 in 2017 (U.S. Department of Homeland Security, 2017; Krogstad & Gonzalez-Barrera, 2018). The largest number of refugees in 2016 came from countries that were at war or engaged in political unrest, including the Democratic Republic of the Congo (19%), Syria (15%), Myanmar (14%), Iraq (12%), and Somalia (11%) (U.S. Department of Homeland Security, 2017).

The most controversial immigration issue in the country is that of unauthorized immigrants, who made up 3.4% of the nation's population in 2015 (López & Bialik, 2017). Seven percent of K–12 students have at least one unauthorized immigrant parent (Passell & Cohn, 2016). Some unauthorized immigrants originally entered the country as travelers or on student or other visas. They extended their stay beyond the authorized date and may be eligible to have their status reclassified as legal at some point if they meet the requirements for employment-based visas, if they are classified as refugees, or if they are sponsored by a family. The number of unauthorized immigrants from Mexico has been on the decline since 2007, with half of the unauthorized immigrants in 2016 being from Mexico and the number from Central America and Asia on the increase. Two in three of the unauthorized immigrants have been in the United States over a decade. Six of ten unauthorized immigrants live in six states— California, Texas, Florida, New York, New Jersey, and Illinois (Krogstad, Passel, & Cohn, 2017)— with the metropolitan areas of New York City, Los Angeles, and Houston being home to the largest concentrations of unauthorized immigrants (Passel & Cohn, 2017).

In 1975, the Texas legislature decided to withhold funds from local school districts for children who were not legally admitted into the United States. The act also allowed school districts to deny enrollment to unauthorized children. When the Supreme Court was asked in *Plyler v. Doe* (1982) to determine the constitutionality of the Texas statute, it ruled that a state cannot deny unauthorized students a public education. School officials cannot ask parents for their immigration status, their Social Security numbers, or other documentation that might expose their status.

Racial and Ethnic Diversity in Schools

The U.S. population is currently predominantly white (61.3%), but less so each year (U.S. Census Bureau, 2017e). By 2060, 44% of the population will be white, and the Latino population will have nearly doubled, comprising 28% of the population (Vespa et al., 2018). The school population reflects the growing diversity of the country more profoundly than the general population because a large number of immigrants are Latino and Asian, and the average age of those groups is younger than whites, resulting in a larger proportion of births. Students of color were 35% of the school-age population in 1995, but were 52% in 2018 and projected to be 55% by 2026, as shown in Figure 2.1 (Snyder, de Brey, & Dillow, 2018). The percentage of African American and American Indian students will remain about the same, while the number of Latino and Asian American students will continue to grow over the next four decades.

The chances that you will teach students from diverse ethnic and racial groups depend on the location of your

"Just how long do you illegal aliens plan on staying in our country?"

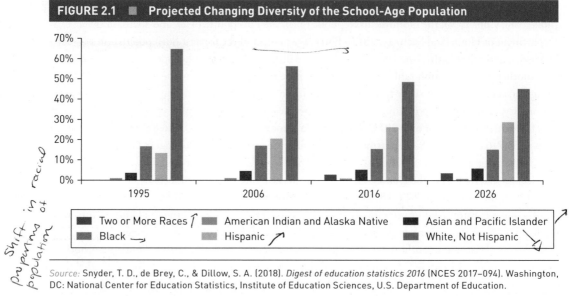

FIGURE 2.1 ■ Projected Changing Divsersity of the School-Age Population

Source: Snyder, T. D., de Brey, C., & Dillow, S. A. (2018). *Digest of education statistics 2016* (NCES 2017–094). Washington, DC: National Center for Education Statistics, Institute of Education Sciences, U.S. Department of Education.

school. The largest concentration of students of color is in the western part of the United States, and the Midwest is the least diverse. The highest concentration of African American students is in the South, where they make up 24% of the student population. Latino students make up 42% and Asian American students 9% of the student population in the West. Already, more than 60% of the public school students in Arizona, California, the District of Columbia, Florida, Hawaii, Maryland, Nevada, New Mexico, and Texas are students of color. Over half of the student population in Delaware, Georgia, Louisiana, Mississippi, and New York are students of color, and the number is approaching 50% in 11 other states (Snyder et al., 2018). Students of color also are the majority of the population in many urban schools across the country.

As shown in Figure 2.2, the diversity of teachers in the nation's schools does not match the ethnic and racial diversity of the student population. Four in five public school teachers are white, and three in four are women (Snyder et al., 2018; Taie & Goldring, 2017). Not all teachers understand their students' cultures or have any experience with them. In these cases, teachers and students may misunderstand each other's cultural cues. Teachers may accept the negative **stereotypes** of students from ethnic and racial groups different from their own. Our "interpretations of student behavior can be misinformed and unnecessary conflicts can result" (Milner, 2015, p. 123). Students and parents may come to believe that the teacher does not respect or value their cultures and experiences. They may feel that the only way to be successful in school is to adopt the teacher's culture, which may lead to the denigration of their own culture. Some adolescents of color resist the dominant culture of schools and sometimes label academically successful peers as "acting white."

Teaching Students From Diverse Racial and Ethnic Groups

How should educators respond to the ethnic and racial diversity in their schools? Many teachers say they are **color blind**, meaning that they don't see the race of their students and treat all students the same. The problem with this approach is that the curricula and activities of most schools predominantly reflect the cultures of European Americans and do not effectively integrate the cultures of students of color. Teaching everyone in the same way does not seem to be working, as shown in the great differences in academic achievement among groups as measured by standardized tests. Instead, you should recognize and integrate the cultures, histories, and experiences of multiple racial and ethnic groups into the curriculum and your instruction so that all students see themselves represented and respected in the classroom.

The Opportunity Gap

Disparities in the academic performance and achievement among groups of students are referred to as the **achievement gap**. Although some students from all groups perform at high levels, achievement

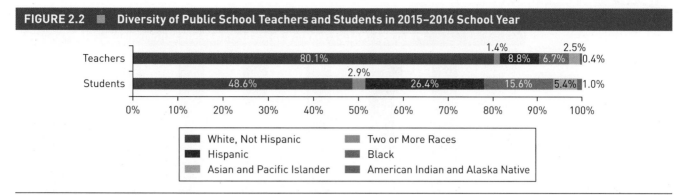

FIGURE 2.2 ■ Diversity of Public School Teachers and Students in 2015–2016 School Year

White, Not Hispanic

Hispanic

Asian and Pacific Islander

Two or More Races

Black

American Indian and Alaska Native

Source for Student Data: Snyder, T. D., de Brey, C., & Dillow, S. A. (2018). *Digest of education statistics 2016* (NCES 2017–094). Washington, DC: National Center for Education Statistics, Institute of Education Sciences, U.S. Department of Education.

Source for Teacher Data: Taie, S., & Goldring, R. (2017). *Characteristics of public elementary and secondary school teachers in the United States: Results from the 2015–16 National Teacher and Principal Survey First Look* (NCES 2017–072). Retrieved from https://nces.ed.gov/pubsearch/pubsinfo.asp?pubid=2017072.

data show that students from white and Asian American families are more likely than other students to score at high levels, graduate from high school and college, and attend professional schools. African American and Hispanic students, and students who live in poverty, do not have the same educational opportunities as students from affluent families. Their Grade Point Averages are lower than those of other students. Their performance on standardized tests is lower, they are less likely to take rigorous courses, they are disproportionately placed in special education, and they are less likely to finish high school in four years.

Another way of looking at academic differences among groups is the availability of opportunities to learn. This **opportunity gap** begins early in the lives of children. Some families are able to provide their children with numerous educational resources and opportunities to travel and participate in education programs during their early years and throughout the school year, especially during summer vacations. Other children have access to few educational resources and suffer from poor health care and nutrition, which can affect their ability to concentrate and focus on school work or even attend school every day. Peer pressure, **tracking** practices, negative stereotyping, test bias, and many other factors also contribute to the achievement opportunities among students. Although poverty is a major factor in the opportunity gap, students of color at all income levels are more likely to experience inadequate or insufficient educational opportunities. Another critical factor in the opportunity gap is that students in poverty and students of color often attend high-poverty schools where more than 75% of the students are eligible for Free or Reduced-Price Lunch (McFarland et al., 2017), and student achievement on standardized tests is more likely to be lower than in other schools.

One of the major challenges for educators is to increase the achievement opportunities for students from different racial and ethnic groups. Schools are required by a federal law, the Every Student Succeeds Act (2015), to annually test public school students to determine if they are meeting state standards in reading and mathematics and report student performance for subgroups of students (e.g., racial and ethnic groups, English Language Learners [ELLs], students from low-income families, and students with disabilities). Students' achievement on standardized tests is the indicator most often used when the achievement gap is being discussed. Although the gap between students of color and white students decreased between 1970 and 1990, it then leveled off, and has not improved significantly since 1990 (Musu-Gillette et al., 2016). An example of the differences in academic performance among ethnic and racial groups of students is shown in Figure 2.3. The challenge for an educator is how to eliminate this achievement gap.

The Children's Defense Fund (2015), an advocacy group for children from low-income families and families of color, reports that many children from families in poverty score lower on measures of cognitive development than affluent children beginning as early as nine months. They enter PreK with lower levels of academic readiness. These gaps grow larger as students continue through school. By the 12th grade, 83% of African American students are not reading at the proficient level, and 93% are

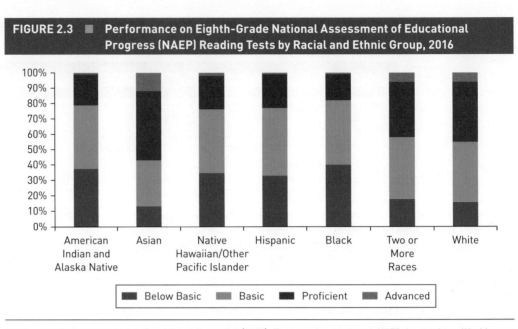

FIGURE 2.3 ■ Performance on Eighth-Grade National Assessment of Educational Progress (NAEP) Reading Tests by Racial and Ethnic Group, 2016

Source: National Assessment of Educational Progress. (2017). *The nation's report card: NAEP data explorer.* Washington, DC: U.S. Department of Education. Retrieved from https://www.nationsreportcard.gov/ndecore/xplore/NDE.

not doing math at the proficient level. Hispanic and American Indian students perform at somewhat higher levels, but still at 18 or more percentage points less than white students (National Assessment of Educational Progress, 2015a).

Elimination of the opportunity gap will require a deliberate effort to provide personalized attention, expert teachers, high-quality curriculum, and more and better learning resources (Darling-Hammond, 2013). Recommendations for reform to improve academic achievement have included reducing class sizes, expanding early-childhood programs, improving the quality of teachers, encouraging more students of color to take high-level courses, and using **culturally responsive teaching** practices in the classroom.

You are likely to be engaged in the work of eliminating the achievement gap, particularly if you teach in a high-poverty school. You may be involved in writing a comprehensive support and improvement plan for your school. You may be working with other teachers and administrators to analyze the test scores for your school and hopefully support each other in helping all students learn at higher levels. In schools where the gap has been eliminated, educators have stopped blaming students and parents for low achievement. Instead, they have taken responsibility for ensuring that students develop the expected outcomes (Boykin & Noguera, 2011). The school districts that have made the most progress in closing the achievement gap in recent years have had educational leaders who prioritize the learning needs of the most vulnerable students (Boykin & Noguera, 2011). Having such a positive impact on a group of students should be celebrated. When students aren't learning, the challenge is to figure out what changes we can make to engage them in their learning.

Race in the Classroom

Race has a profound effect on the life experiences of the U.S. population. The fact that African American and Hispanic students continue to achieve at lower levels than their white peers has become so normalized that many educators have become comfortable with their underperformance, expecting no better. Even some students of color become accustomed to failing grades and may avoid academic pursuits or rigorous courses. When failure becomes so normalized by both educators and students, it becomes extremely difficult to change the outcomes (Boykin & Noguera, 2011). The first step is recognizing the problem. Your job as a teacher will be to do all you can to eliminate the ways that racial identity and the stereotype of failure are reinforced and reproduced in your classroom (Steele, 2010).

The inequitable educational outcomes for students of color are a function of the social context—in this case, their unequal access to key educational resources such as quality teachers and quality curricula (Darling-Hammond, 2013). We need to "embrace students' race and culture as central to their identity and as assets to build on" (Mitchell, Hinueber, & Edwards, 2017, p. 26). Students of color do not always trust teachers from racially privileged groups because those teachers are more likely not to understand the impact of race on their lives (Howard, 2014). Racism's impacts on interactions in the classroom, the curricula, and school policies have often been ignored or not validated by educators.

Schools that have been successful at achieving academic results for African American students don't avoid addressing race directly (Mitchell et al., 2017). Specifically, they focus on increasing the academic achievement of students of color. They teach about race, culture, class, and power and their impact on making communities vulnerable. They "foster strong relationships between educators and black students" (p. 24). Finally, classroom environments promote excellence and support students in taking responsibility for their own learning.

Eliminating racism in schools and society requires the involvement and action of citizens from diverse racial and ethnic groups.

iStock/Alexander Gouletas

Well-known psychologist, author, and president emerita of Spelman College Beverly Daniel Tatum (2017) says that we need "meaningful, productive dialogue [about race] to raise consciousness and lead to effective action and social change" (p. 331). Race and racism are topics not easily discussed in most classrooms. Students of color almost always have experienced racism and discrimination, whereas few white students have direct experiences with racism and sometimes don't believe it exists. Students of color generally are more comfortable talking about race and racism. White students may be more reluctant to join those discussions because they fear they will say the wrong thing or they have limited knowledge about the topics (Tatum, 2017). Discussion can evoke emotions of anger, guilt, shame, and despair. Most students think of the United States as a just and democratic society. Therefore, it may be difficult for them to confront the contradictions that support racism. Nevertheless, we need to confront our own racism and students' racism to begin to overcome the racial gaps that exist in society.

HOW DOES FAMILY INCOME AFFECT A STUDENT'S SCHOOL EXPERIENCES?

Schools generally reflect the income and wealth of the families of their students. More-affluent families have more economic, social, and political resources and, as a result, better schools. Even within a school, students are sometimes classified and sorted by their economic conditions, giving the advantage to students from higher-income families. As the nation has moved away from efforts to desegregate schools, students are increasingly segregated by economic levels with a disproportionate number of Hispanic and African American students enrolled in high-poverty schools. In Ms. Maschari's third-grade classroom, these economic differences can become quite clear in the students' morning meeting when, for example, an affluent student reports that he and his father went to the Wimbledon tennis tournament in London over the weekend.

Economic Diversity of Students

The lack of family resources affects the quality of housing and the environment in which students live, the food they eat, the way they dress, and the educational resources to which they have access. These economic conditions can also have a great impact on the quality of education they receive. Their schools may not have up-to-date laboratories and technology. Their teachers may not have majored in the subjects they are assigned to teach, and they may have a higher absentee rate than students in schools that serve more-affluent communities. With the opportunity gap with which these students enter schools, they need the best teachers and a great deal of support from school officials and the community to ensure they learn at the same levels as their more-affluent peers. However, they are more likely to attend schools with unlicensed teachers, teachers who are not prepared to teach the subjects they are assigned, and fewer resources for enrichment activities that support critical thinking and expand their experiences with the latest technology and arts to nurture their creativity.

Students in Low-Income Families

Family members with low incomes may be temporarily unemployed or working at low wages because of a family illness or because they have lost a job as a result of economic conditions. A very small portion of the population is persistently poor as measured by living in poverty for eight or more years. However, there are many working poor who hold part-time jobs or full-time jobs that pay the minimum wage of $7.25 per hour or $15,080 annually, but who can't pull themselves out of poverty with such a low income. Work in minimum-wage jobs can be sporadic, and unemployment is unpredictably affected by the economy. Fringe benefits usually are not available, leaving many of these workers without health insurance or vacation time.

Poverty differs by age, race, and ethnicity, as shown in Figure 2.4. Although the number of whites in poverty is greater than any other group, the percentage of all whites in poverty is less than other groups, with a larger percentage of Native Americans being in poverty than any other group, followed by African Americans and Hispanics. Generally, the poverty rate for Asian Americans is near that of whites, although some Asian ethnic groups have high poverty levels.

Because families of color generally earn less than white families, their children are more likely to be impoverished. Thus, the rate of poverty is greater for children of color, with 35% of American Indian, 34% of African American, and 28% of Latino children living in poverty, as compared with 12% of white and Asian children (Koball & Jiang, 2018).

One in four public schools is a high-poverty school in which more than three in four of the students live in families that are in poverty. African American and Latino students are six times more likely than white and Asian American students to attend high-poverty schools. As you might guess, a majority of

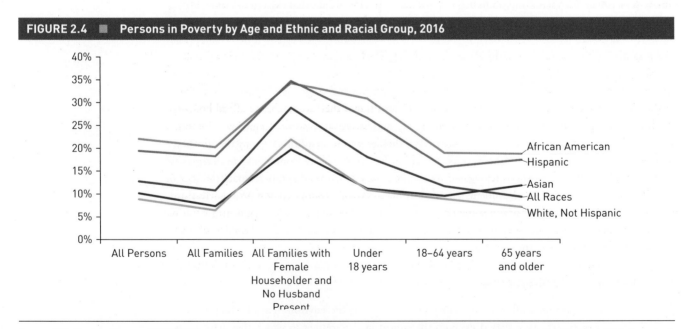

FIGURE 2.4 ■ Persons in Poverty by Age and Ethnic and Racial Group, 2016

Source: U.S. Census Bureau. (2016b). Historical poverty tables: People and families—1959–2016. *Current Population Survey: Annual social and economic supplement.* Retrieved from https://www.census.gov/data/tables/time-series/demo/income-poverty/historical-poverty-people.html.

students in city schools attend high-poverty schools, while a majority of suburban students attend low-poverty schools (McFarland et al., 2017).

Schools classify students as low income by the criteria that make them eligible to participate in the Free or Reduced-Price Lunch program. To be eligible for a Free or Reduced-Price Lunch, family income must fall below 130% of the federal poverty level, or $32,630 for a family of four in the 2018–2019 school year (Federal Register, 2018). For a subsidized lunch, family income must fall between 130% and 185% of the federal poverty level, or between $32,631 and $46,435 for a family of four. Half of all public school students in the United States were eligible for Free or Reduced-Price Lunch in 2015 (Snyder et al., 2018).

When students from low-income families are the majority of the students in a school, they are more likely to have low test scores, unsafe and unattractive schools, and less-than-stimulating schoolwork that has little meaning for their lives. From the beginning of their school career, they are too often not expected to go to college. They are not proportionately picked to lead groups, assigned to AP classes and gifted and talented programs, or encouraged to participate in extracurricular activities other than specific sports. You could conclude that these students are being prepared for jobs that more-affluent people are unwilling to take.

What does living in a low-income family mean for children and teenagers? For one, they are in poorer health than students in higher-income families. They have a greater incidence of vision and hearing problems, especially those caused by ear infections. They lack dental care, leading to tooth-aches. They have greater exposure to lead in water pipes, which affects their cognitive functioning and behavior. They are more likely to have asthma, especially when living in densely populated neighbor-hoods. They are less likely to have regular medical care and may lack health insurance. They suffer from food insecurity, and their nutrition is often poor. The lack of affordable housing results in their families moving from one school district to another. All of these factors affect school attendance and their ability to concentrate and attend carefully to their work when they are in school (Rothstein, 2013).

As a result, students in low-income families are also less likely than those in higher-income families to graduate from high school and pursue postsecondary education. Only 67% of the students from low-income families are enrolled in a two-year or four-year college immediately after high school, as compared to 83% of the students from high-income families (Snyder et al., 2018).

Students Who Are Homeless

Nearly 3.5 million children and young adults in the United States were homeless at some time during the previous year. One in ten young adults between the ages of 18 and 25 was homeless or **couch surf-ing** over a 12-month period. The rate of homelessness was less for adolescents ages 13–17, but was still 1 in 30 adolescents (Morton, Dworsky, & Samuels, 2017). The National Alliance to End Homelessness (2018) reports that in 2016, "half a million people in families stayed at a homeless shelter or transitional housing program—292,166 were children, and 144,991 were under the age of six" (para. 2). Homeless people are not always unemployed: Some work at such low wages they are unable to afford housing. Other homeless people have lost their jobs or have become estranged from their families. Homeless women may have left home to escape violent relationships. Homeless teenagers may have left home to avoid abuse and severe family dysfunctions.

Public schools must provide educational rights to homeless children and youth. The **McKinney–Vento Homeless Assistance Act** requires school districts to provide transportation for homeless stu-dents to stay in their schools of origin if their parents request it. Enrollment cannot be denied because homeless students do not have their school records, immunization records, proof of residency, or other documents. The school district's liaison for homeless students is expected to advocate for them, helping them access available services in the school system and community. The U.S. Department of Education reports that over a million homeless children and youth are enrolled in school (Paulson, 2014).

Middle-Class Families

Many Americans identify as middle class. It is a category that often includes everyone who works steadily and is not a member of the upper class. It ranges from service workers to well-paid professionals.

Many students identify themselves as middle class, which generally means that one or both of their parents are working and their family is buying a home or has stable living arrangements.

This group includes white-collar workers who work in offices as secretaries, administrative assistants, and managers. It also includes many blue-collar workers who are involved in manual labor. Middle-class workers generally have greater job security and better fringe benefits than low-income workers. However, many families live from paycheck to paycheck, not earning enough to accumulate wealth. Both parents often work to make ends meet.

The number of African Americans and Latinos who are in the middle class has increased over the past five decades, but whites and Asian Americans continue to have disproportionately high representation in this group. The upper middle class usually has high educational expectations for its children, expecting them to attend college or receive training after they finish high school. Families are more directly engaged with schools than most less affluent families.

Families with higher incomes can choose to send their children to private schools or contribute to school funds to pay for art, music, and additional teachers. They not only have computers at home but also ensure that their children have access to the latest technology. When their children are not learning at the level expected, they hire tutors. Their children participate in enrichment activities such as academic summer camps when they are not in school. Income provides the advantages to ensure that the children of higher-income families are able to achieve at high academic levels and attend college.

Providing Equity in Schools

Most students who live in poverty have learned how to live in a world that is not imaginable to most middle-class students and teachers. However, their knowledge and skills do not always fit into the middle-class orientation of schools. Students should see ordinary working people as valued members of society. They should see low-income families as contributing members of the school community, rather than as second-class citizens who are not expected to be involved in their children's education.

TEACHERS' LOUNGE

STUDENTS DON'T CARE WHAT YOU KNOW UNTIL THEY KNOW THAT YOU CARE

It has been my experience while teaching middle and high school that students from diverse groups do not care what you have to say until they know that you care. Teaching is getting students to do what you want them to do while having them think it is their idea, because everybody loves their own ideas. This takes me into my experience with two of my middle school students in Henderson, North Carolina. Teaching math to students when it is not their favorite subject can be a bit of a task. I had one student in particular who was having problems, and I tutored him after school. We began to develop a student–mentor relationship that was of significant importance because the student lacked any male guidance. His family welcomed my relationship with the student. As a result, I was granted permission to take the student and his brother for an afternoon out on the town. We went to the movies and had dinner in a nice restaurant and spent time enjoying each other's company at my expense. At the time, this did not seem to be a big deal to me; however, it was a huge deal to the students. The students became ambassadors for me at the school and model students. The students realized that I really cared about them and that I wanted the best for them. The new challenge was that every student wanted to go to dinner and a movie with me now. You never know what you may be to a student and what need you fill. When you let them know you care, they will allow you to lead them where they need to go.

Peter M. Eley, PhD
Fayetteville State University
Fayetteville, North Carolina

One of the first steps to ensuring you serve students from low-income families is to reflect on your perceptions of these students and their families. Do you think they will attend college? Do you think their families value education? Do you think they are likely to use drugs or participate in other harmful behaviors? Do you believe they are lazy and want to take advantage of government benefits? Negative stereotypes can affect your ability to work effectively with students who live in low-income families and help them achieve at high levels.

Teachers are critical in ensuring that students from low-income families are provided all of the opportunities possible in the classroom. They are assisted in this process by schools that have created a culture for what Budge and Parrett (2018) call "disrupting poverty." These schools are "places where people (adults and students) authentically [feel] they belong, [have] a purpose, [are] empowered and supported, and [know] they [are] safe" (p. 12). Budge and Parrett have found that the teachers in high-performing, high-poverty schools care about students and intentionally foster relationships with students. They also have empathy for students, understand the challenges they face, and believe they can meet high standards with appropriate support. Teachers provide opportunities to help students achieve at levels equal to their more advantaged peers. Teachers take responsibility for student learning. When students are not learning, teachers reteach lessons using different instructional strategies to make the content meaningful to students. Finally, teachers continue to confront their own biases and have the courage to try to overcome the barriers to learning that some students face.

Teacher Expectations

Sociologists have documented the classification and segregation of students based on their race and economic status beginning in their first days of school. Most teachers can quickly identify the **cultural capital** that students bring to school. At the same time, many teachers develop expectations for their students' behavior and academic achievement. Often unknowingly, they then develop instruction and interactions with their students that ensure they will behave as the teachers expect—a phenomenon called the **self-fulfilling prophecy**.

If a teacher's goal is to spend extra time with students who are struggling with academics with the intent of ensuring that they develop the academic skills necessary to move to a higher level, a grouping strategy might be successful. The problem is that too often students identified as having lower academic ability at the beginning of the year end the school year with little improvement in their skills, just as the teacher had projected early in the year. Unfortunately, their lack of academic growth during that year usually follows them throughout their school career.

When teachers make such judgments about students based primarily on their social class status, they are preventing them from having an equal opportunity for academic achievement (Gershenson & Papageorge, 2018). In these cases, a teacher's expectations for student achievement lead to the confirmation of the self-fulfilling prophecy. The practice is not congruent with the democratic belief that all students deserve equal education opportunities. One of the joys of teaching is to overcome the odds against students whose families are low income by guiding them to academic performance at the same level as their more-affluent peers. You should expect all of your students to meet rigorous academic requirements regardless of the income of their families. If you require less of low-income students, they may think that you don't think they are as capable as the other students.

Tracking

Tracking is an educational strategy that separates students for instruction, primarily based on their academic abilities. Students may be placed in a specific education track based on their native language or disability. Students may choose or be assigned to a college, vocational, or general track that determines the courses they take. However, these assignments are sometimes based on teachers' or counselors' judgments of a student's future potential. Some students are placed in gifted programs and others in programs that are clearly designed for low-ability students.

SES matters in tracking practices. Test scores, which may be used to track students, are more closely correlated to the education level, or social class, of students' parents than to their academic potential. The same pattern applies to placement of students in high-ability classes. Students in high-ability courses and programs are academically challenged with enrichment activities that improve their intellectual and critical-thinking skills. Courses for students classified as low ability are often characterized as uninviting and boring. They include oral recitation and structured written work that are related to low-status knowledge. In addition, many teachers in these classrooms spend more time on administration and discipline than actually teaching the subject matter, keeping students at the lowest level of academic achievement. These students are most likely to be taught by the least qualified and least experienced teachers in a school. Students from low-income families are also disproportionately assigned to low-ability groups. They also are more likely to be classified as mentally challenged than are their classmates from more-affluent families.

Tracking has led to the **resegregation** of students based on race, class, and language into separate programs within the school (Tyson, 2013). White middle-class students are disproportionately represented in gifted and talented programs, while African Americans, Latinos, students from low-income families, and ELLs are the majority of the students in low-ability classrooms and special education programs. Schools could be accused of discriminatory practice in placing these students in low-ability courses and programs because they are limiting students' educational opportunities and potential for later occupational and economic success.

THINKING DIFFERENTLY
MIX IT UP!

ERIC SEALS/KRT/Newscom

How can you encourage students to interact with students from cultures, religions, and socioeconomic levels that are different from their own? This goal is a longtime project, but you can start the process in your own classroom as you promote and support intergroup activities. As you assign students to groups, you can ensure that students are interacting with both boys and girls, with students from different racial, religious, and socioeconomic groups, and with students who have different native languages.

Over a decade ago, the Southern Poverty Law Center and its Teaching Tolerance project initiated an activity at the school level to improve intergroup relations. Mix It Up at Lunch Day was designed to encourage students "to identify, question, and cross social boundaries." This activity has two goals for students: (1) meet someone new and (2) engage in positive conversations. It does take planning to make the activity work, but the Teaching Tolerance team recommends the following six steps to make it happen:

1. Create a Planning Team that includes enthusiastic students and adults in the school community, including parents and custodians.

2. Determine a Lunchtime Activity that will ensure that students meet someone new and have a positive conversation.

3. Make It Festive by having a theme, decorating the tables, and having fun activities.

4. Publicize the Event using email, calendars, newsletters, morning announcements, posters, fliers, and social media so that everyone in the community knows the details.

5. Capture the Day in photographs and with interviews that can be shared. Alert the local TV station or newspaper.

6. Evaluate, Debrief, and Follow-up by collecting data from students through a show of hands in an elementary classroom or an electronic survey in middle and secondary classes after the event. Review these data in a post-event planning meeting to share what worked and what you would do differently next year. Plan two follow-up activities to sustain good intergroup relations.

For more information on Mix It Up at Lunch Day and other resources related to issues addressed in this chapter, Google Teaching Tolerance at Southern Poverty Law Center.

WHAT IF STUDENTS' NATIVE LANGUAGES ARE NOT ENGLISH?

Language diversity is valued in most countries of the world. The populations of many European, Middle Eastern, African, and Asian countries are bilingual or multilingual. In today's global world, in which many companies operate internationally, employees who know more than one language and culture can be an asset to the company, especially in its interactions with other nations in the areas of commerce, defense, education, science, and technology. Bilingualism is also an asset for jobs such as hotel clerks, airline attendants, social workers, nurses, teachers, and police officers, who may be interacting with individuals who speak little or no English.

Language Diversity of Students

More than 63 million residents of the United States speak a language other than English at home (U.S. Census Bureau, 2016a). Many are recent immigrants whose children are learning English in school. Nearly four in five U.S. residents speak only English. Of the one in five people who speak a language other than English at home, more than half of them report that they speak English "very well" (U.S. Census Bureau, 2016a).

Three in four of the ELLs receiving ELL services in public schools speak Spanish (Snyder et al., 2018). Over the past decade, the percentage of Hispanic students who speak Spanish at home has been declining, due in large part to the decline in immigration and the growth in the number of U.S.-born Hispanics. Ninety-seven percent of new immigrant families speak Spanish to their children, but that drops to 71% in second-generation families with one immigrant parent, and to less than half of third-generation families (M. Lopez, Krogstad, & Flores, 2018). Other languages spoken most often at home by ELLs are Chinese, Tagalog, Vietnamese, French, Korean, German, and Arabic (U.S. Census Bureau, 2016c). Between 30% and 45% of the population in California, Texas, New Mexico, New York, New Jersey, and Nevada speak a language other than English at home, as shown in Figure 2.5. Other than Florida, most southern states have a limited number of non-English speakers (U.S. Census Bureau, 2016a).

FIGURE 2.5 ■ Percentage of Population Speaking a Language Other Than English at Home, 2016

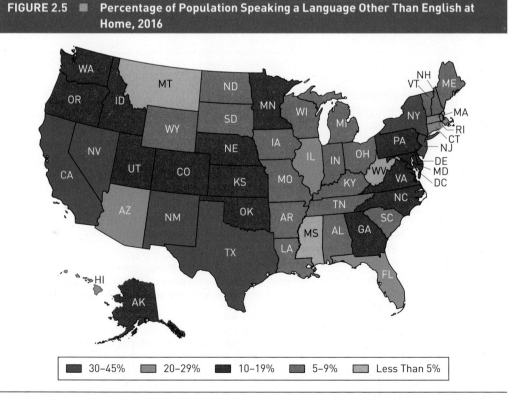

Legend: 30–45% | 20–29% | 10–19% | 5–9% | Less Than 5%

Source: U.S. Census Bureau. (2016a). Language spoken at home. *2012–2016 American Community Survey 5-year estimates.* Retrieved from https://factfinder.census.gov/faces/tableservices/jsf/pages/productview.xhtml?pid=ACS_16_5YR_S1601&prodType=table.

Teaching English Language Learners (ELLs)

Immigrants come to the United States with different levels of education. Almost as many of the foreign-born population hold bachelor's degrees as the native population. At the same time, 3 in 10 foreign-born adults do not have a high school diploma—three times as many as the native-born population (U.S. Census Bureau, 2016d). Immigrants come from different socioeconomic levels, some entering the country with limited economic resources and some entering with enough resources to invest in or begin a business. Their education credentials and economic status in their home countries may give them the social and cultural capital that makes it easier for them to fit into the dominant society (Kubota & Lin, 2009).

UNDERSTANDING AND USING DATA
ELL PERFORMANCE ON A STANDARDIZED TEST

Earlier in the chapter, you learned that students from some racial and ethnic groups are more likely to score at high levels than students from other groups on the National Assessment of Educational Progress (NAEP) tests that are given to a sample of K–12 students every three years. Let's now analyze the most recent NAEP data on performance on mathematics tests by ELL status and family income.

| Grade | English Language Learner | | | | | Not English Language Learner | | | | |
	%	below Basic	at Basic	at Proficient	at Advanced	%	below Basic	at Basic	at Proficient	at Advanced
4th	11	47	39	13	2	89	17	39	34	9
8th	6	71	23	5	1	94	27	36	26	11
12th	4	79	15	5	#	96	37	38	22	3

\# Rounds to zero

| Grade | Eligible for Free or Reduced-Price Lunch | | | | | Not Eligible for FRPL | | | | |
	%	below Basic	at Basic	at Proficient	at Advanced	%	below Basic	at Basic	at Proficient	at Advanced
4th	51	31	44	22	3	43	9	34	43	14
8th	46	45	37	15	3	47	18	35	32	16
12th	40	54	35	10	1	52	28	40	28	4

% does not add up to 100 because information was not available for all students

1. Overall, how are students performing at the three grade levels (e.g., are they improving as they progress through school)?

2. What is the gap between the performance of ELLs and non-ELLs? What is it between students eligible for FRPL and those who are not eligible?

3. What is the relationship of proficiency levels for ELLs and students eligible for FRPL? Based on the information in this chapter, why are ELLs performing at such a low level on this mathematics test?

4. If these were the proficiency levels for students at your school, what do the data suggest for you as a teacher at the level that you plan to teach even if you are not planning to teach math?

The children in immigrant families also have different educational experiences. Some have never been in school and know no English. Metropolitan areas with large numbers of immigrant students may have established special schools or newcomer programs for those students to learn English and be introduced to the U.S. culture. Other children have strong educational backgrounds and are fluent in English. Some families work hard to retain the native language from one generation to another, using their native language at home or sending their children to classes to learn their native language and culture. They are helped in this process when they live in communities that value bilingualism.

Your major challenge in working with ELLs will be to ensure they are learning the content that you are teaching. An advantage to being able to use the native languages of students in the classroom is that students can use resources in their native languages, and you can check their understanding in their native language if you, a teaching assistant, or a volunteer speak that language. The primary reason that ELLs do not perform as well as some of their peers on standardized tests is that they do not possess the English proficiency to understand the content that is being taught in the classroom. Although students can become orally proficient in three to five years, it generally takes four to seven years to develop the academic English used for many assessments (Hakuta, Butler, & Witt, 2000). In addition to the opportunity gap of limited academic English proficiency, many of these students are members of families with low incomes and attend high-poverty schools that further limit their access to the enriched educational resources that would provide the necessary support to develop their knowledge and skills to the same level as their more-affluent native-English-speaking peers (Gándara, 2013).

Bilingual Education

Programs for ELLs vary across school districts, with differences often based on the desires of the immigrant families or politics of the area. Bilingual education, which uses students' native languages and English in instruction, is the most controversial because it values the native language and supports its use in school. Bilingual programs require teachers or teachers' aides who speak the native language to ensure students are understanding concepts and developing academic skills while they learn English. The goal of two-way immersion, two-way bilingual, or dual-language programs is students' development of strong skills and proficiency in both the home language and English (National Clearinghouse for English Language Acquisition [NCELA], 2017).

Other programs that focus on students developing literacy in two languages include transitional or early-exit bilingual education programs. Instruction in these programs is in the home language while English is introduced to help ensure that students are learning academic content. Although these students are gradually moved into English-only classrooms, they continue to receive support for their native language development (NCELA, 2017).

The Office of English Language Acquisition at the U.S. Department of Education also offers grants for the study of indigenous languages. The program supports the preservation and revitalization of the native languages of American Indians, Native Hawaiians, and Native Pacific Islanders while encouraging a focus on developing English proficiency to meet state academic standards (U.S. Department of Education, 2016).

Immersion classrooms use both the home language and English for instruction with the goal of students becoming bilingual. Students in developmental or maintenance bilingual programs share the same native language. In two-way immersion and two-way bilingual programs, English-speaking students are learning a second language while ELLs are learning English. Some school districts offer other immersion programs in elementary schools for English speakers to learn and use a second language such as Chinese, French, or Spanish.

Many classrooms across the country include students who are foreign born or who have one or more foreign-born parents.

iStock/FatCamera

English as a Second Language (ESL) is the most common program used in schools. Students' native languages are not used for instruction in ESL; instruction is provided only in English. Sheltered English instruction or content-based ESL programs usually include students from multiple linguistic and cultural backgrounds in the same class. Visual aids and the home language are used to help students learn English. Students in Structured English Immersion (SEI) programs are usually all ELLs who are learning English. Other programs for developing English fluency include the pullout ESL or English Language Development (ELD) programs. Students are pulled out of the classroom for English instruction that focuses on grammar, vocabulary, and communication skills. In the push-in ESL program, ELLs are in a regular English-only classroom where an ESL teacher or teacher's aide translates if needed and uses ESL strategies to help students learn the content (NCELA, 2017). Newcomer programs for immigrant students who know limited English use ESL to help students learn English, the content, and the common culture (Short & Boyson, 2012).

As the population of the United States becomes more diverse, with larger numbers of people speaking languages other than English, teachers will need to know how to teach ESL. Most universities offer one or more courses on ESL or SEI that could expand your skills and make you more attractive to school districts with growing ELL populations. Speaking a second language that is common in the area in which you plan to teach can also provide you with an advantage when seeking a teaching position.

WHAT IS THE RELATIONSHIP OF GENDER AND EDUCATION?

Men and women often segregate themselves at social gatherings and participate in gender-specific leisure activities. Boys and girls generally choose different games to play. Sometimes students are segregated by sex in schools or school activities, especially sports. We often hold stereotypical perceptions of ourselves and the other sex. We disproportionately enter different occupations and have access to different financial opportunities. These differences are reflected in what is studied in school, how students interact with each other, and how teachers interact with students. In this section, we will explore how education is affected by gender and how teachers can ensure they provide an equitable education for their female and male students.

Differences Between Females and Males

Sex is the term used to identify ourselves as male or female based on biological differences, while *gender* refers to the socially constructed roles, behaviors, and psychological traits typically associated with our sex or our gender identity. Gender today is no longer viewed as simply the male or female binary. It is more of a spectrum based on our sex at birth, which could be both male and female; our personal gender identity; and our gender expression.

Physical differences between males and females can usually be determined by appearance alone. Before age 8, boys and girls have similar hormonal levels and similar physical development. During puberty, hormonal levels of estrogen and testosterone change; these hormones control the physical development of the two sexes. However, physical differences between the sexes, such as upper body strength, can be altered with good nutrition, physical activity, practice, and different behavioral expectations (Eliot, 2012).

Intelligence tests show no differences in the general intelligence between males and females, but studies

David Grossman/Alamy Stock Photo

Most observers of children, including parents and teachers, see differences in the behavior of boys and girls in classrooms, on the playground, and at home.

have found some gender differences in mathematical, verbal, and spatial skills. Psychologist Michael Gurian, physician Leonard Sax, and other popular writers have been reporting for many years that differences between boys and girls are due to innate biological differences. They argue that females favor the left hemisphere of the brain associated with intuitiveness and creativeness, while males tend to favor the left, having greater right-hemisphere specialization that supports logical and analytical reasoning and skills. However, neuroscientists have not found these left-brain/right-brain differences, and they don't connect the subtle differences that do exist to the differences between males and females (Eliot, 2012; Fine, 2011; Jordan-Young, 2011; Kosslyn & Miller, 2013). Nevertheless, proponents of brain-based differences based on sex have had an influence in schools. They have argued that teachers who know these hemispheric differences have a better understanding of why boys and girls behave the way they do in classrooms (Eliot, 2012; Fine, 2011). They report that teachers design lessons and organize their classrooms based on the way that girls learn, which they argue leaves boys academically behind their female peers.

Other researchers attribute most male and female differences to the environment and socialization patterns learned from their parents, relatives, teachers, and peers (Eliot, 2012; Fine, 2011). Schools historically reinforce society's view of gender. Girls are expected to display feminine traits and boys masculine traits. In school, girls are expected to be quieter and better behaved than boys. Girls are more likely than boys to be encouraged to break out of their stereotypical modes. Many parents today tell their daughters that they can be whatever they want. They play on sports teams, are the leaders in many school activities, and attend college at higher rates than boys. Women and girls may struggle to develop a balance between their femininity and their participation in a masculine world.

Young men are generally encouraged to be independent, assertive, leaders, self-reliant, and emotionally stable. They are pushed toward these characteristics, in part, to prevent them from being labeled *gay* or a *sissy*, which could lead to harassment by others. As a result, they sometimes go overboard in proving their masculinity (Kimmel, 2009). The problem is that not all males fit the masculine stereotype: Some are empathic and caring, which are commonly recognized as feminine characteristics. Some critics of feminism declare that boys have been harmed by all of the attention on the education of girls and women, which they think has led to the lower participation of young men in college. It is true that some young men are not adjusting well, as shown in the statistics on their high rates of suicide, binge drinking, and steroid use; they are also more likely to be victims of homicide and car crashes. Psychologists do not always agree on the reasons why a number of boys and young men seem to be at risk today. Some argue that boys are programmed for a culturally determined masculine identity with little room for divergence.

Ms. Maschari indicated that she has observed over her career that girls and boys begin to segregate in the second grade: "By the third grade, they are definitely segregating themselves by sex in the classroom, in the lunchroom, and at recess. I mix them up for group work. When we line up for different activities, I line them up by birthdays and other factors, but never by sex or gender."

Delivering an Equitable Education for Girls and Boys

Teachers are expected to treat all students equally and to encourage academic excellence in all of their students. Whether a student exhibits masculine or feminine characteristics or both, a teacher has the responsibility to exhibit unconditional positive regard for him or her, to recognize the student's special talents and needs, and to provide a learning environment that fosters acceptance and understanding.

Federal legislation governing elementary and secondary education includes Title IX of the Education Amendments of 1972, which makes it illegal to treat students differently or separately on the basis of gender. It requires that all programs, activities, and opportunities offered by a school district be available equally to both males and females. You should be concerned about the academic performance of both boys and girls. You should be asking why so few girls are majoring in computer science and engineering in college, and you should be developing strategies for increasing their participation in those fields. The fact that boys are not performing as well on reading tests suggests that new strategies for involving them in reading and language arts are needed to ensure they are reading at grade level or above. You should wonder why boys are not graduating from high school and not enrolling or finishing college at the same

CHALLENGING ASSUMPTIONS
MYTH: TEACHERS INTERACT WITH ALL STUDENTS IN THE SAME WAY REGARDLESS OF RACE AND GENDER.

The Research

Drawing on 20 years of fieldwork in 11 elementary classrooms in the Midwest and South, a researcher traced the origins of school experiences for students of different races and genders. She also explored the implications of how teachers and students interacted based on their race, gender, and status.

White girls had the most positive interactions with teachers. They received frequent praise from teachers for their good behavior and academic work. In addition, teachers chatted with them about personal issues. For the most part, white girls understood the classroom routine and rules, followed the rules, and focused on the teachers.

Black males, on the other hand, had limited interactions with teachers, and those interactions were almost always negative and initiated by the teacher, not by the boys and young men. Teachers tended to monitor or criticize their behavior or academic work. Black boys were much more likely to interact with their peers than with their teachers. White boys and black girls had a more balanced ratio of interactions with teachers and peers. Their relationships with teachers were cordial, but not as close as those of white girls.

The researcher concluded that schools do more to enhance than to diminish gender and race differences among African American girls, white girls, African American boys, and white boys. Although teachers do not appear to consciously intend to support white girls more than other students, such practices help ensure inequality in a classroom.

Source: Adapted from Grant, L. (2004). Everyday schooling and the elaboration of race-gender stratification. In J. H. Ballantine & J. Z. Spade (Eds.), *Schools and society: A sociological approach to education* (2nd ed., pp. 296–307). Belmont, CA: Wadsworth/Thomson.

rates as girls. Increasing the graduation rates of young men would be another challenge in which you could become involved when you begin teaching. Engaging in activities that keep young men in school and open academic fields such as Science, Technology, Engineering, and Mathematics (called STEM) to more girls and students of color is another way to bring joy to your teaching.

HOW IS SEXUAL ORIENTATION ADDRESSED IN SCHOOLS?

Discussions about sexual orientation are no longer hidden in society. In fact, nearly two in three Americans now support same-sex marriages (Masci, Brown, & Kiley, 2017). The support for equal rights of gays and lesbians has grown as cities, states, and school districts have expanded their policies on equality to include sexual orientation. Even with these changes, some school districts continue to struggle with how to handle diverse sexual orientations in the curricula and in student clubs.

However, **heterosexism** continues to exist when people believe that opposite-sex sexuality is the only acceptable sexual orientation, and all others are abnormal and morally wrong. This behavior can lead to discriminatory practices and harassment against Lesbian, Gay, Bisexual, Transgender, and Queer or Questioning (**LGBTQ**) individuals who continue to face discrimination in housing, employment, and social institutions in some communities. Heterosexism can result in violence against anyone who is identified by his or her assailer as LGBTQ, which is still tolerated in some areas of the country and in some schools. Society's prejudices and discriminatory practices result in many gays and lesbians hiding their sexual orientation and establishing their own social clubs, networks, and communication systems to support one another.

Sexual Identity

What is sexual orientation? The American Psychological Association (2018) defines it as an "enduring pattern of emotional, romantic, and/or sexual attractions to men, women, or both sexes," and further indicates that different sexual orientations are normal forms of human bonding. The sexual orientation of the majority of the population is heterosexual or straight, which has become the norm against which everyone else is measured. In a famous study of the sexual behavior of thousands of white adults in the 1940s and 1950s, Alfred Kinsey reported that 10% of the males and 2% to 6% of the females were more or less exclusively homosexual (Kinsey Institute, 2017). Based on a 2016 Gallup Poll, it is estimated that nearly 10 million Americans, or 4.6% of the U.S. population, identify as LGBTQ, with young people born between 1980 and 1998 twice as likely as people at other ages to indicate they are LGBTQ (Reynolds, 2017).

The term *gay* is sometimes used more generically to refer not only to gay men, but also to lesbians and bisexuals. Transgender persons identify their gender as different from the sex they were assigned at birth. The *Q* in LGBTQ refers to *queer*—a term used to negatively label gays and lesbians in the past, but that is now used as a political term that rejects assimilation into a heterosexual world. The *Q* can also mean *questioning*, to include individuals who are not sure of their sexual orientation. Terms related to sexual orientation and gender identification are always evolving. In addition to the ones in LGBTQ, others used in 2018 included *transsexual, two-spirit, intersex, asexual, ally, pansexual, agender, gender, bigender, gender variant,* and *pangender* (OK2BME, 2018). As you work with students and adults, remember that it is important that they identify their own gender identity and sexual orientation and are not labeled by others. As a teacher or a friend, you should respect their self-identities.

Many LGBTQ adults report feeling different from their siblings or peers from early in life. By the time they reach puberty, most students begin to feel an attraction to the same, opposite, or both sexes. Most students struggle with their identity during middle and high school. However, LGBTQ students usually have a more difficult time, especially with their sexual identity. They may question their sexual feelings but not be sure if they are LGBTQ. If they show signs of being LGBTQ, even if they are not, they may be subjecting themselves to harassment or bullying by their classmates. During this period, they may feel isolated and might not know to whom they can turn for information and support, especially when their family will not accept their sexual orientation. LGBTQ students comprise a disproportionate percentage of homeless students on the nation's streets, in part, because they are not accepted by their families.

Supporting LGBTQ Students

"That's so gay" is a common phrase in the hallways of schools. *Gay* is used as a derogatory term against heterosexual students as well as a reference to students perceived to be LGBTQ. This name-calling begins in elementary schools and increases as students move through school, but it appears to be most prevalent in middle schools. In her experiences in four different schools, Ms. Maschari found that students begin to call others "gay" with a negative connotation around the fourth grade. The teachers at her school use these opportunities to confront these unacceptable behaviors at morning meetings with students. Ms. Maschari has also found that her current school is very accepting of LGBTQ parents, who are warmly welcomed and who actively participate in school activities.

Teachers and other educators can play a very important role in eliminating such harassment and bullying in schools as well as educating students to respect all students. Over half of LGBTQ students fear for their safety in schools, with over four in five of them being verbally harassed at school (Kosciw, Greytak, Giga, Villenas, & Danischewski, 2016). If gays and lesbians openly acknowledge their sexual orientation or appear to be LGBTQ, they are likely to be harassed and face reprisals from peers and, sometimes, from school officials. A school and school personnel do not always provide the same kind of support to LGBTQ students as they do to other students.

LGBTQ students feel more comfortable and safer in schools when faculty and staff are supportive, LGBTQ

Education & Exploration 3/Alamy Stock Photo

LGBTQ students report that schools feel much safer when they know there are safe zones and they can trust specific educators. Safe zones stickers and posters in the school signal a supportive school climate.

The families of students practice many different religions. Educators should be sure they do not discriminate against students whose families practice a religion different from their own.

people are portrayed in the curricula, gay–straight alliances or similar clubs exist, and a comprehensive policy on harassment is enforced (Kosciw et al., 2016). You may know little about LGBTQ history and experiences. You may have had few or no contacts with LGBTQ people who are out, or open about their sexual orientation. Without a better understanding of sexual orientation, you may find it difficult to work effectively with LGBTQ students or the children of gay and lesbian parents. However, you always have the responsibility to provide a safe environment for students, which includes intervening when students are harassing their peers because of their sexual orientation, gender identification, or sex.

HOW DOES RELIGION IMPACT THE CLASSROOM?

Religion has a great influence on the values and lifestyles of families and plays an important role in the socialization of children and young people. Religious doctrines and practices guide how and when one worships, but they also guide beliefs about many aspects of daily life, including the roles of men and women, birth control, child rearing, friendships, and political attitudes. Some religions in the United States also promote patriotism, often displaying the American flag in their places of worship. A religious doctrine can also dictate a family's expectations for teachers and schools. When the religious perspectives and school expectations differ, numerous challenges arise for educators.

Religious Diversity

The United States has strong Judeo-Christian roots. Some Christians believe that God led the European founders to establish this country as a Christian nation. An increase of Asian and Middle Eastern immigrants after the 1960s made the United States more religiously diverse. Mosques and temples have been built in communities that were formerly all Christian. Most urban and suburban areas are home to numerous religious groups and beliefs. Metropolitan areas may have a number of megachurches with thousands of members and their own schools.

Seven in ten Americans identify themselves as Christian, with Protestants currently representing 48% of the population. Catholicism grew greatly after Southern and Eastern Europeans immigrated to the United States in the twentieth century, and now makes up one-fifth of the population (Pew Research Center, 2018). Within all religious groups are liberal, moderate, and conservative or fundamentalist sects. The fundamentalist groups believe in the literal translation of their holy documents (e.g., the Bible, Qur'an, and Torah). Liberal religions, on the other hand, accept the validity of diverse perspectives that have evolved from different historical experiences. One in four people describes himself or herself as **born again** or **evangelical** (Pew Research Center, 2018) and is often identified as a member of the religious right. The religious affiliations of the U.S. population are shown in Figure 2.6.

Although Jews, Protestants, and Catholics once were expected to marry only members of their own faith, marriage across those three groups is fairly common today. Time will tell whether the borders against intermarriage with members of non-Western religious groups will also be permeable.

Addressing Religion in Public Schools

If you teach in an urban or metropolitan area, you can expect to have students from a number of different religious groups. Even smaller midwestern and western towns have had an influx of Asian,

FIGURE 2.6 ■ Religious Preference in the United States

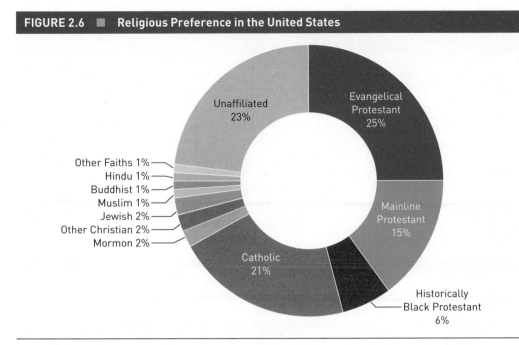

Source: Adapted from Pew Research Center. (2018). Religious landscape study. Retrieved from http://www.pewforum.org/religious-landscape-study.

African, or Middle Eastern immigrants who are bringing their cultural versions of Christianity, Islam, Hinduism, and Buddhism to communities that previously had only a few different Christian denominations.

Accommodations will be needed in schools to respect the religious diversity of the community. Christian holidays are already acknowledged through school holidays and the singing of Christian songs at some school convocations. Jewish students will not attend school during Rosh Hashanah and Yom Kippur. Islamic students will fast during the month of Ramadan and are expected to have daily prayers. Policies that prevent the wearing of a hijab or yarmulke discriminate against Muslim women and Jewish men. School officials could involve the parents of their religious communities to provide Professional Development about their religious traditions and cultures as well as advice for guaranteeing that the **civil rights** of their children are not violated.

Religion is very important to some families and of little or no importance to others. In some communities, religion plays a major role in the lives of families, requiring attendance not only on a specific day but also at services and activities throughout the week. Religious stories reinforce the values of the religion in Sunday school, Bible classes, and other organized religious education programs. Parents in these communities may expect schools to reflect those same values, sometimes enrolling their children in private Catholic, Jewish, Islamic, or Christian schools that reinforce their values and teach their religious doctrine. They may decide to homeschool their children to ensure they are not exposed to values of which they disapprove.

Students whose religious beliefs differ from the majority in the community may be ostracized in school and social settings. Jews, atheists, Jehovah's Witnesses, Pentecostals, Muslims, and Sikhs are among the groups whose members are sometimes shunned and suffer discrimination in the United States. Educators must be careful that their own religious beliefs do not interfere with their ability to provide equal educational opportunities to students whose families are members of other religious groups.

CONNECTING TO THE CLASSROOM

This chapter has introduced you to the students who will be in your classrooms of the future. We have examined the diversity of their group memberships based on ethnicity, race, socioeconomic status (SES), native language, gender, sexual orientation, and religion. Below are some key principles for applying the information in this chapter to the classroom.

1. Curricula and instructional strategies should be relevant to the lives of students, drawing on their ethnic, racial, and cultural backgrounds and experiences to help them learn.

2. Teachers should be aware of biases they have about students based on their SES and ensure they have high academic expectations for all of their students.

3. Schools must provide language programs for English Language Learners to assist them in learning English and having full access to the curriculum.

4. Girls and boys can be taught to develop the skills and behaviors that are usually attributed to the other sex.

5. Teachers should be supportive of LGBTQ students and intervene when they are being harassed to create a safe climate for LGBTQ and other students.

6. Teachers should be aware of the religious groups to which their students belong and make appropriate accommodations in their classrooms.

SUMMARY

This chapter has explored the diversity of students who will be in your future classroom. Six major topics were addressed:

- Students come to your classroom with racial and ethnic heritages that should be recognized, respected, and integrated into the curricula.

- Students' families experience very different levels of economic stability that can affect their capacity to access resources that are needed for their children to be successful within a specific school context.

- In some communities in the United States, numerous languages other than English are spoken across a school district. Schools have the responsibility to ensure that ELLs have access to the content to be able to learn the content at the same level as their native-English-speaking peers.

- Attitudes about gender roles and responsibilities run deep in society, and teachers must constantly be careful not to reinforce stereotypes that might inhibit a student's chance of reaching his or her highest potential.

- Students whose sexual orientation is not heterosexual are often victims of bullying and do not always feel safe or supported in the school environment.

- Christianity has historically been valued in school, but today's student population is becoming increasingly religiously diverse, which can impact the way some topics such as sexuality are addressed and requires a climate that is supportive of students of all faiths.

KEY TERMS

achievement gap 42
assimilation 57
born again 58
civil rights 59
color blind 42
couch surfing 47
cultural capital 49
culturally responsive teaching 44
culture 38
disability 38
ethnicity 38

evangelical 58
gender 38
heterosexism 56
indigenous 39
LGBTQ 56
McKinney–Vento Homeless Assistance Act 47
opportunity gap 43
pan-ethnic 39
race 38
racism 40

refugees 41
resegregation 50
self-fulfilling prophecy 49
sex 38
sexual orientation 38
socialization 55
socioeconomic status (SES) 38
stereotypes 42
tracking 43

CLASS DISCUSSION QUESTIONS

1. The curricula of many schools privilege European American culture and history. How will you ensure that the cultures and histories of diverse students will be incorporated into the curricula? Why should all students know about the cultures and histories of other ethnic and racial groups as well as their own?

2. Half of K–12 students are eligible for Free or Reduced-Price Lunch, indicating that their families have low incomes. What impact does poverty have on the education of students? What accommodations will you make so that the curriculum is more relevant and meaningful for students from low-income families?

3. More than one in five students has one or more foreign-born parents, many of whom speak a language other than English at home. Schools generally use bilingual education or ESL to help students learn English. Which program do you think more effectively serves the need of students and families in your community, and why?

4. Females today are attending college at higher rates than males. What are the reasons for this unequal participation in higher education? What could you do in your classroom to increase the participation of male students?

5. Many LGBTQ students feel very isolated in schools because teachers, students, and counselors do not understand them and provide little or no support for them. What role are you willing to take on to support the psychological and emotional development of LGBTQ students?

6. Religion can influence what families think should be taught in schools. In some religious communities, evolution and sexuality are taboo topics. How will you know how important a role religious groups have in the community in which you are teaching?

SELF-ASSESSMENT

What Is Your Current Level of Understanding Today's Students?

One of the indicators of understanding is to examine how complex your thinking is when asked questions that require you to use the concepts and facts introduced in this chapter.

Answer the following questions as fully as you can. Then use the Assessing Your Learning rubric to self-assess the degree to which you understand and can use the ideas presented in this chapter.

1. How can you bring the cultures of your students into the classroom?

2. What impact does the socioeconomic status of students' families have on teachers' expectations for the academic performance of students?

3. What is the teacher's responsibility for teaching students who are not authorized to be in the country?

4. How can boys and girls be damaged with education that focuses on the stereotypical roles of females and males?

5. What can teachers do to help LGBTQ students feel safe in school?

6. What are some ways in which the religious diversity of a community can be integrated into your classroom?

Assessing Your Learning Rubric

	Parts & Pieces	Unidimensional	Organized	Integrated	Extensions
Indicators	Elements/concepts are talked about as isolated and independent entities. Some important names are provided in isolation.	One or a few concepts are addressed, while others are underdeveloped, or not mentioned.	Deliberate and structured consideration of all key concepts/ elements.	All key concepts/ elements are included in a view that addresses interconnections.	Integration of all elements and dimensions, with extrapolation to new situations.
Relationships between the diversity of students and teaching and learning	Identifies the types of student diversity that exist without being able to explain the relationships to teaching and learning.	Describes a few of the impacts that diversity has on teaching and learning.	Provides examples of how student diversity can influence teaching and learning across cultural groups.	Analyzes the role of the teacher in using student diversity effectively to help students learn.	Explains how teachers can adjust their teaching to use student diversity positively to improve learning across cultural groups and develops a plan for increasing his/her knowledge about cultural groups with which he/she has limited knowledge.

FIELD GUIDE
FOR LEARNING MORE ABOUT . . .

Today's Students

To further increase your understanding about today's students, do one or more of the following activities.

Ask a Teacher or Principal	Ask one or more of the teachers in the schools you are observing how they differentiate their instruction to serve students from different ethnic, racial, socioeconomic, and language groups. What are their greatest concerns about providing equity across groups? What do they suggest that you do to prepare to work in a school with diverse student populations?
Make Your Own Observations	When visiting a school with English Language Learners, observe two different classrooms. What are the native languages of the students in the two classrooms? What is the level of the ELLs' English proficiency? What ELL program is being used for instruction in the two classrooms that you observed? Ask the teachers why they are using a specific approach.
Reflect Through Journaling	This chapter indicates that some students are being better served by some schools than by others, as measured by achievement on the standardized tests required by the Every Student Succeeds Act. In your journal, write why you think students from low-income families are not performing as well on these tests as students from more-affluent families. What difference do you think teachers can make in increasing the achievement of students from low-income families on standardized tests?
Build Your Portfolio	The degree of diversity at a school differs greatly across the country. Choose a school in the community in which your university is located or in which you grew up and describe the cultural makeup of the community and student population in the school, including individuals' racial, ethnic, socioeconomic, religious, and language backgrounds.
	Schools or school districts should have policies on the provision of safety for students. Compare the policies in two school districts and determine what students are included in the policies. Identify how the policies incorporate LGBTQ students.
Read a Book	For ideas from educators on how to make students and their families feel respected and valued, read the special issue of *Rethinking Schools* (Fall 2017) on "Making Black Lives Matter in Our Schools."
	A former student and teacher in an urban school, award-winning educator Christopher Endin calls for a new approach to teaching in urban schools in his book, *For White Folks Who Teach in the Hood . . . and the Rest of Y'all Too: Reality Pedagogy and Urban Education* (Beacon Press, 2016).
	Tales of Two Americas: Stories of Inequality in a Divided Nation by John Freeman (Penguin Books, 2017) includes powerful stories, essays, and poems that demonstrate how boundaries break down when the authors share their stories of the inequalities that have affected their or others' lives.
	The focus on LGBTQ students in this chapter was on safety, but that is only the beginning of the ways that schools should acknowledge and support these students. In the book, *Safe Is Not Enough: Better Schools for LGBTQ Students* (Harvard Education Press, 2016), Michael Sadowski highlights how educators can also support the positive development and academic success of LGBTQ students through LGBTQ-inclusive curriculum, a whole-school climate, and community outreach programs.
Search the Web	**Rethinking Schools:** To help you think about the issues raised in this chapter and read how teachers are addressing them in their classrooms, visit the website of Rethinking Schools (www.rethinkingschools.org).
	Teaching Tolerance: To learn more about incorporating diversity into the curricula and developing a classroom climate that supports students from diverse groups, visit www.splcenter.org/teaching-tolerance.

STUDENT STUDY SITE

⑤SAGE edge™

Get the tools you need to sharpen your study skills. **SAGE edge** offers a robust online environment featuring an impressive array of free tools and resources.

Access practice quizzes, eFlashcards, video, and multimedia at **edge.sagepub.com/hall3e**.

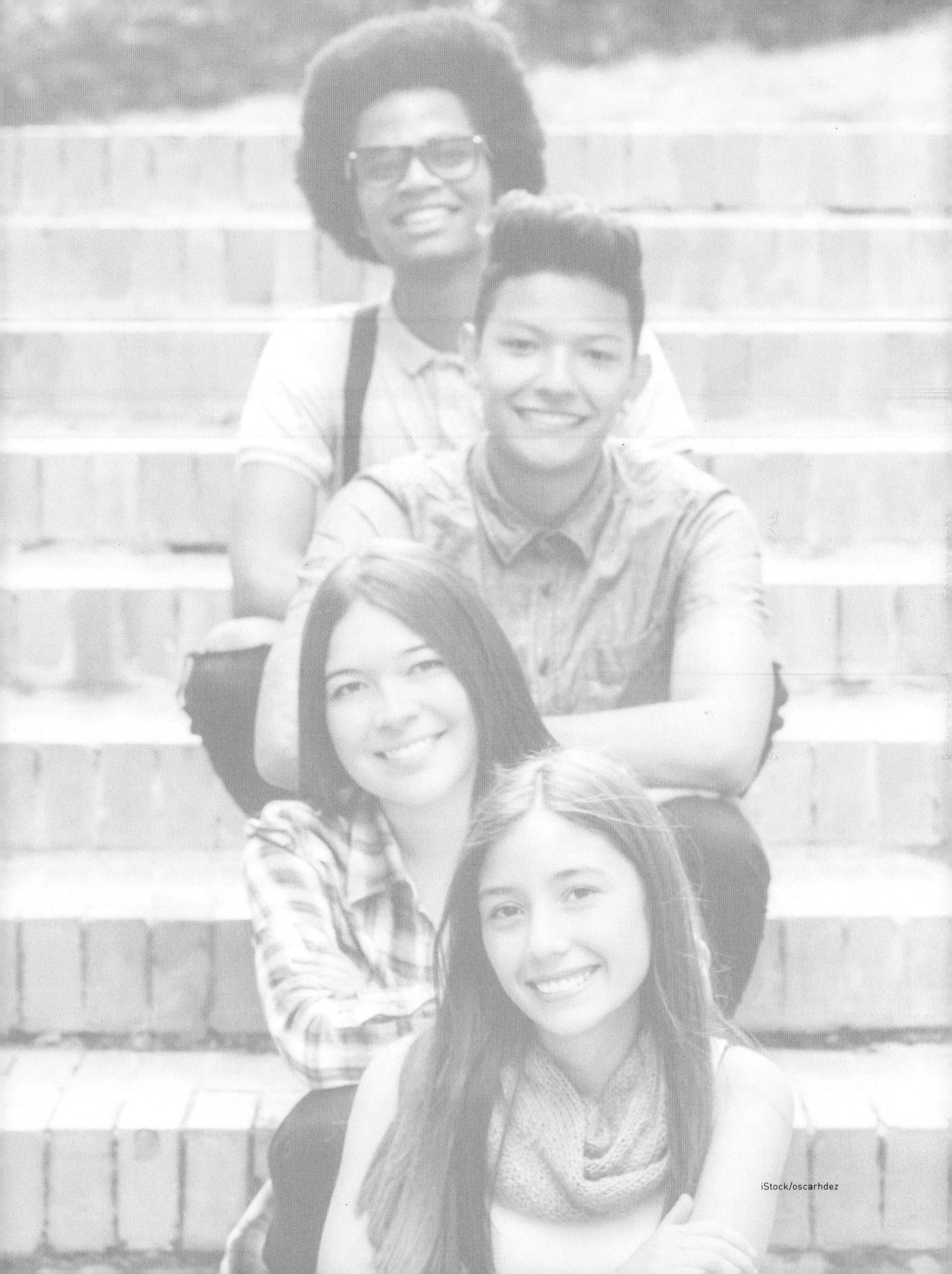

iStock/oscarhdez

EXCEPTIONAL LEARNERS

TEACHER INTERVIEW

Ms. Kia Glimps-Smith

© Kia Glimps-Smith

Ms. Kia Glimps-Smith is a fourth-grade special education resource teacher at Mirror Lakes Elementary School in Lehigh Acres, Florida. She grew up in Detroit, Michigan, and now lives in the quiet suburban area where she teaches. She has been nominated and recognized by her students and peers for the Golden Apple Teacher Recognition Program™ six years in a row.

Q: What is the diversity of the students in your school?

A: The demographics of the school do not match the middle-class neighborhood that surrounds it. When I first started teaching at Mirror Lakes in 2007, the school had just about 800 students. Now, close to 1,300 students attend. Since 2013, the student population has changed from a middle-class majority to a majority of students from low-income families. The school is currently a Title I school with a student population that is 50% Hispanic, 23% black, and 22% white. While our students may be financially challenged, they come to school with smiles on their faces and are welcomed with warm hugs every school day.

Q: What do you do as a special education resource teacher?

A: This is my first year as a resource teacher. Previously, I was in a self-contained classroom where I had the impression that resource teachers only focused on gathering data. I didn't understand the children with disabilities in the general education classroom. I could see firsthand what it took to be a self-contained teacher, and it was a lot. Now that I am a resource teacher, I have learned that the children with disabilities who are in the general education classrooms include children with health impairments, learning disabilities, and emotional and behavioral disabilities. In my district, I provide services based on the IEP goals of the children. I try to push in instead of pulling the children out of the classroom. I try to do inclusion and collaboratively teach with the general education teacher. I work with a small group of six for 30 minutes at a time. Then, I go to the next classroom and the next classroom. I do that throughout my day. I have a caseload of 16–18 students with IEPs whom I support throughout the school

LEARNING OUTCOMES

After reading this chapter, you should be able to do the following:

1. Apply the ways that children and adolescents learn at different stages of development to teaching and learning.

2. Contrast the advantages and disadvantages of distinguishing intelligence as one ability versus multiple abilities.

3. Create a classroom that is welcoming and supportive of students with disabilities.

4. Identify struggling students and appropriate intervention strategies to support their learning.

5. Examine how differentiated instruction, personalized learning, Universal Design for Learning, and culturally responsive teaching can contribute to meeting the needs of every student.

year. Some schools in our district have a resource room where the students go to work with the teacher, but schools generally are pushing for more inclusion.

Q: How do you work with the general education teacher?

A: I work with six or seven different teachers in the fourth grade. Our department is departmentalized with a reading teacher and a math teacher. With the reading teacher, I may co-teach a lesson. For math, I may work with a small group. The teacher may also work with a small group, and the rest of the students will be doing centers. In another classroom, I work with a group on my own lesson, and then send them back to their classroom when we are done.

Q: What brings you joy in teaching?

A: Teaching students with disabilities based on their strengths instead of their disability brings me the greatest joy. It brings me joy to see the progress they make as a result of my teaching and their perseverance. For the past eight years, I was a life skills primary teacher of students with cognitive disabilities. Now, I am a special education resource teacher in several general education fourth-grade classrooms. I teach students with specific learning disabilities. It brings me great joy to know that they are learning to fluently read, write, memorize math facts, become critical thinkers, and think independently. Being a special education teacher brings me joy!

Q: What advice do you have for future teachers?

A: The best advice I can give is to build a positive relationship with your students. Relationship building fosters a positive self-esteem within all students. Be that "popular teacher" whom all the students enjoy talking to and being around in a positive and appropriate way. Consider yourself a mentor and help shape and mold your students' lives positively through education. Every chance I get, I coach/mentor my students when they are frustrated, sad, or happy. At the very least, I will say good morning to them, or at the end of the day, I'll ask my students, "What did you enjoy about your day?" Building relationships is such an important role in education because it allows teachers to get to know their students' families, provides listening time between the teacher and student, and encourages trust.

Questions to Consider

1. In what ways do you think Ms. Glimps-Smith sees each student as exceptional?

2. How is Ms. Glimps-Smith working with the general education teachers to help meet the needs of students in inclusive classrooms? What other cooperative strategies have you observed in schools?

3. What does Ms. Glimps-Smith think is a critical skill in working with students with disabilities?

INTRODUCTION

What were your thoughts when you first read the title of this chapter? Did you think something like "Yeah, sure, another simplistic education slogan"? Or did you think something like "Well, I suppose in some way(s) each student can be thought of as a unique or exceptional individual"? Thinking about student learning in terms of how each student is unique or exceptional is essential to becoming an effective educator.

In this chapter, we will introduce a variety of ways for viewing each student as exceptional. Some of these ways come from research, some are based in laws, others are based on characteristics of students, and a few are drawn from interesting ideas about how to best facilitate learning for all students. Keep in mind that these really will be "introductions." Later on in your teacher education program and as your career unfolds, you will learn more about different ways of seeing each student as exceptional.

The key objective for this chapter is to help you begin developing a repertoire of ways to see each student as unique. As you will hear often, teachers should differentiate instruction. This means customizing your teaching in ways that facilitate learning for each of your students. One important challenge for you will be to determine the basis for the differentiation. Will you look only at students' past grades? Will you consider family backgrounds? Does it make a difference if the subject is reading, mathematics, or science? What about their performance in your class? Some students will grasp new ideas quickly, and others will struggle. Which indicators will you emphasize as you explore how each of your students is exceptional and how you can best help all of them learn at high levels?

DIFFERENTIATE

DO ALL STUDENTS DEVELOP IN THE SAME WAY?

What are some terms you would use to characterize students who are in early-childhood, elementary, middle-level, and secondary classrooms? Each of these stereotypes probably emphasizes specific characteristics about the way students behave or think at different ages in school. However, as with all generalizations, you need to be careful when applying them to individual students. At the same time, to what extent do you think your descriptions of typical students are valid? What these descriptions reflect is a developmental model of how children grow and how they learn. In other words, there are predictable phases and stages to child and adolescent development. As a teacher, you should plan to adapt instruction in ways that recognize and build on students' developmental stages or what is called developmentally appropriate practices for each student.

Stages of Cognitive Development

In your psychology courses, you will study different models and theories about how thinking develops as children grow up. Most of these developmental models evolved from the work of Jean Piaget, who documented the way children's thinking changes in major ways as they move from infancy through adolescence. According to Piaget, the way that thinking changes as a child grows older is genetically programmed. Parents and teachers cannot have much effect on this maturation. Providing safety and keeping children healthy are important supports, but the ways children think will develop at the pace that is set biologically.

Piaget saw children as intrinsically active. They are not passive in their learning; they learn by interacting with their environment. Infants, for example, are limited in their ability to interact due to not having developed muscular control and having limited eyesight. As their neuromuscular system develops, their interactions with their environment become more dynamic and their thinking changes as a result. Children are curious. They are not satisfied with what they know; they want to know more.

As you may recall from your psychology courses, Piaget identifies four stages of cognitive development: sensorimotor, preoperational, concrete operations, and formal operations. Within each stage, the way in which children reason and think is different. It is important to keep in mind that Piaget sees that all children will go through these four stages in sequence. They will not skip a stage. Also, there are age ranges associated with each stage although some children go through them at a faster pace.

Sensorimotor Stage (0–2 Years)

This is the stage when infants rely on their basic senses to learn. Seeing, hearing, touching, tasting, and smelling are the main sources of information. At the earliest part of this stage, infants think of objects as only existing when the object is present. Later on in this stage, children are able to purposefully interact with objects in their environment. These are physical interactions. In other words, they can "reach out and touch something."

Preoperational Stage (2–7 Years)

Being able to recall what happened in the past, keeping track of information, and planning for the future are important parts of thinking. These skills have to be learned. These are mental processes, not physical ones. Developing the ability to use words and gestures is part of the preoperational stage.

Learning words that represent objects happens during this stage. The tendency is to focus on one element only, such as height and not width. At this stage, children's thinking is mainly self-centered, inasmuch as children often hold the assumption that others feel as they do.

Concrete Operations Stage (7–11 Years)

The indicators of students at this stage include their coming to understand that changing the shape of a material still keeps the material the same. They also understand that such changes can be reversed. Another aspect of student thinking at this stage is the ability to classify, such as placing cities within states and states within countries. Furthermore, students can see different ways to classify objects such as by shape or by color.

Formal Operations Stage (11 Years to Adult)

At this stage, students continue to have all of the ways of thinking that they developed during the earlier stages. Now they can imagine what might happen. They can do deductive reasoning: "If college graduates earn more money, then I should go to college." They can think inductively, such as constructing generalizations: "The kids in theater and band are doing things besides going to subject classes." At this stage, they can do what we call "thought experiments": They can imagine what an action or activity might entail and what would happen if it were to take place.

Development of the Brain

Understanding the development of the brain is another useful way to think about how best to help students learn. Not that long ago, neuroscience research offered little that teachers could apply in their classrooms. Now, it is a popular source of research respected by teachers and parents alike with significant implications for thinking about teaching and learning. The findings from neuroscience research also represent new ways to see each child as exceptional.

The basic metaphor in neuroscience for talking about thinking and learning is called **brain architecture**. At its simplest, we are talking about how the brain is wired. As the brain develops throughout childhood, cognitive and motor skills appear in an orderly fashion. Infants crawl before they walk. They babble before they speak words. They begin to read between the ages of 5 and 7. The brain continues to change dynamically into adulthood and, even then, remains plastic or malleable across a lifetime. It turns out that brain architecture is not just a matter of genetics. Researchers have established that cognitive brain development is enhanced by enriched and stimulating environments in which we interact with peers and adults as well as the environment.

Another basic finding from these studies is that there are certain developmental stages or **sensitive periods** where certain experiences have specific effects on how the brain develops. With infants, for example, basic sensory, social, and emotional experiences are necessary. Furthermore, at each sensitive period, development of different parts of the brain is more affected. During this sensitive period, the brain incorporates information from the environment and "locks in" that information. Deprivation of social contact during those periods can affect neural and cognitive development (Banich & Compton, 2018).

Development of Neural Circuits at Different Ages

Brain architecture is composed of neural circuits. Interestingly, these circuits are organized in hierarchies. In other words, some neural circuits have to be in place before others can develop. Also, the circuits within each hierarchy process certain kinds of information. For

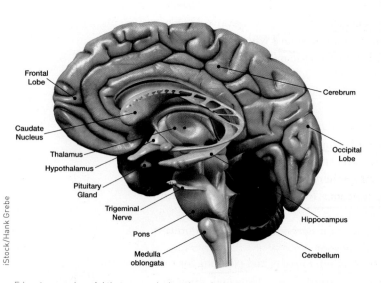

Frontal Lobe
Cerebrum
Caudate Nucleus
Thalamus
Hypothalamus
Pituitary Gland
Trigeminal Nerve
Occipital Lobe
Pons
Hippocampus
Medulla oblongata
Cerebellum

iStock/Hank Grebe

Educators are hopeful that research about how the brain develops will help them develop more effective teaching practices that promote higher-level learning.

FIGURE 3.1 ■ Human Brain Development

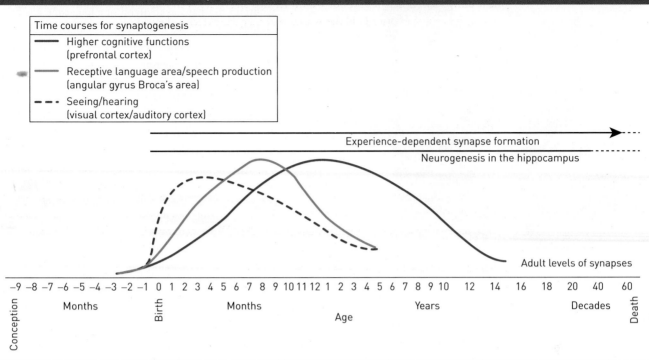

Time courses for synaptogenesis

— Higher cognitive functions
(prefrontal cortex)

— Receptive language area/speech production
(angular gyrus Broca's area)

– – Seeing/hearing
(visual cortex/auditory cortex)

Experience-dependent synapse formation

Neurogenesis in the hippocampus

Adult levels of synapses

-9 -8 -7 -6 -5 -4 -3 -2 -1 0 1 2 3 4 5 6 7 8 9 10 11 12 1 2 3 4 5 6 7 8 9 10 12 14 16 18 20 40 60

Conception   Months   Birth   Months   Years   Decades   Death

Age

Source: Charles A. Nelson, University of Minnesota (2000).

example, one hierarchy has the set of circuits for analyzing visual information. Another set of neural circuits processes auditory information. There are other circuits for learning a language, planning next steps, and interpreting emotions. The development of particular neural circuits occurs at different ages. For example, low-level circuits such as analysis of sensory stimuli develop around the time of birth. High-level circuits such as those that process complex information develop much later.

The research findings related to brain architecture have been organized around three mental capacities. The first to develop are the neural circuits related to visual and auditory interactions. Second is the development of networks related to learning and speaking languages. The third area of learning has to do with higher-order thinking and problem solving. A visual summary of the findings about development of brain architecture in relation to these capacities is presented in Figure 3.1. Notice how significant the early years are for the developing brain.

Long-Lasting Effects of Stress

The findings from brain research document that excessive stress disrupts the early development of the brain, and those effects can be long lasting (National Scientific Council on the Developing Child, 2014). When there is not a positive and appropriately stimulating approach to social, cognitive, and language development, neural networks may not develop fully or in the same ways. This risk is especially problematic during the sensitive periods. In the first three years of life, the neural networks are growing even more rapidly. If there is extreme stress, for example, the functioning and architecture of particular neural circuits can be altered. The result can be that the brain does not process basic information as well or as completely. In a hierarchical model, if the foundation is not strong, the higher functions will be less efficient, or perhaps will not work well at all. When limited or incorrect information is being produced at the lower levels, then the higher levels of brain functioning may not receive complete or accurate information. This can result in higher cognitive functions not working efficiently.

istock/SilviaJansen

Contrary to what many people have believed, the adult brain has the capacity to continue to learn.

The Plasticity of the Brain

Contrary to what was thought for a long time, the brain architecture and its neural circuits continue to adapt throughout adulthood. In other words, even when there was not an optimal environment during the sensitive periods, there is a continuing capacity to learn. However, at these later times, the experiences have to be customized more carefully and targeted toward the particular neural circuits. Another way to think about this is that the architecture of each student's brain is exceptional. When teachers strive to address each student's way of functioning, more learning will be possible. This is not always easy, but teachers most certainly need to understand that learning always is possible and learning can be a lifelong process.

Neuroscience and Education

Because education focuses on developing cognition such as learning, memory, reasoning, and critical thinking, educators have a natural inclination to use neuroscience research to improve their practice. While some educators are optimistic about how the findings and principles of neuroscience can inform the practice of teaching, others argue that no educational practice to date has its origins in neuroscience (Almarode & Daniel, 2018). Nevertheless, a number of so-called experts promote brain-based teaching and learning, and a number of teachers and school districts have adopted those practices. As a result, a number of myths such as left-brain and right-brain learning and differences in male and female brains have been attributed to neuroscience research. Neuroscientists generally urge caution about jumping onto one of the brain-based bandwagons. Most of the studies have not yet been designed to determine classroom implications or interpretations (Almarode & Daniel, 2018).

Implications of Developmental Models for Teaching and Learning

Hopefully, you are seeing some of the similarities across the developmental models. Each has phases. Each has a predictable sequence, and these sequences cannot be skipped. Development is related to chronological age and is based on interactions with the environment. Also, there is extensive research behind each model.

Often, policy makers, administrators, parents, and even some teachers will start pressing for ways to speed up a child's development. The story is often told that when Piaget was questioned as to how to do that, his response was to label it as "the American question." Regardless of the developmental model, the experts report that little can be done to accelerate development. What they will emphasize is that children who have caring, supportive, nonstressful, and rich environments in their early years will be ready for school and will progress well.

These developmental perspectives offer important ways for teachers to see each student as exceptional. Each student is developing at his or her own rate based on experience and age. Past experiences affect development, and if those experiences include toxic stresses, such as extreme poverty or abuse, then the brain architecture may be different (National Scientific Council on the Developing Child, 2014). As a teacher, you need to appreciate that your students will bring different cognitive, emotional, and social capabilities to school based on their past experiences. Your task is to understand where each of your students begins and to differentiate your instruction in ways that build from there. Do not assume that any of your students cannot continue to develop. They may be ahead or behind in terms of developmental perspective, but as the neuroscience findings indicate, our brains have plasticity. It is our task to provide a supportive and rich instructional environment so that each student can continue to develop, as Ms. Glimps-Smith did when she taught life skills to children with Down syndrome and visual and physical disabilities. She reported that

My peers felt like these children should be in a special school because they couldn't read, they couldn't learn, or they couldn't speak. So I made it my duty to prove them wrong. I had students go from limited communications to verbal communication, from not being able to recognize a letter to being able to read. I wanted to prove people wrong. Even the parents would complain that my expectations were too high, but the principal would say "give her time." By the end of the class, they were in love with me. They still drop by my classroom today. Their children are probably in high school now. They still call me; they send me Christmas cards. Their child has really changed; they really see the potential of what their child can do despite the disability.

WHO ARE EXCEPTIONAL STUDENTS?

Exceptional students are generally defined in education circles as students with disabilities. However, the authors of this book recognize each student as exceptional for his or her unique strengths and/or experiences. Exceptional students include students who are labeled as gifted and talented as well as students with disabilities. They include students who do not have an Individualized Education Program (IEP), but are struggling in school, perhaps because of a recent traumatic event in their life. It includes all of those students who come to school almost every day, but do not excel in an area commonly recognized by the school. In other words, we believe that all students are exceptional.

Exceptionality Based on Intelligence

For better or worse, most teachers probably first think about students being exceptional in terms of their intelligence. They may think of some students as being smarter than others. This really is too simplistic a view. Think about your own academic ability and that of some of your classmates. Some will be better with language arts while others will be better with math or science. Each has strengths in terms of learning certain subjects. There will likely be some other areas where learning is more difficult. Simplistically, we can talk about these differences in terms of intelligence. However, as we describe next, the meaning of the term *intelligence* is complicated.

In the past, there was a tendency to see intelligence as a single score on a special test. For example, when the authors of this textbook were in school, we took an Intelligence Quotient (IQ) test, which was the dominant way at that time of determining a student's ability to learn. Neither we nor our parents were likely to be informed of the results, but schools would group students based on their IQ scores. We and our parents would speculate about our IQ score based on what we thought of the other students in the same class. Today, scholars and teachers consider multiple ways to think about the meaning of intelligence. It can refer to how easy it is for particular students to learn new material. Or it could refer to how much a student knows. Other aspects of intelligence could refer to creativity and problem solving, or one's ability to be reflective about one's learning.

Intelligence as One Ability

Over the years, psychologists have examined intelligence in many ways and in relation to many types of tasks. Those who view intelligence as a single ability refer to it as general intelligence. This ability entails information processing and would be used with all types of cognitive tasks. However, for any particular tasks, there are likely to be specific abilities, such as language development, memory, and auditory perception. General intelligence as it relates to learning in school is measured with standardized tests.

The story of how these tests became a part of our system of education dates back to the early 1900s. The

Sometimes an effective strategy for increasing learning is to group students with similar interests and assign them a special project.

iStock/Ridofranz

Minister of Public Instruction in Paris wanted to determine a way to identify students early on who would need extra help in their schooling. In response, Alfred Binet developed a battery of tests for students between the ages of 3 and 13. Students' scores on these tests could then be compared with how well other students of the same age had done.

The label of IQ or Intelligence Quotient was added when the tests were revised at Stanford University, becoming known as the Stanford–Binet Intelligence Scales. IQ then became a comparison of a student's score with that of others in the student's age group, with the score of 100 being the average. Interestingly, in its original forms, this test was administered orally, rather than by having students read and write. In general, a higher IQ score does correlate with higher achievement in school. Contrary to what you might think, when the number of years of education and IQ scores are compared with accomplishments as an adult, the correlations are not very high. Other abilities can play a major part in success in the real world.

Multiple Intelligences (MI)

As you can quickly see, the construct of intelligence can be very complicated. More than 70 specific abilities have been identified by research psychologists. For teachers, a more useful approach is the **Multiple Intelligences (MI)** theory of Howard Gardner. Gardner theorized that there were seven abilities or intelligences as shown in Table 3.1. Later, he added an eighth ability, naturalistic intelligence, which designates the human ability to discriminate among living things and be sensitive to other features of the natural world. Each person will have strengths in some abilities and weaknesses in others (Gardner, 2011).

Gardner's theory has not been accepted widely by psychologists. However, teachers can use the MI theory as a useful framework for seeing each student as exceptional in one or more ways. You can begin by thinking about the students in your class and which of the Multiple Intelligences they possess. How could you differentiate your instruction to most effectively build on the strengths and interests of your students and keep them actively engaged in learning?

TABLE 3.1 ■ Howard Gardner's Theory of Multiple Intelligences	
Verbal/Linguistic Intelligence	Involves sensitivity to spoken and written language, the ability to learn languages, and the capacity to use language to accomplish certain goals.
Logical/Mathematical Intelligence	Consists of the capacity to analyze problems logically, carry out mathematical operations, and investigate issues scientifically.
Visual/Spatial Intelligence	Involves the potential to recognize and use the patterns of wide space and more-confined areas.
Bodily/Kinesthetic Intelligence	Entails the potential of using one's whole body or parts of the body to solve problems. It is the ability to use mental abilities to coordinate bodily movements.
Musical/Rhythmic Intelligence	Involves skill in the performance, composition, and appreciation of musical patterns.
Interpersonal Intelligence	Is concerned with the capacity to understand the intentions, motivations, and desires of other people. It allows people to work effectively with others.
Intrapersonal Intelligence	Entails the capacity to understand oneself, and to appreciate one's feelings, fears, and motivations.

Source: Gardner, H. (2001). *Frames of mind: The theory of multiple intelligences.* New York, NY: Basic Books. Copyright © 2011 Howard Gardner. Reprinted with permission of Basic Books, a member of the Perseus Books Group.

UNDERSTANDING AND USING DATA
USING MULTIPLE INTELLIGENCES TO DEVELOP AN INSTRUCTIONAL MATCH

Although there are criticisms of Howard Gardner's MI model, it provides a way of thinking about the importance of teachers matching their instructional approach to the different ways that students learn. There are several free questionnaires on the web that can be used with students to determine which of the Multiple Intelligences they prefer.

Intelligence of Students in One Class

Part I

Study the data presented in Table A with this question in mind:

1. What do you see as the overall distribution of students in terms of their intelligence?

TABLE A ■ Distribution of Student Multiple Intelligences (1 = Low, 5 = High)							
Student	Verbal/ Linguistic	Logical/ Mathematical	Visual/ Spatial	Bodily/ Kinesthetic	Musical/ Rhythmic	Interpersonal	Intrapersonal
Anne	2	1	3	3	2	4	5
Bill	1	2	4	2	1	2	2
Charlie	5	3	2	2	2	1	2
Elizabeth	4	3	5	3	3	3	2
Fran	4	3	4	1	4	3	2
Juan	4	4	3	1	2	1	2
Maria	3	2	5	3	1	2	2
Roberta	4	2	3	4	2	3	4

Do not read further until you have developed your answer to the question above.

Part II

Read the rest of this feature only after you have developed your analysis of the MI distribution in Table A.

One way to summarize the student information is to count how many of the students had high and low scores for each intelligence. For example, in Table B, how many students scored high (4 or 5), and how many students scored low (1 or 2) on each intelligence?

TABLE B ■ High and Low Multiple Intelligences Scores for Students in One Class							
Number	Verbal/ Linguistic	Logical/ Mathematical	Visual/ Spatial	Bodily/ Kinesthetic	Musical/ Rhythmic	Interpersonal	Intrapersonal
High	5	1	4	1	1	1	2
Low	2	4	1	4	6	4	6

Matching Instruction to MI

The underlying importance of using the MI model is to have you think more carefully about the extent to which your instructional strategies match up with students' intelligences. When there is a match, there should be greater learning. Now that you have studied the students in Table A, consider the following questions:

1. In developing several weeks of instruction, which styles would you want to strive to match more, and which less?

2. What instructional strategies would you use to have a greater match?

Do not read further until you have developed your answer to these questions.

Matching Instruction to MI Scores

One place to start your lesson planning would be to look for those intelligences where the students scored lowest. Of the eight students, six scored lowest on Musical/Rhythmic and Intrapersonal, which would strongly suggest that matching

(Continued)

(Continued)

instruction to these intelligences would be less likely to be successful.

Five students scored highest on Verbal/Linguistic, and four scored highest on Visual/Spatial. Having lessons that are based in reading, writing, and talking would match up. In this case, having students active and moving around would seem to be less important.

Another important consideration is the subject being taught. These students would be ready for language arts and English classes. However, if these students were in a math class, there would likely be difficulties since only one indicated

that she was Logical/Mathematical. It would be very important to take advantage of the higher scores on Visual/Spatial by using many manipulatives, charts, diagrams, and pictures.

This discussion is only meant to be illustrative. In your teaching, it will be important to be aware not only of how your students score in terms of intelligences, but also of how you score. For example, for the students presented here, if you are predominantly Logical/Mathematical, you would need to be careful not to have your main approach to instruction always be based in this intelligence.

"I'm not daydreaming, Ms Howard. I'm reviewing my intellectual properties."

© Chris Wildt

There are several simple-to-use tests of MI that can be found easily on the Internet. Several of these are free for you to use, as long as you are not copying them for publication. You will immediately see the logic behind each test question: for example, asking whether you have music going on in your head, or if you like to be physically active. Two words of caution in regard to these tests: First, there is little research evidence to support their validity, and second, the responses are simple ratings along a continuum, from low to high. In your teaching, you can more accurately check your students' intelligences through interviewing and observing them at work and at play.

Gifted and Talented Students

One of the challenges facing each teacher, school, and community—as well as the nation—is how to enhance learning for the brightest students. Giftedness in children, as adults, is manifested in intellectual, creative, artistic, or leadership domains, or specific fields such as language, arts, mathematics, or science (National Association for Gifted Children [NAGC], n.d.). According to the NAGC, children in the top 10% of a national and/or local norm are generally considered gifted.

Offering programs for gifted and talented students is the responsibility of local school districts. Over 3 million U.S. students (i.e., 6.4% of the total public school population) are enrolled in gifted and talented programs in public schools (NAGC & Council of State Directors of Programs for the Gifted, 2015). Male and female students participate at about the same rate in these programs, but white and Asian students are overrepresented in these programs.

What do you think happens when gifted students are not challenged? Surprisingly, many of them drop out of school. Researchers have identified several predictors for gifted student dropout, which are discussed in the Challenging Assumptions box.

Implications of Academic Abilities for Learning and Teaching

Clearly, intelligence and academic ability are important factors for teachers to consider. But be careful not to think about intelligence as one simple idea or score on a test. In terms of Gardner's Multiple Intelligences, each of your students will have a different profile. Many will be excellent at speaking and writing (Verbal/Linguistic), some will be good at understanding mathematics and science (Logical/

CHALLENGING ASSUMPTIONS
ARE GIFTED STUDENTS AT LESS RISK OF DROPPING OUT?

The Assumption

Much has been written about the risk of students from low-income families dropping out of school. They are more likely to experience stress as a result of trauma in their lives. Expectations are often lower about the possibility of attending college. Gifted students certainly are smart enough to do well in school, so it would seem that they are less likely to drop out of school. Of those who do drop out, are their reasons the same as or different from the reasons of the less academically able?

Researchers have identified some common experiences of gifted students who later drop out of school. These students report being bored in school; they are often put in classes that are not challenging and filled with busy work that is "intellectually insulting." They report they sleep in class, do a poor job on homework and class assignments, and are likely to skip class and have higher absentee rates. It is not surprising that these students also have more behavior problems and spend time with other students who drop out, and who use illegal drugs and alcohol. Many students feel as if they don't fit in at school.

Implications

The first very important implication for teachers is to not assume that just because one of your students is bright, she or he will not be at risk of dropping out. In some ways, the indicators of being at risk that have been identified for regular students seem to apply for gifted students. Developing supportive relationships, knowing family backgrounds, and establishing a classroom climate that is safe will be effective for all of your students.

Source: Landis, R., & Reschly, A. (2013). Re-examining gifted underachievement and dropout through the lens of student engagement. *Journal for the Education of the Gifted, 36*(2), 220–249.

Mathematical), and others will be fully engaged with music (Musical/Rhythmic). Your challenge will be to devise instructional approaches that take advantage of the rich diversity of all your students. Do not teach as your authors regularly find teachers doing: students seated in a block, the teacher standing and talking at the front, short teacher questions followed by right or wrong student answers, and students then completing desk assignments. This might be all right once in a while. Unfortunately, we see too many teachers using only this approach and doing it the same way every day. Exceptional students should have effective teachers who take into account their differences in intelligences, lived experiences, and cultures.

Exceptionality Based on a Disability?

Thirteen percent of the school population has an identified disability, which is defined as a long-lasting condition such as visual or hearing impairment or a condition that substantially limits basic physical, emotional, or mental activities (National Center for Education Statistics [NCES], 2018). The nation's Individuals with Disabilities Education Act of 1990 (IDEA), originally enacted by Congress as the Education for All Handicapped Children Act of 1975, was established to make sure that children with disabilities had the opportunity to receive a free and appropriate public education. IDEA requires that students with disabilities be educated with regular students whenever possible and in as normal an environment as possible. IDEA guides how states and school districts provide special education and related services to the 6.7 million children between the ages of 3 and 21 who were eligible for those services in 2015–2016 (NCES, 2018).

All teachers are expected to implement an IEP for each student with identified disabilities in their classrooms. The IEP is developed by parents, teachers, special educators, and other specialists, such as a school psychologist or occupational therapist, and indicates the **accommodations** and special services that must be provided to that student. IEPs are updated annually by appropriate school professionals.

Providing services to students with disabilities usually involves a team of professionals and assistants, depending on the severity of the disability. The special educator may team-teach or co-teach a class with a regular teacher or serve as a resource teacher who works with students on the development of skills. Students with severe disabilities such as physical conditions that require feeding tubes are usually supported by a teaching or health assistant to help provide the necessary accommodations.

Students with disabilities will likely need accommodations at least some of the time.

iStock/huePhotography

Identifying Students With Disabilities

You may be asking yourself, "How does a student get identified as needing special education services?" That process is defined in IDEA and must be carefully followed. First, a teacher or other education professional can refer a student for an evaluation. Often, a student who is not making progress, even after several different strategies have been tried (see the information on Response to Intervention later in this chapter), is referred for an evaluation. A parent who is concerned about his or her child can also request an evaluation verbally or in writing. A school may not do the assessment before the parent has given permission.

The evaluation must be completed in a reasonable amount of time after a referral has been made. The child must be assessed in all areas of the identified disability. For example, a child who may have a visual disability would have the appropriate type of vision assessment. A child who may have a learning disability would take assessments designed to evaluate that disability. Once all the assessments have been completed, a group of professionals, along with the child's parents, weigh the results and determine if the child meets the definition of a disability as outlined in IDEA. If the team decides the student meets the criteria, the student becomes eligible for special education and related services such as speech–language therapy, psychological services, school nurse services, transportation, and/or occupational therapy that are necessary to help a child benefit from special education.

Within 30 calendar days after the determination is made, an IEP team must meet to write an IEP for the child. To do this, a team of educators, related service personnel, and the parents meets. The student can also be a part of this team when appropriate. The team meets at a time agreeable to the parents and to the school and discusses the child's assessment results, the child's progress in school, and any other relevant information. Based on this discussion, the team develops and writes an IEP that includes annual goals for student progress. (See a section later in this chapter for more information about what is included in the IEP.) If the parents do not agree with the IEP, they may go through an appeal process. The school is responsible for making sure that everything listed in the IEP is carried out.

Categories of Disability

School professionals categorize children with disabilities to determine the most appropriate services for a child. Figure 3.2 shows the number of students being served for each disability category. More than one in three students receiving special education services have a specific learning disability, which makes it difficult for them to read, write, or compute. The second-largest group of students receiving services is composed of students with speech or language impairments.

This section provides a brief introduction to the categories with the largest number of students. You should take at least one course during your teacher preparation program to provide an overview of these disabilities and understand the accommodations necessary to help students with disabilities learn.

Learning Disabilities

Students with learning disabilities usually comprehend the material being studied, but it takes them more time or they need a different strategy to access the information. The problem is that they can't easily understand or use spoken or written language, which affects their ability to listen, think, speak, read, write, spell, or do mathematical calculations. This category includes dyslexia, perceptual disabilities, and developmental aphasia. These students are in regular classrooms with accommodations, which are purposeful additional supports or adjustments in instruction. Their IEP will specify the accommodations to be used in the classroom and in testing situations. In mathematics, it could allow the student to use a calculator. Student work might be modified with fewer questions or a shorter

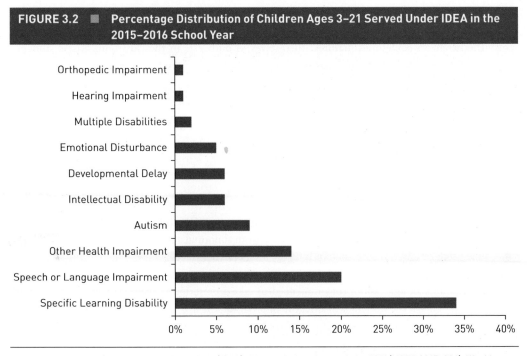

FIGURE 3.2 ■ **Percentage Distribution of Children Ages 3–21 Served Under IDEA in the 2015–2016 School Year**

Source: Snyder, T. D., de Brey, C., & Dillow, S. A. (2018). *Digest of education statistics 2016* (NCES 2017–094). Washington, DC: National Center for Education Statistics, Institute of Education Sciences, U.S. Department of Education.

Note: "Other health impairments" are due to having limited strength, vitality, or alertness due to chronic or acute health problems such as a heart condition, rheumatic fever, sickle cell anemia, leukemia, or diabetes. Deaf/blindness, traumatic brain injury, and visual impairments each account for less than 0.5% of the children served under IDEA and are not shown in this figure.

reading assignment. Extra time may be required to complete an assignment, or the student could be allowed to use a computer for writing assignments.

Speech Impairment

Speech impairment is a communication disorder. A student might stutter or be unable to produce certain words or sounds. Some students cannot process language (i.e., they can hear directions but cannot repeat them), preventing them from following the teacher's directions for an assignment. Students may be able to comprehend at the same levels as other students, but they may not be able to put their thoughts into words due to difficulties with word retrieval and recall. They may have trouble understanding directional prepositions such as *under* and *above*. These students should be receiving support from a speech pathologist. In the regular classroom, teachers may have to allow additional wait time for the student to process the question and to respond to it. Just because these students take extra time for processing or speaking does not mean that they do not comprehend and will not perform well academically.

Intellectual Disability

Students with this disability have significant problems in cognitive functioning and in using socially appropriate behaviors for their age. The most severely affected of these students participate in life skills classes to prepare them to function independently as adults. The majority of these students are classified as mildly intellectually disabled and spend most of their school time in regular classrooms. The IEPs for these students require work modified to their skill level, more repetition of work, and shorter time periods for work with breaks built into their schedule.

Emotionally Disturbed

Students who are emotionally disturbed exhibit behaviors that impact their ability to learn, and that cannot be explained by other intellectual, sensory, or health factors. They have trouble maintaining appropriate interpersonal relationships with their classmates and teachers. They may always be unhappy or depressed. They may develop physical symptoms and fears associated with personal or school problems. The behaviors sometimes manifest themselves in outbursts in the classroom. These students' behaviors may be evaluated by professionals who may indicate the need for therapy. Many of these students have experienced abuse or family problems, or another traumatic incident that has affected their behavior. Students with severe behavior problems that interfere with their learning and the learning of their classmates may be removed from classrooms until they are stabilized.

Autism Spectrum Disorder (ASD)

Rather than being a narrow set of factors that can be easily classified, the **autism** label represents a range of factors and variations in intensities that are referred to as a spectrum. Autism is a developmental disorder that appears in the first years of life. Parents may find that their two-year-old has difficulties with social interactions and/or with verbal and nonverbal communication. The child may be slow to develop language and may not play with others. Autism is related to an abnormal development of the brain. Although vaccines are widely linked to autism, there is no research evidence that they are a cause of autism.

An early diagnosis is important, and treatment programs are intensive. If school-age children have atypical irritability or aggression, they may need to take a prescription drug. Teachers need to work closely with parents; if the student is in a treatment program, the teacher needs to be sure to know about it and to use complementary strategies in the classroom.

TEACHERS' LOUNGE
ABI SPEAKS

© Julie J. Conn

Teaching children puts forth new adventures, delights, and challenges every day. Finding and utilizing the best curriculum and instructional materials for children is critical—particularly as they mature and become fixed in their ways and habits. It can indeed be difficult for any of us to learn new material and new ways, but for a child with Autism Spectrum Disorder (ASD) who is functionally nonverbal, the word *difficult* might well be replaced with *impossible*.

I teach a class specifically designed for providing intensive instruction to children with ASD. My students exhibit a range of interference with communication, social skills, and academics. Abi, diagnosed with ASD and functionally nonverbal, radiated facial expressions of sheer joy when she saw digital photo stories I had created with her classmates' photos and voices. The digital stories utilized creative photoshopped pictures of the child displayed in a storyboard format. The child recorded the story line (which used words from Abi's reading vocabulary) over the pictures to produce a digital story that she could view and hear. It is important to understand that the child must be able to speak into the microphone to create these verbal digital stories!

At the end of the third year of working on many words with the now 10-year-old Abi, she could see and say (with some interference help) the words *horse*, *a*, *car*, and *ball*. I upped the ante to get a few more words from Abi by collecting photos of some of her favorite items and people. I took pictures of Abi, her toy dog Pete, her mother, and a few other animals that had made their way to the class's show-and-tell (a bunny, a horse, and a skink, which is a type of lizard).

This is where I must tell you that Abi's mother had never heard Abi call her *Mom*, or any other name, for that matter. The closest Abi had come to saying *Mom* was an "mmm" sound! We worked day after day on trying to have Abi say the correct word with each picture. I promised Abi she could make a photo story if she would keep working hard to voice out and pronounce the words.

Finally, the day came when I thought I could get a controlled voice from Abi! I arranged the photos in no particular order in the digital photo story web tool and sat Abi in front of the microphone. She looked at each picture and excitedly spoke one by one: "me," "Momma," "Pete"! The first three words were absolutely beautiful! She continued to do her best to say "bunny," "horse," "lizard," "skink," and "The End." We projected the story on the whiteboard screen, and the whole class watched as Abi spoke! Abi watched the children and was excited at their reactions. What an amazing postproduction party we had!

Abi went home from school. In the course of the evening, she looked at her mother, and said, "Momma." I know this because her mother, in tears, immediately called to share the historic event! Abi's mother had waited more than 10 years to hear that word!

"Never give up the dream." As a teacher, you are charged to find just the right ingredients to make sure each child grows and flourishes!

Abi's photo story is available as a YouTube video titled "Abi Speaks."

—Julie J. Conn
Teacher of Exceptional Children
Sugarloaf Elementary School
Hendersonville, North Carolina

Other Disabilities

These categories include students who are blind, deaf, or deaf/blind or who have Attention Deficit Hyperactivity Disorder (ADHD), physical impairments, seizure disorders, traumatic brain injury, or cerebral palsy. The number of students in each of these categories accounts for less than 0.5% of the students served by IDEA (NCES, 2018). These students should be part of the regular classroom as much as possible. Students with the most severe disabilities may receive much of their instruction in a special education classroom and join students without disabilities at lunch and during specials such as music, art, and physical education. The multiple disabilities included in this group are more likely to be determined by medical evidence than by other forms of evaluation.

Twice Exceptional (2e)

Yes, there are many factors and categories that teachers can use to see each of their students as an exceptional individual. In Chapter 2 and throughout this chapter, concepts, models, indicators, and research findings have been introduced for seeing each student as an individual. More than likely, each student represents a unique combination of these factors and categories. One such case is the student who is gifted in one area, such as mathematics, and at the same time is behind in reading, or can't sit still. These students are twice exceptional or 2e. They are academically able in some areas, and they also have an identifiable disability. Often, teachers fail to understand that just because Sarah is quick to understand a science concept doesn't mean that she can easily manage her ADHD.

HOW SHOULD SCHOOLS SERVE STUDENTS WITH DISABILITIES?

If you are preparing to be a general education teacher, you are quite likely to have students with disabilities in your classroom throughout your career. A critical factor in working effectively with these students is to remember that they are more like other students than unlike them. However, you will have to make accommodations or modifications to promote their learning. They will have a formal IEP, which could include an aide. The school should have special educators available to advise you on the implementation of students' IEPs.

One of the problems is that most schools have not been designed for some of the needed accommodations. Whiteboards may be too high and desks too low for students in wheelchairs, and ramps are not always available. Computers, amplification devices, books in Braille, and other educational resources will provide students with disabilities the opportunity to learn at the same level as their peers.

Inclusion

Inclusion is the integration of students with disabilities into the regular classroom. The goal is to ensure that students "who have been traditionally excluded from and marginalized from schooling are able to access, participate, and engage in the full range of educational opportunities made available within learning environments such as classrooms, schools, and school systems" (Gonzalez & Mulligan, 2014, p. 109). Students with disabilities and without disabilities are in the same class, but they do not always work in the same way, depending on the nature and severity of the disability. The curriculum may be adapted and instruction modified to allow access to learning for all students. Teaching and medical assistants may be assigned to work on skills development and accommodations with the students with disabilities in the classroom. Special educators may provide services to the students at defined times during the school day.

About 95% of school-age students with disabilities in the fall of 2015 were enrolled in regular schools (NCES, 2018). In full inclusion, students with disabilities and other special needs receive all of their education in the regular classroom. They are never pulled into settings in which all of the students are students with disabilities. In reality, three in five students with disabilities spend most of their school days in regular classrooms, being pulled out periodicaly for special services from a special educator, a speech–language pathologist, a school nurse, or a school psychologist. Students who are most likely to be placed in segregated special education classes are students with intellectual disabilities and students with multiple disabilities (NCES, 2018).

Most teachers will work in an inclusive classroom that includes students with disabilities and students without disabilities who share the learning space and collaborate in the learning process.

However, students should not be pulled out of the regular classroom during language arts and mathematics lessons. For example, if students are pulled out during reading instruction to be tutored in reading, they are not getting more reading instruction. Instead, they are receiving alternative reading instruction. Because music, art, and physical education classes also provide the opportunity to develop social skills with students without disabilities, students with disabilities are almost always integrated into those classes.

Some people question whether there is a negative impact on general education students when students with disabilities are included in their classrooms. In an analysis of more than 100 research articles focused on this issue, one group of researchers found that in the overwhelming majority of cases (81%), there were either positive or neutral effects for students without disabilities (Kalambouka, Farrell, Dyson, & Kaplan, 2007). In a more recent study, Fruth and Woods (2015) found that there was no significant difference in the performance of students without disabilities in inclusive classrooms compared to that of students in noninclusive environments in reading, science, and social studies.

Individualized Education Programs (IEPs)

The purpose of an IEP is to set reasonable learning goals for a child and to clearly state the services that the school district will provide for the child. Because it is individualized, each IEP is unique, but all IEPs contain specific types of information, including (but not limited to) the following:

- The child's Present Level of Educational Performance (sometimes called PLOP or PLP). This section describes how the student is performing in school and includes information on district-wide and state-wide testing. It explains how the disability impacts the student's ability to learn the general education curriculum and handle functional activities such as socializing.

- Annual goals for the child. Team members decide what they think the child can reasonably accomplish in a year. These goals should be realistic and measurable.

- The special education and related services to be provided to the child, including supplementary aids and services (such as a communication device or speech therapy).

- A description of the accommodations or modifications that will be provided to the student. Accommodations are changes in how a child shows what he or she has learned. Modifications are changes in what is taught to or expected of a student.

- How much of the school day the child will be educated separately from nondisabled children or will participate in extracurricular or other nonacademic activities such as lunch or clubs. IDEA requires participation at the fullest level possible. This is called the **Least Restrictive Environment (LRE)**.

- How (and if) the child is to participate in state-wide and district-wide assessments, including what modifications to tests the child needs.

- When services and modifications will begin, how often they will be provided, where they will be provided, and how long they will last.

- How school personnel will measure the child's progress toward the annual goals and how they will inform parents of their child's progress.

- When a student turns 16, the IEP must include a plan for postgraduate transition. The transition plan outlines the services that will be provided to the student to help him or her graduate from high school and achieve post–high school goals.

A student's IEP is reviewed by the IEP team at least once a year, but it can be reviewed more frequently if the parents or school asks for a review. The same process for the initial development of the IEP must be followed when it is reviewed.

At least every three years, the child must be reevaluated. This evaluation is often called a triennial, and includes the same kinds of assessments used in the original determination evaluation. The purpose of the triennial is to find out if the child continues to be a "child with a disability," as defined by IDEA, and what the child's educational needs are. However, the child must be reevaluated more often if conditions warrant or if the child's parent or teacher asks for a new evaluation.

The development and regular reviews of an Individualized Education Program must involve professional educators and parents.

Accommodations and Modifications

A critical component of special education is the individualization of instruction to meet the specific needs of each student. Different terms are used to describe changes that may be made—*accommodations* and *modifications* are the most commonly used terms to describe ways that instruction may be changed so that children with disabilities can be successful. These terms are often used interchangeably, although there are some differences in their meanings.

In general, an accommodation refers to a change that helps a student work around or overcome a disability. The change is in how a child does his or her work at school, not in what is being taught. For example, a student who is deaf may have an interpreter in the classroom, signing so that the student always understands and is a part of what is happening in the classroom. A modification, however, refers to changes in what a student is taught or expected to learn. For example, a modification for a student with a mental impairment could be changing an assignment to make it less demanding and more appropriate for the student's ability level. Modifications or accommodations are generally made in the five areas outlined in Table 3.2.

What is most important to know about modifications and accommodations is that both are meant to help children improve their learning.

Parental Involvement

We know that one of the most effective means of helping students succeed is to engage families in their children's education. This is even more important when a student has a disability. Parents of students with disabilities must be involved with school professionals in the process of determining the best treatment for their children. Classroom teachers need to work closely with all the parents.

In surveys of parents of special education students, parents generally indicate that, for the most part, they are satisfied with their students' educational experiences. Families of most students with disabilities are involved in supporting their children's educational development at home, especially through homework support. Parents' involvement with the school includes attending meetings, parent–teacher conferences, supporting classroom activities, and volunteering. Many families of youths with disabilities hold high expectations for the children's future success, which has been shown to relate to higher engagement and achievement among these students.

Not all families have such positive evaluations of the services provided their children with disabilities. Low-income families and families of color are more likely to feel their children are being ignored

TABLE 3.2 ■ Common Modifications or Accommodations for Students With Disabilities			
Scheduling	• Giving the student extra time to complete assignments or tests	Instruction	• Using more than one way to demonstrate or explain information
	• Allowing the student to take frequent breaks		• Reducing the difficulty of assignments
	• Breaking up testing over several days		• Reducing the reading level
Setting	• Working in a small group		• Using a student/peer tutor
	• Working one-on-one with the teacher		• Providing study guides or review sheets
	• Providing special lighting	Student Response	• Allowing answers to be given orally or dictated
	• Allowing the student to use a separate room or place to study		• Using a word processor for written work
Materials	• Providing audiotaped lectures or books		• Using sign language, a communication device, Braille, or native language if it is not English
	• Giving the student copies of teacher's lecture notes		• Using a modified answer sheet
	• Using large-print books, Braille, or books on CD (digital text)		

or not adequately supported by educators. They feel that school officials place them in subordinate or inferior roles as the parents try to advocate for their children. Educators, on the other hand, view the families' resistance as disinterest or a threat (Graff & Vazquez, 2014). Building trust with families of color and low-income families will be critical in being able to collaborate to serve children effectively. Parents know their children and must be provided equal input in discussions about the actions to be taken to support their children, including approaches that are culturally based. Parents must believe that their contributions and expectations for their children's well-being are valued and respected by the educators with whom they are working

Disproportionate Placement

Continuing concerns exist about the overidentification of students with disabilities that is based on the students' ethnicity or family background. For example, students receiving special education services are disproportionately male, African American, Latino, American Indian, English Language Learners (ELLs), and whites from low-income families. Students being served under IDEA include 16% of African American students, 17% of American Indian/Alaska Native students, 14% of white students, and 7% of Asian students (NCES, 2018). Educators should monitor their consideration of making referrals of students to be tested for placement in these classes to be sure that there is a clear learning need rather than an underlying bias of some sort.

HOW CAN WE IDENTIFY AND SUPPORT STRUGGLING STUDENTS?

There will be times as a teacher when you will have a student who should be learning, but is not. This can be perplexing and frustrating. Based on what the student has done in the past, you are certain that she or he should be doing well now, but something has changed. Students can be struggling for many reasons. If adjusting instruction doesn't work, then you need to look farther afield.

Some students struggle due to not having the required prior knowledge. Students who are new to the school, or new to your classroom, may not know how things are done at the new school and struggle in adapting to the new culture. In other cases, a family situation such as a divorce or a parent losing a job can be a cause. Most students will struggle at some time. When you detect that a student is struggling, you should strive to find out what's going on.

Effective teachers have high expectations for the academic performance of all of their students, believing that all students can learn. They do not give up on students. You will have to be careful not to stereotype the academic ability of students based on their race, socioeconomic status, gender, family background, or the presence of a disability.

At the same time, some very real differences exist in the experiences of students based on opportunity gaps they

All students will struggle at times. Teachers need to be ready to reach out with support and encouragement.

have experienced. A good teacher seizes on these differences as keys to helping each student learn, rather than as levers that discount a student's potential. Most students will face some academic or other challenges as they progress through school regardless of their cultural group memberships. It is the job of the teacher to know when students are struggling and to intervene as soon as possible to help them get back on track.

Signs of Struggling Students

Another major grouping of students is those who are **at risk**. This includes students who are performing below grade level, are not engaged in classroom activities, and are not interacting appropriately with classmates. They may have fallen behind in learning; they may be at risk of dropping out of school. For you as a teacher, this is another way that some of your students may be exceptional: They are struggling in one or more area that needs a teacher's attention and intervention.

The reasons come right back to the ways outlined in this chapter and the importance of seeing each student as exceptional. For example, students from low-income families are more likely to exhibit elevated stress levels (Center on the Developing Child at Harvard University, 2016). Students who move a lot and do not stay in one school are at risk. Students in schools where the environment is not safe, and may be toxic, are at risk. Very bright students may be bored with the level of assignments. Other students may be bored with the repetitive, uninteresting, and unmeaningful work they are assigned. Family issues, threats in their communities, missing meals, and health problems also can place students at risk.

In this section, we will explore the impact of these challenges on learning and the possible outcomes for students. We will also review a program that is designed to identify struggling students early and develop appropriate interventions for keeping them engaged in the learning process.

The Impact of Trauma

A significant number of children and youth have experienced adverse childhood experiences (ACEs) that affect their behavior and learning in school and throughout life if not treated (Plumb, Bush, & Kersevich, 2016). Research has found that exposure to violence and chronic stress can disrupt the process of normal child development, "producing negative changes in the structure and function of the brain that are pervasive and lasting" (National Association of School Psychologists, 2015, p. 2). These traumas include losing a parent or guardian, neglect, abuse, abandonment, family conflict, betrayal, economic instability, homelessness, the loss of a friend or family member by murder or a car accident, time in a war zone or refugee camp, and many other life-altering events. A traumatic event has been experienced by 43% of youth by the time they are 18 years old (Craig, 2017).

As teachers, we may not know the trauma faced by our students. Unless you have developed a positive relationship with students, they are likely not to share with you a traumatic event because they don't know how you will respond or they think you won't care. If you are perceptive, you can see that a student is acting differently than normal. You may sense that something has happened to lead to the student being fidgety, not being able to concentrate, lashing out at a peer, or being very distracted. These traumatic events can be very disruptive to the learning process. Understanding that there is a reason for the student's behavior will help you develop an intervention or accommodation to help the student through this period. A discussion about trauma-sensitive schools in Chapter 4 will provide you more guidance on working with students who are experiencing trauma in their lives.

Early Warning Signs of Students Dropping Out

A key time of risk for students is when there are **transitions** from one school to the next. The move from elementary school to middle school is a risky time, as is the transition to high school. One of the authors was working with a high school in California that was able to identify 108 students who disappeared between the spring of eighth grade and the following fall's beginning of ninth grade. No one had any idea what had happened to those students.

Many opinions are offered to explain why students drop out of school, and many solutions are proposed for fixing the problem. Most of these address some characteristic of schools ("High schools are too large"), blame someone else ("Well, if they had learned to read in elementary school, we wouldn't have this problem"), or advocate a particular solution (e.g., small learning communities, homeschooling, more/less technology). The contributing factors can be different for each student; however, for students in general, there are several predictors that you should keep in mind.

THINKING DIFFERENTLY
THERAPY DOG AS EMOTIONAL SUPPORT FOR A SCHOOL

Roxanne James

Meet Rigley and Principal Roxanne James, both of whom are at Jerome Mack Middle School in Las Vegas, Nevada. Mack MS has nearly 1,300 students, 75% of whom are Hispanic and 93% of whom receive free or discounted lunch. The school has 60 teachers, 28 support staff, and 4 administrators. The school community deals with many stressors on a regular basis, including stress related to socioeconomic issues and mental health stresses, such as student suicides. The school scores low on standardized tests and is ranked low in comparison to other middle schools.

In response to all of these stressors, Mrs. James and her staff go the extra mile and strive to think of different ways that they can support student learning. They have implemented a variety of activities and programs to support students, parents, and the community. One of Mrs. James's most recent initiatives was to have a therapy dog for the school. She sought out a puppy that would have the right temperament and be friendly and easygoing. His name is Rigley, after a certain baseball field. However, out of respect for that ball field and as a devoted Cubs fan, Mrs. James adjusted the spelling. He has been training to be a certified therapy dog.

While service dogs are trained to do tasks and work for their handlers, therapy dogs are trained to provide psychological support. Therapy dogs generally visit schools, but Rigley is a full-time member of Mack MS. He is based in the school's main office. He seems to sense when someone is stressed out. He will go to the person, put his head on his or her lap, and stay with him or her as long as is needed. Rigley not only supports students and staff; when a discouraged parent or other school visitor arrives, he will walk right up to them. From time to time, Rigley will be mentioned on the homepage of the Mack MS website.

Researchers at Johns Hopkins University found that the following three indicators could predict an eighth grader's potential to drop out of school within four years of starting the ninth grade (Everyone Graduates Center, 2018):

- Attending school 80% or less of the time

- Failing mathematics in the eighth grade

- Failing English in the eighth grade

Other studies have found that higher dropout rates are also linked to "weak school engagement, increased student academic expectations, reduced support from teachers, problematic or deviant behavior, work or family responsibilities, moving to a new school in grade 9, and attending a school with lower achievement scores" (Stoker, Liu, & Arellano, 2017, p. 2). In addition, students who have strong noncognitive skills that allow them to control their academic behavior, study effectively, and feel a sense of belonging in the school have a better chance of completing high school on time.

The ninth grade has been found to be a make-or-break year for students. More students fail ninth grade than any other grade in high school, and the students who are held back are more likely to drop out. Research in large urban school districts has shown that there are two powerful indicators of whether a student will complete high school (Faria et al., 2017). The first is course performance, including course credits earned and course grades, during middle and high school. The second most powerful indicator is the attendance rate. The biggest risk factor for failing ninth grade is the number of absences during the first 30 days of high school (Heppen & Therriault, 2009). Students who miss over two days in September are five times more likely to be chronically absent for the year than those students who miss two or fewer days. Students who miss more than four days in September are 16 times more likely to be chronically absent from school (Olson, 2014). Intervening early with these students can be the difference in their completion of high school.

An important implication of this research is that as early as first grade, teachers have a responsibility to be sensitive to the risks of their students dropping out in the future. Reducing the risk of students dropping out is not something that can be left solely to high school teachers and administrators. A number of states, as well as many schools and school districts, are now tracking these kinds of indicators to develop an early warning system to identify students who are at risk of dropping out. With this information, teachers and administrators hopefully can intervene in effective ways to make it more likely that all students will graduate from school.

The Importance of Vocabulary

A major theme in neuroscience is the critical importance of the first five years in a child's development (see Figure 3.1). Researchers in other fields have identified related patterns that are important indicators of a child's cognitive development that also are indicators of the child's readiness for school. One of the most important of these is vocabulary.

The findings from studies about the size of vocabulary of young children are summarized in Table 3.3. The overall patterns and themes that emerge from these studies are profound. Children in extreme-poverty families are exposed to significantly fewer words than are children in working-class families. The number of words heard doubles again for children in professional-class families. Keep in mind that these studies are for groups of children. The findings may, or may not, apply to the students you teach, even if they fall in a particular economic category.

Look at the last column in Table 3.3. The accumulating effect is that across the first four years of life, children from higher economic classes generally hear millions of words more than their peers from low-income families. This is a characteristic of how each of your students is exceptional that requires you to develop in-depth understanding about how best to design instruction. Please keep in mind that the implications of these differences apply all the way through high school. It is not only teachers in elementary schools who need to consider the size of vocabulary. Secondary teachers also need to be aware of differences in vocabulary size and be sure to address the development of academic vocabulary

TABLE 3.3 ■ Vocabulary Development in the Early Years			
In a typical hour, the average child hears:			
Family Status	**Actual Differences in Quantity of Words Heard**	**Actual Differences in Quality of Words Heard**	**Words Heard in 4 Years**
Welfare	616 words	5 affirmations, 11 prohibitions	13 million
Working class	1,251 words	12 affirmations, 7 prohibitions	26 million
Professional	2,153 words	32 affirmations, 5 prohibitions	45 million

Source: Adapted from tables in University of Oregon. (n.d.). *Big ideas in beginning reading.* Center on Teaching and Learning, University of Oregon, Eugene.

within each lesson. Based on these data, one important question is "What could society and educators do to dramatically increase the vocabulary of students who have not had opportunities to develop the vocabulary that is necessary for academic success in schools and the economy?"

Take a close look at Table 3.3. The significant differences in the quantity of words heard are not the only pattern in the data. Depending on family economic status, there are significant differences in what is said to children. Distinctions are made between affirmations—offering positive comments and supports—and prohibitions—that is, rebukes, or telling the child not to do something. Notice how the proportions of affirmations and prohibitions change across the three family statuses. The quantity changes, but the real significance is that the ratio changes—prohibitions are a relatively small proportion of the words heard by children in the professional families. We need to ensure these patterns do not continue in our interactions with students in classrooms.

You might think that even if some students begin school with a more limited vocabulary, they will catch up. Unfortunately, the vocabulary gap based on family status does not shrink as students move through elementary school. Instead, it increases. It is estimated that a child's vocabulary doubles between Grades 3 and 7. The problem is that if some third-grade students begin the year with a vocabulary size that is half that of others, doubling it does not lead to their catching up. Instead, they are falling farther behind.

An obvious implication from the data presented in Table 3.3 is that you will need to be cautious in making predictions about the size and type of vocabulary your students bring to your classroom. Regardless of family status, your students will each have heard a different quantity of words. They also will have heard words of different quality.

Those of you who plan to teach in middle and high school cannot escape the vocabulary gap and its consequences. Students who leave elementary school with half the size of vocabulary of their peers will most certainly have trouble keeping up when they are in high school. Without adequate vocabulary size, students cannot solve mathematics problems, read literature, or engage in safe science laboratory investigations. All teachers need to post key vocabulary for each lesson and need to continually work on reducing the vocabulary gap.

Here is an example of a successful strategy used by one high school: One year in a high school in Douglas County, Colorado, all of the teachers agreed to work together on increasing the vocabulary size of all their students. A list of words was established for each week, and all the teachers engaged in helping students understand and use the words. They did this because the previous year's students scored lower on the verbal part of the SAT than the staff thought they should. What do you think happened? Yes, the following year, SAT verbal scores were up.

If you are not careful, the vocabulary gap can be used to "sort, distance, and distinguish between families that academically supported their children and those that did not" (Adair, Colegrove, & McManus, 2017). Rather than actively promoting vocabulary development and engaging all students in stimulating and productive discussions and projects, it can become an excuse for lower academic performance. The students' families are blamed for their children's poor performance. As a result, we could revert to low expectations for these students and stop challenging them to perform at high levels.

We must use multiple dynamic and meaningful learning experiences to ensure students are using stronger vocabularies. Encouraging students to talk with you and each other in small groups and full group discussions will contribute to the development of vocabulary (Adair et al., 2017).

Response to Intervention (RTI)

When you visit classrooms, it is likely that you will see students performing at different levels; some will be struggling. There will be a variety of reasons—maybe they have had a lot of absences, maybe they have learning difficulties, maybe they are ELLs, or maybe they are suffering from a recent trauma—and maybe they haven't had consistent teaching. For whatever reason, they are beginning to fall behind. A process called **Response to Intervention (RTI)** has been implemented in many schools as a strategy for identifying these students and to help them before they get too far behind. This process can also prevent many of these students from being identified as needing special education services when that is not the case.

The RTI process begins with screening of all children in a regular classroom. Interventions are provided to struggling learners at increasing levels of intensity (often called *tiers*). Progress is carefully monitored and based on individual student response to the intervention.

In the earliest or lower tier of RTI, many students who may be having some difficulties will be given small interventions. Most of these students will improve, and no other interventions will be needed. However, if they don't show progress, a more intensive set of interventions will be applied. For those small number of students who still do not show progress, additional interventions will be administered. Often, but not always, these will be done through special education services.

Although there are many ways to implement RTI in a school and classroom, its purpose is to make sure that each student is evaluated individually, that struggling students are identified early, and that all students receive what they need to be successful in school. Some school systems have adopted a similar system called a Multi-Tiered System of Supports (MTSS). Acronyms of programs related to exceptionality that are commonly used in schools are listed in Table 3.4. We will describe RTI more fully in Chapter 13.

TABLE 3.4 ■ Common Acronyms for Programs Related to Exceptionality	
LRE	Least Restrictive Environment
MTSS	Multi-Tiered System of Supports
PBIS	Positive Behavioral Interventions and Supports
RTI	Response to Intervention
SEL	Social and Emotional Learning
UDL	Universal Design for Learning

Labeling of Students

Another all-too-frequently used strategy for characterizing students is to label them as being representative of a certain stereotypic group: "She should be in the GATE [gifted and talented education] program." "He is homeless. You know he's living in a car!" Other students will be labeled as at risk, or as having limited English proficiency, or for having an IEP. All too often, these labels are used as rationalization for a student not doing well in school. At the same time, these labels represent another set of categories that can be useful in considering ways that each student is exceptional.

One of the authors of this text had an experience related to this type of simplistic labeling. While studying implementation of a standards-based approach to teaching mathematics in one of the U.S. Department of Defense school districts based in Germany, he heard teachers refer to "those Abrams children." Several teachers went on to exclaim, "Well, you know those kids can't learn this way." Not knowing if these children were from a particular part of Germany, or who they were, the author asked a colleague to explain who/what were Abrams kids. It turns out that there is a type of armored vehicle that is called the Abrams tank. Some teachers had decided that the children of the military personnel who worked with these tanks were not as able to learn through a standards-based approach. They were categorized as being less able to learn simply because of the work of their parents.

HOW CAN SCHOOLS MEET THE NEEDS OF ALL STUDENTS?

The concepts, descriptions, and study findings we've discussed in this chapter make it clear that students can be exceptional in many different ways. Each of these descriptions and categories can be a

Each student brings a unique set of knowledge and experiences to the classroom that can be used to enrich learning.

helpful guide for teachers to teach in ways that greatly increase student learning. At the same time, overuse of labels and making simplistic generalizations can be harmful. We always need to keep in mind that generalities will not nicely fit each individual student. For example, gifted students can be at risk, and ELL students can excel. There are many possible factors that can contribute to each student succeeding or failing to achieve at grade level and with each subject. Also, the fact that a student is currently struggling academically, socially, emotionally, or physically does not have to result in that student being a failure in school. It should be seen as a challenge that can be overcome.

You as the teacher will be making the difference. You as a teacher need to use all of the indicators and your own observations and assessments to identify the different ways that each student is exceptional. Regardless of his or her entering profile, it is your job to devise ways to match instruction with each student's ways of learning. Outstanding teachers are aware of each student's potential, as well as any at-risk indicators. They will use all of these concepts and insights as information to help construct a classroom learning environment that is safe and centered on everyone's learning.

Differentiated Instruction

As has been emphasized throughout this chapter, not all students learn in the same ways. They are not all ready to learn at the same level at the same time or even at the same grade level. They have different interests and intelligences. Therefore, we can't teach them all the same thing in the same way throughout a school year. An educational leader who has synthesized hundreds of research studies on what we know about student learning in classrooms, John Hattie (2009), found that many students are not engaged in their learning. Some cannot keep up. Some lose interest or are bored because the content is not challenging. Nearly two in three students reported that teachers did not care about their learning success.

Differentiated instruction is an approach that provides multiple options for learning based on the learning needs, learning preferences, interests, and readiness of each student (Tomlinson, 2017). It attends to the need for accommodations and modifications for ELLs and students with disabilities. It should ensure "that struggling, advanced, and in-between learners; students with varied cultural heritage and children with a broad array of background experiences all grow as much as they possibly can each day, each week, and throughout the year" (Tomlinson, 2014, p. 3). It encourages students to interact with the content in different ways, submit different types of projects, and become engaged and responsible for their own learning. It models student-centered learning by placing students and their needs and interests at the center of instruction in an environment where the teacher is also a learner.

Most students struggle at some point in some subject as they progress through school. Some students have more aptitude in mathematics, science, reading, or music than other students. Some students need more assistance in learning a new concept or skills while other students are ready to work on advanced projects. You can learn about a student's readiness to learn by conducting formative assessments and then adjusting your instruction to meet their needs. Knowing the interests of your students will help you develop activities and representations that keep them engaged in their learning and make it meaningful for them. Their interests span a broad range of areas such as sports and other activities in which they participate or follow; books, music, and movies that spark their interest; and social and political issues that they support. Planning instruction that recognizes students' different learning profiles will allow students to learn in ways that take advantage of their intelligence preferences, gender, culture, and other factors that influence their learning (Tomlinson, 2017).

You may wonder how you can meet the needs of each student in a classroom. How will you have enough time to differentiate lessons? For one, not every lesson has to be differentiated. You will have to decide when it is most appropriate. Don't be afraid to start differentiating your lessons. You will learn from your mistakes and become better at meeting the needs of your students. Your chances of being successful will be increased if you have a nurturing classroom environment in which your students know that you care about them, and they feel respected and valued.

Personalized Learning

A number of schools are reinventing their curriculum and instruction to place students at the center of learning and tailor instruction to the individual needs of students using technology to develop a customized educational experience. An example is Teach to One, a middle school mathematics program. It was started in New York City in 2009 as the School of One by the nonprofit New Classrooms and has now expanded to other areas of the country. A classroom could have up to 90 children with multiple teachers who support students as they work at their own pace at computers through algorithm-generated programs that help them increase their knowledge and skills (Harold, 2016).

Other schools encourage students to explore areas of interest and produce related projects. Students make gearshifts and remote-control cars out of LEGO blocks, create computer-animated drawings, figure out how algae could immobilize heavy metals in water, and learn to code, among many other activities (M. Davis & Loewus, 2017). The classes are often blends of traditional classes, online learning, and working on their own. Other schools use software programs, especially in mathematics and reading, to help individualize instruction for students at different levels of readiness.

One of the concerns about this **personalized learning** approach is that the use of technology sometimes becomes the focus rather than the students' needs and interests (M. Davis & Loewus, 2017). A RAND study of personalized learning found that current models focus more on meeting individual needs and less on keeping students on pace to meet grade-level standards (Harold, 2017). As technology for learning evolves, students and teachers will learn how to use it more effectively to personalize learning in interesting and engaging ways that contribute to meeting standards.

Universal Design for Learning

Universal design refers to the creation of buildings, environments, and products that are accessible to students with a wide range of abilities and other characteristics. We see examples of universal design in the dropped curb that allows wheelchairs to easily cross the street, ramps next to steps for moving from one level to another, differences in the textures of surfaces in subway stations to assist persons with visual disabilities, and low-floor buses that "kneel" to allow persons with physical disabilities to access public transportation. Over time, universal design has been extended to the use of technology to provide greater access to learning, jobs, and everyday activities. Although many of these changes were made initially to improve the access of persons with disabilities, the changes have also improved the access of persons without disabilities.

Universal Design for Learning (UDL) extends universal design to education to make learning accessible to both students with disabilities and students without disabilities. Classrooms include desks that are accessible to a student in a wheelchair, whiteboards positioned at a level that can be used by all students, books in Braille and computers that allow the type size to be enlarged so that students with visual disabilities can read, interpreters for students with hearing disabilities, software programs that help students with learning disabilities and students who are struggling with mathematics or reading access the content, and technology that allows students who have lost a hand, arm, or leg participate in sports and other activities. Teachers use IEPs and intervention strategies to create flexible learning environments and instructional practices to support the learning of all students (Degner, 2016; Redford, 2018). We make modifications and accommodations in our instruction and assessments to help students learn. UDL is one way of differentiating instruction based on the abilities and academic readiness of students. It focuses on making both the classroom and instruction accessible to each student rather than forcing all students to interact with the teacher, their peers, and the environment in the same way.

Adopting UDL for your classroom is part of differentiating instruction with a focus on making all aspects of the environment and instruction accessible to each student. Opening access to students who have historically been denied that access generally improves education for all students. Columbus, Indiana, fifth-grade teacher Kyle Redford (2018) reported that "when I adapted the delivery of my content, introduced assistive technology for school work, or granted an assessment accommodation for one student, it usually became a helpful practice for many . . . solving an issue for one student often becomes an improved practice for the rest of the class—which is a central tenet of UDL" (para. 7–8).

Intersection With Culturally Responsive Pedagogy

Some groups with disabilities see themselves as cultural communities. Persons who are deaf, for example, share sign language and share cultural characteristics as a community with its own language and experience. A number of them have attended residential schools in which their primary interactions were with peers who also had a hearing impairment. Although most persons with a disability do not identify themselves as members of a cultural group based on their disability, they often have been defined by others by their disability. As a group, they historically have been discriminated against, being segregated in special schools or institutions and denied access to learning with students without disabilities. Students' ability or disability is an essential component in the construction of their cultural identities and intersects with their race, gender, and class (Waitoller & Thorius, 2016).

Today, students with disabilities are attending the same schools, and most of them are learning in classrooms with their nondisabled peers. Although they still face discrimination in schools and communities, the focus on differentiated learning and UDL is contributing to reducing barriers to learning and increasing access to equitable environments and high-level learning. Culturally responsive pedagogy, as discussed in Chapter 2, incorporates the intersection of disability/ability with our membership in other groups such as race, gender, and class. As teachers, we can contribute to dismantling forms of oppression such as racism and ableism as we organize our classrooms, create positive and accessible environments in the classroom where students value and respect each other, and figure out how we can make learning more accessible to all students.

CONNECTING TO THE CLASSROOM

This chapter introduced you to a number of ways to address exceptionalities and the individual needs of students. The research and theories related to the social, emotional, and academic development of children and youth can be very helpful to teachers as they get to know their students and draw on their strengths and special needs to help them learn. They connect to classrooms in the following ways:

1. Children move through the same stages of learning and development although some children develop at a faster rate than others.

2. There are multiple ways to think about intelligence that do not limit it only to academic achievement.

3. Understanding the different types of disabilities helps teachers determine the most appropriate accommodations and modifications for helping students with disabilities learn at high levels.

4. Integrating students with disabilities into the nation's classrooms is the goal of inclusion in which all students learn together and work together to support each other.

5. Early identification of students who are struggling academically, socially, or emotionally allows educators to develop intervention strategies to support these students as they move through difficult periods of their lives.

6. Vocabulary development should be a key component of lessons for all students.

7. Differentiated instruction, personalized learning, universal design for learning, and culturally responsive pedagogy are approaches to teaching that build on the exceptionalities of all students to develop their learning potential.

SUMMARY

The major theme of this chapter has been the importance of seeing each student as an individual and exceptional in some ways. The major points addressed in the chapter include the following:

- The brain develops in stages from before birth through a lifetime with the greatest development before age 5 and extending through adolescence. Neuroscience research, which provides ways to understand how the architecture of the brain relates to learning, is not yet able to tell us the instructional strategies that are more effective than others.

- The passage of the Individuals with Disabilities Education Act (IDEA) in 1990 led to students with disabilities being defined by their disability for the identification of appropriate accommodations and modifications to give them access to the curriculum and school environment in the Least Restrictive Environment.

- Although most students with disabilities attend school with students without disabilities in inclusive classrooms, they must have an Individualized Education Program (IEP) that describes the modifications and accommodations that teachers and other professional educators should follow to support these students effectively.

- Early interventions with students who are struggling in school can prevent them from falling behind academically and dropping out of school. RTI and MTSS are programs used by schools for this purpose.

- The unique needs of each student can be supported through differentiated instruction, personalized learning, universal design for learning, or a culturally responsive pedagogy. These teaching approaches remove barriers to the access of learning and attend to the interests, readiness, and learning preferences of students to engage them actively in their learning.

KEY TERMS

accommodations 75

affirmations 86

at risk 83

autism 78

brain architecture 68

developmental model 67

developmentally appropriate practices 67

differentiate 67

differentiated instruction 88

general intelligence 71

inclusion 79

Individualized Education Program (IEP) 71

Intelligence Quotient (IQ) 71

intrinsically active 67

Least Restrictive Environment (LRE) 80

maturation 67

modifications 79

Multiple Intelligences (MI) 72

personalized learning 89

prohibitions 86

Response to Intervention (RTI) 87

sensitive periods 68

specific abilities 71

student-centered learning 88

transitions 84

twice exceptional (2e) 79

universal design 89

Universal Design for Learning (UDL) 89

vocabulary gap 86

CLASS DISCUSSION QUESTIONS

1. What do you see as implications of the various developmental models of children's growth for the organization of the curriculum, the design of instruction, and the structure of schools? How would you know that your classroom environment and curriculum are developmentally appropriate for your students?

2. A sampling of the different ways that students can be categorized as exceptional has been introduced in this chapter. How would you describe yourself as exceptional?

3. Collaboration with parents contributes greatly to serving students with disabilities effectively. What can you do to build the trust of the parents of students with disabilities

in your classroom, especially when the family is from a cultural group different from your own?

4. Thinking about one of the subjects that you plan to teach, how could you differentiate a lesson to build on the cultures or other interests of students? What would you need to know to differentiate lessons for English Language Learners and a student with a learning disability or other disability?

5. What are some of the major factors that contribute to students dropping out of school? What signs of potential dropping out should you be able to observe as a teacher? What steps could you take to help prevent a student from reaching the stage of leaving school?

What Is Your Current Level of Understanding and Thinking About Addressing Learners' Individual Needs?

One of the indicators of understanding is to examine how complex your thinking is when asked questions that require you to use the concepts and facts introduced in this chapter.

Answer the following questions as fully as you can. Then use the Assessing Your Learning rubric to self-assess the degree to which you understand and can use the organization ideas presented in this chapter.

1. Use several of the concepts introduced in this chapter to describe ways that you see yourself as exceptional. How have teachers used, or ignored, these factors in relation to your learning?

2. Risk factors have been identified as strongly predictive of students not graduating from high school. What are implications of these factors for instruction and different levels of schooling?

3. General intelligence and Multiple Intelligences were introduced in this chapter. What are some of the implications of these with regard to organization of the curriculum and design of instruction?

4. You can expect that you will have several students in your classroom who have a recognized disability. In order for you to be effective in instruction, what will you need to know about the way each of those students is exceptional?

Assessing Your Learning Rubric

	Parts & Pieces	Unidimensional	Organized	Integrated	Extensions
Indicators	Elements/concepts are talked about as isolated and independent entities. Some important names are provided in isolation.	One or a few concepts are addressed, while others are underdeveloped, or not mentioned.	Deliberate and structured consideration of all key concepts/elements.	All key concepts/elements are included in a view that addresses interconnections.	Integration of all elements and dimensions, with extrapolation to new situations.
Identifying characteristics of exceptional students	Names one or two indicators, such as low-income family or failing a subject, without placing them into an overarching category.	Describes only one way that a student can be exceptional, such as gifted.	Describes and compares several ways that students can be exceptional and compares one to the other.	Describes and compares several ways that students can be exceptional and suggests their implications for classroom culture and instruction.	Presents an integrated view of different ways that each student can be exceptional, describes implications for classrooms and instruction, and identifies areas where she or he plans to develop more in-depth understanding.

FIELD GUIDE
FOR LEARNING MORE ABOUT . . .

Addressing Learners' Individual Needs

To further increase your understanding of the different ways to see each student as exceptional, engage in the following field activities.

Ask a Teacher or Principal	Ask a teacher or principal to describe how RTI or MTSS is used in the school and how effective it has been in assisting students who are struggling.
	Ask a teacher when she or he differentiates instruction, for what students, and in what ways.
Make Your Own Observations	Talk to a well-regarded teacher about the ways that she or he strives to learn about the background and interests of each student. Then inquire about examples and strategies the teacher has used to engage students using the interests and backgrounds of the students.

	When you are assigned field experiences, check out the neighborhood around the school. What are the typical homes and businesses like? Do you see indicators in the community that the school and learning are important? What ideas does your walking around give you for examples and community features that can help you make connections with all of your students? During your observations or field experiences in a school, identify a student with disabilities in a class that you are observing and record the modifications and accommodations the teacher uses to ensure that the student is actively engaged in learning. How is this student interacting and working with other students in the classroom?
Reflect Through Journaling	The premise in this chapter is that teachers need to see each student as being exceptional. In other words, each student is special and unique and brings to learning a particular set of background knowledge and experiences. A good place for you to start your journaling following the reading of this chapter is to address this question: *How do you feel about the following statement*: "Teachers should understand that each student is exceptional in unique ways and should use that information when they plan instruction"? Many teachers will not be comfortable with this idea. Also, many teachers will be at a loss to think of a broad spectrum of ways to consider each student as exceptional. Therefore, the second part of your journaling task is to make your own list of indicators and categories for seeing each student as exceptional. Next to each indicator, note ideas for how you could take advantage of each student's exceptionalities to facilitate his or her learning.
Build Your Portfolio	With a teacher education classmate, identify two or three students who recently dropped out of school. Interview them about their reasons for leaving. How do their reasons relate to the major factors identified in the Heppen and Therriault (2009) report? What do they suggest would be necessary for them to return to school? Write a blog about how the classrooms you have been observing could implement Universal Design for Learning (UDL) to give better access to learning to all of the students. Reflect on the values of UDL to both students with disabilities and students without disabilities.
Read a Book	For strategies on using the theory of Multiple Intelligences in the classroom, read *Multiple Intelligences in the Classroom* by Thomas Armstrong (ASCD, 2018). Many teachers struggle with figuring out how to effectively and efficiently differentiate instruction for each student. The internationally recognized leader on differentiated instruction, Carol Ann Tomlinson, describes many ways to meet the individual needs of students, including lesson plans, in her latest book, *How to Differentiate Instruction in Academically Diverse Classrooms* (ASCD, 2017).
Search the Web	**The Renzulli Center for Creativity, Gifted Education, and Talent Development at the Neag School of Education:** Planning instruction for the more academically able students takes special effort. In anticipation of your becoming a teacher, take the time now to develop a two- or three-week set of lessons that will be purposely aimed at gifted students. You will find many sources on the web that can help with this assignment. One good place to start the search is the Renzulli Center at the University of Connecticut. **Gardner's Multiple Intelligences:** Explore some of the websites related to Gardner's Multiple Intelligences (MI) theory. Assess yourself by taking some of the MI tests. What emerges as your strong and weak intelligences? How strongly do you agree/disagree with these scores? Keep in mind that these are just general estimates. **International Society for Technology in Education (ISTE) website:** Review the ISTE standards that are used by many school districts. See "Turn Your Classroom Into a Personalized Learning Environment" by Robyn Howton (2017) for suggestions on personalizing the classroom to meet the individual needs of students.

STUDENT STUDY SITE

⑤SAGE edge™

Get the tools you need to sharpen your study skills. **SAGE edge** offers a robust online environment featuring an impressive array of free tools and resources.

Access practice quizzes, eFlashcards, video, and multimedia at **edge.sagepub.com/hall3e**.

4 THE SOCIAL CONTEXT OF SCHOOLS

© Nicole McGill

TEACHER INTERVIEW

Ms. Nicole McGill

Beginning her career as a teacher of drama and theater, Ms. Nicole McGill switched to teaching science after the Washington, DC, schools eliminated theater programs. She is now in her fifth year of teaching sixth-grade earth science at Charles Hart Middle School where she has been rated as a very effective teacher for the past four years.

Charles Hart Middle School is located in an impoverished neighborhood in southeastern Washington, DC. With the exception of a few Hispanic students, the students at the school are African American. One in four of the students receive special education services, and all of the students eat breakfast and lunch for free at the school.

LEARNING OUTCOMES

After reading this chapter, you should be able to do the following:

1. Identify the most pressing social context issues challenging students and educators in today's schools.

2. Analyze how curricula used in your state or school district is influenced (or not influenced) by the social context of the communities in which the school is located and local, state, and/or national politics.

3. Compare approaches for supporting students who are struggling with social and emotional issues in their lives.

Q: What brings you joy in teaching?

A: My joy in teaching comes from understanding the cycle of being a lifelong learner. As teachers, we are continuously learning. When we learn something new, we then teach others so that they can continue to teach, and so on and so on. Watching my students feel accomplished when they have learned something fills me with pride. Once they become eager to teach someone else, then I know that my job as a teacher has been accomplished.

Q: How do you know that each student is learning?

A: When my students are able to teach or demonstrate in their own way. It is very exciting to give them materials, give them directions, and say, "Go for it." They don't have to teach it the way I taught it. They teach it in the way that they understand it. When you allow yourself as a teacher to be a facilitator and use questions to guide students' thinking instead of trying to just give them the answer, that's when you realize they are learning because they can justify what they have done and why they did it.

Q: Provide an example of how you learn and what you are learning at this time.

A: I am a kinesthetic learner and a theater director by design. As Shakespeare said, "To thine own self be true," and I bring my learning style into all that I do in the classroom. You can expect my students to be acting as the planets, the Sun. Students will be writing dialogue for clouds and the ocean to demonstrate their understanding of the water cycle. Students will also learn real career opportunities and apply real-world applications in the classroom. They will never just be students. They will be engineers—using insurance claims/policies to build earthquake-proof structures, lobbyists—arguing to protect natural environmental processes, and astronauts—seeking to find a new planet in the galaxy. I know that I learn best when I am applying my knowledge. So I make sure my students apply science and other life skills as they are learning.

Q: **What advice do you have for those who are studying to become teachers?**

A: "It is never too late to be great!" During my first year of teaching science, I was horrible. Class was a mess. I had fights break out in my class all the time. My classroom and behavior management was nonexistent. I had all boys in my class. I had never taught science before, so I was also learning the curriculum myself. I had no problem admitting that I was struggling. We had a great instructional coach at my school who said, "Yes, you are struggling. Let me help you." He started with the basics: writing clear objectives, behavior management, and backwards lesson planning. My principal said, "You have a theater background. I am expecting your class to be like Ms. Frizzle," and I just started laughing. I hadn't even thought about *The Magic School Bus*. He said, "Be you, break the mold you have created in your mind, and be great. Give them science, the way you want to be taught science." It was right before Christmas break, and I literally used that whole break to revamp everything. I thought about the next unit and what theater and drama games and activities I could use to teach science. It was a smooth-sailing third quarter as I learned that I could teach science.

Q: **Why is it important for teachers to understand the social context of the students in their classrooms?**

A: When you know the social context of your classroom, you are able to build a community within the four walls you control. Many of my students do not have a strong support system. Many of them have more negative than positive influences. I know that many of them get attention when they do something unfavorable rather than what is expected of them. So in knowing this, I sweat the small stuff. I make sure that I praise them for the small things, and when the big things happen, I go all out! Pizza party for coming on time to class! Lunch with me for turning in homework; and for having zero referrals for a month, let's go to a basketball game! They rarely are praised. And when they are praised, it is short lived. I have to maintain a positive community within my classroom because it may be the only time they will receive admiration within their day.

When schools take the time out to focus on students becoming self-aware, owning self-management skills, becoming socially aware, building relationship skills, and showing responsible decision making, they produce global citizens who are about giving back to their community. I have incorporated the 21st century skills of communicating, critical thinking, collaborating, and being creative into every lesson. I ensure that there is a moment for all students to reflect on their actions, biases, and thoughts as they pertain to their peers. They also get a chance to try things differently if they didn't go well. I build social-emotional skills into my lessons through their text, through their hands-on experiences, and through the use of their Microsoft tablets. I also have partnered with organizations like 100 Black Men of Greater Washington, DC, to help in developing Science, Technology, Engineering, and Mathematics (STEM)–social-emotional opportunities for our sixth-, seventh-, and eighth-grade students. I strive for my learning environment to be stable, nurturing, and supportive.

Q: **How do you incorporate the cultures and experiences of your students and their families in your instruction?**

A: My goal in life was always to educate others on the power of drama and theater to ignite social awareness and change. When I was teaching drama and theater, I used Shakespeare to hone in on reading, writing, and social-emotional skills by taking *Macbeth* to Africa and

Julius Caesar to the Harlem Renaissance. I brought hip-hop to *Hamlet*. I understood that Shakespeare had to be relevant to my students. My students' culture of locks, cornrows, Notorious BIG, Langston Hughes, and "chicken wings with mambo sauce" was important, special, and unique and needed to be honored. When I decided to incorporate drama, theater, and culture into teaching science, students became more engaged in learning.

Questions to Consider

1. How do the challenges faced by students at Charles Hart Middle School compare to the schools with which you are familiar? What are the similarities and differences in the schools and communities?

2. What are some of the challenges that the teachers at Charles Hart Middle School face as they try to engage students in school and help them learn?

3. Ms. McGill's advice to teachers is "It is never too late to be great." What does she mean by this statement?

INTRODUCTION

Social context is based on the sociocultural forces that shape our day-to-day experiences, which directly and indirectly affect our behaviors. It includes the physical and social setting or environment in which we are living and interacting at a specific time. It may differ depending on the social organization in which we are currently participating. For example, we may behave differently when we are at school, home, a club with our friends, or a protest march. The social context in which we find ourselves affects not only our lived experiences but also our learning, behavior, and participation in society. Common factors that impact our interactions and relationships within a social organization include our economic conditions, racial and ethnic memberships, cultural backgrounds, and religions or beliefs.

Education does not take place in a vacuum in which the only tools a teacher needs to be successful are lesson plans, a textbook, and organizational skills. The social context—including the characteristics of a school, community, and culture in which teaching and learning take place—shape all aspects of the teaching and learning experience. These factors affect the available resources, the curriculum, school activities, technology, parental involvement, and community support that will be available to you and your students.

The social contexts of communities and society impact the performance and outcomes of both educators and students (Milner, 2010). First, students who attend public schools (approximately 90% of the total) are impacted by disparities in school funding. Because 91% of public school budgets are derived from revenues produced by state and local taxes (McFarland et al., 2017), schools located in low-income communities and states are less likely to have the same level of personnel, technology, and other resources as are available in schools in affluent states and communities. Class sizes, the ability to hire educational specialists and resource teachers, and the resources to pay for new textbooks or curricula upgrades are determined by the revenues available to a school district. Most significantly, underresourced school districts are more likely to have lower salary scales and less ability to attract and retain highly qualified teachers. To offset the impact of some of these disparities, the federal government contributes 9% of public school funding (McFarland et al., 2017) to supplement needs such as food insecurity through the National School Lunch Program, which is funded and administered by the U.S. Department of Agriculture.

Second, schools located in less affluent states and communities are more likely to have higher concentrations of **high-needs students**, defined by the U.S. Department of Education (n.d.) as "students at risk of educational failure or otherwise in need of special assistance and support." Although poverty is the predominant characteristic in the federal definition, other factors include learning and physical disabilities, limited English proficiency, below-grade-level academic performance, and measures of family instability. Underresourced school districts are also more likely to have a larger number of high-poverty schools, commonly defined as those in which more than three-fourths of students are from low-income families.

Another important component of social context, in schools and communities, is the range and distribution of population groups across racial, ethnic, cultural, and religious identities. In many schools, you will find great pride in the identification of how many national flags are represented in the cultural heritage of their student body. As a teacher, you should learn to celebrate your school's ethnic diversity and use it as a learning tool. You will also need to learn about the cultural norms of population groups represented by students in your classroom, while at the same time avoiding stereotypical assumptions.

HOW DOES SOCIAL CONTEXT IMPACT STUDENTS' PHYSICAL, SOCIAL, EMOTIONAL, AND COGNITIVE DEVELOPMENT?

Learning is affected by many factors beyond intelligence. The conditions students encounter in their families, communities, and society can have positive and negative impacts on their physical, social, emotional, and cognitive development. Most students are dependent on their parents or other legal guardians, who usually support their growth, development, self-esteem, and academic progress. Nevertheless, children face numerous developmental and societal challenges as they mature to adulthood. Other adults—such as teachers, mentors, coaches, and counselors—are vital in helping children and adolescents make sound choices, as well as recover positively from inevitable poor decisions they will make on the path to adulthood. Caring adults can provide children with different perspectives, self-affirmation, recognition of talents or potential, and links to opportunities. As the proverb states, "It takes a village to raise a child."

National education associations such as ASCD (2018) and the National Education Association (2015) have called for schools to adopt a whole child approach to attend not only to the intellectual development of children and youth but also to their physical, social, and emotional development. The implementation of this approach requires an equity of resources to provide students with mentors, counselors, and other resources to meet their individual needs; engage them actively in learning; and ensure they feel safe and secure in schools. Preparing the whole child requires the collaboration of parents, communities, educators, and education support professionals such as teacher assistants, custodians, cafeteria personnel, bus drivers, and security personnel. In this section, we will examine some of the social context factors that can impede children from being fully engaged in schooling and some strategies for addressing them.

Physical and Emotional Safety

One of the tenets of whole child education is that students must feel safe and secure in their school environment in order to be fully engaged in learning. Educators must be advocates for children who may be endangered or improperly cared for outside of school. Middle and high school students may fall prey to gangs, substance abuse, or other circumstances caused by poor decisions and unwholesome influences. Advocacy can take many forms but requires being alert to behavioral and academic downslides, or other signs that a child is ill, suffering, or stressed, and then taking appropriate action (e.g., calling parents, sharing your concerns with a school counselor, or simply letting a child know that you care and are concerned).

Maltreatment of Children

The Centers for Disease Control and Prevention (CDC) divides the maltreatment of children into two categories: (1) child abuse, which is a crime of commission that is deliberate and intentional, and (2) child neglect, which is a crime of omission that fails to provide for a child's basic needs or to protect a child from harm. In 2015, 3.4 million children were referred to social service agencies for abuse or neglect. Seventy-five percent of the victims were neglected, while 17% were reported for physical abuse and 8% for sexual abuse. The victimization rate is the highest for children under three years old (National Institute on Drug Abuse, National Institutes of Health, U.S. Department of Health & Human Services, 2017).

Teachers must learn the warning signs of child abuse and neglect and be prepared to take appropriate action. In nearly all states, educators are legally required to report suspicion of maltreatment within 48 hours of observation. Although teachers may be reluctant to make a report for fear of making matters worse for a family or child who they understand is already under stress, the follow-up by a social worker is likely to result in offers of help, counseling, or other supports, and is unlikely to result in punitive action or removal of a child from the home unless warranted for the safety of the child.

Abused and neglected children and youth may arrive at school hungry, bruised, or depressed. They may find the school a safe haven, arriving early and staying late, or may have excessive absences. They sometimes blame themselves for the abuse they receive and are reluctant to acknowledge the abuse by their parents or caretakers. Some may have been warned to deny or hide signs of abuse from teachers so they don't get taken away from home and put in foster care; others might be more afraid of the punishment they will receive at home if they "tell" than they are of the daily consequences of maltreatment. Some abused youth run away from home, choosing to be homeless or to seek assistance in a shelter.

Bullying

The behavior known as **bullying** has been reconsidered in recent years as an aspect of school behavior that needs to be addressed and contained, and not merely tolerated as a form of mischief or a childhood rite of passage. One of the unfortunate byproducts of social media is the creation of new avenues for bullying behavior (**cyberbullying**) that allow for both anonymity and widespread dissemination of derogatory comments, digital images, and threats. Because even elementary-age children are now likely to have smartphones, laptops, or tablets available for their exclusive personal use, the role that digital media plays in childhood socialization and interaction cannot be underestimated. Parents and teachers may not have the technology skills to monitor what children are doing online or how they are using their devices. Although children who have grown up with technology are likely to have sophisticated skills in a range of applications, they may not have the judgment to use technology safely and responsibly.

Bullying is a form of abusive behavior characterized by (1) a power imbalance between the perpetrator and his or her victim, (2) repetition of behavior, and (3) intentionality (Englander, 2013). Despite the stereotype of a bully as an oversized boy lying in wait to pummel a smaller one, traditional (face-to-face) bullying is more often carried out in a manner other than physical aggression (e.g., it is more likely to be shunning, gestures, or comments) and by girls as well as boys. Unlike those who enact some other forms of aggressive behavior, bullies seek to harm safe targets who are vulnerable to abuse, and who will not or cannot retaliate.

Marginalized social groups or individuals are frequently the target of bullying. Students who are members of underrepresented ethnic and religious groups; students who identify as Lesbian, Gay, Bisexual, Transgender, or Queer or Questioning (LGBTQ); students who are obese or have physical disabilities; and students with exceptional learning needs are more likely to be victims of bullying than other students. According to a survey of high school students, 20% of high school students were bullied on school property in 2015 (U.S. Department of Health & Human Services, Centers for Disease Control and Prevention, 2016). Other studies have found that 33% to 50% of all students have been involved in bullying that ranged from being physically bullied to verbal abuse to social abuse such as being excluded or ostracized (deLara, 2016).

Girls and young women are also victims of bullying. At school, they are most commonly verbally harassed with unwelcome sexual comments, jokes, and gestures. They are more likely than boys to report that the harassment had a negative effect on them, causing them to have trouble sleeping and not want to go to school. Being called gay or lesbian in a negative way is experienced equally by boys and girls (Hill & Kearl, 2011).

Best practices in bullying prevention stress development of a school-based plan and teamwork, with active monitoring of the social climate and enforcement of antibullying rules and policies. Particularly at the elementary school level, strategies include awareness and intervention of "gateway behaviors" such as rudeness or other hurtful acts that may or may not be manifestations of active bullying.

Schools should be safe for children and youth. However, some students find schools unsafe and dangerous. Educators play an important role in limiting and eliminating bullying and other youth violence in schools. Many schools have adopted antibullying programs, but successful strategies require a commitment by teachers, administrators, and parents to change the school climate and norms related to bullying.

Gangs

Gangs do exist in schools, but the percentage of students who report gangs in their schools has been decreasing. In 2015, 13% of high school and 7% of middle school students reported the presence of gangs or gang members in their schools. Gangs are more likely to be in urban schools (15%) as compared to suburban schools (10%) and rural schools (4%) (National Center for Education Statistics, 2017). Middle and high schools should have practices in place to both intervene in and prevent student gang participation. Networking with local police may be useful in educating teachers and parents about local gang activity and how to work with police for effective and positive intervention. Since young people join gangs for reasons ranging from a need for physical protection in their neighborhood to a desire to belong to a social group, schools can do many things to fill that void, including networking with other agencies and volunteers to ensure students have safe and supported places to go outside of school hours. Schools with strong mentoring, counseling, and other support services are also more likely to be successful in the intervention and prevention of gang membership. Antigang curriculum such as Gang Resistance Education And Training (G.R.E.A.T.), which involves police officers as instructors, is sometimes used to educate younger students about gangs.

School Safety

You probably know immediately the meaning of 13 at Columbine, 26 at Sandy Hook, and 17 at Marjory Stoneman Douglas. Although serious violent crime in schools is actually quite rare, incidents of physical violence and murder in schools have become, tragically, part of our national cultural fabric since the shootings at Columbine in 1999. Following the February 14, 2018, shooting at a high school in Parkland, Florida, the *Washington Post* (Cox & Rich, 2018) reported an average of 10 school shootings each year since Columbine. Even more disturbing is the fact that there had already been 11 shootings in schools in 2018 before the end of March. They have occurred in 36 states and the District of Columbia, in cities, small towns, affluent suburbs, and rural communities. Mass shootings occur at predominantly white schools, but students of color are far more likely to experience gun violence in their schools. Targeted shootings occur in schools three times as often as mass shootings.

The damage of these shootings in our schools is far beyond the 130 students, teachers, and others who were killed before April 2018. At least 254 people were injured, and more than 187,000 students who were attending those schools have had to deal with the posttraumatic effects similar to being in a war zone. Many students are dealing with the traumatic impact of the violence for months and years later; others are impacted many years later (Cox & Rich, 2018). Other students around the country worry that their schools could be attacked as well. As a result, students around the world were shouting "Enough" as they gathered for the March for Our Lives in Washington, DC, and other cities on March 24, 2018.

In many schools located in high-density areas, school lockdowns occur routinely whenever a police search is under way in the school vicinity. Fake bomb threats or warnings of potential mayhem are also relatively common. It is important for schools to have protocols in place to protect students from actual harm, but also to provide assurance of safety and protection whenever school routines are interrupted. Teachers must be able to remain calm and redirect students so they do not succumb to fear, while at the same time abiding by emergency protocols in place for the school.

Mental Health

Undiagnosed mental health disorders such as depression, anxiety, Attention Deficit Hyperactivity Disorder (ADHD), bulimia, and anorexia are also prevalent among students, especially among older children who may have developed symptoms later in childhood or who were not diagnosed earlier.

Fifty percent of lifelong mental health disorders appear by age 14, and 75% by age 24 (Kessler et al., 2007). A study at Johns Hopkins University (Merikangas et al., 2010) found that one in four adolescents in the United States suffer from a mental illness. Strategies for improving mental health care for children include providing treatment and counseling in schools and routine mental health screening as part of pediatric care. Without treatment, such disorders can lead to or coexist with substance abuse, poor academic performance, suicide, or other acts of violence. Social workers, school counselors, and community organizations that provide assistance to students and families are important resources that can support teachers as they work with students to help develop their academic, social, emotional, and physical potentials.

Suicide

The prevalence of suicidal behavior (thoughts, plans, attempts) is higher among middle-aged adults than young adults and adolescents, but it is the second leading cause of death for youths and young adults 10 to 34 years old, behind car accidents (National Vital Statistics System, National Center for Health Statistics, Centers for Disease Control and Prevention, 2014). Female teenagers are twice as likely as males to attempt suicide, but males are four times as likely to commit suicide. Hispanic, American Indian, and Alaska Native high school students are more likely to attempt suicide than are students in other groups (Centers for Disease Control and Prevention, 2015). As a teacher, you may see signs of depression and changed behavior that could be precedents to suicide attempts. You should report these signs to appropriate school officials.

Trauma-Sensitive Schools

What are **trauma-sensitive schools**? They are safe zones to "buffer students from external forces that threaten their potential, while at the same time fostering the skills [they] need to regulate internal emotions and drives" (Craig, 2017, p. 5). Educators in these schools understand the vulnerability of students to traumas that are generally out of their control and exceed their capacity to cope. They "recognize the frustration and hopelessness that motivates traumatized students, and they take active steps to help students address these feelings" (Craig, 2017, p. 7). One of the first steps is to understand that academic work under these circumstances may seem overwhelming and trigger an inappropriate response from a student. The situation calls for a teacher–student relationship that is collaborative and

THINKING DIFFERENTLY
MINDFULNESS IN THE CLASSROOM

Shut your eyes . . . breathe deeply. Teachers and schools are teaching students to practice **mindfulness**, which requires paying attention to their thoughts, feelings, and body sensations in a given moment without judging them. In some schools, students and teachers reduce their stress by combining yoga and mindfulness. In other schools, time is set aside for meditation.

Why are educators adopting this therapeutic practice in the classroom? Many students of all ages are experiencing sensory overload, attention difficulty, and anxiety. A 2013 survey by the American College Health Association, National College Health Assessment, discovered that about half of college students experience "overwhelming anxiety." The American Psychological Association (2013) found that 27% of teens experience "extreme stress" during a school year and another 55% experience "moderate stress." Mindfulness provides a time for calmness. Research studies suggest that "it improves attention, reduces stress, and results in better emotional regulation and an improved capacity for compassion and empathy" (L. Davis, 2015, para. 15).

Second-grade teacher Ms. Becca Wertheim says that mindfulness is "challenging. It takes practice. It takes patience." But it is worth it. She reports that "rather than being quick to judge or assume, [her students] became better listeners. They listened more attentively to [her], they listened to their peers, they listened to themselves" (Wertheim, 2017, para. 5–6). Secondary English teacher Mr. Argos Gonzalez uses mindfulness with his students in one of the most impoverished schools in New York City. He says, "My intention as a mindfulness instructor is to give students some very simple and basic tools so they can learn to self regulate" (L. Davis, 2015, para. 32).

encourages meeting agreed-upon goals. Making harsh judgments about students based on their behavior is replaced with learning more about them and what is happening in their lives. Students need to feel that a teacher cares about them and that they can trust the teacher.

Developing a social and emotional learning curriculum is an important step in meeting the needs of all students (Plumb, Bush, & Kersevich, 2016). Instructional strategies also make a difference in working with traumatized students (Craig, 2017). Relating new information to existing knowledge is helpful. Activities that incorporate collaboration with peers positively support learning. Integrating concepts and ideas across disciplines promotes more active engagement by students. Discipline should be proactive to prevent as many problems as possible while helping traumatized students learn to monitor their own behaviors (Craig, 2017). Understanding how to de-escalate a situation when a student is having a crisis or a behavioral outburst that needs attention will be important. A school crisis plan would assist all educators in handling these situations (Plumb et al., 2016).

Trauma-sensitive schools commit to creating an inclusive climate throughout the school that celebrates individual differences (Craig, 2017). You should get to know the strengths and weaknesses of your most problematic students. You should listen to your students and develop a safe and caring community for them. You should create opportunities for students to interact with you and their peers and make meaningful contributions to their classroom community (Craig, 2017). Working with traumatized children and youth is not easy. It requires resiliency on the part of teachers and the skills we expect of students: good coping skills and self-regulation. Believing that you can create change in the lives of students also contributes to helping students feel empowered and respected (Craig, 2017). A resource that you might find helpful is the 2015 film, *Paper Tigers*, which chronicles a year in the life of Lincoln High School in Walla Walla, Washington, as educators and students created a trauma-sensitive school.

Sexuality

One of the major challenges for youth is making the transition to adult sexuality. At all stages of childhood and especially during puberty, students' sexual curiosity is natural and appropriate, while the forms and acceptable responses to curiosity and behaviors change across developmental stages. Young people can become confused by the mixed messages they receive from parents, their religious and cultural affiliations, friends, peers, media, and popular culture about appropriate ways to express or understand feelings of arousal, attraction, and sexual orientation. Furthermore, the role, focus, and extent of sex education in schools has historically been controlled by legislators as well as by community debate over what children are taught about sexuality in public schools. In nearly every state, regulations specify whether sex education can include information on contraception, sexual orientation, and sexually transmitted diseases (STDs). As of 2018, 24 states and the District of Columbia require sex education to be taught in public schools; 22 of those states require the teaching of both HIV and sex education. Thirteen states allow sex and/or HIV education to be taught only if it is "medically accurate." Parents in 36 states and the District of Columbia have the right to remove their children from sex education programs. One of the more controversial issues related to sex education is the role of abstinence in the instruction. Twenty-six states require that abstinence be stressed in sex education (Guttmacher Institute, 2017). As a result, schools face a dilemma about how to help students understand their sexuality. It is often left to the students to sort through the mixed messages and, as a consequence, be deprived of responsible adult guidance in learning life skills, values, and self-understanding in this important area of development.

Sexual Behavior

Teachers at all grade levels are confronted by inappropriate sexual behaviors and will need to learn ways to respond, redirect, and intervene. Appropriate responses become more complicated when a child's behavior impacts another student in the form of harassment, exhibitionism, or physical contact. Research shows that childhood sexualized behavior is most likely the result of social skill deficits or poor impulse control, and not necessarily a sign that a child has been sexually abused (Minahan & Rappaport, 2013). A child's choice of words or actions may suggest he or she is copying behaviors learned at home or from the media and may not clearly understand the sexual nature of his or her actions. Repeated behavior of this type should lead to a conference with the family before further intervention occurs. However, since teachers are mandated reporters of suspected child abuse—as well as responsible for the safety of all children in the classroom including the child who is of concern—it is important to be vigilant, share concerns with other school professionals, and know your school's protocol for dealing with related incidents.

Sexual behaviors at the middle school level and above may involve experimentation, including sexual intercourse. Although fewer than 2% of children report having had sex before age 12, the likelihood of sexual activity increases rapidly in subsequent years. Approximately one in four teenagers have engaged in sex by the age of 16, over half by age 18, and over 70% by age 20 (Guttmacher Institute, 2017). Overall, today's teens are waiting longer to have sex for the first time than two decades ago. One in three high school students were sexually active in 2014 (Henry J. Kaiser Family Foundation, 2014). The good news is that the use of birth control has increased dramatically since the 1980s with 86% and 93% of females and males, respectively, reporting that they use contraceptives when they have sex (Guttmacher Institute, 2017).

Risks and Consequences of Sexual Activity

Approximately 85% of high school students nationwide report having been educated about HIV and AIDS. In spite of the high level of HIV awareness among teens and young adults, they are disproportionately likely to contract HIV and other STDs than are other sexually active age groups (Henry J. Kaiser Family Foundation, 2014).

Another risk of sexual activity is pregnancy. Adolescent pregnancy rates have been on a steady decline for several decades across all racial and ethnic groups. Approximately 5% of teenage girls aged 15 to 19 became pregnant in 2013 with three in four of the births among 18- to 19-year-old women. Although the pregnancy rates for teenagers have declined by 64% over the past 25 years, the rate in the United States continues to be among the highest in developed countries. Fewer pregnancies are largely attributed to easier access to and education about birth control. Of teens who do become pregnant, approximately 61% gave birth, 24% ended in abortions, and 15% had miscarriages (Guttmacher Institute, 2017). Teenage mothers are much less likely to finish high school or obtain a GED by age 22 than are their peers. Only 2% of women who have children before they are 18 earn a college degree by age 30 (National Conference of State Legislatures, 2013).

Recent attention to incidents of rape and other sex crimes on college campuses and in society in general suggest that more education is necessary on the topic of sexual violence and what constitutes sexual consent between partners. The victims of sexual violence are predominantly female, and the perpetrators are most likely to be male, most often someone who is known by the victim. Although sexual violence includes attacks by strangers and the sex trafficking of women around the world, it also occurs in homes, at school, and on college campuses. Nearly 11% of female teenagers report experiencing physical or sexual violence while dating (U.S. Department of Health and Human Services, 2016). Twenty percent of undergraduate women reported being a victim of sexual violence while they were in college (Krebs, Lindquist, Warner, Fisher, & Martin, 2009).

In collaboration with community organizations and families, schools can contribute to the reduction of sexual violence. The CDC recommends that educators and other professionals

iStock/quavondo

Teenage mothers are less likely to complete high school and college than are other teens. Assisting these young mothers in finishing their education will have benefits to both them and their children.

1. promote social norms that protect against violence,

2. teach skills to prevent sexual violence,

3. provide opportunities to empower and support girls and women,

4. create protective environments, and

5. support victim/survivors to lessen harms. (Basile et al., 2016, p. 11)

These strategies include helping students understand their role as a bystander, mobilizing men and boys as allies, incorporating social-emotional learning in education, strengthening economic opportunities for girls, improving safety and monitoring in schools, and providing victim-centered services.

Substance Abuse

Some young people experiment with alcohol, cigarettes, and drugs as early as elementary or middle school, usually as a result of both peer pressure and availability. Children identify the use of tobacco, drugs, and alcohol as desirable adult behaviors and at the same time as acts of rebellion against adult control over their actions. All too often, substance abuse is a contributing factor to impaired judgment in other realms of adolescent decisions. Drugs and alcohol may also be used by students to self-medicate mental health problems such as depression and anxiety.

The public believes that the use of drugs and violence in schools is the fourth-greatest problem faced by public schools behind the lack of funding (22%), standards (9%), and lack of good teachers (7%) ("The 49th Annual PDK Poll," 2017). At the same time, the National Institute on Drug Abuse, National Institutes of Health, U.S. Department of Health and Human Services (2017) reports that the use of illicit drugs other than marijuana by youth is "holding steady at the lowest levels in over two decades" (para. 1). Even the use of opioids such as prescription pain relievers and heroin is on the decline among teenagers at the same time that it has become an epidemic at other age levels (NIDA Blog Team, 2016).

As you can see in Figure 4.1, the most popular addictive drug among teenagers is alcohol. At the 8th and 10th grades, there are few differences in use of illicit drugs by male and female students, but males are more likely than females to use them by the 12th grade and into young adulthood. Frequent alcohol use, daily cigarette smoking, and use of electronic vaporizers also are more prevalent among males. The percentage of white students using alcohol and illicit drugs is generally higher than that of African American and Hispanic students. Hispanic students have the highest prevalence of the use of marijuana (Miech et al., 2017).

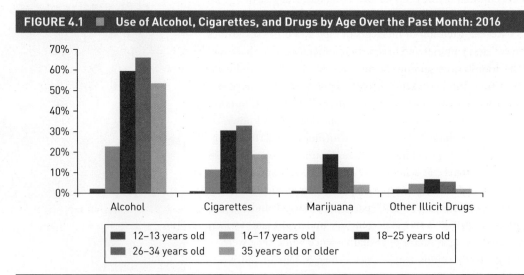

FIGURE 4.1 ■ Use of Alcohol, Cigarettes, and Drugs by Age Over the Past Month: 2016

Legend:
- 12–13 years old
- 26–34 years old
- 16–17 years old
- 35 years old or older
- 18–25 years old

Source: Johnston, L. D., O'Malley, P. M., Miech, R. A., Bachman, J. G., & Schulenberg, J. E. (2017). *Monitoring the future national survey results on drug use, 1975–2016: 2016 overview, key findings on adolescent drug use.* Ann Arbor: Institute for Social Research, University of Michigan.

Overall, teenagers under 18 years old smoke cigarettes, drink alcohol, and use drugs less than most other age groups (National Center for Health Statistics, 2016). Nevertheless, it is important for educators and parents to help young people understand both the dangers of impaired judgment caused by intoxication and the long-term consequences of drug use and addiction.

Health and Fitness

The importance of teaching children about healthy lifestyles—and giving them opportunities to practice healthy behaviors based on informed choices and exposure to a range of physical fitness options—cannot be overestimated. Teaching children about health and fitness should be a responsibility for all teachers in designing lessons and units of instruction, and not only be relegated to physical education or health education teachers.

Nutrition

We live in a time where children are bombarded by media and advertising at unprecedented rates. The idealized, unrealistic, and often unhealthy images of what constitute desirable physical and sexual attributes and glamorous lifestyle choices can have a dangerous impact on children. The advertising of snack foods and other processed food products that are high in sugar, sodium, or saturated fats (e.g., fast foods, many cold cereals, and some frozen or boxed instant meals) is often targeted specifically to youth media markets with catchy jingles and colorful packaging. As parents become more concerned with health and nutrition, advertising often includes references to products with whole grains, organic ingredients, no high fructose corn syrup, and other misleading indicators of their nutritional value. Some educators fight back against misleading food advertising by teaching students how to read federally required nutritional labeling

Girls are not the only ones concerned with how they look. Rather than being obsessed with weight and beauty, boys are more likely to be concerned with muscles.

"The school is serving more nutritious meals, so I've started to bring my own lunch."

on packaged items to assist them in knowing which food choices have the best nutritional value. During President Barack Obama's administration, First Lady Michelle Obama promoted good nutrition for children, which led to the passage of the Healthy, Hunger-Free Kids Act of 2010 and the following changes in school lunches:

- New nutritional standards for all food sold in schools during the school day, including bake sale and vending machine offerings

- Strengthening school wellness policies by providing resources, training, and technical assistance to review or develop fitness and exercise programs

- Improvement of the nutritional quality of school meals, augmented by increased support of farm-to-school partnerships, school gardens, and nutritional education (National Alliance for Nutrition & Activity, 2010)

Obesity

Increases in childhood obesity and related childhood illnesses such as hypertension and diabetes have reached epidemic levels. Obesity nearly doubled over the past 30 years, from 23% to 37% among adults and from 10% to 17% among children and adolescents (National Center for Health Statistics, 2016). Seven in 10 adults in the United States are overweight or obese (National Center for Health Statistics, 2016) as compared to one in three children and youth under 20 years old (U.S. Department of Health & Human Services, 2016). In addition to the health risks of childhood obesity, overweight children are likely to suffer from the emotional consequences of obesity. In a society that puts a premium on thinness, children who are overweight are much more likely to be bullied, to be discriminated against by peers and adults, and to suffer from depression and low self-esteem.

Poor nutrition and lack of physical activity are the main culprits that have led to the obesity epidemic. Since fewer and fewer household economies can accommodate the role of a full- or part-time homemaker whose primary responsibility is the care and feeding of family members, there is ever-greater reliance on ready-made or processed foods that do not require preparation. The widespread availability and affordability of fast-food restaurants increases the likelihood that parents pressed for time will make poor nutritional choices on a regular basis, especially when feeding a family ready-made burgers and fries is likely cheaper than the cost of preparing a nutritious meal from scratch. And in low-income urban neighborhoods, there may not even be access to fresh meats and vegetables.

Physical Activity

Another critical aspect of good health is regular physical activity. The American Heart Association (2013) recommends that children aged two and older should engage in 60 minutes of enjoyable, moderate-to-intense aerobic exercise daily. In support of that recommendation, NFL players are promoting the PLAY 60 Challenge to inspire children and youth to engage in physical activity for 60 minutes a day. However, 15% of the high school students in a national survey "did not participate in at least 60 minutes of physical activity on any day during the 7 days before the survey" (Centers for Disease Control and Prevention, n.d.). Most children spend nearly half of their time outside of school hours engaged in sedentary activities such as watching TV, playing video games, and doing homework. In some urban neighborhoods, parents are afraid to allow their children to play outside without supervision, which increases the likelihood of sedentary behavior and habits.

Researchers have found that daily physical exercise, in addition to promoting health and physical fitness, can have positive effects on children's readiness to learn. However, physical education is not always required in schools. Only one in four high school students participate in physical education on a daily basis (National Physical Activity Plan Alliance, Centers for Disease Control and Prevention, 2016). On the plus side, physical education classes have expanded in recent years to introduce children to a wider range of physical activities such as dance, aerobics, and yoga. As a teacher, you will be in a good position to be an advocate for a range of learning and physical activities that can promote wellness habits for children, both during and after school hours.

HOW DOES SOCIAL CONTEXT INFLUENCE LEARNING?

The demographics of the school district and individual school in which you teach will have a major impact on the challenges, skills, and sensitivities you will need to call on as a teacher. The challenge for schools and educators is how to engage all students in learning. In most middle-class and in aspiring immigrant working-class populations, the community expectation is that schools must prepare their children for higher education. High schools are expected to have structures in place (e.g., Advanced Placement [AP] courses and a sufficient number of guidance counselors) to ensure their children have optimal opportunities for college admission. In working-class communities, the value of hard work and skilled craftsmanship learned on the job—enforced by membership in a labor union or the prospect of self-employment in a trade—may be espoused as the key to economic success. Not all families trust or understand the current focus on higher education as a means to the same end in an economy driven by different labor needs. In this section, we will explore some of the challenges that you and your colleagues may encounter as you try to help all students learn at higher levels. It will require the understanding and respect for the culture and values of the communities whose children you are privileged to teach.

The Sociopolitical Context of Education

Schools are greatly influenced by the sociopolitical context in which they operate. Since the U.S. Constitution includes no provisions for the education of its citizenry, public education has historically been under the jurisdiction of state and local control. As a result, elected state and local officials have great influence over what students are taught and what levels of proficiency they must attain in order to meet educational benchmarks. Local or state regulations may also impact policy decisions such as the number of charter schools, bilingual education, school reading lists, and what can and cannot be taught about sexual health and behavior.

Accountability for Academic Performance

Although the goal of teaching has always been to help students learn, today's teachers are being held accountable for the level of their students' learning. It is no longer enough to ensure that the large majority of your students learn enough to pass to the next grade. Your evaluations will be based partly on how well your students have learned the **Common Core State Standards (CCSS)** or other state learning standards assigned to your subject and grade level. To improve student learning, students need to be invested in their education (Boykin & Noguera, 2011). Families who have not benefited from formal education as a generator of their own economic gains may not see the payoff in instilling good educational habits in their children, such as studying hard, doing homework, regularly attending school, and being on time to class. One of our challenges as teachers is to help parents become invested in the very real benefits of their children achieving educational success, even if they have not had the same experience or support in their own lives.

When the Elementary and Secondary Education Act (ESEA) of 1965 was reauthorized by Congress as the No Child Left Behind Act of 2001, the federal government for the first time held schools accountable for student achievement as measured by state tests. The goal was to improve the academic achievement of all students as well as achievement equity across racial and economic lines. States were required to disaggregate and publish school test scores by specific student characteristics, including race, gender, economic status, native language, and disability. This goal continued with the 2015 reauthorization of ESEA as the Every Student Succeeds Act (ESSA). States must identify schools whose students are the lowest 5% of performers in the state and intervene to improve student performance. States must also identify and intervene in high schools with a graduation rate of 67% or less (Klein, 2016). As a result, teachers and principals may feel a great deal of pressure to produce higher test scores.

Effective teaching matters. You are taking the first step in becoming a teacher who helps students learn regardless of the social contexts that may impact their progress. You can make a difference to the children you teach. You will be expected to help students achieve the learning goals to which you and they are accountable. You should strive to challenge and support each student in your classroom to meet learning objectives in ways that are tailored to their personal and academic needs, skills, and talents. Your challenge will be to help all students achieve academic goals to the best of their ability. Even in your first year of teaching, your payoff will be the glee on the face of the student who "gets it" and is thus empowered to take the next step in his or her unique learning journey. As Ms. McGill indicated in the opening to this chapter, you should become a more effective teacher with practice and support of colleagues.

Teacher quality has a great impact on the academic, social, and emotional development of students.

iStock/Christopher Futcher

Inequities in Academic Achievement

One of the primary goals of ESSA is to create equity in academic achievement by students across racial, ethnic, and socioeconomic groups. However, according to the Nation's Report Card released in 2015 by the National Assessment of Educational Progress (2015b), while overall student achievement improved between 2009 and 2015, only scant improvement has been made in closing the performance disparities between white students and African American, Hispanic, and American Indian/Alaska Native students.

The creator of the common school movement, Horace Mann, wrote that education is the "great equalizer." However, educators have long understood that not all children have equitable opportunities for academic success. Pierre Bourdieu, a 20th-century French sociologist and anthropologist, coined

UNDERSTANDING AND USING DATA
ANALYZING TEST SCORES

The review of test scores based on characteristics of students can help educators understand the opportunity gap that exists in most schools. The federal government monitors student achievement primarily through tests of mathematics and reading administered by the National Assessment of Educational Progress (NAEP) every two years to 4th-, 8th-, and 12th-grade students in a representative sampling of schools across states. The table below provides mean NAEP scores for selected groups in 2015.

Grade and Subject	Sex		School Lunch Eligibility		Race						
	Male	Female	Not Eligible	Eligible[1]	Amer. Indian/ Alaska Native	Asian	Black	Hispanic	Native Hawaiian/ Other Pacific Islander	Two or More Races	White
Mathematics											
4th Grade	241	239	253	229	227	259	224	230	231	245	248
8th Grade	282	282	296	268	267	307	260	270	276	285	292
12th Grade[2]	153	150	NA	NA	138	171	130	139	NA	157	160
Reading											
4th Grade	219	226	237	209	205	239	206	208	215	227	232
8th Grade	261	270	277	253	252	281	248	253	255	269	274
12th Grade[2]	282	292	NA	NA	279	297	266	276	NA	295	295

[1]Students whose families meet federal income criteria qualify for Free or Reduced-Price Lunch. The percentage of qualifying students is commonly used as an indicator of school poverty level.

[2]All scores except for 12th-grade mathematics are based on a 0–500 scale. Twelfth-grade math scores are based on a 0–300 scale.

1. What differences do you see in the scores attained by students of different genders, income levels as indicated by eligibility for school lunch and parent educational levels, and race? What are the differences in students' performances on reading and mathematics tests?

2. What do these test scores suggest for your own teaching?

3. What should be the purpose of teachers and school administrators annually reviewing their students' achievement on NAEP and/or state tests?

the term *cultural capital* to refer to the advantages possessed by individuals from a culture's **dominant social groups**. These advantages provide social, economic, and academic leverage in terms of social mobility. For example, a middle-class child who shares the language, mannerisms, and **knowledge** of common symbols and norms held by the teacher—and reinforced in textbooks and learning materials—possesses more cultural capital at school than a child from a cultural or language background different from the teacher. Children from low-income families and children of color are generally expected to conform to the expectations of the dominant culture to be successful, even when those students represent the majority of the school population.

Students whose families have cultural capital are more likely to live in communities with schools that are attractive and sparkling clean, have qualified teachers, have low student-to-teacher ratios, and are rich in technology and other resources that support learning at high levels.

Deficit Ideology

It is human nature to assume that the positive values and norms we have learned—from our parents, cultural heritage, and the dominant culture in which we live—represent the strengths or ideals to which all people should aspire. When we think about individuals or groups of people who do not share our beliefs, it is tempting to think of their differences as weaknesses, or as problems to be overcome by opportunities or exposure to our own value systems. When we blame low-income people for their own economic disparities or consider them intellectually or culturally inferior, we are projecting a **deficit ideology** (Gorski, 2013).

Assumptions based on a deficit ideology can have a negative impact on teaching and learning in many ways. For example, some teachers may assume that students and families who speak a dialect or who come from single-parent or foster homes are less capable of academic achievement. A deficit ideology is reflected in the belief that students of color and English Language Learners (ELLs) are not achieving at grade level on standardized tests because they are intellectually inferior (Milner, 2010). It justifies inequalities in schools as being caused or perpetuated by the perceived deficiencies of students and their families. A deficit ideology is reflected in the language that educators sometimes use to describe students: at risk, remedial, culturally deprived, or disadvantaged (Gorski, 2013). Recognizing when a deficit ideology is consciously or subconsciously impacting your work as a teacher is a first step toward changing dispositions and behaviors toward students and allowing you to develop high expectations for them regardless of their social contexts.

Stereotyping

Stereotyping is one of the outcomes of a deficit ideology. Stereotypes are an exaggerated, and generally biased, view about a group based on unfounded assumptions. When we consciously or unconsciously maintain stereotypes about a group, we tend to project our preconceived ideas about them onto the students from those groups. Stereotypes can sound positive such as expecting African American students to excel in athletics or performing arts or viewing Asian American students as the **model minority** because a large number of them achieve at higher academic levels than other groups. However, those stereotypes do not describe every African American or Asian American. Most stereotypes reflect negative portrayals of groups of people who are different from ourselves. One of the dangers of stereotyping is that a negative or a false stereotype can both damage a child's sense of self-worth and limit opportunities provided to the child to develop to his or her fullest, and unique, potential. We should be alert to the stereotypes we bring to teaching or have developed over time to ensure they do not interfere with our ability to help all students learn.

It is not just a teacher's stereotyped perspectives toward his or her students that affect student behavior and learning. Common stereotypes that have been perpetuated over time influence how we see ourselves and perceive our own identity. Social psychologist Claude Steele (2010) has identified this stereotype threat as impacting the academic performance of students of color, female students, and students from other groups. These students are well aware of common stereotypes about their group memberships and may internalize or respond to those stereotypes in complex ways. For example, some students of color who have both the cultural capital and the potential for academic success may underperform because they perceive academic achievement as a "white" value or goal that is antithetical to their own sense of cultural loyalty. Female students may not achieve their potential, in part, because of internalized beliefs that competitiveness or having an interest in mathematics and sciences is unfeminine. Students may have experienced interactions with teachers or counselors who reinforced the internalization of learned stereotypes or behaviors.

The good news is that research shows we can change students' negative stereotypical perceptions of themselves by treating students as capable and talented. We can have a positive impact on students by removing the threat of the stereotype from the way they see themselves. Strategies that will help teachers accomplish this goal include the following:

- Provide critical feedback to all students

- When possible, ensure that students are not assigned to classrooms in which they are the only child from a specific cultural, ethnic, or language group

- Foster intergroup conversations among students from diverse groups

- Encourage students to affirm their sense of self

- Allow students to express frustration about their experiences with racism or ostracism in ways that contribute to positive engagement and success (Steele, 2010)

These strategies will help students improve their comfort, sense of belonging, trust, and academic achievement in the classroom. By not reinforcing negative stereotypes and holding all students accountable for meeting established learning goals, a teacher can begin to change the academic performance of students who have believed they aren't capable of intellectual achievement. In the next section, we will explore why some students are not engaging in school and the negative results.

Leaving School Early

In 1990, President George H. W. Bush and the nation's governors developed six National Education Goals to be reached by the year 2000. One goal was to reach a high school graduation rate of 90% and eliminate the high school graduation gap between white students and students of color. Not only did we not meet that goal by the year 2000, but the most recent available data show that 84% of the students in the 2015–2016 school year graduated with a regular high school diploma within four years of starting the ninth grade (ED*Facts* Data Groups 695 and 696, 2017). The good news is that the four-year graduation rate has improved since the president and governors set the 90% goal in 1990, but the gap between groups remains, as shown in Figure 4.2.

The socioeconomic status (SES) of families also correlates with high school graduation, as shown in Figure 4.2. Students whose parents finished high school are more likely to complete high school than those whose parents did not graduate (Rumberger, 2011). Students from families whose incomes are in the lowest quartile are over four times more likely to drop out of high school than are students from families whose incomes are in the highest quartile (Snyder, de Brey, & Dillow, 2016). A study by the Annie E. Casey Foundation confirmed the link between family income and high school graduation, finding that children who live in poverty and read below grade level by third grade are three times as likely not to graduate from high school as students who were born into families with incomes above the poverty level (Hernandez, 2011).

Why Students Drop Out of School

Students drop out of school because of individual and contextual factors. These students face challenges such as economic hardships, housing instability, homelessness, health issues, family dysfunction, and

FIGURE 4.2 ■ Graduation Rates Within Four Years in 2015–2016 by Student Characteristics

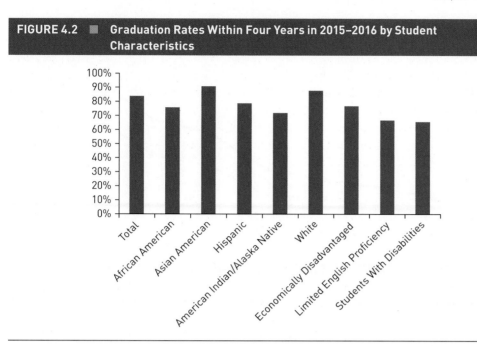

Source: ED*Facts* Data Groups 695 and 696. (2017, October 25). Table 1. Public high school 4-year adjusted cohort graduation rate (ACGR), by race/ethnicity and selected demographic characteristics for the United States, the 50 states, and the District of Columbia: School year 2015–16. Washington, DC: National Center for Education Statistics, U.S. Department of Education.

bullying (Feldman, Smith, & Waxman, 2017). Some students report that they leave school because of family or work responsibilities. Absenteeism, low educational aspirations, moving from school to school, not passing a grade, suspensions, and pregnancy are among the contributors to the decision to leave school (Rumberger, 2011). A majority of the youth who stop attending school experienced academic challenges that were exacerbated after they left elementary school. As they failed to achieve academically, they began to feel more helpless and hopeless while skipping more and more classes and days at school (Feldman et al., 2017). Other students are "pushed out" of school by disciplinary policies that rely heavily on suspension and expulsion as opposed to remediation measures. Peer choices and conditions in the community and family can also influence a student's decision to drop out of school (Rumberger, 2011).

The Cost of Dropping Out

In today's economy, students who do not finish high school have limited chances of finding a job that will enable them to earn enough to support a family. Even traditional working-class jobs (factory worker, truck driver, heavy equipment operator) are now likely to require a high school diploma or even an associate's degree. Although people without a high school diploma can usually find minimum-wage jobs in the service sector (cashiers, fast-food servers, hotel workers), such jobs may be offered only part-time—exempting employers from requirements to provide benefits to the employee. Furthermore, state minimum wages are set so low that unskilled service employees usually need to work well over 40 hours a week, sometimes at several jobs, to support a family.

In 2016, male high school dropouts earned $7,379 a year less than high school graduates and $41,958 less than their peers with a bachelor's degree (U.S. Census Bureau, 2017f). The difference among women is smaller but significant, as shown in Figure 4.3.

According to Civic Enterprises and the Everyone Graduates Center at the School of Education at Johns Hopkins University, there are four major reasons for increasing the number of students who graduate from high school with a diploma (DePaoli, Balfanz, Bridgeland, Atwell, & Ingram, 2017). Graduates are more likely to be employed and earn a higher income. They are less likely to be

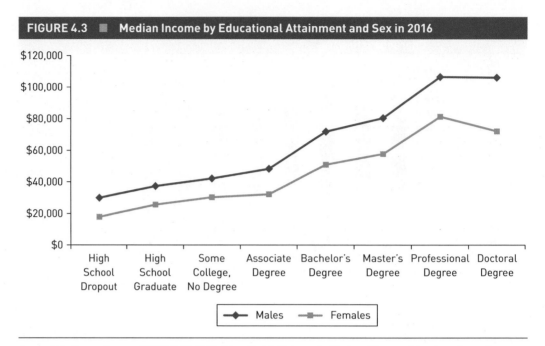

FIGURE 4.3   ■   Median Income by Educational Attainment and Sex in 2016

Source: U.S. Census Bureau. (2017f). Table P-20. Educational attainment—Workers 25 years old and over by median earnings and sex: 1991 to 2016. *Current population survey, annual social and economic supplements.* Washington, DC: Author.

Police officers provide security for schools to support educators in maintaining discipline. However, the disciplinary policies and practices of a school district sometimes lead to students being arrested even for minor infractions.

©Bob Daemmrich/Alamy

involved in criminal behavior or need social services. They have better health and higher life expectancy. Compared to peers who dropped out of school, graduates are also more likely to be active citizens who vote and volunteer.

School-to-Prison Pipeline

Research shows that high school dropouts are more likely to be incarcerated than are their peers who earn a diploma. Some schools rely on harsh or exclusionary forms of discipline such as arrest, expulsion, or suspension for infractions that do not put staff or students at risk. These practices contribute to a **school-to-prison pipeline**, in which students who are most vulnerable to dropping out of school are criminalized, instead of given the supports and intervention needed to remain on track to complete their schooling.

Zero tolerance policies, which have been practiced in a number of schools for the past 25 years, call for automatic punishment when a school rule is broken, without regard for extenuating circumstances, misunderstanding, or innocent mistakes. Although the intent of "no excuses" disciplinary codes is to maintain a safe environment conducive to learning for the majority of students, such policies have led to a significant increase in the number of students being suspended and expelled since the 1970s (Losen, 2011). Although suspensions or expulsions are required by law for infractions such as bringing a gun to school, many infractions are for less serious rule-breaking, such as possessing over-the-counter drugs such as Advil or Midol.

CHALLENGING ASSUMPTIONS
RETHINKING ZERO TOLERANCE

The Assumption

Tough school disciplinary codes create a more conducive environment for student learning. Expelling or suspending students for infractions of school rules ensures the safety of students, teachers, and other school personnel.

Background

More rigid approaches to school discipline, commonly known as zero tolerance policies, gained widespread use toward the end of the millennium, particularly after the enactment of the Gun-Free Schools Act of 1994, which requires a one-year expulsion for students who bring a firearm to school. Schools were encouraged by that legislation to create broader formulaic policies for disciplinary infractions, ranging from classroom misbehavior to possession of weapons or drugs. The hallmark of such practices is that they do not allow school personnel to make exceptions for extenuating circumstances and most often stipulate the removal of the student from school via suspension or expulsion. The rise in rigid disciplinary codes was accompanied by an increase in the assignment of police officers and security guards to school grounds, particularly in urban high schools. The number of schools staffed by law enforcement or security personnel tripled between 1996–1997 and 2007–2008 (Kang-Brown, Trone, Fratello, & Daftary-Kapur, 2013).

What the Research Shows

Twenty-five years later, research indicates that zero tolerance has not created safer schools, nor has it been effective in changing student behavior. Data reveal that African American students are three times as likely to be suspended or expelled as white students, and that students with exceptional needs have disproportionately high rates of disciplinary action (U.S. Department of Education, 2014). Although most of the attention on disproportionate suspensions, expulsions, and arrests has focused on African American and Latino males, African American females also are disproportionately victims of this criminalization. They "are 16% of the female student population, but nearly one-third of all girls referred to law enforcement and more than one-third of all female school-based arrests" (Morris, 2016, p. 3).

Studies show that disciplinary actions that disrupt schooling have a negative impact on students' likelihood of obtaining a high school diploma. Nearly 70% of the prison population does not hold a high school diploma (Amarao, 2013). In 2014, the U.S. Department of Education issued guidelines for reducing racial disparities in suspensions and expulsions, and creating alternatives to punishment-based approaches to management of school climate in ways that encourage positive behavior (Berwick, 2015). More states and school districts are rethinking approaches to school discipline, especially in light of research showing that zero tolerance policies, coupled with the likelihood that a disciplinary violation may result in arrest or court referral, has helped to create a school-to-prison pipeline.

Alternative Approaches to Discipline

The U.S. Department of Education and others have called for schools to take steps such as the following to improve school climate and address student behavioral problems:

Positive Behavioral Interventions and Supports (PBIS). Positive Behavioral Interventions and Supports (PBIS) is a three-tiered approach to school discipline. At the school-wide level, the focus is on defining and modeling positive behaviors by staff. The other two tiers are classroom-level attention to groups of students requiring behavioral monitoring and support, and one-on-one support and interventions for individual students. Additional focus is given to working in collaboration with community mental health agencies.

Emphasis on social and emotional learning. Increasingly, academic curriculum is being supplemented by practices intended to help students develop social and personal abilities for self-development and living in a community. Spending time during the school day on activities that focus on sharing feelings, discussing values, role-playing skills for positive social interaction, and holding class meetings to discuss problems or tensions can help children develop inner traits that will help them resolve conflicts in positive ways.

Restorative justice. Restorative justice practices are designed to reintegrate a student who has caused harm back into the community that has been harmed. As a philosophy, this practice emphasizes that a person who has done a bad thing is not a bad person. Restorative justice circles bring together the wrongdoer, the victim, and other key individuals whose role is to support both the victim and the person who has caused harm. Most often, the person or persons harmed negotiate a reparation agreement with the wrongdoer. Schools that have instituted a restorative justice framework also use circle practice to solve or prevent other breaches in community relationships, as well as to create feelings of trust and caring in the classroom community. Although the practice of restorative justice is relatively simple, it calls for a deep-seated and long-term commitment to creating a culture of community building and support (Cavanagh, 2018).

HOW DOES SOCIAL CONTEXT INFLUENCE WHAT IS TAUGHT?

Parents send their children to school to acquire the knowledge and skills they need to be productive members of society. However, what students bring to school in terms of home experience and background, not to mention what children absorb from friends and classmates, social media, and popular culture, is also part of every student's learning experiences. Successful teachers learn as much as possible about individual students' families and the range of cultures and heritages represented in their classroom, as well as student interests. That knowledge can be used to develop positive relationships with students and create learning activities that build on the expertise and cultural backgrounds that students bring to the classroom. Although saying we are "celebrating diversity" is a well-worn cliché, the diversity of family cultures and experiences should be a source of wealth to any teacher.

Social context also plays an integral role in instructional decision making. Even the geographic location of the school in which you teach will impact the vocabulary as well as the conceptual knowledge that students bring to learning activities such as comparing and contrasting like objects, solving word problems, or comprehending a literary text. Although progress has been made in updating textbooks to include children's photographs and names to represent a range of ethnicities, textbooks are still likely to include homework questions, or word problems, that presume a commonality of conceptual knowledge that is not shared by all students. (At an early age, rural children may have no clue as to what an apartment building or a subway is, while urban children may have little understanding of gardens or farms.) Many other factors (e.g., the racial and ethnic makeup of your school, the number of students who are ELLs, the number of students who qualify for Free or Reduced-Price Lunch) will also impact decisions, such as requiring the use of the Internet for homework, assigning group projects that require students to meet outside of class, and making sensitive choices in terms of textbooks and materials used.

Social Construction of Knowledge

Knowledge is the information, facts, and ideas that have been learned through formal education or lived experience. However, the knowledge valued by one group may be viewed by another group as inaccurate, unimportant, or not relevant to their lives. In the United States, the focus of both PreK–12 and higher education curricula has been and largely remains the Western canon, based on the presumption that Northern and Western European heritage, experiences, literature, and scholarship represent the body of knowledge that should be the scholarly foundation for students educated in the United States.

A growing body of scholars and educators, however, argue that from its beginning the United States has been a multicultural society, and that school and university curricula must incorporate the experiences of people of color, the labor class, women, and non-Christian religions. Multicultural scholars believe that U.S. curricula should more accurately reflect the histories and cultures of the many groups that populate our nation and that they should explore multiple perspectives on the content being taught.

It is not just educators and scholars who debate what should be taught in schools: Parents, school boards, community activists, and politicians also present a range of opinions on what should be included in or excluded from public school curricula. These differing perspectives on what should be taught lead to controversies about the teaching of ethnic studies, class differences, evolution, sex education, ethical or moral education, and other controversial topics. Some families protest that content taught in school infringes on the values they want to inculcate in their children, or claim their parental rights to protect their children from mature topics have been violated. Other families may request that the curricula, texts, and assigned readings in their school be more reflective of the racial and cultural heritage of the student body and nation. As teachers, we should bring an understanding of local community history, current events, and religious and cultural values to the educational choices we make on a daily basis.

Whose Knowledge?

What is taught in schools is generally determined by standards adopted by the state. State boards of education or local school districts select curricula and textbooks that they think will help students meet state standards as well as reflect their own values and beliefs. Some state legislatures set parameters on the content that can be taught in public schools. For example, some states allow creationism to be taught alongside evolution in public schools. Only one state, California, has mandated the inclusion of LGBTQ history as part of school curriculum, while in most states or school districts, efforts to add LGBTQ content to the curriculum have been rejected.

We generally think that what we are taught in school represents an objective body of knowledge and that it is a balance of viewpoints and scholarly consensus as to what an educated student at each grade level should know and be able to do. It may come as a surprise to learn that knowledge is actually socially constructed. Decisions about what is taught in schools and written in textbooks are influenced by the dominant opinions, interpretations, and values of experts in the field, as well as by state and federal policy makers who wish to influence what students are taught or not taught.

A common topic of debate is the extent to which textbooks and curriculum should include a focus on negative aspects of American history or culture, versus focusing solely on topics that inspire patriotism and civic engagement. For instance, some educators and parents object to the presentation of historical information that sugarcoats reality (e.g., downplaying the role of slavery as the root cause of the Civil War). In some cases, authors of textbooks or other educational materials are required to add or remove content in their manuscripts at the request of a state board of education, even though the requested changes may result in a biased or incomplete version of information. In 2010, Texas Board of Education members engaged in a contentious debate about the standards for social studies textbooks that would be used by 4.7 million high schoolers. They disagreed about the portrayal of the separation of church and state; the portrayal of the role of discrimination in society; the prominence given to civil rights leaders of color, including Cesar Chavez and Thurgood Marshall; and hundreds of other details (Robelen, 2010). In 2014, adoption of new textbooks in that state was preceded by another round of controversy on ideological topics, including the portrayal of Islam and global warming. In the current climate of division among groups, the content of the curriculum is likely to remain a contentious issue in some school districts and states.

Because the scholars who have codified the curricula that have been taught in U.S. schools and colleges over the centuries have predominantly been white, upper-middle-class, Protestant males, the perspectives of the powerful in society are generally reflected in their work. A belief widely held by historians is that history is written by the winners, or those who profit from the outcome of historical events and economic progress. Increasingly, scholars and writers from other nationalities, ethnicities, classes, gender identities, and religions are developing a body of work that is broadening the range of art and scholarship available for teaching and learning. Rapid advances in information technology have also dramatically increased our access to human experiences in the rest of the world, so even children who live in socially homogeneous communities are privy to cultures and societies that differ from their own. Although the Western canon retains a dominant presence in U.S. curriculum, the perspectives of women and other social groups and cultures are playing a larger role in what is being taught in our nation's schools.

Multiple Perspectives

Some of your students' families may have recently immigrated to your community from another country; some may have spent periods of time in refugee camps. Some of your students may be living in a car or homeless shelter, or in households that are food insecure. Other children may live in affluent conditions, but in families that are impacted by addiction, domestic violence, or illness. Some of your students may be struggling with their sexual identity, or with depression, anxiety, or an undiagnosed learning disability. Students from different racial and ethnic groups may struggle with both real and perceived racism, as well as hostility among ethnic groups. Even if the students in your classroom appear to belong to the same ethnic group, they may not share the same religion, and some may be more financially secure than others.

iStock/kali9

A diverse group of students provides a rich resource for incorporating multiple perspectives into the curriculum.

How each student and his or her family see the world is unique. Their cultures and experiences impact their perspectives, which could be different from your own perspective especially when your culture does not match your students' cultures. As teachers, we should listen and learn from our students, their families, and their communities. We should encourage multiple perspectives in our classroom by validating student voices and creating a safe environment in which students are encouraged to share family stories, cultural celebrations and customs, favorite foods, music, and greetings from different languages as well as their experiences with racism, sexism, ableism, classism, heterosexism, and intolerance of differences. Above all, children should be taught to celebrate diversity, while at the same time learning that we are much more closely defined by our similarities than by our differences.

Multicultural Education

Multicultural education is a framework or philosophy of education that prepares all students with the intercultural knowledge and skills to thrive in a pluralistic society. Multicultural education embraces the diversity and uniqueness of all students, and holds the view that academic success is not dependent on assimilation to cultural norms represented by the dominant population. It also promotes **social justice**. Multicultural educators are concerned with providing equity of learning opportunities; using a **multicultural curriculum** that includes a range of cultural, gender, and class perspectives; and creating cultural balance, openness, and sensitivity in relationships among teachers, students, staff, parents, and communities. Multicultural educators view all aspects of the educational process through a critical lens that has the needs and learning of students at the center so that lessons are planned to help all students make connections to the learning objectives presented.

Multicultural curricula include the infusion of art, literature, scholarship, history, and current events from a variety of cultures to meet learning objectives across content areas. Multicultural educators also seek ways to teach cross-cultural communication skills across grade levels, including the ability to discuss difficult issues within a safe and respectful environment.

In a school that promotes multicultural education, the curricula, bulletin boards, posters, artwork, textbooks, and other curricular resources incorporate accurate and positive references to diverse groups. School events—from back-to-school gatherings and parent–teacher conferences through holiday concerts and graduation day—are organized to ensure inclusivity and recognition of all groups represented in the school community. Library collections, summer reading lists, field trips, assembly topics, and guest speakers are chosen to represent a diversity of cultures and experiences. In designing lesson plans in all subject areas, care is taken to include activities, depictions, examples, text, and media that represent human diversity. The study of literature and social sciences is inclusive of the experiences and perspectives of women, as well as of underrepresented ethnic, racial, and socioeconomic groups. Multicultural educators learn about the range of family structures, religions, and special circumstances of their students' backgrounds (e.g., some of your students may be foster children, live with grandparents, or have been interracially adopted), and make sure assignments are modified so as not to exclude or cause discomfort to any child.

Some educators might assume that only students of color benefit from multicultural knowledge, believing that white students do not need to explore issues such as racism and discrimination. However, multicultural education is important for all students, regardless of their group memberships. Most textbooks today refer to diverse ethnic and racial groups, and most teachers include information about groups other than their own in lessons, particularly during the months that have been highlighted for African American, Latino, or women's history. However, in some schools, attention to multiculturalism takes the form of isolated or mainly symbolic activities (e.g., creating a poster to commemorate Martin Luther King Jr. Day, or a Parent–Teacher Association [PTA]–sponsored potluck featuring international foods).

Culturally Responsive Teaching

The real-life experiences that students bring to the classroom are often given little credibility in curriculum and instruction. However, each student brings a unique set of behavioral styles, expectations, and expertise to the classroom based on ways he or she has learned to survive and thrive in his or her family and community. All students have rich experiences to share, grounded in their cultural heritage, family stories and traditions, lived experiences, and community and religious affiliations. A multicultural educator will look for ways all students can learn about and share their family heritage that will contribute to the multicultural tapestry of the typical U.S. classroom.

Culturally responsive teaching, introduced in Chapter 2, is based on the premise that culture influences the way students learn (Gay, 2018; Hollins, 2011; Nieto, 2018). Culturally responsible teachers perceive the cultures and experiences of students as strengths, and use their students' cultural heritages as resources to strengthen and enrich the curriculum. Students learn to be proud of their own ethnic and cultural identities, and to value and take pride in the range of cultures of their classmates.

Culturally responsive teachers are careful to examine their teaching practices to ensure they do not unwittingly favor the culturally influenced behaviors of some students over others (e.g., enjoyment of competition, willingness to make eye contact, fear of displeasing adults). Learning is enhanced when teachers choose representations, texts, and media that familiarize students with both their own and other cultures as part of the learning experience. In planning lessons, a culturally responsive teacher considers factors that might present barriers to understanding or engagement for some students. For example, if a math exercise uses pizza and pizza toppings as a representation for division problems, teachers may need to consider whether all students know what a pizza is, and further consider ways of introducing pizza and common toppings to the class without embarrassing students. Lesson content in the sciences, mathematics, the arts, and physical education should include contributions that have been made to those fields by non-Western cultures.

Culturally responsive schooling helps expand students' knowledge of the world's complexities, and uses developmentally appropriate ways to help students process concepts that may be painful or controversial. Teachers must develop strategies and tools for helping students discuss difficult topics in ways that are respectful, encourage deep listening, and allow for safe expression of different opinions. Students of all racial and ethnic groups should develop critical-thinking skills that push them to question and investigate what they read, see, and hear in textbooks, the mass media, and discussions with friends. A curriculum for equality encourages students to identify inequities across groups, ask why they continue to exist, and work to eliminate the inequities.

Social Justice Education

The philosopher and educator John Dewey (1997) called for social justice in education when he said, "What the best and wisest parent wants for his [or her] own child, that must the community want for all of its children" (p. 3). A belief in social justice impels educators to intervene and advocate for children whose families are not ensured adequate shelter, food, and health care. No matter one's political beliefs as to personal versus societal responsibility, a child who is denied access to basic human rights is a child who does not have equal access to educational opportunities.

Confronting the inequities in society and working toward eliminating them undergirds teaching for social justice. Socially just teaching examines and critiques equity across groups. It confronts the social and economic inequities that prevent students from learning and participating effectively in schools (Burant, Christensen, Salas, & Walters, 2010).

Social justice education has applications for both learning and teaching. At the curricular level, learning activities and community service projects allow students to make contributions toward addressing inequities in their own communities, such as collecting canned goods for food banks or

TEACHERS' LOUNGE
MORDIDA!

© Amanda L. Glaze

My second year of teaching was a busy one. I was teaching two courses at two different levels in an inner-city school with about 2,000 students. Many of my students were ELLs struggling through complex science courses while just beginning to learn the language. One particular class of mine was made up mostly of these students, and we learned very quickly that science is especially difficult when you don't understand the language. To help my students, I purchased resource books to translate scientific terms from English to Spanish, used an online program to make loose translations of the notes, and practiced conversational Spanish with them so that I could speak with their families when needed. On my birthday, I came into the classroom after lunch to a big surprise. The students in that class had arranged a special party to celebrate, bringing balloons, snacks, ribbons, and a homemade *tres leches* cake—a big deal since so many of them had so very little. To make it even more special, when cake time came, I was asked to "bite the cake," or "*Mordida!*" as they chanted. In Mexican and other Latino cultures, this is a tradition where, when you lean down to bite, they push your face into the cake! I later learned that this is something you do with family, and their inclusion of me in this tradition was something very special. In return for simply caring for them, they brought me into their culture with a birthday experience I will never forget!

—Amanda L. Glaze
Jacksonville State University
Jacksonville, Alabama

© jupiterimages/Creatas/thinkstock

Social justice education teaches students to identify social inequities and participate in actions to alleviate the injustice.

organizing a fund-raiser for a cause selected by the class. Community service projects can be integrated with academic objectives, including but not limited to researching and/or providing information on the inequity being addressed; discussing causes and solutions; using math and literacy skills to set goals, plan, advertise, and tally donations received from a fund-raiser; or writing about a volunteer experience. In teaching social studies or history, teachers can seek opportunities to explore the causes and impact of institutional racism, in order to help students understand why racism and other forms of discrimination are not resolved by shifts in individual attitudes, or by charitable giving, but instead require societal change.

Schools can also eliminate barriers to equitable learning in the classroom and become advocates for services for students whose potential for learning is impacted by poverty, disabilities, or other circumstances. Some schools have created partnerships with health and social service providers and volunteer organizations to provide wraparound services for children and their families. In this model, teachers and professionals network to address needs any one child and his or her family may have for health care, counseling, after- and before-school programs, or tutoring (National Education Association, 2013). These connections can provide valuable insight into specific challenges and opportunities to link parents with services that can help. In schools with substantial numbers of students from low-income families, teachers should also examine their own practices in terms of assigning projects that rely on home support for optimal success, or assuming all parents and children have Internet access at home.

CONNECTING TO THE CLASSROOM

This chapter has provided you with some basic information about the role of social context in understanding schools and students. Below are some key principles for applying the information in this chapter to the classroom.

1. Teachers should be aware of the social contexts that can have positive or negative influences on student behavior and learning in the classroom, and be ready to apply that knowledge to all facets of instruction.

2. Teachers should be sensitive to the traumas that their students experience and the impact they have on their learning and behavior in the classroom to maximize their learning potential.

3. Teachers must be aware and self-reflective about the harm caused to students by the unconscious

application of a deficit ideology and stereotypes. Holding high expectations for student achievement can overcome the negative influence of stereotype threat.

4. Teachers should be aware of the social context of the community and its political and social culture as they determine how to teach controversial and meaningful lessons to students.

5. Teachers should practice culturally responsive teaching, which incorporates the culture and experiences of students and their families into curriculum and instruction, to make content relevant to students' lives.

6. Teachers and parents can have a positive influence on the choices that students make about sex, drugs, and other potentially harmful choices.

SUMMARY

This chapter focuses on the social contexts in which teachers, students, and communities interact. Three major topics were addressed in this chapter:

- Schools must consider the whole child, and not only the achievement of academic objectives, in designing curricula and allocating resources. Students need an adult support system that extends beyond their parents or guardians in order to help them make good choices and to provide intervention and advocacy when needed.

- Contextual factors inside and outside of school contribute to students' academic performance and behavior in classrooms and play an important role in instructional decision making.

- Learning standards, textbook choices, and what can and cannot be included in a school's curricula are impacted by political decisions made at the state or district level, and primarily reflect perspectives of the dominant cultural groups in any society.

KEY TERMS

bullying 99
canon 114
Common Core State Standards (CCSS) 107
cyberbullying 99
deficit ideology 109
dominant social groups 109
high-needs students 97
high-poverty schools 98

knowledge 109
mindfulness 101
model minority 109
multicultural curriculum 116
multiple perspectives 114
Positive Behavioral Interventions and Supports (PBIS) 113
restorative justice 113
school-to-prison pipeline 112

social justice 116
stereotype threat 110
trauma-sensitive schools 101
whole child approach 98
zero tolerance policies 112

CLASS DISCUSSION QUESTIONS

1. Through your state department of education's website, locate the most recent school report card for a school or school district in which you will be doing field experiences. What patterns are evident as they relate to achievement gaps across grade levels, gender, income, race, and socioeconomic levels of students? What patterns concern you?

2. Peruse a PK–12 textbook that has been published in the last five years—preferably one that is used in your state/district. How well does it incorporate multicultural perspectives in ways that are more than superficial (e.g., more than in illustrations, photos, and ethnic names given to hypothetical students)? Provide specific examples of where the textbook does a good job of representing viewpoints and experiences from nondominant cultures, and/or where you would need to enhance your lessons/teaching materials in order to incorporate the same.

3. The concept of whole child education includes the premise that children cannot achieve their potential unless their physical, social, and emotional well-being is ensured. What steps should a teacher take when a child in his or her classroom is showing signs of distress?

SELF-ASSESSMENT

What Is Your Current Level of Understanding and Thinking About the Social Context of Schools?

One of the indicators of understanding is the complexity with which you respond to questions that require you to use the concepts and facts introduced in this chapter.

Answer the following questions as fully as you can. Then use the Assessing Your Learning rubric to self-assess the degree to which you understand and can use the organizational ideas presented in this chapter.

1. What social contexts challenge teachers as they try to engage students in school and academic work?

2. How have political decisions in recent years influenced the curricula in the state/district in which you intend to pursue teaching licensure or certification?

3. How can teachers support students in making appropriate decisions about issues such as health, sexuality, and peer associations—decisions that can have a long-lasting positive or negative effect on their lives?

Assessing Your Learning Rubric

	Parts & Pieces	Unidimensional	Organized	Integrated	Extensions
Indicators	Elements/concepts are talked about as isolated and independent entities. Some important names are provided in isolation.	One or a few concepts are addressed, while others are underdeveloped, or not mentioned.	Deliberate and structured consideration of all key concepts/elements.	All key concepts/elements are included in a view that addresses interconnections.	Integration of all elements and dimensions, with extrapolation to new situations.
Social contexts of schools	Lists a few social contexts that can impact student learning.	Identifies social contextual characteristics that generally support student learning and students' engagement in school.	Describes how educators can support students whose social contexts may not support positive educational engagement.	Analyzes educational strategies that improve school attendance and keep students engaged in school and learning.	Develops and tests lesson plans that are culturally responsive and designed to engage students from diverse groups actively in the content being taught.

FIELD GUIDE
FOR LEARNING MORE ABOUT . . .

The Social Context of Schools

To further increase your understanding of the social context of schools, do one or more of the following activities.

Ask a Teacher	Ask experienced teachers to reflect on the contextual factors of the school in which they teach, and how those factors impact their work. In preparation for your interview, examine data about student characteristics and enrollment; test data; and dropout, suspension, and expulsion rates (if applicable), which are available on your state's department of education website. Be prepared to ask questions that are prompted by your research. Record each teacher's response (with permission). Provide a written transcript of your interview(s).
Make Your Own Observations	One of the goals of culturally responsive teaching is to connect concepts being taught to students' lives. The teachers that you are observing may use different strategies to make the curricula authentic and meaningful to their students. As you visit classrooms, look for evidence of how the teachers are connecting the curricula to students' lives by using the following rubric from the *Five Standards for Effective Pedagogy and Learning* of the Center for Research on Education, Diversity & Excellence (n.d.). Based on your observation of a specific teacher, choose one of the four rubric levels that best describes his or her performance on the standard listed in the first column. Provide a rationale for your choice based on the rubric description.

School:

Location of School:

Race and Gender of the Teacher:

Race, Gender, and Native Language of Students, by Number and Percentage of Whole Group:

Standard	Emerging	Developing	Enacting	Integrating
Making Meaning—Connecting School to Students' Lives	The teacher (a) includes some aspect of students' everyday experience in instruction, or (b) connects classroom activities by theme or builds on the current unit of instruction, or (c) includes parents or community members in activities or instruction.	The teacher makes incidental connections between students' prior experience/ knowledge from home, school, or community and the new activity/ information.	The teacher integrates the new activity/ information with what students already know from home, school, or community.	The teacher designs, enacts, and assists in contextualized activities that demonstrate skillful integration of multiple standards simultaneously.

Comments:

Reflect Through Journaling	Describe in one or two sentences the contextual factors that describe your background, with consideration of race/ethnicity, parental levels of education and socioeconomic status, and any other significant factors. Can you think of any times in which your background played a role in how you were perceived and treated by teachers in comparison to children from a different background who were in your classes? Support your answer with a few specific examples.
Build Your Portfolio	When you begin teaching, you may have a class with students from ethnic or racial groups with which you are not familiar. You should be able to incorporate information about your students' cultures into the curriculum and draw on their cultures to provide examples to help them learn. To provide you a beginning, identify instructional resources on African Americans, Asian Americans, Latinos, or Native Americans that can be incorporated into your lesson plans for the future.
Read a Book	For tips on implementing trauma-sensitive schools, see *Trauma-Sensitive Schools for the Adolescent Years* by Susan E. Craig (2017, Teachers College Press). Each chapter includes a feature on "What Teachers Can Do."
	Do you sometimes wonder if you can make a difference with the struggling students who are your greatest challenge? The book, *Hanging In: Strategies for Teaching the Students Who Challenge Us Most* by Jeffrey Benson (2014, ASCD), profiles challenging students who needed caring teachers with tenacity to help the students eventually take advantage of schooling.

(Continued)

(Continued)

	Students who have dropped out of school tell their own stories about their path to that decision in *"Why We Drop Out": Understanding and Disrupting Student Pathways to Leaving Schools* by Deborah L. Feldman, Antony T. Smith, and Barbara L. Waxman (2017, Teachers College Press).
	To learn about successful practices in schools and classrooms that are improving students' engagement in learning and their academic performance, read *Creating the Opportunity to Learn: Moving From Research to Practice to Close the Achievement Gap* by A. Wade Boykin and Pedro Noguera (2011, ASCD).
	Bullying and Cyberbullying: What Every Educator Needs to Know by Elizabeth Englander (2013, Harvard University Press) provides a wise and readable analysis of bullying behavior and strategies for effective responses.
Search the Web	**Reporting Child Abuse:** Most states require teachers to report child abuse if they suspect it. Check the U.S. Department of Health and Human Services' Child Welfare Information Gateway or Scholastic's "What Should You Do When You Suspect Child Abuse?" for assistance on identifying and reporting child abuse.
	Restorative Justice Practice: The Oakland City (California) Public School District has for years been at the forefront in using restorative justice practice in its schools. "Restorative Welcome and Reentry Circle," produced by Cassidy Friedman, is a particularly moving video in which an Oakland high school student is welcomed back to his school community after being incarcerated. The video is available on YouTube.
	Stop Sexual Violence: For classroom resources on reducing sexual violence, visit the Centers for Disease Control and Prevention's Sexual Violence Prevention Technical Package.
	Teaching About Substance Abuse: For classroom resources on substance abuse from the National Institute on Drug Abuse, Google National Institute on Drug Abuse for Teachers.

STUDENT STUDY SITE

⑤SAGE edge™

Get the tools you need to sharpen your study skills. **SAGE edge** offers a robust online environment featuring an impressive array of free tools and resources.

Access practice quizzes, eFlashcards, video, and multimedia at **edge.sagepub.com/hall3e**.

5 FAMILIES AND COMMUNITIES

© Rose Yazzie

© James Hernandez

TEACHER INTERVIEW

Ms. Rose Yazzie and
Mr. James Hernandez

Ms. Rose Yazzie has taught fourth grade for three years at Rose Park Elementary School in Salt Lake City, Utah. Before returning to the Salt Lake City area where she grew up, she taught at Tse' Biindzisgal School in the Navajo Nation on the border of the Navajo reservation and Utah. With an ethnic background of Diné (Navajo) and Mexican American, she can relate to the cultural backgrounds of many of the families in this diverse community with white, Latino, African American, Navajo, Pacific Islander, and refugee families.

Mr. James Hernandez worked with Ms. Yazzie when he was the outreach worker for the Granite School District, tutoring American Indian students in five Title I schools. Mr. Hernandez identifies himself ethnically as American Indian from Mission San José in San Antonio, Texas.

LEARNING OUTCOMES

After reading this chapter, you should be able to do the following:

1. Analyze public perspectives about the quality of schools and teachers.

2. Respect the diversity of students' families and understand the importance of not stereotyping students based on their family structure and size.

3. Assess the impact of family culture on the learning and teaching process.

4. Analyze the influence of religious beliefs and native language on curriculum and instruction in your school.

5. Evaluate the school choices available to families in many communities.

6. Create strategies for effectively working with families and the community to support student learning.

Q: What brings you joy in teaching?

A: (Ms. Yazzie) I really like to have children foster empathy with each other and build strong relationships in which they are able to communicate honestly with each other. Like if James drank all the coffee, I can be honest: "James, I am upset that you drank all of the coffee because you know that I love coffee in the morning. I need you to remember that the next time you drink all of the coffee." And James is just like "Oh, sorry, I didn't even realize I did it." It gets solved; the emotions are addressed, and we both have a stronger relationship because we were able to communicate about it. That is something that extends not to just small things like "You drank all of the coffee," but to bigger things like "Oh, I think James said something about me in his language." And being able to say, "James, when you said that, did you know you made me feel like this? Is that what you meant to do?" I want my students to be able to address those kinds of racial microaggressions and other issues with kids in an honest, empathy-driven kind of way.

A: (Mr. Hernandez) I had a group of four boys, and one of them said, "Can we watch this [video]?"—an educational video about drugs. It was about three minutes long, and one of the students said, "You know what? My uncle died of an overdose last year." It took a year for him to tell me, but that really stuck with me because it just came out of nowhere, and I didn't know what was going on. There was another instance after Christmas break when a boy in kindergarten said, "Oh, you came back." He was surprised, and I started tearing up. I said, "Of course, I would," but his face was like "You actually came back." Those things made me feel good because I felt like they trusted me and my presence was making a difference.

Q: **How do you know that each student is learning?**

A: (Ms. Yazzie) When students internalize things. When they have inquiry around things. If I am teaching the water cycle, I can use worksheets, but when we go to the Jordan River that is 10 minutes away from our school and the kids are doing these experiments, they start to ask, "Why is the water going that way when the mountain is going that way?" They start having their own questions around things, and then they actually internalize enough that they want to go home and Google the answers. They come back to school with "Hey, Ms. Yazzie, I found out why the water goes that way." Those kinds of moments go above and beyond the curriculum books that teachers have been given. A lot of texts support them, but kind of constrict them a little bit. These are those teachable moments. When my students have inquiry and when they internalize it or bring it back to their own lives or their own knowledge systems, I know they are learning.

Q: **How are you interacting with the families of students in your classroom?**

A: (Ms. Yazzie) At the Back to School Night, I have centers where the families are able to communicate with me a little bit more instead of just "I'm Ms. Yazzie, and here's my PowerPoint." They're more center based where the parents can do an art project to tell me about the places they call home. Right away, I know the family members and whether their home is on the reservation or they live here in Salt Lake. Or maybe their home is the place where they were before they went to a refugee camp. By being able to hear their stories and their experiences through that art, and then showing them my own home, I get to know them, and they get to know me. Another activity is the aspirations the families have for their children. I have the kids and the families work together on what they want their child to do in the future, like what dreams do they have? One that is always kind of funny is when the kids want to be YouTube famous, and the parent is saying, "You're going to be a lawyer." These introductions make it easier to talk about issues like immigration and mass shootings that are happening because we are on similar wavelengths.

I also do home visits throughout the school year to strengthen the bond we built at the beginning of the year. These visits also help me know more about the families and students in their comfortable setting versus being at the school. That's so much fun. Last year, the members of a Burmese family ended up inviting me back to their apartment for a feast. They had butchered the meat and were telling me about all of the different things they do to prepare the food. Those activities really build strong connections with families and make teaching so much fun.

Q: **What advice about working with families would you give to the readers of this book?**

A: (Mr. Hernandez) You should be persistent with families. When you are supposed to meet with families or students and they don't show up, you should take it as an opportunity to grow. What is happening in your students' families? You should try to understand the situation rather than blame or be judgmental. You should be persistent, and sometimes insistent on understanding where the families are coming from. As a teacher, you are in a unique spot. You have a class for an entire year and have a great opportunity to really learn families and really learn students very well and to make a big positive impact on them.

A: (Ms. Yazzie) Start with understanding your privileges and where you are coming from. For example, I am a Diné woman and grew up lower class, but I still have privileges because I was able to go get a master's degree. I was able to walk up the stairs today. I need to recognize those privileges and how I navigate them and use them to help people or maybe learn how I don't use them to help people. But hopefully, teachers are using them to help. Our PTA teacher said, "When we meet our parents, it is kind of like a first date." You want it to go well. You want to be happy when you see these people. You want to be able to have tough conversations when needed. You know that this is going to be a commitment to these families.

Questions to Consider

1. What does understanding your own cultural background and privileges have to do with developing trust and positive relationships with the families of your students?

2. What are the advantages of teachers being engaged with their students' families?

3. What are some innovative ways you will engage families in their children's learning?

INTRODUCTION

The school is much more than the educators and students who populate it. A good school contributes to the health of a community by nurturing its children and preparing them to contribute to society in the future. Families, of course, are critical supports in their children's education, which is enhanced when families and educators work together to help children and youth learn. In addition, involved community residents, public agencies, and officials who serve the community, businesses, and other organizations all play roles in making schools successful.

When they have a choice, families choose to live in communities in which schools have created high-quality learning environments. These schools provide a safe place for their children, have qualified teachers who are committed to student learning, and have a record of preparing graduates who are successful, contributing adults. They value the input of families and both encourage and support family involvement in the schools. Yet most communities have some schools that have become isolated from the community. They do not provide pleasant or engaging environments, and they too often are not safe havens for the students who attend them. Many of their teachers are not fully qualified or may not appear to care about their students' social, psychological, or academic growth. In some cases, it may seem that the community has given up on its schools and their inhabitants. In this chapter, we will explore the involvement of families, communities, and educators in making schools work for students. We use *families* and *parents* interchangeably to refer to anyone who shares responsibility for the well-being of students. It could be a mother or father, both parents, grandparents, an aunt or uncle, a guardian, and/or another adult.

HOW DOES THE PUBLIC VIEW EDUCATION IN THE PUBLIC SCHOOLS?

Almost everyone has an opinion about schools and how they could be improved. Public attitudes about schools can and do influence educational policies and practices. When the public is upset with the quality of schools, politicians may respond with demands on teachers and school administrators for reform. Educators and policy makers use survey results to determine agreement or disagreement with current and proposed policies and practices. What are some of the public's, educators', and parents' views of education that may impact your work in schools?

The Quality of Our Schools

Forty-three percent of the respondents to the annual PDK (*Phi Delta Kappan*) Poll of the Public's Attitudes Toward the Public Schools ("The 50th Annual PDK Poll," 2018) gave their local schools an A or B. Public school parents grade their public schools higher than the general public grades them, with 70% of those parents giving an A or B to their local schools. Affluent adults and respondents with a college degree were more likely to give high marks to their community schools. In another national poll, 64% of African Americans, 45% of Hispanics, and 40% of Native Americans thought that their children had less of a chance of receiving a quality education than white students (National Public Radio, Robert Wood Johnson Foundation, & Harvard T. H. Chan School of Public Health, 2017).

Teacher Quality

In the 2011 State of the Union address, President Barack Obama declared that "after parents, the biggest impact on a child's success comes from the man or woman at the front of the classroom" (White House, 2011). Parents and community leaders agree that the quality of schools is measured, in great part, by the quality of the teachers in the schools. Parents and students know who the effective teachers are. A number of parents do everything possible to ensure their children are in those teachers' classes and to steer their children away from classes taught by ineffective teachers. They clearly know the value of an effective teacher to the potential success of their children.

Although teaching was the tenth most prestigious occupation in 2014, it was no longer ranked in the top 10 by 2016 on a list that ranked doctor, scientist, firefighter, military officer, engineer, nurse, architect, emergency medical technician, veterinarian, and police officer in the top 10 (McCarthy, 2016; Smith, 2014). At the same time, grade school teachers were rated the third most honest and ethical professionals behind nurses and military officers (Brenan, 2017).

Teachers and principals in high-poverty schools are less likely than those in **low-poverty schools** to be rated as excellent (48% vs. 73% for teachers, and 51% vs. 75% for principals) (MetLife, 2013). On the positive side, eight in ten (79%) parents rate their child's teachers as excellent or good at effectively engaging them in their child's school and education (MetLife, 2012). Engagement is much stronger at the elementary and middle school levels. Parents of high school students are less likely to agree that their child's school helps all parents understand what they can do at home to support a student's success in school (MetLife, 2012).

Concerns About Schools

The public also has views about the major problems in schools. By far, lack of financial support continues to be the number-one challenge facing public schools. In the 50th Annual PDK Poll (2018), over one in five respondents (26%) identified funding as a major problem. The next most common concerns mentioned by 10% of the respondents were general student discipline and bullying. However, subgroups of the general population have a different set of concerns based on their own experiences and needs. Some African American parents speak about not feeling welcome at their children's school and feeling intimidated by administrators. Some parents worry that speaking up could lead to possible negative consequences for their child (Bridges, Awokoya, & Messano, 2012).

WHO ARE THE FAMILIES OF OUR STUDENTS?

The population is getting older as large numbers of baby boomers reach retirement age while the percentage of children and young people continues to decrease. Fifteen percent of the U.S. population was over 65 years old in 2016 while 23% of the population was under the age of 18, which represents a 3% increase in the number of people over 65 since 2000 and a 3% decrease in the student population during the same period (U.S. Census

"I've lost track, am I taking you to basketball practice, hockey practice, wrestling practice or band practice?"

© Dave Carpenter

Bureau, 2001, 2016). Just over 40% of U.S. families have children under the age of 18 (U.S. Census Bureau, 2017d). By 2035, the number of people age 65 years and older will surpass the number under ✸ the age of 18 (U.S. Census Bureau, 2018b). These changes in the demographics of age impact educational policy. Families without school-aged children are not always advocates for education and social programs for children, especially when it comes to providing additional financial support for education.

Family Structures

Families today are different from those in which your grandparents and great-grandparents were raised. Seventy years ago, couples married within a few years after they finished high school. The typical family included both mother and father and two or more children, with the father usually working outside the home while the mother stayed at home to raise the children. Children were more likely to be born to married women, and divorce was rather rare.

Families in the United States today are very diverse. They include mothers working outside the home while fathers stay at home with the children, stay-at-home mothers, single-parent families, two working parents, remarried parents, married couples without children, families with adopted or foster children, gay and lesbian parents, extended families, grandparents raising grandchildren, and unmarried couples with children. Nearly two in three children (64%) live with both of their married parents. Nearly one in four children live with their mother only, but that number grows to almost one in two for African American children (U.S. Census Bureau, 2017a). Overall, single mothers, single fathers, grandparents, and other guardians raise more than one in three children in the United States, as shown in Figure 5.1. As teachers, we should be careful not to judge students based on the structure of their families (Cohen, 2017).

Today, there are more women who are not married than ever before. Two in five children are born to an unmarried mother, but some of those mothers are living with a partner (Pew Research Center, 2015). Although children are advantaged when they live with two caring and loving parents, living with two parents is not essential for success in school and life. Problem behavior and lack of academic success are more directly related to poverty, conflict, and instability in families than to marriage status.

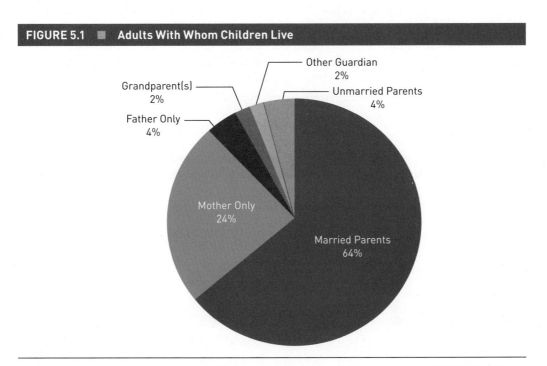

FIGURE 5.1 ■ Adults With Whom Children Live

Other Guardian 2%
Grandparent(s) 2%
Unmarried Parents 4%
Father Only 4%
Mother Only 24%
Married Parents 64%

Source: Compiled from U.S. Census Bureau. (2017a). America's families and living arrangements: 2017 (C tables). *Current population survey, 2017 annual social and economic supplement.* Retrieved from https://census.gov/data/tables/2017/demo/families/cps-2017.html.

Nearly one in four children live in a single-parent household, which is a factor that could negatively affect their economic well-being.

Unfortunately, poverty is a prevalent factor in families headed by single mothers. Ten percent of children in married-couple families are living in poverty, compared with 43% in female-householder families. Poverty can lead to children suffering from inadequate health care and hunger that results from poor housing conditions and not enough money to support basic needs. Eighteen percent of children are living in households classified by the U.S. Department of Agriculture as food insecure or lacking access to affordable, nutritious food on a regular basis. In addition, three in five children live in communities with poor environmental conditions such as poor air quality (Federal Interagency Forum on Child and Family Statistics, 2017).

During your career in schools, you may have students whose parents are gay or lesbian. Most of these parents are married or have made a commitment to their partner and have decided to raise children. Because of the prejudice against Lesbian, Gay, Bisexual, Transgender, and Queer or Questioning (LGBTQ) individuals in some communities, young students may not understand a family with parents of the same sex and ask you questions about why a student has two mommies or two daddies. Some heterosexual couples with children in your classroom may ignore LGBTQ couples or refuse to work with them. In other communities, families will be very accepting of the diversity of students and families that make up the school. Nevertheless, you should be prepared to help students understand and accept families that are different from their own, and be welcoming to all parents and guardians who will be your partners in helping their children learn.

Family Size

The size of families is influenced by societal factors such as women's participation in the labor force and higher education, as well as improvement in contraception and fewer marriages (Pew Research Center, 2015). These factors contribute to lower fertility rates and, thus, smaller families. Although some families in the United States have many children, the majority of women in the United States have two or fewer children, as shown in Figure 5.2. The 2011 general fertility rate was the lowest ever reported for the United States, at 63.0 births per 1,000 women aged 15–44. In addition, the birth rate for teenagers aged 15–19 was 29.4 per 1,000—also the lowest rate ever reported for the United States, with the greatest drop among African American teenagers (Martin, Hamilton, Osterman, Curtin, & Matthews, 2013, 2015).

Low birth rate 2011

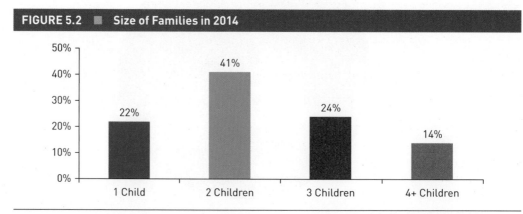

FIGURE 5.2 ■ Size of Families in 2014

1 Child	2 Children	3 Children	4+ Children
22%	41%	24%	14%

Source: Adapted from Pew Research Center. (2015, December 17). *Parenting in education: Outlook, worries, aspirations are strongly linked to financial situation.* Retrieved from http://assets.pewresearch.org/wp-content/uploads/sites/3/2015/12/2015-12-17_parenting-in-america_FINAL.pdf.

WHAT DOES CULTURE HAVE TO DO WITH EDUCATION?

Our culture defines us. It guides our way of thinking, feeling, and behaving in our families and communities. Members of a group develop behavior patterns that help them understand each other and live together in relative harmony. We are comfortable with the members of our cultural group because we know the meaning of their words and actions. However, we may misunderstand the cultural cues of members of a different cultural group. We grow up thinking that everyone thinks and acts like us, not realizing that the experiences and conditions of other groups could lead to different **values**, behaviors, and knowledge. As a result, we may respond to differences as personal affronts, rather than cultural differences. These misunderstandings may seem insignificant, but they can carry important cultural meanings to members of groups. These differences vary from how loud is too loud, to how close to stand to someone without being rude or disrespectful, to how to raise children. You can gain the respect of or offend parents by raising your palm to greet them or by raising your eyebrow. These are some of the many culturally determined behaviors with meaning to members of specific groups.

Culture is learned, shared with others, adapted to the circumstances, and dynamic. We learn our culture from our parents and caretakers. It is reinforced at places of worship, community events, and ethnic celebrations. We acquire our culture and become competent in its language and ways of behaving and knowing through a process called **enculturation**. We learn the social norms and expectations of society through the process of socialization (see Chapter 2). Thus, we learn what it means to be a wife, husband, parent, student, or friend, as well as the meaning of occupational roles such as teacher, businessperson, custodian, and politician. Nurses, physicians, teachers, neighbors, and religious leaders assist parents in enculturating and socializing children by modeling appropriate behavior and rewarding children and youth for acceptable behaviors.

Over time, cultures adapt to environmental conditions, available natural and technological resources, and their relationship to the larger society. Eskimos who live with extreme cold, snow, and ice develop a culture different from that of Pacific Islanders, who have limited land, unlimited seas, and fewer mineral resources. The culture of urban residents differs from that of rural residents, in part because of the resources available in the different settings. Cultures adapt as technology forces changes in available jobs and communication. The cultures of groups that suffer discrimination in society respond to the power relationships within society in ways that are different from how the dominant group responds.

The Role of Culture

Cultural relativism is not judging other cultural groups by our own cultural standards, but rather trying to see the second culture as a member of that group sees it. In developing these multiple perspectives, we might come to understand that the way of doing things in a second culture has validity. As countries and cultures around the world become more interdependent, cultural relativism provides a lens through which we can learn to respect other cultures and avoid relegating them to an inferior status. This stance is particularly important in schools as students from cultures different from our own enter our classrooms.

Cultural relativism does not apply only to cultures outside the United States. Some people judge the cultures of many groups in the United States as inferior to their own culture. We are likely to find children of parents who have immigrated from non-European countries and students of color in our classrooms. What do we really know about their cultures and experiences in the community? When we expect students from diverse cultural groups to act, think, and know as we learned in

Our culture has a great impact on how we interact with each other in our everyday living. We do not always realize that different patterns exist in other cultures.

iStock/MarkBowden

our own culture, we are placing a burden on the students to learn our culture. You will gain respect in communities as you learn about and interact with the cultures of your students and their families. You will not only begin to understand why you and they sometimes behave and think differently, but also be viewed as someone who cares about and respects other cultures and experiences.

We are all multicultural because we are members of more than one identity group within our culture. We behave and think about ourselves and the world based on our gender, ethnicity, race, language, religion, socioeconomic status (SES), and abilities. We may act and speak differently in a professional setting than we do when we are interacting in the community in which we grew up. Males and females often exhibit different behaviors in social settings. As we grew up, we learned the behaviors appropriate in our multiple identity groups. We can also learn the history, experiences, and cultures of other groups, becoming bicultural or multicultural and bilingual or multilingual in the process.

Because most schools reflect the dominant society, students may feel forced to adopt the dominant culture to be academically successful. In contrast, students from the dominant group find almost total congruence of the cultures of their families, schools, and workplaces. Persons of color, immigrants, and persons with low incomes generally need to become bicultural to fit in at work or school, maintaining their own cultural patterns at home and the cultural patterns of the dominant group at work and in school.

When our cultural differences result in one group being treated differently from another, **cultural borders** are erected between groups. Crossing these borders can be difficult, especially when behavior valued on one side of the border is denigrated or not tolerated on the other side. Borders are sometimes drawn in schools around speaking one's native language or dialect in school or around wearing a hijab, yarmulke, or cross. Cultural borders are established in classrooms when we ground all activity and communications in our culture alone. Being able to function comfortably in different cultures allows us to cross cultural borders, incorporating our students' cultures and experiences into the curriculum and classroom activities. It also allows us to model respect for cultural differences and the cultural borders some students must cross on a daily basis.

School Culture

Schools have their own culture with rituals, rules, academic and social expectations, teaching practices, dress codes, and social interactions between students and teachers and among students. The school culture gives a school its own unique look and feel. It could be friendly, competitive, caring, elitist, inclusive, or intolerant and racist. The culture can support academics, sports, bilingualism, and/or the arts. Some schools have established nurturing environments that value and care about their students as individuals. Others have environments that are toxic. They may be very authoritarian with strict rules and hierarchies to reinforce the rules, or staff may have a very negative attitude about students as well as the school's operations and other staff members (Gruenert & Whitaker, 2015). The school culture can impact student learning, helping to improve it or dampen it. Schools that are successful in helping students learn have positive school cultures in which students, families, and the communities are valued and respected.

Although they differ across schools and communities, students and educators practice many common rituals in athletics, extracurricular clubs, graduation exercises, and school social events. The rituals and ceremonies of schools promote national identity formation as students recite the Pledge of Allegiance and sing patriotic songs. The signs and emblems of the individual school culture are displayed in school songs, colors, and cheers. Traditions in the school culture are associated with regional influences, the social structure of a community, and location in a rural, urban, or suburban area. Some schools are influenced greatly by the religion of the children's families, others by the presence of a large military base.

iStock/monkeybusinessimages

Most schools participate in competitive sports events. These events are used to develop school spirit that brings students and the community together.

Schools develop histories that are transferred from generation to generation. Extracurricular activities, proms, award and graduation ceremonies, fund-raisers, school plays, step dance competitions, bands, clubs, athletic games, and school trips take on different degrees of importance from one community to another and from one family to another. Some graduates retain lifelong feelings of pride about their schools. Others have less lofty memories.

HOW ARE STUDENTS' CULTURES REFLECTED IN SCHOOLS?

The cultures of their families have shaped the beliefs and values of the students who appear at the school door every fall. However, their cultures may not align with the cultural patterns of the school, sometimes leading to conflicts between families and teachers and school officials. As a teacher, you will need to be aware of your students' cultures as you choose what to teach and how to teach it. In this section, we will explore issues related to the religious and language diversity of communities.

Religious Diversity

Students' and parents' religious orientation may strongly influence their perceptions of objectivity, fairness, and legality in schools. Some families have removed their children from public schools because they believe that the school does not reflect their values of appropriate student dress, language, and behaviors. Some families support prayer in school and at school events. Some families complain that the curriculum and assigned readings are too secular and do not reflect or even acknowledge their beliefs. Non-Christians accuse schools of not respecting religious diversity, scheduling important assignments and celebrations on their religious holidays, singing Christian hymns during convocations and concerts, and expecting their daughters to attend coed physical education classes. They believe that schools already reflect Christian perspectives, which they feel denigrate their religious beliefs.

Understanding the importance of religion to students and their families provides an advantage to educators in developing effective teaching strategies for individual students. We should avoid stereotyping students based on their religious heritage or lack of religious beliefs. Within each religious group are differences in attitudes and beliefs. Members of the same religion may be a part of a liberal or moderate group, whereas others would be identified as very conservative or fundamentalist. Although teachers have a right to their own religious convictions, they cannot proselytize or promote their religion in the public school classroom.

Many believe that religion is losing its influence on American life. Religious leaders find this very worrisome. They and their adherents may blame many of the problems experienced by families and schools on a perceived lack of morals. They have campaigned to elect school board members who will push schools to teach alternative theories of evolution, for example. They may also reject the introduction of multiple perspectives that validate religions or cultures other than their own. These issues can cause tension in a school regarding curriculum, student behavior, and school activities.

Prayer in School

In 1963, the Supreme Court ruled that prayers could not be organized or required by school officials. However, the law allows voluntary prayer by teachers and students. Individuals can say a private prayer before a meal, between classes, and before and after school. Generally, students can initiate prayer at school events as long as school officials have not endorsed or encouraged it. Schools cannot support a moment of silence because the motivation for the moment of silence has been to encourage prayer. Because U.S. law separates religion from state-sponsored activities, including school, public group prayer is not permitted in school or at school events such as a convocation or football game.

Censorship

Some families are concerned that the books their children read in school are immoral or inappropriate. For example, parents of some religious groups do not want their children to read the Harry Potter books because they perceive them as promoting witchcraft and wizardry. However, the most frequent reasons for requesting a book be banned are based on sexually explicit content, offensive language, or the belief that the book is not suited to the age group to which it is assigned (American Library Association, n.d.). In some cases, books and curriculum are banned because of their multicultural content, such as ethnic studies, the exploration of racism, gay and lesbian issues, and world religions. Although some people or groups pressure school libraries, video stores, or art galleries to remove books, music, videos, or artwork from their shelves or walls, the American Library Association (2017) reports that efforts to ban books are on the decline. In 2013, only 323 books were challenged, as compared with 646 in 2000.

Schools and school libraries are the most vulnerable for challenges by parents, who question books more often than all other individuals and groups together (American Library Association, 2017). However, the Supreme Court ruled in *Board of Education v. Pico* (1982) that books could not be removed from school libraries simply because someone does not like the ideas in the books. Families have also sued school districts because the curriculum or textbooks reflected **secular humanism** or the content was offensive to their religious beliefs, but the courts have ruled that the curriculum includes important secular values such as tolerance and self-esteem and does not have to be revised to accommodate specific religious beliefs.

Calls for censoring books sometimes split communities. Not all families agree that a specific book should not be read, leading to caustic relationships in some communities. Both sides are very sincere about their cause. One side believes the censorship is just and moral. Supporters believe that the objectionable materials will contaminate the minds of their children and contribute to the moral decay of society. On the other side, parents want their children exposed to the real world and multiple perspectives. They do not find the materials objectionable to their religious beliefs. Instead, they find that the books help their children explore reality and think critically about important issues in society. Educators should share with families the objectives of the curriculum. Communication with families is critical in reducing possible alienation between educators and parents over the inclusion of what might be viewed as controversial content in the curricula. You will need to know your community and gauge people's reactions before introducing a book or curriculum, such as sex education or evolution, that might be controversial. School department chairs and other school leaders can guide new teachers in these areas.

Language Diversity

English Language Learners (ELLs) are the fastest-growing segment of the population. More than one in five students in K–12 schools spoke a language other than English at home in 2015. Over nine in ten of those students speak English well or very well (Federal Interagency Forum on Child and Family Statistics, 2017), but one in ten of these students is participating in ELL programs in the nation's schools (Snyder, de Brey, & Dillow, 2018).

Many ELL students whose families have recently immigrated must not only learn a new language but also adjust to a new school system in a foreign setting. You can imagine what it would be like to have to move to another country and attend school when you do not have a firm grasp of the language or culture. A first obvious but sometimes overlooked step is to ensure that you pronounce your students' names correctly. Practice until you can say the names as your students pronounce them; this is a first sign of respect for their unique identity. In class, ELL students may nod or smile as if they understand you, but you will want to check and offer individual assistance as needed. Experts recommend assigning a peer partner, especially one who knows the ELL student's native language, if possible. Researchers also recommend posting a visual daily schedule in the classroom so that ELLs who are not comfortable with English can follow the sequence of events during the day, with images next to the words and time of the activity (¡Colorín Colorado!, n.d.).

Your students' cultures should be integrated into the classroom. Learning becomes more meaningful when students can build on their own cultural experiences as part of the learning process (Gay, 2018). Experts recommend that teachers learn about students' native countries and cultures. Once you discover your students' interests, you could tailor your instruction to align with those interests. For example, most students like music and art. You could have students bring music that they enjoy at home and have them explain what it means to them and their families. You could incorporate art by asking older students to select pieces of art depicting a historical era in their country of origin; writing assignments in English and history could be built around these types of activities. Asking students to research climate and geography of their native countries will fit into a social studies unit. Many libraries now have multicultural collections. Collaborate with your school librarian to have resources on your students' native countries available, and incorporate them into literature, history, and social studies lessons. The point is to bring students' cultures to the classroom by connecting your teaching to artifacts and experiences that are familiar to your students and their families. You should consult more than one Internet or library resource per topic. Experts caution against expecting a student to be the sole authority on his or her cultural background. Learning about other cultures and countries is important not only to ELLs, but also to native English speakers.

Programs for teaching immigrant students are influenced by local and national politics related to immigration and the use of languages other than English for instruction in schools.

Having the ability to speak English does not necessarily mean that students can function effectively using academic language in English. Most students can become conversationally fluent within two or three years, but they may require five to seven years to reach the proficiency necessary for success in academic subjects such as social studies and English (Hakuta, Butler, & Witt, 2000). However, students who are conversationally fluent may be assigned to English-only classrooms without appropriate support to ensure they can function effectively in academic work. In this case, these students may fall further behind their classmates in understanding the subjects being taught.

The Supreme Court ruling in *Lau v. Nichols* (1974) requires school districts to offer language programs to help ELLs learn English. This case was brought on behalf of Chinese American students in San Francisco who argued they were being deprived of equal education because they could not understand the English being used for instruction. To help ELLs learn English and progress through school, schools most often offer either **bilingual education** or **English as a Second Language (ESL)**, which is sometimes called **English for Speakers of Other Languages (ESOL)**. Teachers are expected to use the program that the school or school district has adopted to teach ELLs.

When children speak little or no English when they enter a classroom and neither the teacher nor the teacher assistant speaks their native language, they may feel alienated and can become quite frustrated. Usually, other children become teachers' first allies as they try to communicate with ELLs using signs. When you enter your classroom as a teacher, you may have a number of students who speak languages other than English. School administrators and other resource people in the school district can help you understand the approved programs for helping these students learn both English and the academic content. Being responsive to cultural and linguistic diversity and collaborating with specialists are important steps for improving instruction for ELLs. In the next section, we will look at the differences between the most popular programs for ELLs.

Bilingual Education

Bilingual education uses both English and the students' native language as the mode of instruction. It requires either the teacher or an assistant teacher to be bilingual. In bilingual education, the academic subjects are taught in the native language, giving ELLs the opportunity to learn at the same pace as their English-only classmates. Most schools offer transitional bilingual programs that move students from their native languages to English as soon as possible, usually in one to four years. Over time, more and more of the instruction is conducted in English.

Although the majority of bilingual education programs for ELLs are transitional, some bilingual programs are designed to help students maintain their native language. These maintenance programs promote the use of both languages and cultures as students become bilingual and bicultural with neither language being dominant. This approach values the language and cultures of the students' families and promotes the development of a positive self-image as a bicultural individual. In these programs, both English and the native language have equal status, and both are used interchangeably for instructional purposes.

Other bilingual programs include dual language or immersion programs that teach literacy and academic content in English and a second language. In these programs, both native English students and ELLs become bilingual as their two languages are used for academic instruction with the goal of helping students "develop high levels of language proficiency and literacy in both program languages, attain high levels of academic achievement, and develop an appreciation and understanding of multiple cultures" (Boyle, August, Tabaku, Cole, & Simpson-Baird, 2015, p. viii). These programs recognize the value and benefits of being bilingual for U.S. citizens as they increasingly interact and work in a global community. A growing number of states support students' access to dual language programs.

English as a Second Language (ESL)

ESL or ESOL promotes English proficiency and is used extensively in the United States. Unlike bilingual education, ESL is conducted totally in English; the native language is not used for instruction. ESL is used in newcomer and sheltered programs for new immigrants who have limited or no experience with English and who sometimes have limited literacy skills in their native language.

CHALLENGING ASSUMPTIONS

MYTH: ENGLISH LANGUAGE LEARNERS (ELLS) ACHIEVE AT ACADEMICALLY HIGHER LEVELS WHEN THEY ARE IN ENGLISH-ONLY CLASSROOMS.

The Assumption

ELLs learn English more quickly if they are immersed into classrooms in which only English is used for instruction.

Study Design and Method

In this five-year study, two researchers reviewed the academic achievement of all ELLs in Grades K through 12. The school districts were located in the northeastern, northwestern, south-central, and southeastern United States. The students represented 80 different languages, but the data analysis in three of the sites focused on Spanish speakers. Findings were tracked by the type of program in which the ELL participated. The programs available to students in these five school districts included approaches that ranged from English-only without bilingual or ESL services to two-way bilingual immersion in which ELLs and students whose native language is English received instruction in the two languages.

Study Findings

The researchers found that the reading and mathematics achievement of ELLs in English-only classrooms without bilingual or ESL services decreased by the fifth grade. The largest number of dropouts had been enrolled in these English-only classrooms.

The ELLs in the one-way developmental bilingual education program with four years of instruction in English and their native language in two high-achieving school districts outperformed the ELLs in all other programs and remained above grade level at the seventh grade. The one-way and two-way developmental bilingual education programs were the only programs that assisted ELLs in reaching grade level and maintaining it through the end of their schooling. These programs also had fewer dropouts.

When ELLs enter English-only elementary classrooms after ESL or bilingual education, they do not perform as well on tests given in English as do their counterparts who have been in English-only classrooms. However, the bilingually educated students reach the same level of achievement by middle school and outperform the monolingually schooled students during high school. Native English–speaking students in two-way immersion programs equaled or outperformed on all measures their comparison group in English-only classrooms. The highest-quality ESL programs closed only about half of the achievement gap.

Implications

The findings of this and similar studies are important to policy makers and educators as they try to determine the best programs for increasing the academic achievement of ELLs in PreK–12 schools. The results of this research suggest that ELLs should be placed in bilingual education programs to improve long-term academic achievement and reduce dropout rates. The researchers also found that students who do not speak English need to be placed in bilingual programs for four years or more. For best results, bilingual and ESL programs must meet students' linguistic, academic, cognitive, emotional, social, and physical needs.

Source: Adapted from Thomas, W. P., & Collier, V. P. (2001). *A national study of school effectiveness for language minority students' long-term academic achievement.* Santa Cruz, CA: Center for Research on Education, Diversity & Excellence.

HOW DOES SCHOOL CHOICE OPEN OPTIONS FOR PARENTS?

All parents want the best possible education for their children. Most parents look for neighborhoods where the schools are highly rated, but not all families can afford to live in those areas. Traditionally, students have been required to attend the school in their neighborhood. But what if that school is substandard? Until recently, poor and low-income families had no choice about the school their children would attend unless they could afford a private school. The chance that a student attending a school in a low-income neighborhood will attend college is less than that for a student living in an affluent neighborhood, highlighting the inequality of opportunity for students in underserved areas.

Beginning in the 1990s, a movement for public school choice emerged in Milwaukee, Wisconsin. The public charter school, discussed further in Chapter 8, has become a common option, especially in underserved communities where a disproportionate number of students in traditional public schools are achieving below a proficient level in reading and mathematics. In some communities, **magnet schools** provide another choice for parents. In this section, we will explore options that parents in a growing number of communities now have in the selection of schools for their children.

Private Schools

Nearly 10% of PreK–12 students are enrolled in private schools. Three in four of the private schools in the United States have a religious orientation, as shown in Figure 5.3. One of the most obvious differences between private and public PreK–12 schools is the cost to a family. However, private schools do offer scholarships and grants, encouraging some low-income families to enroll their children in private schools. Some parents are convinced that a private school is the best alternative for their children and are willing to sacrifice other necessities to pay for a private school experience.

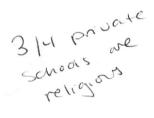

Parents have a variety of reasons for considering private school. They may feel that the neighborhood school may not offer enough advanced courses or a challenging curriculum. Other parents may be concerned that their child will feel lost in a large public school, or perhaps they want their child to receive more individual attention. They may worry about the safety of public schools or the lack of values that they want their children to learn. Some parents believe that their children will be best served with a strong religious education provided in the majority of private schools.

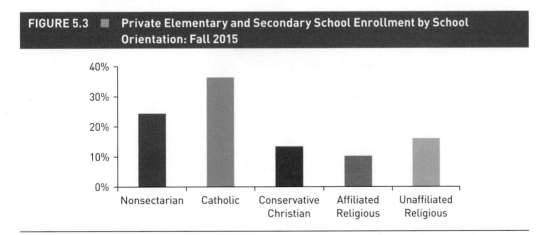

FIGURE 5.3 ■ Private Elementary and Secondary School Enrollment by School Orientation: Fall 2015

Source: Compiled from Snyder, T. D., de Brey, C., and Dillow, S. A. (2018). *Digest of education statistics 2016* (NCES 2017–094). Washington, DC: National Center for Education Statistics, Institute of Education Sciences, U.S. Department of Education.

Note: Catholic schools include parochial, diocesan, and private Catholic schools. Conservative Christian schools have membership in at least one of four associations: Accelerated Christian Education, American Association of Christian Schools, Association of Christian Schools International, or Oral Roberts University Educational Fellowship. Affiliated religious schools belong to associations of schools with a specific religious orientation other than Catholic or conservative Christian. Unaffiliated religious schools have a religious orientation or purpose but are not classified as Conservative Christian or affiliated.

Some private schools are focused on rigorous college preparatory courses that equip students to apply to selective colleges, and a higher percentage of private school students do attend and graduate from college. Private schools generally offer smaller class sizes with 12.2 students per teacher compared to 16.1 in a public school (McFarland et al., 2017). In addition, they may offer newer textbooks, better supplies, greater access to the latest technology, and a more challenging curriculum than many public schools.

School Vouchers

One of the most controversial topics in the education community is **school vouchers**, which are government-funded promissory notes that can be redeemed for tuition at a private school. According to the National Conference of State Legislatures (NCSL, 2018), 27 states allow school vouchers for attendance at private schools or similar type of payment such as tax-credit scholarships or education savings account programs. Legislatures often target subgroups of students as the eligible recipients of vouchers, including students from low-income families, students in very low-performing public schools, students with disabilities, or students in military families or foster care (NCSL, 2018).

Those who support vouchers argue that parents will send their children to the highest-performing school, which may be a private school, when they have a choice. They also believe that vouchers will force low-performing schools to either improve or risk losing students and the funding tied to the students. Those who oppose vouchers argue that moving students from a public school into a private school will decrease public funding for public schools as money is transferred to private schools, leaving the public schools even more poorly resourced. Others have argued that providing public funds to religious schools is unconstitutional, but the U.S. Supreme Court ruled in *Zelman v. Simmons-Harris* (2002) that a voucher program in Cleveland, Ohio, did not violate the U.S. Constitution. However, some states have Blair amendments to their state constitutions that are based on Senator H. H. Blair's proposed amendment to the U.S. Constitution in 1988 that prevented the state from giving financial aid to religious schools.

Charter Schools

A charter school receives public funding but operates independently of the public school system in which it is located. The 2.7 million students in 6,750 charter schools comprised 5.4% of all K–12 students in the fall of 2015 (Snyder et al., 2018). Forty-four states and the District of Columbia allow the establishment of charter schools (National Alliance for Public Charter Schools, 2018). Charter schools were created to help improve the public school system and offer parents another public school option to better meet their child's specific needs. The core of the charter school model is the belief that public schools should be held accountable for student learning. In exchange for this accountability, school leaders are exempted from some of the rules and regulations governing other public schools in order to do what they believe will help students achieve at higher levels.

Charter schools have more autonomy than traditional public schools in that they are free from some state and local regulations as determined by the state (NCSL, 2018). They are judged on how well they meet student achievement goals established in their charter contracts. Charter schools are open to all children, do not charge tuition, and do not have special entrance requirements. When a student transfers from a traditional public school to a public charter school, the funding associated with that student follows him or her to the public charter school.

Approximately 85% of charter schools are nonprofit, with the remainder run by for-profit companies (National Alliance for Public Charter Schools, 2018). Education Management Organizations now manage a large portion of today's charter schools with a common curriculum and teacher training. They often have a major focus on raising students' standardized test scores. The majority of charter schools are in urban areas, but they exist in suburban and rural areas as well. Many charter schools have opened in underserved communities, increasing gradually the number of students of color and students in poverty in charter schools since 2009 (Snyder et al., 2018).

Most charter schools are opened because policy makers, parents, and the public are concerned that student performance in existing public schools is stagnant or well below par, and their goal is to provide

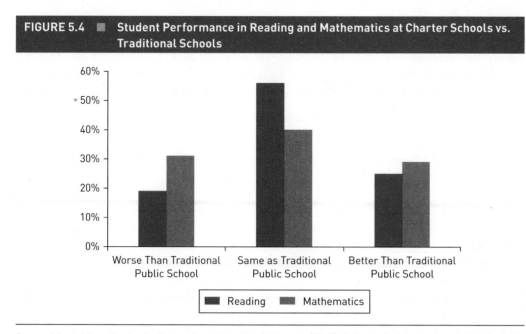

FIGURE 5.4 ■ **Student Performance in Reading and Mathematics at Charter Schools vs. Traditional Schools**

Source: Adapted from Center for Research on Education Outcomes. (2013). *National charter school study.* Stanford, CA: Author.

a new structure that they believe will lead to improved student achievement. Research on the success of charter schools in meeting this goal shows mixed results. Figure 5.4 shows the results of one of the most comprehensive studies of charter schools by the Center for Research on Education Outcomes (CREDO) at Stanford University in which academic results were compared to traditional schools. Achievement levels are still far below satisfactory or proficient levels at some charters just as at some traditional public schools.

The primary reason for the creation of charter schools was to provide parents a choice in the selection of their child's public school. Now that charter schools have existed for nearly 30 years, how are parents perceiving them? In a national survey (Barrows, Peterson, & West, 2017), charter school parents were more satisfied than other public school parents with the teacher quality, school discipline, and character instruction. In addition, private school parents were more satisfied with their children's schools than charter parents. Although charter school parents reported more extensive communications with schools, they complained about the lack of extracurricular activities.

Magnet Schools

Magnet schools are free public elementary and secondary schools that are managed by school districts or a group of districts. These schools are organized according to a theme or themes such as Science, Technology, Engineering, and Mathematics (STEM); fine and performing arts; International Baccalaureate programs; international studies; Career and Technical Education (CTE); world languages (immersion and nonimmersion); and other areas. Most magnet schools do not have entrance criteria. Instead, they often use a random computer-based lottery system for admission. These schools offer additional choices within public schools, and are geared to developing student interests and abilities that correspond with the focused school curriculum.

HOW CAN TEACHERS WORK EFFECTIVELY WITH FAMILIES AND COMMUNITIES?

Families, schools, and communities are the major contexts in which children grow and develop (Edwards, 2016). Ideally, families, schools, and communities would work together to help their children grow and develop in the most positive ways. One of the leading researchers on parental involvement, Joyce Epstein (2018), has identified the following six activities that connect families, schools, and communities:

1. *Parenting*: Assistance to families with parenting skills that prepare their children for school.

2. *Communicating*: Effective school-to-home and home-to-school communications about school programs and student progress.

3. *Volunteering*: Involvement of parents and community members in a wide range of opportunities to support the school.

4. *Learning at home*: Families supporting children with homework and other curricula-related activities and decisions.

5. *Participating in decision making*: Inclusion of parents in the governance of schools and participation on advisory councils, Parent–Teacher Associations, and other groups.

6. *Collaborating with the community*: Coordinating resources and services both from the community and to the community.

Creating Meaningful Partnerships With Families

Trust and respect between parents and schools are critical components of effective school and parent partnerships (Edwards, 2016; Teaching for Change, 2016; Thiers, 2017). In many schools, especially underresourced schools, families may have many reasons for not automatically trusting teachers and school leaders. Their feelings about schools may be grounded in their own negative experiences in school or the community, and they worry that their children's teachers don't really care about them and don't have their best interests in mind. Teachers and administrators can build that trust by reaching out to family members, showing them respect, believing that they can and desire to contribute to their children's academic success, and listening to them. As educators, we need to remember that partnerships require working together in equitable relationships.

The parents with which you work are likely to have different perspectives, beliefs, and abilities to negotiate school on behalf of their children (Edwards, 2016). Knowing the families of your students and the communities in which they live will be helpful in developing effective partnerships. Knowing the capabilities of your students' families will allow you to develop appropriate plans together that build on their strengths. We often make incorrect assumptions about a family's capabilities and then blame the family for not following through on plans. In her book, *New Ways to Engage Parents: Strategies and Tools for Teachers and Leaders, K–12*, Patricia A. Edwards (2016) talks about how frustrated a group of teachers was when the parents wouldn't read to their children at night after the teachers had told them how important that activity was. The problem was that the parents were illiterate, but were too embarrassed to tell the teachers they could not read to their children. If the teachers had known this fact, they could have recommended other ways the parents could support their children's literacy development.

Respecting the cultures of families and making sure they see their cultures represented on the bulletin boards at school, in the books their children are reading, in the curriculum, and in the activities of the school will contribute to the development of trust in the school. "When teachers do not respect what children bring to school, that has direct implications on family involvement. When families feel that teachers are not successfully working with their children, it oftentimes hampers their involvement in the school" (Edwards, 2016, p. 90).

Schools need to be open and friendly places for a diverse group of families (Edwards, 2016). Family members should like visiting school and working with teachers to support learning. They should not be embarrassed because they haven't finished high school or speak limited English. Your goal is to make them feel welcome. Some schools have developed creative ways to actively engage families. The Logan Square Neighborhood Association in Chicago, for example, worked with local schools to create a parent mentor program for the immigrant mothers of their students (Hong, 2011).

THINKING DIFFERENTLY
TELLIN' STORIES TO ENGAGE FAMILIES

iStock/pixdeluxe

Partnerships can be much more than a two-way interaction between a parent and a teacher. They can also help families get to know other families, which can be especially valuable in schools with families from diverse cultural groups. Teaching for Change (2016), a nonprofit community organization in Washington, DC, sees families of color and low-income families as leaders who "have the insight and power to bring about positive change in their children's learning" (p. 40). This organization works with families, teachers, and staff in District of Columbia and Maryland schools to nurture relationships among families and school personnel to support each other and the children and youth in the schools.

Tellin' Stories is Teaching for Change's nationally recognized approach in which parents and educators share their personal stories as they get to know each other. The stories allow all family members a voice. Throughout the year, families become engaged in workshops, community dialogues, learning circles, dances, oral history projects, cultural fairs, parent meetings, and other activities that allow families to bridge differences and work toward shared goals. They learn more about other cultures represented in the school and sometimes begin to learn a second language or assist another parent in learning English. The following signature activities

of the Tellin' Stories approach have been implemented by the participating schools:

- A Welcome Back Breakfast is held at beginning of the school year to welcome families and begin building community among parents and key staff at the school.
- A Story Quilting project brings parents and grandparents together to share personal stories on felt squares. "As these squares are stitched together, so too are the lives of parents who previously had no connection" (Teaching for Change, 2016, p. 7).
- Grade Level Dialogues provide the opportunity for parents and teachers to discuss issues such as literacy or introduce family projects on which families and their children work together.
- The Roving Readers activity involves parents in sharing multicultural children's books that they read to groups of students.
- In a Community Walk, parents lead teachers through the neighborhood around the school to highlight the businesses, churches, and activities that define the community.
- Parent–Principal Chit Chats allow parents to have direct communications with the principal at regularly scheduled meetings.
- Academic Classroom Visits allow parents to visit classrooms during the school day to observe instruction in action.

Viewing diversity as a strength and all parents as resources, Teaching for Change works with schools to engage family members as teachers, supporters, advocates, decision makers, ambassadors, and monitors. This approach has led to increased family participation and advocacy, a more positive school climate, and improved academic achievement (Teaching for Change, 2016).

Although many of these parents had limited English proficiency, they worked with teachers in classrooms. Not only did they learn how to support their own children's academic, social, and emotional development, but they became more confident in their own abilities, with some of them deciding to pursue a teaching career.

Noted school–family partnership advocate Karen L. Mapp (Thiers, 2017) has identified three areas that would help families know that their school is serious about creating meaningful partnerships with them. First, they should be able to see that the school considers them an integral part of their child's development regardless of their race, ethnicity, SES, religion, or sexual orientation. Second, teachers seek knowledge from families about their child that will help engage the student in learning. Third, families in the community feel comfortable in reaching out to their child's teacher and school about working together to support their child.

"I've found that when you have good teachers, loving, caring parents and relatives, you can disappoint a lot of people."

Working With Families as Partners for Student Learning

Teachers and principals perceive parental support as a major contributor to student learning. That's not just a perception; it's a tested reality. Students with involved parents, no matter their income or background, are more likely to

- Earn higher grades

- Finish high school

- Behave appropriately

- Have learning difficulties addressed (Child Trends, 2016)

What does parent involvement mean? Too often, we have defined parent involvement as attendance at Back to School Night soon after school opens in the fall, participation in parent–teacher conferences, and volunteering for fund-raising or school activities, including assisting the teacher in the classroom. In some schools, a high percentage of families are involved with their children's teachers and learning. In other schools, parents are not involved in these ways because of their lack of babysitters, lack of transportation, or work schedules that do not allow them time to meet with teachers during the school day. Parents or other caretakers may feel insecure in meeting with teachers because they do not have a college degree or English is not their native language.

Does a parent's lack of involvement in traditional parent–teacher activities mean that the parent is not supportive of his or her children's education? There are many other ways in which parents support their children's education, from making sure they are at school every day to assisting them with homework to expecting them to achieve at high levels. Vlada Lotkina (2016), the CEO of ClassTag, a free app for communicating with parents, defines effective parent engagement as

> helping children learn and grow in the classroom and at home. It is about bringing everyone closer together by making it easy for parents to know what the child is learning and opening up meaningful opportunities for parents to participate. (para. 10)

It would be a mistake to automatically label parents who can't attend the traditional parent–teacher meeting as uninterested in or not supportive of their children's education.

What are other ways a teacher could engage with these families? Some schools require teachers to conduct home visits to get to know the families and learn more about their child's interest and ways of learning. Ms. Yazzie in the opening interview found home visits not only informative, but also fun. When families believe that you actually care about their child and have his or her best interests at heart, they will be much more interested in joining a partnership in which you and family members work together to support the child's social and emotional development as well as academic achievement. Some schools are supporting regular Homework Nights for students and their parents where the school provides a meal and time for teachers to help parents understand how to support their children with homework.

Parental Involvement in Homework

The National Center for Families Learning (2014) found after conducting a survey that three in five parents admit that their children's homework is a struggle. Some parents of elementary children particularly are allowing their children to opt out of doing homework after school. Some teachers and researchers are not sure of the effectiveness of homework in improving academic achievement. Some educators argue that homework helps students "develop personal responsibility, good study habits, and time management skills" (Weir, 2016, para. 4), but research has not proven these positive outcomes as accurate.

Both the National Education Association and National PTA have recommended the assignment of no more than 10 minutes of homework per night per grade level, which would translate into 10 minutes for a first grader and 2 hours for a twelfth grader (Weir, 2016). However, many parents and teachers are concerned about how much time students are spending on homework. Some elementary teachers are abandoning homework assignments, usually with the support of parents and students (Reilly, 2016), but most students are still being required to submit homework. As you will see in the "Understanding and Using Data" feature, parents and teachers have different perspectives on parents' interactions with students on homework assignments. Your expectations for homework and the involvement of parents is one of the issues you should discuss in a parent–teacher conference.

Communicating With Families

Communications between families and educators are often one-way as families are informed of school activities through newsletters, report cards, websites, and automated phone calls. Today's technology

UNDERSTANDING AND USING DATA
HOW PARENTS HANDLE STUDENT HOMEWORK

Survey data can help educators think about their own practices and perspectives and test them against the perspectives of others. In a survey of parental involvement in schools, Public Agenda asked teachers to consider parental involvement in their children's homework. Parents were asked how they actually handled their children's homework. The following table shows how the two groups responded.

	Teachers' Perspectives on Parental Involvement in Homework	
	What parents should do:	What parents do:
Check the work to make sure it was done, and done correctly	57%	10%
Get involved in helping the student do the work	30%	6%
Ask the student if the work has been done, and leave it at that	9%	34%
Leave it up to the student	2%	44%
% of parents saying they have done the following:		
Have had serious arguments with the child when there was yelling or crying over schoolwork		50%
Have walked away and let the child deal with the consequences of not doing his or her schoolwork rather than dealing with the child's constant stalling		49%
Have done part of child's homework because it was too difficult for the child or because the child was too tired		22%

Source: Adapted from Farkas, S., Johnson, J., & Duffett, A. (1999). *Playing their parts: Parents and teachers talk about parental involvement in public schools.* New York, NY: Public Agenda.

Your Task

As you examine the responses about homework from teachers and parents, respond to the following questions.

1. What does the information above tell you about the perceptions of teachers and parents regarding parental involvement in students' homework?

2. Why do teachers think that some parents are not assisting their children appropriately with their homework? What actually may be happening at home?

3. What do the data suggest about parent and teacher relationships and communication?

supports efficient and timely communications with parents. Almost all parents or caretakers have a cell phone, which allows teachers to leave voice mails, text messages, and emails. Many schools use an online learning management system to post homework assignments for students and provide updates on field trips and school events. At the same time, two-way communications in which educators and parents interact are critical in developing effective partnerships. They are most effective when family members are equal partners in conversations with teachers and other school officials. In this case, teachers cannot do all of the talking; they need to ask questions and listen to the answers to learn more about the children and youth they are teaching.

Being in touch with families on a regular basis will be important. You will also need to be attentive to the native languages of your students. Communications may need to be written in the home language to facilitate positive communications and to show respect for the language and culture of students' families. In some programs such as Head Start and special education for preschoolers, teachers or school social workers conduct home visits. Some schools have expanded home visits beyond these preschool programs.

The availability of translators and translated materials for parents with limited English proficiency makes a significant difference for schools with ELLs. If family members do not speak English or have limited proficiency, you should have a translator with you during parent–teacher conferences and other meetings with parents. Your school may have translators who can assist you. Parent or community volunteers often serve in this role as well.

Parent–Teacher Conferences

Back-to-school nights and regularly scheduled parent–teacher conferences are the most common format employed by schools to arrange for teachers to meet parents, share the academic and social progress of their children, and discuss strategies for improving student learning. If your school does not require

TEACHERS' LOUNGE
"I THINK YOU'RE LOOKING FOR ME"

© Meggie Schultz

One of my favorite things as an educator is seeing my students and their parents out in public—although it can sometimes be a bit awkward, especially if you're wearing grubby, paint-covered sweatpants and a Mario Bros. T-shirt (yes, this happened once, and it was an added bonus that this student's parent also worked on campus).

A few weeks ago, my husband and I were at my local gas station after school, buying waters and a snack before going home, and a few people ahead of me in line was one of my students and a woman I assumed to be her mother. They were having some difficulty at the register, and I was trying to determine the right moment to say hello and introduce myself, if this was even the best time. During their transaction, my student kept catching my eye and smiling, so I was certain an introduction would happen soon, but after they finished, they headed for the door.

I turned to my husband and had just begun to say, "I'll just say hello when she comes in for conference next week," when suddenly I heard a woman calling, "Ms. Schultz!" Looking over at the entrance, I saw the woman I assumed was my student's mother rushing toward me, but then she suddenly stopped, grinning at a much older woman wearing a nurse's outfit. My student's mother grabbed the woman's hand and began shaking vigorously, saying with a wide smile, "Ms. Schultz, it is so nice to meet you! I'm Razjona's mom! Razjona has told me so much about you!" while the poor nurse stood there, dumbstruck. Slowly, I leaned over and said politely, "I think you're looking for me."

The student's mother immediately burst into laughter and apologized to the nurse, then invited me outside to chat, apologizing for and giggling over her awkward mistake. We spoke for a bit, but I must admit it was very difficult to focus on what we were saying, because I could see Razjona in the back seat of the car, shaking her head and trying desperately not to make eye contact with me while she sent her mother embarrassed looks. The next day, I rushed up to her in the hallway, grabbed her hand, and began shaking it as I told her how delighted I was to meet her mother.

—Meggie Schultz
Ninth- and Tenth-Grade English Teacher
Natomas High School
Natomas, California

parent–teacher conferences, you may want to schedule them yourself to learn more about your students from their parents' perspectives and to develop partnerships for students' growth. Parents may also initiate the request for a conference to check on their child's progress.

The meeting with a parent or guardian should be collaborative in nature, with time for questions and discussion (Hoerr, 2014). Beginning and ending the meeting on a positive note is important. Taking notes shows that you value what the parent is saying about his or her child. Asking the parent if there are topics that need more explanation is a way to invite conversation. The end of the meeting can focus on planning new strategies and setting up a time for the next communication (Hoerr, 2014).

As you work with families, remember that the parents were the child's first teachers. They have the well-being of their child in mind when they push for services and attention to their child. In most cases, they are anxious to help their child do well in school. Family involvement in schools and with teachers has proven to be an important variable in supporting student learning and successful school experiences.

Because some parents have a difficult time arranging to meet with teachers about their children's progress, some schools have tried various strategies to support the attendance of low-income families at school events. For example, providing transportation, child care, and a meal may increase attendance. Provision of translators for parents who have limited English skills may make the school setting more comfortable for some parents. There may be cases in which meeting the parent in a neutral spot outside of school will contribute to effective communications.

Parent–Teacher Organizations

The relationship between families and schools is not always positive and supportive, especially when trust is lacking and families do not agree with the decisions being made about their children, the curricula, or other school policies. Over time, however, families have allowed most of these decisions to be made by professional educators rather than by parents. At the same time, most parents want to be involved in their children's education. They know that their children's education is not just the responsibility of schools. Most parents know that what happens at home also affects student achievement. The problem is that some parents do not get involved in schools on their own, requiring educators to figure out how to engage them.

In many areas of the country, the families of students might be unauthorized or undocumented, which could make it more challenging to involve parents in school activities. One structured way of involving some parents is a Parent–Teacher Organization (PTO). Parents trust the advice of parent organizations on the public education system and school reforms more than other sources, such as the news media and other community organizations. They are also more likely to attend meetings of a parent organization than other activities to support schools, although volunteering in them is not far behind.

The most well-known parent organization is the National PTA, which was founded in 1897 by Alice McLellan Birney and Phoebe Apperson Hearst as the National Congress of Mothers. In its early days, the organization led efforts to create kindergarten classes, establish child labor laws, initiate hot lunch programs, develop a juvenile justice system, and require mandatory immunization (National PTA, n.d.). Anyone who is an advocate for students may join the National PTA. Local chapters can be found in many of the nation's schools, with the goal of promoting partnerships between educators and families to be advocates on behalf of children. Another option for parents and teachers is a PTO, which is an independent organization at the local school level that is not connected to a national organization.

Parents can be involved in the schooling of their children by volunteering to help the teacher in the classroom, helping at school events, or assisting their children with homework.

School and Community Relationships

When the community cares about and is actively involved in education, schools serve the community, families, and students well. When schools and communities work together,

- Families are strengthened, resulting in better support for student learning

- Families access community resources more easily

- Trust is built among the community partners and schools

- Businesses help connect education programs with the realities of the workplace

- Students serve and learn beyond their school involvement (Henderson & Mapp, 2002)

When teachers do not live within the boundaries of the school community, they are often not familiar with the leaders, businesses, churches, and community organizations with which they could partner. Teacher Ms. Nicole McGill reported that this was the situation in her school in southeastern Washington, DC:

> *The principal organized a community walk in which the teachers, counselors, social workers, and administrators walked the entire community—a 10-block circumference around the school. We visited barber shops, community centers, and churches and talked with people in the community. The goal was to get the community more involved in the education of their children. Ward 8 has not had the resources or opportunities like other wards in the city. There are no healthy food choices in the neighborhood. The fast-food restaurants like McDonald's and Kentucky Fried Chicken have no air-conditioning in the summer. Families don't feel anyone is investing in their neighborhood or their children. They have been let down for so long, promised so many things.*

The goal of school–community partnerships should be to improve the academic achievement and positive development of young people in the community. Partners should make an investment of time, money, people, and expertise as appropriate. Potential partners include businesses, the local chamber of commerce, charitable organizations, churches, civic groups, foundations, local government, local media, museums, military groups, nonprofit associations, senior citizens, and youth groups. The partners provide support to schools in a number of ways, which could include assigning some employees or volunteers to work with the school, encouraging employees to assist teachers and administrators, and contributing equipment and other resources.

School and community partnerships should be two-way. While the community contributes resources and expertise to schools, the school should help families know more about available resources in the community. Schools can distribute to families information about activities and agencies in the community. They can encourage community members to volunteer in schools. Finally, they can encourage both students and their families to be more involved in community service.

Community Schools

Using public schools as hubs, community schools bring together families, educators, and the community to work together to develop the whole child through the development of cognitive, social, emotional, civic, and ethical competencies by offering a range of supports and opportunities to children, youth, families, and communities. Community schools focus on student learning by creating engaging learning experiences inside and outside the classroom to help students develop the knowledge and skills for working and living in tomorrow's world. Educators, families, and communities collaborate "to help create a safe and supportive culture for learning in the school, at home and in the community" (Jacobson & Blank, 2015, p. 3). Schools provide students and their families enrichment and mentoring opportunities for learning and developing new skills. Schools become centers of the community and are open to everyone all day, and in the evenings, and on weekends. For example, community schools may host family/community resource centers; early childhood development programs; coordinated health, mental health, and social services; counseling; and/or other supports that enhance family life. Nearly 8% of today's U.S. public schools are community schools (Institute for Educational Leadership & Coalition for Community Schools, 2017).

Community schools focus on supporting teaching and learning in underresourced communities through the following research-based opportunities:

1. *Powerful learning.* The curriculum of these schools is student centered and is designed to provide meaningful, authentic, and challenging experiences during and outside the regular school day.

2. *Integrated health and social supports.* Health care, eye care, social and emotional services, and other wraparound services are available in the school building or within walking distance for the full community.

3. *Authentic family and community engagement.* Schools promote the active involvement of the full community in prioritizing the resources needed in the community and being engaged in civic and educational work. (Jacobson, Villarreal, Muñoz, & Mahaffey, 2018)

According to the 49th Annual PDK Poll (2017), three in four of the respondents strongly supported after-school services and the provision of mental health services at school. Two in three of the respondents strongly supported providing health services at school. Building on this public support for integrated health and social supports in schools, the Every Student Succeeds Act provides funding for the development of community schools, a community school coordinator, and reporting on chronic absence, school climate, and safety (Institute for Educational Leadership & Coalition for Community Schools, 2017).

Evaluations of community schools confirm that they have a positive impact on student learning, attendance, and behavior (Oakes, Maier, & Daniel, 2017). In addition, parents' and families' engagement in their children's schooling increases through more opportunities for interaction (Institute for Educational Leadership & Coalition for Community Schools, 2017). A Child Trends (2018) study on Integrated Student Supports (ISS), a central component of community schools, confirms that the ISS model

> may help increase high school graduation rates and may offer a strong return on investment to society. For every dollar invested in ISS, a return of at least $3 and up to $14 can be expected—with students having less grade repetition and fewer problem behaviors. (para. 6)

Bringing the Community Into the School

As a teacher, you can bring the community into your classroom in a number of ways. The parents and grandparents of your students are resources and assets for their children and grandchildren. They can be excellent teachers of their own traditions and histories. You might consider asking a Muslim parent to explain to the class the meaning of Ramadan, a Jewish parent to talk about Rosh Hashanah and Yom Kippur, and a Christian parent to discuss Easter. Immigrant parents could talk about their country of origin and why they immigrated to the United States. Parents can be invited to talk about their jobs or a community project. Parents, of course, are not the only community resources. Employees at local businesses, museum staff, and staff at community agencies have valuable information to share in classrooms. Public officials such as firefighters and police officers could be invited to talk about their roles, safety issues, or community involvement.

When the community becomes actively involved in its schools and with the students in those schools, education programs can be strengthened and student learning improved.

iStock/undefined undefined

Field trips provide another opportunity to know the community. Many students don't have the opportunity to attend concerts or visit museums, fire stations, the zoo, or historical sites except through field trips. A school district should have guidelines for selecting and conducting field trips. Families must be made aware of field trips and give written permission for their children to participate.

Through school projects, students can learn to be involved in community projects that range from planting trees to cleaning up a park to assisting elderly people and younger children. Students, especially older ones, might conduct research on a community need that could lead to action by a city council or state legislature. Some schools require students to provide community service by volunteering in a nursing home, child-care center, nonprofit association, health clinic, or governmental agency. These projects help students understand their responsibility to the larger community.

CONNECTING TO THE CLASSROOM

This chapter has introduced you to public perceptions of schools and the importance of understanding the influence of culture on teaching and learning. Understanding communities and working with your students' families will be important for student learning and development. Below are some key principles for applying the information in this chapter to the classroom.

1. Awareness of the public's perception of public education helps educators reflect on their own practices.

2. All students can achieve at high levels regardless of the structure of their families.

3. The cultural diversity of families is an important asset in the learning and teaching process.

4. Teachers can build the trust of families by authentically caring for their children and respecting their cultures and their contributions to their children's learning and development.

5. Teachers must not promote a religion in their classroom or school activities.

6. Bilingual education encourages English Language Learners (ELLs) to be literate in both English and their native language, whereas English as a Second Language (ESL) education immerses ELLs into English for all instruction.

7. School choice in many school systems provides families the opportunity to select schools to meet the needs of their children, including the option to move their children from schools in which students are not performing well academically.

8. Effective partnerships between schools and families support and improve student learning.

9. Regular teacher outreach to and effective communications with families is an important aspect of a teacher's job in today's schools.

SUMMARY

This chapter focused on how the public and families view schools and how they can be engaged in schools and supporting students and the community. This chapter has explored six major topics:

- **Public perceptions of schools, teachers, and standards.** Less than half of the public gives an A or B to their local public schools, but 70% of parents give the local schools an A or B. Parents of African American, Hispanic, and American Indian parents do not rate their local public schools as highly.

- **Students' families.** Two in three students live in a family that includes two parents. Most other students live in single-parent families, most often with their mother. Other students live with gay or lesbian parents,

some live with their grandparents or other relatives, and others live with foster parents or other guardians.

- **Influence of culture on education.** Culture provides the blueprint for how we live, which differs from one region of the country or world to another. We learn cultural norms from our parents and the community in which we live, including behavior, communication patterns, language, values, and the way we think.

- **Students' cultures in schools.** The religious beliefs of families and communities sometimes lead to cultural clashes around issues such as prayer and assigned readings. Schools are required to provide language programs for English Language Learners, but the type of program differs from one community or school to another.

- **School choice.** In many of today's school districts, parents have options beyond their neighborhood public school. Private schools, which may be religious in orientation, have always been an option for families but may be beyond their economic means. Charter schools are public options that allow parents to move their children to schools they think will better meet the needs of their children.

- **Working with families and communities.** Positive and supportive communications and interactions with students' families contribute to building trust between teachers and families and increase the chances of students having productive experiences in schools. Businesses and community agencies can also support schools and students through formal or informal partnerships. Community schools serve as a hub within the neighborhood or community, and can increase parents' involvement in their child's education as well as offer wraparound assistance such as child care and health services.

KEY TERMS

bilingual education 135

cultural borders 132

cultural relativism 131

dual language education programs 136

enculturation 131

English as a Second Language (ESL) 135

English for Speakers of Other Languages (ESOL) 135

immersion 136

low-poverty schools 128

magnet schools 137

proselytize 133

school vouchers 138

secular 133

secular humanism 134

values 131

CLASS DISCUSSION QUESTIONS

1. The 50th Annual PDK Poll (2018) found that less than half of the public thinks public schools are doing a good job. What steps do you think schools could take to improve that rating?

2. Not all communities are supportive or accepting of Lesbian, Gay, Bisexual, Transgender, and Queer or Questioning (LGBTQ) people. How will you respond when you meet LGBTQ parents the first time at a parent–teacher conference? How will you react when one of your students makes fun of a student with LGBTQ parents?

3. There are many similarities and differences across cultures that bind us together and make us unique. How can you become more familiar with the cultures of your students?

4. Religious diversity in the United States is expanding beyond the Judeo-Christian heritage that has long been reflected in textbooks. What can you do to ensure respect for and inclusion of Muslim, Buddhist, Hindu, Jewish, and other non-Christian students in your classroom?

5. The number of charter schools has expanded greatly across the country since they were created in the 1990s. How popular are charter schools in your state? What is the cultural background of the families enrolling their children in charter schools in your state? What are the reasons that families select charter schools?

6. Research indicates that the engagement of families in the education of their children is important for student achievement. What is the appropriate role of teachers in contacting parents about the behavioral and academic performance of their children? What strategies will you use to promote a positive, collaborative relationship with the parents of your students?

SELF-ASSESSMENT

What Is Your Current Level of Understanding and Thinking About Families and Communities?

One of the indicators of understanding is to examine how you synthesize information when asked questions that require you to use the concepts and facts introduced in this chapter.

After you answer the following questions as fully as you can, rate your knowledge on the Assessing Your Learning rubric to self-assess the degree to which you understand and can apply the ideas presented in this chapter.

1. What are differences between becoming partners with families and meeting with parents or caretakers periodically at parent–teacher conferences?

2. What components of effective partnerships with families are most supportive of student learning?

3. Why is building trust with families so important in developing effective partnership?

4. What is the value of developing positive relationships with the community? How and with whom would you initiate community contacts and interactions?

Assessing Your Learning Rubric

	Parts & Pieces	Unidimensional	Organized	Integrated	Extensions
Indicators	Elements/ concepts are talked about as isolated and independent entities. Some important names are provided in isolation.	One or a few concepts are addressed, while others are underdeveloped, or not mentioned.	Deliberate and structured consideration of all key concepts/ elements.	All key concepts/ elements are included in a view that addresses interconnections.	Integration of all elements and dimensions, with extrapolation to new situations.
Identifies components of effective communications with parents and caretakers	Identifies issues to address in meetings with parents, but is unclear about how to meaningfully engage parents in those meetings.	Knows how to set up a parent–teacher conference but is not comfortable interacting with parents, especially when they are from different cultural groups than the teacher's.	Interacts comfortably with parents on a regular basis about the academic and social progress of their children.	Proactively establishes positive partnerships with parents from diverse cultural groups to promote student learning.	Has developed the trust of parents from diverse groups and interacts authentically with them and others to support student learning and development.

FIELD GUIDE
FOR LEARNING MORE ABOUT . . .

Families and Communities

Ask a Teacher	Language diversity in schools is being addressed in different ways depending on state or district policies. What are the policies and practices in the state or district in which you plan to teach? Ask one or more teachers in a school with ELLs whether the school offers bilingual or ESL programs. What accommodations does the teacher make to ensure that ELL students are learning the content being taught? In what ways does the school demonstrate that it values language diversity? How does the teacher incorporate the cultures of students in instruction? How do teachers communicate with parents who do not speak English? What advice does the teacher have for working effectively with ELLs?
Make Your Own Observations	New teachers report that communicating with families is one of their most challenging tasks. Being able to observe parent and teacher interactions in your field experiences should reduce your concerns about working with parents. Ask the teacher or principal in one of the schools in which you are observing for permission to observe a parent–teacher conference and/or a PTA/PTO or other parent meeting. Determine how the contact with families was made and by whom. In your notes, describe the structure and focus of the conference or meeting. Also record how active the family members were in the conference or meeting and the nature of the interchange with the teacher(s). What strategies did the teacher or principal use to make the conference or meeting helpful to parents? What would you have done differently? How closely did the conference or meeting reflect the recommendations discussed in this chapter?
Reflect Through Journaling	A critical part of working with students from diverse cultural backgrounds is to know yourself. In your journal, describe your own cultural background. For example, what influence has the ethnic background of your family had on your choices of food, entertainment, sports, books you read, where you live, and so on? How does your culture influence your politics or religious beliefs? How were the child-rearing practices of your family different from those of other families you know? What do you particularly like about your cultural background? How effective are you in interacting with members of a different ethnic or cultural group?

Build Your Portfolio	Public and parental perceptions of the quality of their public schools influence state and local policies on issues such as support of teachers, teachers' unions, charter schools, school vouchers, teacher evaluations, and merit pay. Check with your state department of education to discover information relating to the quality of schools in your area. Then search the local papers for articles related to the quality of public schools in your community. Are the two sources in alignment? Prepare a table that indicates the stance of different members of the community on school quality and reform efforts that they support. Write an analysis of your findings and the policy changes that could result from the public's perceptions of schools.
Read a Book	Check out *LGBT Families* by Nancy J. Mezey of Monmouth University (2015, SAGE) to understand the formation, experiences, and strengths of LGBTQ families from diverse racial and socioeconomic groups as well as the challenges they face. Are you wondering how you can effectively engage with parents who are from different cultural groups than your own? See Patricia A. Edwards's *New Ways to Engage Parents: Strategies and Tools for Teachers and Leaders, K–12* (2016, Teachers College Press) for numerous suggestions and examples.
Search the Web	**Religion in the Classroom:** To see guidelines and resources for teachers on religion in the classroom, go to the First Amendment Center website at the Newseum Institute website (www.freedomforuminstitute .org/first-amendment-center/). **Banned Books:** For a list of award-winning books that have been banned by school districts, visit *Banned Books That Shaped America* at the website for Banned Books Week (www.theeagle.com/gallery/featured/ banned-books-week-books-that-shaped-america/collection_e1dc7aa8-a3af-11e7-9825-aba3b5eecab5 .html). **Bilingual Education:** To learn more about bilingual education, two-way immersion, immigrant education, dialects/Ebonics, and ESL, visit the website of the Center for Applied Linguistics (www.cal.org). **Working With Families of Students:** For assistance in working with the families of the students in your classroom, check the National PTA (www.pta.org) and PTO's (www.pto.org) websites. **Family Engagement in Learning:** To learn about the latest research and projects on family involvement in learning, check the Global Family Research Project's website (https://globalfrp.org), which includes publications that cover topics from engaging families in STEM education to strategies that promote educational equity.

STUDENT STUDY SITE

$SAGE edge™

Get the tools you need to sharpen your study skills. **SAGE edge** offers a robust online environment featuring an impressive array of free tools and resources.

Access practice quizzes, eFlashcards, video, and multimedia at **edge.sagepub.com/hall3e**.

PART II

THE FOUNDATIONS OF EDUCATION

iStock/wwing

6 HISTORY OF SCHOOLS IN THE UNITED STATES

TEACHER INTERVIEW

Ms. Martha Brice

© Martha Brice

A third-grade teacher, Ms. Martha Brice began teaching kindergarten in Washington, DC, over 50 years ago. She also taught in Chicago early in her career, returned home to teach in the District of Columbia, and now teaches in Prince George's County, Maryland, just east of the District. Located near the stadium for Washington's National Football League team in Landover, Maryland, her current school, William Paca Elementary School, serves more than 600 African American and Hispanic students who live nearby. The number of Hispanic students, whose families are primarily from El Salvador and Guatemala, increased dramatically when two schools merged a few years ago. The school also has had a recent influx of refugees from Afghanistan, Iraq, and Syria, and a few students have parents who emigrated from Nigeria.

Q: What historical events have had an effect on your work in schools?

A: I experienced major changes in the educational system from the time that I attended segregated schools in Washington, DC, during the 1940s and 1950s, through the desegregation of schools, and now the resegregation of many schools across the nation. When Reverend Martin Luther King Jr. was assassinated in 1968, I remember picking up my daughter after teaching all day and driving through the city as African Americans reacted to the news. Conditions for blacks have changed since the 1960s, and race relations have improved, but a great deal of prejudice remains in society and in schools.

Q: What do you find joyful about teaching?

A: I love to see the students who enter my classroom in the fall with low academic skills flourish in January. I also enjoy listening to my students discover their needs. You would be surprised to find out why students have problems. Eating lunch with them provides so much information. I encourage them to leave me a note that I can respond to. It is one way to discover what students need. I love their reactions when they find a new coat, shoes, or graduation dress in their desk the next day.

LEARNING OUTCOMES

After reading this chapter, you should be able to do the following:

1. Discuss reasons that states established free and universal education in the 1800s and how that goal aligns with U.S. schools today.

2. Analyze some of the historical events that have resulted in different educational experiences among students from diverse racial and ethnic groups.

3. Describe some practical and pedagogical reasons for the establishment of schools by the age of children.

4. Analyze the people and events that have been influential in determining school curricula in the nation's schools and reflect on how the cultures of those people have impacted today's curricula.

5. Reflect on the differences in the professional lives of teachers between the 19th century and now.

Questions to Consider

1. How can learning from the past help you reflect on the histories and experiences of the students in your classroom to help you serve their needs?

2. What curriculum or instructional strategies do you recall from your own school days that have now been repackaged as today's reforms?

3. What are some creative and hands-on strategies that you can use to engage students in learning and being excited about learning? What do we know from history about this approach to learning?

INTRODUCTION

Knowing the past helps us plan for the future. Since the Boston Latin School was established in 1635, the nation has adopted universal schooling for all children, established a public education system, desegregated schools, and opened postsecondary education to almost any student who desires it. In studying the history of education, we find that some educational practices appear cyclical, reappearing in a different form every few generations. Movements such as progressivism, even though it fell out of favor by the 1950s, have had a lasting effect in some aspects of schooling. Reforms of schools come and go as school administrators and policy makers strive to find the magic curriculum, teaching strategies, and system that will ensure that students learn at high levels.

HOW DID PUBLIC SCHOOLS COME TO BE?

The United States has had a long history of providing a **free and universal education** for its children. Many hard-fought political and legal battles over the past four centuries have led to universal education for all students regardless of their race, ethnicity, socioeconomic status, or native language. However, this has not always been the case. In colonial times, access to schooling in basic literacy and numeracy was available only to the affluent. Critical themes in these early debates were around the rights of individuals to decide for themselves whether to attend school and the basic requirements necessary for all citizens in a democracy.

As with many other aspects of early society in the colonies, the Puritans transferred their views and expectations for education from England to the United States. Who should be educated and the purposes of education were hot topics across Europe in the 1600s. Academic and political leaders were asking whether all children should attend school and whether girls as well as boys should attend. They were also asking what students should learn, how long they should attend school, who should pay, and whether school attendance should be compulsory.

Schools in the Colonies

Before communities built schools, children were often taught by women in their neighborhoods who established dame schools in their homes. Most schools were established and controlled by churches, where religion was taught along with reading, writing, and arithmetic. Locally controlled schools were first established in the New England colonies where the *New England Primer* was the first widely used textbook. It included the Lord's Prayer, the Ten Commandments, and a list of the books of the Bible. Students were asked to memorize the primer's **catechism**, which was a series of questions and correct answers that taught the Protestant faith (Spring, 2018).

The Massachusetts Bay Colony is credited with first requiring all children to receive a formal education. The Massachusetts School Law of 1642 called for children to learn to read so they could understand the Bible and the country's laws. A 1647 statute, the Old Deluder Satan Law, established schools by requiring towns with 50 or more families to appoint a teacher and collect taxes to support schools. Connecticut established its own school statutes in 1650. Other colonies were slower to engage with these core issues, and the South continued to resist the establishment of schools for anyone other than aristocrats.

Although the early Massachusetts and Connecticut statutes made reference to the importance of reading the Scriptures, they also implied that the state would be better off with educated citizens. This view had been championed by leading philosophers, scientists, and politicians in Europe for several centuries. Jean-Jacques Rousseau, Francis Bacon, Thomas Hobbes, René Descartes, and John Locke argued in the 18th century that there was a public interest in having all citizens educated. They believed that citizens had to have skills in literacy and numeracy for a democracy to thrive and that education should be available to all children and youth (Urban & Wagoner, 2009). Most leaders in the United States agreed that a free and universal education was a cornerstone of democracy.

Around the time of the Revolutionary War, the concept of secular schools emerged. Some leaders were concerned that religious control of schools could limit political freedom and the scientific revolution. Thomas Jefferson, for one, believed that freedom of thought and beliefs was key to a republican society. This concern led to the adoption of the First Amendment to the Constitution, which prevents the establishment of a state religion. The focus on freedom of ideas during this period opened the door to teaching more than religion, morals, and civil obedience. Education began to be seen as providing intellectual tools based on science that would help create a better society (Spring, 2018).

Creating a System of Public Education

That the states should be responsible for education was seen as important even before the Constitution was written. During the Revolutionary War, the Continental Congress passed several ordinances related to the opening up of lands in the West. The Land Ordinance of 1785 required each new state to form a central government and address education as a component of its founding laws. It also required each township in the new territories north and west of the Ohio River to designate one section (one square mile) of its 36 allocated township sections for public schools. Two years later, the Northwest Ordinance encouraged the establishment of schools because religion, morality, and knowledge were critical for a good government (Urban & Wagoner, 2009).

When the U.S. Constitution was adopted in 1789, it made no reference to education. Even though some of the founders wanted education to be a federal responsibility, the Tenth Amendment made it clear that education would be the responsibility of states: "The powers not delegated to the United States by the Constitution, nor prohibited by it to the States, are reserved to the States respectively, or to the people." Thus, state legislatures became responsible for establishing education policies and financing a public education system.

As the 1800s unfolded, school debates focused on whether attendance should be compulsory and how schools should be supported and managed. Gradually, a consensus emerged that each state would set expectations for public schools, that towns were responsible for the operation of schools, and that schools would be financed through taxation. Concerns about the quality and rigor of education across the states led to a system of education that was somewhat uniform in the organization and operation of public schools. By the 1830s, children were attending public primary schools called common schools.

Massachusetts enacted the first compulsory attendance law in 1852, requiring 12 weeks of school. By the end of the 19th century, 27 states had compulsory attendance laws, with all 48 states passing them by 1918 (Urban & Wagoner, 2009). However, the establishment of attendance laws did not come about without objections. There were competing interests for what children should be doing at a specific age, which sometimes meant working instead of attending school.

Teachers in the one-room schools of the past served not only as the teachers, but also as the custodians, nurses, secretaries, and principals.

By the end of the 19th century, children were a large component of the rapidly growing industrial labor force, especially in the textile mills. Three in 10 mill workers in the South were under 16 years of age, and 75% of the spinners in North Carolina were 14 or younger (Woodward, 1971). They worked long hours in dark, dirty, and dangerous conditions, which eventually led to child labor laws. However, these laws were slow to happen, especially in the South. It was not until 1912 that Southern states prohibited night work for children and set age and hour limits that were as low as age 12 and 60 hours per week.

By the beginning of the 20th century, most 7- to 13-year-old children attended school. However, only 10% remained in school beyond age 14, and fewer than 7% of the 17-year-olds graduated from high school (Olson, 2000). As the 20th century unfolded, the combination of child labor laws and compulsory attendance laws was increasingly effective in pushing young people into school.

Important dates in the development of a system of education are outlined in Table 6.1.

HOW HAS THE EDUCATIONAL SYSTEM CONTRIBUTED TO EQUALITY?

An examination of how different groups have experienced our educational system over the past four centuries provides insights into the importance of education in the struggle for equality in the United

TABLE 6.1 ■ Significant Events in the Development of the U.S. System of Education	
1635	The Boston Latin School was established in Massachusetts.
1647	Massachusetts's Old Deluder Satan Law required establishment of schools.
1785–1787	The Northwest Ordinances passed, supporting schools in new territories.
1789	The U.S. Constitution was adopted without reference to education.
1821	The English Classical School, the first high school, was established in Boston.
	The Troy Female Seminary in New York first prepared teachers for certification.
1825–1826	The first known child care center opened in New Harmony, Indiana.
1827	Massachusetts law established high schools.
1837	Massachusetts established the first state board of education, and Horace Mann was appointed the first secretary.
1839	The first public normal school for preparing teachers opened in Lexington, Massachusetts.
1848	Quincy School, based on grades, was established in Boston.
1852	Massachusetts established the first compulsory attendance law.
1872	The Kalamazoo School Case made it possible for public high schools to be supported by taxes.
1873	St. Louis, Missouri, opened the first public kindergarten in the United States.
1918	Compulsory education was required in all states.
1965	The first Elementary and Secondary Education Act (ESEA) was passed by Congress as part of President Lyndon B. Johnson's "War on Poverty."
1979	The U.S. Department of Education was established by President Jimmy Carter.
2001	ESEA was reauthorized under President George W. Bush as No Child Left Behind (NCLB), requiring accountability based on student test scores.
2015	ESEA was reauthorized under President Barack Obama as the Every Student Succeeds Act (ESSA).

States. All groups have fought for quality education for their children. The progress toward ridding the nation of inequality and providing equal education for all students has involved committed people of color as well as whites. The joy in this sad history of discrimination and inequality is that much has improved, especially in the past 60 years. Importantly, teachers are key in providing a quality and equitable education for all students. Our understanding of how we got to where we are today should encourage us to make a commitment to ensure that all of our future students have every possible opportunity to learn.

First Americans

European colonists thought that American Indian leaders should be educated in the schools of the colonists for the purposes of learning Christianity and the Anglo-Saxon culture, with the goal of replacing their native cultures and languages. When Virginia's College of William and Mary was established in 1693, a part of its mission was the education of American Indian students (Glenn, 2011). New Hampshire's Dartmouth College had the same goal when it was established in 1769, but most of its students were white (Spring, 2018).

Resistance to Conversion

The conversion of American Indians to the Anglo-Saxon culture met with great resistance from tribes and their members. Conversions that did occur were most often among the families formed by marriages of whites and American Indians. Because the government's plans for deculturalizing American Indians were ineffective, Congress passed the Indian Civilization Fund Act of 1819 with the explicit purpose of culturally transforming the native population, especially the southern tribes. To move the effort forward, the Superintendent of Indian Trade encouraged the establishment of tribal schools with missionary teachers. The Protestant churches that joined this effort believed that the spread of Anglo-Saxon culture around the world was part of the nation's manifest destiny. The goals of most American Indian families who participated in the missionary schools were different from the goals of the federal government. The families were interested in literacy, not the extinction of their cultures or the adoption of Christianity (Spring, 2018).

One of the federal government's goals for the tribes in the South was to persuade tribal members to divide tribal lands into private property that could then be sold to Anglo settlers—a goal that was reinforced by the missionary schools. When few American Indians were willing to sell tribal lands, Congress passed the Indian Removal Act of 1830, authorizing the president of the United States to set aside land west of the Mississippi River for American Indians, who then were living in the southern states east of the Mississippi River. Within a few years, the Cherokees, Creeks, Choctaws, Chickasaws, and Seminoles were forcibly moved to the new Indian Territories. During the Trail of Tears, one in four Cherokees died on the trek west from their ancestral homeland in Georgia. In the new territory, which is now Oklahoma, the Cherokees and Choctaws established their own school systems. By 1848, the Choctaws had opened nine boarding schools with many Choctaw teachers. The Choctaws also established segregated schools for the children of freed slaves after the Civil War, as well as a system of schools that included academies that were sometimes separate for boys and girls (Spring, 2018).

Boarding Schools

Still trying to convert American Indians, the 1867 Indian Peace Commission said that American Indians could become citizens if they gave up their native religions and ways of life. Again, education was to play an important role in this process. The charge to schools was to replace native languages with English, destroy tribal customs, and develop allegiance to the federal government. The new strategy called for boarding schools, requiring the removal of children from their families at an early age to isolate them from the language and customs of their parents and tribes. Between 1879 and 1905, 25 boarding schools were located far from the reservations (Spring, 2018). Thousands of young American Indians from the Dakotas were boarded at the Carlisle Indian Industrial School in a Pennsylvania army barracks (Glenn, 2011). Parents and tribes continually complained about the boarding schools, how their children were being treated, and how their native cultures were being denigrated.

Federal policies removed many American Indian children from their homes to attend boarding schools into the 20th century.

Children continued to be removed from their homes and placed in boarding schools at the time citizenship finally was granted to American Indians in 1924. Not until then did concerned citizens seriously investigate the horrible conditions in these schools. Red Cross investigators found that children at the Rice Station Boarding School in Arizona survived on bread, black coffee, and syrup for breakfast; and bread, boiled potatoes, and milk for dinner and supper (Meriam, 1928). The poor diet and overcrowded conditions contributed to the spread of diseases such as tuberculosis and trachoma (Spring, 2016). Investigators found that boarding schools were supported by the work of students who attended classes half the day and worked the other half. The 1928 *Meriam Report* by Johns Hopkins University attacked the government's policies of removing American Indian children from their homes. Following the release of this report, the government began to support community day schools and native cultures (Spring, 2016).

American Indian Control

When John F. Kennedy was elected president in 1960, the Bureau of Indian Affairs (BIA) began to involve American Indians in policy decisions. With the Office of Economic Opportunity, the BIA supported the creation of the Rough Rock Demonstration School on the Navajo reservation, in part to preserve the Navajo language and culture. In addition, Navajo parents were again able to control the education of their children.

As the civil rights movement grew in intensity in the 1960s, America Indian tribes began to participate in a pan-Indian movement that recognized that tribes shared a common set of values and interests. The American Indian Movement (AIM) and the Indians of All Tribes led demonstrations demanding self-determination. At the same time, a Senate report, *Indian Education: A National Tragedy—A National Challenge*, condemned previous federal educational policies for American Indians. The report said that "a careful review of the historical literature reveals that the dominant policy of the Federal Government toward the American Indian has been one of forced assimilation . . . [because of] a desire to divest the Indian of his land" (Senate Committee on Labor and Public Welfare, 1969, p. 9).

Federal policy began to change. Title VII of the Elementary and Secondary Education Act of 1968 provided support for bilingual programs in American Indian languages and English. In 1975, Congress passed the Indian Self-Determination and Education Assistance Act, which gave tribes the right to operate their own schools. The Tribally Controlled Schools Act of 1988 gave grants to tribes to manage and operate their own schools. In a complete switch of earlier policy for assimilation and the destruction of native cultures and languages, the Native American Languages Act of 1990 promoted the preservation of traditional American Indian languages.

African Americans

The education of African Americans is also built on a history of discrimination, but their relationship with the European colonizers was different from that of the American Indians. They were not the native inhabitants of the United States. They had not chosen to immigrate to the United States, but entered involuntarily by force. They did not own land that the settlers wanted, but they were a critical source of labor necessary for the Southern economy. Most African Americans were considered to be property and were owned and sold with little control over their own lives. Until the early part of the 20th century, most African Americans lived in the South, where before the Civil War it was illegal for them to attend school. Although literacy was a punishable crime for African slaves in the South, at least 5% of them were literate by the outbreak of the Civil War (Anderson, 1988).

John N. Choate/Stringer/Getty Images

African American children in the North most often attended segregated and inferior schools. **Charity schools** for freed slaves opened at the end of the 18th century in Philadelphia, New York City, and Baltimore (Kaestle, 1983). African American children could attend Boston schools at that time, but most did not because of their poor economic situations and the hostile reception of them in schools. In 1798, a group of black parents petitioned the Boston School Committee for a separate school to protect their children from the hostile environment. The School Committee did not accept the parents' proposal at first, but it changed its position in 1806 and opened a public segregated school with support from white philanthropists (Spring, 2016).

By the 1820s, black parents decided that the segregated school was providing an inferior education for their children and began to demand better conditions and teachers. They petitioned the Boston School Committee in 1846 to desegregate schools. Even though the School Committee found the segregated schools unacceptable, it took no action to change those conditions or to require its public schools to be open to African American children. In response, Benjamin Roberts sued the city for excluding his daughter from all-white schools near their home. He lost his case before the Massachusetts Supreme Court when it ruled that the city had provided a separate but equal school for his daughter. Not long afterward, in 1855, however, the state legislature passed a law that prevented the segregation of schools based on race or religion, making Massachusetts the first state to outlaw school segregation. The Boston schools were integrated that year (Spring, 2016).

Education in the South

Before the end of the Civil War, former slaves in the South were fighting for universal education. They craved literacy and were unwilling to wait for the government to provide schools. They established and staffed their own schools with African American teachers throughout the South. The African American teachers, school officials, and other leaders adopted the common school ideal with the New England classical liberal curricula. The curricula in elementary schools included reading, spelling, writing, grammar, diction, history, geography, arithmetic, and music. Black colleges were established to prepare exceptional African American students to become the leaders in their communities. The curriculum was a classical liberal education in which students studied Latin, Greek, mathematics, science, and philosophy (Anderson, 1988).

To pursue the goal of universal education, the former slaves sought the help of Republican politicians, Northern missionary societies, the Union Army, and the Freedmen's Bureau, which had been created by Congress in 1865. However, it was very important to them that they control their own education, which was sometimes difficult as Northern missionaries moved into the South to establish schools. When John W. Alvord was appointed the national superintendent of schools for the Freedmen's Bureau in 1865, he discovered a system of at least 500 African American schools as he traveled across the South (Anderson, 1988). These schools had been established and were being managed by former slaves who were committed to ensuring that African American children and adults would learn to read and write as soon as possible. In some communities, black churches developed Sabbath schools that offered literacy instruction in the evenings and on the weekends. In these schools, the speller was as prevalent as the Bible (Anderson, 1988).

Most planters resisted universal education for former slaves and impoverished whites. Their opposition was, in part, due to economics. The planters needed a workforce that would work for low wages; they depended heavily on child labor, which led to schools being opened as late as December. They supported low taxes, opposed compulsory school attendance, and discouraged universal public education. Eventually, they began to provide schools for low-income white students, but they failed to provide schools for black children in most communities. The gains made by African Americans in the 1860s were quickly stymied, and the portion attending school began to drop (Anderson, 1988).

Education at the Beginning of the 20th Century

Although ex-slaves had founded their schools with classical curricula, some leaders questioned the need for such advanced study. They argued that black children would be better served with training for the

New York World-Telegram and the Sun newspaper

Schools segregated by race were the norm in the United States for much of the 20th century.

trades and learning their appropriate role in the Southern culture. With this goal in mind, Northerner Samuel Chapman Armstrong founded Hampton Institute in Virginia to prepare teachers. Most of Hampton's early students had completed only the eighth grade. They were required to work long hours in a sawmill, on the school's farm, or in the school's kitchen or dining room to develop the ethic of hard work that Southern landowners expected of their laborers. One of Armstrong's top students, Booker T. Washington, founded Tuskegee Normal and Industrial Institute in 1881 to extend Armstrong's pedagogy.

Most African Americans had a different vision for their education. They saw Washington giving in to the white demands of industrialists who wanted a steady, complacent workforce at low wages. The primary spokesperson for a different vision, W. E. B. Du Bois, wanted no compromises with the powerful white elites. Instead, he wanted to challenge the oppressive Southern economy. He argued that black education should be about preparing the African American leaders of the future. He supported the classical education that was available in black colleges like Atlanta University and Wilberforce College. While Washington supported segregated schooling, Du Bois became one of the founders of the National Association for the Advancement of Colored People (NAACP)—the organization that spearheaded the effort to desegregate schools later in the century. By 1915, the Du Bois supporters had prevailed, and the Hampton-Tuskegee model began to lose favor among its previous supporters.

At the beginning of the 20th century, most African American children did not attend elementary school because no schools existed for them, and they were not allowed to attend the schools that white children attended. If they wanted a school, African American families in the South often had to build their own schools even though they paid local and state taxes to support white segregated schools (Spring, 2016). When African American children could attend school, their schools were usually inferior to those attended by white students. The schools lacked equipment and supplies. They were allocated textbooks after they had worn out their usefulness in the white schools. Families and leaders in the African American community turned to the courts for support in accessing resources for the education of their children.

When Ms. Brice, the teacher whose interview began this chapter, grew up in Washington, DC, the schools were segregated. When she began high school, her parents sent her to Notre Dame High School in Baltimore with primarily white students. However, she returned to Washington, and graduated from Dunbar High School, which was named after the distinguished African American poet and was the first public high school for blacks. Dunbar's teachers were African Americans with advanced degrees who were well known for preparing the majority of their graduates for college prior to the desegregation of schools (Stewart, 2015). She prepared to be a teacher at the historically black West Virginia State College, which had been integrated by the time she enrolled in the late 1950s.

School Desegregation

Nearly 100 court cases from 20 states and the District of Columbia were filed for equal education in the 19th century. African Americans in the North won a majority of their cases, prohibiting segregation in their public schools (Hendrie, 2000). Nevertheless, segregation continued in the South. After Homer Plessy was arrested for refusing to ride in the "colored" section of a train in Louisiana, he argued that his **Fourteenth Amendment** rights had been abridged. The U.S. Supreme Court disagreed, ruling in its 1896 *Plessy v. Ferguson* decision that "separate but equal" facilities were legal. This decision supported the segregation of schools and other public facilities for the next six decades.

The NAACP decided to pursue a legal path toward desegregating public schools. Five cases from South Carolina, Virginia, Delaware, Kansas, and the District of Columbia were percolating in the lower courts in the mid-1940s. The first four cases were argued before the U.S. Supreme Court in 1952 and 1953 by Thurgood Marshall, who later became the first African American Supreme Court justice. In 1954, the Court declared, "In the field of public education the doctrine of 'separate but equal' has no place. Separate educational facilities are inherently unequal" (*Brown v. Board of Education of Topeka*, 1954). The fifth case, *Bolling v. Sharpe* (1954), declared that the federal government could not segregate schools in the District of Columbia.

Most school districts did not respond to this mandate until after the passage of the Civil Rights Act of 1964. Many white families fiercely resisted the desegregation of their schools. In cities like Little Rock, Arkansas, federal troops protected African American students who were entering white schools for the first time. Virginia's Prince Edward County School Board resisted desegregation, closing its public schools for five years. White families established private Christian schools or moved to the suburbs where the population was primarily white to avoid integration. The 1971 *Swann v. Charlotte-Mecklenburg* decision moved desegregation efforts to another level when it upheld district-wide busing to overcome segregation.

As schools were desegregated, many African American teachers and principals who had worked in segregated schools were not invited to teach in the integrated schools, leaving many of them without jobs. However, the race of the students in schools did change in the three decades following the *Brown* decision. In the mid-1960s, only 2% of black students attended integrated schools; by the late 1980s, 44% of them were in integrated schools (Orfield & Frankenberg, 2014). During this period, rural and small-town schools across the South were integrated. The achievement gap between black and white students closed substantially, students of color had greater access to quality schools and college admission, and students were better prepared to work and interact in a multicultural society (Boger & Orfield, 2005). Even more dramatic than the desegregation of schools during this period was the dismantling of *Plessy v. Ferguson* and its resulting Jim Crow laws, which prohibited African Americans from using the same facilities as whites.

By the mid-1980s, federal court sanctions for integration began to be lifted. After the Supreme Court allowed federal courts to end desegregation plans with *Board of Education of Oklahoma City v. Dowell* in 1991, many federal courts prohibited school districts from voluntarily using race-conscious assignment policies to maintain diversity in their schools (Orfield & Frankenberg, 2014). Because of de facto segregation in many communities (see Chapter 9), neighborhood schools were often made up of students of the same race. Segregation in schools began to return to pre-1970 levels. By 2015, African American and Latino students were nearly eight times more likely than white students to attend high-poverty schools (McFarland et al., 2017). Half of the nation's schools are highly segregated white schools, and the degree of poverty in those schools is considerably less than those schools attended by students of color. Although the ability to attend schools that are less impoverished provides all students a better chance at being successful in school and in life, the onetime goal of integrating schools based on race has been abandoned. A chronology of significant events in providing equality for students is shown in Table 6.2.

Latinos

When the Treaty of Guadalupe Hidalgo was negotiated at the end of the Mexican–American War in 1848, the Mexican government demanded that its citizens in what had been northern Mexico (i.e., Texas, New Mexico, Arizona, California, Nevada, Utah, and parts of Colorado) become U.S. citizens. Although they were granted citizenship, they were viewed as inferior by the Anglo Americans in the region and were treated as second-class citizens. Even in the 1930s, Mexican Americans who had been born in the United States were being deported to Mexico (Spring, 2018). The hope of these new citizens was to reap the benefits of U.S. citizenship while maintaining their native language and culture. As with other non-European groups, the U.S. government intended for them to assimilate into the Anglo American culture of the dominant group and eliminate their ties to Spanish and Mexican culture (Spring, 2018).

Whether Mexican American students could attend the same schools as whites depended on whether they were classified as white. There was no common agreement on the race of Mexican Americans. In

TABLE 6.2	■ Significant Events in the Movement Toward Educational Equality
1855	Massachusetts outlawed the segregation of schools.
1896	The U.S. Supreme Court found "separate but equal" laws constitutional in *Plessy v. Ferguson.*
1905	San Francisco schools were desegregated, allowing Chinese youth to attend regular high schools.
1915	A student strike in Puerto Rico supported instruction in Spanish.
1918	Texas made it a criminal offense to use any language other than English for instruction.
1928	The *Meriam Report* attacked government policies of removing American Indian students from their homes and sending them to boarding schools.
1934	The Padín Reform in Puerto Rico restricted English instruction to high schools.
1940	A federal court required equal salaries for African American and white teachers in *Alston v. School Board of City of Norfolk.*
1947	The federal appeals court struck down segregated schooling for Mexican Americans in *Méndez v. Westminster School District.*
1951	Puerto Rico gained greater control of its school systems after being granted commonwealth status.
1954	The U.S. Supreme Court made school segregation unconstitutional in *Brown v. Board of Education*, overturning *Plessy.*
1956	The Virginia legislature called for "massive resistance" to school desegregation.
1958	In *Cooper v. Aaron*, the U.S. Supreme Court ruled that fear of social unrest or violence does not excuse state governments from complying with *Brown.*
1959	Officials closed public schools in Prince Edward County, Virginia, rather than integrate them.
1964	Congress passed the Civil Rights Act, which prohibits discrimination in school programs and activities that receive federal assistance.
	The U.S. Supreme Court ordered Prince Edward County, Virginia, to reopen its schools on a desegregated basis.
1965	In *Green v. County School Board of New Kent County*, the U.S. Supreme Court ordered states to dismantle segregated facilities, staff, faculty, extracurricular activities, and transportation.
1968	Title VII of the Elementary and Secondary Education Act supported bilingual programs in native languages and English.
	Congress passed the Handicapped Children's Early Education Assistance Act.
1971	In *Swann v. Charlotte-Mecklenburg Board of Education*, the U.S. Supreme Court approved busing, magnet schools, compensatory education, and other tools as appropriate remedies to overcome the role of residential segregation in perpetuating racially segregated schools.
1972	Congress passed Title IX of the Education Amendments Act outlawing discrimination based on sex in any federally funded education program or activity.
1973	The U.S. Supreme Court ruled that education is not a "fundamental right" and that the Constitution does not require equal education expenditures within a state in *San Antonio Independent School District v. Rodriguez.*
1974	The U.S. Supreme Court blocked metropolitan-wide desegregation plans to desegregate urban schools with high minority populations in *Milliken v. Bradley.*
	In *Lau v. Nichols*, the U.S. Supreme Court stipulated that special language programs are necessary to provide equal educational opportunity to students who do not understand English.
1975	Congress passed the Education for All Handicapped Children Act.
	Congress passed the Indian Self-Determination and Education Assistance Act.
1978	The U.S. Supreme Court ruled that race can be a factor in university admissions, but it cannot be the deciding factor, in *Regents of the University of California v. Bakke.*
1982	The U.S. Supreme Court rejected tax exemptions for private religious schools that discriminate in *Bob Jones University v. U.S.* and *Goldsboro Christian Schools v. U.S.*

1986	A federal court found that a school district can be released from its desegregation plan and returned to local control after it meets the *Green* factors in *Riddick v. School Board of the City of Norfolk, Virginia*.
1988	The Tribally Controlled Schools Act gave grants for tribal schools.
1990	The Native American Languages Act promoted preservation of American Indian languages.
1996	The federal appeals court prohibited the use of race in college and university admissions, ending affirmative action in Louisiana, Texas, and Mississippi, in *Hopwood v. Texas*.
2003	The U.S. Supreme Court upheld diversity as a rationale for affirmative action programs in higher education admissions but declared point systems inappropriate in *Gratz v. Bollinger* and *Grutter v. Bollinger*.
	A federal district court case affirmed the value of racial diversity and race-conscious student assignment plans in K–12 education in *Comfort v. Lynn School Committee*.
2007	The U.S. Supreme Court struck down the use of race in determining schools for students in *Parents Involved in Community Schools Inc. v. Seattle School District* and *Meredith v. Jefferson County (Ky.) Board of Education*.
2014	In *Schuette v. Coalition to Defend Affirmative Action*, the U.S. Supreme Court upheld a Michigan constitutional amendment that banned affirmative action in admissions to the state's public universities.
	The U.S. Supreme Court upheld the decision of the Court of Appeals for the Fifth Circuit in *Fisher v. University of Texas at Austin*, which had ruled in favor of the university, writing that "universities may use race as part of a holistic admissions program where it cannot otherwise achieve diversity."

1897, Texas courts declared that Mexican Americans were not white, but they were classified as white in California until 1930, when the attorney general recategorized them as American Indians (Spring, 2016). Because the courts did not consider that they were white, most Mexican American children attended segregated schools through the first half of the 20th century. The same separate but equal laws applied to them as to African Americans.

The Battle for the Use of Spanish

In addition to being in segregated schools, Mexican American students often were not allowed to speak Spanish in school. To ensure that teachers would deliver instruction in English, states passed laws to that effect. In 1918, Texas made it a criminal offense to use any language other than English for instruction. Often, students were forbidden to use Spanish at any time while they were in school. In the last half of the 19th century, Mexican Americans sent their children to Catholic or nonsectarian private schools, both of which were more likely to provide bilingual instruction, to escape the anti-Mexican attitudes of public schools (Spring, 2016).

Many Mexican American children were not attending school at the beginning of the 20th century, in part because farmers were not willing to release them from work in the field to attend school. On the other hand, many school officials wanted them in schools to Americanize them and rid them of their culture and language (Spring, 2016).

Concerned about discrimination against Mexican American students in public schools, the League of United Latin American Citizens (LULAC) called for bilingual instruction and the maintenance of Mexican cultural traditions in schools as early as 1929. However, the English-only laws were not repealed until 1968, when the federal government supported bilingual education as an option for teaching English Language Learners (ELLs) (Spring, 2016). As the federal policy has moved away from support of bilingual education in recent years, some states have now returned to laws prohibiting bilingual education and the use of any language other than English for classroom instruction.

Mexican American families were fighting for the right to attend white schools at the same time that African Americans had turned to the courts for assistance. In the 1930s, the Texas courts upheld the right of school boards to provide segregated education for Mexican Americans. The first breakthrough for integration occurred with the 1947 *Méndez v. Westminster School District* decision, which required a California school district to allow a Mexican American girl to attend the white school. The Mexican American Legal Defense and Educational Fund (MALDEF) was established in 1967 to continue suing for the civil rights and equality of Mexican American students. Court cases since then have focused on discriminatory practices in the funding of schools, the sole use of English in classrooms, and the disproportionate placement of Spanish-speaking children in special education classes as a result of biased tests or tests being given in English. Latino students are now the most segregated students in the country (Orfield & Frankenberg, 2014), and nearly half of them attend high-poverty schools (McFarland et al., 2017).

Equity for Puerto Ricans

Education for students in Puerto Rico has been entangled with a history of occupation by the United States. Puerto Rico had just received its autonomy from Spain when it came under the control of the United States as part of the spoils (along with the Philippines and Guam) from the Spanish–American War at the end of the 19th century. With the Foraker Act of 1900, Congress established a colonial government to replace military rule in Puerto Rico and appointed the first U.S. Commissioner of Education for Puerto Rico. Just as with American Indians, the federal policy was to Americanize Puerto Ricans through education. Because the language of instruction was to be English, and many Puerto Rican teachers spoke only Spanish, teachers from the United States were hired. Not only were students expected to learn English; they were also expected to learn the Anglo culture. Educational policies required celebration of the U.S. patriotic holidays, such as the Fourth of July. Students were required to pledge allegiance to the U.S. flag and to study U.S. heroes. Local textbooks were replaced with U.S. textbooks (Spring, 2016).

Puerto Ricans were not interested in becoming Americans and losing their own native language and culture. In 1912, the Puerto Rico Teachers Association began to defend Spanish as the language of instruction. When a student at San Juan's Central High School was expelled in 1915 for collecting signatures in support of instruction in Spanish, a student strike was sparked (Spring, 2016). Calls for nationalism and independence were common. Congress granted Puerto Ricans citizenship in 1917, which obligated them to serve in the military but did not grant them the right to vote in elections.

Tensions increased in the 1920s when a Puerto Rican who supported the United States' assimilation policies became the commissioner of education. He pressed his predecessor's policies even further: High school seniors had to pass an oral English examination before they could graduate. He banned school newspapers in Spanish. Teachers were required to use English in teacher meetings and informal discussions with students. Protests by teachers, professors, and college students expanded. College students were expelled for participating in anti-American marches, and professors were warned about their support of student protests (Spring, 2016).

After José Padín had been appointed Commissioner of Education by President Herbert Hoover in 1930, the school language policy was reconsidered. By 1934, Padín had reversed the English-only policies of his predecessor and restricted English instruction to high schools. Spanish was to be used through the eighth grade. However, textbooks continued to be printed in English. After the Puerto Rico Teachers Association had successfully lobbied the Puerto Rican legislature to pass a bill requiring the use of Spanish in 1947, President Harry Truman vetoed it. Puerto Rico was granted commonwealth status in 1951, and Puerto Ricans gained greater control of their school systems, restoring Spanish as the language of instruction (Spring, 2016).

Asian Americans

The first Chinese immigrants arrived in California in the 1850s to join the gold rush. However, Japanese were prevented by their government from immigrating to other countries until 1867 when Hawaii planters were allowed to recruit 100 workers (Spring, 2016). Koreans, Filipinos, and Asian Indians did not begin immigrating to the United States in significant numbers until early in the 20th century. All of these groups faced a great deal of hostility and discrimination from the dominant white population. The courts considered Asian immigrants as having the same status as American Indians, and they were not eligible for citizenship.

Although Chinese and Japanese immigrants were recruited by companies to fill labor needs, it was not long until the dominant Anglo population no longer wanted them. Like other groups that weren't white, they were viewed as inferior to the white race. In 1882, Congress passed the Chinese Exclusion Act, preventing immigration by Chinese laborers until the law was rescinded in 1943, allowing Chinese immigrants the right to become naturalized citizens (Spring, 2016). All immigration from Japan was prohibited by 1924. Even when Chinese were allowed to immigrate again and had the right to become a citizen, quotas limited immigration to 105 people per year. Similar quotas applied to Filipinos and Asian Indians (Spring, 2016). It wasn't until 1952 that the McCarran–Walter Act removed the racial restrictions for naturalized citizenship.

The early Chinese American immigrants demanded access to public school for their children and created their own privately funded Chinese language schools to help their children develop "a positive appreciation of Chinese cultures and identity" (Au, Brown, & Calderón, 2016, p. 63). Japanese Americans also created Japanese language schools to ensure their children learned their native language and culture. Some citizens viewed these language schools as preventing Chinese and Japanese students from being Americanized and adopting the dominant Anglo culture. As a result, California enacted the Private School Control Law in 1921 to prevent the growth of language schools in these Asian communities (Au et al., 2016).

When the court ruled in 1885 that native-born Mamie Tape had equal access to public schooling, the California legislature responded by allowing school districts to establish segregated schools for Asian Americans. By 1905, the segregated system in San Francisco was broken as Chinese youths were admitted to the regular city high school (Spring, 2016). Southern courts retained Asian American children in segregated schools attended primarily by African Americans. The family of a Chinese American girl argued that she was not black and therefore should be able to attend the white school. However, the court ruled in 1924 that she was not white and gave schools the authority to determine the race of their students (Spring, 2016).

After the passage of the Immigration and Nationality Act of 1965, the number of Asian immigrants began to grow. Schools in cities like San Francisco were faced with a growing number of students who spoke languages other than English. Because the language of instruction was English, parents worried that their children were not able to achieve at the high academic levels they expected. They sued the San Francisco school system and, in 1974, won the right to have their first language used in instruction in *Lau*

CHALLENGING ASSUMPTIONS
MYTH: ASIAN AMERICANS ARE A MODEL MINORITY.

The Research

The label *model minority* was first popularized in a 1960 *Time* magazine article on the high academic achievement of Japanese and Chinese American students. The image of a model minority was based not only on high achievement as measured in high Grade Point Averages (GPAs) and test scores but also on the hard work of Asian Americans that helped them overcome the adversities they faced as new immigrants or members of a pan-ethnic group of color with a long history of discrimination against them in the United States. It also sent a message to other racial and ethnic groups that they could succeed in the United States if they just tried harder and held Asian American values about education.

Suzuki (2002) was one of the first researchers to debunk the stereotype of Asian Americans, which he found invalidated the group's claims of persistent discrimination and social injustice. Data do show that as a pan-ethnic group, Asian American students score at levels equal to or above white students on standardized tests. However, this pan-ethnic group includes at least 48 countries. The overall census data on academic achievement, income, and unemployment mask the lower scores and economic outcomes of the less populous Asian ethnic groups. "For example, three-quarters of Asian

Indians have at least a bachelor's degree and over two-thirds are in management or professional jobs, but Vietnamese are less well positioned. One-fifth of Vietnamese Americans have less than a high school diploma, and similar numbers are in low-paying personal care and service jobs" (Simms, 2017).

Asian American students from many Asian ethnic groups are not performing at high academic levels, finishing high school in four years, or attending college. Although Asian American students are enrolled at disproportionately high rates in our selective universities, the majority of Asian American postsecondary students are enrolled in community colleges (Teranishi, 2010). Many Asian American students find the school climate unwelcoming. Young people from Southeast Asian ethnic backgrounds (e.g., Cambodians, Laotians, and Hmong) report being profiled by police and other security personnel on a regular basis. Even some high-achieving Asian American students are stressed by the pressure to be "perfect," but they are less likely than other students to seek mental health services (Cheang, 2018). When we aggregate all students from Asian ethnic groups together, those students who have the greatest needs are often forgotten when we apply the model minority stereotype. Sociopolitical factors such as discrimination continue to impact the lives and school experiences of all Asian American students.

v. Nichols. The court said "under state imposed standards, there was no equality of treatment merely by providing students with the same facilities, textbooks, teachers, and curriculum; for students who do not understand English are effectively foreclosed from any meaningful education" (*Lau v. Nichols,* 1974).

WHY ARE SCHOOLS DESIGNED AROUND THE AGE OF STUDENTS?

Early in the 18th century, educators and policy makers envisioned schools as a way to overcome poverty and crime by inculcating a good moral character into students who the reformers believed lacked appropriate parental guidance. Many students from low-income families, including African American students in the North, attended charity schools, while more-affluent children attended private or public schools (Spring, 2018).

The first schools built in many rural communities were one-room schools with a teacher who taught all subjects to students who sometimes ranged in age from 5 to 17. These schools generally had desks or long benches on which students sat together. A popular instructional method was recitation, in which pupils stood and recited the assigned lesson. Values of punctuality, honesty, and hard work were stressed in these rural schools (Gutek, 2002).

In the 1830s and 1840s, Horace Mann was concerned with divisions between social classes and saw mixing the social classes in the common school as one way to reduce the tensions between groups. Mann applied his ideas to schools when he became the first secretary of the Massachusetts Board of Education in 1837. His concept of the common school became the tax-supported, locally controlled elementary schools that dominated U.S. education in the industrial era.

The curriculum of the common school emphasized the skills needed for everyday life, ethical behavior, and responsible citizenship, but it also included standardized subject matter in reading, writing, arithmetic, spelling, history, and geography (Cremin, 1951). Common schools were expected to create conformity in American life by imposing the language and ideological outlook of the dominant Anglo American Protestant group that governed the country. Education in common schools was seen as a venue for upward social and economic mobility for native whites and European immigrants in the United States. Both girls and boys attended the common schools, usually together, but laws prevented children and young people of color from attending school, especially with white students.

Elementary Schools

The elementary school curriculum in the first half of the 19th century was influenced greatly by spellers and textbooks written by Noah Webster. His influence was not only on schools: He also wrote an American dictionary with which you may be familiar. Webster was a schoolmaster who, in 1779, had an idea for a new way of teaching that included a spelling book, grammar book, and reader. When he finished writing the books five years later, he became an itinerant lecturer, riding through the country selling his books. He was a good salesman, selling 1.5 million copies in 1801 and 75 million by 1875. Webster's books contained catechisms, but he did not limit the recitation to religion. He included a moral catechism and a federal one that stressed nationalism and patriotism (Spring, 2018).

Many urban schools prior to 1850 had classrooms for more than 100 students. One teacher managed the classroom with the assistance of student mentors who were selected from the better students. In this Lancasterian method, developed by Englishman Joseph Lancaster, students sat in long rows, and the teacher sat at a desk on a raised platform at the front of the room. When it was time for instruction by the teacher, students marched to the front of the room. Afterward, they were replaced at the front of the room by another group. The first group of students moved to another section of the classroom for recitation and drill with one of the mentors. Throughout the day, students moved from one part of the room to another to work with different mentors with several recitations occurring simultaneously in the room. Many educators and politicians of this era saw this very structured and orderly learning environment as the panacea for efficient schooling of the masses (Spring, 2018).

UNDERSTANDING AND USING DATA
PUBLIC SCHOOL STATISTICS FOR 1879

The federal government has collected data on the population and institutions for over 140 years. These data provide demographic information, but they also assist policy makers and other leaders in planning for the future. The following statistics on the school populations in selected states were reported by the federal government in 1879.

State	School Age	School Population	Number Enrolled in Public Schools	Average Daily Attendance	Average Duration of School in Days
Alabama	7–21	376,649	174,585	112,374	84
California	5–17	216,404	156,769	98,468	149
Colorado	6–21	29,738	14,111	10,899	89
Florida	4–21[a]	72,985[b]	36,964[a]	3,933[a]	105.8[a]
Illinois	6–21	1,000,694	693,334	404,479	150
Kentucky	6–20[c]	539,843	227,607[d]	160,000[d]	110[d]
New York	5–21	1,628,727	1,030,041	570,382	179
Pennsylvania	6–21	1,200,000[e]	935,740	587,672	149
Texas	8–14	208,324	192,616	—	80
West Virginia	6–21	206,123	135,526	90,268	100.76

[a]In 1878. [b]In 1876. [c]For colored [sic] population the school age is from 6 to 16. [d]In 1877. [e]In 1873.

Source: U.S. Census Bureau. (1880). Total population of school age, according to state laws, with the enrollment, attendance, teachers, income, expenditure, and school-fund for the public schools of the states and territories of the United States, for each school year, from 1871 to 1879, inclusive. *Statistical abstract of the United States: 1880* (No. 149). Retrieved from https://www2.census.gov/library/publications/1881/compendia/1880statab.pdf.

Your Task

Using these statistics, answer the following questions to compare attendance and length of school years in 1879 to today.

1. How do the ages of students in 1879 compare with the ages of students in schools today?

2. What percentage of the school-aged population was enrolled in schools in 1879 in the states above? How does this compare to today's enrollment?

3. How many months did students in schools in 1879 attend school? How does the length of the school year compare with the time spent in schools today?

4. What percentage of the enrolled students in 1879 attended school daily? How is this pattern similar or different from today's school attendance?

The first school based on grades, Quincy School, was established in Boston in 1848. Teachers had their own separate classroom, and each student sat at a desk in classrooms designed for 56 students. Within seven years, all Boston schools were graded. Other cities and communities soon adopted the Quincy model, setting the stage for the graded schools of today (Spring, 2018).

By the beginning of the 20th century, the standard classroom had rows of desks bolted to the floor. As the century progressed, many educators moved from lecture and recitation to student-centered activities, which called for smaller classes that allowed experimentation and flexibility. New York City classrooms, for example, averaged 50 students around World War I; by 1930, the average was 38 students (Spring, 2001).

The Lancasterian classroom was designed for one teacher to manage the education of as many as 100 students at one time in the same room.

The Webster spellers were replaced in the last half of the 19th century by the McGuffey Readers, written by William Holmes McGuffey. The readers provided moral lessons for an industrialized society. The leading characters in the readers were stereotypically male (Spring, 2018). Although the stories were more secular than those in earlier textbooks, religious selections were included, along with stories focusing on moral character and the importance of charity. The McGuffey Readers sold more than 120 million copies between 1836 and 1960 (Urban & Wagoner, 2009). Textbooks in the last third of the 20th century became much more secular, to the chagrin of some church leaders, who sometimes suggested that the nation would be better off if textbooks and schools returned to their Puritan roots. The "Dick and Jane" readers, which were popular from the 1930s through the 1950s, reflected idealized white middle-class lifestyles and behaviors (Kaestle & Radway, 2009).

Early Childhood Education

Throughout history, some mothers have had to work outside the home to support their families. Almost always, they have had to leave their children with someone, often a relative or a neighbor. Some women in the neighborhood watched several children, but organized schools with child care providers were not available until the 19th century. Robert Owen opened the first known child care center at a mill in New Harmony, Indiana, in 1825–1826 with more than 100 children (Prochner, Cleghorn, & Drefs, 2015).

The first kindergarten was opened by Friedrich Froebel in 1837 in Germany for three- and four-year-old children. He believed that the kindergarten teacher should not be **authoritarian**, but instead should guide children's learning through their own play, songs, stories, and activities (Gutek, 2012). The first public kindergarten in the United States opened in St. Louis, Missouri, in 1873 to serve children in poverty. Children were to learn the virtues and manners, moral habits, cleanliness, politeness, obedience, promptness, and self-control that would prepare them for elementary school. By the 1880s, Froebelian kindergartens had become popular across the United States (Spring, 2018).

By the beginning of the 20th century, about 6% of the kindergarten-aged population was enrolled in kindergarten. It was at this time that the work of G. Stanley Hall established child development and child psychology as fields of study. He defined childhood as the years between four and eight, which remains the general range for primary education today. The focus of a kindergarten class was on creating order and discipline in the child's life, but continued to encourage children to play and be creative. During this period, the age for kindergartners in public schools was raised to five. Approximately 90% of five-year-olds were attending kindergarten in the 1980s at the time that curricula were beginning to shift from being child centered to academics (Berg, 2003).

High Schools

During the colonial period, a struggle for intellectual freedom was under way in England to expand education beyond the classical study of Latin and Greek. Dissenters believed that schools were limiting the freedom of ideas by teaching students to be obedient to a church or the government. The scientific revolution fueled the debate, and intellectuals such as Francis Bacon argued that education should provide the intellectual tools and scientific knowledge required to create a better society. This

Early nursery schools were developed in the 1920s and 1930s based on the emerging field of child development and psychology.

movement led to the development of what was called dissenting academies (Spring, 2018).

When the idea crossed the Atlantic Ocean, the academies became a popular alternative to the Latin grammar schools. An early model of a high school, the academies taught ideas and skills related to the practical world, including the sciences and business. They provided useful education and transmitted the culture that helped move graduates into the middle class. Sometimes the academies were considered small colleges, at other times high schools (Spring, 2018).

The English Classical School was founded in Boston in 1821 as an alternative to boarding schools and the Boston Latin School, which provided a classical education. Curricula included English, geography, arithmetic, algebra, geometry, trigonometry, history, navigation, and surveying. A few years later, it was renamed English High School, becoming the first high school in the United States (Spring, 2018). Within a few years, Massachusetts passed a law to establish high schools across the state. Other states followed suit, but not without resistance. One of the most famous cases against public high schools was the Kalamazoo School Case in the 1870s, the result of a lawsuit brought by three prominent citizens who believed that high schools should not be supported with public funds. The courts did not agree, settling the question about taxes supporting high schools.

"Sitting at a desk all day and bringing work home is how schools prepare you for a career."

As high schools were established in small towns and cities, debates about the purpose of high schools were similar to those that led to the development of academies during the colonial days. Some people argued that the high school should develop a well-disciplined mind in the tradition of the old grammar schools. Others believed that curricula should prepare students for the practical world and occupations. Most of the early high schools ended up focusing on advanced science, math, English, history, and the political economy, but curricula were generally determined by the textbooks of the period. Admission required passing rigorous examinations; only 4% of eligible students were enrolled in a high school in the 1870s. Fewer than one in three of the admitted students completed high school. Those who didn't complete the four-year curricula entered business or taught elementary school (Cuban, 2004).

The National Education Association (NEA), which today is the largest teachers' union in the United States, formed the Committee of Ten on Secondary School Studies in 1892 to develop uniform requirements for college admission. Instead, its final report identified goals for secondary education, recommending that the children of wealthy and low-income families take the same course of study, regardless of whether they would attend college. The Committee called for at least four years of English, four years of a foreign language, and three years each of mathematics, science, and history (Spring, 2001).

The number of high schools grew dramatically at the turn of the century. Seventy percent of the students entering college in 1872 were graduates of academies; by 1920, 90% were high school graduates (Alexander & Alexander, 2001). High schools at this time were beginning to sort students for specific roles in society. When the NEA's Commission on the Reorganization of Secondary Education published its 1918 report, *Cardinal Principles of Secondary Education*, the high school was redesigned to meet the needs of the modern corporate state, impacting the high school curricula for the next 50 years. The proposed comprehensive high schools were to teach English and social studies to promote unity among students from different socioeconomic, ethnic, and language backgrounds, but also included vocational programs in agriculture, business, industry, fine arts, and the household. The purpose of high schools was expanded from a narrow focus on academics to also attend to the socialization of students by encouraging their involvement in common activities such as athletics and extracurricular activities such as student government, the student newspaper, and clubs. The report also called for high schools to promote good health through physical and health education (Spring, 2018). During this

© Chris Wildt

"This is kindergarten, Mason. You can think outside the box, but you'd better color between the lines."

period, high schools developed an academic track for students who were encouraged to attend college. All other students were guided into general or vocational tracks that would prepare them for jobs immediately after high school. Over time, fewer and fewer students took the academic courses.

It was not until after World War II that the need for a high school education became widespread. By the 1950s, a majority of teenagers were earning high school diplomas. Although more students were attending high school, not all of them were happy with the curricula and the way they were treated. By the end of the 1960s and into the 1970s, students of color were disrupting many high schools as they confronted discrimination and demanded that their cultures be included in the curricula. High schools entered the 1980s more peacefully, but with more rights for students, in part due to a number of court cases that had been brought by students. The curricula and textbooks began to incorporate content on the experiences and history of people beyond the white, Anglo-Saxon, Protestant male.

Middle-Level Education

At the beginning of the 20th century, psychologist G. Stanley Hall argued that early adolescents were neither children nor adults. He believed that separate education would better serve students between elementary and high school (Beane, 2001). A second reason for the creation of this new level of schooling was to prepare young people for the differentiated comprehensive high school in which they would be sorted into academic and vocational tracks (Urban & Wagoner, 2009).

The first junior high school was established in 1909 in Columbus, Ohio, followed by one in Berkeley, California, in 1910. The number of junior high schools grew over the next few decades, primarily in response to social conditions. Elementary schools were overcrowded with the large influx of immigrant children and the increasing number of students not being promoted to the next grade (Beane, 2001). Four in five students were attending junior high school by 1960 (McEwin, Dickinson, & Jenkins, 2003). For the most part, they had become miniature high schools that were not effectively serving young adolescents.

Still believing that early adolescents deserved an education that was different from that provided in elementary and secondary schools, middle-level educators proposed a new structure. Like junior high schools, middle schools evolved, in part, because of the practicalities of the times. By the late 1950s, the baby boom generation was overcrowding elementary schools, which suggested building more elementary schools. Another option was to add a wing to the high school, move Grade 9 to it from the high school, and move Grades 6–8 from the elementary school. Some communities built a new high school and remodeled the old one for Grades 6–8. Sometimes Grade 5 was also moved into the new intermediate schools.

Middle school advocates argued that schooling for young adolescents should focus on their developmental as well as academic needs. Rather than a large, departmentalized school like high school, their vision was smaller clusters of teachers and students. Teachers and other school professionals in these schools were to provide guidance to help students maneuver through their changing social and physical development. Educators were to be more affectionate and sensitive to young people.

As the popularity of junior high schools declined, the number of middle schools grew quickly from just over 2,000 in 1971 to more than 13,000 by 2015 (Snyder, de Brey, & Dillow, 2018). With the national focus on academics in the 1990s, middle-level educators pushed for curricula that would provide access to academic subjects in a positive and nurturing climate. Teachers were encouraged to use collaborative and cooperative learning with interdisciplinary teams of teachers and block scheduling.

Advocates promoted eliminating the tracking of students and creating heterogeneous groups in which cultural diversity was celebrated and diverse learning styles were recognized.

How to best serve preadolescent students remains an unsettled issue. Critics charge that the middle school philosophy focuses on self-exploration, socialization, and group learning to the detriment of academics. These charges are fueled by poor showings of eighth graders on national and international tests where they rank lower than fourth graders, suggesting that they are losing ground as they progress through the middle grades. Some research suggests that these students would be better served in K–8 schools (Meyer, 2011). You are likely to be engaged in discussions about the value of middle schools as you proceed through your teaching career.

WHAT HAS INFLUENCED THE SCHOOL CURRICULUM?

Curricula have gone through major changes since the first schools were established in the Plymouth colony. They no longer have the religious and moral overtones of the past. However, curricula have been influenced by the changing needs of businesses and evolving new technologies. The intensity of debates among educators, politicians, business leaders, and the public about what should be taught and how it should be taught continues, as reflected in numerous national and state reports about the state of education. Educators today are concerned about the academic performance of their students and providing equal access for all students to learn. In this section, we will examine how curricula have evolved in different historical periods.

The Industrial Revolution

As industrialization took hold in the northeastern cities of the United States at the end of the 19th century, schooling was greatly influenced by the need to help new immigrant populations become literate and disciplined workers. Education was becoming more standardized, compartmentalized, and centralized. The Lancasterian system was promoted as an inexpensive solution for the education of the masses.

The move toward preparing young people to contribute effectively to the Industrial Revolution was assisted by the work of psychologists at the turn of the century. Harvard philosopher and psychologist William James found evidence that the stimulus–response, or behavioral, concepts of learning could be used to help children develop desirable habits. His ideas were expanded by Edward Thorndike, whose ideas of teaching as a science and behaviorism influenced education for the next few decades (Spring, 2018). He also promoted testing as a way of determining which people are suited for which social roles. Thorndike's principles were applied to schools in the popular textbook *Classroom Management* by William Chandler Bagley in 1907, who believed that schools should help students develop the industrial habits needed for the assembly line.

Progressivism: Curricula for Reform

In *Emile*, first published in 1762, European philosopher Jean-Jacques Rousseau questioned education's focus on memorization and the subordination to authority. He thought that learning occurred through experience and discovery. He also believed that moral education should occur in adolescence, not childhood (Urban & Wagoner, 2009). Influenced by Rousseau, Johann Pestalozzi of Switzerland introduced a teaching approach in 1781 that used teaching objects from the real world, learning by doing, and activities rather than seatwork (Urban & Wagoner, 2009).

A philosopher who integrated psychology and pedagogy into his thinking about education, John Dewey opened his laboratory school in Chicago in 1896 to test his progressive ideas about child-oriented curricula. His classrooms had movable tables rather than individual desks to encourage group work and learning (Spring, 2018). Unlike most of his colleagues, Dewey saw education as critical to changing society and preparing students to participate in a democratic society (Urban & Wagoner, 2009).

A colleague of Dewey's at Columbia University, William Heard Kilpatrick, introduced in 1918 the so-called project method that was widely adopted by school districts. The project method developed school activities that were meaningful to students and relevant to society (Urban & Wagoner, 2009).

The progressive movement led to movable furniture, small-group work, and more hands-on work in classrooms.

In the eyes of progressives, traditional curricula with an emphasis on lecture and recitation could not possibly address students' individual needs and learning styles. Progressives believed that curricula must be moderated through activities directed by the learner.

Student-centered instruction had become good practice by the 1940s, and schools were more humane by the 1950s. As progressives pressed for reformed schools that they believed could solve societal problems, they became more vulnerable to criticism for neglecting academic subjects (Urban & Wagoner, 2009). Not to be kept down, progressive thought reappeared in the 1960s and early 1970s, but it was confronted by the **back-to-basics** movement at the end of the 1970s. Nevertheless, it continues to reappear. The progressive ideology continues to be reflected today in charter schools and other schools of choice that have some freedom from the central-office-driven culture.

Many of the practices of the progressive movement are now taken for granted by educators as they rearrange movable furniture, place students in small work groups, and teach an integrated curricula.

TEACHERS' LOUNGE

IT'S OK TO "KID" AROUND

Being a teacher at a school of struggling learners has always been a passion of mine. I love finding new opportunities to connect with my students, and some of my most treasured relationships were built from very rocky beginnings. For the 2013–2014 school year, I entered my first teaching position at a continuation high school in the East Bay [in the San Francisco, California, area]. My students, despite being in English 1 and English 2, ranged from age 16 to 20, with many of them looking over the age of 21. Now, the major concern my family had with me moving three hours away for this position was that I would get chewed up and spit out by these rough-and-tumble kids, especially since I don't look a day over 17. Personally, I was more worried about finding ways to bring positive change and future goals into these struggling students' lives.

Within a few months of school starting, I leapt forward with my first school-wide community-building activity; I encouraged all of the staff to email me responses to several questions about why they taught at the school and how they had struggled as students, and with this information I made personalized posters for every teacher's door. These posters started conversations in every classroom, bringing students and teachers together through their common struggles and through humor, as each poster also included a fun fact about that teacher. (Mine was that I've gone shark fishing in a 10-foot metal canoe, and boy, oh boy, did this spark their interest!)

After seeing how successful this activity was, I was ready to spread more joy, and I had a team of students who were now just as excited as I was about making connections on campus. By the time the school year ended, we had a variety of successful activities, including a Halloween face paint day, where students and teachers arrived two hours early to make up the students who could not afford costumes, and a school-wide anti-bullying day celebrating student differences.

Most important to me, however, was our fund-raiser for the Leukemia and Lymphoma Society. While I was a teacher at the school, my grandmother passed away from a very long battle with lymphoma; this fund-raiser gave me a great opportunity to connect with students and support a great cause. During this fund-raiser, students donated money for two purposes: to raise money for our fund-raiser and to see a teacher kiss a goat. For this fund-raiser, I sat out at lunch with cups that had pictures of each teacher making a goofy "kissing" face, and the students would place their donations in the cup for the teacher they wanted to see kiss the goat.

By the time it was over, our principal and one of the more-popular-for-being-less-popular teachers were tied with me in third. As the last donations came in, I realized the other two staff members weren't so inclined to give that goat a kiss, and I persuaded several students to place their donations in my jar. So during the last week of school, I drove to a friend's house who owns a goat, puckered up, and took a "kiss" for the team. The photo was shared with students school-wide. Not only did we raise over $2,000 for the Leukemia and Lymphoma Society, but our school worked together as a community to make a difference, and have a good laugh.

—Meggie Schultz
English Teacher, Grades 9 and 10
Natomas High School
Natomas, California

Sputnik I

An urgent demand for new curricula and teaching techniques emerged after the Soviet Union launched the first satellite, *Sputnik I*, on October 4, 1957. U.S. leaders were determined to do whatever it would take to regain their nation's scientific and technological supremacy over the Soviet Union during this Cold War period. Congressional resistance to financially supporting education disappeared with the passage of the National Defense Education Act (NDEA) of 1958 to improve curricula and teaching of science, mathematics, and foreign languages. The law also included support for guidance, counseling, testing, and identifying the brightest students. The development of more scientists, mathematicians, and engineers was seen as critical to U.S. prominence in the world, and the federal government began to take its first step toward national curricula (Kliebard, 2004).

The National Science Foundation (NSF) was charged with developing curricula for science and mathematics. Professors in major research universities, rather than professional educators, designed the new curricula that would transform the teaching of science and math in the nation's schools. "New math" was one of the outcomes of this work that changed how math was taught in schools. Math teachers participated in professional development workshops to learn the new math and how to teach basic concepts such as set theory and functions. Although the public generally supported the new focus on reforming schools, they questioned the need for the new math as they struggled to help their children with their homework (Spring, 2018).

New formats for textbooks and ideas for the presentation of relevant subject matter emerged from these projects. Teachers were suddenly presented with an avalanche of choices regarding what and how to teach. There were attribute games and tangrams. Elementary school science packages offered Petri dishes full of fungi and amoebas on order from the local science laboratory (Spring, 2001). Reading texts were organized around literary themes and generalizations relating to the students' own lives. Many teachers benefited from the programs that taught new math and introduced them to new curriculum materials.

The curricula reforms after *Sputnik I* continue to resurface in the nation's discourse about improving education. Today's critics once again are concerned that the United States is falling behind other countries in scientific and technological advances. As a result, achievement on standardized tests is of utmost importance to policy makers. The federal government has called for the recruitment of more students in Science, Technology, Engineering, and Mathematics (STEM). Finally, the Common Core State Standards for mathematics and reading have been adopted or adapted by most states to improve the academic achievement of students and the prominence of the United States in these fields.

Cultural Diversity

As indicated at the beginning of the chapter, the first schools established by the Europeans in the United States were based on the Anglo curricula with which the teachers were familiar. Until the late 19th century, the books and instruction were explicitly based on the Protestant bible. After protests by newly arrived Catholics in the mid-19th century, the curricula and related books became more secular but maintained the Christian values and traditions that continue to be reflected in today's schools.

It was not just the Protestantism that permeated the curricula that was contested by new immigrants. Most ethnic groups that did not have roots in northern or western Europe never saw themselves or their ethnic histories, culture, or traditions in the school or the curricula. In fact, state governments and school officials expected all new immigrants to be Americanized or assimilated into the dominant cultural group. They were expected not only to learn the Anglo culture but also to give up their native culture and language and adopt the Anglo culture as their own. Their native cultures were sometimes denigrated or totally ignored in the curricula. The Americanization program began when the early political leaders planned to "educate" American Indians with the goal of eliminating their American Indian cultures and converting them to Christianity. Many American Indian tribes fought these reeducation programs by establishing their own schools. Other immigrant groups were expected to lose their native cultures and languages when they entered the country, and schools were charged to carry

THINKING DIFFERENTLY
GIRLS CAN CODE TOO

iStock/izusek

Whatever subject or grade you plan to teach, you can be encouraging girls to be involved in Science, Technology, Engineering, and Mathematics (STEM) fields. Computer science is one of the STEM fields in which girls have shown little interest; fewer than one in five of the computer science bachelor degrees in the United States were being earned by females in 2016. Even though tech jobs are among the fastest growing, girls are not being prepared for them, and their interest in computer science drops off as they progress through school.

Punahou School (K–12) in Hawaii reports that the school has been able to increase the number of girls in computer science classes from near 0 to 35% (Kiang, 2018). Female role models have been key in attracting girls to these classes. Having female computer science teachers is one step. Another is having guest speakers meet with students via Skype discussions. They have included females who work as programmers with companies like Microsoft, web developers, and app developers in areas that are of interest to many female students. Designing computer science classes that are appealing to girls as well as boys helps as well. "Emphasizing the purpose of the course (create music) over the tools and language (learn EarSketch or Python) made a big difference" (Kiang, 2018, para. 8).

You can encourage girls as well as boys in your classes to develop the skills for pursuing any of the STEM fields regardless of the socioeconomic status of their families or their racial or ethnic identity. Girls are now learning the basic skills for coding in after-school programs and summer programs/courses offered by Girls Who Code (https://girlswhocode.com), which is available in all 50 states. Black Girls Code (www.blackgirlscode.com) began introducing coding to girls in underrepresented communities through workshops and after-school programs in San Francisco, but has now expanded to seven states and Johannesburg, South Africa. Girls Who Code reports that its alumni are majoring in computer science at a rate 15 times higher than the national average. You can make a great difference to the girls in your classroom and their future careers by helping them become interested in computer science and other STEM fields and letting them know that they too can develop these skills.

out that goal even when African American, Latino, and Asian American students were forced to attend a segregated school.

Not until the civil rights movement in the 1960s and 1970s did curricula begin to reflect cultures other than Anglo American. College students organized campus protests and sit-ins at the offices of university presidents, calling for the recognition and inclusion of their cultures in college curricula. Civil rights activists called for a revision of school curricula to include the cultures and perspectives of the diverse ethnic groups that comprised the U.S. population. Colleges and some schools added ethnic studies courses and programs to the options that students could select along with women's studies and world religions. It has taken much longer to integrate curricula in ways that incorporate the histories and contributions of diverse groups as part of the cultural narrative to which all K–12 students are exposed.

These cultural wars over the content of the curricula continue today as some state and local school boards reject the inclusion of specific people from groups other than European Americans or refuse to include or discuss important events such as slavery and institutional discrimination in accurate and meaningful ways. On one side, citizens still believe that all citizens must adopt the Anglo culture and that the inclusion of the cultures of other citizens will lead to a divisive society. On the other side, citizens value and respect our cultural diversity and see it as a strength as we learn from each other to build a stronger and integrated society.

HOW HAVE TEACHERS EVOLVED?

The role of women in teaching defines the profession. Because of their traditional roles as nurturing mothers, women have been seen as the natural teachers of children. Historically, they have provided a stable, inexpensive, moral teaching force for the country. However, women have not always been the majority of teachers. During the colonial period, teachers were men except in the dame schools. After the Revolutionary War, females began to be recruited as teachers. Teachers today are even more likely to be women than in the 19th century, which may contribute to the lower status attributed to teaching due to the sexism that exists in society.

The emerging pattern in the 19th century was men administrators managing women teachers. The leadership of the NEA was male school administrators, college presidents, and professors throughout most of its first 100 years. Women teachers had to seek permission from the male leadership to speak at the business meetings of the annual conference. The American Federation of Teachers (AFT), on the other hand, evolved from the Chicago Federation of Teachers, where two activist women teachers—Margaret Haley and Catherine Goggin—joined forces with organized labor because they felt they shared the same interests as workers (Spring, 2018).

Teacher Preparation

Teachers of children in the 1700s had not always finished elementary school, although teachers of adolescents may have attended college. The amount of education increased in each century that followed. In the 1800s, a growing number of elementary school teachers completed high school and began to attend teacher institutes and normal schools to further develop their knowledge of the subjects they were teaching as well as their teaching skills. It was not until the mid-1900s that most teachers completed a four-year college, which is now a minimum requirement for a teaching license. Into the mid-1900s, teachers had more education than most members of their community. However, by the beginning of the 21st century, a larger portion of the population had a bachelor's degree than in previous centuries.

To ensure that teachers taught the curricula that educational leaders desired, teacher education programs were developed early in the 19th century. Reverend Samuel Hall is credited with establishing one of the first institutions for preparing teachers in 1823 in Concord, Vermont, but Emma Willard had opened the Troy Female Seminary in 1821, in which women earned the certification that many school boards required. However, certified teachers were not readily available in many rural areas for another century (Spring, 2018).

Normal schools were established in 1839 in Lexington, Massachusetts, to prepare teachers for elementary schools. Most students in normal schools were women who had completed elementary or common schools, but who had not completed high school. Curricula in the normal schools required one to two years of study in which the elementary school curriculum was reviewed, classroom management studied, and teaching methods taught. Many of today's state colleges and universities began as normal schools. They changed their names and expanded their missions beyond the preparation of teachers in the mid-1900s. Today, they continue to prepare the majority of teachers in the country.

Teacher Behavior

Teachers have long been under the control of school boards and administrators. Not only did administrators oversee the work of teachers and select their textbooks, but they also monitored their personal behavior. Teachers were expected to live exemplary moral lives. Their social activities were monitored by school officials throughout the 19th century and into the 20th. Horace Mann in 1840 indicated that a teacher should have "perfect" knowledge of the subject being taught; an aptitude for teaching, which he believed could be learned; the ability to manage and govern a classroom and mold moral behavior; good behavior as a model for students; and good morals (Spring, 2018).

Teachers in the 19th century were predominantly women who were expected to be single and follow strict codes of behavior set by local school boards.

Fotosearch/Stringer/Getty Images

Even though morals were only one of Mann's five qualifications, it appeared to be one of the most important to school superintendents and school board members. Contracts for women teachers did not allow them to socialize with men or be married. The emphasis on high moral character continued into the 20th century as teachers were warned that they should be very careful about their dress and behavior. Although moral character is not included in today's teacher contracts, teachers are still expected by the public to be models of high moral character.

CONNECTING TO THE CLASSROOM

This chapter has provided you with some basic information about how schools and the education of students have evolved to the schools we know today. Below are some key principles for applying the information in this chapter to the classroom.

1. The history of education helps us understand teaching practices that have been tried previously by educators, the reasons for their falling out of favor, and their evolution into new and refined pedagogical strategies.

2. Understanding, respecting, and valuing the histories and experiences of the families of your students will contribute to developing the trust of the families and their children.

3. Teachers in primary, middle, and high schools are expected to provide age-appropriate education or developmentally appropriate education for students based on research on child and adolescent development.

4. Good teachers are able to analyze and evaluate the different curricula packages their school districts are likely to impose on them during their careers and make wise, pedagogically sound decisions about their use in their classrooms.

5. Throughout history, families and the public have expected teachers to be model citizens of high moral character whom children and youth can look up to.

SUMMARY

This chapter reviewed key developments over the past four centuries that established public schools and influenced the schools you know today. The following five major topics were discussed:

- **Establishment of public schools in the United States.** By omitting mention of education, the Constitution gave the responsibility for education to states, which were expected to provide education for their children.

- **Education and equality.** When students of color began attending school, they were enrolled in segregated schools, which did not change until schools were desegregated in the 1960s. The civil rights movement of the 1960s and 1970s was the foundation for ensuring that an equal education could finally be accessible to all children regardless of their race or ethnicity.

- **Schools designed by students' age.** As scholars learned more about child and adolescent development, schools were divided into grade levels to meet the needs of early childhood, elementary, middle-level, and high school students.

- **Historical influences on school curricula.** Curricula were influenced by the country's needs during the Industrial Revolution in the 1800s and the launching of the first satellite by the Soviet Union in 1957. In addition, curricula in today's schools were influenced by the progressive movement in the early 1900s and the incorporation of diverse cultures in the last quarter of the 20th century.

- **The evolution of teaching.** The preparation of teachers has evolved from the requirement for completion of elementary school in colonial days to a college degree and specialized training today.

KEY TERMS

authoritarian 170
back-to-basics 174
catechism 156
charity schools 161
common schools 157

deculturalizing 159
Fourteenth Amendment 162
free and universal education 156
integration 163
Jim Crow laws 163

manifest destiny 159
morals 157
naturalized citizenship 167

CLASS DISCUSSION QUESTIONS

1. Public schools were established in 1635, but there is a movement today toward the privatization of schools. What is the relationship of this issue to debates today about vouchers to attend private schools, charter schools, and decreases in state support of public education? What would be your argument for or against the privatization of schools?

2. Historically, not all children have had access to the same quality of education, sometimes through laws that did not allow children of color either to attend school or to attend school with white students. What factors led to the changes in equal educational opportunity that occurred in the 1960s and 1970s? Identify two to three principles that will guide you in providing equal educational opportunity across the racial and ethnic groups in your classroom.

3. You have probably decided that you want to teach students of a specific age. How should your curriculum and instruction differ from that for older or younger students than the students whom you plan to teach? Why do you want to work with children of this age, and how will you learn the age-appropriate strategies for these students?

4. The Industrial Revolution, progressiveness, *Sputnik I*, and the inclusion of multiple cultures are among societal changes that have impacted school curricula over the past 200 years. What remnants of these events are reflected in today's schools?

5. The education level of today's teachers is much higher than in the past. What conditions appear to remain little changed from the past?

SELF-ASSESSMENT

What Is Your Current Level of Understanding and Thinking About the History of Schools in the United States?

One of the indicators of understanding is to examine how complex your thinking is when asked questions that require you to use the concepts and facts introduced in this chapter. After you answer the following questions as fully as you can, rate your knowledge on the Assessing Your Learning rubric to self-assess the degree to which you understand and can apply the ideas presented in this chapter.

1. Who are some of the key educators and scholars who contributed to the establishment of the common schools in the 1800s and the early childhood and middle school movements in the 1900s?

2. How has the field of child development contributed to the types of schools that exist today?

3. Why were high schools initially established? Why and how have they changed since those early days?

4. What is your current level of understanding of why schools developed into educational settings for students of different age levels?

Assessing Your Learning Rubric

	Parts & Pieces	Unidimensional	Organized	Integrated	Extensions
Indicators	Elements/concepts are talked about as isolated and independent entities. Some important names are provided in isolation.	One or a few concepts are addressed, while others are underdeveloped, or not mentioned.	Deliberate and structured consideration of all key concepts/elements.	All key concepts/elements are included in a view that addresses interconnections.	Integration of all elements and dimensions, with extrapolation to new situations.
Understanding of history of schools by age	Identifies some of the key people involved in establishing common schools, early childhood education, and middle-level education.	Identifies the role of child development in creating the type of schools that exist today.	Describes the development of schools based on the age of students.	Discusses the development of schools based on the age of students and the work of the scholars and educators who contributed to their development.	Explores the major developments over time of the level of the school in which he or she plans to teach and discusses the major issues faced at that school level today.

FIELD GUIDE
FOR LEARNING MORE ABOUT . . .

The History of Schools in the United States

Ask a Teacher	Identify a teacher who has been teaching for more than 10 years and ask him or her to describe some of the curricula packages or programs the school system has asked teachers to use over the years. How long did most of them survive? Why were they successful or not successful? What does the teacher think are keys to a curricula package being successful?
Make Your Own Observations	When you begin teaching, you will probably work in a preschool, a kindergarten, or a primary, elementary, middle, or high school. Your teaching license may allow you to teach at two or more levels. The levels are different not only in the curricula taught but also in the organization of a school day and the interactions of students and teachers. As you observe teachers in schools at two different levels (e.g., middle and high school), make notes of the similarities and differences between the levels. You could organize your notes into a table or narrative. Write a brief paper on what level you would prefer to teach and why.
Reflect Through Journaling	Expectations for education have changed greatly since colonial times. Take a few minutes to reflect in your journal on what has changed and remained the same since the primary goal of education was to learn to read the scriptures and be a moral and patriotic person. In your opinion, what should be the goals of education today?
Build Your Portfolio	What is the largest group of color in your community or state? What do you know about the historical educational experiences of this group in your community or state? Write a brief paper on the historic and current segregation or integration of schools in your area.
	Teachers have a history of not being included as members of committees or panels developing policies to reform education. Why are they not included? How could teachers become more involved in these activities? Prepare a brief paper about the importance of teacher involvement in policy groups that are making recommendations for improving teaching and public schools and how you could become involved in that work.
Read a Book	To gain an understanding of the histories of American Indians, Asian Americans, Latinos, and African Americans that have not made it into the curriculum of most U.S. schools, read *Reclaiming the Multicultural Roots of U.S. Curriculum: Communities of Color and Official Knowledge in Education* by Wayne Au, Anthony L. Brown, and Dolores Calderón (Teachers College Press, 2016).
	In their novel for adolescents, *All American Boys* (Simon & Schuster, 2015), Jason Reynold and Brendan Kiely tell the story of two teenagers—one black and one white—who struggle with the issues of race and police brutality. This book can help young people tackle racism, white privilege, and the stereotypes they have developed from their own experiences.
Search the Web	**U.S. Constitution:** Check out the references to the Constitution of the United States, including the amendments mentioned in this chapter, at www.archives.gov/founding-docs.
	Brown v. Board of Education of Topeka: Listen to NPR's discussion and background on the historic Supreme Court case *Brown v. Board of Education of Topeka* by historians, political leaders, and educators at www.npr.org/news/specials/brown50/.
	Video History of America's Teachers: To review the history of America's teachers in video clips and articles, visit www.pbs.org/onlyateacher/about.html.

STUDENT STUDY SITE

⑤SAGE edge™

Get the tools you need to sharpen your study skills. **SAGE edge** offers a robust online environment featuring an impressive array of free tools and resources.

Access practice quizzes, eFlashcards, video, and multimedia at **edge.sagepub.com/hall3e**.

7 DEVELOPING A PHILOSOPHY OF TEACHING AND LEARNING

© Matthew Balaban

TEACHER INTERVIEW

Mr. Matthew Balaban

Meet Mr. Matthew Balaban. Mr. Balaban is definitely a teacher of global dimensions. His desire for adventure and learning about other cultures took him to Bangladesh, where he taught English classes to seventh, eighth, and ninth graders. He then moved from Dhaka to the American International School of Niamey in Niger, West Africa. There he taught middle school and high school math classes, high school science classes (biology, chemistry, and AP physics), AP psychology, and global leadership to the 30–40 students who made up Grades 6–12. While living in Niger and adjusting to unexpected power cuts, excessive heat, Internet outages, and ever-changing security concerns, Mr. Balaban completed a master's degree through summer courses at the College of New Jersey in its Bangkok offsite program. From Niamey, Mr. Balaban moved to the American International School of Kuwait with over 2,000 students, where he currently teaches mathematics.

Q: What were your school communities like?

A: In Dhaka, my morning and afternoon shifts involved eight or nine daily classes. I like to believe I was able to bring something special to the classroom, especially because native English was so hard to come by there. My students were all Bangladeshi and came from similar backgrounds. In Niamey, students at the American International School mostly came from African nations, but many other countries were represented as well. Because the school was so small, it required me to assume roles other than that of teacher, so I rehearsed music, participated in the facilities committee, and coached softball as well. The American International School of Kuwait is certainly much different from what I experienced in Africa. The students at AIS-Kuwait are primarily from the Gulf countries, with the Kuwaiti population being the largest group. I am curious about how my ideas of effective teaching will grow and about what my future aspirations will look like when my chapter at this school is also complete.

Q: What do you do to make sure that all of your students are learning?

A: In the multi-grade-level classes in Niamey, it was important to group students through differentiated content, depending on their readiness. Before units, I would give pretests I could use to organize the students into content groups and then deliver material through instructional videos I made that the students would watch at home. That way, while groups were learning different things, everyone could still be practicing simultaneously in class.

More generally, I often pursue teaching that's rooted in inquiry in order to bring about learning. Whether it's a crowded Bangladeshi classroom or a conversation about the nuances of trigonometry problem-solving strategies, it always seems that one of my most important jobs is asking good questions. When questions allow us to dig into what we perceive, to access prior "knowledge," to analyze the elements we can tease out, to compare and contrast, to generate implications and predictions, to create conclusions and evaluations, to find and articulate our voices as thinkers—these are the questions that the teacher can use as guides in the dynamic and unsettled process that learning follows. The conclusions that are eventually reached are owned by the learner, but the shared interaction in the classroom plays an unmistakable role in bringing it about.

Q: What brings you joy in teaching?

A: Having studied neuroscience and music in college, I was surprised to find how much I enjoyed discussing the ideas in the short stories we read in the English classes I taught in Bangladesh. Using questions to pick apart thinking and to reveal fundamental underlying understandings was something I found to be fueling and invigorating. Discussions while teaching resulted in powerful moments where I could sense two things simultaneously: a sense of grounding that came from clear shared understanding built up from the very basics and a sense of liberation generated through witnessing all the possible results of our thinking.

Q: Give one example of how you learn as a teacher.

A: Among the many things that made the three years in Niamey memorable, being in a position to continually learn comes to mind first. I learned how to make instructional videos and structure a flipped classroom to meet the varied skill sets of a multi-grade classroom. I revisited material in science and psychology I hadn't seen since high school or college. I engaged in course work to earn my master's degree and interacted with fantastic educators and mentors along the way. Learning keeps us cognitively alive, and for me, this is one of the most important aspects of how I understand teaching and learning.

Q: What stages or phases did you go through in establishing your personal beliefs regarding teaching and learning?

A: Throughout my years as a teacher, I don't think I've undergone major paradigm shifts in the way I approach teaching and learning, but I have certainly gotten the chance to structure my thinking about it. *Constructivism* is one of the many terms that seems to take on various meanings depending on who's talking about it. My favorite take on constructivism is the collection of three premises I came across while doing some research: (1) Understanding emerges through our interactions with the environment, (2) cognitive conflict or "puzzlement" both stimulates learning and determines what is learned and how it is mentally organized, and (3) social negotiation is the main determiner of what we call knowledge by subjecting it to evaluation and discussions of viability. The picture this paints about how we create understanding is an often messy and occasionally uncomfortable one; I think it's important that education acknowledges the value of cultivating in our students the fortitude to navigate the cognitive turbulence of experiencing something not yet understood, guided through reason and discussion that eventually leads to satisfying resolution.

Q: Have your attitudes changed throughout your teaching career?

A: Although we bring our perceptions and past experiences to the table every day when we're asked to learn something new, being presented with something not yet understood inherently results in dissonance with a current mental schema, and maybe that's the true role of our past context in forming new understanding. Maybe foundational knowledge doesn't stay the same, as the foundation of a building does; perhaps instead our old knowledge evolves more dynamically through the "puzzlements" we encounter, resulting in understanding that might look quite different from what we started with. I find it interesting how so many teachers have such a variety of understandings about what education is all about. Discussing them is one reason I like being in education. As long as I'm continuing to evolve my understanding through the negotiation between prior context and novel experiences, I'm both sharing in what students undergo and continuing to enjoy what brought me into education in the first place—the satisfaction of learning something new.

Questions to Consider

Mr. Balaban's personal beliefs regarding teaching and learning did not go through any major paradigm shifts, but he was able to structure his thinking about his beliefs through his various teaching assignments. We all have some predetermined attitudes and beliefs about teaching and learning that will evolve and develop as our teaching experiences change.

1. What are your attitudes and beliefs about teaching and learning?

2. How might you articulate your personal beliefs to another person?

3. What basic educational philosophies would you consider as the basis for your own beliefs?

4. What one way of learning is most enjoyable to you?

5. How do you know that you are learning?

6. What other ways, besides the ones Mr. Balaban mentioned, can teachers use to know if their students are learning?

7. How do you anticipate finding joy in teaching?

INTRODUCTION

Life changes us. Though much of what we believe and the way we act is the result of our genetic code and our early upbringing, experiences do challenge us to change. Being a teacher changes us even more. Every group of students we meet pushes us to change in thought and action. Mr. Balaban sought out circumstances beyond his formative years in order to expand his knowledge and to test his beliefs and attitudes about teaching and learning. While there may not have been a drastic change in his attitudes, he clearly modified them with each new teaching assignment.

It is always a good idea to enter a classroom with a mental picture of yourself as a teacher and learner, your sensitivity to others' codes of conduct, your understanding of what schooling is and what you believe it should be, and, most important, your ability to put your own needs and desires behind those of others. One way you can examine the assumptions you have about teaching and learning is through creating your own educational philosophy. Knowledge about teaching and learning is most useful to teachers when past knowledge is constantly rearranged and integrated with new ideas and new experiences. The knowledge, skills, attitudes, and opinions we all bring to any situation have a powerful influence on our behavior and expectations. What we have learned and practiced, and what we have gained from experiences both favorable and not so favorable, causes us to create a personal perspective toward life (*isms*, if you will) that influences everything we think and do.

Naturally, what teachers know and are able to do has changed over time, but teachers are always motivated by their assumptions (e.g., Do you believe there is some knowledge that all students must learn? Should there be a greater emphasis on the arts in the school curriculum? Is the well-being of students more important than what they learn?). Learning to teach and how to apply what you know about your assumptions toward students and schooling is truly a developmental process. In this chapter, you will begin to understand why it is important for teachers to confront the assumptions that guide their behavior and practice in classrooms.

HOW DO TEACHERS DEVELOP PERSONAL PHILOSOPHIES TOWARD TEACHING AND LEARNING?

Everyone operates from a personal philosophy. We know what makes sense to us, what is important, and what is good. When you become a teacher, you take your personal vision of the world into the classroom with you. This personal vision affects everything you do in your classroom and with your students. It is necessary to understand your philosophical perspectives so that you can understand and reflect on what you are doing and why you are doing it. Teachers who do not know or understand themselves can be of little service to the students in their classrooms. Or as Confucius put it, "What has one who is not able to govern himself to do with governing others?"

Neil Bright begins the preface of his book, *Rethinking Everything: Personal Growth Through Transactional Analysis* (2015), with a quote from Friedrich Nietzsche: "We knowers are unknown to ourselves, and for good reason; how can we ever find what we have never looked for?" In looking for ourselves, Bright introduces us to Eric Berne's theory of transactional analysis. The tenets of this theory may help teachers to develop positive communication with their students as well as increase their potential as effective teachers. Knowledge of what we can achieve is certainly an initial step in achieving it.

Developing a Personal Philosophy of Teaching

An educational philosophy consists of the beliefs and principles that guide teaching and learning practices. Teacher education candidates are usually asked to draft a statement that organizes their thinking about how students learn and how teachers should teach. Revisiting this original philosophy statement over time throughout your program and throughout your career is one way you can keep track of your growth as a professional. As you acquire more wisdom and encounter new ideas, you will develop new attitudes and opinions that will cause changes to your personal philosophy. Understanding can be achieved only through an examination of what you have learned about teaching and learning and how well you are able to articulate your perspectives. Figure 7.1 is an example of one teacher's effort to come to grips with the curriculum she is asked to teach and her philosophical perspective on teaching.

FIGURE 7.1 ■ A Personal Philosophy Example

Studying curriculum development has activated a completely different learning experience for me, as an educator. I began to realize teachers have a big voice in the modeling of curriculum and can be fully involved in the decision of developing or predetermining the curriculum used in the classroom and/ or school. As I reflected on my personal philosophy of teaching, I began to understand the influence a school and community can have on your strengths or weaknesses. For example, I fell heavily on the belief of essentialism because I immediately understood I needed to meet certain requirements and criteria as a teacher from administration, the community, parents, and of course my students. Within my belief of essentialism, my role as the teacher is to provide the essentials asked to teach by the community, families, administration, and the school district with the resources, knowledge, and values I am given or seek out. Essentialism made me understand the demands this profession requires, but I have become interested in the progressive view on education.

Progressivism aligns with my belief of what the nature of the learner is. Learning increases when students undertake meaningful activities (Dewey, 1963). I have experienced while I am implementing and trying to follow through with the curriculum design that interaction between students and students or students and teacher is what allows the engagement of the learners to increase. So I do think my instructional practice has changed during this semester because of the reflection of my own educational philosophy, the research on the models of curriculum, and the constant study of efficient curriculum design.

The demands are high as an educator and especially as a curriculum developer. I have become more collaborative within my school meetings in regards to curriculum because I feel more confident after taking this course. I have also begun to increase the implementation of student discourse, modifications of curriculum to meet the needs of my diverse learners, and piecing together my own resources to develop higher engagement and proficiency in my classroom. So far, the rewards are great. My students' test scores are increasing every month on math and reading. My intrigue in more involved collaboration has led to some great co-taught lessons and data collection as a grade level to decide on a curriculum design.

The most beneficial reflection I've had this semester was because of John Dewey. I strongly believed that the three philosophies I chose at the beginning of the semester would educate me on "fixing the traditional" education. But after reading Dewey's Experience and Education, *I understood the break in my own thinking. Progressive education argues that experience is the answer to reinventing education from the traditional framework, but Dewey argues that there was never an issue of not having experiences in the traditional education, but that those experiences were wrong. It's okay to modify traditional experiences like student discourse, but doing that with technology is where essentialism and progressivism come into play.*

—Raquel Cordova, Second-Grade Teacher

I know an English composition teacher who requires students to attach all previous drafts of a composition to the final copy that is being submitted. This allows the teacher to evaluate students' growth in writing ability and also to see whether students have incorporated or learned from the teacher's editorial comments. The final packets can be rather substantial, but they do illustrate effort and the process of coming to a final product. Keeping copies of your original and subsequent philosophy statements will provide you with a graphic representation of the changes in your thinking as you become more knowledgeable about teaching.

Whether it's fair or not, you will be expected to do the same job on your first day of work as a veteran of 5 or 10 years. Logically, this doesn't seem possible, but who can argue with the fact that the children in your classroom deserve no less than the children in Mrs. Z's room even though she has been teaching for 20 years? Beginning teachers may react to this dilemma by performing certain actions that make them appear capable of keeping up with their more experienced colleagues, even when those actions don't exactly mesh with their own personal philosophy of teaching. Nothing can be more exhausting than maintaining a false front or upholding the assumptions of others. Ideas need time to percolate in the reality of full-time teaching.

Questions that you might be expected to respond to when you are asked to develop your personal attitude/beliefs statement about teaching and learning include the following:

- What is the role of the teacher?
- What is the role of the students?
- What is the purpose of schooling?
- What curriculum should be taught in schools?
- How should this curriculum be taught?
- What is the point of learning?

Once you have responded to these questions, you will have a beginning point from which to revise your responses based on any changes in philosophical perspective. If you are in a practicum experience and having opportunities to teach, think about how your philosophy of teaching is incorporated within your teaching behaviors.

There are always more questions than answers in life, but as your answers to the above questions begin to take shape, your idea of who you will be as a teacher will fall into place. You will also begin to understand the many ways your opinions can shape your teaching behavior and practice. Knowing why you are doing what you are doing will give you confidence. Having a firm belief regarding your place in the teaching profession will provide you a solid foundation from which to try out new ideas—something teachers are always challenged to do. Anyone attempting to cross a rushing stream on rocks must make sure his or her footing is secure before taking each step. Believe it or not, sometimes classrooms can resemble rushing streams.

The Influence of Stories in Building a Personal Philosophy of Teaching

There are defining moments in everyone's life. We tell stories about them. Stories are powerful. We all remember a good story, whether true or not. Stories can alter our perception of things. That's one reason the news media and television are so powerful. The stories we hear and tell can frighten us or evoke courage. Sooner or later, the stories we tell about our lives become our lives. We can make the stories we tell about our lives healthy or destructive. The choice is ours. Stories provide us with ideas, actions, and tools for working toward goals. Stories are what Robert Coles (1989) refers to as "reservoirs of wisdom" (p. xii).

Many of the professors in the institution where you are preparing to be a teacher have been classroom teachers or still are. They may work in classrooms, serve as mentors for new teachers, or work with teachers in Professional Development seminars. They have had the benefit of experience to help them mold their philosophies of teaching. They have no doubt kept track of their professorial careers through portfolios and tenure and promotion files. Talk to them about the defining teaching moments in their lives that helped them construct a specific approach to teaching. Teaching is a people profession. People like to talk and tell stories about their lives.

Researchers and writers have looked at teachers and listened to their stories of teaching to unravel the mysteries of the profession (Lieberman & Miller, 1984; Lortie, 1977). Clark and Peterson (1986) listened to teachers talk about planning. They then mapped these stories into flowcharts for new generations of teachers to follow and learn from. Ester Wright (1999) says, "There is a moment when the struggle to master an activity or subject ceases and the action becomes familiar and regimented. Teaching is hundreds of such moments, strung together to create a career" (p. 11). As you try out your ideas, you will become more familiar and therefore comfortable with what works in a variety of contexts. You are fortunate to be learning to teach in this period of time. Life is full of choices, and many of those choices add depth and breadth to your ultimate practice in the classroom. What happens in classrooms will continue to accommodate evolving ideas and trends about which learning is of most worth.

Defining Events in Building a Personal Philosophy of Teaching

Certainly, high-profile events on the education scene affect the type of teaching and the content you are required to study. Knowing the effect certain events have had on teaching and learning when you were a student will help you better understand your own philosophical perspectives toward schooling. There have been defining moments in society as well as in our own lives. We learn about defining moments in the world of education in history and foundations of education courses. Defining moments change the way we go about our business. In many ways, the launch of *Sputnik* in 1957 was a 9/11 of the mind. It changed the ways Americans thought about the future. It initiated a reexamination of the purpose of schooling and school curriculum. The National Science Foundation (NSF) made millions of federal dollars available for the development of modern science, mathematics, and engineering programs and materials. Another defining moment was the publication of *A Nation at Risk: The Imperative for Educational Reform* (National Commission on Excellence in Education, 1983), which prompted a renewed focus on student achievement and the condition of schooling in America. In hindsight, the reaction to some events may seem ludicrous, but at that moment in time, politicians and policy makers believed certain actions were mandatory.

Keeping a record of your own stories of teaching and events in a journal or diary can also help you build a data reference system for comparing new ideas you encounter with the old ones you have used. The act of looking back to remember which way you've come is a device that has been used by travelers and learners for centuries. From time to time, you need to revisit your journey to becoming a teacher with a critical eye. By checking where you've come from, you will have a better idea where you are headed. Looking back can help you assess the defining moments in your Professional Development and prepare for the future.

Teaching should not be slap dash or something you might be rushing to get done with while you are thinking of something else. Teaching must be focused, done with purpose and with a clear understanding of who you are and your beliefs about what teachers should do, what students should do, what schools should be, what curriculum should be taught, how it should be taught, and what the purpose of learning is.

Taking Stock of Your Beliefs

Teachers can become exhausted operating under expectations counter to what they believe. For many first-year teachers, discouragement raises its ugly head about mid-December when they begin to realize that the theories they have put into practice are not working. Formulating who you are going to be as a teacher will prepare you to act on your beliefs and assumptions rather than someone else's. When you do this, you increase your chances of success and happiness as a teacher.

All teachers have some idea of how their future classroom will appear.

Using tenets of known philosophies as keystones for developing your own philosophy about teaching and answering some of the questions these philosophies pose can help you decide who you will be as a teacher. Do you think that the world is an orderly, logical place, or do you see it as chaotic and random? Obviously, these two views would have a strong influence on how, for example, you arrange your classroom and lessons. Do you learn by repetition or by connecting new information to what you already know? Do you prefer to discover information for yourself or have it delivered to you in an organized outline? What senses do you find most important? In other words, how do you learn about the world around you?

Do you believe there are clear rights and wrongs in life (black and white), or is life a series of slightly differing shades of gray? Do you feel it is possible to understand everything if enough intelligence and logic are applied, or do you believe some things must simply be taken on faith? Are you an abstract or random learner? Linear or global? There is so much to learn and so little time.

Taking Stock of Your Students

Every child is an individual, a smaller-sized person than most of the people you socialize with, but no less individual in opinions and thinking. Any toddler will in some ways represent the adult he or she will become. We all have a friend who can't follow the simplest directions, or one who asks the same question over and over until you answer it in a way that makes sense to her, or one who never shows up on time and may even forget the day you were supposed to meet. Frustrating, at times, yes, but we try to understand them and help them understand us. Humans (friends, relatives, and students) have so much to learn that any single theory or simple approach to helping them just won't do. Teacher-focused and student-focused approaches to teaching and learning combined can encompass the spectrum of philosophical perspectives that underpin decision making and curriculum in education. It is teachers' responsibility to continually question what to teach and how to teach it, and to learn about and develop skill in using methods that have their roots in philosophical approaches to teaching that may differ from their own.

When classroom teachers puzzle over which educational goals should be met and how these goals might be achieved through teaching practices, they are dealing with questions about knowing, learning, and teaching. In Plato's discussion of epistemology, he argued that in order to grasp reality or knowledge, individuals use understanding, reason, perception, and imagination.

Teachers implement Plato's ideas of knowing when they plan and structure lessons and decide which methods are most appropriate to a specific learning task. As you progress in your teacher education course work, you will no doubt become very familiar with the theory of constructivism or constructivist teaching. When you study this approach to teaching and learning, think of it as an epistemological view. Constructivist approaches to teaching take into account the ways that children learn and what conditions are necessary to promote such learning. The theory of constructivism ponders how knowing is achieved.

HOW DO STUDENTS LEARN?

Mr. Balaban engaged students in discussions of short stories they had read to help the students "navigate the cognitive turbulence of experiencing something not yet understood." Through questioning and discussions, he presented the students with ideas that did not mesh easily with their current mental schema and helped them form new understanding. Student learning can be realized when a teacher takes time to understand the students themselves and how they learn as individuals.

Few modern educators would argue that there is but a single way to learn, or a single way to teach the skills, facts, and concepts deemed essential to a contemporary education. However, there are those who would argue

Recognizing the ways students learn can help teachers design engaging lessons.

iStock/Steve Debenport

Plant (metaphor) →

that one particular way of teaching is inherently better or more efficient than another. Listen to teachers talk about how they teach their students to read or spell, and chances are that you will hear quite different philosophies regarding learning, methods, and materials. Such discussions often generate more heat than enlightenment and provide proof of the value we place on our own firmly held assumptions.

Ideas about how students learn are in abundance, and since not all ideas are of equal value, it can be difficult to weed out the good from the bad. Some ideas are priceless. Some are not. Some are in direct conflict with one another. Ideas germinate in knowledge and are driven by opinions, beliefs, assumptions, experiences, and the context in which the ideas blossom. Unfortunately, in education, as in all areas of life, some good ideas are stamped out before they have a time to blossom, while some bad ideas flourish in unguarded cultures.

As you progress through your teacher education program, you will encounter many ideas about how students learn. Such ideas are often based in one or another of the established philosophies of life. There will be more about these established philosophies later in the chapter. Good ideas about how students learn can come out of educational research conducted by professors and research centers dedicated to the study of teaching and learning. Good ideas also emerge from teacher educators and teachers practicing their craft, collecting data, and making grassroots changes in practice. Some of the teachers who have generated great ideas for future generations of teachers and learners are famous. Some are not, but all have, through thinking about teaching and learning, contributed to the profession.

Ideas About How Students Learn

Great minds in American education wrestle with ideas of what should be taught in America's schools, how it should be taught, and when it should be taught. As American education has evolved, a number of approaches and programs to promote students' learning have been tried. Nearly everyone you talk to has some idea about what should be happening in school. The popular press has nearly as much to say about teaching and learning as educators. The range of ideas teachers are confronted with is staggering.

Numerous ideas about structuring curriculum and methods for delivering the curriculum have been tried, revamped, and tried again. Teachers who have been around for any length of time and have experienced the ebb and flow of programs and approaches to teaching will tell you that many of the new programs they are asked to implement are really only revamped versions of tried-and-true methods. The fact is that data collected on some of these tried-and-true methods are frequently used to improve those methods. Constant thinking about teaching can lead to new ideas that will improve education for teachers and learners alike.

While educators know an informed populace helps build a democratic society, they do not know exactly what skills a six-year-old of today will need 30 years down the line in order to be successful and to contribute to the well-being of society. The constant generation of ideas about teaching and learning is one way educators attempt to imagine and prepare for the future. The following sample of individuals who have generated ideas about teaching and learning ranges from the recent past to the present, and from the famous to those who may be known only to a local community or school district. Their ideas provide a cross section of ways thinking about education has affected schooling and how students learn.

The Western world's first great philosophers came from Athens, Greece. The names of three of these philosophers are no doubt familiar to you: Socrates (470–399 BCE), Plato (427–347 BCE), and Aristotle (384–322 BCE). Socrates is famous for creating the Socratic method of teaching still used by many teachers today who ask a series of questions that lead the student to a certain conclusion. Plato believed that each person's abilities should be used to serve society and should be developed to the person's fullest capacity. Aristotle favored the scientific, the practical, and the objective in learning, and believed that the quality of a society was determined by the quality of the education that society promoted.

As you read about the good ideas of the following educators, you might discover similarities among their ideas that discuss ways we learn and should be taught.

John Dewey (1859–1952)

It would be folly to try to adequately cover in this chapter the contributions of John Dewey's ideas to how students learn best. Suffice it to say he was a giant among the thinkers of the 20th century.

For more than 50 years, Dewey's ideas helped shape the destiny of education in America. Dewey's thoughts on pedagogy and epistemology (knowing) and his pragmatic approaches to ethics and aesthetics remain influential in education today. You should become familiar with Dewey's ideas as you progress through your teacher education course work. His ideas can provide a basis for you to establish your own pedagogical vision.

Dewey established the Chicago Laboratory School for the purpose of testing the sociological implications of his educational theories and the effect his theories had on student learning. Dewey called his laboratory school a "miniature society," an "embryonic community" in which children learned collaboratively by working together to solve problems (Martin, 2002, pp. 199–200). Dewey described "the fundamental factors in the educational process as (1) the learner, (2) society, and (3) organized subject matter" (Saylor & Alexander, 1974, p. 7).

Dewey's ideas in *The School and Society* (1943) have remarkable significance for the field of education as we now know it. His ideas about the needs, the problems, and the possibilities of education are detailed in *Experience and Education* (1963), perhaps the most concise statement on education ever written.

Dewey devised a five-step, process-oriented method for students to approach problem solving:

1. Encountering a problem that needs to be solved

2. Defining the problem and asking questions that will help clarify exactly what needs to be solved

3. Collecting information about the problem

4. Making tentative hypotheses and reflecting on possible actions and outcomes

5. Acting on a hypothesis that is likely to solve the problem

Problem solving using the scientific method, action, and empirical testing is considered by many to be the most effective strategy for helping students learn. Dewey believed that schools should teach children not what to think, but how to think through "continuous reconstruction of experience" ("John Dewey," n.d.).

Hilda Taba (1902–1967)

This Estonian-born U.S. educator spent much of her professional career contemplating ideas concerned with the development of thinking skills in students. Hilda Taba believed that information must be organized for students to understand it. She developed concept development and concept attainment strategies to help students learn. Her instructional model is based on three levels of knowledge: facts, basic ideas, and principles and concepts. She based her teaching model on three main assumptions:

1. Thinking can be taught.

2. Thinking is an active transaction between the individual and data.

3. Processes of thought evolve by a sequence that is "lawful." (Joyce & Weil, 2000, p. 131)

According to Taba (1962), "efforts to develop thinking take a different shape depending on whether the major function of education is seen as fostering creative thinking and problem solving or as following the rational forms of thinking established in our classical tradition. As such, differences in these concepts naturally determine what are considered the essentials and the dispensable frills in education" (p. 30).

Taba was famous for her work in concept development in social studies, and her ideas can be easily applied in a classroom to promote student learning.

Jerome Bruner (1915–2016)

Jerome Seymour Bruner was an American psychologist who made significant contributions to cognitive learning theory in educational psychology. He held that the outcome of cognitive development is thinking. The intelligent mind creates from experience "generic coding systems that permit one to go beyond the data to new and possibly fruitful predictions" (Bruner, 1957, p. 234) and become an autonomous learner. Bruner (1962) studied how we acquire, retain, and transform knowledge of the world in which each of us lives—a world in part "outside" us, in part "inside" us (p. 3). He proposed three modes of the ways in which information or knowledge is stored and encoded in memory:

- Enactive representation (action-based information or motor tasks)

- Iconic representation (image-based—storing a mental picture)

- Symbolic representation (language-based—knowledge is stored primarily as words, math symbols, etc.)

Bruner stressed the importance of language that makes it possible for individuals to code stimuli and frees them from the constraints of dealing only with appearances, to provide a more complex yet flexible cognition.

Ralph W. Tyler (1902–1994)

Ralph W. Tyler's innovative ideas made him one of the most influential men in American education. Tyler believed that successful teaching and learning could be determined by scientific study, but he stressed that evaluation should start with objectives and should not rely entirely on a statistical process. His insights into educational evaluation affected the lives of generations of students whose performance and potential are frequently tested. As director of the Eight-Year Study (1933–1941), he helped convince the educational community that schools that offer programs that are interesting and useful to their students can help students become successful in college.

Tyler's 83-page book, *Basic Principles of Curriculum and Instruction*, published in 1949, made an indelible mark on teaching practices in the American public schools. This short text was originally the syllabus for one of Tyler's courses at the University of Chicago. In the text, Tyler espoused four basic ideas for developing a curriculum that would promote student learning. These four basic ideas, listed here, remain as relevant for teachers today as they were 60 years ago, and continue to serve as a framework for selecting appropriate strategies to use to connect the learner with the content:

1. Define appropriate learning objectives.

2. Establish useful learning experiences.

3. Organize learning experiences to have a maximum cumulative effect.

4. Evaluate the curriculum and revise those aspects that do not prove to be effective.

By using Tyler's ideas, teachers become scientific observers of student behavior, checking for evidence of student learning and making modifications to plans when necessary to guarantee results. Tyler's ideas are so powerful, functional, and easy to apply that they are still widely implemented in public schools today.

Robert M. Gagné (1916–2002)

Robert M. Gagné's theory of "task analysis" required that a learning hierarchy be developed by working backward from the final goal of the learning so that each prerequisite for the learning process could be determined and presented in a meaningful sequence. His approach to training using the task analysis model identified the mental conditions necessary for effective learning. Interestingly, pilots for World War II fighters were trained in just this way.

According to Norton and Wilburg (1998), Gagné's (1965) model for design of instruction includes a sequence of nine instructional events and its corresponding learning processes that guide the design of instruction.

Paulo Freire (1921–1997)

Paulo Freire's idea that the process of education can never be neutral and that education should provide nontraditional educational opportunities grew out of his efforts among illiterate poor workers in Brazil. Helping the workers learn to read and write led him to recognize the ways education can result in powerful changes among people and governments. In 1967, Freire published *Education as the Practice of Freedom*, and in 1970, he published the *Pedagogy of the Oppressed* in English.

Briefly stated, Freire posits that education is a political act—the way students are taught and what they are taught serves a political agenda. The purpose of education should be the liberation of the "oppressed" (i.e., those not currently in control of the political agenda) through nontraditional forms and through their own examples, and not through the models presented by the oppressors. Education can help the oppressed overcome their status as long as they play a role in their own education. Freire's ideas encouraged educators to consider the political aspects of the institution of education, thereby bringing a new perspective to teaching and learning in the form of critical pedagogy. Critical pedagogy presents a philosophical perspective toward teaching and learning that seeks to "cultivate in students a healthy skepticism about power, a willingness to temper any reverence for authority with a sense of critical awareness" (Giroux, 2010).

Eleanor Duckworth (1935–)

Eleanor Duckworth, a professor at Harvard Graduate School of Education, grounded her approaches to teaching and learning in Jean Piaget's (1896–1980) insights into the nature and development of intelligence. Duckworth developed Piaget's research methods into a critical exploration approach to helping students learn. According to Duckworth, ideas are the essence of intelligence. Through her research, she has demonstrated that there are many ways of knowing and that different paths can be taken to understanding similar concepts (Duckworth, 1996).

Duckworth's ideas provide exceptional insight into the blossoming of ideas, how they are nurtured, and how they grow. She discusses the detrimental effect teachers who view learning from only one perspective can have on the wonderful ideas of their students. She encourages teachers to explore their students' intelligence rather than turn it off in the pursuit of conventions and standardized ways of thinking. This may seem difficult given the current standardized assessment culture in American education. Duckworth's ideas require that teachers engage in intellectual conversation with their students—that teachers make time to listen to students' explanations so they may recognize the students' wonderful ideas.

[handwritten margin note: there are many ways of knowing]

[handwritten margin note: explore student's intelligence rather than turning it off]

Howard Earl Gardner (1943–)

In his 2011 text, *Frames of Mind: The Theory of Multiple Intelligences*, Gardner presented the idea that intelligence cannot be determined by only one measure. He created a list of seven ways of learning and demonstrated how some are typically valued in school, some are usually associated with the arts, and some are what he termed "personal intelligences." In brief, these are the seven ways of learning defined by Gardner:

1. Linguistic intelligence: the ability to learn, understand, and use language

2. Logical-mathematical intelligence: the ability to think logically and scientifically

3. Musical intelligence: the ability to recognize musical patterns and compose music

4. Bodily-kinesthetic intelligence: the ability to direct bodily movements through mental abilities

5. Spatial intelligence: the ability to recognize dimensions of large and confined spaces

6. Interpersonal intelligence: the ability to understand and work effectively with others

7. Intrapersonal intelligence: the ability to understand oneself and to regulate one's life

By helping educators think about the many ways intelligence can be understood and demonstrated, Gardner provided teachers a rationale for designing lessons in ways that would engage all students in learning.

Grant Wiggins (1950–2015)

Grant Wiggins was perhaps most famous for his ideas on curriculum expressed in *Understanding by Design*, second edition (2005), which he coauthored with Jay McTighe. Understanding by Design (UbD) presents a framework for improving student learning and helps teachers create learning goals, build engaging activities, and develop authentic assessments. Four ideas for improving student learning inherent in UbD are (1) that topics taught should be covered in depth rather than breadth, (2) that goals and assessments should be established prior to instruction, (3) that teachers should collaborate in planning lessons and units for students, and (4) that materials should be adjusted according to student success. One of the subcomponents of UbD is backwards design, encouraging teachers to consider the end goal in deciding what is most important for students to learn. Wiggins's ideas encourage teachers to improve student learning by exploring essential questions and big ideas.

National Teachers of the Year

In Chapter 1 of this text, you were introduced to Sydney Chaffee, 2017 Teacher of the Year. She has lots of great ideas to help her students learn. Visit the website for Teachers of the Year and hear the good ideas these teachers have come up with. These teachers have translated their great ideas into lessons that enrich the lives of students. Hero teachers are teachers who have good ideas, put them into practice, and share them with others. This is not always the easiest thing to do when working on the front lines of teaching, but good ideas should be disseminated to inspire learning and more "good" ideas.

Conflicting Perspectives in Teaching and Learning

There is a back-and-forth nature to the struggle to educate. Perpetual controversy over one or another reigning educational philosophy and the give-and-take regarding ideas about classroom practices often create a cyclical effect. Ideas in education have been batted back and forth like Ping-Pong balls, falling out of favor only to be, at some later date, reembraced as brilliant. Education is neither here nor there, one way or another. It is what works, and what actually works is not always most commonsensical.

During the 1960s, a period of unprecedented upheaval and change in the field of education in America, two men in particular, Jerome S. Bruner and David P. Ausubel, came to symbolize a dichotomy of viewpoints regarding the methods and means of teaching and learning, and, between them, defined the terms of a debate that continues to this day.

For his part, Bruner theorized that by categorizing one's environment, a learner is better able to comprehend it. Bruner's learning theory, which emphasized the structure of disciplines and the use of inquiry—or what came to be called the discovery method—stressed the importance of teaching the sort of thinking skills necessary to the development of problem-solving abilities. His Concept Attainment Theory was based on the technique of combining rules learned by discovery into a concept the learner is desired to understand. This discovery or experience of the learner is the moving force that Dewey described as central to learning.

It was Ausubel's view, on the other hand, that the teacher's major task is to transmit large bodies of already organized knowledge to the learner through a reception–receptive method—the relationship between the way knowledge is organized and the manner in which the mind works to process such information. Ausubel (1967), considered the more traditional of the two thinkers, was opposed to most learning activities that could be described as discovery, and believed that discovery was not an indispensable condition for the occurrence of meaningful learning.

Bruner (1966) was attempting to find new answers to basic questions of how students learn, and from there to lead learners to construct models of reality on their own terms. Ausubel (1963) was adamantly opposed to passive learning on the part of the student, and unyielding in his insistence that receptive learning could be meaningful, arguing that just because learning by reception implies the material is presented rather than discovered does not make it inherently passive and less meaningful.

Oddly enough, within their theories are many broad areas of agreement that have never been of much interest to the warrior-pedagogues of the continuing methods wars. Though Ausubel did not deny the usefulness and practicality of problem-solving skills, he regarded knowing as a substantive phenomenon, not as a problem-solving capability.

The Necessity of Evaluating Ideas

What could be better than always having the right answer? A quick, right answer in the classroom and on timed standardized tests is always appreciated. Unfortunately, quick, right answers measure what students have already mastered, not what they are in the process of figuring out. Learning is, however, the process of understanding concepts; for many of us, the understanding of complex concepts does not take the form of quick, right answers. Think about the process you have gone through in your teacher education course work: Facts and concepts that you learned early in your program will take on more meaning as your experiences with the concepts in action increase. You may have been able to recite ideas expressed by your professors, but ideas do not become part of your teaching schema until you have figured them out through thoughtful action.

Schooling in the recent past put a greater emphasis on a right answer than how the student came to that answer. Currently, the implementation of the Common Core State Standards is an attempt to produce students who are problem solvers and thinkers and not just those focused on the right answer. Schools have so much to teach and so little time to teach it that finding the right answer or solution in the shortest amount of time may seem the direction to take. However, of what value is knowing something if we don't know how to use that knowledge or use it to help us learn more? You will hear a lot about the breadth and depth of knowledge and understanding. One point of view is that if we learn something and learn it through the right process, then we will be able to transfer that process of learning to other tasks.

Unfortunately, society today seems more concerned with how a world-class golfer thinks through a shot to the green or a putt, or how cyclists prepare for different legs of the Tour de France, than how a seventh grader learns to appreciate the elements of literary style in a compelling story about the death of a favorite pet. On more than one occasion, we have posed a question to a group of our friends only to have them turn to their smartphones to see who can come up with an answer the quickest when it was not an answer we were looking for, but rather a conversation. Your mission as a teacher, should you choose to accept it, is to help your students recognize the routes they have taken to finding the right answers, and that those paths represent learning as much as a right answer does.

[handwritten margin note: the path one takes in inquiry is important]

Having a Research-Based Perspective

Some ideas that seem good have been held through long-standing beliefs. They are what we have come to know through experience, and they stick with us regardless of how the facts or our environment change. Jerome Kagan's book *Three Seductive Ideas* (1998) challenges some basic assumptions the social sciences have held about intelligence, child development, and motivation. His arguments are based on research and give teachers, both new and experienced, some ideas to ponder about the way we conduct business in classrooms. William James (1975), a 20th-century pragmatist, said that new knowledge derived from new experiences is absorbed slowly into firmly held prejudices and beliefs so that old knowledge is maintained and unaltered as much as possible to maintain one's equilibrium of thought.

Theory and practice are fundamental to how we organize and think about our intellectual and practical world. Ideas and theories sometimes prevail and sometimes take a back seat to the driving force of practicality. It may be an unfortunate fact that many teachers consider application the only relationship between theory and practice when, in reality, the relationship is ever more complicated. When teachers test ideas, they have a better chance of detecting those that contain flaws based on beliefs and assumptions. Each of us could probably make a list of the bad ideas we have had. Sometimes we're lucky not to put our bad ideas into action; sometimes, after the fact, we have proof that they were bad ideas, and we don't try them again.

Great ideas and grand plans for educating the children and young adults of this country can come from a variety of sources. Such thoughts may spring forth from the minds of the country's leaders, as they did from Thomas Jefferson, or from the minds of business executives such as Andrew Carnegie, or from the minds of thoughtful teachers, or from the minds of leaders in the field of education like John Dewey. While tried-and-true ideas are being implemented, newer and seemingly more radical ideas are being proposed. The continuous flow of refreshing ideas is part of the reason many of us have been drawn to the profession. Teachers constantly work with ideas. Teachers also represent a rich pool of creative thinking that has the power to stimulate major changes in education as well as in student learning. Translating ideas into practice is a heavy responsibility and takes a courageous heart. In order to fulfill this responsibility, teachers must be knowledgeable of the ideas of numerous others who have encountered the same concerns and have established theories that have practical application in teaching and learning.

HOW DOES EDUCATIONAL PSYCHOLOGY HELP TEACHERS UNDERSTAND STUDENT LEARNING?

Knowing stages in a child's development is important to understanding ways students can learn. When fifth graders start the year, they exhibit behaviors that would be considered immature for fifth graders. However, after about six weeks, teachers usually note a big change in the way students act in class: They are more responsible about their work and demonstrate the attitudes and behavior expected of fifth graders. By the end of the year, they are truly ready to go on to middle school.

Since you are studying to be a teacher, you will no doubt take a course in educational psychology. The role of research in educational psychology is to carefully examine certain questions about factors that may contribute to learning. Such research can help you interpret your experiences and understand why you teach and learn the ways you do. Educational psychology is a branch of applied psychology that studies children in educational settings. It deals with the psychological aspects of teaching and learning processes of early childhood, adolescence, and adulthood. Educational psychology is concerned with the assessment of ability and aptitude, and the evaluation of teaching and learning (Lucas, Blazek, Raley, & Washington, 2005).

Research on Teaching and Learning

Perhaps the first research on learning occurred when people began to ask, Why? Why do I know how to do that? How did I learn that? What do I need to know now? Or when philosophers began to ask questions related to the state of knowing. Research that attempts to explain what we know and learn is deeply ingrained in the history of learning. Some important events in the establishment of educational research include, but are not limited to, the following list. Many of the names will be familiar to you.

1690: John Locke publishes *An Essay Concerning Human Understanding*.

1802: Johann Pestalozzi publishes *How Gertrude Teaches Her Children*.

1896: John Dewey establishes the laboratory schools in Hyde Park, Chicago.

1917: The first large-scale IQ testing of American adults occurs.

1921: Jean Piaget publishes his first article on the psychology of intelligence.

1956: Benjamin Bloom publishes *Taxonomy of Educational Objectives*.

1962: Lev Vygotsky's *Social Development Theory* is published in the United States.

1969: Carl Rogers publishes *Freedom to Learn*.

A glance at this short list makes it clear that, as schooling in America has developed, it has been accompanied by researchers documenting its growth through studies and assessments of teaching and learning. Knowledge of past findings can help you understand teachers' roles and responsibilities toward student learning, and it can often illuminate the path of education so past mistakes are not repeated.

Translating Educational Psychological Perspectives Into Teaching Practice

Theories of learning translate into teaching practices as organization of information. Ideas about human development come together to mirror the ideas of the learner, society, and organized subject matter expressed by Dewey. Theorists often differ in their perspective on what provides the optimum setting for student learning, hence the variety of programs and activities that exist in schools today.

Johann Pestalozzi (1746–1827), Jean Piaget (1896–1980), and Abraham Maslow (1908–1970)

Johann Pestalozzi's theories emphasize group and participatory activities. His ideas on recognizing individual differences and grouping students by ability rather than age were considered radical for his time. He felt teachers should allow students freedom to express themselves and develop naturally. He envisioned children learning through observation of the real world rather than from books.

Jean Piaget is best known for his epistemological studies (i.e., how we know what we know) of the intellectual growth of children. Piaget concluded from his studies that human knowledge is constructed through interactions with reality. Piaget's work has had a profound effect on educational theories regarding when students are ready to learn specific information.

Piaget studied the ways children come to know the world about them through their interactions.

Abraham Maslow developed the theory of human motivation now known as Maslow's Hierarchy of Needs. He described the power of human needs and organized these needs into five general categories, from most basic (food, safety) to higher categories of need such as the need for caring relationships and self-worth. Maslow's Hierarchy of Needs became a framework for considering the individual needs of students as indicators of what they were capable of learning when constrained by personal needs.

These different, yet somewhat similar, perspectives have promoted self-actualization and developmental and motivational approaches to instructional practices.

Ivan Pavlov (1849–1936), Edward Thorndike (1874–1949), and Burrhus Frederic Skinner (1904–1990)

Ivan Pavlov demonstrated a form of conditioning in 1927, with the help of a dog and a bell. His experiments on stimulus and response led him to posit that learning required a dependent relationship between an unconditional stimulus (i.e., presenting a stimulus to elicit a reflexive response) and a conditional stimulus to create a conditional response.

Edward Thorndike developed the Law of Effect principle suggesting that responses closely followed by satisfaction are more likely to elicit similar responses when the situation is repeated. However, when a situation is followed by discomfort, the response to the situation will be less likely to occur or will become weakened over time. Thorndike helped lay the scientific foundation for modern educational psychology.

B. F. Skinner based his theories of operant conditioning on the work of Thorndike. He studied observable behavior by looking at an action and its consequences. Skinner believed that the best way to understand behavior is to look at the causes of an action and the consequences of that action and so be able to predict and control behavior.

Each of these theorists believed that behavior can be modified, controlled, or directed when specific stimuli are present or when a behavior is rewarded or depressed. Behavior modification practices that are widely used in classrooms today affect instructional practices and classroom management strategies.

Lev Vygotsky (1896–1934)

Lev Vygotsky presented the Social Development Theory, viewing cognition as the end product of socialization and social behavior. Interactions with more knowledgeable others help students learn.

Vygotsky's theories support the foundations of constructivism. Three major themes in Vygotsky's (1978) Social Development Theory are that (1) development in a child appears first on a social level with others and then inside the child, (2) the child learns from a more knowledgeable other, and (3) learning occurs in a zone of proximal development between the learner's ability to learn with the support of others and the ability to learn independently.

It would be foolish to suggest that the complex theories of these educational psychologists can be explained and discussed in such succinct terms. Detailed information about their contributions to the ways educators perceive student learning is available through the references listed at the end of this book. It is necessary that as future teachers you begin to understand the many ways their ideas have influenced different modes of instruction in schools.

HOW DO PHILOSOPHICAL PERSPECTIVES HELP TEACHERS UNDERSTAND STUDENT LEARNING?

Teaching and learning are a social process and should be shared. Developing a mutual respect with students and creating an environment that is comfortable and relaxed make students eager to share information and stories. Teachers can learn as much from their students as the students learn from them.

You no doubt took a philosophy or logic course as part of the core requirements for your degree. Understanding philosophical thought prepares teachers for critical thinking and reasoning and constructing logically sound arguments. The study of philosophy helps teachers sift through ideas and articulate thoughts in ways that others can follow. Understanding the practices of philosophical perspectives helps teachers learn how to look and listen, how to engage in meaningful discussions, and how to recognize the many ways of thinking about teaching.

We all seek answers to questions in order to make sense of our worlds by developing our own philosophies. The Greek word *philosophia* means "love of wisdom," though it's clear we don't all have the same questions or view wisdom in the same way. Philosophers have thought long and hard about their philosophies and about the implications their perspectives have for learning and teaching.

Metaphysics, Epistemology, and Axiology

Three different branches of philosophy are concerned with seeking answers to different types of questions. **Metaphysics** is concerned with questions about the nature of reality and human attempts to find coherence in the realm of thought and experience. Questions on teaching and learning examined from this perspective explore the relationship between learners and teachers.

Epistemology examines questions about how and what we know, and how knowing takes place. Questions dealt with in the study of epistemology may include "Where do ideas come from?" and "How do we pose and solve problems?" The **axiology** branch of philosophy deals with questions concerning the nature of values. Questions examined from the axiology perspective deal with what should be or what values we hold: "What is good for students?" "How should students behave?" As you can see, the questions that are the focus of each branch of philosophy are related to different aspects of education. Such questions posed by the different branches of philosophy can be found in educational concerns over curriculum, methods, and teaching behaviors.

The Metaphysical Questions of Content or Child

In 340 BCE, Aristotle declared that metaphysics involves intuitive knowledge of unprovable starting points (truths) and demonstrative knowledge of what follows from them. Teachers want to know why some

Teachers must engage in critical thinking to be able to translate ideas so their students can understand complex problems and begin to make sense of the world.

students are successful at particular tasks while other students struggle with the same tasks. Can a child choose whether or not to learn? Is the ability to learn determined by factors outside of a student's control? Is understanding of specific content necessary to a successful life, or is the way in which the content is learned of utmost importance to the learner? The manner in which a teacher approaches the content and the way the child interacts with the content both depend somewhat on the teacher's attitudes about human nature. Children are real. How they develop and learn is, at times, metaphysical.

Ways of Knowing, Learning, and Teaching

In the concern over how students learn, what they should learn, and how they should learn it, educators connect epistemology and education. Epistemology is the study of the origin, nature, methods, and limits of knowledge. Epistemology is the science of how we learn and teach, and encompasses the range of questions educators face in designing the very best schooling for children. Education is focused on how students best learn the knowledge they must have and how teachers learn the necessary behaviors to facilitate student learning.

When classroom teachers puzzle over which educational goals they should meet and how they should achieve them through teaching practices, they are dealing with questions about knowing, learning, and teaching. In Plato's discussion of epistemology, he argued that in order to grasp reality or know, individuals use understanding, reason, perception, and imagination.

You will also learn about Piaget in your course work and how his program of naturalistic research helped teachers understand child development. Piaget was primarily interested in how knowledge developed in human organisms, and he termed his general theoretical framework genetic epistemology.

The Role of Values and Ethics in the Classroom

There are many reasons that parents care a great deal about who teaches their children. Certainly, parents hope for a teacher who is knowledgeable. They hope for one who will be sympathetic to any idiosyncratic behaviors or learning styles their particular child might possess. But probably nothing concerns parents more than the moral values, or ethics, the teachers of their children demonstrate. Parental concern over the moral values of individual teachers as well as those expressed by schools has given rise to an increased interest in homeschooling and school vouchers. As one example, the National Character Education Center relates core values to human anatomy and gets at the heart and mind of values in action. In this approach, the seven virtues attributed to respective body parts are respect (eyes and ears), integrity (mouth), compassion (heart), perseverance (stomach), cooperation (hands), initiative (feet), and positive mental attitudes (mind).

Another initiative to accomplish the teaching of core values is the Institute for Global Ethics. This institute provides guidelines for ethical literacy. The Ethics & Compliance Initiative, a character education website, discusses the questions of whether schools should be teaching values and, if so, whose values should be taught. Ethics is a way of processing behavior. Teachers weight different elements of their own behavior and the behavior of their students differently depending on their own set of ethics and values.

While ethics provides food for thought, not everyone has the same beliefs that public institutions should dictate to individuals what should be considered an acceptable form of conduct. Teachers must negotiate the omnipresent conflict between societal values and individual values in the classroom. A well-informed teacher understands and respects the diversity of cultural and ethnic thought in any community and uses this knowledge to help all students learn. Teachers faced with questions about values are dealing with the axiology branch of philosophy.

Philosophical Perspectives' Influence on Teaching and Learning

Various schools of philosophy seek to answer the broad philosophical questions posed through metaphysics, epistemology, and axiology from differing perspectives. The schools of philosophy most often mentioned in terms of the implications they have for education are idealism, realism, perennialism, pragmatism, progressivism, essentialism, and existentialism. These philosophies represent a broad spectrum of influence on educational practice and thought, and ways of knowing. Some schools

TEACHERS' LOUNGE
THE ONE CONSTANT

© Mary Bauer

Thirty-one years ago, I walked into school with a set schedule, set class list, set curriculum, and set lesson plans . . . or so I thought. Within the first hour, I realized that I would need to change a "few" things. As the day wore on, then the weeks, the months, and the years, I have come to understand that ideas, students, methods, expectations, and anything else related to education is anything *but* set. The commonality for all these things is change. You can't fight it. You can't worry about it. You can only be flexible and open-minded and know, too, that change will be the one constant in your teaching career. I have experienced changes in students and families, changes in discipline, changes in standards, changes in technology, and, well, you get the idea. Sometimes we think we have found a better way only to revert back to the way we did things a decade earlier. Flexibility is being capable of being "bent without breaking." There were many times I thought I would break but didn't. We are a unique group in that way. We contort, give, change, and bounce back. Students need us to be that way, and we hope that if we are, they will learn a very valuable lesson about life through us. I honestly believe as an educator that my philosophy of education has a direct impact on my students' lives. Our greatest responsibility as educators is to be everything we can be, learn everything we can learn, and find and capitalize on the strengths of our students—not for our own benefit, but for the benefit of the lives of students we touch on a daily basis.

—Mary Ella Bauer, as told to William Bauer
Marietta College
Marietta, Ohio

of philosophy give rise to compatible educational theories, while others generate quite opposite and competing points of view. Some of the philosophical perspectives listed below may not be considered schools of philosophy in the truest sense. However, their impact on teaching and learning has given them a relevant stature in the realm of thinking about education. Observance of one or another of these philosophical perspectives, or a combination of two or more, could produce differing school structures, curriculum, instructional methods, and classroom practices for teachers and students. What follows is a succinct description of some of the schools of philosophy teachers should be familiar with as they undertake construction of their own personal philosophy of teaching.

Confucianism

Confucius (551–479 BCE) is in many cultures regarded as the world's foremost and greatest philosopher. Confucius's teachings, a source of perennial good sense, encourage people to lead good lives by doing what is right. At some time in your preservice teacher education course work and during inservice Professional Development, you will no doubt see or hear one of Confucius's many axioms: "I hear and I forget. I see and I remember. I do and I understand." Another is "If you think in terms of a year, plant a seed; if in terms of 10 years, plant trees; if in terms of 100 years, teach the people." Confucius taught that there are three methods to gaining wisdom. The first is reflection, which is the highest. The second is imitation, which is the easiest. The third is experience, which is the bitterest. As a teacher education candidate, you will have the opportunity to use all three methods to gain wisdom.

Idealism and Realism

Idealism, the oldest of the Western philosophies, originated with Plato (427–347 BCE). Idealism refers to a rational world of the mind where ideas or concepts are the essence of all that is worth knowing. The idealism philosophy guides behavior or thought based on the theory that the objects of external perception consist of ideas. Universal and absolute truths offer examples of the ideal to strive for. Since ideas are consistent in an ever-changing world, they should be learned and understood. The ideal should be sought and emulated when found. Georg Hegel's (1770–1831) absolute idealism posits that since ideas about reality are products of the mind, there must be a mind at work in the universe that establishes reality and gives it structure. Idealism is used to refer to any metaphysical theory positing the primacy of mind, spirit, or language over matter.

Realism describes a world in which material objects exist in themselves apart from the mind's awareness of them. Aristotle (384–322 BCE) built on the ideas of his famous teacher, Plato, to describe the realistic world. That world is real and exists whether or not a mind is there to perceive it. Remember the question of the tree falling in the forest that you discussed in your first philosophy class? If a tree falls in the forest and no one is there to hear it, does it make a sound? Imagine the answer from both an idealist and a realist perspective. In realism, laws of nature and the order of the physical world override the idealist notion that ideas are the ultimate reality. In a realist's world, we respond to what is seen and sensed. According to John Locke's (1632–1704) tabula rasa theory, we all begin as blank slates, and our senses help us fill the void with knowledge. Plato's idealistic perspective is that we are full of ideas at birth and that life's experiences help us eventually know these ideas. Is it the teacher's responsibility to bring out the knowledge students already possess or to engrave it on their blank slates?

Perennialism and Essentialism

The roots of **perennialism** lie in the philosophies of Plato and Aristotle as well as of Saint Thomas Aquinas. Perennialism offers a conservative and traditional view of human nature. In this school of thought, human beings do not change much, but they are capable of analytical thinking, reason, and imagination, and should be encouraged along these lines. Through reason lies revelation. When certain perpetual truths are learned, individuals will develop rationality. While human nature is somewhat predictable, it is possible to improve the human condition through understanding of history, the great works of literature, and art.

Essentialism became a popular educational philosophy in the United States in the 1930s following what was considered an excess of progressive education. Essentialists believe there is a fundamental core of knowledge that any functioning member of society must possess. Such knowledge is absolutely essential for an individual to lead a productive life. Learning takes place through contact with the physical world as well as with specific core disciplines. Goodness lies in acquisition of certain essential knowledge. E. D. Hirsch clearly delineated the finer points of essential knowledge in his 1987 book, *Cultural Literacy*, making clear the exact information that every literate person should possess. Teaching the essentials has been, since colonial times, the dominant approach to American education. The testing frenzy of the No Child Left Behind Act of 2001 movement would attest to the staying power of essentialism in American education. "While essentialism reflects the traditional view that the 'real' world is the physical world we experience with our senses, perennialism is more open to the notion that universal spiritual forms are equally real" (Sadaker & Sadaker, 2000, pp. 400–401).

Pragmatism and Progressivism

Pragmatism was first introduced into philosophy by Charles Peirce in 1878. The term *pragmatic* is derived from the Greek word *pragma*, meaning "action," which is also the source for the words *practice* and *practical*. The universe of pragmatism is dynamic and evolving. Change happens, and humans are constantly in the process of becoming, evolving to reach ever-greater understanding. Truth is what works in one place and time, and even if it worked once, it might not work again given different variables. Concepts and outcomes should be tested by their practical results. Maybe your university professor who answers, "It depends," to your questions about what works best is taking a pragmatic point of view. Pragmatism shares some views with Aristotle's realism but is less rigid since in pragmatism experience is of utmost importance. Because of the changing nature of truths, individuals must be flexible and be capable of dealing with change. America was founded on pragmatic ideals. Since the arrival of the first explorers and settlers, Americans have spent a large portion of their energy adapting to one another and to ever-changing environments.

Ancient philosophical ideas are present in current teaching practices.

iStock/1970s

Libraries around the world, such as this one at Trinity College in Dublin, Ireland, contain the wisdom of the ages.

Progressivism, marked by progress, reform, or a continuing improvement, became popular in the 1920s through the work of John Dewey. The tenets of progressivism demonstrate respect for individuality, a high regard for science, and receptivity to change. According to Dewey, human beings are social animals that learn through interaction with one another. Learning increases when we are engaged in activities that have meaning for us (Dewey, 1963). The influence of progressivism helped American educators take a closer look at the role of the learner in any acquisition of knowledge.

Existentialism

Existentialism rose out of the cult of **nihilism**, a philosophical position that argues the world, and especially human existence, is without objective meaning, purpose, comprehensible truth, or essential value, and **pessimism**, a general belief that things are bad and tend to become worse. Existentialism presents a world in which individuals determine for themselves what is true or false. Only through free will can individuals oppose hostile environments. The first principle of existentialism, according to Jean-Paul Sartre, is "Man is nothing else but what he makes of himself." When the caterpillar in *Alice in Wonderland* asks, "Who are YOU?" had Alice been an existentialist, she might have answered, "Yes, who am I, and what should I do?"

Maxine Greene (1988), a longtime professor at Columbia Teachers College, contends that living is philosophy and that freedom means overcoming obstacles that obstruct our attempt to find ourselves and fulfill our potential. The writings of Friedrich Nietzsche (1844–1900) offer a framework for cultivating a healthy love of self. He wanted to help liberate people from the oppression of feeling inferior.

Carl Rogers (1902–1987), the founder of humanistic psychology, made outstanding contributions to the field of education. His writings focus on empowering individuals to achieve their full potential—that is, to become self-actualized. According to Rogers (1969), existential living means living in the here-and-now, being in touch with reality, while learning from the past and dreaming of the future. Though the ideas of existentialism seem radical to many people, Donald Kauchak and Paul Eggen (2005) point out, "Existentialism makes a contribution to education because it places primary emphasis on the individual, and in doing so, it reminds us that we don't teach math, science, reading, and writing; rather, we teach people, and the people we teach are at the core of learning" (p. 214).

There are far more philosophical perspectives than have been mentioned here. When you read of the naturalists or of scholasticism, humanism, or social reconstructivism, you will increase your knowledge of the ideas that have influenced how you may be expected to perform in the classroom. Most philosophical perspectives hold increased knowledge or understanding as good.

Constructivism, a theory of learning and method of education, stresses the importance of how people construct meaning in the world around them; it is embedded with theories developed by Dewey, Piaget, and Vygotsky. The continuous interaction between building on prior knowledge and reflecting on one's environment promotes meaning, allowing the learner to gain knowledge even through mistakes or errors (Heddens, Speer, & Brahier, 2009).

Knowledge of teaching and learning is always incomplete even though there is a wealth of theories to support many of the practices and policies that exist. Knowledge and attitudes about education grow and change as the physical and social world changes. Teachers construct a personal philosophy toward teaching and learning in order to make sense of the complexities of their craft.

Teachers may not be able to name a specific school of philosophy if you ask them to tell you which philosophy they adhere to in daily practice, but they will certainly be able to give you their thoughts on how children learn, what they should learn, and how they should be learning it. Most teachers select ideas from a number of schools of philosophy and apply what works best for them given the requirements of their teaching situation. In order to maintain a sense of humor and hope in teaching, most teachers are pragmatic and operate from a philosophical viewpoint of eclecticism. They select ideas

UNDERSTANDING AND USING DATA
CHANGING VALUES

From 1960 to 2000, American society experienced radical change. Consider the following, and then discuss with your classmates the consequences such changes may have had on American education. How does current American society compare?

1960	2000	Today
Transcendentalism	Instant gratification	
	verty line	
	media	
	al computing	
	ey kids	
	cores	
	ames	
	ty status	

(Handwritten note card overlapping left portion of page:)

MY TEACHING PHILOSOPHY

INQUIRY ORIENTED → ONE OF THE MOST IMPORTANT ROLES IS ASKING GOOD QUESTIONS.

WHAT IS A GOOD Q?
- ask us to dig into what we perceive
- prior knowledge
- analyze elements we can tease out
- compare and contrast
- to generalize implications + predicts

(Right column, partially obscured text:)

he Under-
first con-
pare them
ntury. How
s that took
nces affect
d Twitter?
atch on TV
anged the
tial does it

e life given
t ways can
d teachers
react in a classroom or think about education in general?

Climate change

Terrorism

Social networking/blogs

Political polarization

Obesity

Health care

Your Task

Make a list of your own ideas about the state of American values today. To get you started, here are some ideas:

Teacher-focused approaches to teaching, in which the teacher is master of the knowledge to be learned and dispenses it to all students at a specified rate over a specified period of time, adhere to the essentialism school of philosophy in which learning the content is of major concern. The teacher-focused approach also follows a perennialist perspective, believing that education serves to inform students of knowledge that will remain constant through life (Oliva, 2005). In education, essentialism and perennialism perspectives dictate basic and prescribed subject matter. Learning is transferred in a programmatic fashion from teacher to students.

from various systems in the same way they gather materials from various sources. Such is the practical world of teaching.

The Presence of Educational Philosophies in Classrooms

Sarah E. Brown (2015) has done extensive research in comparing different educational philosophies. Brown posits that "every teacher has a (subconsciously or consciously held) philosophy of education that affects their everyday decision-making and choice of teaching and discipline methods." She suggests that teachers may not know which philosophical perspectives they favor, but teachers do favor specific methods. The educational practices she provides in her synopsis will certainly help direct you to your leanings toward a specific philosophy of education.

Teacher-Focused Classrooms

Room arrangement may not be the best clue as to a teacher's views on what and how children should learn, but it is an indicator. Picture students seated in individual islands separate from other students with eyes directed toward a teacher at the front of the room explaining or demonstrating something the students are expected to remember. The students are quiet. The teacher is talking. We've seen examples of this style of teaching in movies and on television. Unfortunately, in most of these examples, the teacher is oblivious to what the students are doing or thinking. If you haven't watched *Ferris Bueller's Day Off*, do so. The movie is a classic and includes a scene in which a teacher asks and answers his own questions without really being aware of what the students might be learning or doing. Of course, teacher-focused classrooms can be excellent learning situations for students and not at all like they are portrayed in movies.

Student-Focused Classrooms

Student-focused approaches to teaching correspond to pragmatism and progressivism. In education, these philosophical perspectives view the major role of schools and teachers as to create learning opportunities that will enable students to construct knowledge relevant to a specific task or situation through self-interest and dialogue with others. The tenets of a constructivist teaching style are closely associated with progressivism, emphasizing hands-on, activity-based learning. The room arrangement in a student-focused classroom is open and flexible. Students can easily interact with one another. Motivation is encouraged through intrinsic rewards. Teacher and learners share control of behavior and the learning environment. Inquiry is promoted, and divergent points of view are respected. The teacher models participatory evaluation through questioning and student-led discussions of results. The students value themselves as learners and welcome the active role they have in directing their education along the lines of their own interests. In a student-focused classroom, the curriculum should take into account students' interests. Students construct knowledge through interaction with others. See Table 7.1 for ways philosophical perspectives can influence teaching and learning.

TABLE 7.1 ■ The Influence of Philosophical Perspectives on Teaching and Learning					
	Learning Focus	**Teaching Methods**	**Educational Goal**	**Curriculum**	**Assessment**
Perennialism	Students will be prepared for their futures through learning the essential truths identified in idealism and realism.	Teachers use didactic instruction and questioning strategies (i.e., the Socratic method).	Students will develop intellectual skills and demonstrate rational behavior.	The curriculum is focused on the basics and liberal arts through the use of the Great Books series.	Essay exams and objective tests are used to evaluate student learning.
Essentialism	Instruction centers on knowledge and skills with a focus on literacy and history.	Teachers use detailed lesson plans, use lecture as a strategy, and focus on learning competencies.	Students will develop disciplined minds and become literate.	Reading, writing, and mathematics serve as the basis for achieving a basic body of knowledge.	Standardized tests are used to evaluate mastery of content.
Progressivism	Students are engaged in cooperative learning experiences that provide opportunities for them to interact with the environment in solving problems.	Lessons engage students in group work and projects with the teacher as a guide and collaborative partner.	Students will become productive citizens in a democratic society.	Lessons that integrate subject matter and are relevant to social experiences foster group work.	Student progress is closely monitored through formative assessment with frequent feedback from the teacher.

	Learning Focus	Teaching Methods	Educational Goal	Curriculum	Assessment
Existentialism	Students choose subject matter since reality exists in the eye of the beholder and meaning is constructed by the learner.	Students engage in community projects to identify and rectify social problems.	Students exercise critical inquiry and become citizens to challenge established constructs in society.	Curriculum is presented as a model for questioning, critiquing, and analyzing social values and political culture.	Self-assessment of learning is through journaling, writing samples, and portfolios.

Source: Adapted from Webb, L. D., Metha, A., & Jordan, K. F. (2013). *Foundations of American education* (7th ed.). Upper Saddle River, NJ: Pearson.

CHALLENGING ASSUMPTIONS
IS ONE METHOD OF TEACHING READING SKILLS UNIVERSALLY BETTER THAN ANOTHER?

The Assumption

Teacher-focused direct instruction is not as effective as a child-centered, constructivist method in helping children learn, retain, and apply reading skills. Teacher educators, teachers, and school administrators have long debated the effectiveness of a whole language approach versus the direct instruction approach to teaching early reading skills. Critics of the whole language approach blame colleges of education for continuing to advocate a teaching method that does not seem to be working for all students and does not have a foundation in empirical research, while proponents of the whole language approach argue that the direct instruction approach constrains a child's learning style. According to educators who advocate the whole language approach, the child-centered focus of this method introduces students to reading in a way that makes them enjoy reading and become lifelong readers.

The Research

Schug, Tarver, and Western (2001), of the University of Wisconsin–Madison, examined the issue of direct instruction in their study, "Direct Instruction and the Teaching of Early Reading." Their goal was to conduct research on direct instruction in authentic settings using methods that would capture the rich complexity of classroom experience. Six schools in Wisconsin participated in the study. The researchers observed and conducted interviews related to the use of direct instruction programs in these schools. In this qualitative study, teachers and principals reported positive effects from use of direct instruction for both regular education and special education students in reading decoding, reading comprehension, and attitudes toward reading. Teachers also reported other positive effects that included improved writing skills, improved capacity to focus and sustain effort, and, generally, improved student behavior. Teachers also reported no evidence of the various negative effects critics have attributed to direct instruction methods. Understandably, it is impossible to statistically evaluate joy in reading or document lifelong reading.

Implications

Since not all individuals learn, retain, and apply information in the same way, it is important for teachers to use a variety of instructional methods to meet the needs of all students. One approach to teaching reading may gain popularity to the detriment of other equally effective methods. It is important for teachers to be aware of the role of academic fashion in instructional programs and to examine research results.

There are more sites on the Internet for constructivist lesson plans than there are for teacher-focused lesson plans. Does this mean that student-focused approaches to teaching are more popular than teacher-focused approaches in the nation's schools? Or is this an idea that sounds excellent in theory but is difficult to put into practice? Visit www.interventioncentral.org for suggestions using teacher-focused strategies to increase student learning. Then go to www.thirteen.org/edonline/concept2class/constructivism to learn about teaching strategies in classrooms with a constructivist and student-centered focus. Is one type of lesson more appealing to you than the other? Why do you think that might be?

Source: Schug, M. C., Tarver, S. G., & Western, R. D. (2001). Direct instruction and the teaching of early reading: Wisconsin's teacher-led insurgency. *Wisconsin Policy Research Institute Report, 14*(2).

The Changing Focus

In any given day in a classroom, the focus shifts from teacher to students and back again. This is not wishy-washy but rather a fact of the profession. Much as a skilled photographer will shift the focus on a scene to emphasize or pick up an unusual feature, an effective teacher is able to view the classroom as a vibrant life form, taking note of all movement and features. In doing so, the teacher may find it necessary to redirect student attention, or perhaps momentarily call a halt to all activity. Learning how to combine parts of different educational philosophies for the benefit of all of the students may be one of the hardest tasks a new teacher must learn.

Using Philosophy to Problem-Solve

Thinking and trying to find answers to questions are much of what teaching is about. A teacher perplexed by certain student behaviors or by the content of the textbooks mandated by the school district administrators can find comfort in the teachings of philosophers. With a little effort, teachers can use the great ideas from different philosophical perspectives to help them understand human learning, behavior, and value systems. As your knowledge of teaching practices increases, so must your understanding of the basis for such practices. Do not take anything on hearsay. Seek the answers to your questions and build a cognitive framework of theory and practice to rival the architecture of the Taj Mahal. The mind should be a beautiful thing.

Our opinions about public school teaching and learning begin with the very first moment we enter schools as students. Every beginning teacher's knowledge of teaching is more memory than schema. Beliefs are the frameworks that all subsequent knowledge is incorporated into. It is necessary for teachers to categorize their thinking and understand the traditions of practice and the historical circumstances out of which certain kinds of thinking arise.

There are many ways to think about teaching and learning, and because of this, identifying one particular philosophical perspective for your approach to teaching can be like looking for a needle in a haystack. Don't worry. Be happy that there are so many possibilities and ideas. It is important for you to become familiar with a variety of philosophical perspectives in order to organize your own thinking and develop a personal wellspring of original and useful ideas to help your students learn. The more you think about teaching and the more you hear how others think about it, the easier it will be for you to construct your own unique personal philosophy of teaching.

CONNECTING TO THE CLASSROOM

This chapter has provided information on some of the widely held philosophical perspectives that influence attitudes about what and how children are to learn and how teachers are to teach. It is likely that during your teaching career you will have firsthand experience with more than one philosophical perspective. Below are some ways to recognize and become familiar with different philosophical perspectives in instruction and in interactions with students and their families, and with your teacher colleagues.

1. Keep a list of the questions teachers ask during instruction. Do the questions seem to ask for recall of facts, or do they consider the opinions of students? Are students often asked to make inferences, or does the teacher provide conclusive statements for the students to record and remember? At what point do the students seem to be most engaged in answering the teacher's questions?

2. In a previous chapter, it was suggested that you take part in a parent–teacher conference. You can learn much about the philosophical perspective of teachers and parents when observing a parent–teacher conference. Pay close attention to how the teacher conducts the conference. In what ways does the teacher express his or her personal philosophy of teaching? Are the parents given equal opportunity to express their attitudes about what their child is learning in school?

3. When teachers agree with one another and with their administrators, the school climate is pleasant and productive. On the other hand, when there are glaring differences among colleagues regarding content, conduct, and teaching strategies, discord may permeate the school. What actions have you seen teachers and administrators take to alleviate the disagreement among colleagues that stems from belief in the tenets of different schools of philosophy?

SUMMARY

Four major topics were covered in this chapter:

- Developing a personal philosophy toward teaching and learning: Knowing your beliefs and attitudes toward teaching and learning is an important first step in understanding your influence on student learning.

- Student learning: There are a variety of ways students learn and a variety of ways teachers can support student learning.

- Recognizing the connection between educational psychology and student learning: When teachers understand the tenets of educational psychology, they have an improved chance of helping all students learn.

- Philosophical perspectives toward teaching and learning: Using different approaches to teaching and learning is important to help all students succeed since not all students have the same approach to learning.

KEY TERMS

axiology 198

epistemology 198

essentialism 201

existentialism 202

metaphysics 198

nihilism 202

perennialism 201

pessimism 202

pragmatism 201

progressivism 202

schools of philosophy 199

Socratic method 190

CLASS DISCUSSION QUESTIONS

1. Experiences you have had as a student quite likely will shape your attitudes and beliefs as a teacher. Discuss one experience that stands out from the rest. Refer to particular schools of philosophy to explain why this experience was so important to you.

2. Describe stories from your experiences that have shaped your philosophy of teaching. What critical events have given rise to strongly held opinions?

3. In schools where teachers follow the same philosophical perspective as their colleagues or students' families, there is probably agreement with the curriculum that is being taught and the instructional methods that are used to teach it. What issues might arise, however, if many of the teachers followed the tenets of the progressive school of philosophy, while many of the families of the students followed the tenets of essentialism, and the administration mainly expressed a perennialist's point of view?

4. Pick a philosophical perspective. What role might reflection on student achievement play for a teacher from that perspective?

SELF-ASSESSMENT

What Is Your Current Level of Understanding and Thinking About Developing a Philosophy of Teaching and Learning?

One of the indicators of understanding is to examine how complex your thinking is when asked questions that require you to use the concepts and facts introduced in this chapter.

Answer the following questions as fully as you can. Then use the Assessing Your Learning rubric to self-assess the degree to which you understand and can use the ideas presented in this chapter.

1. What are three issues related to developing a personal philosophy of teaching and learning?

2. Why is it important for teachers to have a working knowledge of educational psychology?

3. What are the common educational philosophies teachers should know?

4. Name three ways educational psychology perspectives and educational philosophies can be apparent in classrooms.

Assessing Your Learning Rubric

	Parts & Pieces	Unidimensional	Organized	Integrated	Extensions
Indicators	Elements/concepts are talked about as isolated and independent entities. Some important names are provided in isolation.	One or a few concepts are addressed, while others are underdeveloped, or not mentioned.	Deliberate and structured consideration of all key concepts/elements.	All key concepts/elements are included in a view that addresses interconnections.	Integration of all elements and dimensions, with extrapolation to new situations.
Relationships between educational psychology, educational philosophy, and teaching and learning	Names a few educational psychology approaches without mentioning relationship to schools of philosophy.	Describes only one or two approaches to teaching and learning.	Describes how educational psychology and philosophical perspectives can result in specific teaching practices.	Learner can categorize educational psychology perspective with educational philosophies to provide examples of ways a teacher might plan, implement, and assess lessons.	Explains ways past knowledge and experiences can influence the development of a personal philosophy of teaching and learning.

FIELD GUIDE
FOR LEARNING MORE ABOUT . . .

Developing a Philosophy of Teaching and Learning

At this point in the text, you should have quite a collection of artifacts to add to your personal field guide of learning to teach. Refer back to Chapter 1 for a detailed description of what your field guide should contain and how it can provide opportunities for reflection on your professional growth.

Ask a Teacher or Principal	Ask two separate teachers to share with you their opinions of how students learn. Ask how they know when their students have actually learned the information being taught. Do they believe that learning one piece of information automatically leads to learning a subsequent piece of information? In their opinion, is all learning of equal value? Will knowledge help students lead a better life?
Make Your Own Observations	Classrooms are different. They come in different sizes and shapes, and they are populated by people who also come in different sizes and shapes. It is interesting to compare the way classrooms are arranged, what is being taught, how the teacher interacts with the students, and how the students are expected to interact with one another. Can such observations provide a clue as to the attitudes and beliefs of the teachers regarding how children learn? Is it possible for only one observation to present a clear picture of a teacher's beliefs? How might someone who watched you teach identify your personal philosophy of teaching?
Reflect Through Journaling	Think about the teachers you have encountered over your years as a student in classrooms. Explain why you believe that a specific teacher had a specific philosophy of teaching and learning. What do you remember of his or her actions in the classroom that would lead you to this conclusion? Did you find his or her teaching methods compatible with your style of learning?
Build Your Portfolio	In order to recognize the influence of life events on the adoption of a personal philosophy of teaching, create an educational autobiography by documenting at least three critical events that had an impact on your schooling. Here are some questions you might consider: What were the major events taking place in the world during your childhood years? What were some of the learning experiences you had in school that are still vivid memories? Which of your teachers did you like or dislike the most? Why? Who were your heroes? What was of major importance when you graduated from high school? What did your family expect you to do with your life? At the end of your autobiography, reflect on how your experiences might be like or different from your students' experiences.
Read a Book	*On Knowing: Essays for the Left Hand*, by J. S. Bruner (1962, Harvard University Press), takes a fascinating look at the influence of intuition, feeling, and spontaneity in determining how we know what we know, and how we can teach others what we know.
	Neil Bright's book, *Rethinking Everything: Personal Growth Through Transactional Analysis* (2015, Rowman & Littlefied), provides a refreshing lens through which all learners can find out who they really are.
Search the Web	Visit **www.school-for-champions.com/education/philosophies.htm** for Ron Kurtus's overview of five basic philosophies of education.
	Visit **http://oregonstate.edu/instruct/ed416/sample.html** for two sample philosophy of education statements from Oregon State University education candidates.

STUDENT STUDY SITE

⑤SAGE edge™

Get the tools you need to sharpen your study skills. **SAGE edge** offers a robust online environment featuring an impressive array of free tools and resources.

Access practice quizzes, eFlashcards, video, and multimedia at **edge.sagepub.com/hall3e**.

8

ORGANIZING AND FINANCING SCHOOLS FOR LEARNING

© Michael Weaver

PRINCIPAL INTERVIEW

Mr. Michael Weaver

Mr. Michael Weaver is in his seventh year of being the principal of a very large high school, Mountain Vista High School in the Douglas County (Colorado) School District. *There are approximately 2,330 students this school year. We are projecting an increase to more than 2,360 students next year.* The school has 123 certified staff and 55 support staff. In addition to Mr. Weaver, administrative leadership of the school includes five assistant principals and an athletic director. *Also, we have a group of staff who are not certified teachers. We call them Admin Pro Tech, which includes about 15 people. This group includes computer tech, library media, and intervention specialists. Overall, it is a big place!*

Q: For you as the principal, what are your most important priorities?

A: Establishment and maintenance of culture and climate that works for kids, the staff, and our community has come to be my most important role. As I look at my importance for this big operation, I think setting the tone for culture and climate is my most important factor.

Happy kids come from happy teachers. The work that comes from creating a professionally satisfying atmosphere is critical. Continuing to challenge people to learn and grow and their feeling that they are part of the community and part of the process are huge factors in staff retention and their being in a place to continue to learn and grow.

Q: Would you say a little more about what you mean by "learning and growing"?

A: An underlying theme of my philosophy is that really truly the only thing we can really control is us getting better every day at what we do. The idea of staff being challenged to be the best they can be in the classroom every day. For them to be able to clearly define purpose, to understand relationships with kids will take them further than they ever imagined. For them to be given opportunities to work with each other, to model, to facilitate, to have some input, and wanting to be excited about getting better and better every day. This all centers back on our philosophy that nothing good happens unless it is good in the classroom every day.

LEARNING OUTCOMES

After reading this chapter, you should be able to do the following:

1. Explain the organizational relationships between teachers, the school principal, and other school staff.

2. Summarize important functions and relationships of school districts and state governments as they affect teachers.

3. Describe ways that the federal government influences education and the work of teachers.

4. Recognize the differences between good and bad governance.

5. Describe the different sources of funds for education and issues related to each source.

6. Examine the major ways that funds for schools are spent.

7. Identify key issues with implications for teachers about the organization and funding of schools.

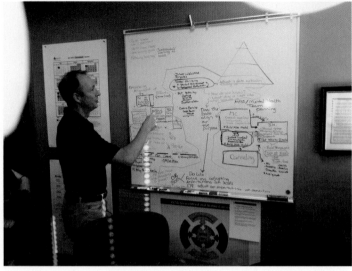

© Michael Weaver

For example, when I approach staff development, I try to present reflective ideas. I don't think innovation is presenting a program and telling them how to do it. Instead, it is presenting ideas and their figuring out how to move kids toward that end result.

Q: **Your school has another full-time professional position called a Professional Learning Specialist (PLS). What is this role about?**

A: Yes, the district provides funds so that we can employ a full-time master teacher to lead Professional Development, mentor new teachers, and be a nonadministrator instructional support for all teachers. She was a highly regarded teacher in terms of instructional expertise, and she walks the walk. All the things we have tried to do, she implemented as a teacher. She worked very hard to do things right. These attributes have carried over into her being a terrific PLS.

To be an effective PLS requires patience, flexibility, and (at times) a thick skin. Sometimes teachers push back pretty hard. Being approachable and relational is one of the important things. You want to be someone people feel safe in coming to. That I taught in this building helps me have some empathy and understanding of what's it like to be a teacher here.

(*Note:* See more about this special role later in this chapter in the section about teachers as full-time instructional leaders.)

Q: **I see that you have a set of notes on the whiteboard. What are those about?**

A: Well, there are three different things on there. One is the alignment for our providing Professional Development time. On the right is kind of the structure for how our mental health support is broken down. We have three mental health people, and this is thinking about how they relate to the counselors. Down the middle with crazy arrows pointing all over is my thinking about how we look at the next two Professional Development days.

Q: **I also see a chart that states another aspect of the school's vision.**

A: Yes, it says, "Sustainable instruction is the catalyst for sustainable learning." This year, we added, "Sustainable learning can be defined simply as learning that 'sticks.'" Below this statement are five Characteristics of Sustainable Instruction & Learning: Student Centered, Balance of Skills and Content, Higher Level Thinking Focus, Constructivist Activities, and Authentic/Real World Context.

Q: **In regard to the school's budget, what are the sources of funds, and how is the money spent?**

A: In theory, we follow a site-based budget process, which means in January we start projecting course needs for the next year. State funding and local funding come into play as the base budget is set. We are about a $13 million building. We then use the master schedule to determine how many teachers will be needed in each department. Our process sets a standard amount for each *Full-Time Equivalent (FTE)*. So, for every hire, that amount is charged in the budget. From there, we look at supplies and operations and try to have enough money to operate a professional business in a professional way. Once it is all said and done, about 85% of the budget is human capital.

We have tried to work with the philosophy that we would love to have our classes with 30 kids or fewer, have every pathway available that we want to offer, have kids be able to take any class they want, and not have the budget or course catalog limit any of those things.

Q: **In a large high school, there are other sources of money such as booster club accounts, gate receipts, donations, and student purchases, including yearbooks and class rings. How are these funds managed?**

A: Also, all of the coaches and the Department Chairs have their own individual accounts to manage. We have a full-time bookkeeper who does a terrific job. Across the contingency budget there probably at any one time are $250,000 to $300,000 that have to be accounted for.

Q: **When you are looking to hire new teachers, what are you looking for?**

A: When any candidate comes in, we will do an Interview Day that has a three-session rotation. One part is the traditional interview with department members, the Department Chair, and an assistant principal. Candidates talk about their background, their instructional strategies, and what their classroom looks like. Another part is a one-on-one session with students, which is our favorite. Then they have a one-on-one session with me.

I, first and foremost, look for personality presentation that I think will connect with kids. I'll ask about a passion for the profession. One of my favorite questions is to have candidates talk about who their favorite educational role model was. And, what have they attempted to emulate from that person? It is interesting to hear what things have made an impact on them and the kind of educator they wish to be. Out of these questions, the conversation can go into what role they take in team meetings, and communication with all stakeholders.

Q: **What brings you joy?**

A: Playing a positive role and having positive relationships is the thing that I gain the majority of my satisfaction from. In my role, I am going to multiple events most nights of the week. People will ask, "Gosh, aren't you tired?" Those things aren't tiring, because you see kids in their most passionate roles. They are truly doing high school things that they love to do. Being able to play a role in a culture that allows those kids to have those pathways and opportunities makes me feel really good.

Also, over the years I continue to be in education, I am taking more and more pride in the educators that I have influenced in some way—in flashing back about the number of people I had a role in hiring and who are doing great things. The people in the building who are some of the best of the best and who I had some role in being a model for and supporting—that is bringing me as much satisfaction and joy as anything.

Questions to Consider

1. What key themes do you hear in the expectations that Mr. Weaver has for teachers and students?

2. What is your impression about the size and items in the school's budget?

3. What would you say in response to Mr. Weaver's teacher interview questions?

4. In what ways would you expect to see joy in Mountain Vista High School?

INTRODUCTION

Becoming a successful teacher entails understanding teaching, standards, students, parents, and learning. Becoming successful also requires beginning teachers to understand how schools are staffed, organized, and paid for. It is especially important to be clear about the principal's expectations for student and teacher learning.

You may have never thought about schools being organizations, but they are. Just like businesses, schools comprise workers who produce a product or service. To be successful, all organizations must structure the work and arrange employees so that their product or service can be produced efficiently and effectively. A unique characteristic of schools as organizations is that not all of the workers are paid a salary. Teachers, principals, custodians, cafeteria workers, and other adults receive paychecks. Students are workers, too, but their "pay" is in a different form: Rather than receiving money, students are rewarded in other ways, including the joy of learning, the satisfaction of participation, feedback on assignments, grades, a diploma, and ultimately a better life.

Another special characteristic of schools as organizations is that the largest component of the labor force is composed of professionals: teachers. Professionals have higher levels of education and expect to have more autonomy in organizing and doing their work than would be acceptable for other types of workers. Professionals also expect to have strong input into how the whole school is organized and which tasks they will do. Since they are staffed by professionals, schools are unique organizations in many ways. The organizational structures, the degree of employee involvement in decision making, and the way the work is done, as well as how the money is spent, are different from what would be true of a manufacturing business or a bank.

In this chapter, learning about schools as organizations is the topic. One way of understanding schools as organizations is learning about their structure. The differences in authority of teachers, principals, teacher leaders, and other personnel can be described and charted. The second important topic is learning about the sources of funds and how the money is spent. The money has to come from somewhere, and there always will be disagreements about how the funds should be spent. Also, schools should not be thought of as isolated and autonomous. Instead, schools are clustered into school districts and are part of each state's education system. In addition, over the past 60-plus years, schools have become increasingly accountable to the federal government. Each of these ways of understanding schools is presented in this chapter. The final major section of this chapter will introduce a number of issues and implications of viewing schools as the workplace for students and teachers.

HOW ARE SCHOOLS STAFFED AND ORGANIZED?

When thinking about schools as organizations, the first place to start is with identifying the different roles of the adults including teachers, principals, secretaries, and Department Chairs. There are structural concepts that are important for you to understand, including areas of responsibility, line and staff relationships, and chain of command. In its purest form, the structural view of schools does not deal with workers' feelings and perceptions. Instead, the focus is entirely on the work at hand, how tasks are organized, who does what, and who is responsible.

Roles of the Adult Workers in Schools

Role differentiation is the primary way to understand the organizational structure of schools. All of the adults do not do the same things. Instead, roles are defined in relation to the accomplishment of organizational tasks. The two most obvious roles for the adults in schools are administrators and teachers. However, there are a number of other important roles to know about, including resource teacher, curriculum specialist, counselor, secretary, cafeteria worker, and custodian. A key to beginning-teacher success is getting to know these other school-based staff since they see students in other settings. There are a number of additional roles outside the school that directly impact what teachers do—for example, the school psychologist, coordinator of special programs such as those for English Language Learners (ELLs), and the school–community liaison. School bus drivers and Human Resources personnel are important, too.

Principals

The administrator with final authority over everything that goes on in a school is the principal. In most schools, principals have a major say in who is hired. They supervise all teachers and the other school-based personnel. The principal is charged with the responsibility for evaluating all teachers, especially beginning teachers. Earlier in their careers, nearly all principals were teachers. Therefore, it is assumed that principals are experts in curriculum and instruction, and that they know about all of the aspects of running a school as an organization. In addition, principals are in charge of safety, enforcing rules of student behavior, and making sure that all of the employees and students obey all laws, statutes, policies, rules, and regulations. Principals also work with parents, community groups, and the various committees that are established for involving teachers, students, parents, and others in doing the work of the school.

Principals have their own technology tools. Asked what forms of technology he uses, Dr. Trevor Ellis, principal of Carmen Arace Middle School in Bloomfield, Connecticut, answered:

Oh, wow, I have a list!

You probably have not thought about principals using technology. Actually, they use many forms. Just as we expect teachers to use technology to closely follow students' learning progress, principals do this, too. Principals also use other technologies for their administrative work. Take a look at Table 8.1. This is a list of typical technology resources principals use. How well does this list match with your expectations for what a school administrator would use? What are implications for you as a teacher?

TABLE 8.1 ■ Typical Technology Tools Being Used by School Principals	
Technology	**Principal Ellis's Descriptions of Purpose**
SchoolMessenger (Reliance Communications)	You need a way to advertise and communicate with parents and the community. There are many reasons, from safety to engaging parents in an activity in the school. It's an automated system that is both online and on the phone. You can text. You can use multiple languages and can choose to communicate with only eighth-grade parents, for example.
Student Information System	This is a web-based student information system that includes student assessment data, where students live, their phone numbers, how to contact their parents, student schedules, student grades, whether each student lives in a single-parent home, and parental rights, special needs, and transportation services. It is an excellent tool for finding out what you want to know about each and every child.
SWIS (School-Wide Information System) (Educational and Community Supports)	This is another online data system for tracking discipline data, suspensions, and referrals.
Parent Participation	We track the level of engagement of parents, such as how often they come to school and engage in other ways. You would be amazed at the smiles when we give incentives at the end of the school year for the level of parent participation.
Standardized Testing Database	This provides one-point access to high-stakes testing data, summative data, and formative data.
Digital Resource Library (Technomic)	This is an online source that has the Common Core State Standards, reference books, graphic organizers, and other state standards.
Curriculum Mapping	Curriculum is a living document. As teachers change their lesson plans, their unit plans, and assessments, they upload them to Curriculum Connector.
Other technologies	Other technologies include SurveyMonkey and Google Docs.

Assistant or Vice Principals and Deans

As the brief summary of the principal's role suggests, the job expectations cover more areas and tasks than one person can do. The organizational structure solution to this problem has been to create another administrator role: assistant or vice principal. Depending on the size of the school, there may be one, two, or no assistant/vice principal(s). For example, elementary schools will typically need to have more than 600 students before they will have an assistant principal. As high schools increase in size from under 1,000 to 2,000 or 3,000 students, the number of assistant/vice principals and other administrators such as deans will increase from one to four or more. Typically, the individuals in these roles share in accomplishing the tasks that are formally the responsibility of the principal. Assistant/vice principals and deans may evaluate teachers, although normally not **probationary teachers**. Assistant/vice principals and deans may have full responsibility for certain tasks, such as discipline or managing aspects of the school's budgets. They also will assume authority for the school during times when the principal is out of the building.

Teachers

The other obvious worker role in the organizational structure of schools is that of teachers. Here, too, there is differentiation within the role. In your experience as a student, you will have seen many of these teacher roles.

- **Grade level(s):** One form of differentiation is by the level of schooling where the teacher works. Elementary and secondary teachers are viewed as specialists within that level of schooling. There are other ways that the teacher role is differentiated. For example, elementary teachers are classified as **primary** (Grades K–3) or **intermediate** (Grades 4–5 or 6), while **secondary** teachers are either junior high school (Grades 6 or 7–8), middle school (Grades 6–8 or 9), or senior high school (Grades 9 or 10–12). Teachers also may specialize in other ways:

- **Subject(s) taught:** Specializing in terms of subject(s) taught is the regular pattern in secondary schools. For example, teachers are specialists in teaching mathematics, English, social studies, science, physical education, music, or technical areas. Increasingly, there is specialization in elementary schools; for example, some teachers become literacy or math specialists and work across grade levels to teach the language arts or math.

- **Types of students taught:** Teacher roles may be specialized according to the needs of particular students, such as resource teachers (for students with special needs), bilingual or ELL teachers for students whose first language is not English, and Title I teachers who teach students who are from low-income families and may be at risk of falling behind.

On a regular basis school staffs meet to review data about student progress and to refine Action Steps in the School Improvement Plan (SIP).

- **Additional outside-the-classroom responsibilities:** In most schools, teachers will have additional responsibilities. For example, in most secondary schools, teachers will be expected to supervise an extracurricular activity such as yearbook, pep squad, theater, or a music program. Elementary school teachers may be expected to offer tutorials before or after school, do bus duty during the morning arrival and afternoon departure of students, and/or supervise the lunchroom.

Department Chairs and Team Leaders

As schools have grown in size, the role of Department Chair, team leader, and/or grade-level leader has become a regular part of the school organization chart. The most common staffing pattern in secondary schools is to have teachers organized into departments by subject matter (e.g., science department, language arts department, and mathematics department). One of the teachers will serve as Department Chair (DC). At a minimum, this way of structuring workers facilitates communication between teachers within the subject area. Typically, the DCs will meet regularly with the principal and serve as a communication channel for passing on information from the principal to the teachers. In most schools, DCs are teachers, not administrators. In other words, they have no role in the evaluation of teachers; their primary tasks are to facilitate communication and coordination of teacher work within the particular subject area. DCs also are important sources of ideas and assistance for new teachers. A similar coordination and communication role will be assumed by grade-level teacher leaders in elementary schools.

Teachers as Full-Time Instructional Leaders

Some school districts will have another important role that can be especially important for beginning teachers. This role is that of a full-time instructional specialist increasingly being called **teacher leaders**. In some districts they will have a different title such as **onsite staff developer**. These professionals are master teachers who serve as mentor, model teacher, peer coach, and planner of teacher Professional Development within a school. Often, they specialize in supporting the teaching of a particular subject such as literacy or mathematics. They will teach a teacher's students in order to model an instructional strategy, but they will not have a class assigned to them full-time. They do not have a teacher evaluation role. Instead, their primary responsibility is to serve all teachers by helping them increase their knowledge and skill in ways that will lead to increases in student learning.

This is the Professional Learning Specialist role at Mountain Vista High School in Douglas County, Colorado, that Mr. Weaver mentioned in the introduction to this chapter. Before becoming a PLS, Rachael Matthews spent 13 years as an English teacher at Mountain Vista. She is in her second year as a PLS.

Q: As the PLS for Mountain Vista High School, what does your job entail?

A: My role is about supporting teachers and supporting their growth. I coordinate and plan all Professional Development for the building. I work with new teachers in the process of induction. Also, I work closely with the Building Leadership Team, which is a team of eight teachers and a counselor. They help facilitate and coordinate Professional Development. They are an additional resource and help for teachers, especially new teachers. Each one has adopted a new teacher and checks on him or her regularly. They are strong teachers who also are collaborative.

School secretaries and other noninstructional staff are important to teacher and student success.

Principal Michael Weaver and Professional Learning Specialist Rachel Matthews review plans for the next professional development day.

Q: What advice do you have for people who are preparing to be teachers?

A: *I wrote down four things:*

- FIND YOUR PEOPLE. I think teaching can be a really isolating thing. You have got to find the right people. Find the people who are happy to be here, positive solution oriented, and encouraging.

- THINK OF IT AS A JOURNEY OR EVOLUTION. You don't have to get it right the first time. In the first year of teaching, you are going to make a lot of mistakes. Think of it as learning as you grow.

- SET BOUNDARIES. Have a balance and say, "I am done working for today, and now I am going to do life and be well." Otherwise, you will burn out.

- STAY GROUNDED. When I was a first-year teacher, a teacher asked, "What do you believe about teaching? Are you doing those things?" Stay grounded in who you are and stay connected to what you believe and give yourself permission to do those things.

Other School-Based Staff

It takes more than teachers and administrators to run a school. In addition to making sure all the necessary forms are completed, office managers and secretaries greet students. Library/media specialists increasingly are another instructional resource for teachers. Custodians keep the campus clean and the plumbing/heating/cooling working. Cafeteria workers not only prepare meals; they also see students daily. Another position increasingly found on school staffs is the **School Resource Officer (SRO)**. Their primary role is to enhance safety and security. These professionals may be district employees or representatives of the local police force. Either way, SROs will be visible and work closely with the school staff and students. A key to beginning-teacher success is getting to know all of these school-based staff since they will be seeing your students in other settings and can be of help to you. There also will be regular visitors from the district office.

Organization Charts

Another regularly used way to understand schools as organizations is to see the **organization chart**. This is a graphic that depicts the formal relationships between different roles and positions. An organization chart for a typical school is presented in Figure 8.1. A number of the important characteristics of organizational structure are represented in this type of chart. One that is very important for beginning teachers to understand is the difference between line and staff relationships. **Line relationships** are those where one position has direct supervisory authority over another. In the organizational structure of schools, the principal is in a line relationship with all teachers, the assistant/vice principals, and all other school-based personnel. **Staff relationships** are those where one position does not have direct authority over another but where there is an expectation that the two positions will communicate, coordinate, and work together. For example, in secondary schools, there will be a staff relationship among the various Department Chairs, and in all schools, assistant/vice principals are in a staff relationship with teachers. Teachers are in staff relationships with other teachers.

Communication Within the School as an Organization

One of the reasons schools are structured as they are is to facilitate communication. There is a continual risk that teachers will become isolated within their classrooms, grade levels, or departments and not be aware of school-wide needs and district initiatives. The reverse risk also is very real: One teacher, a team, or a department may be doing something very wonderful, but without communication, the rest of the organization does not learn about it. Two types of communication are built into the structure of the school organization chart, vertical and horizontal. **Vertical communication** is communication that moves down, and up, the organization chart. This is where the phrase "the lines of communication" comes from. An important responsibility of people in each role is to initiate and facilitate communication up and down the lines of authority. In business and military organizations, a frequently used phrase to refer

FIGURE 8.1 ■ School Organization Chart

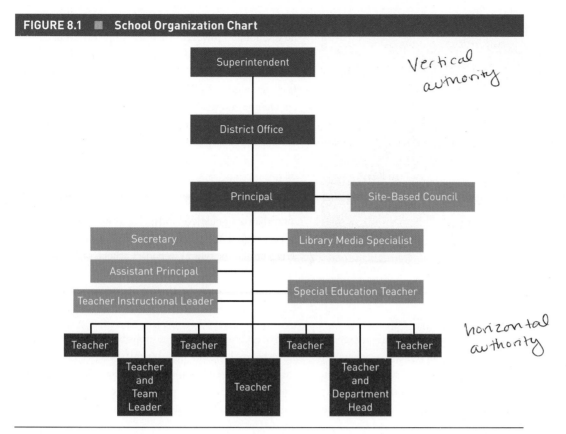

Vertical authority

horizontal authority

Source: Adapted from Johnson, J. A., Musial, D., Hall, G. E., Gollnick, D. M., & Dupuis, V. (2005). *Introduction to the foundations of American education* (13th ed.). Boston, MA: Pearson/Allyn & Bacon.

to the up/down line relationships in an organization chart is **chain of command**. As a teacher, it will be very important that you understand vertical communication. You will need to follow this chain one level at a time when you have a question, a concern, or a suggestion.

In most organizations, including schools, vertical communication is not sufficient, so there also needs to be communication *across* the various levels in the organization chart—in other words, **horizontal communication**. One example of horizontal communication is when a veteran fourth-grade teacher tells a first-year fourth-grade teacher about an upcoming Professional Development workshop. Another example would be when one Department Chair tells another about an interesting idea that the principal proposed in an informal conversation. In schools that are more successful, there will be more vertical *and* horizontal communication.

Variations in Teachers' Role and Responsibilities

Up to this point, the description of the organizational structure of schools has been about the typical way schools are staffed and how the different roles relate to each other. There are many other ways that teacher assignments and responsibilities can vary.

Self-Contained Classroom

In most settings, **self-contained classroom** means that one teacher stays in a classroom and is assigned responsibility for teaching all subjects to one set of students. The self-contained classroom

"They meet in there. Some kind of support group."

© Martha Campbell

Chairs, tables, storage, and the walls of a classroom can be used to group students in a variety of ways to facilitate group work.

continues to be the dominant structure for U.S. elementary schools. However, an interesting variation on the meaning of self-contained classroom was tested recently in some high schools in New York City. In this variation, the students stay in one classroom, and the teachers change rooms. This variation seems to be reducing the isolation that so many students experience in high schools, especially those with thousands of students.

Teaching More Than One Grade or Subject

Most secondary school teachers will be expected to teach more than one grade level and perhaps more than one subject. For example, a math teacher may teach general math as well as algebra. In the typical secondary school, each teacher will have contact each day with more than 100 students. Learning the names and needs of each student is an important task.

Departmentalization

In both elementary and secondary schools, instead of each teacher being responsible for one group of 25 to 35 students for all subjects, teachers will specialize by teaching one subject to all students. For example, one teacher teaches mathematics while another teaches social studies and another specializes in language arts. A variation on this staffing model is to have one teacher lead in the preparation of the instruction for a subject; each teacher then uses the same lesson plan and materials to teach his or her class.

Looping

In **looping**, teachers follow their students to the next grade. For example, the teacher of a first-grade class one year moves to teaching second grade the next year and keeps the same students. An obvious advantage is that the teacher knows the students and the students know the teacher, which means less time lost to diagnostic assessments at the beginning of the year. Of course, looping also requires teachers to develop lessons for use in both years.

Team Teaching

Team teaching is a staffing plan that has two or more teachers working together to plan and teach a common group of students. Team teaching is used in many configurations in both elementary and secondary schools. For example, in middle schools, there will be grade-level interdisciplinary teams. Each team will have a language arts, social studies, science, and math teacher. Each team is assigned a large block of students, and it is responsible for all of the instruction and for most of the day. Team teaching also is frequently applied in elementary schools.

Another frequently found variation is to have teachers team-teach part of the day and then teach their "own" students for the remainder of the day. The organizational support of teachers to do teaming will vary, too. In some schools, teams have to do their planning before and after school. In other schools, there will be a scheduled team planning period. Another variation is to have an early-release day: On certain days, students leave school early in order to provide time for teacher teams to plan.

Teacher Leadership Beyond the Classroom

All teachers have responsibilities outside of their classrooms. In addition to leading student extra curricula activities such as pep squad and chess club, teachers will have important roles and responsibilities with the other adults. For example, they serve as mentors for beginning teachers. They help plan for and lead Professional Development sessions. They serve on committees, such as the School Improvement Committee, facilitate discussions about student data, and help develop plans for next steps in instruction.

TABLE 8.2 ■ Themes in Professional Learning Communities
Supportive and shared leadership requires the collegial and facilitative participation of the principal who shares leadership—and, thus, power and authority—by inviting staff input and action in decision making.
Shared values and vision include an unwavering commitment to student learning that is consistently articulated and referenced in the staff's work.
Collective learning and application of learning requires that school staff members at all levels be engaged in a process that collectively seeks new knowledge among staff and application of the learning to solutions that address students' needs.
Supportive conditions include physical conditions and human capacities that encourage and sustain a collegial atmosphere and collective learning.
Shared practice involves the review of a teacher's behavior by colleagues and includes feedback and assistance activity to support individual and community improvement.

Source: Adapted from Hord, S. M. (2004). *Learning together, leading together: Changing schools through Professional Learning Communities* (p. 7). New York, NY: Teachers College Press.

Professional Learning Communities

An increasingly common approach to organizing the teachers in a school is through what are called **Professional Learning Communities (PLCs)**. There are two general approaches to PLCs: (1) A scheduled time is set each week for teachers to meet as PLCs, and (2) a school-wide effort is focused on developing a collaborative culture around student *and* adult learning. In the first approach, the primary purpose of the meetings is to discuss data about student learning and to plan next steps for instruction. In the second approach, the aim is for all day, every day, adult and student interactions related to everyone learning. In the past 15 years, there has been extensive study of PLCs, their characteristics, and what it takes to develop and sustain such an ideal organizational culture. One of the researchers, Shirley Hord (2004), has identified five themes or dimensions of PLCs (see Table 8.2).

As important as each of these themes is individually, additional importance comes from the ways that they become intertwined in a live PLC. For example, without supportive leadership, it is very difficult for teachers to be collegial and collaborative. Collective learning of the adults in the organization is possible only when there is shared practice. Developing and sustaining a PLC is hard work. All of the adults and students in the school must participate. In an earlier study of school organizational culture in Belgium, Dr. Katrine Staessens (1993) identified a culture that is very similar to the PLC, which she named "the school as a professional organization." She also described the importance of the principal in this type of school:

> In this type of school, the teachers characterize the principal as an architect. He [*sic*] is a well-read person, is well-informed about the recent developments in the different domains, and often talks about these with his staff. . . . The norm is created whereby the school is a place where teachers can learn something, and can become better teachers by bringing up professional concerns. To be isolated in one's classroom is not accepted. The proposition that everything can always be improved appears to be a fundamental belief of this principal. (Staessens, 1993, p. 119)

Organizing Students for Their Work—Learning

Organizing the adults in the school seems relatively easy in comparison to organizing the students. A variety of organizational structures, methods, and student groupings have been tried. (For many of these structures, there are continuing debates about their effectiveness. For example, study the

Challenging Assumptions box about student grouping.) Curiously, some of the structures for organizing students seem to have become fixed in concrete.

The First Factor Used to Group Students Is . . . ?

Think about it: What is the first step in organizing school students for doing their work? What characteristic of students is determined first in deciding their placement? This characteristic of students is not used in any other type of organization as the basis for organizing the workers. It is their age! Students cannot begin schooling until they have passed a certain birthday. Students cannot leave school until they have reached a particular birthday. At their simplest, grade levels are groupings of students by their age. There are a number of additional ways that should be considered in regard to organizing students to do their work.

What Are Some of the Ways of Grouping Students?

Continuing the use of the metaphor of students as workers leads to examining some of the ways they can be grouped for learning. Table 8.3 presents a brief summary of some of the ways that students can be grouped. At different times in your career as a student in schools, you will have experienced each one of these, and you probably prefer some ways over others. Each of these ways brings with it important consequences for the teacher, as well as for student learning. For example, presenting a lecture to the whole class provides the teacher with a way to cover the content, but brings with it very limited opportunity to check for individual student understanding.

As another example, think about the different ways of organizing small groups. The teacher role needs to change dramatically from dispenser of information (or giving directions) to monitor and facilitator of group work. Each time a lesson is planned, the teacher has to decide how the student workers will be organized. Table 8.3 will help you as you begin thinking about how you want to organize the student "workers" in your classroom.

TABLE 8.3 ■ Ways of Organizing Students to Do Their Work

Structure	Description	Advantages	Teacher Challenge
Whole class	All students are taught as a single, intact group.	The lesson is presented at the same time to all students.	It is difficult to address individual differences in understanding.
Small groups	Typically, there are three to five students per group.	There is more opportunity for each student to participate.	Some students may do most of the work, but it is difficult to determine each student's effort.
Dyads/pairs	Two students work together.	Each student has an opportunity to participate.	It is difficult to manage and monitor all dyads at the same time.
Individuals	Each student does his or her own work without dialogue with others.	Students can learn at their own rate.	It is difficult to manage and monitor each student closely.
Homogeneous	Like students are grouped together.	Students can progress at the same rate.	There is the risk of labeling and neglecting "fast" and "slow" groups.
Heterogeneous	Mixed-level students are grouped together.	Students can learn from what each brings to the group.	"Slow" and/or "fast" students may be neglected.
Fixed groupings	The same students stay together over an extended time.	Students and teachers know what to expect.	Fixed groupings do not make adjustment for different students' rates of progress.
Flexible groups	Students routinely change group membership.	Each new grouping provides fresh opportunities.	It is difficult to monitor students to know when to regroup.
Cooperative groups	Each group member has a prescribed role (e.g., facilitator or note taker).	Students learn roles for facilitating group work. Some research suggests students learn more.	Students have to be trained in doing roles.

THINKING DIFFERENTLY
WHAT SCHOOL START TIME MAKES THE MOST SENSE?

A widely held experience is that teenagers are sleepyheads, while elementary school children wake up early and are ready to go. What would happen if the school start times were adjusted to take into account the natural sleep patterns of the students? In a report, the Centers for Disease Control and Prevention points out that too many adolescents are sleep deprived. This leads to less physical activity, health risks, and poor academic performance. A later start time addresses all of these symptoms. A few school districts are making this change. For example, in the La Joya Independent School District (Texas), elementary schools start at 7:30 a.m., middle schools at 7:45, and high schools at 8:30.

Source: Centers for Disease Control and Prevention. (2018, July 30). *Schools start too early.* Retrieved from www.cdc.gov/features/school-start-times/index.html; Centers for Disease Control and Prevention. (2018, February 5). *Sleep in middle school and high school students.* Retrieved from www.cdc.gov/features/students-sleep/index.html

CHALLENGING ASSUMPTIONS
SHOULD GIFTED STUDENTS BE GROUPED TOGETHER?

Student Grouping: Which Is Best: Tracking or Mixed Ability?

Teachers, parents, school leaders, and policy makers have long debated which is best—homogeneous or heterogeneous grouping of students. The debate can focus on what a teacher should do in grouping students for a day's lessons, or how students should be grouped for an entire school year. When students are grouped according to ability for a semester or longer, it is called tracking (see Chapter 2).

What is your current position about this important question? Do you believe that students will make greater progress if they are placed with like students so that all can move at the same pace? Or do you believe that students can learn from each other and that it is not fair to label some as being in the "slow" group?

Findings From Research

Although there have been hundreds of studies, there still are not definitive simple answers to the overall question. There are some research findings related to these subquestions: (a) In which grouping pattern do students learn more? (b) What difference do grouping patterns make in students' attitudes about learning and self-perceptions? and (c) What difference do teachers make in determining the effects of grouping arrangements?

Well over three decades ago, Oakes (1985) and Slavin (1987) argued for all students being placed in heterogeneous classes. A main theme in their position is that a democratic ideal is not to create different categories of people, and there needs to be equal opportunity for all students. They also reported that there was no clear pattern of gains in student learning with homogeneous grouping.

The grouping question is so important that it is a continuing topic of inquiry in other countries and is a component of the Trends in International Mathematics and Science Study (TIMSS) research as well. For example, in a study of grouping of fifth- and eighth-grade students in Canada, Shields (2002) reported that the academically talented self-contained classes had higher student achievement. However, there was "considerable overlap (from 46% to 88%) in the scores of the two groups" (Shields, 2002, p. 117). In other words, students in both the gifted and heterogeneous classes were achieving. (An important contextual factor to keep in mind is that Canada has offered self-contained programs for elementary school academically able students since 1934.)

Although the findings about perceptions and attitudes were more complicated, Shields (2002) drew the following conclusion:

> These data do not suggest that the needs of all students would be better served if they had all been grouped in a single heterogeneous class; rather, in this study, homogeneous grouping for academically talented and gifted students was associated with positive student perceptions of themselves as learners and of their total school experience. Likewise, students placed in a heterogeneous classroom demonstrated similarly positive attitudes and perceptions. (p. 118)

Across the many studies of student grouping, a key factor is the teacher's attitudes and teaching approach; this is probably the most significant of all the factors. When the teacher sets high expectations for learning and presents all students with the same curriculum, students learn in either grouping arrangement. Student attitudes and perceptions can be positive in either grouping arrangement, again dependent on the teacher's attitudes and expectations. Still, much of the research indicates that placing more academically able students in a homogeneous group advances their level of achievement while not diminishing other students having success in heterogeneous groups.

Sources: Oakes, J. (1985). *Keeping track: How schools structure inequality.* New Haven, CT: Yale University Press; Shields, C. M. (2002, Spring). A comparison study of student attitudes and perceptions in homogeneous and heterogeneous classrooms. *Roeper Review, 24*(3), 115–120; Slavin, R. E. (1987). Ability grouping and student achievement in elementary schools: A best-evidence synthesis. *Review of Educational Research, 57,* 347–370.

WHAT IS THE RELATIONSHIP OF SCHOOLS TO SCHOOL DISTRICTS AND THE STATE?

Schools are not independent, isolated, and autonomous organizations. Instead, schools are clustered to form school districts, also called **Local Education Agencies (LEAs)**; above them is the **State Education Agency (SEA)**; and above the state(s) is the federal government. The primary factor for determining an LEA is geography: School districts typically encompass all of the public schools within a certain area such as a city or county.

Organization of School Districts

Mapping the geographic area covered by a school district is one way of understanding its size. Another is the levels of schooling that are covered. For example, most school districts encompass all public elementary and secondary schools within a certain geographic area. However, in some states, such as Arizona, some school districts are responsible for elementary schools only, with a separate school district responsible for the secondary schools. Another way to understand the size of a school district is to find out the number of schools within the school district. Very small districts may have as few as one or two schools. The largest school districts will have 200 or more schools.

School District Organization

An organization chart for a typical school district is presented in Figure 8.2. One of the first impressions from studying this chart should be the fact that there are many roles and functions that are not directly related to teaching and learning. As is true for organizations in business and industry, a number of support functions must be addressed and staffed. A **Human Resources (HR)** department is needed to hire employees, to see that they are paid, and to see that they have health and retirement programs (benefits). Organizations need specialists to manage and audit the budgets. Other typical school district departments include maintenance/facilities and grounds, a transportation department to operate the buses, and legal counsel.

A number of functions are unique to schooling, such as the various special services for students and their families. Another unique district department will be for federal programs: School districts receive federal funds through grants and contracts, to support different functions such as special education and ELL programs. Districts also have many required reporting tasks. Of course, the instructional support function must be staffed as well. A function that has grown significantly in importance is the assessment office. Given the heavy focus on testing, experts are needed to organize test administration and to analyze test data. As never before, teachers, administrators, parents, policy makers, and the public are demanding quick turnaround and understandable reporting of data about student achievement.

School District Superintendent

The Chief Executive Officer of the school district is the **superintendent**. This person has the overwhelming responsibility of leading the entire school district. As is reflected in the organization chart (Figure 8.2), all of the district office and school personnel are in a line relationship with the superintendent. As President Harry Truman would say, "The buck stops here." In the end, the superintendent is accountable for everything that happens, should happen, and should not happen within the school district. In a large school district, with many layers to the organization chart, holding the superintendent responsible for everything is very unrealistic; however, in the structural view of organizations, that is the reality.

The superintendent must communicate well with teachers, the school board, the public, and the media.

FIGURE 8.2 ■ School District Organization Chart

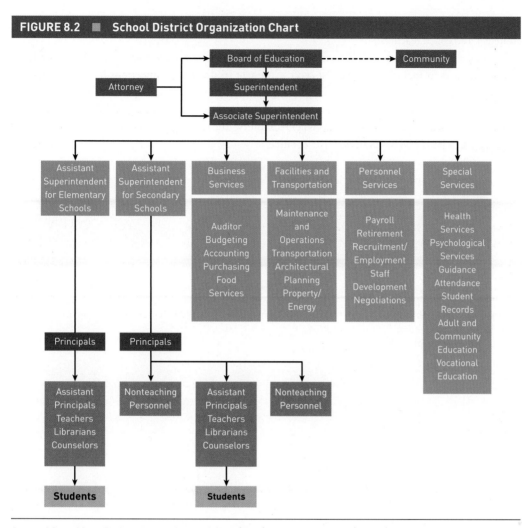

Source: Adapted from Parkay, F. W., & Stanford, B. H. (2004). *Becoming a teacher* (6th ed.). Boston, MA: Allyn & Bacon.

Most superintendents are appointed and will have a contract for one to three, and in some cases four to five, years. There are some exceptions, such as Florida and Indiana, where some superintendents are elected through a community-wide vote. One of the consequences of their being elected is that the individual may not have any background in education as either a teacher or an administrator. In some cities, the superintendent is appointed by the mayor.

Superintendents do not have tenure in the position and may be removed at any time. One unfortunate consequence of this fact is that there is a large turnover in the superintendency each year. Some years, a state will have one-third or more of the school district superintendents change. In urban school districts, the average longevity of superintendents is less than three years. One important consequence of this rapid turnover is that with the arrival of each new superintendent, the strategic directions and priorities within the school district change. This leads to another consequence: District and school administrators, as well as teachers and families, are unable to develop and sustain initiatives and directions across the three to five to eight years it takes to make meaningful changes. This places significantly heavier responsibility on principals and teachers to maintain a focus on the most essential long-term efforts that will benefit students the most.

District Office–Based School Support Personnel

There are a number of education professionals in district offices whose role is to support instruction across all schools and classrooms. For example, curriculum specialists in literacy, mathematics, science, and ELL provide district-wide leadership in their specialty areas. They also develop Professional

Development sessions. Many not only will visit schools but also are willing to model instructional strategies and coach teachers.

School district support staff increasingly include data analysis specialists who assist school leaders and teachers in making sense of test scores and help in drawing connections between standards and individual student performance. Experts in special education are another important district office resource. You will work with them when you have a student with an Individualized Education Program (IEP) or refer a student for testing for a possible disability. The testing will be done by a licensed school psychologist, who is also based in the district office.

UNDERSTANDING AND USING DATA
DIFFERENCES IN SCHOOL STAFFING

You might want to consider a number of readily available statistics as you look ahead to your first teaching position. How important to you is the size of the school? What about class size? Would you prefer to be teaching smaller classes, or does it really matter that much? Also, what about the diversity of students?

Study the table below. What information can you draw from these data? Which school would you expect to be most challenging? In which school would you most want to teach?

Descriptive Statistics for High Schools					
School	No. of Students	No. of Teachers (FTE)	Student–Teacher Ratio	Free Lunch Eligible	Reduced-Price Lunch Eligible
Adams High School	2,572	114	22.6	1,212	127
Jefferson High School	2,583	102	25.3	1,074	121
Lincoln High School	1,636	80	20.5	182	64
Washington High School	907	96.3	9.42	307	33

Note: FTE = Full-Time Equivalent.

Data like these for real schools can be found within the National Center for Education Statistics (NCES) site. Visit https://nces.ed.gov/globallocator/ and type in the name of a school or college. For this table, the author of this chapter pulled up these statistics for the high school he attended and for three other schools where he has conducted research. Of course, the names of the schools have been changed.

In which of these schools would you want to teach?

Be careful about drawing conclusions about each of these schools based on these data alone. Still, these are the facts, as far as they go. Here are some guiding questions:

- Which school has the largest student population? Which the smallest?
- An important indicator of diversity is socioeconomic status (SES). The federal government indicator for

poverty in a school is how many students are eligible for Free or Reduced-Price Lunch. What does this indicator suggest about these four high schools?

- If you want to teach in a school with small class sizes, which school would you pick?

One of the patterns within these data is that the two largest high schools have the highest student–teacher ratios. You might expect that larger schools would have more teachers and could have lower student–teacher ratios. In this case, it is likely that each of these schools has smaller class sizes for some special offerings and offsets these with large class sizes in other areas. A factor that is not reported in this table is the funding for each school. A useful statistic for comparing funding is the amount of dollars per pupil. If you were to know that Adams and Jefferson High Schools are in a state that is relatively low on funding, how would this affect your thinking?

A New Role: Chief Academic Officer

Many school districts are now establishing a new top-level position, Chief Academic Officer (CAO). This position provides district-wide leadership in relation to instruction, assessment, curriculum, and improvement of the overall quality of educational services. The CAO reports directly to the superintendent and is responsible for seeing that all resources and personnel are aligned to support the learning of all students.

School Boards

The school district governing body is the **school board** or **board of trustees**. School boards typically consist of five to seven members. (The reasoning behind having an odd number of members is to reduce the chance of having tie votes by the board.) In most communities, school board members are elected by voters in a designated geographic part of the community or by the community at large. In some cities, such as Chicago, Illinois, and Hartford, Connecticut, the mayor or the city council will appoint some or all of the school board members.

In 1988, Downey identified two major obligations for school boards, which still hold true today:

1. To process the values, needs, and demands of society and, in so doing, to determine which of these are to be accepted as the official guidelines for the educational system

2. To set the guidelines for action that are, in effect, the directions or general rules for the operation of the school system (p. 18)

School Boards as Policy Bodies

Policies are the official stated overarching parameters for what can and cannot be done within an organization. Policies are guidelines that can be **prescriptive** by setting limits and specifying the procedures that are to be used, or they can be **empowering** by identifying the target or vision and leaving open the means for achieving the desired end. In school districts, the board is the overarching policy-making body.

For example, a school board could set as policy that the school district should achieve a 10-point increase in the percentage of high school graduates who go on to some type of postsecondary education. This would be an empowering policy. District administrators and teachers would be expected to devise the steps to be taken to achieve the goal. If the school board established a prescriptive policy, it would specify the approach to be used, such as "no pass, no play," or enact a rule that all eighth-grade students must take Algebra I. With prescriptive policies, administrators and teachers have little or no say in the strategies to be used and instead are charged with implementing the policy mandate.

Keep in mind that school boards can only set polices for the district as long as these are not inconsistent with state and federal policies. For example, a school board could require a longer school year, but it couldn't set a minimum number of days fewer than the number required by the state.

School Board Responsibilities

One of the most important school board responsibilities is hiring the superintendent. Another is approving the employment of all district personnel, including teachers. Beginning teachers will turn in their signed employment contract to the district office of Human Resources, but the contract is not official until it has been approved by the school board.

School boards are responsible for oversight of all administrative and educational matters, including review and approval of the district budget, large purchase orders, student band trip travel support, and review of test scores. Boards also evaluate the performance of the superintendent. In the ideal setting, the board will turn to the superintendent, as the Chief Executive Officer, and trust him or her to lead the day-to-day operations of the district.

Unfortunately, in too many instances, school board members are not satisfied with limiting their role to establishing policy and oversight of district operations. Many board members seem to be most interested in pushing a pet agenda, such as use of a particular curriculum approach or hiring/firing of a particular district employee. Many boards also have a tendency to become overly involved in the day-to-day operations of the district—that is, **micromanaging**. School boards' involvement in these daily operations has become a significant contributing factor to the high rate of superintendent turnover.

Intermediate Units

Intermediate units are part of the organization of education in most states. They have different names, such as BOCES (Boards of Cooperative Educational Services) in New York, County Offices in California, and Regional Service Centers in Texas. These units will serve several school districts by providing joint purchasing, special education services, Professional Development, and some types of data analyses. In some cases, initial teacher and administrator preparation programs are offered as well.

School Choice Shifts the Public Education Landscape

So far, we have described the more typical ways that schools and districts are organized. However, we would be remiss if alternative organization structures were not overviewed. In the distant past, the deeply held belief was that all children should receive a public supported education. The assumption has been that having a well-educated citizenry was fundamental to continuing the democracy and having a strong economy. It also was assumed that through public schools, all children would have equal opportunity. These assumptions and expectations have been explicit in one way or another in each state's constitution. These assumptions and expectations are so important that attending school is **compulsory**.

However, over the last 20 to 30 years, these assumptions have been overridden by a movement to establish alternatives to the neighborhood public school. One theme in this movement is the argument that public schools are not doing the job and, just as in business, there needs to be *competition*. A second theme is that parents need to be able to *choose* the school their children attend, not be forced to attend the nearby public school.

By far, the majority (some 90%) of students attend regular public schools. As a result of questioning the traditional public school, now, in most communities, parents have one or more alternatives to their neighborhood public school. The alternative could be a public school in a different neighborhood, or a school that is not operated by the school district. There are different labels used in the alternative school movement. The following terms represent key concepts. As you study this list, keep in mind that each term is not tightly defined and mutually exclusive of other terms. In practice, any one school may incorporate overlapping terms. Another aspect to keep in mind is that any particular alternative school may be fully within, partially within, or completely outside the local school district.

Choice has a three-part definition. First, the term is used to represent the menu of alternative schools that might be available. The second part of the definition is about parents having the option of selecting an alternative to the regular public school. The third part, which is more complicated, is the expectation that public school funds will follow the student to the alternative school.

Private schools are organized and operated outside the public school system. These schools do not have direct public funding. They are financed through tuition and donations. Some 80% of these schools have a religious orientation. The most recent data indicate that 42% are Catholic and 40% non-Catholic religious-oriented, with 18% nonsectarian (National Center for Education Statistics, 2016). One trend in recent years has been a decrease in the number of Catholic schools. Many of these are located in urban areas. The cost of operations has continued to go up while low-income parents have limited ability to pay the tuition.

Charter schools are public schools that are open to all students, with no special admission requirements. These schools are expected to meet the same student learning outcomes as regular public schools. The leadership of the school is given more freedom to configure curriculum, instruction, and staffing. There also is an expectation that charter schools will share what works with other schools. Each state has established its own regulations for how charter schools can be established, which has resulted in variations from state to state.

Home school, as the term states, is schooling at home. Normally a parent, or in some cases a tutor, will be the teacher. Most states require that the teacher be certified. For the 2011–2012 school year, the last year for which there are statistics, 3.4% of the school-age student population were being home-schooled. Eighty-three percent of the students were white (Ray, 2016).

Virtual school is another alternative. Online courses are regularly offered for advance study and credit recovery. It also is possible to be a full-time online school student. The virtual school calendar typically parallels the traditional school year. The students receive instruction, do assignments, and interact with certified teachers online and use related technologies. The necessary curriculum materials and other resources will be delivered to the student's home. Students do not come to a campus; instead, they access schooling from wherever they are located. These schools will be accredited, and students will take the normal state-required assessments.

Vouchers represent a financial strategy for supporting choice. The student's parent receives a certificate for a certain amount of funds. These dollars can be used for tuition at a private school. The funds may come from the school district or in some cases the state. The amount of the voucher does not cover all of the costs for a student to attend an alternative school.

An **Education Management Organization (EMO)** is a private company that receives payment to manage private, charter, other public, and virtual schools. Most of the EMOs are for-profit companies. There will be a multiyear contract between the EMO and the school district. The EMO may only be responsible for day-to-day operation of the school. The EMO may also have full authority over all aspects of the school, including employment of teachers and the principal. The contract agreement usually includes the expectation that student outcomes will be higher than they were in the past.

Organization of Education at the State Level

In the distant past, the governance of schools was primarily a matter of local control. School boards set most policies and obtained financial support locally. In the past 60 years, much of the control has shifted to the states. This shift has come about in part because the funding of public schools has become a very large part of state budgets. For sure, state policy makers have a right to take an active interest in education. In fact, all state constitutions have articles related to the responsibility of the state to ensure that all citizens have access to education. Some examples from state constitutions follow.

Arkansas

Intelligence and virtue being the safeguards of liberty and the bulwark of a free and good government, the State shall ever maintain a general, suitable and efficient system of free public schools and shall adopt all suitable means to secure to the people the advantages and opportunities of education. (Arkansas State Constitution, Article 14, Education, Sec. 1, Free school system)

California

The Legislature shall provide for a system of common schools by which a free school shall be kept up and supported in each district at least six months in every year, after the first year in which a school has been established. (California Constitution, Article 9, Education, Sec. 5)

Vermont

The right to public education is integral to Vermont's constitutional form of government and its guarantees of political and civil rights. Further, the right to education is fundamental for the success of Vermont's children in a rapidly changing society and global marketplace as well as for the state's own economic and social prosperity. To keep Vermont's democracy competitive and thriving, Vermont students must be afforded substantially equal access to a quality basic education. However, one of the strengths of Vermont's education system lies in its rich diversity and the ability for each local school district to adapt its educational program to local needs and desires. Therefore, it is the policy of the state that all Vermont children will be afforded educational opportunities which are substantially equal although educational program may vary from district to district. (Vermont: Added 1997, No. 60, 2, eff. June 26, 1997)

Today, all three branches of state government—legislative, administrative, and judicial—are extremely active when it comes to public education. Figure 8.3 is an organization chart for state government.

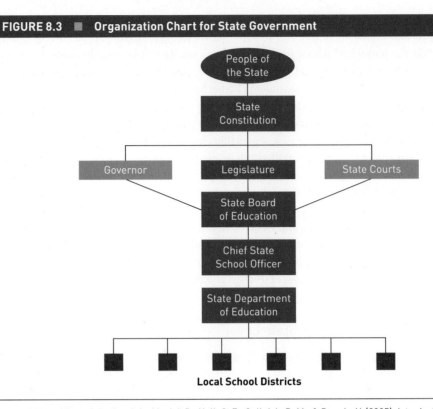

FIGURE 8.3 ■ **Organization Chart for State Government**

Source: Adapted from Johnson, J. A., Musial, D., Hall, G. E., Gollnick, D. M., & Dupuis, V. (2005). *Introduction to the foundations of American education* (13th ed.). Boston, MA: Pearson/Allyn & Bacon.

Executive: State Governors

Since citizens are concerned about the quality of schools and the costs of education, it is logical that to some degree state political leaders would be attending to education problems and needs. In the past, the phrase *education governor* was applied frequently. However, since 2008 and the Great Recession, many governors have cut the support for public education. Recently, in states including Wisconsin, Ohio, and Florida, the governors have openly attacked teachers and other public employees. This is a new phenomenon in the United States, and different from the tendency in some communities and other countries to hold teachers in high esteem.

Governors are able to establish aspirations and visions for a state's education system. In some states, they have a major say over the state budget, and in all states, governors can propose changes in state policies that they believe will improve schools. In some states, the governor appoints members of the state board of education and/or the state superintendent. In other states, the legislature may appoint or will need to approve appointment of the state superintendent and state board members.

Legislative: State Legislatures

The primary policy-making body for education at the state level is the state legislature. State legislatures can create new education policies in any area, from student discipline to curriculum to specifying how teachers and administrators are evaluated. A very significant responsibility of state legislatures is to establish the state budget for education, which necessarily is linked to state sources of funds such as income and sales taxes. Within whatever limits have been set by a state's constitution, the legislature can prescribe what the state board of education and other education agencies can and should do.

Judicial: State Courts

As the cost of public education has increased and as concerns about the adequacy of schools has grown, the courts have become more instrumental in shaping the directions of education. In the past, the courts were most frequently asked to address contractual issues and to make determinations about the rights of students. In the past 30-plus years, the courts have been asked to address issues of funding adequacy and equity. In fact, most of the states have had, or now have, lawsuits related to the funding of education.

The precedent-setting case was filed in the 1980s in Kentucky. Using the wording in the Kentucky Constitution, the Kentucky Supreme Court ruled in 1989 that the entire system of public education in Kentucky was inadequate. Going even further, the court ruled that the entire system and organization of the State Education Agency and the Local Education Agencies were unconstitutional. The court then directed the governor and the legislature to develop a new system of education.

The result was the Kentucky Education Reform Act (KERA), which was passed in 1990. KERA identified a number of important reforms, including integrated primary school–based management councils, major changes in high schools, and a system of annual standardized testing of students. Since KERA was passed, many other states, including Arkansas, Kansas, Ohio, and New York, have had state courts review and rule on the quality and adequacy of the state's education system. However, to date, no other state has been as ambitious in its attempts to redress past inadequacies and to implement dramatic changes in practice as Kentucky.

State Boards of Education

State boards of education have become very important bodies. As the legislators and governors have become more engaged with education issues, the state boards of education have been given more authority and charged with greater responsibilities. The state board and the staff of the state education department must ensure that all school districts and schools are performing in compliance with state policies and statutes. Other responsibilities include setting standards for teacher licensure, establishing processes for developing and approving curriculum standards, and organizing test data and other data from schools in order to prepare reports about school and student performance for the legislature, the public, and the federal government. State boards are also the body to review cases of teacher malpractice and the revocation of teacher licenses. Most states' board members are either elected or appointed by the governor.

Chief State School Officer

The **Chief State School Officer (CSSO)**, state superintendent of public instruction, or commissioner of education is the Chief Executive Officer for the state board of education. This person is responsible for supervision of the staff and work of the state education department. The CSSO also plays a key leadership and advocacy role for education with the legislature, the governor, school districts, and the state at large. In some states, chiefs are elected at large; in others, they are appointed by the state board of education or by the governor.

WHAT IS THE ROLE OF THE FEDERAL GOVERNMENT IN EDUCATION?

Feds [officials of the federal government] *give us money and the state gives us money. That's important. They lay out certain policies nationally, for example, testing. The states have to abide by the feds, and the districts have to abide by the states. They have a very strong impact. The teacher has [his or] her classroom of kids, the administrator has his or her school of teachers and employees, the state has their districts, and the feds have their states.*

—Dr. Italia Negroni, Former Assistant
Superintendent, Wethersfield, Connecticut

So far in this chapter, the overall structure of schools, school districts, and State Education Agencies has been described. The other major organization affecting schooling is the federal government. Since World War II, the federal government has had an ever-increasing influence over education. In the following pages, we will explain how this has happened.

Although the federal government provides a very small proportion of the funds (around 10%), its influence over states, districts, and schools has been steadily increasing over the past 60 years. Each of the three federal branches of government—the executive, legislative, and judicial—are having direct influences on schools. The president can give a speech, or propose a new statute, with the intent of influencing education. Legislation, such as each reauthorization of the Elementary and Secondary Education Act (ESEA), when passed by both houses of Congress and signed by the president, can have major implications for schools. Also, when the U.S. Supreme Court rules on an education-related case, there will be immediate consequences for schools.

Three Parts of the Federal Government: Three Sources of Education Policy

As you learned in social studies, the U.S. Constitution specifies that the federal government comprises the executive, legislative, and judicial branches. The architects of the Constitution strove for balance and equality in power among the three. Although at times in history there have been imbalances, in general the three-way approach has been maintained.

Executive: President of the United States

Most presidents in the past 60 years have had a strong interest in public education. For example, in 1965, as one of the major pieces of legislation within his Great Society program, President Lyndon B. Johnson led the passage of the first Elementary and Secondary Education Act (ESEA). This act established a number of national priorities for improving schools and education. Federal funds were targeted to improving libraries, teacher Professional Development, improving teacher education, supporting bilingual and special education, developing national statistics about education, and, through the National Assessment of Educational Progress (NAEP), measuring student learning within each state.

ESEA has been reauthorized every four to eight years since that time. The 2001 reauthorization by President George W. Bush, called No Child Left Behind (NCLB), had a much longer life. The next reauthorization of ESEA, now called the Every Student Succeeds Act (ESSA), was not signed into law until December 2015 by President Barack Obama. There will be some carryover of requirements with each reauthorization. For example, some of the elements of NCLB have continued in ESSA including the mandate to test students each year in reading, math, and social studies. Also, some presidents will establish their own education initiatives. For example, during the time of the Obama administration, there was the Race to the Top initiative, which provided multimillion-dollar grants to selected states to bring about statewide reforms.

Legislative: U.S. Congress

Many members of the House of Representatives and the Senate have very strong interest in schools and education issues. Both the House and the Senate have committees with responsibilities related to education. As a result, in most sessions of Congress, there are a number of education bills and statutes proposed. Of course, each does not become law until passed by both houses and signed by the president.

An important understanding related to legislative bodies, such as Congress, is that two pieces of legislation are needed to accomplish a change. First, a bill must be passed to authorize the program or activity. This bill does just what its name implies: It places into law authorization for schools, or any other body, to engage in a specified activity. No dollars are provided with authorization, although frequently the bill will set a limit on how much can be spent. Funding for an authorized activity or project comes through separate budget legislation. Although the major budget bills for the federal government are supposed to be approved by Congress early in the year, it seems to be typical to have them not approved until well into fall, or not at all. When the fiscal-year budget bills are not passed, the typical move is to have a continuing resolution, which leaves funding at the same level as the previous year. A regular occurrence in the budget process is that an education activity that was authorized earlier will not be funded, or the budget bill will include funding far below what was authorized and desired.

Judicial: U.S. Supreme Court

At the top of the judicial branch is the U.S. Supreme Court. This court is the highest court in the nation and has the last word on any legal issue in the United States. Over the years, the Court has reviewed many cases and made a number of significant decisions that have had a direct and long-lasting impact on schools, students, teachers, and communities. We will go into detail about Court decisions in Chapter 9.

U.S. Department of Education

The federal government comprises the various departments and offices that, in theory, are part of the executive branch. We say in theory because in many ways these departments develop their own directives through the establishment of regulations, rules, and procedures,

U.S. Government, Architect of the Capitol

Over the past 60 years the federal government has played an ever-increasing role in setting directions for schools.

which are called administrative law (see Chapter 9). When Congress and the president pass a bill, it becomes federal law. Implementation of the law becomes the responsibility of the various federal agencies and departments. The same is true when the Supreme Court makes a decision: One or more offices of the federal government will be responsible for drawing up the steps to be taken to implement the decision. The Education Department, for example, will develop the rules, procedures, and guidelines for implementing each newly passed education statute. In many ways, developing administrative law is more important than is the official passage of the statute. These rules and procedures specify what states, schools, teachers, and others must do.

A number of other federal agencies and departments have authorities and responsibilities related to schools, but the largest and most visible is the U.S. Department of Education (DOE). Major program offices of the DOE include the Office for Civil Rights, the Office of Safe and Healthy Students, the National Center for Education Statistics, and the Office of Special Education and Rehabilitative Services. Each of the offices, initiatives, and institutes has its own home page, and all can be found within the home page for the DOE.

HOW IS GOVERNANCE DIFFERENT FROM THE STRUCTURES OF GOVERNMENT?

When asked about school boards, Dr. Italia Negroni, former assistant superintendent in Wethersfield, Connecticut, said the following:

> *The meetings should be short and regular. They should have goal-setting meetings and annual retreats. It is important that they get on the same page as the superintendent. It is important especially for the chair of the board and the superintendent to be working together. I have seen board chairs and superintendents work well, and I have seen the process deteriorate.*

> *When there are good connections and communication, they make good decisions. You have to have policies, money, people, and support. If they have good control of those areas, they should be able to implement their vision.*

There is one other aspect of the organization of education that needs to be addressed. This is the process by which decisions are made. Each of the deliberative bodies, from a team of four first-grade teachers to a congressional committee, has to develop ways of working together and coming to a decision. The general term for this is governance. Governance is the functions, the processes, and the various roles that must work well together in order to have sound decisions and actions. Although

Governance is the process of involving a variety of interests in making decisions.

we are talking about governmental entities, such as school boards and Congress, the idea of governance also can be applied to a family, a church, a school, or some other organization such as a bank or manufacturing company.

How well a school board meeting runs, who gets to speak, whether there is consensus, and how public the discussion is are all elements of the processes of governance. In other words, the quality of the decision making, as well as the consequences of the decisions, is related to governance.

Surrounding the governance process is politics. Mentioning politics makes many teachers uncomfortable. They do not want to think that politics is a part of education. But it is an inescapable component of educational governance, just as politics is infused into any other governing body.

Governance Can Be Good or Bad

In an earlier interview, we posed a question to Bloomfield, Connecticut, middle school principal Dr. Trevor Ellis: "Governance is such an abstract concept for future teachers to understand. How does it work with your school board?"

First of all, nowadays the federal government is mandating that districts and schools, especially those that are low performing, have in place governance teams. Whether new teachers know about it or not, it will come their way.

My vision is that the school board is supposed to plan and support student achievement. The board also is supposed to incorporate what the community thinks students should know and be able to do. The board needs to be accessible to the public and accountable for the performance of its schools. It needs to ensure that students get a good education for the tax dollars spent.

Governance is partnering and collaborating to ensure student achievement.

In and of itself, the idea of governance is not good or bad. At the same time, we tend to think more about our experiences with a governmental body that is not working well. Just reflect on the polarization between congressional Republicans and Democrats. The only agreement is to disagree. For example, in the summer of 2011, there was ongoing disagreement about raising the debt ceiling. In December 2012, Congress disagreed about the "fiscal cliff." In 2015, there was another shutdown threat over raising the debt ceiling. The election of President Trump has added another loud voice of decisions having to be "my way" or not at all. These are not positive processes. A governing body cannot function well unless there is dialogue, understanding of the views of others, and compromise that leads to a consensus decision.

Fortunately, there are many examples of governing bodies working well together, debating openly, and in the end developing powerful decisions for the better. One clear example from the recent past would be how so many governmental agencies and corporations from several countries worked together in 2010 to rescue 33 Chilean miners trapped a half-mile underground. Various long-established governmental entities, national and international corporations, and other national governments—each with its own structures (policies, procedures, and leaders) and politics—worked across their structures and together committed experts and resources to address an urgent problem. The whole world watched over the two months it took to drill a new hole more than a half-mile into the ground. In the end, all of the miners were rescued. This story is a wonderful example of how the processes of governance can be used to work through the many rules, regulations, and silos of different government entities and interests to solve a pressing problem.

Characteristics of Good Governance

What was Dr. Negroni saying above about the characteristics of a good school board? It isn't just a matter of structure, or a district having a certain number of board members, a chair, and a superintendent. What's important is how they work together. Efficiency in use of time is important. Having both short-term objectives and long-term strategic goals is important. Having clear and open communication between the board and superintendent is important. Being able to listen and advocate are important skills. All of these are indicators of good governance, which entails conducting affairs in public, managing resources well, and keeping in mind core values and what will be best for the people in the long term. These characteristics can be applied to state legislatures, Congress, boards of corporations, and school committees. In many ways, they are universal indicators.

The universality of the interest in and concern about the need for good governance is reflected in Figure 8.4. This figure is from a United Nations document, but each of the characteristics is directly applicable to a school board, a state legislature, and Congress. As you read each of the following characteristics, keep in mind that each also applies to well-functioning teacher committees and other groups.

- **Participatory:** Participation includes men and women, and provides freedom for every person to express his or her views.

- **Follows the rule of law:** The **rule of law** is enforced equally for all.

- **Transparent:** Transparency means that the decision-making process, the reasoning, and the output are open to the public and freely available.

- **Responsive:** Responsiveness entails establishing time frames that are reasonable and at the same time sufficiently long so that all necessary information is available.

- **Consensus oriented:** Governance is **consensus oriented** if decisions are made through open dialogue, rather than resorting to ultimatums and refusals to negotiate.

- **Equitable and inclusive:** Equity and inclusion mean that all groups have open access.

- **Effective and efficient:** Effectiveness and efficiency mean that time and resources are used purposefully and well.

- **Accountable:** Accountability is demonstrated through decisions, actions, and evaluations, confirming to the various constituencies that there has been careful consideration of the alternatives and that there is wise use of public resources.

FIGURE 8.4 ■ Characteristics of Good Governance

Source: United Nations Economic and Social Commission for Asia and the Pacific. (n.d.). *What is good governance?* Retrieved from https://www.unescap.org/sites/default/files/good-governance.pdf

Achieving and maintaining each of these characteristics is a major responsibility of all governing bodies. As you can quickly see, these characteristics ask a lot of the participants, whether they be state legislators or teachers serving on a school-based council. Achieving and sustaining good governance are not easy.

Characteristics of Bad Governance

Oh, the stories people tell. You heard hints of our interview with school leaders such as Dr. Ellis and Dr. Negroni. Another observation of Dr. Negroni's was this:

> *Often politics and personal interest get in the way with the result being that we don't always do what is best for kids. When I am in schools, I see the inequities between classrooms. And across districts, there will be inequities from school to school. I am sure there are inequities from state to state. There should be better ways to address these problems without causing such turmoil.*

When one or more of the characteristics of good governance are violated, there can be loss of the strategic vision and an increasingly narrow focus on short-term actions and reactions. Trust gets lost. As the tensions increase, there is greater impatience to fix things, which usually results in the organization establishing shortsighted directives and narrow mandates. In recent years, this consequence is regularly observed in education. Instead of supporting teachers, several state governors have led initiatives to cut their bargaining rights. Teacher and administrator evaluations (and pay) are mandated to be tied to increases in test scores. Federal legislation mandates tests for all students whether or not from the teachers' perspective it makes sense. **No pass, no play** laws are passed by state legislatures. School boards ban certain books, movies, and websites. The increasing polarization within so many governing bodies and the failure to come together and strive to make important decisions through consensus most certainly illustrate the absence of many of the characteristics of good governance.

There Always Will Be Politics

By now, you are probably thinking, but what about politics? As we said earlier, there is no escaping politics, which is the means through which the governance process operates. For example, in most governing bodies, the final decision is made by a vote. A key step that effective leaders take before there is a vote is "vote counting." They survey in advance to see which way each member will vote, checking to see if their side has enough votes.

The idea of "sides" hints at another aspect of politics, **interest groups**. These are individuals who have joined together around a shared agenda that they want to see implemented. For example, a teachers' union may want more planning periods built into teachers' contracts. At the same time, a business association doesn't want to pay more taxes. Adding a planning period would most certainly increase personnel costs, and could result in higher taxes. The school board has to make a decision. It is time for vote counting to see which side appears to have the majority vote. Which board members are friends of the teachers, and which are business owners? Through good governance, there would be an open sharing of information, and a compromise would be reached.

Frequently, interest groups will join together to form a **coalition**. By joining forces with one or more other interest groups, they will have a larger numbership and can have more influence on how the board votes. In the example above, other interest groups that might join in could be parents (supporting teachers) and the police officers' association (that wants to have a tax increase to hire more police). Keep in mind that quite often coalitions are made up of interest groups that in general have

Debate and passion are two important characteristics of politics in government, in education, and elsewhere.

iStock/Wavebreak

different and even opposing purposes. This can result in strange marriages of convenience, such as Ducks Unlimited (which wants more ducks) forming a coalition with the National Rifle Association (which wants more hunting). What could possibly be their shared agenda? Having Congress protect more wetlands will provide more habitats for ducks, and so more ducks to hunt. It is a win–win situation (except for the ducks).

This is not a far-fetched example. Interest groups form coalitions all the time. In a high school, the science teachers join with the math teachers to get more computers, while the coaches join with the theater and band directors to change the end of the school day. Teachers must understand that politics is not about right or wrong—it is about getting what you want through the governance process. Teachers have to not only accept that education is politics but also develop the knowledge and skill to be political. Hopefully, you will engage in politics for the right reasons.

HOW ARE SCHOOLS PAID FOR?

We asked Dr. Ellis, "What are the key sources of funding for your school/district?"

In Connecticut, funding is a combination of local and state based on the size of the community, income, and property taxes, which are the key sources of our district's money. We do supplement a lot of our programs with grants. For the school, it is an enrollment-driven budget. The more kids you have, the larger your budget. As a principal, I have a little discretion over how to fill the positions I have, but if enrollment goes down, I have a smaller budget.

In learning about the financing of education, you must consider two important questions:

1. Where does the money come from to pay for schools?

2. How is the money spent?

As obvious as these questions may seem, as you might expect, the answers are complicated. Here we will sketch the big picture of school finance. We will leave the details for you to study in graduate school.

As Dr. Ellis pointed out, the funds for schools come from three main sources: the local community, the state, and the federal government. There are other sources of funds, but these tend to provide much smaller proportions of school budgets.

Paying for all of the schools and school districts requires that a large amount of money be found each year. In the last year for which the statistical analysis was done, the 2013–2014 school year, approximately $632 billion in revenue was collected. Notice in Figure 8.5 that the federal government was only about 9% of this total. These funds were for elementary and secondary public schools only. Of course, the amount of revenue raised within each state varies, depending on a number of factors, such as the size of the state, the health of its economy, and the political party in power. For example, the high was California, which had revenues of around $66.445 billion, while the low was North Dakota, with revenue of $1.361 billion (U.S. Census Bureau, *2014 Annual Survey of School System Finances*). As is displayed in Figure 8.6, once the funds are raised, states, school districts, and schools spend the money, with most of it being spent on instruction.

Finding the Money to Pay for Schools

The money for the funding of schools comes from a number of different sources. The obvious sources are income, sales, and property taxes. There are several other sources, including estate taxes and lotteries. As schools' need for funds has increased, a number of additional sources are being tested. In the chapter opening interview, Mr. Weaver pointed out some of the other sources of funds. Still, in most states, half of the funding for local schools comes from the state.

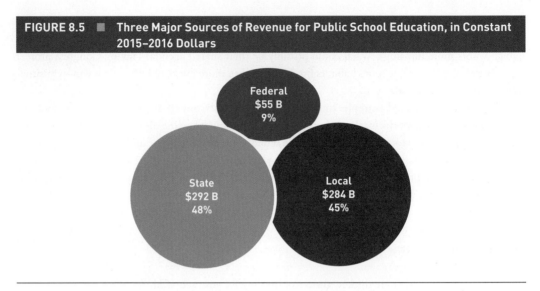

FIGURE 8.5 ■ Three Major Sources of Revenue for Public School Education, in Constant 2015–2016 Dollars

Source: U.S. National Center for Education Statistics. *Public School Revenue Sources* (updated March 2017).

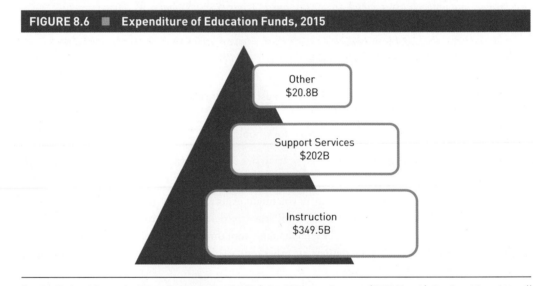

FIGURE 8.6 ■ Expenditure of Education Funds, 2015

Source: National Center for Education Statistics, Public School Revenue Sources. (2017, March). Retrieved from https://factfinder.census.gov/faces/tableservices/jsf/pages/productview.xhtml?src=bkmk; Cornman, S. Q., Zhou, L., Howell, M., & Young, J. (2018, January). Revenues and expenditures for public elementary and secondary education: School year 2014–15 (fiscal year 2015). *U.S. Department of Education.* Retrieved from https://nces.ed.gov/pubs2018/2018301.pdf

Income Tax

The first thought by most of us when we hear the word *taxes* is income tax. Implicitly, we are thinking about **personal income taxes**, which are the taxes individuals pay to the federal and state governments based on their level of income. What is not thought about is that businesses also pay a **corporate income tax**. Governments rely heavily on these two forms of income tax. One of the important features of income taxes is that those with higher levels of income pay more. The term for this kind of income tax is **progressive**. In other words, the tax is graduated, with those having a higher level of income paying a larger amount. The assumption is that a progressive tax is correlated with the ability to pay and that there will be less impact on those with less income.

Property Tax

Property taxes are those paid on tangible and intangible property. Tangible property includes real estate, vehicles, boats, computers, livestock, and equipment, while intangible property consists of those forms of wealth that do not have a physical existence, such as stocks, bonds, and savings. Property taxes, especially real estate, have been a primary source of funds for public schools. Advantages of this form of taxation are that the property can be objectively evaluated and a tax rate determined. Property also doesn't move away or have its value change very rapidly, so there is a predictable evenness to the revenue over time. A disadvantage is that only those who own property pay the taxes. For example, apartment renters do not directly pay property taxes.

Another very significant disadvantage of the property tax is that the value of real estate is not the same for every community, which limits the ability of each school district to raise the money that it needs. For example, a school district that has a popular shopping mall in its tax district will have a significant source of revenue in addition to the property tax on homes. But a

In many communities there have been taxpayer revolts that have raised questions about how to pay for public institutions such as schools.

school district that has a high proportion of older homes where the only local industry is a closed manufacturing plant will not have the same ability to raise revenue through a local property tax. As will be discussed at the end of this chapter, these local differences in ability to pay for schools have led to school finance lawsuits in most states.

Sales taxes are based on consumption. When various products and some services are purchased, the vendor may add a certain percentage to the price as a sales tax. The dollars from sales tax typically go to the state; however, in some localities, a proportion will become a source of local or regional revenue. For example, the total of the sales tax may be 7%, with 5% the state sales tax and 2% a local city tax. This form of taxation is **regressive**, which means that it proportionately costs more for those with lesser ability to pay.

Federal Government Sources of Funds

We asked another school leader, Dr. Kim Friel, who had been principal of Sawyer Middle School in Las Vegas, Nevada, about the proportion of the school budget that came from federal funds.

> *We are 67% Free or Reduced-Price Lunch, which qualifies the school for Title I funds. Interestingly, in our state, the state education department pretty much told us how the funds could be spent. These funds can be spent on tutoring, staff development, and we were able to hire two additional staff to make class sizes smaller.*

As can be seen in Figure 8.5, about 10% of the funding for schools comes from the federal government. The U.S. Department of Education, the U.S. Department of Labor, the National Science Foundation (NSF), and other federal agencies provide funding. Most of the funds are tied to particular needs, such as providing more instructional supports and free meals to children of poverty. Other programs provide grants to obtain technology, provide in-service training for teachers, and support the needs of special education and ELL students.

Given all of the forms of taxation, including a number not mentioned above, such as the federal excise tax on car tires and phone calls, it is not surprising that many citizens are unhappy with the current tax system. As a result, various forms of tax rebellion, such as citizen referenda and the underground economy, have been growing. The now infamous Proposition 13, which reduced property taxes by about

57%, was passed by the voters of California in 1978 (Moore, 1998). Similar referenda have since been replicated in a number of other states, such as in the Colorado Taxpayer Bill of Rights of 1992 (TABOR).

Citizen initiatives begin with seeking signatures of voters and placing on the ballot a constitutional referendum that, if approved by the voters, sets a cap on tax rates and/or government spending. Typically, these initiatives sound very good to frustrated taxpayers and in the short term appear to work well. Depending on the size and rate of growth of a state's economy, as well as the restrictions in the referendum, a state may be able to continue for quite some time before the unintended consequences become visible. For example, it took some 30 years for the long-term consequences of California's Prop 13 to become visible. A key reason for California's recent serious financial problems and the sad decline in the quality of its schools can be traced back to the reductions in property tax revenues that resulted from passage of Prop 13. The consequences were observed sooner in Colorado, where recently there have been local and statewide efforts to override the TABOR caps.

Seeking Additional Sources of Funding for Schools

Even with the funding provided by the established sources, education systems across the United States are short of dollars. Costs keep going up, aging buildings need maintenance, and class sizes have gotten as large as can be tolerated, but growth in revenue has not kept pace. This has been an increasing problem due not only to the recent economic struggles but also to conservative politics and the unwillingness of many taxpayers to pay more.

Income, property, and sales taxes are direct forms of taxation. Everyone has to pay them. So policy makers have been turning to sources of revenue that are "voluntary." In other words, the financial situation has led policy makers to seek additional forms of revenue enhancement, especially forms that are less direct and more open to citizen discretion.

Student Fees

In the past, participation in after-school programs such as sports and theater were incorporated into the regular school budget. However, over the past several decades, student fees have become commonplace. Fees are charged not only for participation in extracurricular activities, including sports, but also for costs related to academic classes. Schools are charging lab fees, tech fees, and in some cases even textbook fees.

Possible Sources of Revenue That Were Never Considered Before

When it comes to conflicts between the need for more revenue and traditional values, a majority of policy makers—and voters—seem to be willing to take the money. A frequently used euphemism for this is **sin taxes**. For example, in 1933, Prohibition was ended, and along with alcohol consumption came the revenue from taxing it. There have been sin taxes on tobacco for a long time. Fifty years ago, lotteries and gambling were illegal everywhere except Nevada. Now there are only two states where neither of these sources of revenue is legal: Utah and Hawaii.

Lotteries

Lotteries have become an additional source of revenue in all but seven states. Beginning in the mid-1960s, New Hampshire and New York established lotteries. Over the 55-plus years since, 44 states have established their own or participated in a multistate lottery. In lotteries, a portion of the funds received through sale of tickets is used to pay for the prizes. There also are administration costs. The remainder becomes revenue for the state.

Initially, in each state, the proponents of lotteries promised new funds for schools and other well-thought-of needs. For example, the original intent in Florida was that the lottery profits would be used for add-on and special projects in schools. However, very quickly in a tight budget year, the legislature rolled lottery revenues into the base funding for schools, leaving no extra funding for special projects. This has been the trend across the country. Very quickly, the promised extra revenues from lotteries and gambling have become absorbed into the regular budgets and are used to offset, or even reduce, past levels of spending. In addition, although the revenues from lotteries sound large, in terms of the overall budget for schools, the revenue is at best 1% or 2% of the total budget.

Gambling

Recently, more states are turning to gambling as another source of revenue. With the exceptions of Utah and Hawaii, all states have some form of gambling. This is another form of revenue gain that is voluntary. People do not have to gamble in casinos or play video poker. For those who do, there is a tax on the casino's take and a licensing fee for each machine. In addition, in states with an income tax, winners must pay state as well as federal income taxes.

Downside of Lotteries and Gambling

Critics argue that lotteries and gambling are played most by those who can least afford to spend their money that way. Low-income adults play more than the well-to-do. Other critics are concerned about the many who become problem gamblers. Also, the odds of winning are infinitesimally small. People have a much higher probability of being hit by lightning than of winning a lottery. Still, the states have become addicted to these indirect sources of revenue, and the direct forms of taxation have not had to be raised as much to cover the level of services provided.

Legalization of Marijuana

The newest and rapidly increasing source of tax dollars is coming through the legal sale of marijuana. As of 2018, 30 states and the District of Columbia have made prescriptions for medical marijuana legal. Many states are following Colorado and Washington State's lead and moving rapidly to legalize recreational use of marijuana for those 21 years of age and older. Clearly, the revenue gain is significant. In its first year, 2014, the tax revenue for Colorado was $60 million. In July 2017, the first month of legal sales in Nevada, the tax revenue was $3.68 million. The potential social costs and the risk of school students accessing marijuana are yet to be determined.

Finding the funds to maintain schools is a continuing challenge.

iStock/Steve Weinik

Creative Sources of Funds for Individual Schools

Given how tight school district budgets have become, educators too have become creative about fundraising. Each school has to engage in its own fund-raising activities. For most schools, the need for discretionary dollars is so great that bake sales are no longer sufficient. Now there are fees for participating in athletics, and product advertising will be painted on the sides of school buses. Even the Cola War is being played out in school districts with the decision to allow only one or the other brand to be available. Of course, each of these decisions has a price.

School Carnivals, Field Events, and Parent–Teacher Organizations (PTOs)

As schools seek additional funds, one activity is to have a carnival or special field day. The activities and events may be entirely organized by the school staff and students, or an outside vendor may be contracted to organize and manage the day. **Parent–Teacher Organizations (PTOs)** may be major organizers of fund-raisers. Parents also join booster clubs that raise funds for extracurricular activities, such as football, baseball, and band.

School–Business Partnerships

Neighborhood businesses and branches of national companies are partnering with specific schools. At the simplest, a business pays for an advertisement in a school publication or for a sign on the athletic

Schools have had to seek a variety of new sources for funding. Some have even begun placing advertisements on school buses.

field. More serious partnerships will have the business providing employee time to help students learn to read or to paint a classroom. Too often these partnerships seem to be one-way, with the business partner providing resources and services to the school. When it is a two-way partnership, the staff and students will be engaged in service to the business. For example, a high school history class could take on a project of developing a written or oral history of the business. Students could shadow business employees and in some businesses help employees use a new technology.

Each of These Fund-Raising Activities Has a Price

Critics of these innovative approaches to fund-raising have some serious concerns: The school is no longer objective or independent of particular commercial interests. The particular products or services that are advertised on campus will have an edge over those that are not advertised. Business partners might expect favoritism in the assignment of students to teachers. And parents may be concerned about the too-ready availability of junk food.

HOW DO SCHOOLS SPEND THE MONEY?

In Broomfield, you would be amazed; we actually spend a lot per kid. We spend about $21,000 per kid! But, we cannot maintain that level of funding with declining enrollment. The size of the district's budget each year is determined by the Town Council.

—Dr. Trevor Ellis, Principal, Bloomfield, Connecticut

Dr. Friel described some of the parts of her school's budget when asked, "Does your school have a budget?"

We have several. The budget for personnel salaries is kept by the district. The school receives a set amount from the district based on the number of pupils. This budget is for teacher supplies, books, janitorial supplies. Within this budget, I can determine how it is used. For example, if I get $150,000 for textbooks, I sit down with the staff, and we decide what to buy. Another budget is student generated, which comes from fund-raisers, vending machines, and so on. These funds are spent on students for awards, field trips, and teacher incentives.

Distribution of Revenue

Once the funds have been collected and allocated to school districts and schools, budgets are constructed, and the funds are spent. There are several ways to analyze and summarize the way that the money is spent. One is to compare how much is spent on instruction versus administration. Another commonly employed statistic is comparisons of the amount of money spent per pupil.

Spending by Major Functions

Clearly, the most important component of spending should be directly related to instruction. Teacher salaries, curriculum materials, technology for instruction, and school library resources are some of the direct costs for instruction. Figure 8.6 (see page 238) represents the national averages for current expenditures by function in 2015, the last year for which data are available. Don't forget that there are other expenditures, such as payments on school construction bonds, in addition to those identified in Figure 8.6.

In Figure 8.6, the category of Instruction represents three-fifths of the budget. Although this is a large proportion, it actually is a conservative estimate since the definition of what is included in this category is very restrictive. It relates only to teachers and direct resources for classrooms. The principal's salary and that of the school secretary, as well as the cost of the library, are included under Support Services. Other items included in Support Services are student counseling and transportation, which most school and community members see as having a direct influence on instruction and student learning. Thus the Instruction statistic is very conservative. Overall, it is clear that at least 90% of a school district budget is directly related to teachers and what they do in the classroom. From this perspective, another way to summarize the information in Figure 8.6 is to say that very little of every education dollar is spent on something that is not related to instruction.

Per-Pupil Expenditure

In his interview, Dr. Ellis referred to **per-pupil expenditure** for his school. This statistic is frequently used to compare how much different districts and states spend for each student. This statistic is derived by dividing the total number of dollars spent by the number of students. The national mean in 2015 was $11,454. Per-pupil expenditure is used regularly as an indicator of a community's commitment to and support of public education. As can be seen in Figure 8.7, per-pupil expenditure is also useful in comparing each state's investment in its schools.

FIGURE 8.7 ■ Per-Pupil Expenditure by State, 2015

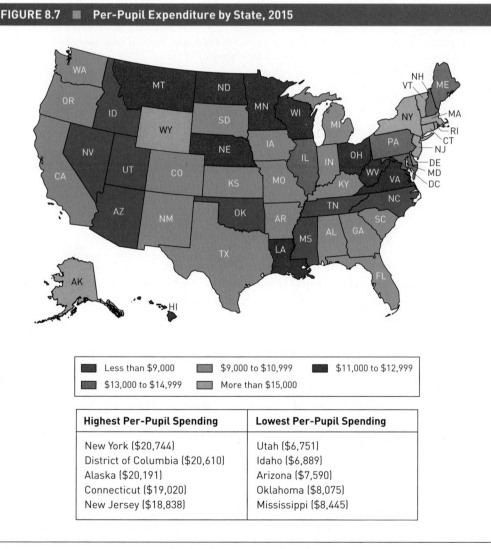

| Less than $9,000 | $9,000 to $10,999 | $11,000 to $12,999 |
| $13,000 to $14,999 | More than $15,000 | |

Highest Per-Pupil Spending	Lowest Per-Pupil Spending
New York ($20,744)	Utah ($6,751)
District of Columbia ($20,610)	Idaho ($6,889)
Alaska ($20,191)	Arizona ($7,590)
Connecticut ($19,020)	Oklahoma ($8,075)
New Jersey ($18,838)	Mississippi ($8,445)

Source: Cornman, S. Q., Musu-Gillette, L., Zhou, L., & Howell, M. (2018, January 8). National spending for public schools increases for second consecutive year in school year 2014–2015. *NCES Blog.* Retrieved from https://nces.ed.gov/blogs/ nces/post/national-spending-for-public-schools-increases-for-second-consecutive-year-in-school-year-2014-15; Cornman, S. Q., Zhou, L., Howell, M., & Young, J. (2018, January). Revenues and expenditures for public elementary and secondary education: School year 2014–15 (fiscal year 2015). *U.S. Department of Education.* Retrieved from https://nces .ed.gov/pubs2018/2018301.pdf.

UNDERSTANDING AND USING DATA
ANALYZING A SCHOOL BUDGET

Parents are not the only ones who need to understand the basic financing of schools. Teachers also need to understand where the money goes. The table presented here is a summary of the budget for one school.

Gold Flake School, Enrollment: 1,657	Amount
Instruction	$5,876,265
Instructional Support	$1,923,388
Operations	$2,524,402
Other Commitments	$0
Leadership	$772,706
Total School Expenditures	$11,096,761

Some people easily understand tables of numbers. Others find it easier to understand a summary number, such as a ratio. An even easier way to understand numbers, for those who are visual, is to see the same information in a graph. For example, the budget numbers for this school could be presented in some other ways that might make more sense. The ways data have been displayed in the figures in this chapter provide good models.

Per-Pupil Expenditure

One very common statistic that is used to understand and compare the funding for schools is to determine how much is spent for each student in the school. There are 1,657 students in Gold Flake School. Simply divide the total dollars in each budget line item by the number of pupils, and you will have determined the per-pupil expenditure.

Graphing the School Budget

The budget for Gold Flake School can be displayed as a pie chart. The information could be placed in a bar graph too, but it would not be as easy to see the whole. How does the per-pupil expenditure for Gold Flake School compare to your state's expenditures in Figure 8.7?

Balancing the Budget in Tight Times

School districts, and states, are required to balance their budgets each year. In times of tight budgets and tax limitations, very difficult choices have to be made. Reductions in funding of schools was a serious consequence of the 2008 Great Recession. Even now, districts are just returning to the level of funding that was in place before then.

Addressing funding shortfalls and budget cuts is hard. Districts have to decide where to make cuts and where to reduce services. A general guiding principle is to make the cuts first in areas that will not directly affect classrooms. One of the first steps that will affect classrooms is to increase class size. Increasing the average class size by one student across all schools will save significant dollars by reducing the number of teachers that need to be employed. Building maintenance may be deferred, and computers kept for another year. In extremely difficult financial times, districts will turn to a number of more severe money-saving strategies.

Outsourcing/Privatizing

Instead of having district employees do a particular function, such as cleaning buildings or driving school buses, contracts are made with outside companies to provide these services. This is known as **outsourcing** or **privatizing**. The district then can reduce the size of its payroll and hold the outside contractor accountable for the quality of service. Unfortunately, this strategy, as well as across-the-board budget cuts, likely means that a number of district employees will lose their jobs. Another consequence is that the quality of service is not of the same level as before. For example, the district-employed high school custodian will note when an outside door is left open at the end of the day and know that it

TEACHERS' LOUNGE
INCOME VIA EXTRA-DUTY ASSIGNMENTS CAN BE COSTLY

Revenue Codes	General Description	Example
100–199	Local District Funds	Revenue from local school support taxes
200–299	State Funds	Revenue from state school support taxes
300–399	Federal Funds	Revenue from federal sources—grants, special education, etc.
400–499	School-Generated Funds	Income generated from school-sponsored sports, student activities, and fund raising

Michael S. Robison

Schools receive funds from different sources including tax funds raised locally and by the state government (sales taxes, property tax, etc.). In addition, schools often generate funds to support school activities via ticket tales, raffles, gate receipts, and so on. Each source of revenue requires the school to account for the expenditures made from each fund.

The base operating budget for each school can be significant considering it includes salaries and facilities costs. To put this in perspective, a school with 2,000 students can deal with a yearly budget of over $15 million in tax-supported revenues. This does not include school-generated funds that can accumulate in excess of hundreds of thousands of dollars.

School-generated funds generally are accrued in the form of cash and checks, while tax revenues are managed via purchase orders. This brings about extra precautionary procedures to ensure the funds are properly managed. Even with the strictest of written procedures, problems can arise when managing cash collections and check withdrawals.

Teachers are called upon to help with fund-raising activities. They are the lifeblood of a school's support system. Without their support and time, many of the activities students are involved in would not exist. Our schools look to their employees to fill in. They are asked to donate their time, or in some cases, teachers are paid for taking extra-duty assignments.

One such extra-duty assignment is selling and taking tickets at the home football games. This extra-duty assignment includes extra-duty pay for the time spent. In one high school, this opportunity drew the interest of a couple of young teachers. Because they were young and needed extra income, this assignment was appealing.

As the football season unfolded, the athletic department began to notice that the attendance at home games did not generate the expected ticket sales. Nor did the volume of ticket sales match the recorded game attendance. Following some discussions, a district athletic administrator decided to watch the ticket sales process. For the next home game, he sat in his district car in view of the ticket booth and entrance gate.

After watching several transactions, it was noted that the employee who served as the ticket taker, under the watchful eye of a security guard, would take the tickets she had collected and return them to the ticket booth. The standard process required the employee to tear the ticket in two and deposit one half in the ticket box and return the remaining half to the paying customer. However, that night, an alternative process was used. Instead of returning half the ticket to the customer, the whole ticket was collected and returned to the ticket booth for resale.

One could call it double dipping—paid by the hour for services rendered and then receiving a self-imposed tip from the ticket resales.

In order to document the action, the administrator returned the following week. He again sat in a marked district car and used a video camera to document the process accurately.

An embarrassed administration, athletic department, and a few teachers were subsequently faced with financial losses and damaged reputations.

—Dr. Michael S. Robison, Retired
School and District Administrator

needs to be closed. The outsourced employee understands that his or her job description is to sweep the floor. Nothing is in the contract about keeping doors closed.

Unpaid Furlough Days

Following the beginning of the Great Recession in 2008, many states, school districts, and municipalities required employees to take one or two days a month off without pay, or **unpaid furlough days**. At the same time, there was an unwritten expectation that there would not be interruptions in services. For school and college teachers, there has been no way to accommodate both of these conflicting expectations.

Reduction in Force (RIF)

As a last resort, balancing the budget has been done by **Reduction in Force (RIF)**—that is, by giving some employees pink slips. These are official letters informing certain employees that due to budget cuts they may not have a job for the next school year. Unless there has been a different agreement, in most school districts the teacher contract will specify that the last person hired will be the first to be laid off. There may be exceptions for certain areas, such as for mathematics and special education teachers, which are always in short supply.

WHAT ARE SOME OF THE KEY ORGANIZATION AND FINANCE ISSUES AND CHALLENGES?

Up to this point, we have been introducing basic ideas about the organization and financing of education. We have described schooling in terms of roles, authority, and responsibilities. We introduced the primary sources of funds and described how the money is spent. What was not done within each of these descriptions was to point out some of the many related tensions, debates, and unresolved issues. The remainder of this chapter introduces a number of these issues.

What Are Some Key Questions About the Organization of Schools?

The structure of schools, school districts, and state education departments is well established and has been pretty much the same for the past 100-plus years. Still, there are questions, issues, and debates about the best ways to organize schools.

Class Size: What's Best?

Teachers and parents regularly express concern about the number of students in classes. The general belief is that smaller classes are better. In fact, this belief is so widespread that between 1990 and 2008 all but six states adopted some form of class size reduction policy (Mitchell & Mitchell, 2003). It is believed that with smaller classes teachers will be able to spend more time with each student. One obvious consequence of going to smaller classes is that the cost of staffing the school will go up; smaller classes mean more teachers. At some point, the school will not have enough classrooms, and there will be the added cost for constructing more classrooms. Due to the Great Recession of 2008 and the significant budget cuts that followed, the trend toward smaller class sizes has now been reversed. As the economy continues to improve, class size reduction will again be a topic of debate.

Why Are Schools Organized the Way They Are?

In many ways, the organization of schools at this time is a direct result of the Industrial Revolution. Think about the photos you have seen of factory workers standing at their stations on the assembly line that produces the Ford Model T, textiles, or soft drinks. For the assembly line to work well, each worker must do a prescribed job. There are supervisors and managers, too, doing prescribed jobs. Even the timing of tasks and the workday are specified. Many of these ideas about how to structure an organization are now institutionalized in schools. Line and staff relationships, organization charts, position descriptions, and 50-minute class periods with bells ringing are well-defined components of nearly all schools.

Think about the typical middle/junior high school and high school. Each teacher is a specialist in a subject, the bells ring at specified times, and the students are on conveyor belts moving to their next workstation. The principal and assistant principals monitor the movements and press to make sure everyone is at the right station for the next 50-minute period. The structural view of schools continues. Is this industrial model best for adult and student workers in the 21st century?

What Should Be the Role of School Boards?

In the past, school boards were the major policy bodies for governing their school districts. Today, much of the governance role has been assumed by governors and state legislatures. An important question now is, What is the appropriate role for school district school boards? In most communities, school boards are no longer solely responsible for determining local taxes for schools, as they receive most of their funds from the state. Curriculum, standards, and even many personnel and student behavior policies and procedures are dictated by the state and federal governments.

So what should school boards be doing? Or do we need local school boards any longer? It is easy to find individuals to argue on all sides of these questions. Some strongly believe that school boards are essential as representatives of the citizens in local government. Others are concerned about the willingness of many boards to engage in determining the details of day-to-day operations of the school district—in other words, micromanaging. Many believe that school boards are no longer needed and that they should have no role beyond selecting the superintendent and approving the annual district budget.

What About School Safety?

One of the most challenging problems for today's schools is safety. Before learning can take place, schools need to be safe and secure places for students and adults. The concern and challenges related to violence, bullying, and disasters are so complex that all levels of the education system are pressed to address the problem. Teachers are responsible for having a safe classroom. Schools are responsible for having safe facilities, including the grounds. Many school districts now have their own police forces, and all schools and district administrators have to coordinate closely with the local police agencies. State and federal policy makers are engaged by passing laws, such as those that require that any student who brings a weapon to school be expelled (e.g., Gun-Free Schools Act of 1994). No matter the circumstances, teachers, principals, and school district personnel have no option—state law mandates the response.

Being prepared and knowing what to do ahead of time are essential. One important response is for schools to have established procedures for what to do in the case of an emergency. Table 8.4 illustrates the kinds of steps that teachers, students, and administrators should have in place and practice—just in case.

Is There a Best Balance Between Centralization and Local Control?

Another important theme and source of debate through the past 100 years concerns the balance between having decisions made by those people close to home versus having decisions made by those who are more removed but have a broader view. **Local control** is the term used when the authority for decision making is in the hands of those nearest the site, whether it is the district or a school. At this time, local control has been eroded not only by the states but also by the federal government.

As described above, as the state portion of the education budget has increased, so has the interest of state policy makers in making education decisions. Also, over the past 60 years, there has been increasing involvement of the federal government in making decisions about education for the whole nation—in other words, increasing **federalism**. NCLB was by far the most far-reaching and, many would say, the most top-down education policy initiative ever for the federal government. The pattern over the past 60 years is clear: Local control of schools and education has been dramatically diminished.

How Should the Dilemmas of School Choice Be Addressed?

As wonderful as the arguments in support of choice sound, as with other strategies, there are serious consequences with whichever approach to choice is taken. One important issue has to do with

TABLE 8.4 ■ School Emergency Action Plan

Fire Drill	Lockdown	Shelter-in-Place
• Students exit room with no talking and proceed to designated area.	• Everyone moves inside to a safe location.	• CLASSES FOLLOW SAME PROCEDURES AS LOCKDOWN.
• Teachers take Emergency Folder.	• If students are with special teachers, they stay there.	• In addition to lockdown procedures:
• Teachers turn out lights.	• Teachers lock all doors and DO NOT OPEN FOR ANYONE.	○ Teachers place a piece of masking tape on classroom window.
• Teachers close and lock door.	• Teachers take attendance.	○ Teachers locate plastic sheets and flashlight.
• Teachers take attendance at designated area.	• Teachers report any missing students to the office via intercom.	○ In a real emergency, teachers use plastic to cover and tape all vents and doors.
• Teachers immediately report any missing student by holding up red card.	• Everyone stays away from doors and windows.	○ NO ONE IS TO USE CELL PHONES.
• An administrator will announce when it is clear to reenter building.	• Teachers use intercom for emergencies only.	○ Teachers wait until an administrator has given the "ALL CLEAR" before unlocking door.
• Teachers and students return to classroom quietly.	• Teachers wait for "ALL CLEAR" before unlocking door.	

funding. Vouchers do not provide all the money that is needed to support operation of an alternative school. Additional funding has to come from somewhere. In the 49th annual PDK Poll (September 2017), several questions were asked about the support for vouchers. One of the respondents asked what if the full cost were covered. Sixty-one percent of the respondents preferred funds to only be used for public schools. Thirty-four percent supported public funds being used to fully fund vouchers. On the other side, vouchers draw funds away from the school district, which means less funding for the public schools. Another issue has to do with access. Parents in a particular neighborhood may have access to several alternative schools, while parents in another community have no alternatives within reach. Another important issue has to do with student learning. The research findings are unclear. In the end, the individual differences of each school, public or alternative, are determinant.

What Are Some of the School Finance Issues and Challenges?

Securing sufficient funds for schools and deciding how the available dollars will be spent are serious activities. Many actors are involved, and many more have opinions about what should be the major sources of funds (e.g., no increases in [my] taxes) and in what ways schools should spend the funds (e.g., too many administrators). Table 8.5 lists key questions that have to be answered in relation to finding the funds and deciding how the obtained funds will be spent. The debates and final decisions related to each of these questions require becoming informed and participating in the decision-making processes—which is why a major topic of this chapter is governance. No individual has the final say. Many individuals and agencies contribute to the debates, and in the end, schools and teachers have to live with the final decisions. There are many pressing issues related to governance and school finance. A few key ones are introduced here.

School Finance: Equal and Enough

The school finance suit in Kentucky that resulted in KERA was only the first of its kind. Since that time, more than 40 states have experienced lawsuits related to the funding of schools, and others are

TABLE 8.5 ■ Key Questions About School Finance That Policy Makers, School Administrators, Teachers, Parents, and Community Members Need to Consider
1. How much funding per pupil is really enough?
2. What sources of funds should be used to pay for increasing quality?
3. Should high-stakes test scores be the only determinant of teacher and/or school quality?
4. When there is a low level of student and/or teacher performance, should there be sanctions, or should there be additional investment?
5. Who should decide how schools are financed? Should it be mainly policy makers at the state or federal level, or should it be experts at the local level? To what extent should citizens have a role in making those decisions?

under threat of having suits filed. There are serious differences in funding and spending. For example, you do not have to look very far in a community, across a large city, or across a state to see dramatic differences in the quality of school facilities. Some districts, typically in the suburbs, have brand-new buildings, while other school districts, typically in the inner cities and rural areas, have old buildings. As an aspiring teacher, you likely already can name those school districts that pay teachers higher salaries. These dramatic discrepancies in the quality of facilities, teacher salaries, and per-pupil expenditures provide ripe conditions for school finance lawsuits.

Two Fundamental Finance Questions

One form of **accountability** that clearly is a state responsibility has to do with how schools are financed. When some perceive that the state has not been doing its job, they may turn to the courts. The exact basis for the funding lawsuits has varied by state. Each lawsuit is carefully crafted to take advantage of whatever that state's constitution says about that state's responsibility for education.

Two general models are being used to test the constitutionality of school finance, equity and adequacy:

Equity school finance suits test whether there is equal funding given to all schools and/or students.

Adequacy suits argue that the needs are different in different districts and for different students. The question is raised as to whether sufficient funds are being provided so that all students have a reasonable opportunity to learn.

In the 1980s and 1990s, most of the finance suits were based in questions of equity. It was clear that within each state there was unequal funding of school districts. Now, most of the finance suits are based in questions of adequacy. One main theme in these court challenges is that simply providing the same number of dollars to each school district and school does not provide the same level of opportunity for students to learn. Plaintiffs argue that it costs more to educate students from poor families, students with special needs, and those who are ELLs. In other words, schools that have higher proportions of needy students are not adequately funded, and students in those schools therefore do not have an equal opportunity to learn.

Opponents of this view argue that it is not the state's role to determine how the funds are spent. As long as all school districts receive the same number of dollars per pupil—that is, equity—it is the district's responsibility to use those funds in ways that will help their particular mix of students succeed. As you can see, it is not easy to answer the key policy questions about the financing of education listed in Table 8.5. What do you think are good answers to each of these questions?

CONNECTING TO THE CLASSROOM

The organization of schools, school districts, and state education systems and the ways schools are paid for have been described in this chapter. School finance, taxation, and how the money is spent are three other main topics in this chapter. Another is the importance of having good governance. Learning about organization structures and education finances may seem remote for candidates who are at the beginning of their teacher preparation program. However, each of these topics will become increasingly important as you begin having clinical and field experiences, and as you have conversations with parents and community members. These topics also are important for you to understand as a taxpayer and parent.

1. The processes by which agencies make, implement, and evaluate decisions constitute governance. Good governance is transparent and participatory and follows the rule of law. Teacher participation is an important component of good governance.

2. In many ways, schools are professional organizations. One consequence is that teachers have more autonomy and greater responsibility than is possible for workers in most businesses. Teachers must be very careful to demonstrate that they are ready and able to be effective given this higher level of self-responsibility.

3. Keep in mind that teachers and schools are not autonomous, but rather are subparts of school districts and each state's education system.

4. The principal is the one administrator who is in a line relationship with teachers.

5. The three main sources of funds for schools are income, property, and sales taxes.

6. The federal government is playing an increasing role in public schools, as was demonstrated in the No Child Left Behind Act of 2001 (NCLB) and the current Every Student Succeeds Act (ESSA) legislation. However, only around 10% of the funds for schools comes from the federal government.

7. Be respectful of the fact that a large portion of the taxes you and others pay is used to fund schools. People work hard and want to know that their taxes are being spent wisely and well.

SUMMARY

The first part of this chapter presented different ways that schools are viewed as organizations. Of course, the work of teachers is teaching, and the work of students is learning. But teachers and students do their work in an organizational setting. The second part introduced major topics related to the sources of funds and how the funds are spent.

Key topics about the organization of schooling that have been addressed include the following:

- The adults and the children in a school have to be organized in effective ways to do their work.

- Schools are organized into districts (Local Education Agencies, or LEAs), with school boards and a superintendent.

- Each state has ultimate authority for its public education system.

- Issues and problems include class size, the role of school boards, and safety.

- School choice does provide alternatives to the regular public schools, but also creates questions about equity and relative effectiveness.

- Revenue: The funds that pay for schooling come from several sources including income, property, and sales taxes.

- Expenditures: By far the largest item in the education budget is for instruction and instruction-related expenses.

- Federalism: The federal government influences education by tying funding with requirements for schools to implement certain activities.

- Current issues: Tighter definitions of accountability and who pays are two of the most challenging issues.

KEY TERMS

CLASS DISCUSSION QUESTIONS

1. When you are a beginning teacher and you have a concern about a student or some problem within the school, whom do you talk to?

2. As a teacher, how important will it be to you to know who the superintendent is and to learn about what she or he thinks is important?

3. The role of school boards has been reduced in many ways. Some argue that local school boards are no longer needed. Others argue that school boards are an important component of democracy and that having local citizen representation is very important to the process. What do you say?

4. The funding of schools is heavily dependent on property taxes. Do you think this is fair? If not, what other sources of revenue for schools do you think should be used instead?

5. One of the embedded themes in this chapter is the need to accept and understand politics. How do you feel about this recommendation? Are you ready to engage in politics with your current activities? Are you ready to engage in politics in your future life as a teacher?

SELF-ASSESSMENT

What Is Your Current Level of Understanding and Thinking About Organizing Schools for Learning and School Finance?

One of the indicators of understanding is to examine how complex your thinking is when asked questions that require you to use the concepts and facts introduced in this chapter.

Answer the following questions as fully as you can. Then use the Assessing Your Learning rubric to self-assess the degree to which you understand and can use the ideas presented in this chapter.

1. How would you explain to a friend the authority of the school principal?

2. What is the difference between line and staff relationships?

3. What is the relationship of teachers to the school district superintendent?

4. What role do you think school boards should have?

5. What education problems would you like to see your state address with policy that could significantly improve student learning?

6. What are the key sources of revenue for schools, and what are the strengths and weaknesses of each source?

7. What's wrong, and what's right, with relying on property taxes to pay for public schools?

8. What do you see as implications of the trend toward increasing federalism in education?

9. What do you see as being the most pressing issues related to the governance and financing of education? Why do you think these are significant?

Assessing Your Learning Rubric

	Parts & Pieces	Unidimensional	Organized	Integrated	Extensions
Indicators	Elements/ concepts are talked about as isolated and independent entities. Some important names are provided in isolation.	One or a few concepts are addressed, while others are underdeveloped, or not mentioned.	Deliberate and structured consideration of all key concepts/ elements.	All key concepts/ elements are included in a view that addresses interconnections.	Integration of all elements and dimensions, with extrapolation to new situations.
Organization structure	Names a few roles and organization concepts, without explaining relationships.	Describes school-based role and line relationships for the principal, but not LEA or SEA; no ideas about what the state or federal policy makers should do.	Describes school-based, LEA, and SEA roles and relationships; provides very general idea for needed policy.	Describes role, line, and staff relationships at all levels and issues related to communication; identifies one education problem that policy makers should address—the identified problem may have limited implications for student learning.	Describes role, line, and staff relationships at all levels and issues related to communication; identifies one education problem that policy makers should address—and draws connection between the problem, the proposed solution, and its implications for student learning.
Finance	Describes in general terms that taxes are how schools are funded.	Sources of funding are identified, but little is said about how the money is spent.	Different sources of funds are described, and the three major ways that the money is spent are described.	Interrelationships and implications of different sources of funds and the adequacy of funding are described.	Sources of funds are interrelated with how the funds are spent with identifying implications for teaching and learning.

FIELD GUIDE
FOR LEARNING MORE ABOUT . . .

Organizing and Financing Schools for Learning

To further increase your understanding about schools as organizations and school finance, do one or more of the following activities.

Ask a Teacher or Principal	Ask a veteran teacher about the relationship with his or her principal. When is the principal clear about there being a line relationship? How much autonomy as a professional does the teacher have?
	Study the organization chart for a school. Are the various relationships clear? Are there roles named that you had not thought of?
	For a school district where you would like to be a teacher, take a look at the district's budget. Which items are the largest? Are there budget items that you had not expected to see?
Make Your Own Observations	When you are visiting a school, seek out the school's organization chart. How does it compare with the chart in Figure 8.1? Is it drawn so that line and staff relationships are clear? Ask different staff members where they see themselves within the school's organization. Are they clear about who is in a line relationship with them and who is in a staff relationship? For example, many teachers will see the assistant principal as their supervisor. However, in most schools, the assistant principal is officially in a staff relationship with teachers. How do teachers and administrators relate within these different formal relationships?
	When you are visiting a school, inquire about how decisions are made to spend the funds. What are the sources of funds? To what extent are teachers involved in making the spending decisions? Listen for the characteristics of good governance that are embedded in the allocation process.
	Attend a school board meeting and observe the processes of governance firsthand. How many of the characteristics of good governance (Figure 8.4) do you see in action? Is there a characteristic that seems to be employed less?

| Reflect Through Journaling | In the past, local control was an important argument against state and federal governments intruding on what were seen as local issues, such as selection of curriculum and determination of the qualifications of teachers and principals. Now, the state and federal governments are making most of the decisions about schools. For you as a teacher, what do you see as being gained? What is lost with the current trend toward increasing centralization?

Summarize your notes about school finance. What are the key themes for you? What are the implications for you in terms of what you need to learn more about before you enter your classroom as a first-year teacher? |
|---|---|
| Build Your Portfolio | Find the website for the school district where you would like to teach. Review the organization chart for this district. Note the name of the superintendent. Also, check within the HR office for directions about applying for a teaching position. You should keep copies and make notes about information you will need to have when you apply for that teaching position. Also, develop a checklist of things in the position description and note things you will need to work on so that you will be well qualified for a teaching position.

You can do a similar activity and self-assessment by reviewing the website for particular schools where you would like to teach. Who is the principal? How has the school been doing on the annual reporting of test scores? Find the school improvement plan and see what action steps the school is implementing this year. Do you already know about the strategies, or are these areas where you need to learn more? Either way, adding information about the strategies to your portfolio will have you better prepared when the time comes to apply for that special teaching position. |
| Read a Book | To learn more about schools as Professional Learning Communities, read *Guiding Professional Learning Communities* by Shirley M. Hord, James L. Roussin, and William A. Sommers (2010, Corwin).

A very interesting and informative source for learning more about schools as organizations is *Reframing Organizations: Artistry, Choice, and Leadership* (6th ed.) by Lee G. Bolman and Terrence E. Deal (2017, Jossey-Bass).

School finance is a very important and complex subject. One straightforward resource is the book *Sound School Finance for Education Excellence*, by Stephen Coffin and Bruce S. Cooper (2017, Rowman & Littlefield). When you want to learn more about finance and budgeting, this book will be a good place to begin. The first chapter sets the stage with "four words": *equity, equality, efficiency,* and *effectiveness.* Each chapter is a survey of basic topics including models for developing school budgets, taking into consideration enrollments and special needs students, and the relationships to state and federal funding. |
| Search the Web | **Organization Charts:** Go to the website for a school or school district where you would like to become a teacher. Look for the organization chart(s) and identify the key office and individuals that are related to the employment of teachers.

Professional Qualifications: Review the website for the State Education Agency (SEA) in your state. Find the name of the Chief State School Officer/state superintendent. What are the person's professional background and qualifications for this important position? Also, review the qualifications of the members of the state board of education. How do their qualifications compare?

Statistical Information: This chapter has included many statistics about revenue, expenditures, and the size of schools and school districts. Two useful resources for finding statistical information related to your state and to compare your school district or school to national norms are the U.S. Census Bureau and the National Center for Education Statistics. Within these sites, you can find funding information for each state, each school district, and in some ways each school. One check would be to see how your state's per-pupil expenditure compares to the national average.

Go to the website for a school or school district where you would like to become a teacher. Find the minutes of the school board meetings. Which budget topics seem to be most discussed? |

9

THE LAW AS IT RELATES TO TEACHING AND LEARNING

© Kristy Anderson

EDUCATOR INTERVIEW

Mrs. Kristy Anderson, General Counsel, Maryland State Education Association

Q: What is the Maryland State Education Association?

A: We are a union—some would like to say professional association—representing public employees. We represent everyone from custodians, to bus drivers, to anybody who is in the classroom or school building, including central office personnel. They could be instructional leaders, Department Chairs, or curriculum writers. We represent all public school employees. The superintendent is exempt, of course. We also represent principals and administrators. All employees who are permitted by law to be placed in the bargaining unit are included.

Q: What does representation of members entail?

A: We provide services as they relate to individuals' employment. If it occurs on the job, we are going to represent our members. So, anything that occurs during the course of your normal workday will be covered. For example, if there is a criminal charge for assault or child abuse, we provide representation. Also, we enforce the collective bargaining agreement. If they are recommended for suspension, recommended for termination, or reprimanded, we represent members through the appeal process. For any type of disciplinary action, we are going to provide representation. Or, at least, we meet with our members and discuss what their options are under the circumstances.

Q: In the big picture, in what ways are unions proactive?

A: Although unions are likely to be dealt a blow by the Supreme Court in *Janus [at the time of this interview, an impending Supreme Court decision; see page 285]*, which will prohibit the collection of a fee from nonmembers of the bargaining unit, creating free riders, I believe that unions will continue to exist and to be a critical player in education. Unions not only advocate for employees but also support quality schools. It is through unions that individual power can be increased through collective action of the masses—such collective action gets the attention of public officials charged with providing a free and appropriate public education.

LEARNING OUTCOMES

After reading this chapter, you should be able to do the following:

1. Discuss the role of the U.S. Constitution as it relates to education.

2. Identify emerging legal issues in education related to uses of social media, particularly in terms of privacy, harassment, and discrimination.

3. Describe the themes within major issues that although addressed in the past continue to be major topics within the legal system.

4. Analyze key aspects of students' rights and the implications of those rights for teachers.

5. Provide examples of teachers' responsibilities, rights, and liabilities.

Educators in many states are resorting to such collective action through the unions carrying out strikes in order to demand fair and just salaries. Enough is enough, and educators are demanding more: more salaries, more resources, and more time in order to do their jobs effectively. Through unions, educators are connecting to the community and community organizations that support similar goals—ideally, when educators are satisfied with their working conditions, it leads to an environment that fosters student success in the school.

Q: **Given all of that, when it comes to future teachers, what key topics do they need to understand right now?**

A: We are at a point in time in which we're struggling to have teachers treated as the professionals that they are. Similarly situated individuals with a college degree are treated better than public school teachers. A lot of teachers' discretion is taken away because of administration. We are almost at a turning point, because of the high expectations for teacher and student performance. Teachers must be vested with the discretion to determine the best or most effective instructional strategies to implement with their students. Increasingly, the public sees that it is the teacher who makes the decisions and has the greatest singular impact on student learning. Teachers make, or break, a child in terms of his or her success and ability to stay with learning and to make good choices. They are a critical piece, and a role model for the kids.

I think one of the biggest struggles for new teachers is understanding that they are held to extremely high standards. They have to be incredibly cognizant of this when they are in public, generally. If you are going to go out and have a drink after work on a Friday afternoon, don't go to the local community neighborhood bar. You are going to see a parent, or someone from the community, who is going to judge you differently as a result. Go somewhere else. While you are of age and allowed to drink, don't do it in the same neighborhood where you work.

New teachers must have an appreciation for the position they hold. New educators come out of school thinking they can do whatever they want, and there is no appreciation of the important role they play in a child's life and how that role permeates every aspect of their personal life as well. Whether in the classroom or the community, you are still a teacher. You are an educator. You work with people's children. So, you need to be superhuman. More and more, I try to impress on teachers going into the classroom that this is an incredibly important job.

We are on the verge of having teachers paid for this very important job. In some states, we are further along; in some states, we are regressing. For example, in North Carolina, teachers have to punch a time clock. But where there is collective bargaining, such as Maryland, we are making some strides and getting educators where they should be in terms of salary and professionalism.

Q: **You have described important topics in relation to the profession overall. Are there specific areas that future teachers need to attend to now?**

A: Social media is forever going to be an issue. Understanding that students should never be on a teacher's Facebook page, an educator should always use the professional means of communicating, which consists of school email accounts or sites. Do not let students/parents bleed into your personal life. All too often, that is where you end up with allegations of child abuse or sex abuse. Unfortunately, the way public officials and the media treat educators, any time you have an allegation against you, 9 times out of 10 you are going to be pulled out of the classroom. Right there, it is your reputation. You are going to be interviewed by the police and the school system. If you are cleared, you might be able to go back to the classroom, but it will be months later, and your reputation will be severely damaged.

Q: What other topics do you see emerging right now?

A: We have a lot of issues with inappropriate communication, generally—the lack of classroom management, a lack of understanding or ability to deal with all walks of life. The kids in classrooms are not uniform; they are not widgets. You have to be nimble and quick in dealing with different ethnic backgrounds, race, and poverty. Some teachers don't understand or appreciate the personal life struggles of students. We are seeing a lot of student discipline referrals and administrators pushing back. Student discipline is a huge problem. Students have little respect for authority, and that plays out in the classroom.

Similarly, new educators walk into the classroom and think they can say and do whatever they want—they are just teaching students—and they think they have rights, including free speech rights. They think, "It is my classroom," and "If I feel it is necessary, I can deviate from the curriculum to discuss a current event or what I think is important." No, this is not okay. The Supreme Court says you are a public employee, and the employer controls your speech when you are in front of the classroom.

Q: What brings you joy?

A: My family and their successes. Also, being able to achieve a positive outcome for some of our members who don't get the fair shake they are entitled to. I spend a lot of time working and with my family. So it is somewhat equal although the positive outcomes for educators are often hard fought and, therefore, the joy is sweet.

Q: Anything else for beginning teachers?

A: Respect yourself, respect the position, and understand and appreciate the high regard in which you are viewed and held. Follow the Mom Rule: If your mother would not like to see something on your Facebook page, then don't put it there. And, always be prepared to ask questions and seek out the right people to get support in those first critical and trying years—education is a team sport, after all.

© Michael Simpson

INTERVIEW WITH A SECOND LEGAL EXPERT

Mr. Michael Simpson

Throughout this chapter will be quotes from a second education law expert, Mr. Michael Simpson, now retired, who was assistant general counsel at the National Education Association (NEA) in Washington, DC. For more than 30 years, he was an adviser to attorneys around the United States who were working on legal issues and cases for NEA members.

Q: What do you see as being important legal implications of the widespread use of social media?

A: If you read the papers, virtually every day there is a story about some school employee getting fired for posting something inappropriate on Facebook or Myspace. These are not just teachers, but principals and other staff as well.

So many of the young teachers in particular are so active in using social media that they think nothing of putting up stories about themselves on their own Facebook pages. My stepdaughter has more than 2,000 Facebook friends. Her page might as well be open to the public.

Using social media responsibly is really important. The irresponsible use of such media can cause an uproar in the community, which can cause and has caused the termination of school employees. For example, there was a case from Georgia a couple of years ago where a probatory teacher posted a picture of herself having a glass of wine in France. She certainly was of age. She got fingered by a parent; the administration told her to "resign now, or we will fire you." So she resigned.

Q: **What other topics are important for future teachers to know about?**

A: They need to know how to identify and put an end to sexual harassment in schools. We have had a number of our members sued for damages because they witnessed instances of harassment and didn't step in and stop it. This includes harassment based on sexual orientation, and not just gender-based harassment. The courts are quite sympathetic to students who are bullied at school or harassed when the adult has the power and the obligation to step in and stop it and doesn't do anything at all. Future teachers need to know their responsibilities about intervening when they witness harassment or bullying.

Q: **What do you see school leaders looking for in new teachers?**

A: I have found that the best teachers are the ones who are empathetic with students and who have the capacity to engage them. As we know, student engagement is the single most important factor in learning. Teachers who understand their role, which is more than just providing information, and enjoy that role certainly will get a joy out of teaching.

Questions to Consider

1. How aware have you been of the importance of the legal aspects in teaching?

2. What have you seen on social media that, if done by a teacher or fellow teacher candidate, could cause a legal problem?

3. What do you know about the rights of students?

4. What do you know now about the rights of probationary teachers?

5. Are your various social media posts ready for the Mom Rule?

At this point, you likely have a very limited understanding of how the legal system relates to your developing career. However, now is the time for you to learn the basics, especially since, if not already, very soon you will be in schools and classrooms as part of your professional preparation and you will need to be certain to perform in ways that are within the law.

As stated by the two legal experts interviewed above, teacher education candidates must consider legal aspects of their activities every time they are in field settings and whenever they are in contact with students, parents, other teachers, and administrators. You most certainly must understand student rights, including the right for students' records to be protected; you also must understand your responsibility for student safety. Additionally, teacher education candidates need to learn about the liabilities and protections afforded to beginning/probationary teachers. Although first-year teachers have the same professional responsibilities as tenured teachers, they do not have all of the same protections, especially related to nonrenewal and dismissal.

INTRODUCTION

Probably, your beginning thought about the legal system is an image of the court as seen on television, with a judge and jury. Actually, much is done before an issue is the subject of a court case. The first step is for a legislative body, such as Congress or a state legislature, to pass a statute. This law is the formal statement of what is not, or in some cases what is, permitted. The wording in most statutes sets the general boundaries and some of the limits, but not the specific details. Normally, developing the details for implementing the statute is done by the executive branch of government. For education statutes at the national level, the U.S. Department of Education develops the rules and procedures, which are called administrative law. In your state, the state education department will most likely establish the rules underlying new education statutes.

The courts do not become involved until there is a disagreement. An individual or a group may see an action taken by others as a violation of a statute or its related rules and procedures. In other instances, some may disagree with any or all of a particular legislative agenda and question its correctness. When there is a dispute, the courts become the decider. The resulting decisions through the courts are called case law. In this chapter, we will introduce some of the key education questions that have been addressed through the courts, especially questions addressed by the U.S. Supreme Court. We also will reference selected pieces of legislation, since in many instances these statutes become important bases for determining what teachers, students, and schools should do.

The U.S. Supreme Court's nine justices have the final say when there are legal questions with regard to the educational system in the United States.

The U.S. Constitution and the States' Responsibility for Education

Since the United States is a nation of laws, the U.S. Constitution is the first and final guide for what is, and is not, legal. Nested beneath the U.S. Constitution is each state's constitution. All decisions made by the courts consider first what is stated in the U.S. Constitution, and then what is stated in relevant state constitutions. Subsequently, courts consider past case law and related statutes. Ultimately, Supreme Court decisions are final.

For any level of government, the role and authority of all bodies (executive, legislative, and judicial) is derived from what is stated in the related constitution. Curiously, the U.S. Constitution includes no statements about expectations or responsibilities for education. Through interpretation of what is said, the states have been assigned responsibility for education. As a result, each state's constitution sets the beginning expectations for education. However, over the past 70 years, all three branches of the federal government have increasingly become engaged with and increasingly directive about what states, school districts, and schools should be doing.

The U.S. Constitution comprises six articles. Shortly after it was approved, the Bill of Rights was added. The Constitution itself has been stable over time. However, over the past two centuries, 27 amendments have been added. As is frequently stated, the U.S. Constitution is the law of the land. All other laws and statutes, each state's constitution, and the actions of governments at all levels must be consonant with the U.S. Constitution. As we said, since the U.S. Constitution does not directly address education or schooling, several of its amendments have been interpreted by the U.S. Supreme Court and various governing bodies in ways that assign responsibility to the states. The Tenth Amendment is the key.

The Tenth Amendment— Grants Responsibility to the States

The Tenth Amendment was adopted in 1791 in order to make clear that the civil rights of citizens would be protected against state actions. The Bill of Rights protected citizens against actions of the federal government, but not necessarily actions of a state. The Tenth Amendment states,

> The powers not delegated to the United States by the Constitution, nor prohibited by it to the States, are reserved to the States respectively, or to the people.

Since education is not mentioned in the U.S. Constitution, it is "reserved to the States."

The First and Fourteenth Amendments of the U.S. Constitution also continue to be of major importance to schools, teachers, and students.

As with all political processes, the writing of the Constitution included debate, passion, and compromise.

The First Amendment—Freedom of Speech and Religion

Passed in 1791, the First Amendment states,

> Congress shall make no law respecting an establishment of religion, or prohibiting the free exercise thereof; or abridging the freedom of speech, or of the press; or the right of the people peaceably to assemble, and to petition the Government for a redress of grievances.

Two clauses in the First Amendment have become central to the role of schools, and the rights of teachers and students:

- Interpretation of the Establishment Clause, "Congress shall make no law respecting an establishment of religion," has today taken center stage as various individuals and groups become advocates for prayer in schools and use of public dollars to fund educational activities in buildings and programs sponsored by religious groups. The Founding Fathers had serious concerns about the possibility of government supporting a religion or punishing citizen participation in a religion. There has been continuing debate about how to balance what government can do with the need to provide educational opportunities for all students without those opportunities being seen as government support of a particular religion.

- The Free Speech Clause has been used to challenge a variety of topics such as the extent of teacher academic freedom, the amount of freedom of school-sponsored student newspapers, and dress codes. Since there have been a number of past Court decisions, there are fewer questions in this area at this time.

The Fourteenth Amendment—Due Process

Passed in 1868, the Fourteenth Amendment states in part,

> No State shall make or enforce any law which shall abridge the privileges or immunities of citizens of the United States; nor shall any State deprive any person of life, liberty, or property, without due process of law; nor deny to any person within its jurisdiction the equal protection of the laws.

Due process is an important right granted to all citizens, including students in public schools. There are two components: substantive due process and procedural due process. **Substantive due process** has to do with protection against the loss of the rights granted in the Constitution, such as freedom of expression. Government cannot be arbitrary, capricious, or unreasonable in its actions relative to the rights of all citizens, including educators and students. Administrators can enforce rules of behavior, but all students must be treated similarly. **Procedural due process** deals with whether or not a person has been treated fairly and proper procedures have been followed. Procedural due process has been at the center of many student suspension cases.

"You're sure one of the three branches isn't the media?"

Elementary and Secondary Education Act (ESEA) Past, Present, and Future

A major component of President Lyndon Johnson's Great Society initiatives was directly aimed at improving education. In 1965, Congress passed and President Johnson signed the Elementary and Secondary Education Act (ESEA). At the time, he stated that Congress should set "full educational opportunity as our first national goal" (Johnson, 1965). ESEA had several parts, or titles. The law provided grants to school districts to serve low-income students. It established special education centers and provided books for libraries. Since 1965, ESEA has been reauthorized every eight years or so.

2001 Reauthorization of the Elementary and Secondary Education Act (ESEA) Was Called No Child Left Behind (NCLB)

The No Child Left Behind Act of 2001 (NCLB) was the education legislative initiative of President George W. Bush. Many of the ideas were derived from his earlier initiatives in Texas when he was the governor. The expressed intent was to raise student achievement, increase teacher quality, and make schools safer. This reauthorization of ESEA was passed by both houses of Congress in 2001 and signed into law in January 2002 by President Bush.

NCLB represented the most significant federal intrusion into public education. Within its 2,100 pages, the statute set expectations for levels of teacher qualifications, student performance, and activities by each state. The statute backed these expectations with an array of mandates for states, school districts, schools, and teachers. The overall aspiration was admirable: to have all children proficient by 2013–2014. NCLB included penalties and sanctions for schools, districts, and states that did not reach this goal. However, as the school year 2013–2014 got closer, everyone had to face the hard facts: All children, schools, districts, and states were not going to have all students proficient. Since Congress was in gridlock, there was no new reauthorization of ESEA until 2015. This led to each state having to negotiate with the U.S. Department of Education for a waiver from the NCLB mandates and to implement changes related to the identified areas of low performance.

Elements of No Child Left Behind (NCLB) Are Still With Us

Three important areas of NCLB mandates continue to have direct consequences for states, schools, and even teacher education candidates. These are highly qualified teacher (HQT), Adequate Yearly Progress (AYP), and Schools in Need of Improvement (SINOI). Within each of these components were many expectations and explicit directives that had all of the nation's schools, teachers, and administrators struggling to comply. An added observation about NCLB, which is true of many other pieces of federal and state legislation, is that the act was not funded at anywhere near the level that would be necessary to make total compliance a reality. In other words, in part, it was an unfunded mandate.

Highly Qualified Teacher (HQT)

NCLB set specifications for what it means to be an HQT. Note that the term is *highly qualified*, not *high quality*. The intent was to ensure that all classrooms would be staffed by teachers who have met a set of minimum criteria. The HQT criteria are now reflected in what candidates have to do to receive a teacher license:

- Teachers should be fully licensed by the state and must not have any certification requirements waived on an emergency or temporary basis.

- Teachers should have at least a bachelor's degree and demonstrate competency equivalent to a major in a graduate degree or advanced certification.

- New teachers must pass a state test of subject matter knowledge and teaching skill.

- School districts must notify parents of the availability of information on the professional qualifications of the student's classroom teachers and whether a particular teacher meets state qualification and licensing criteria. In other words, when you become a teacher, your district has to inform any parent who asks about your professional qualifications.

As with many other parts of NCLB, the states were mandated to determine the details of what HQT meant. For example, in most states, before being licensed, aspiring teachers must pass a test. In many states, there is a test upon entering the teacher education program and another at the time of program completion. However, the test score that a candidate needs to make can vary by state, since each state can set its own cut score (see Chapter 1). A few states do not rely on a single high-stakes test and instead use multiple measures, such as teacher portfolios or work samples. If you have not already done so, very soon you should seek out the criteria that have been established for teacher licensure for the state in which you plan to teach.

Another significant NCLB component had to do with student achievement as measured on standardized tests. The AYP mandate included these stipulations:

- All Grade 3–8 students must be tested annually in math and reading/language arts. All Grade 10–12 students must be tested at least once.

- For each school and school district, student test performance must be disaggregated using a number of demographic factors—for example, boy/girl, ethnicity, special education, and English Language Learner (ELL).

- Students in each of the subgroups must make progress each year.

- Ninety-five percent of all students in a school must be tested.

- In addition to states implementing state-wide annual testing programs, in each year between 2002 and 2014, schools were to make special efforts with all students who scored below the proficient level.

Schools in Need of Improvement (SINOI)

Another element of NCLB is what happened to schools that failed to have the mandated increases in test scores. These became SINOI and faced a set of escalating consequences for each year that the test scores did not increase by a sufficient amount. The NCLB expectations included these:

- Students in all schools must make AYP in each of the subgroups that have been identified.

- Failure to make AYP in any one category means that the school will be placed on the list of SINOI.

- A report card must be prepared and disseminated to parents and the public that
  - names each SINOI;
  - provides the number and percentage of SINOIs and how many years they have been on the list; and
  - compares the SINOI student achievement to achievement in the district and the state.

Although the aspirations in NCLB were admirable, the act required a great deal of additional work on the part of teachers, administrators, districts, states, and students. There has been significantly increased pressure on teachers, administrators, and students to do well on each year's tests. Then the 2013–2014 school targets were missed. This situation led the Obama administration to allow states to apply for waivers and introduced new strategies for improving schools.

Reauthorization of ESEA (2015–2016): Every Student Succeeds Act (ESSA)

Historically, ESEA had been reauthorized every four to six years. On this schedule, NCLB would have been replaced in 2007. However, the reauthorization effort dragged on much longer.

In late 2015, both houses of Congress and President Barack Obama came to an agreement on the new reauthorization, called the Every Student Succeeds Act (ESSA). In response to the experience with NCLB, some of the requirements were dropped, such as the penalties for not maintaining AYP. In this reauthorization, states are given more discretion in some areas, such as setting cut scores. Some of the elements of ESSA that will have direct implications for you include the following:

- All students must be taught to high academic standards that will prepare them to succeed in college and careers.

- Annual testing is required in Grades 3–8 and once in high school.

- Academic factors (e.g., tests and graduation rates) weigh more than other factors (e.g., climate, safety, teacher engagement).

- States are required to adopt challenging academic standards but not necessarily the Common Core State Standards.

- States are allowed to develop their own state-based accountability systems.

- States must report disaggregated data by breaking out test scores for subgroups and must report proficiency levels.

- District, school, teacher, and administrator incentives and evaluations must include student academic factors.

- States must provide targeted support to the lowest-performing 5% of schools.

- States must help support and grow local innovations—including evidence-based and place-based interventions developed by local leaders and educators.

- States must sustain and expand investments in increasing access to high-quality preschool.

As you can see, there are strong parallels between directions set in NCLB and what is now set in ESSA. However, one underlying shift is laying more responsibility upon each state. For example, the annual testing and data disaggregation mandates are continued, but each state decides the details. But there is the caveat that the U.S. Department of Education must approve what each state plans to do. Completing the planning, review, and approval processes has taken years.

LEGAL ISSUES AND THEIR DELIBERATIONS: USES OF TECHNOLOGY AND SOCIAL MEDIA

I have given a number of presentations around the country on the social media problem. I tell them up front: Do not ever text your students unless you are using your school district server and your school district email account, and you are only talking about class work, study questions, or something like that. Don't ever "friend" students on social media, and certainly don't text them. Maintain a professional relationship.

—Mr. Simpson

The rapid development of new technologies certainly is an area where teachers, school administrators, and parents need to think carefully about what is appropriate use. However, use of technology is but one of many contemporary problems being addressed through legislation and the development of new rules and procedures and being tested through court challenges. Bullying of students and school safety in general are other important problem areas. Also, the increasing ease with which technology makes it possible to access information is generating new questions related to protection of copyrights and fair use.

These topics illustrate the continually evolving need for new legislation and emerging questions that have to be addressed by the courts. Many other questions have been decided in the past and need to be understood by today's teachers. Keep in mind that different lower-level courts may reach different decisions. Until the U.S. Supreme Court decides—and, ultimately, each state's statutes reflect what is prohibited and permitted—it is very important for you to be extra careful about what you do and don't do.

Teachers and students should be very careful about what they share through social media.

iStock/elenaleonova

Social Media: Uses, Misuses, and Issues

Teachers and administrators need to consider carefully what are acceptable uses of new technologies as well as older technologies such as cell phones, digital cameras, and the Internet. Recently, courts have been addressing various questions related to rights of privacy, consequences of distributing certain types of information, and legality of searches.

Teachers' Use of Myspace and Facebook

Do teachers have guaranteed First Amendment free speech rights to establish social media profiles and make these available to students? No. In the fall of 2005, Jeffrey Spanierman, a nontenured English teacher in Connecticut, set up a Myspace account called "Mr. Spiderman." He used the account to communicate with students about homework as well as more personal issues including casual comments and pictures of naked men. Several students complained to a counselor, who referred the matter to the principal. An administrative investigation was conducted with the conclusion being a letter from the assistant superintendent that the teacher's contract would not be renewed. Mr. Spanierman filed suit in federal court. The federal district court's decision supported the school district's decision in seeing the Myspace profile as disruptive and stated that it was "reasonable for the Defendants to expect the Plaintiff, a teacher with supervisory authority over students, to maintain a professional, respectful association with students" (*Spanierman v. Hughes, Druzolowski, & Hylwa*, 2008).

Cyberbullying

Are there any limits on what students can create and distribute about school officials and students from home? Yes and no. Two of the major questions related to cyberbullying are "When does the exercise of free speech become bullying?" and "Under what conditions can a school district suspend a student for cyberbullying?" Each of these questions is being addressed by lower courts through a variety of cases.

Keep in mind that cyberbullying can be directed toward adults as well as students. For example, in two 2010 cases in Pennsylvania (*J. S. v. Blue Mountain School District* and *Layshock v. Hermitage School District*), students were suspended for having created offensive fake Myspace profiles of school officials. One eighth-grade student called her principal a "hairy sex addict" and a "pervert." In the other case, a high school senior had called his principal a "whore" who used drugs. In both cases, the students had been using home computers. Both cases were appealed to three-judge panels of the U.S. Court of Appeals for the Third Circuit. The two panels rendered opposite decisions. The *J. S.* case was seen as proper while the *Layshock* case was seen as not having established a sufficiently close connection to be disruptive. The full Third Circuit Court of Appeals reheard both cases and ruled that the students' off-campus behavior was not disruptive to the school and therefore was protected under the First Amendment.

In a recent case in West Virginia (*Kara Kowalski, Plaintiff, v. Berkeley County Schools*, No. 1098, July 27, 2011), the Fourth Circuit Court of Appeals ruled that a school district had the right to suspend a senior who online had called another girl a "slut" with venereal disease. School officials labeled this a "hate website" that violated school policy against harassment and bullying.

As you can see, different courts are making different decisions. As the process continues to unfold, one or more cases will be appealed to and accepted by the U.S. Supreme Court. Also, as the process unfolds, there will be gradual clarification of what is considered cyberbullying and under what conditions school officials can suspend or expel students. One possible emerging direction from the cases cited here is that school officials may have more authority to suspend students when the victim is a fellow student. They may have less authority when the offensive activity is done away from school. Another important element is the extent of disruption of school activity.

Sexting

Is it okay for students to take and share explicit photos of themselves? No. **Sexting** is the act of using a cell phone or other technology to send or receive sexually explicit pictures, video, and/or text. This act can

TEACHERS' LOUNGE

THE PITFALLS OF SOCIAL MEDIA FOR TEACHERS

Stacey Snyder was an education major at Millersville University in Pennsylvania. During the 2006 spring semester, she enrolled in the university's student teaching program and was assigned to Conestoga Valley High School. She anticipated that when she completed her student teaching successfully, she would graduate in May 2006 with a bachelor of science in education. During the orientation to student teaching early in the semester, university officials discussed the use of personal web pages and warned the student teachers about posting information about their students or teachers on social media sites. Later, Stacey recollected that the university's student–teacher coordinator had told her not to post information about her students or her cooperating teacher on her social media.

After Stacey began her student teaching placement at the high school, she disregarded the directions from university personnel and began posting personal comments with her students on her personal Myspace page. She told her students in class that she used Myspace and told her classroom supervising teacher that many of her students also used Myspace. Her supervising teacher cautioned Stacey that she should not discuss her social media account with her students, and told her that she should avoid allowing her students to get involved in her personal life.

Early in May, the final month of her student teaching, two of Stacey's personal posts on her Myspace page began a series of events that resulted in her being terminated from her student teaching by school administrators. One of her Myspace posts confirmed that she was sharing personal information about her work and her students in defiance of directives from university administrators and her supervising teacher. In addition, the message mentioned that someone at the high school was causing her problems. When one teacher showed her post to her supervising teacher, the supervisor believed that Stacey was referring to her as the one causing her problems because of her critical evaluations of Stacey's work during the student teaching placement. Stacey's Myspace page also included a photograph of her captioned "drunken pirate." The photo showed her wearing a pirate hat and holding a plastic cup, which Stacey later said contained a "mixed beverage."

Together, these two posts on Stacey's Myspace account, along with some negative performance evaluations by her university supervisor and classroom supervising teacher, resulted in school administrators immediately removing Stacey from her student teaching placement. Because she did not complete her student teaching, the university could not award academic credit. Consequently, Stacey was not eligible for a teaching certificate from the Pennsylvania Department of Education. Stacey sued Millersville University and several university administrators in federal court for allegedly violating her First Amendment free speech rights, among other things.

After the trial, the federal district court judge determined that while Stacey was a student teacher, her role was more like a public employee than a student. In addition, the judge determined that Stacey's Myspace posts did not touch on matters of public concern, but were personal in nature. Thus, the university administrators did not violate her First Amendment speech rights by not allowing her to complete student teaching and not awarding a bachelor's degree in education.

It should be noted that the university allowed Stacey to withdraw from student teaching rather than giving her a failing grade, and allowed her academic credits to be applied to a bachelor of arts in English, which she did receive at the end of the semester.

—Mr. William E. Sparkman, Professor
University of Nevada, Reno

Source: *Snyder v. Millersville University*, 2008 WL 5093140 (E.D. Pa. 2008).

be consensual or nonconsensual. One of the earliest sexting cases (*Miller v. Skumanick*, 2009) developed in Pennsylvania. Teachers discovered pictures of three topless 13-year-old girls on the cell phones of boy classmates. School district officials confiscated the phones and turned them over to the district attorney, who determined that the images were provocative and that the girls were accomplices in the production of child pornography.

The district attorney threatened charges against the girls as well as the boys for distribution unless they participated in a counseling remediation program. The boys agreed, but the girls refused and filed a lawsuit (*Miller v. Mitchell*, 2010) alleging violation of their First Amendment right to free expression. Following two years of legal procedures, the Third Circuit Court of Appeals ruled that the photographs did not constitute child pornography and that the girls were protected under the First Amendment.

Although in *Miller v. Mitchell* (2010) the students were not taken to criminal court for either the production or the distribution of pornography, in other states and other school districts, similar charges and the related challenges are wending their way through the courts. Fortunately, state legislatures are now developing laws that distinguish between crimes related to child pornography—a felony—and the unwitting behaviors of minors, which in many cases can be considered a misdemeanor. Regardless of the intent, teachers and their students need to be sensitive to the actions that can be construed as sexting, as well as the legal and emotional consequences.

Copying Documents and Other Material From the Internet

The use and misuse of social media is just one of the areas currently being examined by the courts. Table 9.1 is a summary of selected court cases related to social media and a number of other contemporary legal questions. As you will read below, many of the current questions have to do with uses of the Internet, which has most certainly brought us into the Information Age. Teachers and students can access all sorts of documents, pictures, sources, and resources by simply hitting a few keys and accessing a search engine. Students today seem to think nothing of downloading for free music and videos. Teachers can be all too casual about copying text and other resources. But what about downloading and using digital material that is protected and/or has a copyright? By law, a potential user, including teachers or students, is required to seek permission from the source before distributing said material.

Accessing Material on the Web That Has a Copyright

Is all information on the Internet considered public domain? No. There are federal, state, and international laws that govern copyright practices. In general, they are designed to protect the rights of scholars and artists while preserving the public's right to benefit from the works of those same creators. Copyrights protect the imagination of individuals.

Searching for and finding a juicy piece of information to complement any work in progress is a satisfying process. The accessibility of the web even makes it convenient. What is not so clear, given the ease of downloading artifacts or evidence from the web, is just how closely protected web-based sources are, and what the requirements are for using such sources in your own work.

Federal law (U.S. Copyright Law: Title 17 U.S.C. Section 101 et seq., Title 18 U.S.C. Section 2319) protects copyright owners from the unauthorized reproduction, adaptation, performance, display, or distribution of copyright-protected works. Penalties for copyright infringement differ in civil and criminal cases. Civil remedies are generally available for any act of infringement without regard

---

TABLE 9.1 ■ Social Media Questions Being Considered by the Courts

Question	Case	Decision
Do teachers have First Amendment protections in their use of Myspace?	Teacher Free Speech *Spanierman v. Hughes et al.* (2008)	Not when what they do is considered to be disruptive.
Are students protected when they post uncomplimentary descriptions of school personnel or students from home?	Cyberbullying *J. S. v. Blue Mountain School District* (2010) and *Layshock v. Hermitage School District* (2010)	It is okay if posts are about students. It is probably okay when it is done off-campus and about school personnel.
Is sharing photos of topless girls the production and distribution of pornographic material?	Sexting *Miller v. Skumanick* (2009)	Yes, in some states.
Can teachers take and use whatever they find on the Internet?	Taking Material off the Internet U.S. Copyright Law	No. Be careful when thinking that you are covered by fair use. Check the source carefully.

to the intention or knowledge of the defendant or harm to the copyright owner. Criminal penalties are available for intentional acts undertaken for purposes of commercial advantage or private financial gain. Private financial gain includes the possibility of financial loss to the copyright holder as well as traditional gain by the defendant.

Is there information regarding copyright that will help teachers understand what they can and should do? Yes. Following are a few examples:

Everyone, including teachers, can be prosecuted for violating copyright laws.

- Given the easy access to digital media by students and teachers, one important resource is the website of the Recording Industry Association of America. Two important tabs to check out under the main tab Resources & Learning are "Parental Advisory Label" and "For Students and Educators."

- Commonsense media offers a variety of curriculum resources for teachers and information for parents about how to use media in safe and responsible ways.

- At Brad Templeton's web page, "10 Big Myths About Copyright Explained," he explains 10 myths about copyright in ways that teachers and students can understand.

- Among the teacher resources of the U.S. Library of Congress is a page titled "Copyright and Primary Sources" that addresses the importance of teachers using primary sources in legally correct ways.

- The Electronic Frontier Foundation has developed a unit, "Teaching Copyright," that consists of five 60-minute lesson plans, including quizzes, handouts, and notes for the teacher.

Copyright Guidelines for Teachers and Students

Are there some exceptions to copyright laws on the Internet? Yes. **Fair use** criteria can create some exceptions to copyright laws for teachers and students. However, keep in mind that there are no absolute guidelines for fair use in educational settings. According to the Stanford University Libraries website, the only way to get a definitive answer on whether a particular use is a fair use is to have it resolved in federal court. Judges use four factors to resolve fair use disputes:

1. The purpose and character of your use
2. The nature of the copyrighted work
3. The amount and substantiality of the portion taken
4. The effect of the use on the potential market

Copyright and fair use guidelines for teachers have been summarized by various agencies. One very useful summary has been published by Xavier University, www.xavier.edu/library/about/documents/Copyright_9-23-08.pdf. These guidelines are not directly part of the Copyright Law of 1976 or its subsequent amendments, but they should be studied carefully before embarking on any major use of copyrighted material.

Too many teachers and most students tend to treat the Internet as an open source. There is all too frequently the philosophy of "If I find it on the Internet, I can use it for free." This is not necessarily so. Internet users, including teachers, are accountable to copyright laws in the same way that they are when accessing and using information in the real world. Since April 1, 1989, every communication (words, photos, music, or art) produced on the Internet is copyrighted by default.

Is it true that as long as you don't use the material for commercial purposes, you are not breaking any laws? No. Be safe. Ask the source for permission when using any material produced by anyone else.

Finding Out If Something Has a Copyright

You may not be in the habit of scrolling down to the bottom of any web page that you access, but in the future, click on the disclaimer and copyright information posted at the bottom of nearly every web page. You'll find out quickly how much of the information on that website is available for public use. In most cases it's zilch, but there is usually a place where you can contact the designers or owners of the website to see if they will let you use some of the information they have organized. Most would be more than happy to give permission to educators.

CONTINUING LEGAL DILEMMAS: RELIGION, SCHOOL FINANCE, AND SEGREGATION

Given the hundreds of years of history related to the identification of problems, development of laws to address each problem, and the arbitration of disputes by the courts, you might think that all the questions from the past would have been addressed and solutions established. However, this is not the case. There are a number of questions for which there seems to be no final answers. Several of these related to education are highlighted next.

One idea that might help you understand why each of these areas has been so enduring is to make a distinction between something that is a **problem** and something that is a **dilemma**. By definition, a problem has a solution. Once a problem is defined, one or more solutions can be devised to fix it. Most of the time, when something stops working on your car, a mechanic can fix it. A problem is identified (it won't start), there is a diagnosis (the battery is dead), and a new part is installed (a new battery). Sometimes the car still won't start, and all are puzzled—in other words, it's a dilemma. Dilemmas do not have simple solutions. In fact, dilemmas are so complex that there is no single solution. The enduring legal topics described herein are dilemmas. Although there have been legislative actions, statutes approved, and court cases conducted, the problem has morphed into a dilemma, and persists. It is likely that elements of each of these enduring topics will still be in debate at the end of your teaching career.

Separation of Church and State

We all learned in school that one reason the Puritans traveled in tiny ships across the Atlantic to a new country was to escape religious persecution. When the U.S. Constitution was written, this concern was addressed directly in two clauses within the First Amendment.

There are continuing questions and challenges related to the separation of church and state when it comes to education. For example, can tax dollars be used to pay for student transportation to Catholic schools?

Establishment Clause: "Congress shall make no law respecting an establishment of religion."

Free Exercise Clause: "Or prohibiting the free exercise thereof."

These two clauses would seem to be straightforward. At the time, Thomas Jefferson talked about a wall of separation between church and state. Until some 70 years ago, this view was pretty much accepted—in other words, it was not a problem. A 1947 Supreme Court decision (*Everson v. Board of Education*) is now seen as the beginning of the creation of a dilemma.

Using Public Funds to Pay for Transportation to Catholic Schools

New Jersey had a statute that allowed for reimbursement of public bus transportation costs to parents who sent their children to Catholic schools. The question asked in *Everson v. Board of Education* (1947) was whether these payments were a violation of the Establishment Clause. A divided Court ruled that it was not a violation. The reasoning was that the payments were not direct support to parochial schools but a general program of support to assist parents of all religions. The door was now open to test the limits of using public funds for schools in conjunction with religious activities.

Two Continuing Questions

In many ways, *Everson v. Board of Education* broke a logjam. Since 1947, there have been continuing debates, actions that challenge the boundaries, development of various statutes, and publication of various rules and procedures, all of which were intended to either stay clear of or test where the boundary now is between church and state.

Two questions that can be used to understand elements of what is now a dilemma are these:

1. In what ways and to what extent can public funds be used in association with religious schooling and not be in violation of the U.S. Constitution?

2. What types of religious activities can and cannot be done, within and around public schools, and not be seen as a violation of the U.S. Constitution?

Since 1947, there have been many court challenges and decisions relative to the ways that public funds can be used in association with nonpublic schools. Table 9.2 includes a summary of selected cases. Each decision has provided more guidance but also led to new questions.

TABLE 9.2 ■ Legal Dilemmas That Continue to Be Addressed by the Courts That Have Major Implications for Schools, Students, Teachers, and Communities

Question	Case	Decision
Separation of Church and State		
Can state funds be used to reimburse parents for bus travel to Catholic schools?	*Everson v. Board of Education* (1947)	Yes. The statute did not pay money to parochial schools, nor did it directly support them.
Can public funds be used to pay for teachers in nonpublic schools?	*Lemon v. Kurtzman* (1971)	No. This would be a violation of the Establishment Clause.
Can student-led prayer be a part of school activities?	*Santa Fe Independent School District v. Doe* (2000)	No. This would be a violation of the Establishment Clause.
Can religious holidays be observed in public schools?	*Florey v. Sioux Falls School District* (1980)	Yes, as long as the celebration is secular.
Can religious student groups meet at a public school?	*Board of Education of the Westside Community Schools v. Mergens* (1990)	If one noncurriculum-related student group is permitted to meet at a public school, then the school may not deny other clubs.
Desegregation and Integration		
Is separate but equal constitutional?	*Plessy v. Ferguson* (1896)	Yes.
Is separate but equal constitutional?	*Brown v. Board of Education of Topeka* (1954)	No.
School Finance		
Can local property taxes be used to pay for schools?	*San Antonio (Texas) Independent School District v. Rodriguez* (1973)	Yes.
Do the states have to fund all schools efficiently?	*Rose v. Council for Better Education* (1989)	Yes, in Kentucky. Many other states also have had to reconfigure their funding of schools, based on how education is addressed within each state's constitution.

Can public funds be used to pay for teachers in nonpublic schools? No. In *Lemon v. Kurtzman* (1971), the Court was asked to decide whether public funds could be used to pay for teachers and textbooks for secular subjects in nonpublic schools. The Court ruled 8 to 0 (for various reasons, sometimes a justice will not be voting) that state financial aid of this type was a violation of the Establishment Clause. Additionally, Chief Justice Warren E. Burger stated a three-part test for laws to be constitutional. This test has become known as the Lemon Test. The three parts are that (1) the statute must have "a secular legislative purpose," (2) it must neither advance nor hinder religion, and (3) it must not encourage "an excessive government entanglement with religion."

As you can see in studying Table 9.2, there has been a continuing circling around the central question of to what extent and in what ways public funds can be used in conjunction with nonpublic schools and not run into violation of the Establishment Clause.

The Place of Religious Activities in Public Schools

Tests of the free exercise clause have been equally extensive. A year does not go by without reports in the news in which another student at his or her graduation ceremony prays, or a teacher is reported to be proselytizing, or a governing body mandates that the Bible or a topic such as creationism be part of the public school curriculum. The central question then becomes "Is not permitting the activity prohibiting the free exercise of religion?" Of course, allowing it may be seen as a violation of the Establishment Clause. Table 9.2 includes selected cases and Court decisions related to religious activities in public schools.

Prayer at School Events

Can students lead a prayer at athletic events, graduation ceremonies, and other school-sponsored events? No. Before 1995, an elected student council member at Santa Fe (Texas) High School delivered a prayer over the public address system before every home football game. It was described as overtly Christian. A Mormon and a Catholic family filed suit. In *Santa Fe Independent School District v. Doe* (2000), the Court ruled 6 to 3 that the policy of permitting student-led prayer at football games violates the Establishment Clause.

But what if there is a period of silent meditation and prayer set aside in public schools? Here, too, the answer is no. In *Wallace v. Jaffree* (1985), the Court ruled that an Alabama statute that authorized a minute of silent prayer, and another authorizing silent meditation, was unconstitutional. The Court concluded that there was no secular purpose and that the intent of the Alabama legislature was to establish prayer in the schools.

Celebration of Religious Holidays in Schools

Can religious holidays be observed at school events? Yes, if the celebration has a secular basis. In *Florey v. Sioux Falls School District* (1980), the Court based its decision on the historical and cultural significance of Christmas and the fact that the holiday was not being observed for the purpose of promoting Christianity. A federal district court in New Jersey allowed a school district to include on the school calendar holidays such as Christmas and Hanukkah "to broaden students' sensitivity toward religious diversity and their knowledge of the role of religion in the development of civilization" (Cambron-McCabe, McCarthy, & Thomas, 2004, p. 38). The courts have ruled that school choirs and assemblies may sing holiday carols, for instance, as long as the performances are not organized for religious purposes.

Some parents have charged schools with promoting the religion of Wicca when they observe Halloween with pictures of witches and goblins. However, a Florida court ruled that such displays did not promote a religion. The U.S. Supreme Court has declined appeals of cases related to the observance of holidays that are perceived by some parents as promoting religion.

Funding of Public Schools: Equity and Equality

Another continuing dilemma has to do with the funding of schools. Over the past 30 years, more than 40 states have had court challenges related to the amount of funding support and/or whether the available funds have been distributed fairly. In *Rodriguez v. San Antonio Independent School District* (1971), the U.S. Supreme Court deferred to the states questions about the funding of schools. Since then, challenges about funding thus have been based in the wording and way the provision of schooling has been addressed in each state's constitution.

What the U.S. Constitution Says About Funding

Is the funding of schools a U.S. Constitution issue? No. The Mexican American Legal Defense and Educational Fund (MALDEF) filed a class action suit on the behalf of a group of Mexican American parents against the inequitable funding of Texas schools. In 1971, the federal district court ruled in *Rodriguez v. San Antonio Independent School District* that the Texas school finance system was unconstitutional based on the Equal Protection Clause of the Fourteenth Amendment. In 1973, the U.S. Supreme Court ruled that school finance was not a constitutional issue, pushing the cases back to state courts for resolution.

View of the States About the Funding of Schools

Could a state supreme court declare the whole system of public education unconstitutional? Yes. This is exactly what happened in Kentucky in the early 1990s. In *Rose v. Council for Better Education* (1989), the Kentucky Supreme Court ruled, "It is crystal clear that the General Assembly has fallen short of its duty to enact legislation to provide for an efficient system of common schools throughout the state." The key term here is *efficient*, which was a stated expectation in Kentucky's constitution. The court went on to say, "Lest there be any doubt, the result of our decision is that Kentucky's entire system of common schools is unconstitutional." The court directed the legislature to develop a new system of public education for the state. The result was the Kentucky Education Reform Act (KERA) of 1991.

Segregation, Desegregation, and the Risks of Resegregation

Another important dilemma that has a long history is achieving and sustaining nondiscriminatory practices in society in general and in schools in particular. Over the past 200 years, the courts have been on both sides of this dilemma. You need to keep in mind two important terms in considering this dilemma: **De facto segregation** refers to segregation that has developed through the facts of a situation, which are outside of the actions of government. **De jure segregation** refers to segregation that is brought about through laws *and* the actions of state and local officials.

Separate but Equal Was Constitutional

In 1896, in *Plessy v. Ferguson*, the Supreme Court ruled that public facilities and services for blacks could be "separate but equal." For the next 58 years, de jure segregation led to dual school systems (one for whites and another for blacks). This included black teachers for segregated schools and white teachers for white students. Mainly, but not only in Southern schools, the state constitutions, statutes, and local school policies reinforced having dual school systems. This also was the time when Southern states adopted Jim Crow laws that required whites and blacks to use separate facilities, including drinking fountains, toilets, hotels, restaurants, and seats on public transportation.

Separate but Equal Becomes Unconstitutional

In 1954, the U.S. Supreme Court in *Brown v. Board of Education of Topeka* reversed its ruling of 58 years before. "We conclude that in the field of public education the doctrine of 'separate but equal' has no place. Separate educational facilities are inherently unequal." In other words, de jure segregation is now unconstitutional. *Brown* dealt only with public schools; however, its consequences have evolved to affect all of American society.

Separate but equal was not equal.

Implementation of *Brown* has continued to require Court engagement. The overall strategy was to achieve **integration** whereby there would not be bias in the distribution of facilities, students, and school personnel. The first strategy of the courts was to direct dismantling of the dual systems of schooling. Another was to bus students from one community to another to achieve racial balance in each school. In many instances, the courts' directive of implementing desegregation with "all deliberate speed" was not resulting in observable movements. So, in cases such as *Alexander v. Holmes County Board of Education* (1969), the Court mandated that districts must immediately terminate dual school systems.

Release From Court Order

Over the intervening years, there have continued to be suits related to progress in achieving integration in schools. Many school systems have been placed under court supervision, and their procedures as well as the assignment of students and personnel have been closely monitored. As the vestiges of the dual systems have been eliminated and the distribution of students and personnel has become equalized—in other words, as integration has been achieved—school systems have been released from supervision by the Court. In many communities, this has been a process that has taken many years.

Risk of Resegregation

Much has been achieved over the seven decades since the 1954 *Brown* decision. De jure segregation has been widely challenged and in most settings eliminated. However, now there is a new risk, resegregation (see Chapter 2). Now most of the segregation in schools and communities is de facto. As the courts directed that schools integrate white and black students, many white families reacted by moving to other school districts. This movement was called "white flight." There also have been economic factors contributing to where people live. As people gain in wealth, they tend to move to areas that are more affluent. More recently, a new trend has been developing—tribalism. With the current extremes in polarity of politics, media, and lifestyles, people are increasingly deciding to live in communities where there are shared beliefs and economic status. They choose to be members of a tribe that has similar values and beliefs to their own. A consequence is more homogeneity within communities (i.e., less diversity). The result can be de facto resegregation.

In Summary: Solving Dilemmas Takes Time

As the dilemmas of separation of church and state, financing of public schools, and desegregation well illustrate, many of today's challenges are not easily addressed. Most certainly, they do not have simple solutions that will bring each to a final conclusion. Instead, each of these dilemmas is enduring and likely to require concerted effort not only by the courts but also by government leaders, citizens, and especially teachers. As is readily seen within each of these dilemmas, the one institution that continues to be seen as a tool for solving them is education.

STUDENTS' RIGHTS AND PROTECTIONS

Another area where beginning teachers can get in trouble is dealing with students with disabilities. For example, there is great controversy around the country now about what is called "restraint and seclusion" as ways of dealing with students who are out of control. Both school districts and individual employees have been sued in recent years either for confining a student with disabilities in a room until he or she calms down (that's called seclusion) or for physically restraining a student, for example, by tying his hands to a chair to keep him from hitting himself or others.

Beginning teachers need to know the ins and outs of how the Individuals with Disabilities Education Act of 1990 (IDEA) works because every new teacher will likely have one or more students in each class with IEPs and BIPs (Behavioral Intervention Plans). Teachers have to sit in on IEP meetings. They really need to have a grasp of what rights students have under IDEA and Section 504, and what their responsibilities are.

—Mr. Simpson

UNDERSTANDING AND USING DATA
ANALYZING SCHOOL-WIDE DATA ABOUT STUDENT LEARNING

As a teacher, you have important opportunities to become involved school-wide. One important way is to work on one of the committees that works with data. Data teams, Response to Intervention (RTI) teams, and the School Improvement Team (SIT) are obvious places to work with data. The SIT, for example, will include teachers, the principal or vice principal, team leaders/Department Chairs, and perhaps an outside resource such as a district office person and/or a university faculty member.

Each year, the SIT reviews the test scores for all students and then develops the School Improvement Plan (SIP) that details the action steps the school will take the next year to improve student learning. Reviewing the data is where the SIT work begins.

For this Understanding and Using Data activity, assume that you are a member of the SIT for a large (2,700 students) high school. The table presents two years of scores for a proficiency test. This is a test that students must pass in order to graduate from high school. It is typically taken the first time at the end of the sophomore year.

Questions

Study the data in the table and answer these questions:

1. What patterns or trends do you see in the data?
2. Are there areas where students improved from one year to the next?
3. Are there areas where students did not improve?
4. Which groups of students would you want the SIP to address in planning for the next school year?
5. Given your developing knowledge of the law, what cautions would you keep in mind in developing the SIP action steps?

Reading	Year 1			Year 2		
Population	Number	% Proficient	% Nonproficient	Number	% Proficient	% Nonproficient
Hispanic/Latino	230	54.5%	45.5%	274	63.4%	36.6%
Black/African American	89	60.5%	39.5%	85	62.0%	38.0%
White	85	73.9%	26.1%	78	76.5%	23.5%
IEP	14	20.9%	79.1%	14	19.4%	80.6%
LEP	144	50.3%	49.7%	209	61.8%	38.2%
FRPL	59	57.8%	42.2%	161	68.8%	31.2%

IEP = Individualized Education Program; LEP = Limited English Proficiency; FRPL = Free or Reduced-Price Lunch.

Answer the Questions

Study the data and answer the questions above for yourself before proceeding to the discussion below.

Discussion

There are several trends in these data. How many of these did you identify?

- Hispanic/Latino students had an increase in their proficiency rate.
- There is no change for black/African American students.
- White students' scores might have increased a little.
- There was no change in the number or proficiency rate for students with IEPs.
- There were significant increases in the pass rates for LEP and FRPL students.

Plans for Next Year

What did you recommend that the SIT address in planning for next year? For example, shouldn't something different be done to address black/African American students? Whatever has been done to help Hispanic/Latino, LEP, and FRPL students probably should be continued. What are your thoughts about serving students with IEPs? Should there be more inclusion? If there isn't co-teaching (where the regular classroom teacher and the special education resource teacher work together), maybe it should be tried.

Legal Cautions

What do you have in mind in regard to legal aspects of the data and an SIP? For example, if your plan would place all of the black/African American students in a special class, would there be potential legal questions? Also, you would want to be cautious about establishing a permanent class of LEP students. This could be seen as discriminatory. One useful step would be to have more data. For example, ask that the test scores be disaggregated by the learning standards, then group students according to the standards where they need extra attention.

In summary, data-driven decision making always begins with looking at and disaggregating the data so that instruction can be customized. At the same time, keep in mind that there may be legal implications if some strategies are implemented without the data to support how student learning will be enhanced.

Although in many ways students have the rights of all citizens, in some ways their rights as students are more prescribed. In the distant past, a commonly held view was that school officials were acting in place of the parents—in other words, in loco parentis. This is no longer the case. Teachers and school administrators have to be careful to protect the rights of students and follow established procedures in all matters, including discipline, searches, bullying, disseminating information from student records, and seeing that students are safe. Table 9.3 presents some of the findings of the courts. These and other cases are described here.

Statutes Related to Students With Disabilities

Statues and administrative laws related to students with disabilities were described in Chapter 3, "Exceptional Learners." Here we begin by identifying legal aspects of students with disabilities. The remainder of the section describes other important aspects of student rights.

The Least Restrictive Environment (LRE)

Not all students have common capabilities for learning. Some students may need more time to learn a concept or skill that will lead to meeting academic standards. Some students may need special instruction or materials and resources to help them process instruction. Laws have been established to regulate and determine the placement of such students in schools. IDEA is the federal law governing the education of children with disabilities. IDEA and its regulations define Least Restrictive Environment (LRE) and require that all states demonstrate they have policies and procedures in place to guarantee they meet the federal LRE requirements (see Chapter 3).

iStock/Kim Gunkel

The Individuals with Disabilities Education Act requires that students with disabilities be included in the regular classroom to the maximum extent that is appropriate.

Does a student with disabilities have an IEP that indicates what the extent of his or her LRE should be? Yes. The 1997 amendments to IDEA require that in a situation where a child will not participate fully with peers without disabilities, the IEP must include an explanation of why and to what extent the child will not be included.

Inclusion

Is inclusion a right? No. People often assume that IDEA regulations require schools to practice inclusion. However, the term *inclusion* is not included in the IDEA statutes. The terms *mainstreaming* and *Least Restrictive Environment* are included in the IDEA regulations; these terms require school districts to educate students with disabilities in regular classrooms with their nondisabled classmates in the school they would attend to the maximum extent appropriate. According to the definition of

TABLE 9.3 ■ Student Rights		
Question	**Case**	**Decision**
Do schools have a free hand in engaging in student searches?	*New Jersey v. T.L.O.* (1985)	No, unless there is reasonable cause.
Can a student be suspended without a hearing?	*Goss v. Lopez* (1975)	Only in an emergency.
May states constitutionally authorize corporal punishment?	*Ingraham v. Wright* (1977)	Yes, and many states have.
May a student's social media posts done away from school be disciplined by school authorities?	*Tinker v. Des Moines* (1969)	Yes, if there is the likelihood of the activity causing a school disruption.

Least Restrictive Environment, a child with a disability may be removed from the regular classroom only when the nature or severity of the disability is such that the education in regular classes cannot be achieved satisfactorily, even with the use of supplementary aids and services. Students with disabilities may at times be removed from the regular classroom to work in a small group or in one-on-one situations designed to provide them with additional education in a specific academic area.

Paying for Special Education

Do parents of students with disabilities have to pay for the special services provided by the school? No. Reauthorization of IDEA in 1997 extended federal funding for special education services to ensure that all children with disabilities were provided with a free and appropriate public education, and that the student's placement and the services he or she receives depend on the student's individual needs, not on administrative convenience.

Student and Teacher Qualifications Under the Individuals with Disabilities Education Act of 1990 (IDEA)

Is there a test to determine a student's eligibility for IDEA services? Yes. In a two-part test, a student's disability must fit within one of the categories of eligibility, and then it must be proven that the child needs special services because of this disability. Not all children with physical or mental impairments will satisfy IDEA's two-part eligibility test, and so not all of them are eligible for IDEA services.

    Are there special requirements for classroom teachers who will teach students with disabilities in the LRE? Yes. All general and special education teachers responsible for providing services to students with disabilities must receive appropriate training, resources, and support necessary to help such students achieve academic goals. Specifications for a teaching certificate require that some college course work related to the special needs of students with disabilities be included on a licensure applicant's transcript.

Student Rights

The rights of students as well as teacher and school responsibilities have been tested in the courts, and in most instances, there are now established policies, rules, and procedures. Now is the time for you, as a future teacher, to begin to understand the rights of all students and your role in protecting those rights.

Family Privacy Rights

Do families have the right to review their child's student records? Yes. In 1974, Congress passed Public Law 93-380, the Family Educational Rights and Privacy Act (FERPA), to protect the confidentiality of student records. It allows parents the right to review their children's records and to file complaints. Non-English-speaking parents must be notified of these rights in their native language. The law requires the withdrawal of federal funds if a school (1) does not allow parents access to their children's records or (2) releases information (with some exceptions) without the parent's permission. FERPA also applies to colleges and universities, but parental approval is not required for students over 18 years old. After age 18, approval can be granted only by the college student.

    Recent Court cases have clarified applicable violations under FERPA. For example, a college student filed for damages in *Gonzaga University v. Doe* because the university had released to the state department of education records indicating an unsubstantiated allegation of sexual misconduct, which led to the denial of a teaching license. The Supreme Court ruled in 2002 that individuals are not entitled to awards of damages under FERPA. In 2002, the Supreme Court also ruled that peer grading practices did not violate FERPA in *Owasso Independent School District v. Falvo*.

    Student records can sometimes be released without parental approval. For example, schools can release official student records to another school to which a student is transferring if the school has a clear policy that it routinely transfers such records. Student records are also made available for accreditation visits and audits and evaluations of federal programs.

Data Privacy

Can teachers decide by themselves what information about a student will be shared? No. As more and more data about individual students are being collected, compiled, and inserted into databases, a new and very important dilemma has arisen: Who should have access to which sets of data, and when? Teachers most certainly should be able to access test scores and other assessment information. As described in Chapter 8 and displayed in Table 8.1, today's principals have access to enormous amounts of data about each student, their families, and teachers. Who else should have access to individual student data? Which data should be made available for teacher and administrator evaluations?

The key statute that addresses this question is FERPA. This statute makes clear that parents/guardians may have access to their child's educational records. Also, their child's educational records cannot be shared with others outside the school/district without written parent/guardian consent.

Related questions about data privacy are beginning to appear in court cases. For example, there are Fourth Amendment questions about the right to be free from unreasonable searches, while school officials have needs to monitor students for misbehavior. More concretely, when is it permissible for school officials to check a student's cell phone or Facebook site? Until the courts, legislative bodies, and administrations work out what is and is not permissible, teachers should be cautious and protective of any and all data they access.

State Interests vs. Individual Rights

Can compulsory attendance laws require all children to attend public schools? No. In 1922, the Oregon legislature passed the Compulsory Education Act, which required the parents and custodians of children between the ages of 8 and 16 to send them "to a public school for the period of time a public school shall be held during the current year." This statute required attendance at public schools only. The Society of Sisters, which had been organized in 1880 to care for orphans, challenged the statute. In its ruling, *Pierce v. Society of Sisters* (1925), the Supreme Court declared that states may require compulsory attendance, but they may not require that all children attend public schools.

Public High Schools

Do states have the authority to establish public high schools? Yes. The answer to this question came in *Stuart v. School District No. 1 of Village of Kalamazoo* (1874). Kalamazoo College, a private academy, had been established in 1855. As demand for preparation for university increased, in 1858 the district superintendent created a union high school. The school was successful. The college was concerned because it pulled some students away, and some taxpayers objected. In 1873, the college and a group of prominent citizens filed suit. The case was decided in support of public high schools by the Supreme Court of Michigan.

Sports for Girls

Can separate playing seasons be scheduled for girls' and boys' teams that are playing the same sport? No. This practice violates the Equal Protection Clauses of federal and state constitutions. Some school districts argue that they do not have the facilities or coaches for both teams to practice and compete during the same season. The courts in Michigan and West Virginia ruled that if the two teams cannot play during the same season, the burden of playing during the off-season must be shared. For example, the boys' team would have to play during the off-season in alternating years.

Undocumented Students

Can the undocumented children of alien parents be denied a public school education? No. In 1975, the Texas legislature decided to withhold funds from local school districts for children who were not "legally admitted" into the United States. The act also empowered school districts to deny enrollment to undocumented children. In *Plyler v. Doe* (1982), the Supreme Court was asked to determine the constitutionality of the Texas statute. The equal protection clause of the Fourteenth Amendment, which says that "No State shall . . . deprive any person of life, liberty, or property, without due process of law; nor deny to any person within its jurisdiction the equal protection of the laws," does not limit protection to citizens.

The Court found that although public education is not a right granted by the Constitution, it is not merely a governmental benefit indistinguishable from other forms of social welfare. Education was found to be important both in maintaining our basic institutions and in having a lasting impact on the life of the child and ultimately having an educated citizenry. In sum, education is seen as having a fundamental role in maintaining the fabric of our society. We cannot ignore the significant social costs borne by the nation when select groups are denied an education. Illiteracy is an enduring disability.

Paradoxically, by depriving the children of any disfavored group an education, we foreclose the means by which that group might raise the level of esteem in which it is held by the majority.

Students' Freedom of Expression

Can students criticize governmental policies or practices in school? Yes. In 1965, three students in Des Moines, Iowa, were sent home for wearing black armbands to protest the United States' involvement in Vietnam. The Supreme Court in *Tinker v. Des Moines Independent Community School District* (1969) ruled that students (and teachers) do not "shed their constitutional rights to freedom of speech or expression at the schoolhouse gate." However, they must present their views in an orderly way and not in a way that could be judged to be disruptive.

The First Amendment allows both students and adults the right to express themselves and the right to be silent. For example, students cannot be forced to salute the American flag or say the Pledge of Allegiance. However, some student expression is not covered by the First Amendment. School officials can take action against a student whose written or oral language is defamatory, shaming, or ridiculing others (remember the social media and bullying discussions at the beginning of this chapter?). The Supreme Court in 1986 ruled in *Bethel School District No. 403 v. Fraser* that school officials could censor lewd, vulgar, and indecent student behavior. Courts have also upheld a school's right to discipline students for inflammatory expression, such as threatening other students or teachers.

Can schools punish students for social media posts that were done away from school? Yes, if there is some connection between the message and the school. Interestingly, although *Tinker* is almost 50 years old, it continues to be a relevant case. In part, the judgment states that "conduct by the student, in class or out of it, which for any reason . . . materially disrupts classwork or involves substantial disorder" may come under school authorities.

Student Search

Is searching a student or student's personal belongings lawful? Yes. It is not uncommon for school administrators to be placed in the uncomfortable position of having to search students or student lockers when there is a suspicion that a student or students may possess some illegal substance, a weapon, or property that is not rightly theirs. When such searches are deemed necessary by administrators or teachers, it is possible that students will complain that their rights according to the Fourth Amendment of the U.S. Constitution have been violated. Courts must then come to a decision about an individual student's right to privacy versus the responsibility of the school administration to maintain a safe and secure school environment for all students.

In 1985, in *New Jersey v. T.L.O.*, the Court concluded that a search of a student's belongings for evidence of cigarettes, which further turned up evidence of drug dealing, did not violate the Fourth Amendment. According to the courts, the search was reasonable, but only because there was evidence that provided a substantial suspicion that the student was indeed in possession of an illegal substance.

Locker Search

Can a student's locker be searched without a warrant? Yes. Courts allow locker searches on the grounds that schools ultimately retain control over lockers as school property. Schools are also held responsible for protecting the educational function of the school and students' welfare. Lockers can be searched to prevent their illicit use.

Lesbian, Gay, Bisexual, Transgender, and Queer or Questioning (LGBTQ) Students' Rights Are an Emerging Topic for the Courts

Statutes, court cases, and the establishment of policies related to protecting students from bullying have become clear and are widely understood.

AP Photo/Kingman Daily Miner, JC Amberlyn

Searches of students and their property at school are legal.

Communities, administrators and teachers, policy makers, and the courts are now addressing questions about school practices and issues related to the rights of Lesbian, Gay, Bisexual, Transgender, and Queer or Questioning (LGBTQ) students. Most certainly, these students must experience safe climates and not be the victims of harassment and/or discrimination. At the same time, new questions are being raised about appropriate policies and practices. For example, in two recent cases, one in Colorado and one in Maine, elementary school biologically male students who identified as females (transgender) were not permitted to use the girls' restrooms. In both cases, the courts decided that the students had the right to use the restroom of their choice.

Here are some of the other questions and issues related to LGBTQ students that the courts have been addressing and that you need to understand: Can students of the same gender hold hands while walking through the school corridors? (They should have the same rules applied as for other students.) Can same-sex students go together to school events such as proms? (Yes, this is within the First Amendment right of free expression.) Can the school make public a student's sexual orientation or gender identity? (No, students have a constitutional right to privacy.) Can a transgender girl or boy be prohibited from wearing a tuxedo or dress to a dance? (No, First Amendment rights again.)

THINKING DIFFERENTLY
"DUTY OF CARE" IS FOR ALL STUDENTS, AND FOR EACH STUDENT

Most certainly, teachers understand that they are responsible for establishing and maintaining a safe and supportive learning environment. However, what is safe and supportive for the classroom overall may be counterproductive for some students individually. Each student will have his or her own approach to learning, as well as behavioral and, yes, medical characteristics. The classroom must be safe all the time and supportive of all students learning. Attending to duty of care means that teachers must simultaneously establish and maintain a safe classroom overall while accommodating each student's individual readiness for and approaches to learning. Teachers need to know if a particular student needs to take a medication during the day, and when support services should be called. At the same time that teachers are establishing processes and procedures for the classroom as a whole, they also must think through the possible ways in which each student will benefit or lose out. From a legal perspective, failure to demonstrate duty of care can lead to charges of negligence.

TEACHERS' RIGHTS, RESPONSIBILITIES, AND LIABILITIES

Although it can be difficult to accept, beginning teachers need to understand that when they are first hired, they have very few employment rights unless the union has negotiated a section in the contract protecting probationary teachers. Currently, many of the rights of even veteran educators are being taken away by a number of state legislatures and governors: Arizona, Florida, Ohio, Wisconsin, and on and on. There are some ways that the union can assist because many states now require a close evaluation of beginning teachers, and if the teacher is found to be deficient in some way, he or she must have an opportunity to improve under a plan of improvement.

> *It also is important to join a union because you get liability insurance. We live in such a litigious society that it is hard to imagine doing a job where you are uninsured, where you can be sued for tens of thousands of dollars and lose your house. NEA, and I am sure AFT (American Federation of Teachers) as well, provides its members with a million-dollar liability insurance policy. If you are sued for something you did on the job, you will be defended, and the insurance will pay up to a million dollars.*

—Mr. Simpson

Mr. Simpson has touched on several aspects of the responsibilities and liabilities related to being a teacher. Now is the time for you to start developing an understanding of teacher-related legal topics including the rights of probationary teachers, employment contracts, liability, and due process. Some of the important cases are presented in Table 9.4. These and other cases are described briefly here.

Teacher Responsibilities as a School District Employee

Teachers are employees of a school district. As such, teachers must follow all of the policies, rules, and procedures that the district has established. For example, teachers do not have complete autonomy to decide what to teach. They must follow state standards and the curriculum as specified by the state and the district.

Determining the Content of the Curriculum

Do teachers have the right to determine the content to be taught? No. There is a never-ending debate about which topics should and should not be taught. One of the most famous cases, *State v. Scopes* (1927), more commonly referred to as the Scopes Monkey Trial, was held in Tennessee in the summer of 1925. This case clearly demonstrates the emotions that discussions of "what will be taught in schools" can evoke. Douglas Linder (2002) has written a fascinating narrative of the trial. He begins his description with the historical perspectives that added fuel to the debate:

> The early 1920s found social patterns in chaos. Traditionalists, the older Victorians, worried that everything valuable was ending. Younger modernists no longer asked whether society would approve of their behaviour. . . . Intellectual experimentation flourished. Americans danced to the sound of the Jazz Age, showed their contempt for . . . prohibition, debated abstract art and Freudian theories. In a response to the new social patterns set in motion by modernism, a wave of revivalism developed, becoming especially strong in the American South.
>
> Who would dominate American culture—the modernists or the traditionalists? Journalists were looking for a showdown, and they found one in a Dayton, Tennessee, courtroom in the summer of 1925. There a jury was to decide the fate of John Scopes, a high school biology teacher charged with illegally teaching the theory of evolution. The guilt or innocence of John Scopes, and even the constitutionality of Tennessee's anti-evolution statute, mattered little. The meaning of the trial emerged through its interpretation as a conflict of social and intellectual values. (Linder, 2002, p. 1)

When Parents Disagree With Teachers

Will parents complain to the school board about what a teacher is teaching? Yes. You might be surprised at what some parents would consider inappropriate content for teachers to teach, as one of the authors of this text experienced when teaching third grade in Beaverton, Oregon.

> I read my students Baum's *The Wizard of Oz*. Parents of a child in my class took umbrage to the text because of the "communistic" overtones it contained. They asked the school district to remove the book from the school libraries and to forbid teachers to share it with their students. I was amazed. I thought the flying monkeys were the worst things in the book. (Linda Quinn, Teaching Notes)

Corporal Punishment

Are there statutory provisions designed to protect teachers and administrators from suits resulting from their administration of corporal punishment? Yes. The use of corporal punishment in this country as a means of disciplining schoolchildren dates back to the colonial period. It has survived the transformation of primary and secondary education from the colonials' reliance on optional private arrangements to our present system of compulsory education and dependence on public schools. In many states, **corporal punishment**, a teacher paddling or spanking a student, is legal and happens regularly.

TABLE 9.4 ■ Teachers' Rights		
Question	**Case**	**Decision**
May teachers criticize a school board and superintendent in a letter published by a local newspaper?	*Pickering v. Board of Education* (1968)	Teachers cannot be "compelled to relinquish their First Amendment rights."
Can school districts have a policy forcing all pregnant teachers to take mandatory maternity leave?	*Cleveland Board of Education v. LeFleur* (1974)	No.
Do untenured teachers have property rights when dismissed?	*Board of Regents of State Colleges v. Roth* (1972)	No.

Signing a contract to teach is a special moment, and comes with accepting important responsibilities.

In 1977, the U.S. Supreme Court upheld the practice of corporal punishment. The law was challenged in *Ingraham v. Wright* (1977), with Justice Lewis Powell delivering the opinion of the Court. Two issues were raised during the court case: (1) Does the punishment represent cruel and unusual punishment in violation of the Eighth Amendment of the U.S. Constitution? and (2) Was prior notice and the opportunity to be heard required? According to the Court, three categories of corporal punishment exist.

> Punishments that do not exceed the traditional common law standard of reasonableness are not actionable; punishments that exceed the common law standard without adequate state remedies violate procedural due process rights;

and finally, punishments that are so grossly excessive as to be shocking to the conscience, violate substantive due process rights, without regard to the adequacy of state remedies. (p. 135)

More than half of the states do not allow the practice of corporal punishment. In some instances, local school boards, in states that allow corporal punishment, have banned or curtailed the practice. Teachers must be aware of any statutory provisions pertaining to corporal punishment in the state where they teach and whether practices within a school district are in conformance with state and local provisions.

Reporting Child Abuse

Can teachers be held liable for not reporting suspected child abuse? Yes. Teachers are among the professionals who are required to report signs of child abuse. Penalties for not reporting include fines and/or prison terms. School districts may also impose disciplinary action. For example, the Seventh Circuit upheld the suspension and demotion of a teacher-psychologist who did not promptly report suspected abuse in *Pesce v. J. Sterling Morton High School District 201, Cook County, Illinois* (1987). School districts usually have procedures for reporting suspected abuse, including to whom the abuse should be reported. In 1998, the Kentucky Supreme Court ruled that once the abuse is reported to a supervisor, the supervisor has responsibility for reporting it to the appropriate authority. However, teachers should follow up to ensure that the appropriate agency has been notified.

The Basis for Student Grouping

Can students be grouped by ability or achievement? Yes, unless it results in discrimination against a group of students. In the most publicized case, *Hobson v. Hansen* (1967), parents in Washington, DC, argued that their children were assigned to lower tracks with limited curriculum and little chance for moving to higher levels. The court found that the testing methods used by the school district discriminated against students of color. Testing instruments used to make decisions about placement must be reliable, valid, and unbiased. They cannot be racially biased or administered in discriminatory ways. They must be administered in the student's native language or with appropriate accommodations for students with disabilities.

Teacher and School Accountability

Can teachers be held responsible for their students not meeting federal standards? Yes. Since the passage of NCLB in 2001, the goals and benchmarks states and school districts set must address the established national standards and federal mandates. It is probably pretty well understood that no school district wants to have any of its schools classified as "in need of improvement" or "failing." It is certain that teachers will not see high status in working at a school that is on a "watch list." In all schools, teachers are expected to assume responsibility for seeing that their students' achievement meets the standards. As the new **value added** teacher evaluation systems come into use, each teacher will be under even more pressure to "raise those test scores." In more and more states, legislatures are mandating that improvement in student test scores will count for as much as half of a teacher's evaluation.

Beginning Teacher Nonrenewal and Dismissal

In New York State for the first three years, teachers do not have much protection. There are two primary forms of protections for teachers. One is the tenure statute in education law. The other is contractual protection, which typically is negotiated by a labor union.

Under the tenure statute, historically during the first three years of employment, a teacher could be discharged, as the saying goes, "for a good reason, for a bad reason, or for no reason at all." In reality, a teacher can be discharged for a good reason, a bad reason, or no reason at all as long as that reason is a legal reason. There are illegal reasons, such as discrimination and retaliation, or in response to a whistle-blowing effort.

Now there is legislation mandating that everybody has to consider student data, and you will be evaluated on those data. In fact, the statute in New York says that the way the teacher uses student data shall be a significant factor in tenure determinations.

Do administrators have to provide reasons for dismissal of a nontenured teacher? No. School administrators have the responsibility for evaluating the fitness of teachers and determining whether their level of performance is satisfactory. They must

Teachers are liable for what happens in their classroom, across the school campus, and during all other school-related activities.

follow the provisions outlined in state statutes; however, the U.S. Supreme Court in *Board of Regents of State Colleges v. Roth* (1972) decided that nontenured teachers need not be given reasons for nonrenewal. Note that this case addressed the dismissal of a college faculty member. As with many other cases, court decisions that have addressed questions related to higher education have been interpreted as applying to public school teachers as well. Each state has statutes that address the dismissal of tenured teachers, or teachers under a continuing contract. These provisions lay out the due process requirements. Grounds for dismissal, such as insubordination, incompetency, failure to comply with reasonable orders, and conviction of crimes involving moral turpitude, are addressed. These same grounds apply to probationary teachers, but in most states, school officials are not required to provide any reasons for dismissal.

Due Process

Note that the idea of due process is referenced in several of the cases introduced here. The term *due process* gets mentioned frequently in social conversations. In the legal system, there are two important meanings. Procedural due process addresses the actions that must be taken to ensure that teachers' and students' rights are protected. As stated in the Fourteenth Amendment, no "State shall deprive any person of life, liberty, or property, without due process of law." A teacher must have an opportunity to be heard, and the procedures must be stated and in place.

Substantive due process directs that the process must be fair. In other words, the actions cannot be arbitrary, unreasonable, or discriminatory. Both meanings of due process must be addressed in school administrative actions and will be considered by the courts. However, as you have read above for students and will read below for teachers, due process rights for each are not fully the same as their rights as a citizen.

Question to Mr. Simpson:	What about the contractual part of teaching, probationary teachers, student teachers, and their rights and responsibilities?
A:	I work for a teachers' union, and we also have support personnel as members. I do think it is important for a number of reasons that beginning teachers join a professional association. If it is not the NEA, it could be the AFT, or some other organization. There's been a real shift in the focus of NEA over the last 15 years away from what I would call hardline unionism to Professional Development. Unions now are taking on the task of helping beginning teachers do better in their teaching. It could be something as simple as negotiating in the collective bargaining agreement to establish a system of master teachers who are assigned to beginning teachers who are often thrown into the classroom with nothing for support. There now is an understanding that the turnover of teachers is so high that we need to do a better job of helping beginning teachers excel and not to be left alone in the classroom.

Individual Teacher Rights and Responsibilities

There are many areas where the actions of teachers have been examined by the legal system. Questions about how to dress, freedom of speech, and drug testing are some of the many topics that have been examined by the courts.

Teacher Freedom of Public Expression

Do teachers have absolute freedom of public expression? No. Historically, teachers were seen as government employees and therefore had less freedom of public expression. This view was formalized at the federal level in the Hatch Act (1939). Since then, there have been continual challenges to the extent of teacher free speech. The definitive case is *Pickering v. Board of Education Township High School District 205* (1968). A teacher (Pickering) was dismissed for writing a letter to the newspaper that was critical of actions taken by his school board. He challenged in court his loss of First Amendment rights as a citizen. The Court stated in part, "The problem in any case is to arrive at a balance between the interests of the teacher, as a citizen, in commenting upon matters of public concerns and the interest of the state, as an employer, in promoting the efficiency of the public services it performs through its employees." Teachers have to walk a very fine line between their being employees and public citizens.

Pickering does not mean that teachers can say anything they want and not have it lead to employment consequences. For example, in *Mt. Healthy City School District Board of Education v. Doyle* (1977), a nontenured teacher, Doyle, had an altercation with a colleague, argued with cafeteria employees, swore at students, and called a radio station and conveyed information in a principal memo about teacher dress codes. He was dismissed. He then alleged that his not being rehired was in conflict with his First Amendment rights. The Court ruled that the school board would not have rehired him regardless of his "protected conduct."

More recently, in *Garcetti v. Ceballos* (2006), the U.S. Supreme Court made clear that within their employment duties public employees' free speech is limited. In these settings, they are seen as speaking not as citizens, but as representatives of their employment agency.

May a teacher speak to the school board as a citizen? Yes, if it is during the time set in the agenda for public comment. This question was addressed in *Barrett v. Walker County (Georgia) School District* (2016). The head of the district employee union, Barrett, was unable to be approved by the superintendent to speak in opposition to a new district grading policy. The federal district court in its ruling emphasized that any policy must be content neutral. In other words, the opportunity for citizens to speak must be open to all points of view.

Teacher Dress

What about teacher dress? Can school districts impose dress standards? Yes. For example, a male high school English teacher in East Hartford, Connecticut, refused to wear a tie. In court, he argued that requiring him to wear a tie would deprive him of his right to free speech. The courts in *East Hartford Education*

Association v. Board of Education of Town of East Hartford (1977) had to balance the policy of the school board, which required teachers to dress more formally, with the teacher's individual rights. In these cases, the courts have weighed heavily the community standards and values as reflected through the school board's policies and procedures. In this case, and others, the courts have supported the school board's interest in requiring a degree of uniformity.

Drug Testing of Teachers

Can teachers be screened for use of drugs? Yes. As drug use has become widespread among students and adults, some school districts have implemented policies related to teacher use of drugs. When teachers have challenged these policies, the courts have had to balance the interests of schools in having a drug-free environment with the Fourth Amendment privacy interests of the teacher. Considerations include how extensive the drug problem is, how intrusive the search, and how significant the action that led to the search. In *Knox County Education Association v. Knox County Board of Education* (1998), the Sixth Circuit Court ruled that the Fourth Amendment was not violated. The school district had a two-part policy: (1) suspicionless drug testing of all candidates for safety-sensitive positions (e.g., teacher and principal) and (2) reasonable suspicion drug testing of individual employees.

Teacher Liability

Can teachers be sued as individuals? Yes. Teachers must constantly be aware of the potential of being personally liable for damages as a result of what they do, or don't do. They must always act in ways that are seen as reasonable and prudent. It is not likely that anything a teacher does will result in a lawsuit, but foolish behavior can possibly lead to unpleasantness in court. Recent cases include a teacher's use of duct tape to quiet a chatty six-year-old, a student injured while jumping from a moving bus in order to avoid being disciplined, a principal pointing a toy gun at a student, and a coach's verbal abuse and comments about a student's weight.

TEACHERS' LOUNGE

AN UNFORTUNATE START TO A WELL-PLANNED FIELD TRIP

Field trips are like vacations to students. They are looked forward to with enthusiasm and excitement. Teachers with years of experience know how to build that excitement so students will profit from an event away from school.

As I listened to two very good teachers tell their tale of how they had prepared their students for a trip to the nature preserve, I thought how a walk through the desert would be uneventful for me, but for their students, it had become an event to look forward to. They had their students prepare for the field trip by reading, drawing, and telling stories about the Gila monster, the horny toad, the desert tortoise, and the roadrunner. They also learned about different varieties of flowering cacti and desert plants that could be used for food.

The teachers met over dinner the weekend before the planned field trip to accomplish the task of writing a note to parents that would accompany the required district field trip permission form. They met Saturday night for dinner and wine. Yes, they said wine! Before dinner, over some red wine, they wrote this elaborate letter telling parents of the upcoming event and encouraged them to join their child on this adventure. They described the children's stories about Gila monsters, horny toads, and cacti to build an interest they hoped would entice parents to join them.

After dinner, they sat and visited over a second bottle of wine! After several hours of laughter and fun, they sat back down to write version 2 of the permission slip with some added humor.

They were quite proud of draft 2. They planned to share this version with a few select friends and colleagues. The revised version spoke of their students not as brilliant and smart but as ornery little snots and monsters of a different type. And yes, a different interpretation of horny toads was included.

Let your mind wander, and you will get a picture of a very embarrassing note that went home to parents. The wine made it sound funny at the time, but just 48 hours later, the humor turned to shame and total embarrassment.

On Monday, they ran off the permission slips and placed version 2 copies in a few mailboxes of their friends. They returned to class to hand out the forms and encourage their students to take them home and bring them back the following day.

After school, the teachers were invited to the office by the principal and were asked for a copy of the field trip form—which they provided, only to hear the principal say, "This is not the form that Mrs. Smooth just read to me on the phone." At this point, the teachers described a burning sensation they felt come across their faces as they realized their grievous error. Horrified and embarrassed, they began the task of dealing with and calling each parent to apologize for their error in judgment. The response to the district office and the news media was left in the hands of their principal.

—Dr. Michael S. Robison, Retired
School and District Administrator

Studies about questions of law generally use a different approach than is typical in regular education research. Instead of using questionnaires, surveys, and interviews, legal research typically involves reviewing what has been stated in statutes and examining previous court decisions. Law journals then report these reviews. In addition, legal scholars and attorneys will add to these analyses in court proceedings, and some will write occasional papers. Law reviews most certainly can incorporate quantitative data, such as crime statistics, the frequency of certain incidents, and dollar costs. However, in general, legal research reports will be based in qualitative analyses. Teachers being sued is another part of the law called **tort law**. This area of law deals with civil wrongs instead of criminal wrongs, although there may also be a criminal component. The plaintiff seeks compensation for a loss or damages. Liability for alleged injury, death, malpractice, or depriving someone of his or her constitutional rights, while under the teacher's or school's supervision, can lead to legal action.

Negligence that leads to a student being injured within a classroom, on the school grounds, or on a field trip can lead to questions of teacher liability. Assault and battery is another area of torts. Threatening a child in anger, even without striking the child, can be interpreted as assault. Striking someone, even without harming him or her, can be interpreted as battery. Teachers can use sufficient force only for self-protection when attempting to restrain a student.

CHALLENGING ASSUMPTIONS
ARE THERE MORE NEGLIGENCE SUITS NOW THAN IN THE PAST?

Studies about questions of law generally use a different approach than is typical in regular education research. Instead of using questionnaires, surveys, and interviews, legal research typically involves reviewing what has been stated in statutes and examining previous court decisions. Law journals then report these reviews. In addition, legal scholars and attorneys will add to these analyses in court proceedings, and some will write occasional papers. Law reviews most certainly can incorporate quantitative data, such as crime statistics, the frequency of certain incidents, and dollar costs. However, in general, legal research reports will be based in qualitative analyses.

The Question

A general perception is that there are now more civil suits against teachers and schools than there were in the past. Another commonly held perception is that most of the time schools and teachers lose.

The Facts

A review by Zirkel and Clark (2008) examined 212 published decisions related to these two assumptions. The cases involved personal injuries to students and covered the 15-year period from 1990 to 2005. The authors examined the frequency of decisions within four-year intervals.

Is the frequency of negligence suits on the rise?

Number of negligence case decisions in four-year intervals			
1990–1993	1994–1997	1998–2001	2002–2005
49	56	49	46

Several themes can be deduced from these frequencies and the related data. First, there is no clear pattern suggesting that the rate of negligence decisions is increasing or decreasing. Within their data, the authors found that, during the 15-year period, 40 of the 212 decisions were in New York State. Louisiana had more decisions that went against schools (9 out of 14 cases). This pattern suggests that there are state-by-state differences.

Who won the majority of cases?

In 63% of the cases, the district won conclusively. In only 9% of the cases did the student win conclusively. A related finding was that there was a higher frequency of cases based in secondary schools. This makes sense, since secondary students are engaged in more-risky activities, including sports, which probably explains why coaches were most frequently named as being negligent. At the same time, elementary school decisions had a higher portion (16% vs. 7%) in favor of the students as plaintiffs.

Regardless of whether you plan to be an elementary or secondary teacher, you need to continually strive to protect students from injury. Your duty to protect includes providing adequate supervision and close supervision when students are engaged in more-risky activities, especially on field trips. Also, be sure to monitor equipment for correct operation and maintenance.

Source: Zirkel, P. A., & Clark, J. H. (2008). School negligence case law trends. *Southern Illinois University Law Journal, 32,* 345–363.

In addition to being aware of district, state, and national statutes regarding what is considered reasonable in managing student behavior, you should consider whether joining a professional association or purchasing liability insurance is a wise investment. Typically, coverage is included as part of membership in the NEA or AFT, as well as in some professional organizations. Or you can protect yourself from monetary loss by obtaining liability insurance.

Right-to-Work vs. Collective Bargaining

Most of the legal topics that have been introduced in this chapter have addressed teachers and students as individuals. There are other topics that affect all teachers and students. One that is receiving extra judicial and political attention now is the place of unions and the extent of authority of unions. Each state has its own labor laws, which in general lead to each being called a "right-to-work" state or one that has "collective bargaining." There are important differences and consequences for teachers depending on how in statute teacher employment is defined.

Collective bargaining is what happens when workers are represented through a union. The union negotiates contracts on behalf of all its members for conditions of employment including pay, benefits, work hours, and job safety. The right to bargain collectively for transportation works was established in the Railway Labor Act in 1926. The 1935 Labor Relations Act expanded the right to most other private sector workers. The right of public employees to bargain collectively is less clear and is treated differently within each state.

Right-to-work laws prohibit agreements between labor unions and employers. There are state-by-state differences in these laws. In some states, the laws apply to all public employees. In some states, some employees (e.g., police) can bargain collectively, but other employees (e.g., teachers) cannot. Since 2012, a number of states, including Michigan, Indiana, and Wisconsin, have passed right-to-work laws.

Public employee union dues are now voluntary. Until 2018, public employee nonunion members could be required to pay dues, called **agency fees**. In a 5–4 decision in June 2018, the Supreme Court ruled this practice unconstitutional. The case, *Janus v. American Federation of State, County, and Municipal Employees, Council 31*, affects public employees in 22 states. The argument in favor of agency fees is based on the assumption that the union represents all employees. The argument against includes the view that employees individually should decide if they want to pay union dues. One immediate consequence will be a reduction in union budgets and therefore their political power.

Teacher Walkouts

To address issues of declining school funding, in 2018, teachers turned to a new form of activism—walkouts. In many states, teachers have received little or no pay increases for several years. When there have been salary increases in some states, the increases have lagged behind the cost of living. As pointed out in Chapter 8, in many places, school facilities have deteriorated to the point of being unsafe. Also, in many districts, textbooks and other curriculum materials are out-of-date. For example, teachers in Oklahoma were using 10-year-old textbooks.

For years, teachers have accepted these conditions with little complaint. However, in 2018, the proverbial dam broke. Teachers came together, along with many administrators, across districts and states for **walkouts** to protest the funding of schools.

Right to Strike. Keep in mind that strikes by public employees are prohibited in right-to-work states. In a somewhat ironic step, West Virginia passed a right-to-work law in 2016, then in early 2018, there was a nine-day statewide teacher walkout. West Virginia teachers are among the lowest paid across the United States. They had not had a salary increase in four years, and the cost of health insurance was increasing significantly. There also were concerns about the inability to hire teachers due to low wages and benefits.

Teacher Activism. Teacher activism through walkouts then spread to other states. Later in the spring and over the summer of 2018, there were statewide protests and walkouts in Arizona, Oklahoma, West Virginia, Kentucky, Washington, North Carolina, and other states. In the early fall, teachers in Hawaii staged a "walk-in" to support a bond election that would raise real estate taxes for education. The teacher protest movement has a much wider scope than salaries—it is about generating support for schools to have up-to-date curricula and facilities, as well addressing issues of safety.

Teacher walkouts have been taking place in many states.

School Safety

It seems likely that over the next several years, school safety is going to be the key subject area for development of new statutes, rules and regulations, and court cases. Given the continuing concern about guns in schools, you might be thinking that this is the primary topic related to school safety. Don't forget other elements including bullying, harassment, student searches, and the presence of other weapons such as knives. There are other aspects of safety including responsible administration of prescription medications, product safety, and "premises liability." Student and employee codes of conduct outline safe procedures. However, against the intentions to prescribe tighter procedures is the need to protect First Amendment rights, including freedom of speech.

Have you thought about the topic of premises liability? Owners and occupiers of land, including schools, are required to keep the premises safe. School administrators and teachers are responsible for maintaining safe conditions and to protect persons from gaining access to risky areas. If injured on the school grounds, students, as well as employees, can sue for damages. Most certainly, teachers are at all times responsible for keeping the premises safe, not just their classrooms.

Product safety is another concern. Classroom furniture, storage spaces, laboratory equipment, playgrounds, plastic containers, and all other school-related items need to be considered in terms of potential for harmful risk. An item may be considered a terrific support for learning, but is it safe? If uncertain, a good first step for guidance is to consult the standards of the U.S. Consumer Product Safety Commission.

The all-too-regularly occurring school shootings have to be addressed more effectively by policy makers, educators, and the courts. The debate about whether schoolteachers and/or administrators should be armed continues. The widespread concern about availability of mental health resources is of concern. The now common training and regular practicing of lockdowns will continue. All of these actions are addressing elements of the problem. None will completely eliminate the risk. So it is very important for teachers to continually stay abreast of the latest procedures and policies, and to always keep in mind what they can be doing to keep schools safe.

Law and Ethics Are Not the Same

An all-too-common view of teachers and citizens at large is to think in some way about law and ethics being the same, or at least interconnected. Actually, they are not the same, and often teachers will find themselves in situations that are conflicted. Under the law, one set of actions will be required, but from a value and belief point of view, the teacher may see an alternative action is needed.

This tension between what the law expects from an employee and what an individual may see as ethical can lead to what a wonderful former colleague, Dr. Joan Curcio, called "crises of integrity." It is likely that within your first several years as a teacher, you will experience one of these moments. The law, rules, and procedures will be directing you to do one thing, but your moral beliefs will be telling you to do something different. Let's consider the two frames separately and then consider some ways to negotiate a constructive outcome.

The Perspective of the Law: Is It Legal?

As you have read in this chapter, through the legislative process, various laws, policies, and procedures are developed. All of these apply to everyone in the affected group, whether they are teachers, public health workers, or all citizens. As a teacher, you must understand what the law expects in terms of your actions and those of your students. Outlining the legal perspective has been the primary objective of this chapter.

The Ethical Perspective: What Is Right?

As you are becoming a teacher, one of your ongoing activities is developing your philosophy of education. An important reason for your reading Chapter 6 (history of schools) and Chapter 7 (philosophies of teaching and learning) was to provide you with information that you can use to refine your own philosophical framework. It is through this framework that you are judging what you think is right and good.

As a teacher, you will not be alone in developing your philosophy. The different education associations have professional codes. You bring with you values related to the American ideals as well as moral codes and standards offered by religion, such as the Ten Commandments, and either implicitly or explicitly, your parents will have brought you up to know the differences between right and wrong. All of these elements of morality and ethics combine in what you will be as a teacher.

Resolving Dilemmas: Legal and Ethical Processes

Earlier in this chapter, the idea of a dilemma was introduced. As illustrated with the dilemmas of school finance, desegregation, and separation of church and state, the legal processes to address each of these has been extensive and continuing. As each process has unfolded, specific problems have been addressed and solutions established. In each instance, there has been processing by both perspectives: legal and ethical. As a simple example, if someone murders, the law will find him or her guilty, and the murderer will have violated one of the commandments ("Thou shalt not kill"). Both the legal and ethical perspectives have made it clear about what to do and what is right.

The problem comes when something new or different occurs. One or both perspectives will be challenged to rethink and determine what is the best course of action. Each frame has a process for review, deliberation, and development of a solution. However, there is a major difference between the two processes. The legal process results in a law that all are directed to follow, while the ethical process results in guidelines or a moral code that each individual may, or may not, follow.

As you have read, the legal system turns to the courts to resolve disputes and to the legislative process to develop new laws. The ethical process is less structured and formal. You as an individual can engage in considerations of right and wrong. Different groups such as church members and physicians can work together to consider what should be done in a critical situation. As another example, professional associations establish committees to develop and update ethical principles and codes of conduct.

As an individual teacher, you have a more private process for review and reflection to determine what you will do in a certain situation. As you experience new problems and dilemmas, you will have to work out what you think is right (and wrong). Furthermore, you will have to decide to take action or delay doing anything.

Making the Final Decision

Ultimately, when confronted with a difficult problem, what you decide will be a product of your basic values and moral compass. The questions in Table 9.5 are suggested starting points for you to consider ahead of time so that you will be better prepared when you are facing one of those crises of integrity. These questions will help you in considering the right thing to do.

TABLE 9.5 ■ Key Topic Areas and Beginning Questions to Consider in Developing an Ethical Framework About Good Teaching	
Education	What do you see as the reason for having public schools? Why are they important to individuals and to society?
Student learning	What are your beliefs about how students learn? How much should learning be teacher directed? Should students have many opportunities to talk out their thinking? Should students work individually most of the time, or is group work important, too?
Teachers as learners	How important is it for teachers to be continuing to learn about and try new instructional approaches? Do teachers learn best individually, or is learning in groups and as a whole staff useful?
Teachers as members of a school staff	What should be the role of the teacher with other teachers? What types of beyond-the-classroom activities and efforts should teachers embrace?
Parents	To what extent and about what topics should teachers communicate with parents? Should parents be involved in your classroom? If so, in what ways?
Policy, laws, and court decisions	Which policies, laws, and procedures apply? What are you required to do?
Hills to die on	Are there any topics, problems, or directives where you would say, "No, I won't do that"?

At the same time, you need to be aware that when legal and ethical questions reach the courts, the judgments are increasingly taking the side of the school district. For example, in *Woodlock v. Orange Ulster B.O.C.S.* (2006/2008), a third-year probationary school counselor was not given tenure. She had repeatedly raised concerns to administration about lack of certified gym and art instructors and escalating safety incidents related to a special education student. She had left messages for administrators and continued to express her professional concerns. She received several disciplinary memoranda for "taking it upon yourself to go out of process." In her eyes, she was guided by the ethical norms of advocacy for students. However, the Court made its decision based more on *Garcetti v. Ceballos* (2006), which held that the First Amendment does not protect statements that public employees make as part of their official duties.

It is in this processing that you as a teacher will decide what you believe is good teaching and how best to help all of your students learn. The more you now think about what you see as important, good, and right for teachers, the clearer you will be about your personal moral code and your philosophy of education.

A Final Thought

The many topics touched upon in this chapter may have you worried. Worry needs to be balanced with keeping the joy of teaching in mind. Mr. Simpson said the following when asked where he saw joy in teaching:

> The quote that I read at my mother's funeral, and I think you ought to put it in your book, is attributed to American scholar and teacher Forest Witcraft:

> A hundred years from now it will not matter what my bank account was, the type of house I lived in, or the kind of car I drove, but the world may be different because I was important in the life of a child.

CONNECTING TO THE CLASSROOM

From the legal perspective, teachers have to continually be thinking about what they are doing and possible consequences for students and/or themselves.

1. Think twice about possible legal implications and consequences before placing anything on your social media sites. Once it is there, you cannot retrieve it.

2. Only communicate with your students about teaching- and learning-related topics, and do this only with school/district media.

3. Student records are confidential and not to be shared outside the school and district, except when parents request to see them.

4. Always consider possible safety risks in your classroom, at school, and especially on field trips. There may be liability risks.

5. Bullying includes more than punching and kicking. It includes verbal insults, both face-to-face and via social media.

6. When grouping students, consider possible subtle indications of discrimination such as mainly having boys in one group and girls in another.

7. Students and teachers do not have complete freedom of expression.

SUMMARY

Given the many tasks and areas of responsibilities that teachers have, it is important that you begin now to understand legal aspects of teaching. These major topics were introduced in this chapter:

- Student (and teacher) uses of social media can be a benefit to learning and at the same time in regard to the law the cause of serious problems.

- Teachers, as well as administrators, must continually keep in mind potential issues related to school safety and bullying for all students and adults.

- There are a number of dilemmas—such as separation of church and state, desegregation, and equitable school funding—that continue to be addressed through the courts.

- Students and teachers have limits to their rights as citizens.

KEY TERMS

Adequate Yearly Progress (AYP) 261

administrative law 258

agency fees 285

case law 259

corporal punishment 279

de facto segregation 271

de jure segregation 271

dilemma 268

fair use 267

highly qualified teacher (HQT) 261

integration 272

mainstreaming 274

problem 268

procedural due process 260

Schools in Need of Improvement
   (SINOI) 261

sexting 264

statute 258

substantive due process 260

tort law 284

unfunded mandate 261

value added 281

waiver 261

walkout 285

CLASS DISCUSSION QUESTIONS

1. Under what conditions can teachers use social media such as Twitter and Facebook to communicate with their students? What is not permissible?

2. What are your thoughts about the proposal for teachers and/or administrators to carry guns in schools? Will this approach make schools safer? What other approaches to school safety would you propose?

3. Which aspects of the rights and protections of students from discrimination are new to you?

4. What are your thoughts about the fact that in most states and school districts no explanation has to be provided when a probationary teacher is not rehired?

5. Have you seen situations where a teacher could have been held liable for something that occurred that placed students at risk? What about safety on the school premises—have you seen examples of unsafe conditions?

SELF-ASSESSMENT

What Is Your Current Level of Understanding and Thinking About the Law as It Relates to Teaching and Learning?

One of the indicators of understanding is to examine how complex your thinking is when asked questions that require you to use the concepts and facts introduced in this chapter. After you answer the following questions as fully as you can, rate your knowledge of school law on the Assessing Your Learning rubric to self-assess the degree to which you understand and can apply the law to yourself as a teacher and future school employee.

1. Name three key questions related to the dilemma of separation of church and state. What has been the legal reasoning underlying the related court decisions?

2. What do you see as implications for you as a teacher of the limits the courts have set in regard to use of social media?

3. How would you respond to a colleague who claims that teachers can freely use copyrighted material as long as it is only for their class?

4. Bullying and discrimination are serious problems. What guidelines do teachers need to keep in mind in efforts to prevent and respond to any instances of bullying and/or discrimination?

5. What are four steps related to safety that schools are taking? In terms of the law, what statutes and cases support each of these steps?

Assess your current level of understanding of how the legal system affects what you do as a teacher and the rights of your students.

Assessing Your Learning Rubric

	Parts & Pieces	Unidimensional	Organized	Integrated	Extensions
Indicators	Elements/concepts are talked about as isolated and independent entities. Some important names are provided in isolation.	One or a few concepts are addressed, while others are underdeveloped, or not mentioned.	Deliberate and structured consideration of all key concepts/elements.	All key concepts/elements are included in a view that addresses interconnections.	Integration of all elements and dimensions, with extrapolation to new situations.
Understanding and applying the law	Names one or two court cases but is unclear about the issues or what was decided.	Describes the elements and decision in cases related to one area, but is less knowledgeable about other areas and related cases.	Names and describes court decisions related to major dilemmas, along with the reasoning for each decision.	Describes the themes across court decisions and explains how these are related to teacher practices.	Presents an integrated description of court decisions, draws clear implications for teaching, and suggests possible directions that might emerge in the near future.

FIELD GUIDE
FOR LEARNING MORE ABOUT . . .

The Law as It Relates to Teaching and Learning

In Chapter 1, you were introduced to the concept of a field guide for learning more about your surroundings. The artifacts and information you will collect for this part of your field guide will involve collecting information related to legal aspects of schooling. Remember to take field notes as you complete the activities suggested here. These notes should include your identifying topics and issues that could have legal implications. Your field notes should also include date, time of day, the grade or group you are observing, and your reflections and aha moments. As was said in an earlier chapter, this form of journaling will help you understand the steps you are taking to becoming a teacher. Remember, also, to collect pictures and samples. A picture can be worth a thousand words.

Ask a Teacher or Principal	Experienced teachers and most certainly principals will be knowledgeable about school problems they have experienced that have had a legal component. Ask them to describe a few examples that have had important legal aspects. What legal resources and counsel do they turn to when a problem with potentially legal implications comes up?
Make Your Own Observations	Legal representation and counsel will be part of many venues. For example, attend a school board meeting and observe the role of the district's attorney and in what ways the law guides proceedings. You also could visit a court and observe the proceedings. The purpose of these observations is to see how the U.S. and state constitutions and statutes provide the framework for the consideration of a question. The particular topic should not be the center of your attention; instead, you are there to watch the legal process.
Reflect Through Journaling	It is very likely that much of the content in this chapter has been new to you. Take some time to think about implications of the legal system for your future as a teacher. Which of the topics and cases did you find most relevant? Construct a table of legal topics. For example, you could label one column "student rights," another "teacher rights," and another "schools and society." In each column, list what you now see as key dos and don'ts for you as a teacher.
Build Your Portfolio	Two useful resources for keeping abreast of legal issues in education are *Education Week* and the *Phi Delta Kappan*. Each issue of *Education Week* will have reports on current court cases and judicial decisions. Most issues of the *Kappan* will have a column called "Ed Law." These columns are easy to read and summarize legal proceedings about a particular topic. Search through several issues of one or both of these publications and develop a set of notes about current issues and implications for yourself as a teacher.

Read a Book	*The Law of Schools, Students and Teachers in a Nutshell*, 5th edition, by Kern Alexander and M. Alexander (2015). The authors are leading national school law experts who cover the rights of students and the constitutional rights and protections of teachers. Employment terms and conditions are also addressed.
	School Law for Teachers: Concepts and Applications, by Julie Underwood and L. Dean Webb (2006, Pearson), is written for teachers. Key topics addressed include teacher and student rights, negligence, discrimination and harassment, and religion in schools.
	Although *Responding to Cyber Bullying: An Action Tool for School Leaders*, by Jill J. Myers, Donna S. McCaw, and Leaunda S. Hemphill (2011, Corwin), was written for school leaders, it still is a useful resource for teachers. In your teaching career, you will most certainly be confronted with bullying in general and through social media in particular. This book reviews student rights and your responsibilities. There are suggestions for how to balance free expression with providing a safe environment. The authors even provide the "Top Ten Rules" for addressing cyberbullying.
Search the Web	**U.S. Supreme Court Decisions:** As with any topic, the web is an important resource for finding information about legal matters. The organization of courts, past decisions, and current cases under consideration can be found. One useful website about U.S. Supreme Court decisions (**www.streetlaw.org**) has been developed specifically to help teachers find resources and activities that can be used in teaching about major Court decisions.
	Supreme Court Case Summaries: Oyez (**www.oyez.org/about**) has easy-to-follow summaries of major U.S. Supreme Court decisions. Each case is presented in a summary format that includes the term, facts about the case, the question, and the decision.
	State Court Case Summaries: You also can find a website for each state's court decisions. For example, the Kansas Supreme Court site describes the number of justices, cases under consideration, and how justices are selected. As an activity, take a look at your state's judicial branch website. Are there current cases related to schools and teaching? What education cases has your state dealt with in the past?
	Archives of News Programs: Another web resource is audio and video archives of news programs. Go to the website for one of the media news sources and search for recent programs related to some of the legal topics introduced in this chapter. For example, PBS *Frontline* has posted "Growing Up Trans," which is a very sensitive interview with one young person dealing with gender identity, school, and discrimination.

STUDENT STUDY SITE

$SAGE edge™

Get the tools you need to sharpen your study skills. **SAGE edge** offers a robust online environment featuring an impressive array of free tools and resources.

Access practice quizzes, eFlashcards, video, and multimedia at **edge.sagepub.com/hall3e**.

TEACHING FOR STUDENT LEARNING

10 STANDARDS, CURRICULUM, AND ACCOUNTABILITY

TEACHER INTERVIEW

Mrs. Donna Jovin

© Donna Jovin

Meet Mrs. Donna Jovin, a teacher of English as a Second Language (ESL) at Oakdale Elementary School in Dedham, Massachusetts. Mrs. Jovin graduated from Merrimack College in North Andover, Massachusetts, with a BA in teaching French. After several years as a French and Spanish high school teacher, she earned a master's of education with a concentration in teaching English as a Second Language. She has been teaching ESL in her current position for the Dedham Public Schools since 1989. Mrs. Jovin works with small, pull-out groups of English Language Learners at Oakdale Elementary School. Oakdale was built in 1902 and is one of the oldest schools in the Dedham Public School District, the first taxpayer-funded public school district in the United States. There are three elementary schools, a middle school, a childhood center, a regional technology school, and two high schools in Dedham.

LEARNING OUTCOMES

After reading this chapter, you should be able to do the following:

1. Describe the purpose and characteristics of standards, benchmarks, and curriculum.

2. Explain ways the focus on standards and benchmarks can improve teaching practices and student learning.

3. Identify the ways that standards, curriculum, and assessment are interrelated in curriculum alignment.

Q: What brings you joy in teaching?

A: I feel joy in teaching when I can help my students become confident in their abilities to succeed academically and socially. Sometimes just a smile, or a hug, or an "I love your class" fills me with joy. I try to laugh every day with my students. Sometimes if a student is upset, I will say something silly or make a funny face. That helps defuse a tense situation.

Q: When you consider "standards," what do you think about?

A: I consider standards as guides for planning curriculum, instruction, and assessment. As an ESL teacher, I use the WIDA English Language Development Standards in planning instruction for English Language Learners (ELLs). These standards focus on the language needed for ELLs to succeed in school. The WIDA standards can be found at *https://wida .wisc.edu/*. The standards help guide instruction by setting expectations for social and academic language and by encompassing all four language domains of reading, writing, listening, and speaking. Expectations are based on English proficiency levels. Each lesson should be planned with these elements in mind.

Q: What does the term *curriculum* mean in your daily work as a teacher?

A: Curriculum gives order and focus to instruction. It helps to standardize instruction across a district or state. I follow a curriculum that was developed by National Geographic for the

Reach series. If and when necessary, I make modifications to the curriculum based on the students' English proficiency levels.

Q: **What do you do to make sure that all of your students are learning? And how do you keep track of each student's progress?**

A: To make sure that all my students are learning, I assess all domains of language learning—namely, listening, speaking, reading, and writing. I do this in a variety of ways. I make sure to have all students tell me what they have learned, we write about what they have learned, we take periodic assessment tests based on our textbook series, and I check in with their mainstream classroom teachers. Information from classroom teachers helps me know if my lessons help make the mainstream curriculum more comprehensible for ELLs.

Q: **What advice would you give a new teacher about developing curriculum and assessing student learning?**

A: My advice to teachers in this age of standardized assessment is to never forget the individual—to always consider where students started out when you first met them and where they ended up when they left your class.

Q: **And finally, give one example of how you learn as a teacher.**

A: As a teacher, I learn by making mistakes and finding a better way, by talking to my colleagues and watching them teach, and by being willing to try something new. If my students are not engaged in a lesson, then I have to consider what I can do to keep their interest and to make them active, engaged learners. This may mean incorporating more group activities, media, games, songs—whatever it takes to stimulate and keep their interest.

Questions to Consider

1. How might knowing content standards help a teacher plan lessons and develop curriculum?

2. One of the ways Mrs. Jovin finds joy in teaching is when she can help her students become confident in their ability to succeed academically. How might a teacher help the students take charge of their own learning?

3. Mrs. Jovin believes that curriculum provides order and focus to instruction. What are some ways teachers might develop curriculum to bring student focus to learning?

4. In what ways can new teachers help themselves be successful during their first year of teaching?

5. Why might creating a portfolio help you grow professionally?

INTRODUCTION

There is a seemingly endless curriculum process from lesson plans, to instruction, to assessment, and around again. In a perfect world, the curriculum would perfectly match instruction. Unfortunately, there is often a "discrepancy between the intentions of the curriculum and what the teacher actually delivers to students" (Wiles & Bondi, 2015, p. 125). This curriculum process is perhaps the most complex and complicated work a teacher must understand. Teachers have to know stuff. They have to know how the students in their care learn and how what these students learn can be connected to what they have yet to learn. Teachers have to be able to teach a fact, an idea, or a concept in such a way that students will delight in learning it, will use it, and will know it forever.

You are starting down the road to becoming a teacher at a time when all eyes—public, political, parental, and even those of your peers—are focused on student learning as something that can be viewed as a direct result of teacher performance. This emphasis on what students and teachers know and know how to do has given rise to all manner of standards, benchmarks, and criteria for determining ways education—and especially teachers—are accountable. Standards have become an integral part of schooling: establishing them, using them to improve schools, using them to improve instruction, and using them as a means toward determining student progress. Teachers who plan for and prepare their lessons to engage students' minds should be well aware of the role standards, curriculum, and assessment play in promoting student learning.

There is an indisputable logic behind having a certain level of achievement in mind when undertaking any project. If you have ever planted a garden, painted a room or house, gone camping, played in a recital, or performed on stage, you didn't start out without some idea

There is always a degree of difference in the ways standards of performance are judged.

of what everything would look or be like in the end. For example, say a Camp Fire leader has decided on a birdhouse project for her group, but doesn't want the project to involve cutting wood or a hammer and nails. So she buys a bolt of heavy twine and three packages of tongue depressors, collects 10 empty one-pound coffee or peanut cans, and demonstrates how to combine all materials into a birdhouse with a roof. The children are amazed and can hardly wait to get started. As the leader watches each child create a birdhouse, she is able to anticipate any major deviation from the standard goal she had in mind in the beginning. With help and guidance, each child is able to build a birdhouse, fill it with the straw the teacher has provided, and anticipate the birds that will make a home there. During the entire project, much discussion takes place of why birds (and other animals) need homes, what might attract birds to a particular ready-built home, which birds live in the neighborhood, and what they look and sound like. This is truly curriculum in action.

WHAT ARE STANDARDS AND BENCHMARKS?

Standards are statements about overarching values in education that the majority of people agree upon. A standard is an acknowledged measure of comparison for quantitative or qualitative value, a criterion, a norm, or a degree or level of excellence that is achieved. Deciding what PreK–12 students and their teachers should know and be able to do is a major concern of educational policy makers as well as of schools and departments of education. Their solution to deciding what teachers should know and be able to do is the development of standards. What should be learned is also of concern to the teachers and students who grapple with standards on a daily basis. A teacher's job is to transform standards into enriched learning experiences that engage the intellect of students.

Standards are necessary in order to measure the learning that takes place in one school or place against other schools and other places. Setting such standards may seem like a simple task, but it was probably easier to standardize the size and width of railroad cars in the 19th century than to standardize anything having to do with education. Performance-based standards are designed to ensure accountability and improve schools by holding students, teachers, schools, and districts accountable for the results of student achievement. Additionally, an underlying agenda of standards is to see that public tax dollars are spent well. Setting standards in education has become a huge undertaking. It is complex, political, and fraught with challenges.

Standards are a general statement of a final goal; benchmarks, introduced in Chapter 1, are specific waypoints, turning points, or landmarks along the way to achieving the goal. Benchmarks denote the measurable stages along the journey to successfully achieving standards. For example, when a stagecoach left St. Louis, Missouri, for Custer, South Dakota, it began with a fast, fresh team of horses. During the trip, however, there were regular stops along the way to refresh the horses or hitch up a new team, and to give the travelers some time to check on their own condition. The stops where this change of horses or taking stock occurred were the benchmarks: measurable, familiar points along the way to reaching the final goal. Each time a new stagecoach left St. Louis, its forward journey was measured by reaching predetermined stage stops. Individual journeys might be filled with novel experiences, but the stage stops, or benchmarks, along the way were familiar and well established.

Characteristics of Standards

Standards are conceptually nothing new. Standards for student achievement have probably existed in this country since the first student had to read from the Bible in the first Massachusetts school, founded in 1635. The General School Law of 1647 definitely set standards for what students of that era were expected to know since it was assumed that one chief aim of Satan was to keep people from knowledge of the Scriptures. Every township of 50 or more families was ordered to appoint someone within the town to provide all children with an elementary education so they could, of course, read the Scriptures.

Benjamin Franklin's 1749 "Proposals Relating to the Education of Youth in Pensilvania" [sic] was intended to make English the standard of instruction rather than Latin and to establish a curriculum that was both scientific and practical. Thomas Jefferson's 1778 and 1780 "Bill for the More General Diffusion of Knowledge" planned to establish cumulative and consecutive levels of education—from elementary schools, to secondary schools, and then possibly on to college. Jefferson's plan also called for control of the schools to pass from the church or the federal government to the states.

The curriculum of the common school movement of the 1800s outlined the skills needed for everyday life, for ethical behavior, and for responsible citizenship (Cremin, 1951, p. 62). President George W. Bush's No Child Left Behind Act of 2001 (NCLB) supported reading instruction to ensure that every child in public schools could read at or above grade level by third grade. NCLB also strove to strengthen teacher quality for public schools by investing in training and retention of high-quality teachers.

The federal Elementary and Secondary Education Act (ESEA) of 1965 stresses access to education, sets high standards for academic performance, and demands a rigorous level of accountability from schools and districts. The Every Student Succeeds Act (ESSA) of 2015 is a reauthorization of ESEA and establishes the federal government's expanded role in public education. Each of these policies—in addition to a multitude of other proposals, bills, and plans—to establish standards and improve American education has contributed to and continues to contribute to setting criteria for a cumulative and consecutive system of universal public education for all children who attend the nation's schools.

While the establishment of standards may appear to be the purview of lawmakers, politicians, and educators, parents also have major concerns about what schools will expect of their children. Parents want some measures of accountability (see Chapter 8). They want their children to succeed in school, and to have rewarding and worthwhile experiences there. Some standards are easy for parents to understand— for example, all children will learn to read—yet some standards are less clear, such as that all children will be ready to learn. Readiness for elementary school is an implicit standard for beginning formal schooling in the United States. Although school attendance is not mandatory in most states until first grade, national surveys of parents of early elementary pupils show that a large majority of primary school children attended kindergarten before entering first grade. Such reports provide evidence that parents are concerned that their sons and daughters will begin school well prepared to meet the standards.

There are standards for content, for student achievement, for teachers, and for teacher education. In Chapter 1, you learned about the Interstate Teacher Assessment and Support Consortium (InTASC) Standards and about national certification for teachers by the National Board for Professional Teaching Standards (NBPTS). You can learn more about the purposes of each of these organizations by visiting their websites. You will become very familiar with the InTASC Standards during your teacher education course work and with the NBPTS later in your career.

Common Core State Standards

At the Council of the Great City Schools website (www.cgcs.org), questions regarding the Common Core State Standards (CCSS) are answered, and you learn that "standards do not tell teachers how to teach, but they do help teachers figure out the knowledge and skills their students should have so that teachers can build the best lessons and environments for their classrooms. Standards also help students and parents by setting clear and realistic goals for success. Standards are a first step—a key building block—in providing . . . an accessible roadmap for our teachers, parents, and students" (National Governors Association & Council of Chief State School Officers, 2015).

The Common Core State Standards Initiative, while coordinated by the National Governors Association Center for Best Practices and the Council of Chief State School Officers (CCSSO), is truly a state-led effort. The CCSS in math and English language arts (ELA) have been voluntarily adopted by 45 states and the District of Columbia. Implementation of the standards in these states is well under way. However, criticism of the Common Core and debates over design, implementation, and purpose of this policy have been waged in legislatures and school district board rooms. A handful of states have backed away from the Common Core, believing, among other concerns, that the decisions about education should be made at the state level and not by the federal government (Lu, 2014).

In 2014, the Bill & Melinda Gates Foundation called for a two-year moratorium on states or school districts making any high-stakes decisions based on tests aligned to the CCSS (Rich, 2014). The following statement, quoted in the *Washington Post*, was issued by Vicki Phillips, the director of education for the Gates Foundation:

> No evaluation system will work unless teachers believe it is fair and reliable, and it's very hard to be fair in a time of transition. The standards need time to work. Teachers need time to develop lessons, receive more training, get used to the new tests, and offer their feedback. (Strauss, 2014)

So it seems that, even with the attention of the nation focused on the Common Core—what the standards mean, how they are to be implemented, and how they may dictate assessment of student learning—the bottom line is how well teachers will understand the standards and be able to develop the curriculum that will help the students in their classrooms learn.

Engage in some research into your state's adoption or refusal of the CCSS. Did the state you plan to teach in take the *common* out of the Common Core and name it something else? Did the state design a separate set of standards and assessments of student learning? What debate emerged over the Common Core in your state? Knowing what legislative actions were taken in your state will prepare you to understand the programs you will be expected to teach and the assessments you will be expected to administer.

The Intent of the Common Core State Standards

According to the CCSSO, the CCSS are informed by the highest, most effective models from states across the country and countries around the world, and provide teachers and parents with a common understanding of what students are expected to learn. It is anticipated that consistent common standards will provide appropriate benchmarks for all students, regardless of where they live. The CCSS developed by each state define the knowledge and skills students should have within their K–12 education so they graduate from high school able to "succeed in entry-level, credit-bearing academic college courses" (Common Core State Standards Initiative, n.d.).

The CCSS are defined for each grade level and subject. For example, ELA standards in Grade 6 are delineated into strands of (a) key ideas and details, (b) craft and structure, (c) integration of knowledge and ideas, and (d) range of reading and level of text complexity. Each strand is accompanied by a list of additional standards that should be articulated through curriculum and instruction.

Teachers often reference standards documents when planning lessons to be sure they have included necessary standards and benchmarks.

The path from standard to curriculum to accountability is clearly marked, so there should be little risk of teachers losing their way. As the CCSS are adopted across the nation, curriculum must be developed to help teachers design appropriate instruction that will match the goals of the standards. This can be achieved only through teachers' knowledge of the Common Core and through their implementation. Teachers must be the voice for their students who may have little voice in what or how they should learn. Teachers shouldn't rely too heavily on established organizations to be the only entity to determine standards. Every day, teachers set standards for attendance and behavior in classrooms. Perhaps it is time for communities of teachers to create school-level and grade-level standards specific to the demographics of their students so each student will graduate from high school ready for academic college courses and workforce training programs.

WHY ARE THERE STANDARDS FOR CONTENT?

In order to help you understand the scope and design of the standards movement, it seems wise to provide you with a brief history of the effort to standardize content goals and establish assessments that are intended to provide accurate data on student performance. The amount of time invested, the workforce needed to staff the numerous committees that were created, and the funding from tax dollars over 15 years make it crystal clear that the establishment of national standards in education was not a frivolous endeavor.

At the beginning of the 1990s, the National Council on Education Standards and Testing (NCEST) was created to make recommendations regarding voluntary national standards. This council in turn proposed an oversight board to establish guidelines for standards setting and assessment development. This board became the National Education Standards and Assessments Council (NESAC); its purpose was to review and evaluate content standards and assessments proposed by specialized professional associations. Of course, before all these councils and boards were created by the federal government, the National Council of Teachers of Mathematics published *Curriculum and Evaluation Standards for School Mathematics*, in 1989, blazing the trail for other content areas to follow.

Many content standards were drafted and finalized during the last decade of the 20th century. Part of the Goals 2000: Educate America Act of 1994, signed into law by President Bill Clinton, created the National Education Standards and Improvement Council (NESIC) to certify national and state content and performance standards. Federal funding was made available to support content-area organizations in creating standards.

Creating standards for each content area in schools is often a controversial task garnering few rewards for the initial designers. For example, the National Endowment for the Humanities and the National Geographic Society worked together on a first draft of history and geography standards. When these standards were released, the history standards were denounced by the U.S. Senate as being unacceptable.

Creating standards for student learning can result in controversy and conflict that will be resolved only through thoughtful discussion.

© iStock/Geber86

Other groups had more success. For example, the Committee for National Health Education Standards was funded by the American Cancer Society. The Consortium of National Arts Education Associations published the arts standards (dance, music, theater, and the visual arts). National standards for sport and physical education were published, standards for foreign language learning were published, national science education standards were published, and the National Council of Teachers of English and the International Reading Association (now the International Literacy Association) also published standards.

Developing the Content Standards

Standards for each content area have seen much revision since the first installments. They have undergone strict scrutiny from peers and from the general public for their cost, for their ability to truly reform education, for their content, and for their voluminous size. The new math standards in the Common Core have been criticized for being a "complete mess"—too advanced for younger students yet not nearly rigorous enough in the upper grades (Rubinkam, 2014, p. 14A). Through the wave of heated discussion, the current standards and assessment criteria have survived and are rapidly becoming a permanent part of the educational panorama. The federal government established grants to support the process of designing standards, and it also withdrew funding for certain organizations when controversy over the standards ran counter to national goals.

Navigating the ocean of standards can sometimes seem like an impossible task for teachers and teacher education candidates, but the thread of content standards in education is strong and easy to follow. The manner in which national standards are articulated can help teachers understand the ways in which courses and subjects are defined. Standards help describe levels of student performance, and they also help determine how student performance is graded and reported. Table 10.1 offers a snapshot of how specific overarching concepts in eight different disciplines are categorized by the standards movement.

TABLE 10.1 ■ Examples of Standards as Lesson Plan Objectives

National Standards	Common Core State Standards	Example of Standards as Lesson Plan Objectives
National Council of Teachers of Mathematics—Algebra Using mathematical models to represent and understand quantitative relationships	Student models problem situations with objects and uses representations such as graphs, tables, and equations to draw conclusions.	Grade 3: Students will determine how many packages each of 18 napkins, 10 plates, 5 cups, and 2 cupcakes they will need to purchase in order to serve a group of 33 guests.
National Standards for History—World History 5–12 Understanding the search for community, stability, and peace in an interdependent world	Student understands how population explosion and environmental change have altered conditions of life around the world.	Grade 11: Students will compare the negative population growth in Russia with the burgeoning population growth in Mexico and draw conclusions about the economic and social development in the two countries.
National Standards for Arts Education—Visual Arts 5–8 Understanding and applying media techniques and processes	Student intentionally takes advantage of the qualities and characteristics of art media, techniques, and processes to enhance communication of his or her experiences and ideas.	Grade 5: Students will create original works of art by applying different media (salt, tissue, plastic wrap) to water colors.
National Council of Teachers of English—K–12 Applying language skills	Student uses spoken, written, and visual language to accomplish his or her own purposes (e.g., for learning, enjoyment, persuasion, and the exchange of information).	Grade 4: Students will develop an infomercial on the causes and possible solutions for the dead zone at the mouth of the Mississippi River.
Science Content Standards—Physical Science 5–8 Developing an understanding of ● properties and changes of properties in matter, ● motions and forces, and ● transfer of energy	Student observes and measures characteristic properties, such as boiling and melting points, solubility, and simple chemical changes of pure substances, and uses those properties to distinguish and separate one substance from another.	Grade 8: Students will describe the changes of properties in relation to heat and temperature, and discover conditions for raising solubility of a solution.
U.S. National Geography Standards—K–12 Places and regions	Student recognizes places as human creations and understands the genesis, evolution, and meaning of places.	Grade 5: Students will produce a presentation or performance describing the unique features of their hometown to welcome visitors.
National Health Education Standards Health information, products, and services	Student identifies characteristics of valid health information and health-promoting products and services.	Grade 3: Students will explain how media influences the selection of health information, products, and services.
ISTE Standards Technology problem-solving and decision-making tools	Student uses technology resources for solving problems and making informed decisions.	Grade 8: Students will use evaluation criteria to locate sites on the Internet that provide useful information and useless information on a predetermined topic.

Organizing the Standards

National standards are intended to serve as frameworks that will assist state departments of education and local districts in organizing knowledge and skills into curricula. National standards do not define a national curriculum per se. They do, however, specify broad areas of agreement on content that all students are expected to be exposed to. Some national standards are divided into grade-level bands (i.e., K–4, 5–8, 9–12) to further articulate content deemed especially relevant to particular grade levels. National standards for social studies are divided into sets of standards for civics, economics, geography, U.S. history, and world history. Each professional association determines the range of its standards and the exact number of standards that will cover the structure of each discipline. Table 10.2 offers a glimpse of overarching concepts captured by the standards movement.

National standards are intended to serve as frameworks that will assist state departments of education and local districts in organizing knowledge and skills into curricula. Each set of national standards provides details for developing student abilities and understandings as well as suggestions for curriculum planning. For example, there are seven broad content areas for science. Each area is separated into grade-level bands. In the Grade 5–8 band for "science as inquiry," it is expected that all students should develop abilities necessary to do and understand scientific inquiry. Examples are provided in the content standards documents illustrating how intermediate objectives might be achieved through lessons. State departments of education and district curriculum committees establish subsets of objectives, and classroom teachers deliver these objectives through instructional practices. The route from the overarching concepts embedded in national standards to a specific objective may be long, but it is clear, and at the end of the journey, it is the teachers who convey all of the standards to the students through curriculum. Since the content of education is of extreme importance to the future of our society, the absence of standards would leave society vulnerable to all manner of misfortune and misunderstanding. The CCSS in math and ELA, and the Next Generation Science Standards (the science equivalent of the Common Core), provide a framework for curriculum development that will lead to optimal student learning.

Using the Standards

Beginning teachers use published standards as a guide for what they can and should do and as a caution against things they shouldn't do. Teachers also depend in some ways on the advice of others who are experienced with the actual ways standards are enforced and assessed. Teachers, both new and

TABLE 10.2 ■ National Standard Concepts				
Physical Education	**Health**	**Science**	**Mathematics**	**Language Arts**
Movement forms	Health promotion and disease prevention	Science as inquiry	Number and operations	Reading for perspective
Movement concepts		Physical science	Algebra	Reading for understanding
Physical activity	Health information, products, and services	Life science	Geometry	Evaluation strategies
Physical fitness	Reducing health risks	Earth and space science	Measurement	Communication skills
Responsible behavior	Health influences	Science and technology	Data analysis and probability	Communication strategies
Respect for others	Using communication skills to promote good health	Science in personal and social perspectives	Problem-solving process	Applying knowledge
Understanding challenge			Reasoning and proof processes	Evaluating data
	Setting goals for good health	History and nature of science	Communication processes	Developing research skills
	Health advocacy		Connections process	Multicultural understanding
			Representation	Applying non-English language perspective
				Participating in society
				Applying language skills

experienced, rely on established guidelines and standards to help them navigate the educational sea without going astray. There are guidelines for professional behavior and for professional relationships between students and teachers. There are curriculum guides that set benchmarks for student achievement. There are standards for attendance, for grading, for discipline, and for dress. There are even standards for textbooks and protocols for the ways states and districts adopt one textbook over others.

Using Benchmarks

Since benchmarks denote stages on the path to achieving standards, it is logical and perhaps more doable that students' progress be assessed at benchmarks rather than at the end of the journey to achieving standards. At benchmarks, administrators and teachers can ascertain whether redirection or reteaching is indicated and determine what steps are necessary to rectify problems. Consider each benchmark as a point of curriculum accomplishment. How each benchmark might look in actual professional practice is determined by the standards each state department of education set for teacher effectiveness. Benchmark requirements for students in Oregon are readily available to students, to their parents, and to their teachers. The Oregon Department of Education website provides information regarding the nine cross-disciplinary skills that students should be developing across Grades K–12.

Schools and classrooms have been likened to eggs in a carton, with each teacher and class in a separate environment having little or no contact with others. The advent of standards across all levels of school, student, and teacher performance has increased the opportunity for teachers to work together to develop strategies for achieving common short-term and long-term goals. Setting measurable goals and benchmarks is an integral part of any school reform planning process.

Teachers create lesson plans that reflect district, state, and national goals for student learning. The process of planning is one of the most crucial ongoing tasks that teachers perform.

Students' achievement can be improved when teachers work together to promote effective instructional practices and establish goals for student learning.

> Studies of high performing schools indicate that school quality is a people process. It requires that teachers collaboratively implement a focused curriculum and clear goals for students, and that teachers continually improve their instructional and assessment methods. Teachers design units and look at evidence of student learning together so that classrooms are no longer separate entities and teachers become learners in the sense of finding better ways to help all students be successful. (C. Robertson, 2004, p. 2)

While standards alone cannot bring about school improvement, they provide useful guidelines for states and local curriculum framework developers to define the knowledge and skills they want their students to have. Standards and benchmarks can help bring coherence to disjointed curricula. They can help planners determine what to teach, how to teach it, and how to assess it. Standards and benchmarks can help define a base for teacher content knowledge and for coordinating Professional Development for teachers. With such guidelines, the task of school improvement can become a well-organized project.

Keeping Track of Benchmarks and Standards in Lesson Planning

Effective teachers know and think about standards every day when they plan lessons and write down what they expect from their students. Standards guide teachers in focusing instruction on the essential knowledge and skills their students should learn. Each teacher becomes responsible for teaching to a standard, measuring student mastery of the knowledge or skill, and reteaching when students don't achieve mastery. Teachers are held accountable through assessments by their supervisors and through the results of student learning.

"In a standards-based system, the end is held constant for all students; each one is expected to meet the standard" (Jamentz, 2002, p. 11). Additionally, in a standards-based system, teachers are expected to articulate how the objectives and assessment of the lesson are tied to local, state, or national benchmarks or standards. School districts develop curriculum documents and standards that teachers must know and refer to in planning and instruction.

In Texas, the state standards for science in Grade 4 are divided into three categories of (1) knowledge and skills, (2) scientific processes, and (3) science concepts. Benchmarks are listed for each category. One part of the scientific processes category states, "The student knows how to use a variety of tools and methods to conduct science inquiry" (Perma-Bound School Library, n.d.). The benchmarks for this standard list the tools students are expected to use in collecting and analyzing information (calculators, safety goggles, microscopes, cameras, sound recorders, computers, hand lenses, rulers, thermometers, meter sticks, timing devices, balances, and compasses). The benchmarks listed for this standard also expect students to be able to demonstrate that repeated investigations may increase the reliability of results.

Computerized software applications can aid teachers in planning lessons. IBM also offers a product for lesson planning for use on iPhone, iPad, and Android-based devices. There are numerous Internet sites to help teachers plan lessons. These sites often illustrate ways standards can be expressed in lesson objectives. An excellent site to begin a search for help with standards, benchmarks, and lesson plans is Education World (www.educationworld.com).

Web-based tools, among other things, enable educators to design lessons and units, map and track standards, and create rubrics. It is important for teachers to be able to explain what the students will be required to do at the end of the unit, and the use of rubrics helps students understand what criteria will be used to judge their performance. Effective planning helps teachers keep track of the benchmarks their students have passed and those they need to revisit.

Knowing the Standards

You may begin to feel overwhelmed with the topic of standards, but if you can talk about standards during your job interview and how they can be integrated into instruction, you may be the top candidate for the job since most schools have adopted a standards-based curriculum (see Chapter 1). It is not only the standards for the students you will be teaching that affect your work; the teacher education program in which you are enrolled should also be standards based. Your program should be preparing you to meet InTASC standards and professional standards for your field (e.g., mathematics or early childhood education). You should become familiar with a range of standards.

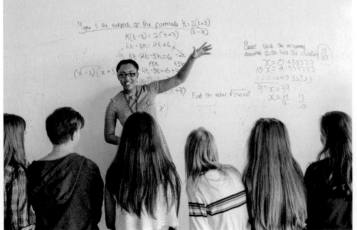

When students are informed of the standards and objectives for a lesson, they have a better idea of what is expected of them.

Standards for Students

New teachers should know the student standards for the subject they will be teaching or the students with whom they will be working. All states have developed student standards that indicate what students at different grade levels should know and be able to do in a subject area.

Mrs. Jovin at the beginning of this chapter uses the WIDA English Language Development Standards in her lesson planning. The tests that students are required to take annually in mathematics, reading, science, and social studies are based on the state standards. Many of the state standards have been adapted from the standards of national organizations such as the National Council of Teachers of Mathematics (NCTM), International Literacy Association (ILA), National Council for the Social Studies (NCSS), and American Association for the Advancement of Science (AAAS). These standards should provide the guide for what you should be teaching in those core curriculum areas. They can be used to develop your own performance assessments, introduced in Chapter 1, to determine what students are learning. The state tests also provide feedback, although it is limited, on what students have learned. State standards can be accessed on the website of your state department of education.

Standards for Teachers

Standards for teaching and for learning to become a teacher are not a new phenomenon. Teachers have always been held to some form of standards and accountability. Even before a degree and graduation from an accredited institution was mandatory, school boards or directors of schools demanded a level of respectability demonstrated by social status, family background, or gender. In 1867, D. W. Fish's *American Educational Series: A Full Course of Practical and Progressive Text-Books; and Almanac* offered a list of 26 suggestions for what a teacher should do (Gutek, 1986, p. 99). Even today, what a teacher knows and knows how to do are fundamental to being employed. They are also keys to success in one's identity as a teacher and level of confidence in teaching. However, what a teacher does with this know-how is far more important to the achievement and success of students than simply having the knowledge.

Teacher education candidates are required to pass standards-based examinations often before they are allowed into K–12 classrooms. Results from such tests help state departments of education and colleges of education determine whether a student is qualified to be admitted to and matriculate through a teacher education program. Some state departments of education require the ETS Praxis® series of tests for licensure, and some states require test results from the Pearson Evaluation Systems. The Florida Teacher Certification Examinations, for example, are administered by the Evaluation Systems group of Pearson. Once the state receives the test results, student scores are compiled in a Title II report that is sent to institutions. Visit the Florida Department of Education website for a summary of certification tests.

Teacher education programs across the nation either require candidates to pass the Praxis II or teacher certification test through the Pearson Evaluation Systems prior to graduation or recommend that it be taken soon after graduation. Test results can help determine whether candidates meet state criteria for licensing.

An example of how standards have become a standard fixture of the professional scene is the way in which the InTASC Standards were conceived, constituted, and connected to every aspect of teacher preparation and performance. The standards were originally created to promote in-district Professional Development of beginning teachers, but these standards have evolved into a system for evaluating teaching performance at all levels. There is no question that standards and accountability will be in your teaching future.

Teacher education candidates should be aware that state departments of education can establish their own pedagogical standards for beginning teachers. Iowa, for example, has identified eight standards for beginning teachers who have earned a two-year initial license. To receive a standard Iowa state teaching license, teachers must be approved by their building principal as passing the Iowa Teaching Standards. You need to become knowledgeable about how the state where you want to teach assesses beginning teachers.

Teachers are held to standards and are required to sit for exams that measure their knowledge of content as well as their knowledge of how to design instruction.

National professional associations have also developed standards that describe what teachers should know and be able to do to teach a specific group of students (e.g., English Language Learners or students with disabilities) or a specific subject such as ELA or physical education. If teachers meet these standards, they should be able to help students meet the student standards.

Standards for Undergraduates

The **National STEM Standards** developed by the Committee on Undergraduate Science Education, in collaboration with the Center for Science, Mathematics, and Engineering Education and the National Research Council, promoted the rise of the standards that serve to increase student knowledge in Science, Technology, Engineering, and Mathematics (STEM). The committee recognizes that achievement of this goal relies in part on precollege experiences that include quality instruction in standards-based classrooms and a clear awareness that achievement in science, mathematics, and technology is a prerequisite for admission to college. In order for teachers to help students engage in STEM subjects, teachers must receive training. Professional Development resources for teachers who are seeking ways to develop curriculum in STEM are provided at www.nea.org/home/stem.html, and recently the federal government provided STEM grants for teacher training and for implementation of STEM curriculum in schools.

Standards for Colleges of Education and Universities

There are also standards for school districts, universities, and colleges of education. Such institutions are expected to meet standards. Through the consolidation of the National Council for Accreditation of Teacher Education (NCATE) and Teacher Education Accreditation Council (TEAC), the Council for the Accreditation of Educator Preparation (CAEP) was created to serve as a single accrediting agency for reform, innovation, and research in educator preparation. In addition to national accreditation agencies, regional agencies such as the Northwest Commission on Colleges and Universities (NWCCU) are recognized by state and federal departments of education as the regional authority on educational quality of higher education institutions in a specific area. These regional agencies establish criteria and evaluation procedures for reviewing institutions and qualify students enrolled in these institutions for access to federal funds to support student financial aid.

Teacher education programs at accredited institutions have been approved by the Specialized Professional Associations (SPAs) and by state departments of education. Candidates at these institutions must pass standardized tests and maintain a required Grade Point Average. Most states with institutions that have received national accreditation have reciprocal agreements with other states for licensure. This means if you get your degree in New York and want to be licensed to teach in Indiana, the Indiana State Board of Education will consider whether you graduated from an accredited institution; if you have, your chances of being granted a license to teach in Indiana will be better than if you graduated from an institution that has not achieved national, regional, or state accreditation. It is in your best interests to become aware of the standards underpinning your teacher education program and do your best to not just meet, but *exceed*, these standards at every opportunity.

Standards for Professional Practice

When you begin your teaching career, you will be evaluated on your performance as well as the achievement of your students. States may develop their own set of standards for evaluating teachers, as Iowa and Nevada have done. The Nevada Educator Performance Framework (NEPF) requires teachers as part of their evaluation by supervisors to provide evidence that their students are learning as a result of their teaching. Some districts rely on published works of experts in the field of teacher practice evaluation. In *Enhancing Professional Practice: A Framework for Teaching* (1996), Charlotte Danielson describes the elements of a teacher's responsibilities that promote student learning. These elements are derived from the findings of research studies on the connection between teaching behavior and students' learning. Danielson's framework divides the complex act of teaching into four domains of teaching responsibility: (1) planning and preparation, (2) classroom environment, (3) instruction, and (4) professional responsibilities; Danielson then describes the distinct features of each domain.

Frameworks such as the NEPF's and Danielson's provide teachers and supervisors with benchmarks by which to document teacher progress toward a specific goal.

After you have taught for three or more years, you may decide to go through the yearlong process for National Board certification. If you talk to a National Board–certified teacher, you will begin to understand how becoming board certified changes a teacher's perspective. If you are truly lucky, you will be able to teach in a school that hosts one or more certified teachers.

The NBPTS expects accomplished teachers to

- be committed to students and their learning,

- know the subjects they teach and how to teach those subjects to students,

- be responsible for managing and monitoring student learning,

- think systematically about their practice and learn from experience, and

- be members of learning communities.

In addition to these general expectations, the NBPTS has standards for teaching each subject area for specific age levels such as early childhood, middle childhood, early adolescence, and young adulthood. Your teacher education program should be helping you develop the foundation to meet these standards during your career. A number of colleges and universities have redesigned their master's degrees to reflect these standards and to help teachers gain National Board certification.

Knowing When Students Have Met the Standards

Lately, it seems that every time students turn around they are being asked to take yet another test. It happens at all levels and in all schools. This increase in testing is part of the focus on accountability, though there is much current debate regarding whether standardized tests accurately reflect student learning. Not too long ago, tests were administered at distant intervals, when students were at a point of transition in developmental levels or at increased demand of content knowledge (fourth grade, seventh grade, or ninth grade). However, now that states and school districts must keep a closer eye on student progress in order to maintain accountability, tests are being administered with more intensity and more frequency. It is not uncommon to have all students, even primary students, taking districtwide competency tests at midpoints in each school quarter.

It would be unnatural if parents and teachers alike didn't question the validity of the increase in testing or ask, "What's the point?" or "When will I have time to teach?" Testing is part of what you must contend with as a teacher. Think of it as a challenge, not as an unsettling catastrophe. Tests can provide teachers with useful data. They can be used to improve, not to condemn. As a new teacher, you will have to understand that testing is a large part of the education scene; reconcile yourself to that fact, and do what you can to make it most effective (Popham, 2011). Your response to the testing of your students is of extreme value to your students' success, to your peace of mind, and to the overall standing of your school.

WHAT IS CURRICULUM?

Curriculum is as old as any education institution. It is a dynamic field, complex and sometimes messy. Descriptions of curriculum range from "everything that happens in a school" to "a set of performance objectives" (Oliva & Gordon, 2012, p. 3). Oliva and Gordon (2012) provide a list of 13 ways curriculum can be described, as well as a quote from Madeleine R. Grumet, who labeled curriculum as a "field of utter confusion" (Grumet, 1988, p. 4). Perhaps the field of curriculum is a bit less chaotic today with the advent of easy-to-understand and easy-to-follow national and state standards and benchmarks. Curriculum is essential to standards and benchmarks, for without curriculum, standards lack movement. While standards and benchmarks provide the goals for education, excellent teaching and the curriculum create the various paths, avenues, and highways to reaching these goals.

Curriculum is one of the key concerns of schooling in the United States. Excellent schools for the future cannot be created without an understanding of curriculum theory and practice. McNeil (2003) says that curriculum is the teacher's initiative. When teachers become active participants in determining the curriculum and the instructional practices that translate it into action, there is a greater chance that excellence will be achieved. Hilda Taba (1962) wrote, "All curricula, no matter what their particular design, are composed of certain elements. A curriculum usually contains a statement of aims and of specific objectives; it indicates some selection and organization of content; it either implies or manifests certain patterns of learning and teaching, whether because the objectives demand them or because the content organization requires them. Finally, it includes a program of evaluation of the outcomes" (p. 11). Even though schools look pretty much the same today as they did at the turn of the 19th century, the present never exactly mirrors the past. Curriculum has gone through some major changes since the first public schools were established in the Plymouth Colony nearly 400 years ago. From schooling in Colonial America to the present day, concerns with teaching reading and equal access for all students to learn (as well as the intensity of debates among educators, politicians, and the population in general about what should be taught and how it should be taught) has never faltered.

Students will always be expected to know the basics, which might include, in addition to reading, writing, and arithmetic, how to conduct a search on the Internet or create a media presentation. Curriculum has been the conduit through which educational ideas and goals become evident in practice and programs. There has always been an ebb and flow to school curriculum as it reacts to the changing pull of American life. In the beginning, the waves of curriculum reform were gentle, while the undertow was hardly noticed. As American society and the American system of education grew in tandem, the pull of new ideas and novel educational practices became stronger and was, in turn, resisted with ever greater force. Curriculum always changes, but a useful and purposeful curriculum is never far removed from the students and society it serves.

Characteristics of Curriculum

To understand the nature of curriculum, it helps to have a framework for thinking about it. Oliva and Gordon (2012) offer a view of curriculum through 10 different lenses termed *axioms*. These axioms provide guidelines for educators seeking ways to improve curriculum and solve curriculum problems. In the following section, we have directed your thinking to something you may have experienced that reflects the intent of each axiom.

Axiom 1: Change is both inevitable and necessary, for it is through change that life forms grow and develop.

Though change is never easy, it is a fact of life. Some of the changes in American education occurred because of social issues, some because of philosophical debates, and some because of new inventions. Think for a moment of the problems a school you are familiar with has faced due to societal or technological influences. Consider any philosophical differences that have risen in the community you are familiar with. Then, ask yourself, in light of these changes, what curriculum changes might benefit the students in the school as well as the larger community?

Perseverance, knowledge, effort, and skill can help teachers overcome any hurdles that the standards and benchmarks might pose for students.

iStock/monkeybusinessimages

THINKING DIFFERENTLY
MAKING A COMPLEX CONCEPT SIMPLE

Some beginning teachers are given a published curricular program to use as the foundation for instruction in the grade level or content that they teach. Others may be presented with a list of standards and be expected to build curriculum and lessons from whatever resources are available. Some teachers will be inducted into a Professional Learning Community with grade-level colleagues or a group of teachers of similar content. Regardless, your first foray into curriculum development and understanding can be overwhelming if not downright confusing.

There are many ways to approach the concept of curriculum, and leaders in the field of curriculum development often have heated debates regarding specific approaches or definitions. The best way to approach curriculum for a new teacher is to think of it as a process whereby choices are made to design a learning experience for students and then those choices are set in motion through a series of coordinated activities (Wiles & Bondi, 2015). The learners, the society in which they are learning, and the subject they are expected to learn are of fundamental importance, not a single textbook or published program. When approaching curriculum from a beginning standpoint, ask yourself, "Who am I teaching, what do they need to know, and how best can I translate the curriculum into meaningful lessons that will help them learn?" That's all you really need to know to get started.

UNDERSTANDING AND USING DATA
ARE STANDARDS FOR AMERICAN STUDENTS SET TOO LOW?

The National Center for Education Statistics (NCES) collects and reports reliable data on student assessments in the United States and other nations in its ongoing examination of education systems around the world. One report, the Program for International Student Assessment (PISA), conducted in 2015, focused on 15-year-olds' capabilities in mathematics literacy, reading literacy, and science literacy. The data presented here represent the combined math, reading, and science scores for each country.

Program for International Student Assessment (PISA) Results, 2015				
Ranking	Country name	Math, mean score	Reading, mean score	Science, mean score
0	OECD average	490	493	493
1	Singapore	564	535	556
2	Hong Kong	548	527	518
3	Macau	544	509	529
4	Taiwan	542	497	523
5	Japan	532	516	538
6	China	531	494	518
7	Korea	524	517	516
8	Switzerland	521	492	506
9	Estonia	520	519	534
10	Canada	516	527	528
11	Netherlands	512	503	509
12	Denmark	500	496	498
13	Finland	511	526	531

(Continued)

(Continued)

Program for International Student Assessment (PISA) Results, 2015				
Ranking	Country name	Math, mean score	Reading, mean score	Science, mean score
14	Slovenia	510	505	513
15	Belgium	507	499	502
16	Germany	506	509	509
17	Poland	504	506	501
18	Ireland	501	523	522
19	Norway	502	513	498
20	Austria	497	485	495
21	New Zealand	500	512	516
22	Viet Nam	495	487	525
23	Russia	494	495	487
24	Sweden	494	500	493
25	Australia	494	503	510
26	France	493	499	509
27	United Kingdom	492	498	514
28	Czech Republic	492	487	493
29	Portugal	492	498	501
30	Italy	490	485	481
31	Iceland	493	483	478
32	Spain	486	496	493
33	Luxembourg	490	488	491
34	Latvia	482	488	490
35	Malta	479	447	465
36	Lithuania	478	472	475
37	Hungary	477	470	477
38	Slovak Republic	475	453	461
39	Israel	470	479	467
40	United States	470	497	496

Source: Jackson, A., & Kiersz, A. (2016, December 6). The latest ranking of top countries in math, reading, and science is out—and the US didn't crack the top 10. *Business Insider.* Retrieved from https://www.businessinsider.com/pisa-worldwide-ranking-of-math-science-reading-skills-2016-12.

Note: The Organisation for Economic Co-operation and Development (OECD) promotes policies that will improve the economic and social well-being of people around the world.

Using the list of combined scores from the countries of the OECD, discuss why you think U.S. standards for student achievement in math, reading, and science might need to be, or not need to be, revised. What do the data mean, and how might you interpret them? Which country does best at reading, math, and science?

Taken at face value, the U.S. ranking of 40th (in 2012 the United States was 39th, and in 2006 it was 24th) among the countries listed indicates that American 15-year-old students' capabilities in math, reading, and science are poor. The data point out a discouraging fact, and one could quickly jump to the conclusion that, yes, standards for U.S. students are set too low. However, the U.S. scores rank above the OECD average, but who wants to be average?

Teachers are often presented with data that provide an overall picture of the state of the profession or the achievement of students. Sometimes such data can be encouraging, and sometimes they can leave us wondering how things could have gone so poorly. Data presented in a simple format like the one provided above require teachers to take a critical look at what important information might be missing. Questions about the missing information should include these:

- What are the requirements for a teaching license in math, reading, and science in each country listed?

- How does the elementary and secondary school curriculum in math, reading, and science in each country compare with that in the United States?

- What is the diversity of the students tested in each country?

- What cultural and linguistic advantages might each country listed have over any of the others?

While the showing of U.S. 15-year-olds is nothing to be proud of, the idea of raising standards to improve these scores does not take into account other variables that might have as great an impact. Teacher excellence is undeniably one of the key components of student success.

Teachers are programmed to recognize the individuality of students and to celebrate student achievements, whether or not a distant set of standards is followed. Sometimes, because of this orientation and the accepting dispositions all teachers are expected to possess, teachers can lose sight of the importance of the nudge they need to exert on all students to achieve to their highest ability. There is a major difference between encouragement and acceptance. Understanding this difference and recognizing ways highly qualified teachers combine the two is a difficult lesson to grasp, but it is within your reach. It is human nature to respond to the raising of any bar as a challenge. We set our own bars and mentally raise them again and again each time we succeed in meeting the goals we have set for ourselves. Standards and benchmarks set the bar for students and teachers alike. Thank goodness teachers have the characteristic of perseverance, and that they continuously help their students over the bars they encounter. When administrators recognize the importance of the teacher's role in implementing standards and benchmarks, and when these administrators support the teachers' efforts, student achievement and school improvement are a likely result.

CHALLENGING ASSUMPTIONS
WILL IMPLEMENTING THE COMMON CORE STATE STANDARDS IN MATHEMATICS HELP STUDENTS BECOME PROBLEM SOLVERS AND THINKERS?

The Assumption

The idea behind the Common Core State Standards for mathematics is to help students understand how numbers relate to each other, and not necessarily to use the tried-and-true methods their parents learned. The Common Core State Standards for mathematics will teach both conceptual understanding and procedural fluency. Supporters of the standards for mathematics insist the standards are developmentally appropriate and driven by research.

The Research

Not all educators, parents, or students are in support of the new Common Core State Standards in mathematics. Some parents say that the math homework expected of elementary students is as complicated as calculus. Parents are confused by their children's homework, and confused by unfamiliar terms and impenetrable word problems. One parent complained her daughter's long-division homework was a foreign amalgam of boxes, slashes, and dots with nary a quotient or dividend in sight.

Stanford University mathematician James Milgram calls the reform math-inspired standards a "complete mess"

(Rubinkam, 2014, p. 14A). To Milgram's thinking, teachers are mostly ill prepared to put the standards into practice. Common Core advocates blame parent and student frustration with the standards on "botched implementation, insufficient training or poorly written math programs" (Rubinkam, 2014, p. 14A).

Implications

Will better-designed programs alleviate confusion? Is it the school's responsibility to do a better job of communicating the purposes of the Common Core to parents? How are teachers expected to help their students understand what they may not understand themselves? Surely students suffer when they are presented with exercises that they do not understand. Will students go from loving math to hating it? There is little doubt that the new math standards seem to complicate what many educators, teachers, and parents view as simple arithmetic. What might be done to ease the new standards into the curriculum spiral that leads and follows students through schooling?

Source: Rubinkam, M. (2014, May 18). Grade-school math has parents flummoxed. Associated Press. Reprinted in the *Las Vegas Review-Journal.*

Axiom 2: A school curriculum not only reflects, but also is a product of its time.

Something happens, then something else happens. Stuff happens. Events overlap. Societies change. People move. Scientific innovations, pandemics, war, and the media change the way we perceive the world. Consider the changes in technology, the environment, and population shifts that have occurred in your lifetime. Did any of these shifts cause a change in the school curriculum?

Axiom 3: Curriculum changes made at an earlier period can exist concurrently with newer curriculum changes at a later period.

You're probably familiar with educational reform being likened to a pendulum. School curriculum swings from one extreme to another, back and forth—from learning basic skills in math, to new math concepts, and back; from emphasis on direct instruction, to classrooms that are student centered, and back; from phonics, to whole language, and back. Ideas fall out of favor at some point and then later are embraced as exactly what is needed. Teachers who have been trained in one method of instruction often resist the newer methods being promoted. New teachers are often eager to try the latest innovation. No doubt you are aware of some of the back-and-forth swing of curricular ideas in your own history of schooling. Ask your grandparents or parents what curriculum was important when they went to school. Is it similar to what you experienced? Dissimilar?

Axiom 4: Curriculum change results from changes in people.

Alice Miel, in *Changing the Curriculum: A Social Process* (1946), wrote, "To change the curriculum of the school is to change the factors interacting to shape that curriculum" (p. 10).

Teachers enact curriculum. They translate words on a page into meaningful lectures, demonstrations, or projects for students. Reading the curriculum for *Sesame Street* and seeing the curriculum come to life through Big Bird and the Muppets are two very different experiences. When educators want the curriculum to be changed, they must also help the teachers who will translate the curriculum to change their instructional practices. Sometimes it is even necessary for parents and the entire community to change their attitudes and beliefs about what should be taught and how it should be taught. Anyone involved in creating changes in curriculum must him- or herself change. Are you aware of any curriculum changes in your high school? If there were changes, how were they received by parents and the community?

Axiom 5: Curriculum change is effected as a result of cooperative endeavors on the part of groups. Teachers, professional planners, and curriculum developers must work together to effect positive curricular change. Significant curriculum improvement comes about through group activity.

Margaret Mead's famous quote, "Never doubt that a small group of thoughtful, committed citizens can change the world. Indeed, it is the only thing that ever has," can be applied to groups of people who come together to develop a curriculum that will meet the needs and expand the learning of students in any specific time or place. Hilda Taba's (1962) idea for a curriculum based on key concepts, organization, and facts was practiced and perfected by groups of educators who saw Taba's ideas as a way to teach critical-thinking skills in social studies to K–8 students. In 1969, this was a positive change in teaching the social studies curriculum, and it was made possible by a "cooperative endeavor on the part of groups" (Oliva & Gordon, 2012, p. 33). Consider how groups of people may have made changes in the curriculum you experienced as a student.

Axiom 6: Curriculum development is basically a decision-making process.

Choices have to be made—what content should be included or excluded? What curriculum best serves the needs of the local society? Decisions about instructional methods need to be made. (How did you learn to read?) The types of programs that will exist in the school must be determined. How will classes and grade levels be organized? How will the teachers work to ensure that all students have an equal opportunity to learn? "What knowledge is of most worth?," Herbert Spencer asked in 1860, and that question has echoed through American education ever since: Policy makers, school administrators, and teachers wrestle with what students should know and be able to do.

Axiom 7: Curriculum development is a never-ending process.

Once you've got it the way you want it, it's time to go back to the drawing board. Curriculum planners must constantly monitor the curriculum they have developed to make sure it is fulfilling its original promise and is not creating unforeseen problems. As you read in Chapter 7, there have been good ideas in teaching and learning and ideas that were not so productive. Keeping track of what a curriculum poses to accomplish and the final results in student learning from that curriculum is of utmost importance in determining if the curriculum should be modified. Students constantly ask teachers, "Why do I need to know this?" When curriculum is well developed, the answer should be easy.

Axiom 8: Curriculum development is a comprehensive process.

Curriculum planning should not be piecemeal, patching, cutting, adding, plugging in, shortening, lengthening, or troubleshooting (Taba, 1962). If one aspect of the curriculum is out of whack, the whole curriculum can be a disaster. Every aspect of the curriculum must be taken into consideration: Oliva and Gordon (2012) advise curriculum planners to be aware of the impact of curriculum development not only on the students, teachers, and parents directly concerned with a programmatic change, but also on the innocent bystanders, those not directly involved in the curriculum planning but who are affected in some way by the results of planning. Can you think of a time in your education when a curriculum seemed confusing or irrational?

Axiom 9: Systematic curriculum development is more effective than trial and error.

Having a final goal in mind, just as state-established core standards aim for a final result, will direct curriculum development to a productive end. The whole picture should be apparent from the beginning. Just as a talented sculptor sees the form inside a block of stone, curriculum developers must be able to see through the existing curriculum to envision something more meaningful, effective, and purposeful, and then follow a specific set of procedures to achieve the desired goal. Results from curriculum changes do not happen overnight or at the rapid pace school administrators would like, so changes in curriculum may occur more often than would benefit any long-range systematic plan. How often did you see curriculum change in your own educational journey?

Axiom 10: The curriculum planner starts from where the curriculum is just as the teacher starts from where the students are.

What has come before should not necessarily be tossed aside. Preexisting ideas and modes of delivery may have some merit that will fit into new ideas for curriculum. Perhaps all that is needed is a reorganization of current practices and future goals. If a spiral curriculum for the development of math skills has been carefully developed, then it will not make sense to eliminate one section of the spiral and expect students to move forward through the curriculum with all the required skills and knowledge. Most drastic changes are caused by trauma. Young students and their teachers do not need to experience the stress that could result from a poorly conceived curriculum.

Viewing curriculum as one side of a coin and instruction as the other side can help you understand the close relationship between the two. One side cannot exist without the other.

Teachers Making Curriculum Come Alive

A very talented teacher you will meet in Chapter 12, Ms. Lynn, is especially able to weave different strands of curriculum through multiple forms of delivery and make learning fun for the students. She combines detailed planning and management to provide her students a hands-on experience in understanding anatomy and other scientific concepts. She plans for extending their newly acquired knowledge and skill through additional curriculum. Both curricular projects require the teacher to preplan extensively and garner a wealth of resources. The lessons are fun and memorable for the students, but more important, they set an example for the students of enjoyable ways to learn, to investigate, and to solve problems. It's likely that the students who participate in these projects learn to be aware of indicators of their own knowledge base and how it is acquired. Translating curriculum into action is similar to writing a lesson plan, though the perspective is not so much on objectives as it is on making ideas come to life, to be intriguing to students, and to motivate them to learn what is required.

TEACHERS' LOUNGE

IS IT *STRONCKIUM* OR *STRONTIUM*?

David Stronck

When I was teaching high school chemistry, I emphasized with my students the need to learn some basic facts. To help them, I often used a little drama and lighthearted discussion to connect with their youthful humor. For example:

1. I explained that many of the recent "man-made" transuranium elements are named after famous recent scientists: curium (for Marie Curie), einsteinium (for Albert Einstein), nobelium (for Alfred Nobel), fermium (for Enrico Fermi), mendelevium (for Dmitry Mendeleyev), lawrencium (for Ernest Orlando Lawrence), and so on.

2. I explained that the most-feared of the common radioactive dropouts from the explosion of an atomic bomb is the isotope strontium 90. The radioactive form of the element strontium can replace the element calcium, which is the next element in its family on the Periodic Table.

3. Strontium 90 can fall on grass, be eaten by cows, become part of milk, and replace calcium in the bones of humans. These humans may eventually die of cancer of the bone.

My students then reported back to me their great fear of "stronckium 90." (My last name being Stronck made for an easy pun. As much as I protested that the element of concern is *strontium* and that there is no element called stronckium, they insisted that since some of the elements are named after great scientists, the correct name must be *stronckium*.)

I lost this argument and was unable to teach my happy students the correct spelling of *strontium*. I admit that I overemphasized some facts because they seemed more interesting to me. Although I failed to teach my students correct spelling, I hope they have remembered more through their playing with words. Perhaps emphasizing fun facts with my students and giving them some freedom to "argue" with the teacher over interpretations have been effective strategies.

Another example of science teaching with humor happened when my colleague, Dr. Michele Korb, asked her students, who are candidates to become elementary school teachers, to draw pictures of their stereotype of a "science teacher." When I walked into the classroom, they immediately saw me as matching their stereotype.

—Dr. David Stronck
Professor Emeritus
California State University, East Bay

Teachers who incorporate engaging curriculum projects and then share them with other teachers are following Hilda Taba's (1962) plan for curriculum development. Teachers may be handed a curriculum guide when they begin their careers, but the lessons they create to help students meet standards and benchmarks can be produced only by spending time with learners, knowing their abilities and interests, and knowing the content.

Accountability Measures Through Standards, Benchmarks, and Curriculum

Schools and, to a greater extent, teachers have always been held accountable in some manner for student learning. Accreditation agencies, local school districts, and state and national departments of education demand some sort of evidence of teacher effectiveness before initial licensure and tenure of teachers. In the past, evidence of teacher effectiveness was based mainly on supervisory reports conducted by administrators and standardized tests of teacher competencies. Now, evidence of student learning based on accountability measures identified through standards and curriculum goals will be used to determine teacher effectiveness.

Value-Added Assessment of Teacher Effectiveness

That teachers are accountable for student learning is a reasonable claim. However, it is difficult to pin down credit for student learning to a specific teacher's actions over a specific period. The variables that determine student academic achievement comprise physical, mental, and emotional aspects that might be, at any given moment, unrelated to a teacher's actions. In value-added assessment of teacher effectiveness, statistics are used to determine an individual student's potential results on standardized tests. In any year that a student's results exceed his or her potential, the teacher is viewed as contributing to the student's academic growth (i.e., being effective). Such statistics can be used by school district administrators and departments of education to determine teacher retention and merit pay for teachers.

The effort to determine the effect of teacher behavior on student academic achievement has been around since 1971. In 1996, Sanders and Rivers stated that effective teachers could be distinguished from ineffective teachers through rigorous research methods. In 2010, the Bill & Melinda Gates Foundation released initial results from a yearlong study indicating that value-added assessments could determine teacher effectiveness. Some school districts have adopted the practice of value-added assessment for teachers though using statistical analyses; the results of student test scores have never had unanimous support. Teachers often respond to claims that test scores can be used to determine their effectiveness by countering that test scores can be influenced by time of day, noise level, hunger, and even the weather. It seems likely that the debate on ways teacher effectiveness can be determined will continue throughout your professional career. Whichever way the debate unfolds, it is in your best interest to recognize the professional standards by which your effectiveness might be judged.

School Accountability

When accountability is not met through standards and curriculum, policy makers must examine current practices and find some way to change or improve existing practices. In 1955, Rudolf Flesch published *Why Johnny Can't Read*. This publication forced curriculum developers to examine current instructional practices in reading. In 1983, Flesch published a second attack on instructional practices in reading, *Why Johnny Still Can't Read*. That same year, President Ronald Reagan's National Commission on Excellence in Education published *A Nation at Risk: The Imperative for Educational Reform*. Such publications did much to heighten professional and public awareness that standards and accountability were necessary in order for the nation's educational programs to improve. As concern over problems in the education system increase, so will efforts to hold teachers and schools accountable through establishment of standards and benchmarks.

Accountability is not an evil construct with which to badger schools and teachers. If we are not held accountable for our actions and for the result of our actions, then what is the value of our efforts? Many believe that education is the great leveler in the field of life. Standards that can help students navigate this field successfully should be embraced. Standards that help teachers become more effective and a greater force in student learning should be met. Standards that can help schools be shining examples of American education should be integrated into every phase of the school curriculum. Accountability is nothing to worry about when standards, benchmarks, and curriculum are designed for student success and are followed with the creative flare only teachers can bring to translating them into instruction.

CONNECTING TO THE CLASSROOM

Students frequently ask, "Why do I have to learn this?"

Explaining that they have to learn something because it will be on the test or that they will use the information sometime in the future doesn't seem to carry much weight with students. When students ask why it is important to learn something, they want to know how it will be important *now*. Effective teachers—teachers who are successful in getting students to learn the standards-based curriculum—are masters at relating whatever content they are teaching to the students' here and now, creating ways to tie the content to students' lives, to make the standards relevant.

When you hear a student asking a teacher, "Why do I have to learn this?" pay attention to how the teacher responds.

1. Does the teacher's response engage the student's thinking?

2. Does the teacher ignore the question and continue on with the lesson?

3. What seems to be the most common teacher response?

4. Following the teacher's response, does the student appear more interested in the content? Why or why not?

SUMMARY

Four major topics have been addressed in this chapter:

- Standards: the statements that indicate what students should know and be able to do at specific points in their education

- Benchmarks: the intermediate goals that guide students toward achieving standards

- Curriculum: one of the key concerns in education, which provides the link between standards statements and instruction

- Accountability: the way schools, teachers, and students can show they have met standards, benchmarks, and curriculum goals

KEY TERMS

National STEM Standards 306

standards 297

CLASS DISCUSSION QUESTIONS

1. Discuss ways teaching with a focus on local, state, and national standards can help students learn specific concepts.

2. Effective teachers must also meet standards for teaching by reflecting on their practice and the behavior of their students in order to improve their instructional practices and student achievement. Name some of the ways focus on teacher standards can affect student learning.

3. Think back to your own experiences as a learner. Describe one time when you were trying to learn something one

way and someone else tried to teach you the same thing in another way. Were you confused by the idea of two different approaches to learning the same thing? Did having another perspective on how to learn it make you understand the concept or idea better?

4. How did your teachers reinforce your new learning? Were you ever aware as a student that the results of your learning were evidence that you were meeting standards and achieving specified benchmarks?

SELF-ASSESSMENT

What Is Your Current Level of Understanding and Thinking About Standards, Curriculum, and Accountability?

One of the indicators of understanding is to examine how complex your thinking is when asked questions that require you to use the concepts and facts introduced in this chapter.

Answer the following questions as fully as you can. Then use the Assessing Your Learning rubric to self-assess the degree to which you understand and can use the ideas presented in this chapter.

1. How many types of standards can you explain?

2. What is the relationship of benchmarks to standards?

3. Why is it important for teachers to understand national, state, and local standards for student achievement?

4. What conditions influence the changing nature of the school curriculum?

What is your current level of understanding? Rate yourself using this rubric.

Assessing Your Learning Rubric

	Parts & Pieces	Unidimensional	Organized	Integrated	Extensions
Indicators	Elements/concepts are talked about as isolated and independent entities. Some important names are provided in isolation.	One or a few concepts are addressed, while others are underdeveloped, or not mentioned.	Deliberate and structured consideration of all key concepts/elements.	All key concepts/elements are included in a view that addresses interconnections.	Integration of all elements and dimensions, with extrapolation to new situations.
Standards, benchmarks, and curriculum	Names some standards and benchmarks without explaining relationships.	Describes basic role of standards but not of benchmarks and curriculum.	Describes multiple roles of standards in curriculum design and implementation.	Describes standards and benchmarks at all levels and relates these standards to present curriculum practices.	Describes ways standards can affect student learning and teaching practices.

FIELD GUIDE
FOR LEARNING MORE ABOUT . . .

Standards, Curriculum, and Accountability

In Chapter 1, you were introduced to the concept of a field guide for learning more about your surroundings. The artifacts and information you will collect for this part of your field guide will involve the evidence of standards-based curriculum in the schools and classrooms that you visit during your teacher education program.

Ask a Teacher or Principal	Ask a teacher to talk about ways standards can facilitate the planning process. How do teachers incorporate the Common Core State Standards into instruction?
Make Your Own Observations	Join a department meeting as the teachers plan a lesson or lessons for a specific content area. Note how often the teachers refer to standards as they plan these lessons. How often do they refer to particular students or groups of students and consider how they may have to differentiate the instruction to meet the learning needs of these students?
	After you have observed the planning session, visit one of the teachers' classrooms to see how the standards and curriculum are expressed through instruction.
Reflect Through Journaling	One of the reasons people give for becoming teachers is the desire to enter a field where their creative talents can be expressed. Discussions of standards-based curriculum can often dampen teachers' creative spirit. Write in your journal about ways you want to express your creative spirit in the classroom and how you might be able to do this even in an environment of standards.
Read a Book	*Creating Standards-Based Integrated Curriculum*, by Susan M. Drake (2007, Corwin), provides a wealth of information on accountability in standards-based curriculum and standards-based interdisciplinary curriculum, and offers a process model for designing curriculum.
	Understanding Common Core State Standards, by J. Kendall (2011, McREL; Association for Supervision and Curriculum Development), offers educators an overview of the ways the Common Core State Standards can improve teaching and learning across the United States.
Search the Web	The website www.corestandards.org explains the Common Core State Standards in an easy-to-follow format. On the **Teachers Pay Teachers** website (www.teacherspayteachers.com), you can view a curriculum map that includes all of the Common Core State Standards for second graders.
	For a small price, CorePlanner, the Common Core State Standards Lesson Planning website at **http://coreplanner.com**, will provide you with the tools to create a lesson plan around Common Core State Standards and allow you to track your lessons.

(Continued)

(Continued)

Standards for Professional Education Areas	• American Association for Health Education (AAHE)—**www.cnheo.org/aahe.htm** • American Association of Physics Teachers (AAPT)—**www.aapt.org** • American Council on the Teaching of Foreign Languages (ACTFL)—**www.actfl.org** • Association for Childhood Education International (ACEI)—**www.acei.org** • Association for Education in Journalism and Mass Communications (AEJMC)—**www.aejmc.org** • Association for Educational Communications and Technology (AECT)—**www.aect.org** • Association for Middle Level Education (AMLE)— **www.amle.org** • Council for Exceptional Children (CEC)—**www.cec.sped.org** • International Literacy Association (ILD)—**www.literacyworldwide.org** • International Society for Technology in Education (ISTE)— **www.iste.org** • International Technology and Engineering Educators Association (ITEEA)—**www.iteea.org** • Modern Language Association of America (MLA)— **www.mla.org** • Music Teachers National Association (MTNA)—**www.mtna.org** • National Art Education Association (NAEA)— **www.arteducators.org** • National Association for Bilingual Education (NABE)— **www.nabe.org** • National Association of Biology Teachers (NABT)— **www.nabt.org** • National Association for the Education of Young Children (NAEYC)—**www.naeyc.org** • National Association for Gifted Children (NAGC)— **www.nagc.org** • National Association for Multicultural Education (NAME)—**http://nameorg.org** • National Business Education Association (NBEA)— **www.nbea.org** • National Council for the Social Studies (NCSS)—**www.ncss.org** • National Council of Teachers of English (NCTE)— **www.ncte.org** • National Council of Teachers of Mathematics (NCTM)— **www.nctm.org** • National Science Teachers Association (NSTA)—**www.nsta.org** • Society of Health and Physical Educators (Shape America)— **www.shapeamerica.org** • TESOL International Association—**www.tesol.org**

STUDENT STUDY SITE

Ⓢ SAGE edge™

Get the tools you need to sharpen your study skills. **SAGE edge** offers a robust online environment featuring an impressive array of free tools and resources.

Access practice quizzes, eFlashcards, video, and multimedia at **edge.sagepub.com/hall3e**.

11 MANAGING THE CLASSROOM AND STUDENT BEHAVIOR

TEACHER INTERVIEW

Mrs. Sara Boucher

Meet Mrs. Sara Boucher. She teaches robotics and computer programming to seventh and eighth graders at Los Lunas Middle School in Los Lunas, New Mexico. Los Lunas is a small village about 30 minutes south of Albuquerque with an estimated population of 15,500. The residents are mainly white and Hispanic or Latino. There are 16 schools in Los Lunas: 1 charter school, 10 elementary schools, 2 middle schools, and 3 high schools. Los Lunas Middle School is the only middle school with fewer than 800 students. The 32 students in each of Mrs. Boucher's classes use an iPad cart or a computer lab for completing their work. Four students are assigned to one Raspberry Pi. This low-cost, credit-card-sized computer uses a standard keyboard and mouse and enables students to learn how to program in languages like Scratch and Python.

LEARNING OUTCOMES

After reading this chapter, you should be able to do the following:

1. Formulate a management approach (style) that is compatible with your personality.

2. Explain the ways classroom management facilitates teaching and learning.

3. Demonstrate how the use of data on student behavior can help teachers determine the effectiveness of their classroom management plans.

4. Show the connection between teacher knowledge and national expectations for classroom management.

Q: What brings you joy in teaching?

A: What brings me the most joy in teaching is the relationships I build with students. I love working with students and having them share all of the amazing things that they do in and out of school. A good teacher is one who can build and maintain relationships with his or her students. I love getting to know my students. When coming back from a break or day off, it is always nice to hear about their weekends or how they did a great job in their classes. It really brings me joy to get to know my students more and more each day.

Q: What do you do to make sure that all of your students are learning?

A: To ensure that all of my students are learning and understanding, I will check in with them as often as I can. We often reflect at the end of class to see how they felt about the lesson and the assignment for the day. I use this time to reflect and see if the students are learning or if we need to reteach. If we do indeed need to reteach, I do my best to reteach the students who need it or the whole class if necessary. My students are the ones who guide my lessons and are the ones who help me understand if they are learning or not.

Q: How do you keep track of each student's progress?

A: I keep track of each student's progress the old-fashioned way with a grade book. Having so many students makes it difficult to reach each of my students during each class period.

I do my best to check in with each student every few days—more if necessary. If I notice a student is not turning in work or is struggling with a specific unit, I will give him or her time to work on it or come in for clarification. We are required by the administration to record two grades a week, so this allows me to visually see how students are doing and help them as soon as I see them struggling.

Q: **What behavior management strategies do you use with middle school students? Which strategies seem to work best?**

A: My behavior management style is based off of Love and Logic (www.loveandlogic.com), and strategies in Lemov's book, *Teach Like a Champion*. I have used these strategies since I started teaching and have found them to be effective no matter the grade level. The strategies I have seen work the best are "Neutralizing Arguments With the Brain Dead Technique" from Love and Logic and "Do It Again" from *Teach Like a Champion*. The Brain Dead technique is when you provide a student who is arguing with a one-liner that reminds him or her that you will not argue. A one-liner I use most often with students is "I know, but what did I say?" so that they understand I will not argue and no convincing on their part will convince me otherwise. The "Do It Again" strategy is when you find their work is not up to standard and you have them do it again until it is correct. I often use this strategy within the first day of a specific lesson to set the high expectations in my classroom.

Q: **How do you manage instruction and the time constraints of conducting multiple classes in a day?**

A: Luckily, I get to teach two different classes where the material is the same for both classes. Within the first few weeks, I figure out if some classes will move along quickly and others will move slower through the material. I adjust my lessons to fit the needs of each of my classes by providing more or less material depending on the needs of the class. My lessons always include a bell ringer, introduction to the material, time to work on the assignment for the day (alone or with peers), and finally a wrap-up of material and standards we went over for the day. During their work time, I come around to help individual students or groups on their work from helping debug coding to showing ways to connect their Raspberry Pis for the lesson. This model of instruction allows me time to see how students are using their time in my class and what parts of a lesson I can adjust for the next class.

Q: **How do you learn as a teacher?**

A: As a teacher, I learn by watching and doing. In our district, I get the opportunity to visit different classrooms to see different teaching styles as well as different ways to manage behavior. After observing other classrooms, I will debrief with a teacher and see how I can incorporate his or her strategies into my own classroom. I also learn by reading blogs and watching videos of other teachers using strategies I am not familiar with. I am a very hands-on and visual learner, so having videos or watching other teachers helps me learn.

Questions to Consider

1. Think back to your days as an elementary, middle, or high school student. What was it about the classroom that was most appealing to you? Why?

2. What does "being in command of the class" mean to you?

3. How might asking your students for input on homework contribute to effective classroom management?

4. What type of feedback would you most like to hear from your students following a lesson?

5. Do you think there could ever be too many organized procedures in a classroom?

INTRODUCTION

Winston Churchill once said, "We shape our buildings and afterwards our buildings shape us" (1943). It is also likely that teachers shape their classrooms and then the classrooms they have created shape the learning that occurs there as well as the behavior of the learners. What every teacher wants is a classroom of students who want to learn, who feel good about being in school and about what they do when they are there. Expert classroom management can make that desire become a reality.

All schools, classrooms, students, and teachers are not the same. What works in one setting or for one group of learners may not work for another. School days begin and end on different notes, and the times in between are strung together by a variety of events that can perplex even the most experienced teachers. Each day in a classroom unfolds through actions and reactions influenced by environmental impacts, emotions, expectations, and sometimes frustration. Some people believe that what happens is inevitable and outside their control. Others may believe they have some degree of control over what happens. A teacher with a strong locus of control probably has a better chance of creating a well-managed classroom than a teacher who believes everything that happens in the classroom is beyond the teacher's control.

Teachers must develop plans for managing their classrooms that create a comfortable atmosphere for the students and teacher to work in that allow for professional and personal choice, and that are acceptable within a given school culture. Any classroom management system must support teaching and learning, recognize individual needs and desires among students, and encourage growth of acceptable behaviors. Every teacher holds an ideal classroom in mind. The challenge is to make that classroom come to life through knowledge of oneself, through an awareness of the wide range of techniques and strategies available for building a management plan, and through communicating with students to inform them of that vision.

Learning about ways to manage a classroom and why certain teacher behaviors can be beneficial while others might be detrimental to teaching and learning will help you begin to articulate a plan for the way you want your classroom to look, feel, and function.

Developing a managing plan requires the same skills you use to plan a lesson. You have to have a goal in mind. You need to establish objectives and implement instruction that will help the students achieve the objectives. There needs to be an assessment of student success in meeting the objectives and reaching the desired goal so that you can evaluate whether the plan is actually working. This chapter will help you begin to envision a management plan.

WHAT IS CLASSROOM MANAGEMENT?

Classroom management covers a wide range of actions and attitudes associated with teaching and learning. Educators discuss classroom management from differing perspectives, but these perspectives all take into consideration the interaction among students, teachers, and the content to be taught in an effective learning environment. The importance of establishing and enforcing rules, of room arrangement, of easy access to materials and resources, and of interactions with parents is seen as part of any well-managed classroom. We learn from Ecclesiastes that there is a time for many events in a person's life. So it is with managing a classroom. There is a time to learn, to laugh, to be silent, to rejoice, to think, and to play. All of the emotions of the students and the teacher become part of the gestalt of classroom management.

iStock/skynesher

There is a world of difference between a well-managed classroom and a chaotic one. Teachers and administrators usually prefer the former.

Will Weber (1994), the late professor of classroom management at the University of Houston, defined classroom management as a complex set of strategies that a teacher uses to establish and maintain the conditions that will enable students to learn. Wong and Wong (2014) view classroom management as everything that teachers do to organize students, space, time, and materials. Iverson (2003) defines classroom management as "the act of supervising relationships, behaviors, and instructional settings and lessons for communities of learners" (p. 4), and views management as separate from discipline in that discipline refers to "teaching students how to behave appropriately" (p. 4). To Evertson and Emmer (2013), classroom management involves a series of decisions teachers make to create classroom communities where students are engaged in worthwhile activities that support their learning. Lemov (2010) views management as teaching students to do something right through building relationships that are "nontransactional."

Establishing and maintaining an effective learning environment through management of space, time, instruction, and behavior requires a teacher to have expert knowledge of the learners, the content, and the context. Teachers' ideas about classroom management often go through a series of transformations as the teachers observe, learn, and reflect on the success of the management plans they have enacted. The way a particular teacher chooses to manage a classroom also derives from a specific system of values and priorities for attending to a range of educational functions. As you develop your personal professional philosophy of teaching, introduced in Chapter 7, you will most likely include some of the ideas you have for managing a classroom.

If one considers the alternative to managing a classroom, which is *chaos*, effective classroom management can be viewed as central to all that is good and right about teaching. Since the responsibility for managing a classroom rests almost entirely on the teacher's shoulders, this is perhaps the main reason that managing a classroom is often cited as the number-one concern of beginning teachers. Such concern is not just a recent phenomenon in education. Consider the following excerpt from D. H. Lawrence's (1915) novel, *The Rainbow*, in which Ursula Brangwen begins her teaching career and is faced with the daunting task of managing the behavior of her students.

> The day passed incredibly slowly. She never knew what to do. There came horrible gaps, when she was merely exposed to the children. . . . Before this inhuman number of children she was always at bay. She could not get away from it. There it was. This class of fifty collective children, depending on her for command, for command it hated and resented. It made her feel she could not breathe: she must suffocate, it was so inhuman. They were so many, that they were not children. They were a squadron. She could not speak as she would to a child, because they were not individual children, they were a collective, inhuman thing. (pp. 355–356)

Ursula's experience may seem a bit extreme and out of the ordinary, but it is a rare teacher indeed who has never felt outnumbered or outmaneuvered by an unmanageable group of students. Teacher education candidates can take comfort in the fact that a modicum of knowledge about human behavior and skill in implementing management strategies can provide even a novice teacher some degree of self-confidence and competence in managing a classroom. It is a huge undertaking, but it does not have to be overwhelming.

Listening as Part of Classroom Management

Perhaps the beginning of any type of management is to listen. We spend so little time, in this age of technology, listening to one another. Conversations, when they happen, are abbreviated to questions easily answered by a quick search on the Internet or by a short phrase. However, children do hear most everything their parents, teachers, and friends say. They may not react to what they hear, but they do listen and begin to form impressions and knowledge from what they have heard. Certainly, students hear what teachers say to one another and listen intently when the teachers are talking to one of their friends. In *Into the Woods*, the Witch sings the song "Children Will Listen" to offer this advice: "Careful the things you say, children will listen. Careful the things you do, children will see and learn." This is certainly good advice to all of us, and especially important for new teachers thinking of establishing management plans. Teachers who are aware of what they say and how it might be interpreted by their students are more likely to build trust with students. A teacher who knows how to listen and then models listening by listening to the students may overcome any barrier there is to peaceful and productive classroom management.

Being a great teacher is about making connections directly with each and every student. If you want to know how to reach, engage, and best teach your students, ask them (Aguilar, 2016). In addition to being a vital social skill, listening is essential to learning. Hudson (2017) lists five reasons why listening is important for teachers: to show respect for and motivate your students; to find out what's really going on with your students; to be an effective role model; to be the best kind of support for your colleagues at school; and to help you with parent conferences.

Mrs. Boucher talks about getting to know her students, finding out what they are doing, and sharing their lives with them. This cannot be accomplished without time spent listening to what they have to say. Classroom management involves all of the tasks that teachers and students perform in any given day, and listening to one another must be part of any classroom management plan.

Using What You Already Know About Classroom Management

In learning theory, the technique of activation or the use of advance organizers helps bring the students' full attention to what they are about to study. For example, if a teacher wants to teach a science lesson about weather, he might ask the students to recall a time they experienced stormy weather. He will talk about the sound of the wind moving objects around or the sound of rain and the smell of ozone or dust in the air. These are all things students will be familiar with, and recalling the memory of them will help students build a **cognitive framework** of weather to include additional information.

Likewise, we've all had some experience with management. If you've ever packed a suitcase, loaded a car, decorated a house or a room, planned a wedding or birthday party, or been shopping, you probably already have a good idea about the importance of organization, time management, and access to resources. If you have spent any time at all working with young children, you no doubt know quite a bit about behavior management. You've also spent considerable time in classrooms observing how other teachers organize tasks and activities and manage the behavior of their students. You've spent time communicating with others regarding ways to manage your actions and the actions of others. You are familiar with all types of management, and it is nothing to fear.

Frameworks for Learning About Classroom Management

Performance in managing a classroom does not rest entirely on rules, routines, rewards, and reprimands, but it is a far more complex combination of all that a teacher is, knows, and does. As an aspiring teacher education candidate, you need to recognize the relationships between teacher dispositions, teacher Pedagogical Content Knowledge that Lee Shulman (1986) termed PCK, and a teacher's management skills. You also need to reflect on your responses to others' behavior. Some behaviors will upset you more than others do. Ask yourself why. Make a list of "What Gets My Goat." Figure out how to respond to these irritations in a professional manner, and you may be surprised how your calm demeanor, in the face of difficulty, will affect the classroom climate and your ability to manage.

Three Areas of Classroom Management

Content management includes planning the physical environment, deciding on the procedures that will occur during the instructional day, and instruction. Planning is the key. Teachers plan during the summer break for the coming school year. They plan on weekends. They plan before and after school, and during free periods. The planning that teachers do has a profound effect on instruction, student behavior, and the relationships that are formed with and among their students. You will learn more about the planning cycle in Chapter 13.

Conduct management is maintained through the establishment of rules and guidelines of behavior. Three to five rules for appropriate behavior seem to be the ideal numbers. How these rules are established depends on grade level, the teacher's philosophy of classroom management, and what is considered acceptable behavior in the school. (See Table 11.1.) "Be nice" is a little vague for a rule. A

TABLE 11.1 ■ Examples of Classroom Rules (Elementary, Middle, and High School)

Some rules of conduct are appropriate for all grade levels—for example, *Treat other students the way you would like to be treated.* Some variations are required to address the specific behaviors and attitudes of different age groups.

Elementary Classroom Rules

Speak softly

Be ready to listen

Ask before you act

Middle School Classroom Rules

Work to succeed

Be on time and tidy

Respect other people's property

Act as if your grandmother is watching

High School Rules

Have high expectations for yourself

Be positive

Respect the rights of others

Use MP3 devices only for academic work

fifth grader might interpret "Be nice" as an invitation to chat with whoever is within earshot, while a high school senior might choose to "be nice" by doing a friend's homework. Rules and procedures must be taught so that students know how to succeed in the classroom.

Children in different grade levels react in different ways to rules, regulations, and procedures, so naturally what works in a kindergarten class to get students' attention may not work in a middle school class. Experienced teachers have found out that each developmental level has a set of typical behaviors that help determine which strategies teachers can use to their best advantage. Third graders tattle. Fourth graders will do everything the teacher does. Middle school students will do whatever their friends do, and high school students usually make behavior choices based on a combination of the norms set by the school administration, their teachers, and their peers. Whatever rules are agreed upon and posted for all to read, they need to be discussed with all students, explained, and reiterated from time to time.

Covenant management is about managing relationships, having highly developed communication skills, and knowing ways the combined effects of content management and conduct management will influence interactions in the classroom. The relationships teachers are able to build with students, their parents, and the other teachers and staff in a school often provide a safety net when management problems arise. Any teacher who uses good listening skills, exhibits a willingness to understand another person's perspective, and treats students with **"unconditional positive regard"** (Rogers & Freiberg, 1994)—letting students know that it is their behavior meeting with disapproval, not them—will be viewed as caring and thoughtful. Teachers who make the effort to build personal relationships are usually given more leeway when they must make difficult management decisions that might clash with what the students desire or what parents consider just. A copy of a checklist for implementing covenant management is provided in Table 11.2.

The Personal and Parental Effect in Classroom Management

From the first day of school, teachers should greet their students by name, make one personal comment to them each day, and note individual efforts and achievements in social, personal, and academic

THINKING DIFFERENTLY
BUBBLE CHAIRS

© Leanne Montgomery

Teachers know that movement is management. Teachers know that it is impossible to keep an eye on each and every student from any one location in a classroom, so they move around. However, while the teachers move, the students are required to be still, pay attention, and not disrupt the class by moving around. Movement is key to both physical and mental health. Every health or sport magazine touts the benefits of exercise and movement for all age groups. Movement is also comfortable and can be refreshing, yet students are often required to sit on hard-surface, straight-backed chairs for extended periods with little relief except maybe to tilt these chairs back on two legs, or to crouch on them to a teacher's dismay. There are some classrooms with a "Sit Anywhere" policy, and thoughtful teachers provide beanbag chairs and carpets for a respite from the institutionally designed hard chairs most classrooms contain. Is it any wonder that when the recess bell rings or the end of the school day comes, most students rejoice with the freedom to move?

Educators from California State University, San Bernardino, presented a paper at the 2018 annual meeting of the American Educational Research Association on ways a classroom might be transformed if each student was given a bubble to sit on—a bubble with a back and legs and wheels. According to the study, the bubble chairs had a positive effect on learning and behavior, and according to the manufacturer, Gaiam, its stability ball chair promotes a healthy posture and keeps the mind focused. Sound like a good thing?

TABLE 11.2 ■ Checklist for Implementing Covenant Management
For solutions to discipline problems
☐ 1. Listen to the student as you discuss the misbehavior.
☐ 2. When it is necessary to discipline a student, focus only on the current behavior.
☐ 3. Elicit student input about the behavior.
☐ 4. Work with the student to develop a plan to improve his or her misbehavior.
☐ 5. Commit to the plan. Shake hands on it.
☐ 6. Sometimes plans go awry. When they do, discuss the misstep and move forward.
☐ 7. Do not punish or criticize the student for failed plans.

Source: Adapted from Froyen, L. A., & Iverson, A. M. (1999). *Schoolwide and classroom management: The reflective educator-leader* (3rd ed.). Upper Saddle River, NJ: Prentice-Hall.

areas. Teachers who make an effort to communicate with parents will learn from the insights parents can provide about their children. Parents should be viewed as being in partnership with teachers in the education of children. Parents love their children and want them to be successful. Let parents know how much you appreciate the gift of their children that they entrust into your care each day. "By 2010, 41 states had adopted licensure requirements that include parent, family, and community components" (National Education Association, 2011).

Suggestions for helping teachers communicate with parents include but are not limited to the following:

- Encourage parents to spend time in your classroom
- Chat with parents when they pick up their child after school

- Invite active parents to bring along another parent when they visit your classroom

- Call a parent you don't know well and ask for help

- Give parents your phone number or email address

The Paradoxes of Classroom Management

In many ways, the concept of classroom management can be seen as paradoxical. It is inconsistent to implement classroom management practices focused on rules, rewards, and punishments when the curriculum encourages problem solving and critical thinking. Students must be orderly but active, be curious but follow the directions of the leader, and be self-motivated but follow established rules and guidelines. Management should be student centered and culture centered yet meet the norms of the local educational community, and build interpersonal relationships yet get the job done. This list of conflicting ideas could be endless.

Effective classroom management requires expert decision making by the teacher, and the multitude of decisions a teacher must make in any given day must be based on a clear understanding of a wide range of educational goals determined by the teacher as well as entities beyond the classroom. Here, then, is another paradox of classroom management: If management is a decision-making process, how can it be reduced to a set of recipes? And if it can't be reduced to some guidelines, what is a beginning teacher to do? It really is difficult to move someone else's experiences into your own instinctive behavior. To do this, you have to work hard at understanding the behavior of others. It is so much easier to learn firsthand with the support of a mentor or expert guide. Think about this: When you take public transportation across a large city unfamiliar to you, you must consult schedules, stops, and routes on your smartphone or with paper maps. If you go with a friend who has made the trip many times before, it's a breeze, and you learn and will be better at making the trip on your own next time.

HOW DO YOU BUILD A PERSONAL PHILOSOPHY OF CLASSROOM MANAGEMENT?

Before you begin to think about building a personal philosophy of classroom management, complete this exercise. Name three things that you would like to change about your own behavior. Describe how you would go about changing the behaviors. Describe a simple technique that you have used to help you relax or relieve stress. Ask yourself if you could practice this technique in a classroom while you were teaching students. Building a personal philosophy of classroom management must naturally begin with a clear understanding of ways you manage your behavior and why you do what you do.

Establishing a personal philosophy of classroom management also requires a certain level of knowledge of some of the common models and theories that surround the concept of classroom management. With an understanding of the basic tenets of numerous models, any teacher education candidate can begin to incorporate specific strategies and key elements from each model into a personalized perspective. Most of us try out new skills beginning with what feels comfortable for us or with what we think might work given past experiences and personal attributes. In that respect, learning how to manage a classroom is not much different from learning how to snowboard. There are certain things you should know before starting out, and there are many things you will learn along the way. Attempting to learn can either meet with resistance or create heat, but both should be fun. Here are some of the theories you should be familiar with when learning about classroom management.

iStock/Steve Debenport

Teachers who spend time listening to their students are able to build personal relationships with them.

Theorists, Theories, and Models

Teachers as well as teacher education candidates have access to a wide range of classroom management methods. While having many choices is nice, making the right ones in a highly charged classroom situation is challenging. The best-prepared teachers become familiar with many approaches and are ready to act effectively when called upon to do so. Each theory or model of classroom management discussed in this section can serve as an advance organizer for a set of strategies and teacher behaviors. You may be learning or have learned some of the philosophical and psychological underpinnings of the theories in course work associated with human learning and development and psychology.

As you read about these models, make notes on which strategies you would most like to incorporate into your own personalized classroom management style. As Madeline Hunter (1994) wrote in response to criticism of her *Instructional Theory Into Practice* model, "Models are judged on their ability to guide behavior, predict outcomes, and stimulate research, not on being the final answer to the establishment of any one method" (p. 36).

Behavior Modification

Behavioral psychology tells us that behavior is learned and can be modified through positive reinforcement, punishment, extinction, and negative reinforcement. Burrhus Frederic Skinner, as discussed by Wattenberg (1967), is most often associated with the ideas of behavior modification in classrooms. The most common use of Skinner's theories is the idea of positive reinforcement—providing students with tangible rewards or praise for completing work or demonstrating acceptable behavior. The expected outcome is that when children are rewarded for acceptable behavior, they will continue to exhibit that behavior, and nonproductive behavior will be "extinguished." Positive reinforcement can be a powerful classroom management tool; however, there is disagreement in the professional community about the effect continued use of extrinsic rewards will have on self-motivation.

One of the most common mistakes in the use of behavior modification strategies by teachers is the practice of taking back a reward once it has been earned. For example, if a teacher distributes "behavior bucks" to students who are following directions and then demands that they be paid back to the teacher when directions aren't being followed, or if marbles are put in a jar when the whole class is doing a good job, working quietly, or staying on task and then marbles are taken out of the jar when the opposite occurs, a reward that has been earned is being taken away. This practice only serves to reinforce a negative attitude in students toward working for a goal. If the goal might be moved or removed entirely, the uncertainty of attaining it would negate even trying for it in the first place. Consider how many of us would run a race without a clear understanding of the finish line. Even a race car driver going around and around the track knows how many laps to the checkered flag.

Assertive Discipline

Lee and Marlene Canter (1992) established a system to manage behavior that relies, in part, on a set of hierarchical consequences. In their **assertive discipline** model, teachers must insist upon responsible behavior from students. The most easily recognized example of assertive discipline in elementary classrooms is the use of a set of colored cards for each student, usually kept in individually named pockets on a wall chart. When students display irresponsible behavior, they are directed to rearrange their individual cards from green, to yellow, or to red. Each colored card represents a corresponding consequence. Ask any student in any classroom in America, and they have probably had some experience with the Canter model of behavior management.

In middle schools and high schools, students are often directed to write their names on the board if misbehavior occurs and to place tally marks after the name if the misbehavior continues. This method makes it easier for middle and secondary teachers to keep track of student behavior over time given the frequent change in class venue. Keeping track of student behavior is a prerequisite to changing it. Tracking behavior and the effectiveness of interventions to improve behavior is a critical aspect of any kind of classroom management plan. And it is one of the most difficult things for teachers to stay on top of in light of their already taxing schedules.

One suggestion for using the ideas behind the Canter model in a more positive manner would be to develop a scale more directed toward building students' control of their own behaviors to emulate

Teachers often use a behavior chart to help students stay on task.

personal learning and success in the classroom rather than to avoid consequences. Such a self-awareness scale might involve different colors and terms that when students are asked to check their behavior they make choices on ways to improve. A general practice is to use green, yellow, and red colors. Students begin each day on green. Infringement on rules or behavior would require the students to switch to a yellow card for caution. Further unacceptable behavior would lead to a red card and some sort of consequence. Some teachers opt to use different colors though the normative colors are green, yellow, and red. For example: I need to listen before I speak, I will follow directions, I should spend some quiet time at my desk, I will finish my work on time, I will do better tomorrow, or I feel good about my behavior today. Mrs. Boucher uses a "Do It Again" strategy to help her students learn new content. The same strategy works wonders to help students learn new behavior strategies. When students know what you expect from them and what they should expect of themselves, they will most often adjust their behavior accordingly.

Social-Emotional and Group Dynamics Management Approaches

Classroom management methods based on the theories of group dynamics and social psychology, and **judicious discipline**, a philosophy that creates an environment respectful of the citizenship rights of students (Gathercoal, 1997), focus on the importance of membership in a group, the need for individuals to control their own behavior, and the need for teachers to provide guidance and create environments conducive to a candid exchange of ideas. William Glasser's (1997) **choice theory** model calls for teachers to help students satisfy their five psychological needs (the need for survival, the need to belong, the need for power, the need for freedom, and the need for fun) so that students can choose appropriate behavior individually and as a group. Glasser believes that performance is raised by doing what's real, responsible, and right (Sullo, 2011).

Quay and Quaglia (2004) suggest providing opportunities for students to be leaders in the classroom and to take responsibility for their choices. For example, when students feel that they are an important part of the classroom, that their opinions matter, that they have the chance to lead, and that they are held accountable for their decisions, increased enthusiasm for learning can be the result.

The **democratic classroom** uses class meetings to engage students in shared decision making and in taking responsibility for building a democratic learning environment. Democratic classrooms depend on a teacher who recognizes the worth and dignity of every person, who can build a sense of community within the classroom, and who has the ability to build positive relationships with students, parents, and members of the professional community. Teachers employing democratic classroom strategies view students as social beings who want to be accepted into the group, and use encouragement rather than praise to direct student behavior. Robert Sylwester (2003) argues that a democratic classroom provides an excellent venue for brain maturation. The Epoch Teacher website (https://epochedu cation.com/) claims to be the number-one resource for culturally responsive teaching.

The Class Meeting

The students in Mr. T.'s second-grade classroom participate in a class meeting every Thursday morning. Students sit around the edges of a large square carpet to one side of the classroom. Since the last class meeting, students have written agenda items on pieces of paper and placed them in a jar on Mr. T.'s desk. These agenda items range from altercations between students, to complaints, to suggestions students have for changes in classroom procedures, to suggestions for topics they would like to study. Before the first topic is pulled from the jar and the meeting begins, Mr. T. reminds students of the procedures for class meetings:

1. The person who placed the topic in the jar will explain why it is important.

2. Three students who wish to react to the topic will be chosen by the class president.

3. These three students will express their comments within the two-minute time limit.

4. At the end of the comments, the topic initiator will be allowed to respond.

5. If a vote is deemed necessary, the class president will ask for a show of hands.

6. The decision of the class is final and must be abided by, except in the case of what to study. What to study is not up for grabs in a student vote.

7. The class meeting will last only 30 minutes.

8. Any issues not resolved at this meeting will be dealt with the following week.

As the meeting begins, Mr. T. moves outside the square of students and intervenes only if students request assistance in resolving an issue. Mr. T. admits that the class meetings take time away from instruction, but he firmly believes that the conflict resolution skills his students are developing along with respect for others is knowledge that all students should learn. Classroom meetings such as the ones in Mr. T.'s second-grade class are an example of the shift from a teacher-centered classroom to a classroom in which the teacher and students share leadership responsibility.

Instruction and Communication Approaches to Classroom Management

Communication models of classroom management rely on the teacher's ability to provide effective instruction and to shape the classroom environment through effective communication that facilitates positive behavior and fosters harmony and cooperation. In such classrooms, teachers talk to their students like the sensitive, intelligent individuals they are. Teachers refrain from using threatening comments and sarcasm, they guide rather than criticize, and they learn to let some misbehavior slip by.

TEACHERS' LOUNGE
CLASSROOM RHYTHMS

© TaLisha Givan

In classroom management, procedures and routines are vital. However, getting to know your students is equally important. I remember in my fifth-grade classroom, I would often use music in order to manipulate the mood of my students. On those days when the sun was blazing overhead and my students were squirming in their chairs while trying to wait for recess, I would use a piano sonata or instrumental saxophone CD in order to calm their mood. And, on those days when it seemed as if they were lacking the amount of energy I needed for a particular assignment or group work, I would use an upbeat, faster-paced music piece in order to pump up the mood. While using music often accomplished my goal, I had a particular student who still, regardless of the music manipulation, lacked any spirit in my class. She was very quiet and very sweet but, despite my efforts, still had no energy.

One morning, I used the old song "Can't Get Enough of Your Love, Baby" by Barry White because of its awesome groove and rhythm. I looked up to see that same student who constantly lacked motivation dancing in her seat. She was alive and had a great smile on her face that I had never seen. I was so excited! I took that "open door" to inquire about why that song made her dance. She stated that that song was her dad's favorite song, and they often danced to that song together before he passed away two years prior. On that day, regardless of our classroom procedures and routines, I had found a way to reach that one student. Mission accomplished!

—Dr. TaLisha Givan
Henderson State University
Arkadelphia, Arkansas

A class meeting is an effective management strategy for helping students solve individual and group behavior problems.

When teachers learn to use Gordon's (1989) **I-messages**, which avoid any negative or neutral use of the word *you*, and to use the principles of **active listening**, by intentionally focusing on whom they are listening to, they show respect for students' needs, interests, and abilities.

D. W. Johnson and Johnson (1999b) advocate cooperation as the key to promoting a well-managed classroom and propose the three *C*s (cooperating, conflict resolution, and civic values) as the basis for effective learning environments. Visit the website of the Cooperative Learning Institute at the University of Minnesota to learn more about the three *C*s of school and classroom management.

For Evertson and Emmer (2013), classroom management becomes routine once rules and expectations are made clear and instruction is well managed and related

UNDERSTANDING AND USING DATA
REVIEWING DATA ON TIME SPENT ON MANAGEMENT TASKS AND ON CLASSROOM INTERRUPTIONS

Teachers have to plan and implement strategies for starting each day, and maintaining a purposeful pace throughout the day keeps students focused on learning and completing required tasks. The Stallings (1990) Time Spent on Organizing and on Classroom Interruption checklist provides teachers with a snapshot of the time that it actually takes to complete certain management tasks as well as tracking instructional time that is lost during interruptions. The checklist is easy to complete and summarize, and analysis of the data provides instant information about events that are, to some extent, out of the classroom teacher's control but influence instructional activities.

Tracking the rate at which instructional time is diminished through poor classroom management can help a teacher gain a greater awareness of the value of efficient and effective routines. Actions or behaviors that infringe on the finite amount

of time for teaching and learning in any given school day can have an accumulative effect on student opportunity to learn. An average school day begins at 8:55 and ends at 3:06. With time reserved for lunch and transition between specialists, the amount of time for classroom instruction is roughly five hours a day.

Your Task

Use the data on the Time Spent on Organizing and on Classroom Interruptions checklist below to analyze approximately how much time can be consumed by management in an average school day. What conclusions can you draw from the data? Is the teacher represented on this checklist an effective classroom manager?

TIME SPENT ON ORGANIZING AND ON CLASSROOM INTERRUPTIONS				
School:	Teacher:	Observer:	Time	Time
Observation of Classroom Organizing				
Taking attendance			8:57	8:58
Collecting lunch money			8:57	9:00
Collecting homework or seatwork			8:57	8:58
Making assignments for seatwork			9:50	9:54

TIME SPENT ON ORGANIZING AND ON CLASSROOM INTERRUPTIONS				
School:	Teacher:	Observer:	Time	Time
Observation of Classroom Organizing				
Making assignments for homework			2:55	3:05
Distributing books and materials			9:05	9:07
Explaining activities and procedures			9:00	9:05
Organizing groups			1:15	1:18
Shifting from one activity to another			10:20	10:22
Disciplining students			9:45	9:46
Students enter late			9:10	9:12
Students leave early			2:30	
Parents enter			2:27	2:30
Administrator enters			11:10	11:15
Other visitors enter		Observer	8:55	
Loudspeaker announcements			9:00	9:05
Special sales		Fifth graders selling tickets to drama extravaganza	2:15	2:25
School events				
Outside noise				

Source: Adapted from Stallings, J. A. (1990). *Effective use of time program.* Houston, TX: University of Houston.

This teacher has spent approximately 30 minutes of the day managing class activities and getting ready for instruction. The short times spent for each management routine add up, and at the end of a week, two and half hours of instructional time have been lost.

Your first question after considering the data could have been "Why does it take the teacher a minute to take attendance?" Good question. Establishing a routine that has students entering the room for the first time in the morning and moving a tag with their name or picture on it to a designated slot would make it possible for a teacher to take attendance at a glance. Homework should also be placed in a designated folder at the same time that each student marks his or her attendance.

A second question about the amount of time spent making assignments is certainly called for. Assignments for seatwork can be on the board or in folders located at centers around the room. And the same goes for homework assignments. Time at the end of the day should be spent summarizing what was learned during the day while homework assignments should be given immediately following the related instructional episode.

Too much time seems to be consumed when moving from one activity to another or getting students ready for group work, in this example. Time can be saved here by well-established routines and procedures. When students know what they are supposed to do when they enter the classroom, arriving late should not cause an interruption, and students who have been taught how to get ready for group work can certainly do so in less than three minutes. Teachers may have little control over the interruptions that come from outside the classroom, but there is no crime in placing a "Do Not Disturb" sign or a "Testing" sign outside the door when the teacher feels any interruption would be detrimental to student learning.

The teacher represented on this checklist is no doubt conscientious and aware of the benefits of a well-managed classroom. Collecting data that would indicate the time actually spent in organizing and in interruptions can only serve to help her improve her professional practice.

to the individual needs and talents of the students. In this well-managed classroom, it is vital that teachers recognize the relationship between their own behavior and that of their students and understand the support classroom management provides for instruction.

Kohn (2006) invites teachers to move beyond rules, to understand the needs of children and how these needs can be met. This seems a reasonable challenge given the diversity of culture and backgrounds represented by students in classrooms today. Visit Alfie Kohn's homepage at www.alfiekohn.org for a better understanding of the ideas of *Beyond Discipline: From Compliance to Community*.

No one shoe will fit all. We learned that from the story of Cinderella. The students you will meet in your future classrooms will possess skills society has only begun to imagine. Additionally, the technology that is shaping student thinking and behavior is creating changes the profession has yet to fully understand. As you meet these children and lead them to ever higher levels of understanding, consider ways that order in your classroom and increased student learning can be maintained by a range of positive approaches.

Principle 5 of the InTASC Standards (see Chapter 1) states that the teacher uses an understanding of individual and group motivation and behavior to create a learning environment that encourages positive social interaction, active engagement in learning, and self-motivation. It is not too soon for you to begin to acquire a more in-depth understanding of the many theories surrounding classroom management.

CHALLENGING ASSUMPTIONS
WHAT MATTERS MOST IN CLASSROOM MANAGEMENT?

The Assumption

Many beginning teachers worry most about their ability to manage the movement and behavior of their students. They have heard horror stories and observed unfortunate examples of teachers who have little or no effect on getting students ready for learning. Having no control over a classroom is a frequent concern of teacher education candidates. Cooperating teachers who work with practicum or student teachers may advise them to begin the year with a stern and strict attitude, and to reserve smiles for later in the year. Experienced teachers often advise new teachers not to become a friend too soon. So what really works in classroom management, and how is a new teacher to approach this aspect of teaching?

The Research

There are probably as many approaches to managing a classroom as there are teachers who implement one course of action or another. What approach works for each teacher really does depend on individual attitudes and capabilities. Certainly, having a high level of self-efficacy is important. Teachers who view themselves as capable of managing a classroom are more likely to be successful doing so than a teacher who is unsure. One way researchers have approached the study of effective classroom management is to observe teacher behaviors and document those behaviors that result in positive student actions and attitudes.

The study cited here looked at two teachers who represented contrasting styles of classroom management. One teacher used

an authoritarian style of classroom management, and the other used a style that encouraged students to take responsibility for their own behavior. Three variables—student interactions (behaviors), teacher questioning, and quality of teaching—were used to analyze the effectiveness of the teachers' management styles. Both teachers used lower-level questioning skills, and it was determined in the study that the overall quality of instruction was poor. The study found that neither of these two teachers' classroom management styles effected "consistent positive student interactions." The study concluded that the "quality of instruction is central to the interplay between student's interactions and teacher's classroom management practices."

Implications

While this study is very small in scope, and perhaps the teachers who participated in the study did not employ the most effective instructional strategies, it does provide a small piece of evidence regarding the connection between management style and instructional practices. When students are engaged in learning, they are more likely to exhibit positive behaviors. The success of the approach a teacher uses for classroom management may be highly influenced by the instructional practices that are in place. Teachers who teach well usually have few problems with classroom management.

Source: Jeanpierre, B. J. (2005). Two urban elementary science classrooms: The interplay between student interactions and classroom management practices. *Education, 124*(4), 664–676.

WHAT CONSTITUTES A WELL-MANAGED CLASSROOM?

Perhaps a well-managed classroom begins by helping students figure out the rules and the consequences for classroom behavior, and by teaching them how to have some control over managing themselves. Most of us want to decide stuff for ourselves. As we're growing up, someone else is always telling us what to do or is giving us advice on what actions we should take. Sure, advice is helpful, but much of the time, it is just annoying. Kids want to try things for themselves. Smart teachers establish some parameters for behavior and then allow a little wiggle room inside the set parameters. They spend a good deal of time watching students interact with others and listening to their conversations. Smart teachers create a community in their classroom where everyone is important and everyone has a role to play. The teachers at my first school as a teacher were required to eat lunch with their students. Each class occupied a long table. Lunchtime was spent in casual conversation with students while we learned important facts about one another and came to see ourselves as a part of a group.

William Morris (1834–1896) might have said that décor is what makes a home a thing of beauty and a joy forever. While students spend almost as much time in school as they do at home, schools are built from a utilitarian viewpoint, with maintenance and durability the determining factors of what goes where. Nearly all classrooms are rectangular in shape. Most have windows, though it is cheaper to build schools without windows. The desks, bookcases, shelves, and tables in classrooms are institutional in style and by themselves don't offer much in the way of décor. Teachers are wonderfully creative people, however, and have the power to turn a somewhat bland environment into a scintillating palace of learning. Wise teachers let the students help build the environment that is the most comfortable for their needs and expressive of their individual and group personalities, while the teacher keeps in mind simply that room arrangement should promote learning in every nook and cranny.

Room Arrangement

The arrangement of a classroom can contribute to the responsibility students may feel toward a specific classroom. If it is a pleasant place to be, a place the teacher seems happy in, a place to be proud of, a place where significant things happen, then students are likely to perform in ways conducive to learning. The placement of furniture and materials in a classroom can also contribute significantly to instruction. Jones (2003) discusses the "interior loop" of a classroom and describes the ways in which room arrangement relates directly to fewer behavior issues.

In order for classroom arrangement to support learning, students need to have a clear view of the focal point for instruction. The teacher must be able to move easily around the classroom to monitor students' work, and materials and resources should be easily available to keep lessons moving. Teachers need to identify traffic routes and be ever on the lookout for obstacles that would impede movement or create a management problem.

Evertson and Emmer (2013) offer five key elements to good room arrangement:

Use a room arrangement consistent with your instructional goals and activities.

Keep high-traffic areas free of congestion.

Be sure students can be easily seen by the teachers (and vice versa).

Keep frequently used teaching materials and student supplies readily accessible.

Be certain students can easily see instructional presentations and displays. (p. 13)

Classroom arrangements are dictated by the size of the classroom, the number of students, and the types of furniture in the room. Teacher education candidates can be asked to draw a floor plan of what they believe would be a perfect classroom and then describe why they arranged it the way they did.

Helping Students Be Comfortable in the Room You Have Arranged

Students need to know what is expected of them, how to act in certain situations, and what instructional purposes are assigned to different spaces in the classroom. Everyone wants to know what is his or hers. So, helping students find their own space and become comfortable in it might be one of the first orders of building a productive teacher–learner relationship. In order for this to happen, students should be taught everything from how to enter the classroom, to where personal possessions should be kept, to how materials should be passed out and collected, to rules regarding the teacher's personal space. When students understand what they must do and why they must do a certain thing a certain way, they have a tendency to do what is expected.

Hardly anyone learns a thing perfectly the first time it is taught. Rules and regulations that are taught and learned on the first day of school or during the first week will no doubt have to be reviewed from time to time to reinforce students' comfort in your classroom. Reteaching can take the form of gentle reminders or practice accompanied by a clarification of the goals and intended outcomes for the procedure. Certainly, some things that were stressed at the beginning of the year may change, but once a teacher has established a process for learning a procedure, future changes to the procedure will be simplified.

Managing Paperwork

Have you ever stood in a post office and watched folks empty out their mailboxes? There is usually someone standing near a huge wastebasket throwing away what is commonly referred to as "junk" mail. Even the advent of the digital age and email has not appeared to reduce the amount of paperwork that floods our lives. As a student, you have more than enough experience dealing with paperwork. Mostly, you learn to organize paperwork in files (paper and digital), notebooks, or stacks. Dealing with paperwork can seem like a never-ending job. One of the benefits of technology is the way it can reduce paperwork, though losing a file on a computer or misplacing a thumb drive can be as easy for the disorganized person as losing a piece of paper.

Developing a plan or system for handling the huge amount of documents and other paper forms associated with teaching is absolutely necessary in order for the management of paperwork not to interfere with effective instruction. The first step in dealing with documents, records, reports, and resources is to create one or more filing systems. Efficient filing systems provide ways of tracking individual student performance and progress, organizing forms and letters that are used on a regular basis, organizing lesson materials (plans, assessment criteria, teacher reflections on success or shortcomings of lessons, student evaluations of lessons, and resources), dating entries, and keeping track of schedules. Technology helps, but teachers have to establish a mental picture of where every item is stored.

Technology for Managing the Classroom

Technology can make managing the classroom a breeze. Paperwork is kept to a minimum, and information is processed and stored without the teacher having to worry about losing data that is supposed to make its way to the central office. Any teacher can develop an electronic format for keeping track of student information. Spreadsheets can be filled out by students at the beginning of the day and entered into a database by an aide, a parent helper, or even a student helper. Teachers and students can keep in touch during the day through Twitter or email. Don't laugh. Twitter or email communication may cut down on interruptions from students when the teacher is working with a small group or with a single student. Teachers often require that students with burning questions ask them of other students in the classroom before they ask the teacher. Putting the question on email would be one additional step in thinking through the question and perhaps coming up with an answer before requiring the teacher's assistance.

Teachers have to keep track of books, supplies, borrowed resources, and schedules. Amazingly, teachers have the capacity to keep all of that information stored in a special part of the brain teachers have for miscellaneous information. Even though teachers can come up with all the right answers at the right times, it would be comforting to know that the information was stored somewhere else and that it could be accessed by other people without the teacher having to stop what he or she was doing or thinking about to find a specific piece of information within a well-developed teacher cognitive framework. Computer programs provide great storage places for documents and information. And, when they are connected to a printer, a clean copy of any document can be produced even if the first one had someone's lunch spilled on it.

Creating a Technology-Rich Learning Environment

Creating a technology-rich learning environment should be part of planning how your classroom will be arranged. Technology can help you easily create spaces that are rich in sound and visual experiences. If a fish tank or pets are not allowed in classrooms, screen savers can provide scenes that are visually calming. A required text for your grade level can be saved electronically on individual tablets and notebooks. Students can read the text aloud to one another or quietly to themselves. No more "I can't find my book!" when students own their personal copies of study material.

Music can be anywhere the teacher wants it to be. MP3 player docking stations can add a dimension of soothing baroque strains to calm the wiggliest students. A teacher might keep a digital camera available for students

Teachers can bring peaceful and inspiring images from the world into the classroom.

to take pictures of meaningful moments, within guidelines of course. There should be areas in each classroom for play, for meetings, and for contemplation. With a little imagination and help from technology, even the smallest classroom can provide a productive learning space for all of the students.

Students Managing Their Own Paperwork

Teach students to manage their assignments. Even first graders can keep a folder of the week's work in their desks. Teach them to arrange items chronologically. This can be done easily on a blog. Students can learn to check their email or the class blog for assignments and return them to the drop box created for electronic documents. Students can be held responsible for making entries in an electronic homework log to assist the teacher in keeping track of individual student progress. Once you have established a routine for handling assignments in hard copy or electronically, you will have more time for instruction, and the students will have more time for learning.

Imagine this:

As students enter the classroom, they approach the classroom computer console and click on the square after their name to mark their attendance in class. The time and date are registered automatically in the teacher's electronic grade book and in the central office of the school. When the students take their seats, homework assignments are scanned and evaluated on their individual desk consoles by programs designed to recognize correct responses. Within minutes of the first bell, the teacher receives a printout showing who has done what and how well. From a technology station at the front of the room, the teacher can post grades and send private messages to students who might need clarification of the grade. The teacher can also schedule times to visit privately with individual students about their work and attendance. While these messages are being sent, the teacher has directed the students to a National Geographic website where they are to read about the Alashan Plateau section of the Gobi Desert as an introduction to the unit on natural deserts. Questions for discussion are listed on the board. Little time is wasted. The students are engaged in learning, and soon a lively, thoughtful, and informed discussion is taking place about barren landscapes, fragile soils, and scarce water sources.

A Multidimensional Look at Classroom Management

Some components of a classroom never change. While the characteristics and behaviors of the students may change as society changes and as digital tools become more commonplace, the dynamics of a classroom of students appear to follow well-established norms. Doyle (1986) described five dimensions of classroom life that provide a framework for theorists, researchers, and practitioners to study the myriad events and interactions that can occur in any given time span in classrooms. Doyle's five dimensions—(1) multidimensionality, (2) simultaneity, (3) immediacy, (4) unpredictable and public climate, and (5) history—can also serve as a guide for teachers to develop and organize a range of management strategies that will address the activities they must orchestrate in any given day.

Multidimensionality

Classrooms are complex, tightly populated social structures. Many events take place, and every single action can result in multiple effects. This variety of events with multiple effects that occur in a classroom can challenge a teacher's ability to keep student attention focused and to manage student behavior. For example, the domino effect of one student reaching down to get something out of a backpack may disturb another student, with the result of an exchange of words that causes a student across the room to stand up to see what is going on. Which action is the teacher to respond to, if at all? Or enthusiastic comments from students working on a group project may create a wave of excitement that draws other students to see what all the talk is about. How does a teacher manage such a situation and keep learning at a peak?

Simultaneity

Many actions occur at the same time in a classroom. A teacher is aware of many actions occurring in the classroom and processes information on student behavior or idleness to adjust lesson pace, input, and interest to keep the attention of all students. Students are also aware of the teacher's response to them. Students make their own adjustments to the events occurring around them, and these adjustments may give rise to additional actions. An effective classroom manager must be aware of what students are paying attention to and constantly be aware of the impact the simultaneousness of events will have on the learning environment.

Immediacy

Life in classrooms is fast paced and up close, and some events must be taken care of immediately. The movement in a classroom is perpetual; some students move at a faster pace than others, but no one really stands still. Immediacy in the classroom can come in the form of a call over the intercom asking someone to report to the office, or students leaving the classroom at odd times for special programs; something is misplaced, a necessary book can't be found, a pencil is broken, or someone gets sick. Each day a teacher must respond to a hundred such interactions that often require immediate attention. Having routines and contingency plans in place can help both the teacher and students adjust smoothly to some of the immediacy of the classroom.

Unpredictable and Public

Everything that happens in a classroom is public, and many of the events that occur are unexpected. An experienced teacher once explained to her practicum students that the first time she meets with parents she tells them that she won't believe anything the children tell her about what happens at home if the parents won't believe anything the children tell them about what happens in the classroom. She was joking, of course, but her humor did illustrate the fact that everything that goes on in a classroom is very public and can be unpredictable. A teacher in a sour mood can overreact to a minor problem, and every student within earshot can hear and be ready to spread the word. Even the way a teacher responds to different students is viewed by many pairs of eyes. The teacher may smile and listen to one student, but turn away from another student in midsentence. Teacher behavior is always public and can have lasting effects on students and their ability to learn.

iStock/patchareporn_s

In a well-managed classroom, students can be engaged in a variety of learning activities while the teacher helps individuals.

History

History is a powerful force in any classroom and is constantly in the making. It takes a strong will and much determination to live down past mistakes or to change direction once a particular path has been chosen. Classroom histories are created as norms, and common understandings develop in a single class over a single year. What happens in the very beginning when a class is formed can have long-lasting consequences. The history of each classroom is often being constructed even before the school year begins. Parents will have swapped details of the teachers their children had the previous year and the classrooms these teachers managed. Judgments are being formed that will be either confirmed or dismissed as the year gets under way. The manner in which each teacher begins the year, how well he or she has planned for the multitude of activities that will take place within the first week, how well organized resources and materials are, and how the teacher deals with minor upsets or behavior malfunctions start a classroom's history.

Management of Movement on School Grounds and in Hallways

Movement in schools is almost constant. Students are moving between their own classrooms and other rooms in the school at regular and irregular intervals. Some schools do not allow students to move around the school alone or unsupervised while other schools may leave student movement outside of the classroom up to the discretion of individual teachers. The advent of school violence and dangerous weapons in the hands of elementary and secondary students has given rise to stricter rules governing student movement outside classrooms and to the utilization of metal detectors to ensure that harmful instruments will not be available to students on school property.

The freedom to move around in the school environment is carefully managed by administrators and teachers in the form of bells and hall passes and the event of a "lockdown." In high schools and middle schools, short periods of time are allocated for students to go from one class to another. Teachers or "hall guards" stand watch at strategic locations throughout the building during the break between classes. In elementary schools, teachers generally lead students to special classes such as music, art, or technology.

Teacher responsibilities include duties assigned by the administration to supervise large groups of students at recess or during lunch. As a teacher, you will spend many hours on the playground watching students interact and play games. You may learn to play four square and tetherball with students from your own classroom and from other classrooms. It is educational to observe the ways students behave outside of the classroom and to have conversations with students in a relaxed atmosphere. Playground, lunch, or hall duty should not be seen as drudgery or a responsibility to avoid but should be welcomed as an opportunity to learn more about your students.

Routines, Rules, and Schedules

Generally, people don't like a lot of rules, and some may say that consequences get in the way of creativity. When students begin to understand and have some role in determining what the consequence might be for a certain behavior, they are more likely to monitor their own behavior so that you can get on with the job of teaching rather than managing. Robert Heinlein has been credited with saying, "Don't spoil your children's future by making their life too easy." There should be rules and responsibilities for students to follow and some work to complete along the way. There are many bumps and pitfalls along the road of life. Students have to learn strategies for navigating these. Almost every day brings a new lesson.

Teachers can learn about their students through play while observing them on the playground.

Routines, rules, and schedules provide the framework in which our actions take place. When a routine is established, some of the uncertainty of life is laid to rest. Rules provide security. Rules and schedules relieve stress. They also encourage responsibility. Routines, rules, and schedules do not discourage spontaneity or creativity. The self-discipline that they encourage can give rise to disciplined expressions of creativity.

Rules provide guidance and clarity to routines. Who makes the rules should be determined for the most part by the person or people who are going to enforce them or monitor students' response to them. Keep in mind that any rule that is set forth may be scrutinized by students, parents, other teachers, and the school administration, and that the First and Fourteenth Amendments of the U.S. Constitution address students' and teachers' rights and responsibilities related to the establishment and enforcement of rules. Rules and procedures should be developed in conjunction with teaching strategies that help students meet their personal and academic needs. Table 11.3 lists specific requirements for classroom rules.

Some rules are predetermined, and everyone at school is expected to follow them. Some rules are determined by space and school structure. In most classrooms, rules are determined by the teacher with input from the students, and the smartest teachers allow the students to believe they are the ones who determine the rules. The possibilities for establishing and implementing classroom rules are endless and result from variables such as standards, student needs, and expectations.

Schedules form a framework for routines. Imagine getting through a day or a day at school without at least the semblance of a schedule. In fact, when schedules at school are interrupted, it doesn't take long for disorder to ensue. Getting from point A to point B in a timely manner depends mightily on a schedule. If a class of sixth graders is to be at an assembly at 9:45 a.m., the teacher had better have them in the gym and quietly seated at the time the assembly is to begin or suffer the consequences of reprimands by the principal or other teachers.

Schedules are usually set by school administrators and to some extent determine ways routines will be enacted in individual classrooms. For example, in a high school with block scheduling, or an A/B class schedule, routines take on quite a different shape than if classes meet every day for 55 minutes. A block schedule also provides extended class time and opportunities to enhance instruction through project work and role-playing experiences, thereby dictating the need for routines governing such activities.

The Characteristics of a Well-Managed Classroom

The characteristics of a well-managed classroom are usually apparent even to the untrained eye. Students are involved in academic work, they know what is expected of them, time in the classroom is used wisely, all work in the classroom is being conducted in a purposeful manner, and students are not disrupting one another. While the elements of a well-managed classroom are easy to understand, translating these characteristics into purposeful actions is a major undertaking for teachers. Just as important as laying the groundwork for a great beginning to the year, teachers have to plan and implement strategies for starting each day and maintaining a purposeful pace that keeps students focused on learning and completing required tasks.

Maintaining on-task behavior when students are actively engaged in learning is one of the most important responsibilities of a teacher. The more time students have to learn, the more chances they have for success. Many events can interfere with students' time to learn, and it is a teacher's job to anticipate and eliminate distractions that interfere with learning time. In

© Shawn Rossi

Rules should be brief, to the point, and posted where everyone in the classroom can see them.

TABLE 11.3   ■   Key Components of Classroom Rules
1. The rule must be publicized to students. Whether it is issued orally or in writing, school authorities must take reasonable steps to bring the rule to the attention of students.
2. The rule must have a legitimate educational purpose.
3. The rule must have a rational relationship to the achievement of the stated educational purpose.
4. The meaning of the rule must be reasonably clear.
5. The rule must be sufficiently narrow in scope so as not to encompass constitutionally protected activities along with those which constitutionally may be proscribed in the school setting.
6. If the rule infringes on a fundamental constitutional right of students, a compelling interest of the school (state) in the enforcement of the rule must be shown. (Reutter, 1975, p. 6)

order to accomplish this responsibility, teachers must possess knowledge of classroom management strategies and be able to implement procedures in an efficient and timely manner.

Students are compelled by law to attend public school whether they want to be there or not, and while at school the U.S. Constitution's Fourteenth Amendment of due process and equal protection under the law protects students in the classroom and ensures their rights to a full range of opportunities. Given that all students must be provided equal and a full range of opportunities to learn, a well-managed classroom may be the first step in making this goal attainable.

WHAT IS THE CONNECTION BETWEEN DISCIPLINE AND MANAGEMENT?

One view of discipline is gaining control by enforcing obedience or order. In this view, teachers are seen as enforcers or controllers. Another view of discipline sees teachers as the trainers or guides that help mold and develop student behavior. Discipline can also be viewed as a way to get students to change their misbehavior. When students misbehave, teachers must make decisions about how to manage the misbehavior. Managing furniture and classroom space is much easier than managing students' behavior. Students talk back. They disagree. They have their own ideas about what should be done and how it should be done. Managing behavior or disciplining students who have misbehaved requires communication and effective interpersonal skills.

Four Stages of Classroom Life That Influence Behavior

The classroom discipline landscape changes constantly throughout a school year. Within the framework of content, conduct, and covenant management described earlier in this chapter, Iverson (2003) describes four stages that can influence management and discipline in a classroom. The stages are (1) forming, (2) storming, (3) norming, and (4) performing. There are a number of effects that can disrupt these clearly delineated stages of behavior. One effect results from the rapidly changing demographics in America's schools. Another disruption can be caused by the frequent movement of students from one school to another. Rapid changes in the growth of students can also disrupt the stages. Fourth-grade students who begin the year as gentle beings may soon begin to show signs of the exuberance and impatience of fifth graders. Likewise, seemingly "out-of-touch" sophomores can become mature, thoughtful seniors. Little ever stays the same in elementary or secondary classrooms, and the more prepared teachers are to respond to the changing environments they will experience, the more competent they will become at exhibiting best practices. If a teacher changes positions or leaves in the middle of a year, the new teacher may find it necessary to revisit all of the stages that influence management and discipline with a specific group of students.

Forming

The forming stage takes place at the beginning of the year, when students are learning information about their new surroundings as roles and procedures are established. In some instances, this first stage presents a sort of "honeymoon" period when, for the most part, everyone is trying to put his or her best foot forward. The more effective the teacher is in content management at the beginning of the year, the longer the honeymoon period can last.

Storming

As the year progresses, students may begin to test the limits that have been outlined and through peer pressure or for some other reason begin to distance themselves from established norms of behavior.

Norming

Somewhere around the middle of the year, nearly all behavioral and management struggles have been reconciled, and the content and conduct standards have been accepted. There are few reasons for behavior problems to interrupt opportunities for students to learn, and both the teacher and students feel a sense of accomplishment.

Performing

During the performing stage, students exhibit self-reliance and self-discipline. They have formed close relationships with their classmates and with the teacher and can rely on support from them when needed. With expert teacher management, it is possible for behaviors associated with the performing stage to be evident throughout the school year. When teachers understand these stages, there is less opportunity to be caught off guard or frustrated by the changing climate of the classroom.

The Importance of Communication in Behavior Management

Most forms of management begin with talk. Teachers explain rules, they correct behavior, they give directions, and they issue instructions. The manner in which teachers conduct their communication with students can have an enormous influence on the ways their students behave. Mr. Spock's trademark salutation of "Live long and prosper" in *Star Trek* conveys an emotional message full of kindness and hope. Teachers should emulate Spock in the ways they communicate their desires and expectations to students.

Large class sizes, the number of details to keep track of, and so little time all contribute to decreasing the amount of friendly and polite conversation a high school teacher can have with students. Because some high schools are as large as towns, once teachers leave their familiar section of the school, they may seldom meet anyone they know. Knowing the names of the students they teach is a challenge in itself, and knowing the names and faces of the other 3,000 students in the school is close to impossible. A high school nurse indicated the number of traumas in any given day in her school far exceeded those cases that show up at a quick care medical facility in the neighborhood. Having the skills to communicate in positive and productive ways becomes exceedingly important in such environments.

All talk contains some type of emotional content. Imagine how boring communication would be if there was never any emotion in what people had to say. When teachers talk to students, when students talk to teachers, and when students talk to one another, the resultant messages are likely to contain emotional content that has the ability to shade the actual meaning of the words being expressed. Certainly, a pouting child or teenager can be

iStock/FatCamera

Teachers must consider tone, facial expression, and body language when communicating with students.

intimidated into saying what a parent wants to hear, but the emotional overtones in such a forced message can speak volumes in resentment and anger.

Every communication you have with your students is filtered through personal sieves woven together of hopes, fears, needs, and intellectual potential. When you talk to students, when you ask them to do something or to behave in a particular way, you must always be aware of the emotional impact your words will have. Learn ways to communicate that show you are aware of students' personal issues and that help the students also understand your concerns. Much of what we communicate to students comes through physical stance and tone of voice and contradicts the words we say.

Teachers must practice the art of giving their full attention to students who are speaking.

Basic Rules of Engagement

Listen, listen, listen, and listen some more. Otherwise, you might not hear what your students are saying. Two students come in from the playground or hallway, yelling and pushing one another, followed by a growing number of spectators. The great lesson you are ready to start will have to be postponed until tempers have cooled and you have defused the anger. What do you do? First, take charge. Give some orders in a low, clear voice. Send students from other classes back to their rooms. Tell your own students to go to their desks. If you are in an elementary grade, you might hold the hands of the two students who created the disturbance, keeping them near you. In high school, you might ask the students to remain standing by the door until you are ready to *listen* to them. State some rules. For example,

Each of you will be able to tell me in your own words what happened.

No one will be allowed to interrupt.

I will talk when you are finished.

Then you magically pull out the small circular disk you have in your pocket (one side heads, one tails), ask one of the students to choose heads or tails, and flip the disk. In a flash, what has happened on the playground or in the hallway becomes of lesser interest to most of the students than what is about to happen in the classroom. The key is that you have made decisions, the students know what to do, and you have not added to either student's frustration or humiliation. Now, do what your mother always told you to do: Take a deep breath, count to three, and listen.

When teachers listen actively to what the students have to say, they use a variety of response strategies. They make eye contact. They nod or make sounds indicating that they are taking in every word. They encourage students having difficulty expressing their thoughts to "Tell me more" or "Go on." Teachers who listen well don't interpret but try to identify with honest labeling the feelings and attitudes they are hearing. Teachers who are good listeners help students recognize how they feel and the ramifications of these feelings for themselves and for others.

HOW DO TEACHERS MANAGE THE STRESS OF MANAGING A CLASSROOM?

Managing a classroom and student behavior often results in stressful interactions and situations. Teachers often talk about the stress of keeping up with demands of their profession such as learning new programs, taking university classes, balancing the instruction and assessment components of student learning, and taking on teacher leadership responsibilities at their schools. They have so much on their minds that they can't fall asleep at night, and so they get up in the morning already stressed by their lack of sleep.

Student failure can cause teachers stress. Students don't know what or where they are going to be two years from now. They don't know how important what you are teaching them will be to their future lives. The learning comes from inside the kids, and they have to want to do the learning. They go to school to be cool, and you have to start from what is cool for the students. The stress of teaching can be relieved when teachers find out what each student can do and work from that point.

Many teachers are parents who have children they must help get ready for school as well as themselves. Some live long distances from their work, and driving to school causes additional stress. Stress can have long-term effects on the heart, mental well-being, and overall health. Teachers have to be healthy. They have to go to school every day, and they have to arrive there with a sense of well-being and mental acuity. Teachers must learn to manage stress as they have learned to manage their classrooms. A little support can go a long way in helping teachers manage their personal stress levels. Once they have managed stress, teachers can manage almost anything else.

Stress comes to students as well as teachers, and management problems can result from a buildup of anxiety in the classroom for no apparent reason. When teachers provide a small amount of time each day for students to take stock of their personal sense of well-being, students can better understand and deal with some causes of stress. Reflection in the classroom can take different forms such as journal writing, class meetings, writing comments for a suggestion box, or experiencing a few minutes of silent reflection time each day. When students are able to manage the stressful situations they encounter, teachers may also experience less stress.

Three Dimensions of Psychological Support for Teachers

The degree of psychological support teachers need in order to be successful, to be able to manage the stress of their profession, and to recognize the joy and rewards that come from teaching is threefold. The three dimensions of this support are emotional–physical, psychosocial, and personal–intellectual. When teachers don't deal with daily stress, it can gradually become overwhelming. Teachers need to be strong in mind and body.

Emotional–Physical Support

The emotional–physical dimension focuses on self-esteem, security, acceptance, self-confidence, and even the ability to resist illness. In psychology 101, we learned that the emotional stability of an individual can have a profound effect on the physical well-being of that person. A mild headache can lead to distraction and irritation at others, and a prolonged illness can render us incapable of coping with even the most routine events. Teachers' self-esteem is high when they know they are doing a good job and others acknowledge their successes. An administrator or fellow teacher who offers congratulations on a job well done is providing necessary emotional–physical support to keep the teachers happy and healthy.

Psychosocial Support

The psychosocial dimension focuses on an individual's need for belonging—for friendship, relationships, collegiality, and interactions with others. Teachers generally like people. They liked going to school as students and enjoyed the interactions they had with classmates and with their teachers. Becoming part of a school faculty and working with other professionals interested in helping children and youth learn can be a rewarding way to balance the stress that is a normal byproduct of living.

Personal–Intellectual Support

The personal–intellectual dimension relates to an individual's desire to grow mentally and professionally. When teachers are encouraged in the belief that they can make a difference in their profession, they assume responsibilities with eagerness and confidence. When teachers have opportunities to learn new methods and strategies to become more effective, they find self-expression in their work instead of stress. Teachers who are inspired by membership in a Professional Learning Community see the horizon, not the trench.

Laughter in the Classroom

There is nothing wrong with having fun in the classroom. Moments of unexpected laughter and fun are the ones we remember. Laughter can ease the strain of following rules and sticking to schedules. It can turn a tense situation into a lighthearted learning experience. It can relieve stress. School should be more fun than playing hooky. It might be okay to smile before Christmas, maybe even laugh a little. It doesn't mean becoming a stand-up comic or running a steady stream of knock, knock or elephant jokes. The line between teacher and student must be maintained. But maybe if your students see you as a happy person, they will be happy to be in your classroom.

CONNECTING TO THE CLASSROOM

Try the visualization exercise (described below) from Stallings's (1990) *Effective Use of Time Program* to create a personalized mental image of a classroom. When you have finished creating a mental image of your classroom, draw a picture of it. Then think about how your choices for placement of desks and other furniture match Evertson and Emmer's (2013) guidelines for effective use of classroom space described earlier in this chapter.

Visualize Your Classroom

1. With your eyes closed, visualize an empty classroom.

2. In your mind's eye, look carefully at the space you have to work with.

3. Imagine a space for the large group, a space for small-group learning, and a space for individual learning (a space where a student can be alone).

4. Decide on a place for your desk.

5. Think about sound: quiet places and noisy places.

6. Consider storage.

7. Think about what will be on the walls.

8. Think about putting some color in the room (red and orange for energy, blue and green for quiet, and purple for deep thought).

Remember that people space is more important than furniture space. Compare your room arrangement to the arrangement of a classroom you have recently visited. What are the differences? The similarities?

SUMMARY

This chapter on classroom management addresses a range of models and approaches to creating and maintaining an effective learning environment. An overarching theme of this chapter is that classroom management does not occur through happenstance. It requires teacher knowledge, skill, and a particular set of dispositions that recognize the individual worth of students and their right to an effective learning environment. Classroom management is also dependent on specific actions by teachers to communicate expectations to students and to enlist student acceptance of these expectations. Life in classrooms is complex and changeable. Developing the ability to manage such a dynamic environment is an essential function of learning to teach.

This chapter addressed five areas of classroom management:

1. The multiple tasks associated with classroom management and ways of categorizing them

2. Models of classroom management that require different teacher actions, and making decisions regarding which of the models will work within your personal belief system, a special group of learners, and the classroom environment

3. The physical and emotional components of classroom management

4. The relationship between management and discipline

5. The ways that stress resulting from managing a classroom and student behavior can be lessened through positive approaches and interactions with other teachers

KEY TERMS

active listening 332

assertive discipline 329

choice theory 330

cognitive framework 325

conduct management 325

content management 325

covenant management 326

democratic classroom 330

I-messages 332

judicious discipline 330

locus of control 323

unconditional positive regard 326

CLASS DISCUSSION QUESTIONS

1. We have all had the experience of managing something. We have organized our personal space and time and have arranged furniture to suit our tastes. Recall a time when you were required to manage something. How successful were you? What do you consider your strengths in making arrangements and in organization?

2. When you have had to include others in your plans, how did you convince them to go along with your ideas? What did you do to enlist their support? If someone disagreed with your plans, what did you do to change his or her mind? How did you make this person comfortable with your expectations?

3. Teachers are required to manage the behavior of students so that everyone in the group has the greatest opportunity to learn. When teachers are faced with difficult behavior issues that infringe on the rights of other students in the class, they must often enforce consequences that might seem harsh and unreasonable to the unpracticed eye. Think about a time when you observed a child or youth being disciplined that made you uncomfortable. How might you have handled the situation differently? What about the situation might have been unknown to you?

4. What about your life is most stressful to you? What do you do to manage that stress? Would this method of managing stress be appropriate for use in a classroom?

SELF-ASSESSMENT

What Is Your Current Level of Understanding and Thinking About Managing the Classroom and Student Behavior?

One of the indicators of understanding is to examine how complex your thinking is when asked questions that require you to use the concepts and facts introduced in this chapter. Answer the following questions as fully as you can. Then use the Complexity of Thinking rubric to self-assess the degree to which you understand and can use the ideas presented in the chapter.

1. Why is it important for teachers to develop a personalized approach to managing a classroom and student behavior?

2. How can building relationships with students and their parents help a teacher manage a classroom and student behavior?

3. What is one framework for thinking about classroom management that you believe matches your personal philosophy of teaching?

4. In what regard is communication a key component of managing student behavior?

5. Why is it important for teachers to learn ways to minimize stress in teaching?

6. What is your current level of understanding? Rate yourself using this rubric.

Complexity of Thinking Rubric

	Parts & Pieces	Unidimensional	Organized	Integrated	Extensions
Indicators	Elements/concepts are talked about as isolated and independent entities.	One or a few concepts are addressed, while others are underdeveloped.	Deliberate and structured consideration of all key concepts/ elements.	All key concepts/ elements are included in a view that addresses interconnections.	Integration of all elements and dimensions, with extrapolation to new situations.
Managing the classroom and student behavior	Discusses frameworks and theories in isolation from one another.	Describes basic approaches to managing a classroom only from a teacher's point of view.	Describes multiple ways classrooms and student behavior can be managed.	Describes multiple ways classrooms and student behavior can be managed for various purposes.	Describes ways the use of certain approaches to classroom management might influence and advance student achievement.

FIELD GUIDE

FOR LEARNING MORE ABOUT . . .

Managing the Classroom and Student Behavior

To further increase your understanding about today's students, do one or more of the following activities.

Ask a Teacher or Principal	Chances are that teachers in most schools lean toward different strategies for handling similar problems. Ask six teachers for advice on how to cope with a specific management problem, and you'll more than likely receive six or seven different responses. This can be somewhat confusing for a beginning teacher or for someone who has not yet developed a personal classroom management game plan, system, or approach.
	In the 1995 film *Dangerous Minds*, the protagonist, LouAnne Johnson, is desperately seeking ways to connect with her inner-city students. One scene shows LouAnne sitting in her apartment, taking notes from a classroom management book and then wadding up her notes and throwing them across the room. This scene could leave viewers with the impression that there was nothing in the book that was going to help LouAnne succeed as a teacher. But, in finally gaining the attention and respect of her high school students, she employs techniques and strategies research has shown to be effective in managing student behavior:
	She made her lessons relevant to the students' lives.
	She piqued their interest so they became engaged in learning.
	She rewarded their efforts.
	She showed them the respect she, herself, so desperately sought.
	Ask the teacher you are observing (or practice teaching with) how he or she addresses the four strategies mentioned above in his or her daily management of the classroom and student behavior.
Make Your Own Observations	Use the following grid to document the ways that the teacher you are observing manages different events during the day. Some—but not all—management concerns are listed on the grid. You may need to add some others that you observe. Choose one of the management strategies the teacher exhibits and ask how he or she learned and decided to use it.
	Events to Manage and How to Manage Them

Event	Management Strategy
Students entering classroom	
Beginning instruction/focusing attention	
Distributing materials/resources	
Monitoring students during guided practice	
Responding to individual requests	
Getting students ready to leave classroom	
Providing individual attention	

Reflect Through Journaling	Learn what experts or researchers have determined are important things to know and to know how to do in regard to classroom management. Include ideas, actual events, and observations in your journal. Write about how a particular teacher handled a particular event. Ask yourself if you would act in the same way. Consider how the students reacted. Mark down what happened, how the teacher handled it, and ways a particular student or many students reacted. There is no lack of information about classroom management strategies available. The teacher's task is to learn enough to know which of the multitude of strategies is worth testing or adapting, and which ones might work best for you.

(Continued)

(Continued)

Build Your Portfolio	What did the classrooms you most enjoyed as a student look like? What kinds of things happened during the day that made these classrooms comfortable places for you to be? Do you remember a teacher who seemed to take care of problems with little effort or without disrupting your learning? Did you have a teacher who made you laugh; made you look forward to each school day?
	Reflect on your responses to these questions and then describe how your ideal classroom might be managed. How might your classroom be arranged? What type of learning activities might take place? How might you interact with each of your students? Give reasons from your personal experiences and from what you have read about classroom management to support your rationale for the classroom you have described.
Read or Listen to a Book	*Setting Limits in the Classroom: How to Move Beyond the Classroom Dance of Discipline*, by Robert J. Mackenzie and Lisa Stanzione (2010, Random House), provides techniques on how to establish structure in your classroom.
	Listen to *Positive Discipline Tools for Teachers: Effective Classroom Management for Social, Emotional, and Academic Success*, an unabridged audiobook by Jane Nelsen and Kelly Gfroerer, narrated by Virginia Wolf, released on June 6, 2017.
Search the Web	The Internet is loaded with sites for teachers seeking information on classroom management and discipline. Conduct a web search to locate at least two sites that have information on different aspects of classroom management that interest you. Briefly describe what information on the sites you think might be of value to you in the future. Include the descriptions of the two sites in your portfolio. For example, you could visit **www.pecentral.org** to find out how to create a positive learning environment. Using the Internet as a resource should become one of your professional habits as a teacher.
Watch a Movie	If you haven't seen it already, you should watch *Dangerous Minds.* Just remember that it is a Hollywood perspective. Some events in the film must be taken with a grain of salt, though overall it does a good job showing some of the management problems teachers might face in inner-city high schools.

STUDENT STUDY SITE

$SAGE edge™

Get the tools you need to sharpen your study skills. **SAGE edge** offers a robust online environment featuring an impressive array of free tools and resources.

Access practice quizzes, eFlashcards, video, and multimedia at **edge.sagepub.com/hall3e**.

iStock/DGLimages

TEACHING STRATEGIES

© Jose Martinez

TEACHER INTERVIEW

Mr. Jose Martinez

Mr. Jose Martinez graduated in 2007 from the University of Northern Colorado with a bachelor's degree in secondary education and endorsements in English as a Second Language (ESL) and leadership education. He began his teaching career at Bear Creek High School in Jefferson County School District where he teaches Honors Government (Grade 9), Honors Geography (Grade 9), Economics (Grade 12), Student Senate (all grades), and a broadcasting class (all grades) that puts out a daily news show to the school. He is also the Social Studies Department Chair, a member of the Bear Creek Technology Team and the PLC Guiding Coalition Group, and the junior varsity boys tennis coach.

Bear Creek High School is located in the foothills of the Rocky Mountains in a city called Lakewood (about 12 miles southwest of Denver). Bear Creek is one of 18 high schools in the Jefferson County School District of over 80,000 students. The demographics of the 1,500-student population of Bear Creek are 48% white, 40% Latino, and 12% other. Bear Creek students also have a 13% mobility rate, a 41% Free or Reduced-Price Lunch rate, and a 93% graduation rate. Seventy percent of the 105 teachers at Bear Creek have advanced degrees.

Q: What brings you joy in teaching?

A: To this day, I think one of the most magical experiences any teacher can have is seeing the light in students' eyes when they truly understand something for the first time. Granted, high schoolers are not as emotive as kids in primary school are when it comes to getting excited about learning, but the "light" still exists. It is such a great feeling to know that you are helping students make sense of the world around them, and the visual sense of gratitude they express as an extension of that "aha moment" is amazing.

I also really find joy in the relationships I have formed with peers. Having school and department faculty who work well together and enjoy time with one another socially makes a huge difference. It creates a unified sense of belonging, and it's nice to know you have the support of others when you need it; plus, being able to work with others and bounce ideas around lends itself to some awesome lessons and projects.

> ### LEARNING OUTCOMES
>
> After reading this chapter, you should be able to do the following:
>
> 1. Describe some of the strategies teachers use to prepare students for learning.
>
> 2. Explain why some teaching strategies might work better with one content area than another.
>
> 3. Determine how to apply different teaching strategies for different purposes and for different students.

Q: **What do you do to make sure that all of your students are learning? And how do you keep track of each student's progress?**

A: As I reflect upon where I am today, I realize that most of my information regarding the progress of my students comes from two different areas. The first is from my relationship with them. I know this sounds a little crazy, but because I choose to get to know all of my students and to interact with them on many levels, I am able to perceive how they are doing because I am able to detect the nuances in their behavior and work. When things start to go off the rails or they get stuck, I use that as a natural teaching point or a place to regroup everyone before we move forward. In addition to these "soft" data, I try to use concrete data to objectively measure their progress along the way. Sometimes it's analyzing a short formative assessment to see where everyone is at. Other times it's a warm-up to determine the level of predeveloped knowledge. I even use already-gathered formative and summative data to observe overarching trends throughout the class and semester. When the data show gaps or abrupt changes, it usually means that a conversation is in order. It sounds very complicated, but it's not. It's just about keeping and understanding those data that most of us are already collecting.

Q: **What advice about teaching strategies do you have for those who are studying to become teachers?**

A: Especially early on in their career, I think the best pieces of advice I can give to teachers is to try and have fun and mix it up as much as you can. You will learn very quickly that your attitude about your teaching and content is reflected back to you by your students. If you are enthusiastic and playful and are having a good time, your kids will inherently find your lessons more enjoyable and will likely perform better. Another way to think about it is, if you aren't enjoying what you teach, why in the world would your students enjoy it?

That being said, I think it's also important to really try tons of different activities and projects and styles of teaching when you first begin. Many of these experiments will end up with less-than-ideal results (things are going to go wrong), but I think the process part is what is so important. The early part of your career is really a time to spread your wings and find your personal teaching style. Doing lots of different activities will also help you gauge what kinds of activities you really enjoy teaching and what activities your students really like completing. The ideal place to end up is somewhere where the two meet, but you will never find that place if you don't try lots of different things.

Q: **In what ways do you use technology (social media) to improve student learning?**

A: Meet kids halfway. My own personal technological journey has been very positive, and it is my goal to do the same for my students. I try to integrate technology into most of what I do simply because it is fun for me and because I feel as though it is a place where my students are comfortable. I have also found that using technology has really ramped up my ability to communicate and give feedback more easily and more frequently. This can sometimes mean that I am pushing myself, but I feel it is important to meet my students halfway, and they are appreciative of that effort. I have tried everything from basic things like various presentation software and video integration, all the way to video editing, website construction, and digital 3D modeling by both myself and my students. In my experience, I have found that technology, if applied correctly, can really harness the creativity and energy of my students. That being said, there are two guiding principles that I hold as I use technology. The first is that when using technology, especially with regard to daily lessons and presentations, I try and make it as seamless as possible (this usually requires lots of practice before I show it publicly). I think technology can be almost magical when it works well, but a huge part of that is making it look easy and flawless for my students. This encourages students to believe in themselves because it models the idea that utilizing the technology is not scary or hard. . . . I mean, if their teacher can do it, it's got to be easy. My other guiding principle is simply to make things look "pretty." It often means I spend 20% to 30% more time creating my technology and lessons, but in my experience, it pays incredible dividends. Not only does it encourage my students to pay attention (because it is visually stimulating), but it also provides a great avenue to discuss the power of going beyond the minimum requirements.

Q: How do you build trust with your students?

A: Trust with students is something that takes time to master, but I think some of the best ways to begin to build it are to be fair, to be consistent, and to be honest. Being fair doesn't mean you treat every student the same; it means that you approach each situation with students differently, considering all the factors at play and then working toward helping individual students in the way that is best suited for them. Being consistent really means following through with what you ask or say, whether it is when assignments are due, what will be counted as a grade, and even what lessons and activities are upcoming. As simple as this sounds, it can be so hard to follow, but being consistent really builds trust with students because it is all about your word and what they can expect. Finally, I am a firm believer in being honest with my students. I am honest about our content and lessons; I am honest about challenges they face or that we all face as a society; I am honest about areas where they can improve and areas where they excel. Doing this builds trust because my students learn that my classroom is a safe place where we are encouraged to think about all aspects of our learning, even if it means to question some of that learning. This can be transformational and empowering for our relationship because it encourages them to take academic risks, which generally improves both their knowledge base and their skill base, all while also building trust with me.

Q: How do you learn as a teacher?

A: When I think about learning as a teacher, I actually think about two things, YouTube and my colleagues. I think the Internet is incredible with regard to how much information is available for anyone willing to look for it. One embodiment of this idea is YouTube, and I am constantly utilizing it to develop my own skills, both professionally and personally. When it comes to my colleagues, regardless of how much experience I have as a teacher, I find that I can always make lessons better by working with colleagues. Whether it is because they teach me about some great new digital tool to aid in my lesson or because they simply give feedback on my lesson that helps fill in gaps or point out areas of improvement, today, working with others and sharing ideas is one of the best ways to learn more as a teacher.

Questions to Consider

1. What did a teacher do to encourage you to learn something?

2. Why might learning be more fun for students who have a trusting relationship with their teacher?

3. Mr. Martinez finds joy in teaching when his students are excited about learning and from the teachers he works and learns with. What do you anticipate will bring you joy in your teaching career?

4. Why is it important for a teacher to know how to use technology when teaching?

5. Have you had a teacher who encouraged you to think about your learning? How did that make you feel?

INTRODUCTION

Every teacher has a mental "rolodex" of ideas, plans, activities, and strategies that have been accumulated over time. When teachers consider the curriculum they must teach, they spin through their mental rolodex to consider possible approaches to lessons, what strategies to use, how to capture student attention, and what student learning should look like. Novice teachers have to start to build their rolodex by keeping track of what they have seen or heard from more experienced teachers, from what they have read, and from the assignments they have completed in their teacher education programs. Organizing ideas for teaching will put the beginning teacher firmly on the path to understanding and using a variety of plans and strategies to make teaching and learning productive for all.

The Art and Science of Teaching

The artistic side of teaching requires a habit of instinctual mindfulness that relies on empathy and quick thinking. You might well ask what that looks like in a classroom: The answer is that it can look as many different ways as the teachers who have developed such habits. Think about instructors you have had who momentarily stopped whatever they were doing and then continued along a different line of explanation with different examples or different demonstrations. Teachers who possess instinctual mindfulness may have noticed a confused look on a student's face or an "I have seriously checked out" look on more than one face in the classroom. Being attuned to students' reactions to the lesson, and being able to shift gears when it appears the lesson isn't going so well, is what thoughtful and quick-minded teachers constantly do. One of our favorite quotes is "Don't finish a lesson that is bombing." New teachers work hard to develop their lesson plans so they may forge ahead with the attitude that "it is my lesson and I am going to finish it" even when the students are not learning. Don't be that teacher. Be aware, be mindful, and be quick to pick up on the subtle and sometimes not-so-subtle messages your students are sending you regarding what may or may not be happening in their heads.

One of the things that makes teaching so much fun is that even though there are recipes to follow, for every group of students, in every place the teacher teaches a lesson, something has to be changed—a new ingredient added or a time changed. Such moments come and go in the blink of an eye, like the Higgs boson. Expert teachers know these moments are always likely to pop up, and they anticipate them and use them to make learning come alive. It's not an easy habit to learn, and it is not a behavior that is easy to see. But it happens in teaching all the time.

This habit of thoughtful quick-mindedness can be developed through a process of reflection that is automatic and continuous, and that draws on all manner of sensory awareness of the multitude of stimuli emanating from learner–teacher interactions. As teachers practice their art and reflect on the outcomes of that practice, they construct a framework for instinctive and spontaneous actions that promote student learning. Although it may seem that spontaneity and quick-mindedness are random, they are not. Some beginning teachers walk into the classroom with a well-developed sense of mindfulness. However, most teachers develop instinctive quick-mindedness from experience and over time. Mr. Martinez works at incorporating technology to make his lessons entertaining and engaging.

Teaching as a science is evident in the strategies that teachers learn to use to achieve desired results in student learning. Strategies are used to capture and hold student attention, to direct that attention to a specific detail of knowledge, or to develop a skill students will begin to incorporate into their own framework for learning. Some strategies help students practice and connect new bits of information to what they already know and to what they will be expected to know in the future. These and other strategies are all part of the science of teaching.

iStock/Jani Bryson

Teachers who are aware of students' perceptions of a lesson are likely to encourage student learning.

The science of teaching is concerned with keeping track of where students are in the **learning cycle** (Kolb & Fry, 1974; Lawson, 1995)—which student has just fallen off the cart and which has already made a leap of learning to dimensions beyond the scope of the lesson. The science of teaching is in the planning, in the tactical adjustments teachers make in action, and in documenting the teachers' own progress and performance and that of the students.

When you ask your college instructor for a definitive answer about what particular strategy will work in a classroom, and the instructor answers, "Well, it depends," your frustration at such an equivocal answer may not be entirely warranted. What your instructor knows is that skill in teaching is developed through experience; since nearly every day in the classroom represents a different set of experiences, how a teacher might respond in any given situation often depends on an unpredictable set of conditions. Your instructor also knows that the science of teaching can be learned, and that what will work for you in a classroom will depend on how well you learn to use a range of teaching strategies and how well you monitor the effects of the applied science of your teaching.

You have probably heard the comment that teachers are born, not made. The truth is that some people are born to be teachers with all the natural talents necessary to produce excellent results in learner achievement. However, most of us must learn to teach by practicing the science of teaching—that is, the skills that together make up the characteristics of excellent teachers. We also learn through persistence, practice, and patience to develop the same art of teaching talent that others may be born with.

This chapter will introduce you to a variety of teaching strategies that work in classrooms, and will help you understand a scientific approach to teaching. You will also learn ways specific strategies can be used to meet the learning needs of the range of student abilities most commonly found in a single classroom. You will develop the art of teaching as you practice these skills in classrooms.

WHAT ARE TEACHING STRATEGIES?

Mr. Jason Choi, a science teacher at Sleepy Hollow High School in Sleepy Hollow, New York, offers his perspective on teaching strategies. "In education, it seems as if every year or two, a new theory or instructional model appears on the horizon. I think it is important to realize that there is no cure-all or panacea for struggling students. I believe that good instructional strategies, whether in science, mathematics, English, or foreign language, all resemble one another. The students are engaged, challenged, and supported; the teachers are passionate, enthusiastic, and believe that teaching is the only profession for them" (Choi, 2012, p. 386). Hear and see more of Mr. Choi on the video and audio links in this textbook.

Any teaching **strategy** certainly falls into the category of something that is carefully planned—a method or a stratagem for reaching a desired goal. The word *stratagem* has a somewhat negative connotation, defined as being a cleverly contrived trick or scheme for gaining a desired end or outwitting an opponent, but effective teachers know they have to invent all manner of activities to encourage their students to drink from the fountain of knowledge. Teaching strategies properly used make it possible for teachers to help students acquire useful and necessary information, sometimes contrary to the students' desire.

Since the emergence of the first human societies, knowledge and skills have been handed down from one generation to another in different modalities. The apprentice model worked for the culture of knights and their squires. Even today, some aspiring potters spend weeks, months, or even years carrying the master teacher's clay from the source to the wheel to the kiln before ever trying to form a pot. In Iran, students learn the Persian alphabet through repetition and spend hours each day at a table writing a single Arabic symbol over and over until it is so etched in the mind that only an act of Allah could erase it. Children in school in China or Japan must learn more than 2,000 ideograms (written symbols) to properly communicate in an educated society; they copy these symbols until every individual brushstroke becomes as natural as taking a breath. Students do not come to your classroom knowing how to participate in the strategies that you will want to use to help them learn the content. You will also have to teach your students the guidelines for behavior inherent in each strategy. A useful rule of thumb when introducing a group of students to new instructional strategies is this: Never teach a new strategy with new content.

Generic Teaching Strategies

In their Framework of Universal Teaching Strategies, Freiberg and Driscoll (2004) describe generic instructional strategies along a continuum that ranges from a teacher focus or teacher-centered perspective to a student focus or student-centered perspective (see Figure 12.1). The strategies are truly universal, cutting across grade levels and content areas. The strategies described by Freiberg and Driscoll consider the context of teaching situations, the curriculum to be taught, and the diverse learners present in classrooms. At the end of this chapter, you will be directed to www.teachingchannel.org/videos to see how teachers learn to use different strategies for student learning.

The lecture is the strategy used most often in classrooms and provides the teacher with the most immediate control over what content the students are exposed to, the expected behavior of the students, and that most valuable commodity—time. When teachers are expected to cover a set amount of curriculum in a specified period, the lecture is often the favored strategy. David Ausubel, an educational psychologist you read about in Chapter 7 of this text, argued that lectures provide the most efficient use of time when trying to impart large amounts of information to a group of students. Since teachers and students have the gift of language, Ausubel's (1963) contention was that teachers should use language to impart knowledge.

At the student-centered end of the strategies continuum described by Freiberg and Driscoll (2004), students interact with books, audio- and videotapes, computer programs, and the Internet. Students use these resources to investigate topics assigned by the teacher or topics that interest them and that they are highly motivated to learn. Nancie Atwell's (2015) writings on teaching and conducting workshops in the Edgecomb, Maine, K–8 demonstration school bring practical application to the idea that if teachers want students to read and write, then they should encourage students to read and write about something that interests them. Using student-centered strategies to help students requires a high level of teacher competence to be able to guide students to resources that will give them adequate, useful, and accurate information.

There is logical organization to the strategies on the continuum. Since students can't be expected to discuss what they know nothing about, inputting information is important, and is usually done most efficiently through lecture or presentation. Group work requires that the students know how to ask questions of one another and discuss topics in a civilized manner. Role-playing and drama require students to demonstrate their knowledge of a subject using higher-level thinking skills. Students who engage in inquiry need to know how to access information, what to do with it, and how to organize and synthesize it. All learning has to begin with some level of knowledge. As you progress through your teacher education program, you will learn more details of a range of teaching strategies and the

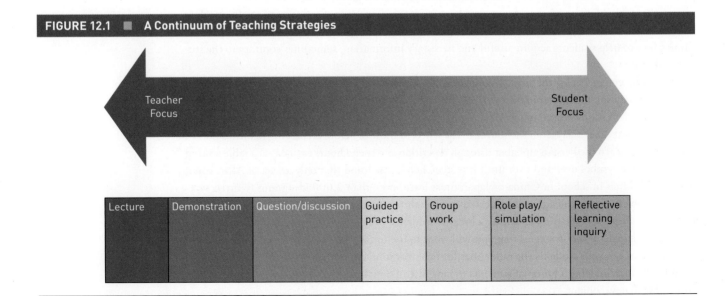

FIGURE 12.1 ■ A Continuum of Teaching Strategies

Teacher Focus

Student Focus

| Lecture | Demonstration | Question/discussion | Guided practice | Group work | Role play/ simulation | Reflective learning inquiry |

optimum application of each for specific content areas. Remember, all instructional strategies resemble one another in some way, but it is the teacher who determines which strategy to use and how best to use it. At www.youtube.com/user/AEA267Iowa, you will be able to view the results that expert use of teaching strategies can produce.

Some learning requires hours of practice: notes, scales, chords, Chopin.

Lecture

We've all had the experience of being talked to. Sometimes we have been inspired by being talked to, and sometimes not. There were probably even times when we had no idea what the lecturer was talking about. Fortunately or unfortunately, the lecture teaching strategy has survived for more than 2,000 years and is used in all content areas and at all grade levels. When the teacher is presenting information through a lecture, the students are in a passive role, and passively receiving information can hinder learning. The one-way communication of a lecture does not allow for any verbal feedback, although students can nod or shake their heads. When delivering a lecture, the teacher must activate instinctual mindfulness to be aware of any student problems with the material and to be able to check for student understanding. While the lecture may not always enjoy a favorable reputation, it can be effective in both elementary and secondary settings.

Teachers talk about the short attention span of their students. There is hardly a classroom that doesn't contain at least one student who has been assessed with Attention Deficit Hyperactivity Disorder. It's highly unreasonable to expect the kid who can't sit still, can't stop talking, and can't stop fidgeting with whatever is within reach to attend to the lecture teaching strategy.

To gain information from a lecture, the listeners must attend to what the speaker is saying and, in the case of a presentation, be able to see what the lecturer is talking about. Think about that demonstration in the supermarket when everyone is crowded around the man with the super juicer. What he is saying and doing doesn't make much sense unless you can see it. Students have to see what is going on as well as hear it. Mindful teachers learn to adjust the length of a lecture to the natural listening ability of their students.

The unfavorable reputation the lecture seems to have as a teaching strategy could be, in part, a result of the failure of teachers to recognize and use the guidelines that help make this teaching strategy effective. Professional speakers would never consider giving a boring speech: Watch Mike Rowe, for instance, the host of the *Dirty Jobs* show on the Discovery Channel, talk about the nature of hard work. Nothing boring there and some surprises. You may have ample opportunities to present information or give a talk on a specific subject during your teacher education program. Think of such opportunities as mini lectures that provide practice for that time you're in front of a truly hard audience (your seventh-grade history class), and take some time to reflect on how successful you are at giving information and telling stories in a lecture format. Some teacher education programs even require that candidates take a speech class to improve their skills in public speaking, and—trust me—there is nothing quite as public as a classroom. Perhaps a debate class or a theater class would also help teachers develop skill in using the lecture strategy.

The research on effective instruction provides guidelines for delivery of lectures and presentations (Rosenshine & Stevens, 1986). For the teacher education candidate or beginning teacher who is just becoming familiar with delivering a lecture or presentation, these guidelines can be reduced to

iStock/Jackf

There are many ways to enhance student interest in a lecture by following the five elements of an effective lecture. The lecture teaching strategy is an expeditious way to impart information to students.

five major elements essential for planning and delivering a lecture that instructs, entertains, and sticks (see Table 12.1).

The following illustrates how a teacher might develop a lecture around these five elements to help students learn.

Audience. A class of fifth graders in St. Louis is learning about the Westward Migration during the 19th century in the United States. The teacher knows that the students will be able to listen for about 10 minutes at the most, and has planned the lesson accordingly. The objectives for this lecture are for the students to learn the major routes followed by the pioneers as they left Independence, Missouri; to recognize and remember place names along the routes; and to understand why certain places along the routes later became settlements.

Focus. To generate interest, the teacher compares how the pioneers prepared for their cross-country trek to how the students might prepare for a vacation or trip to some other part of the country. Details about the rigors of the pioneers' journey are compared to what it might be like for the students to walk across Missouri today, while listing some of the dangers and hardships both sets of travelers might face.

Organization. The teacher gives each student a map with certain wagon train routes marked in dotted lines and with spaces for students to write place names and dates for stops along these routes. As the teacher talks about the major trails pioneers could take—the Oregon Trail, the Santa Fe Trail, the Mormon Trail, and the California Trail—students use the Google GPS app on their phones to mark the starting points for these trails on their individual maps and identify where the trails meet up or split, and the forts the travelers visited along the way.

TABLE 12.1 ■ Know Your Students	
Audience	**Know what is developmentally appropriate for your students. Be aware of their interests, their abilities, and what prerequisite skills and knowledge they need to have to understand what you are talking about.**
Focus	Know your subject, be enthusiastic about it, and stick to it. We all can be seduced into talking about things we really don't know much about. Everyone wants to have an opinion, but an educative lecture should be a learning experience for the listener, not just an opportunity for the speaker to spout his or her opinion. Present ideas in small chunks, one idea at a time. Make sure your students are with you; keep their attention.
Organization	Know how to introduce the topic, to expand on it, and to summarize what has been talked about. Know when to change pace and when to stop.
Clarity	Know how to present an idea from the listeners' perspective. Provide examples that are relevant, and make the subject come alive through explanations that are colorful, unusual, or startling.
Pacing	Know when to shift gears, check for understanding, and bring an idea to its logical conclusion. Make students think about what you are saying by having them take notes—for example, by writing down the names of important people or important dates. Provide students with an outline of your lecture before beginning so that they can follow along and make notations.

Source: Adapted from Rosenshine and Stevens (1986).

Clarity. There is a large map in the front of the room that the teacher refers to during the lecture. The teacher also writes the names of places on the board when the students are expected to mark them on their individual maps.

Pacing. The teacher ends the lecture by asking questions to help students recall the information and extend their thinking. The teacher shows some images of Fort Laramie and encourages students to talk about how the pioneers might have felt as they approached the fort. The teacher has provided resources on the Westward Migration and provides time for the students to browse through them at the end of the lesson.

The lecture strategy can be a very effective teaching tool. Using a lecture makes it possible for teachers to present information in the least amount of time. All members of the class as well as the teacher hear the same information at the same time. And a lecture can be a perfect beginning to a unit, or it can introduce a new concept. However, when using the lecture strategy, it is difficult to address individual needs since the information is presented to all students in the same mode.

A variety of teaching resources can help teachers create images in students' minds to enhance their learning.

Questioning and Discussions

We all learn from the questions we ask and from the questions others ask us. We have questions we want answered, we have questions we are sometimes afraid to ask, and sometimes people ask us questions for which we have no answers. People ask questions to gain information, to increase understanding, and even to draw attention to themselves. Some of the questions people ask are silly, some are shocking, and some are just downright wrongheaded. Sometimes teachers are so concerned with answers that they miss the importance of questions, of asking the right questions, and of listening to and learning from the questions their students ask of them.

Teachers have to know ways to ask questions that will give all students a chance to learn.

Teachers ask questions of their students for many reasons. Questions such as "Have you ever had an alligator nibble at your toes?" are asked to generate interest and gain student attention. Teachers ask questions to check for student understanding, to encourage student thinking, and to structure and redirect learning. Questioning is used by teachers as a diagnostic tool in determining the level of instruction at which students need to begin learning. Questions asked to manage student behavior or classroom organization are usually intended to help students remember rules, while some questions allow students to express their own feelings and opinions. Eleanor Duckworth has said, "Getting people to think about what they think, and asking them questions about it, is the best way I know how to teach" (cited in Kamenetz, 2014).

A Questioning Exercise. In collaboration with one or more of your classmates, write five questions that you believe teachers should never ask students. Then share these questions with the rest of the class and explain why you decided these questions should never be asked. A discussion of the types

THINKING DIFFERENTLY
COMMUNICATING WITH STUDENTS TO DISCOVER "WHY?"

Every teacher has heard students ask, "Why do we need to know this?" Sometimes teachers are just as confused as their kids, and having conversations with your students to explore the why of things might be the first step in helping them recognize a purpose in learning. For ideas on how to answer this age-old question, read "Why Do We Need to Learn This?" by Allen Mendler (2014) at edutopia.org.

Taking a few minutes out of a busy day to work through a math problem or talk about why one sentence clearly communicates an idea while another similar one doesn't might make a huge difference in a student's understanding. Excellent teachers use simple and real-life examples to explain complex concepts, but brilliant teachers work with students to enable them to come up with examples of their own. Encouraging students to use strategic thinking processes to solve problems is something that can be accomplished through thoughtful dialogue.

Having a copy of *How Everything Works* by Louis Bloomfield (2007) or a copy of the National Geographic Kids book *Why? 1,111 Answers to Everything* by Crispin Boyer (2015) as a resource in your classroom might just inspire students to find their own answers to their own questions.

of questions teachers should avoid will help you think about questioning in general. Learning the art of asking the right question at the right time and in the right way can be one of the most challenging aspects of teaching.

Guidelines have been created to help teachers with this task. Decades ago, John Dewey (1933) developed an "Art of Questioning Guide" that still holds true today.

The following guidelines have been reworded from Dewey's questioning guide:

- Questions should direct students to a deep understanding of a subject rather than focusing on facts related to that subject.

- Questions should avoid emphases on literal and direct responses over personal interpretations.

- Questions should be part of sets of questions that spark discussion and lead students to new and more complex questioning.

- Questions should include important points from earlier material to help students incorporate previous information into current content. Teachers should periodically review important points so that old, previously discussed material can be placed into perspective with that which is presently being studied.

- Questions should help students summarize what they learned and think about how the present learning might be integrated into future learning.

- Questions should not elicit fact upon fact, but should be asked in such a way as to delve deeply into the subject—that is, to develop an overall concept of the selection.

- Questions should not be asked randomly so that each is an end in itself, but should be planned so that one leads into the next throughout a continuous discussion.

- Teachers should bring closure to the experience by guiding students to summarize the main points. This is a way of helping students understand.

Other classification systems, taxonomies, have been created to aid teachers in developing questions for multiple purposes. There are multiple ways of organizing questions to encourage higher-order thinking skills, but you will most likely be introduced to Benjamin Bloom's (1956) taxonomy in your teacher education course work, or to Norman L. Webb's Depth of Knowledge (DOK) taxonomy.

The four levels of Webb's DOK taxonomy range from Level 1, Recall and Reproduction; to Level 2, Skills and Concepts; to Level 3, Short-Term Strategic Thinking and Reasoning; to Level 4, Extended Thinking (see Table 12.2 and "Webb's Depth of Knowledge Guide," 2009). Bloom's taxonomy was based on three levels of cognitive processes, from lower-level to higher-level thinking skills.

TABLE 12.2 ■ Webb's Depth of Knowledge Taxonomy		
Question Type	**Student Performance**	**Examples**
Level 1: Recall and Reproduction	List, identify, and define	List 10 elements on the Periodic Table.
Level 2: Skills and Concepts	Summarize, estimate, organize, classify, and infer	What might happen to Peter when he returns to Narnia?
Level 3: Short-Term Strategic Thinking and Reasoning	Analyze, explain and support with evidence, generalize, and create	If all of the students contributed the same amount of money for a field trip, why might the funds fall short of the necessary amount needed?
Level 4: Extended Thinking	Synthesize, reflect, conduct, and manage	Using the attached map, plot a course for the UPS driver to follow so that he covers the least number of miles to deliver the following packages: . . .

Source: Adapted from "Webb's Depth of Knowledge Guide" (2009), http://www.aps.edu/sapr/documents/resources/Webbs_DOK_Guide.pdf.

TABLE 12.3 ■ Bloom's Taxonomy of Question Types		
Question Type	**Student Performance**	**Examples**
Remembering	Retrieve, identify, match, select, label	Name the first four presidents of the United States.
Understanding	Compare, explain, present	Describe the stages of the water cycle.
Applying	Illustrate, demonstrate, use	What is the slope of the following equation?
Analyzing	Organize, attribute, distinguish	When did you know that Goldilocks was tired?
Evaluating	Assess, hypothesize, defend	What is the best air route to take from Tokyo, Japan, to Disney World in Florida? Why?
Creating	Design, invent, compose, revise	If you could build the perfect community, what five organizations would you have to include?

The original six levels of Bloom's (1956) classification system were identified as knowledge, comprehension, application, analysis, synthesis, and evaluation. In 1990, the levels of Bloom's taxonomy were renamed (1) remembering, (2) understanding, (3) applying, (4) analyzing, (5) evaluating, and (6) creating.

Table 12.3 shows the types of questions that elicit different responses from students and that require differing types of cognitive activity.

Of course, as a classroom teacher, the most important questions might be the ones you ask yourself. There are both less-than-productive and unproductive questions. Teachers should never ask unproductive questions. Time for learning in classrooms is at a premium, and not a minute should be wasted. When teachers ask irrelevant questions, questions that are too complex, trick questions, or questions that humiliate, the flow of any lesson is disturbed, and students can become confused and/or embarrassed. A too-complex question can be less than productive because it is usually impossible to answer intelligently during a rapid-paced question-and-answer exchange. Such a question has the negative effect of slowing a lesson down to the point that students' attention drifts. Teacher-answered questions need no explanation. Once a teacher starts answering his or her own questions, it's game over for effective questioning strategies.

An important component of asking questions is wait-time. Sometimes in the fast-paced lives we lead, it is difficult to wait for anything, but effective teachers know that giving students ample time to process a question before they answer it is absolutely necessary. Practice your ability to wait for someone to answer your questions by silently counting from 1,000 to 1,003. Waiting any longer than three seconds is not necessarily productive and may result in your students asking you if anything is wrong. There are two types of wait-time, **wait-time I** and **wait-time II**. Teachers use wait-time I for someone to answer a direct question. Smart teachers then use wait-time II to see if anyone else would like to add something to the first response. Teachers who consistently use the second wait-time during questioning are encouraging a form of mini discussion, and students become comfortable contributing to comments from their peers.

One purpose of asking questions is to promote thought. When teachers ask questions that promote thoughtful responses, the students are encouraged to develop the habit of thinking. Grant Wiggins and Jay McTighe's text *Understanding by Design* (2005) introduces the concept of big ideas and that the questions essential to any unit of study need to be identified before instruction for the unit begins.

From Questions to Discussions. A lot of talk goes on in classrooms. Productive talk in the classroom is structured by the teacher and engaged in by the students. Teachers who understand the art of questioning teach their students how to answer and ask thoughtful questions in a courteous manner. This prepares students to engage in productive discussions with their peers to solve problems, attain goals, develop concepts, and become actively engaged in the content they must learn. Through discussion, students can learn to think and value their own ideas as well as those of others.

Effective teachers prepare their students for participation in discussions. Knowing how to participate in a productive discussion is a necessary step toward learning how to be a productive member of a cooperative learning group. Students may find it difficult to work productively in groups if they do not understand that discussions require active listening, respect for the ideas of others, and noninterference when others are speaking. Even very young students can be taught how to exchange ideas with others if they are given time to practice the guidelines for a successful discussion.

Teachers who want their students to engage in meaningful discussions let them practice the discussion skills. Teachers make certain all students understand the skills they have been practicing by asking the following questions:

1. Were your comments relevant to the current discussion?

2. Were your comments supported by facts?

3. Did you consider the importance of your comment before you made it?

4. Did your comment broaden the discussion or clarify a point being discussed?

5. Were your comments complete and concise?

The Fishbowl. The **fishbowl** gives students the opportunity to be both contributors and listeners in a discussion. What follows is a brief explanation of how the fishbowl strategy can help students learn discussion techniques and see what a discussion should look like. In preparing for the fishbowl, students sit in two circles—an inner circle and an outer circle. The inner circle of students is the discussion circle, and the outer circle is the observation circle.

The steps in setting up a fishbowl are these:

1. Select a topic that allows for multiple perspectives and opinions.

2. Provide space for the fishbowl: a circle of chairs (6 to 12) and room for observers outside the circle of chairs.

3. Once a topic has been selected, allow time for students to prepare ideas and questions.

4. Establish the fishbowl format and rules. (You might wish to have the observers note specific aspects of the process of the discussion.)

5. Have the inner circle hold a discussion while the outer circle observes silently.

6. Debrief the discussion. Provide comments on what was learned, the quality of the discussion, and the behavior of the participants.

Grouping

Humans are not born with the ability to collaborate, though learning to cooperate has been a major factor in the survival of our species. We have to learn how to get along with others even though it may take much energy and patience. Parents remind their children to share, to take turns, and to let someone else be first. Teachers organize classroom activities and playtime so that students have opportunities to practice behaviors necessary for life in a community and in a democracy. Working together may not come naturally for everyone, but through every step of formal education, students are prompted to develop more and more skill at becoming productive members of a group. The seminal research of David W. Johnson and Roger T. Johnson (1990) emphasized that the skills needed to interact effectively with others need to be taught just as systematically as the skills needed for math or social studies.

Human beings are not born with an innate ability to share. Students must be taught and then continually reminded of the guidelines for working peacefully with others.

iStock/evgeny_pylayev

Formal group work has been a teaching strategy used in schools since the early 1800s. Grouping students for instruction usually involves grouping students by age to form grade-level classes and then grouping within classes by ability. (Do you remember the reading group you were in during elementary school? Were you a bluebird or a vulture?) Students can be grouped to study specific subjects, for tutoring purposes, and to learn together (e.g., in cooperative learning groups).

When teachers think of grouping students, it is usually to accomplish a specific goal and to provide students increased opportunity to learn both academic content and group participation skills. Johnson and Johnson (1999a) define cooperative learning as the instructional use of small groups so students work together to maximize their own and each other's learning. Slavin (1993) provided an organizational structure for managing cooperative learning in the classroom. Table 12.4 provides an overview of the characteristics of grouping students for cooperative learning.

Early socializing activities can begin by teachers handing out cards with numbers or symbols. Students find the classmates with the same number or symbol, form groups, and start to get to know one another. An "In the Bag" activity has small groups of students working together to blow a paper cup into bags taped at the edge of their desks or tables. In a strategy called "Number Heads Together," each student in the group has a number. The teacher asks a question and then says, "Put your heads together and make sure everyone knows the answer." Students discuss the answer, then the teacher calls a number, and that student answers.

TABLE 12.4 ■ **Common Characteristics of Cooperative Learning**	
Heterogeneous groups	**Group members represent a mixture of gender, ethnicity, and ability.**
Positive interdependence	Everyone in the group has a meaningful task to complete.
Verbal face-to-face interaction	Students engage in purposeful discussion.
Individual accountability	Each member must complete an assessment appropriate to the group goal.
Social and academic goals identified	Guidelines for group work have been explained and practiced.
Group processing conducted	During group work, the instructor monitors student involvement; at the close of group work, the level of success of the group is assessed.

UNDERSTANDING AND USING DATA
USING THIRD-GRADE MATH SCORES ON A UNIT TEST TO CREATE COOPERATIVE LEARNING GROUPS

The following data provide the individual scores of third-grade students on an end-of-unit test. It has been determined by the teacher that a majority of the students could benefit from review work on regrouping when subtracting three-digit numbers. The teacher has decided to place the students in heterogeneous groups for cooperative group work, or **cooperative learning groups**. The purpose of the group work will be to provide students with the opportunity to ask questions of one another and to practice and develop skill in regrouping.

Student Name	Test Score (Highest Possible Score = 100)
End-of-Unit Test Scores on Regrouping During Subtraction of Three-Digit Numbers	
Carl	96
Lucia	60
Caitlin	100
Tiffany	40
Carla	88
Nancy	24
Neil	76
Pete	68
Andrew	84
Timette	74
Richard	72
Jaylynn	88
Patrick	28
Stacy	68
Kenneth	80
Angelica	64
Marilyn	52
Susan	48

Your Task

Establish cooperative learning groups of three or four students that are heterogeneous, reflecting high- and low-performing students as well as gender differences. Once you have done this, read below about how the teacher of this class actually organized the students into groups.

What Did You Learn From This Exercise?

Teachers must constantly assess student learning through reflection on data and then organize those data in useful ways. The teacher of this class has decided to put the students into cooperative learning groups so that the students can have more practice in using regrouping strategies. Teachers always know, or should know, more about their students than raw data can show, and so they may make decisions based on personal experience rather than entirely on what the raw data indicate. This is a teacher's professional right and one that all effective teachers exercise from time to time.

The teacher of the class has decided to put one high-performing student in each group. There were 25 items on the test, and the teacher also considers the number of questions missed along with the raw score.

- Caitlin missed no problems and works well with all other students in the class, even with Neil, who can sometimes be a behavior problem, so the teacher has placed Caitlin, Neil, and Nancy in one group. The teacher wants Nancy to have as much practice as possible during the group work time and so has decided that a smaller group will be better suited to Nancy's needs. Also, a smaller group may give Neil less opportunity to act out.

- Carl is also an excellent student, though sometimes he disregards others' feelings. The teacher is placing him with Timette, who has a calming personality, and with Patrick, who is Carl's friend, and with Susan. The teacher believes a larger group with numerous interactions will engage Carl's helper potential.

- Carla and Kenneth scored close in their performance on the test and have often helped one another in the past. The teacher is placing Marilyn and Tiffany in this group because all of these students are hard workers and have demonstrated their ability to cooperate during group work in the past.

- Jaylynn and Andrew performed very close on the test, and the teacher feels they will provide great assistance to Angelica and Lucia. Jaylynn also speaks Spanish and will be able to help with translation of any terms that may be unfamiliar to Lucia, who is an English Language Learner.

- Pete, Stacy, and Richard will form a group. Richard scored in the middle range on the test, but he is very thoughtful and patient. The teacher feels that she will be able to spend some extra time with this group if her calculations about the other groups are correct.

In high school classes, students are often given the task of working together to solve problems or complete lab assignments. Group activities of this nature can provide a virtual experience for students' future roles as citizens in the larger community of their city or state or country. Such activities also make learning fun. When students learn the strategies and skills necessary to work together in productive groups, the result can be enjoyable and intrinsically rewarding. Initial group activities should be short and simple and should concentrate on positive social interaction. Assessment of academic work in groups should not be addressed until students have learned to successfully interact with one another.

The Learning Together Model of Johnson and Johnson (1999a) contains five key steps:

1. Teacher presents students with a specific academic learning task.

2. Students understand the social skills necessary to complete the task through group effort.

3. Teacher checks for student understanding of both academic and social skills.

4. Groups work together demonstrating a high level of verbal interaction and positive interdependence.

5. Teacher assesses individual accountability for the academic task and initiates a class discussion of the group process.

The following scenario is an example of how a teacher designs, implements, and coordinates cooperative group learning. Clearly, preparing for effective cooperative learning groups in the classroom is no small undertaking.

A Teacher's Preparation for Group Work. One evening during a unit on anatomy in her seventh-grade curriculum, Ms. Lynn drives across town with two large, well-iced cool cans in her pickup truck. She collects sterilized pigs' hearts from the local meat processing plant through an arrangement she has made with the school administration, the Parent–Teacher Association, the parents and students in her seventh-grade science classes, and the managers of the processing plant. The next day, her students, already aware of their task for the day, don medical gloves and aprons and get into their appointed groups around the tables in the science lab.

Ms. Lynn states the plan for the day, placing special emphasis on the timing of the lesson since there will be no opportunity for students to complete their work at a later date. She questions the students to make certain they understand their assignment and the role each will assume in the group. As the students dissect the hearts and identify the parts, one member of each group uses a scalpel, one takes notes, and another draws pictures, while another offers suggestions from a sheet handed out by Ms. Lynn, asks the other group members questions, and keeps an eye on the clock. Ms. Lynn circulates among the lab tables, stops to praise a group for their progress, prompts them to look at specific areas, and moves on to the next group. She allows the students to work at their task for most of the period, reminding them that they will debrief the lesson the next day.

Cleanup is handled efficiently, with all heart parts placed back in the cool cans. Ms. Lynn tells the class she is checking for fingers and toes before she closes the lids. Just before the bell rings, she asks the students to place their index and middle fingers on the wrist of one of the other members of their group, making a circle of heartbeats. She thanks them for their contribution to today's lesson. As the students leave the lab, there is much chatter and excited energy from the lesson today and even some anticipation of exciting lessons to come.

Before groups of students can work together successfully, they must learn the skills of cooperative work, communication, and division of labor. Before teachers can implement cooperative learning strategies effectively, they must know how to organize materials, equipment, and work space. Teachers must carefully plan and schedule group work. For your benefit, at http://math.sfsu.edu/hsu/talks/asilo-group-thoughts.html, Mr. Eric Hsu, a math teacher, poses and answers questions on teaching with group work.

Marzano, Pickering, and Pollack (2001) say that cooperative learning activities instill in learners important behaviors that prepare them to reason and perform in an adult world. Teachers are expected to pose problems for students to solve. When students can work together to find solutions to problems that may emerge through other sources, they are using critical-thinking skills.

You may have been the member of a group sometime in the past. Was the experience rewarding or frustrating? You may have felt that you had to do most of the work and that other members of your group contributed very little to the assignment. There are probably many reasons why some group members do not perform as readily as others. Knowing more about the processes and purposes of group work should help all participants be more engaged.

Role-Playing, Simulations, and Drama

Teaching strategies that involve students in acting a part or responding to a specific set of circumstances are perhaps the most emotionally charged of all teaching strategies. Role-playing, simulations, and drama allow students to experience tough, real-life problems in a controlled environment. Students in a first-aid class learn to resuscitate drowning victims and administer CPR with the assistance of life-like dummies whose touch and response are similar to those of a living person. Second graders learn to "drop and roll" to extinguish flames on their clothes, and to crawl along the floor of an escape route to exit a burning building.

Through role-playing, we learn how to act in places we have never been and how to negotiate unknown territory. Simulations can help students learn empathy, to understand the predicaments life creates for others. In simulations, students are faced with dilemmas. They must make choices, take action, and then experience the consequences of their actions. Training for medical triage groups and rescue teams relies heavily on simulations and role-playing. Role-playing, simulations, and drama can help students learn by doing, thinking, feeling, or responding and develop their own knowledge, skills, and dispositions. They allow students to have vicarious experiences that can substitute for firsthand experiences that may be impossible to achieve. Teacher education candidates often cite field experience as the most informative and influential part of teacher education course work. Perhaps that's because fieldwork puts them in the "role" of teacher.

The Powerful Effect of Role-Playing and Simulation. An infamous simulation exercise, "Blue-eyed/Brown-eyed," had its birth in 1968, in Jane Elliott's fourth-grade classroom in Riceville, Iowa. Following the assassination of Martin Luther King Jr., when one of her students asked why this had happened, Elliott decided to provide her students with firsthand knowledge of racial discrimination. Since Elliott's students lived and attended school in an all-white community, she had to create a hypothetical situation that would demonstrate to her students what racial discrimination looked and felt like and the demoralizing effects it could have on individuals. Blue-eyed and brown-eyed students in her classroom were assigned to two groups; one group was not allowed to enjoy the benefits enjoyed by others in the classroom, and one group enjoyed all of the benefits plus special considerations. After a time of being in one group, students switched roles.

Elliott's Blue-eyed/Brown-eyed simulation exercise is a classic in teaching about racial discrimination and a perfect example of the impact a well-planned teaching strategy can have on students. Elliott's simulation was such a powerful piece of teaching that her students will always remember it. Read more about Elliott's lesson at www.janeelliott.com or check out stories of Elliott's lesson on racial discrimination, "The Angry Eye," "The Eye of the Storm," and "The Stolen Eye," on YouTube. The website www.virtlab.com/?gclid=CLqzlZbTgcgCFUNcf

iStock/ferrantraite

Incorporating role-playing, simulations, and drama into the classroom can be both simple and elaborate.

godrVYNEw introduces students to a virtual laboratory. Such websites can make it unnecessary for the teacher to create a complete classical lab for experimentation.

Reflective Learning/Inquiry

Discovering something for yourself is intrinsically rewarding because you are actively involved in exploring and manipulating your environment. Most people love a well-planned scavenger hunt and movies that have the hero fight nature, the forces of evil, and doubting Thomases to finally discover some wondrous prize. It's the reason scientists of all kinds spend long hours laboring over test tubes, ancient texts, or computer programs to finally solve a puzzling piece of nature, history, or engineering—to be able to say, "I did it."

Reflective learning strategies deal with a problem or problems the students must solve. In reflective learning, students are often asked to contend with circumstances that lie outside the range of what is commonplace and normal to them. Students involved in reflective learning must discover facts and concepts and knowledge that are new to them. They also have to compile evidence to support or refute a solution. Students must develop hypotheses.

One well-known reflective learning teaching strategy is the Social Inquiry Model, described by Joyce and Weil (2008). This model, specifically developed for the social studies curriculum, has six phases that help students develop cooperation and collaboration skills in addition to the cognitive benefits of the inquiry process:

1. Orientation: Presentation and clarification of a puzzling situation

2. Hypothesis: Development of a hypothesis to structure an exploration of or solution to the problem

3. Definition: Process of defining, clarifying, and understanding the hypothesis

4. Exploration: Looking for the assumptions, implications, and logical validity of the hypothesis

5. Evidence: Assembling relevant facts and evidence to support or refute each hypothesis

6. Generalizations: Arriving at an acceptable solution based on evidence

Viewing Teaching Strategies as Direct or Indirect Instruction

Teaching strategies can also be grouped into two overarching categories of **direct** and **indirect instruction**, sometimes referred to as **explicit** and **implicit instruction**. Explicit instruction can be viewed as instruction that helps students increase and broaden their existing knowledge or skills. Teaching strategies that are explicit or direct are successful in helping students acquire information that is highly structured. Implicit teaching strategies are intended to assist students in thinking about their own thinking (also called **metacognition**), deciding on a specific choice or solution, and acting on their decisions. Each area of instruction requires different behaviors from teachers and responses from students.

Direct instruction represents a teacher-centered approach with the teacher providing the instructional input. The teacher's role in direct instruction is to pass facts, rules, or action sequences on to students in the most direct way possible (Borich, 2011). Direct instruction has been shown to correlate highest with student achievement as measured by standardized tests emphasizing facts, rules, and sequences. Direct instruction strategies make it possible for teachers to serve up information in chunks palatable to students; to make dry, boring information interesting; and to help students master content.

Rosenshine and Stevens (1986) wrote a seminal essay on the power of direct instruction that has provided a

Indirect instructional strategies help students work together to solve existing problems.

framework for understanding the components of direct instruction. Additionally, Carnine, Silbert, Kame'enui, Tarver, and Archer (2012) provide many examples of the use of direct instruction strategies. Remember the lecture on the Westward Migration referred to earlier in this chapter, and the way the teacher provided stimuli to pique student interest and attention.

Indirect teaching strategies encourage students to think beyond the facts given, to draw conclusions, or to make generalizations. Teachers who use direct instruction focus learner attention on a problem and then provide students with background information (Woolfolk, 2004). This approach activates the cognitive processes required to form concepts and to recognize patterns and abstractions. Borich and Tombari (2003) suggest that indirect teaching functions are most useful in providing behaviors that students will use in their adult lives. Reaction to the world outside the classroom requires students to be able to analyze situations, make decisions, organize information, and adapt. These skills are not learned through memorization of rules and facts but must be constructed through experiences demanding higher-level thinking. Learners are using information to think and draw conclusions. When students think well while learning, they learn well.

A Constructivist Approach to Teaching

As you learned in Chapter 7 of this text, a constructivist approach to teaching is built on the idea that each student actively creates, interprets, and reorganizes information in ways that are unique. Present knowledge is used to achieve predetermined educational goals. Students engage in problem-based learning, inquiry activities, and dialogues with others to connect elements in the learning environment. They come together in communities of learners with an opportunity to think critically by challenging and explaining their thinking to one another. Students experience the ideas, phenomena, and artifacts of the discipline before having formal explanations of them.

In a constructivist environment, teachers do not prescribe, but instead are more likely to respond to, the needs of learners, the content, and the context. The teacher's role is that of a facilitator of learning, one who responds to the students' needs in a flexible manner. By allowing students to construct knowledge as learners, teachers help them think critically about concepts, and to design and sequence lessons that encourage learners to use their own experiences to actively construct meaning. Constructivist teaching strategies also work great with technology. Individuals can connect through technology to exchange ideas and solve problems.

There are many constructivist strategies that a teacher might employ when teaching a particular content area. Scaffolding allows the learner to make sense of a complex task. Modeling requires teachers to think aloud about the process they have gone through to solve a problem. Teachers probe students' thinking through coaching, guiding, and advising. To create a constructivist learning environment, teachers must clearly understand how the theory of constructivism translates into practice (Windschitl, 1999).

Activity Learning

Simply put, the activity approach to teaching is exactly what it implies. Students develop understanding of the link between the conscious and the objective world by engaging in activities. Through the manipulation of objects and tools, students can gain knowledge in a variety of domains. Piaget (1932/1985) proposed that individuals gain knowledge through active exploration in which they form schemes, cognitive structures that help them organize patterns, or thoughts to interpret their experiences. A teacher might allow a student to choose either a pictorial or a concrete representation to solve a math problem (e.g., 2 × 3). The student then can either make two groups with three cubes in each group or draw two circles with three boxes in each, thus discovering the answer is 6. The objective of the activity is achieved through a physical or mental product.

When teachers plan an activity for their students, they consider the curriculum objectives for that activity, what resources should be available, and what prerequisite knowledge the students must have to complete the activity. Teachers take into account the context in which the activity will take place.

Teachers know that as students become actively engaged, things will happen that may change the intended outcome, and that sometimes students will come up with solutions or answers that the teacher

TEACHERS' LOUNGE
WHERE ARE YOU FROM?

Having been born and raised in American states that subscribe to a deep, rich Southern drawl, I took my best colloquial pronunciations with me when I left a teaching position in South Carolina to begin teaching over 1,500 miles away in Montana. It is said that the older one gets, the more difficult it is to learn new languages. On the other hand, children with their malleable brains are able to learn second languages quite readily. Therefore, I remained steadfast in speaking and teaching with my Southern drawl, while my fifth-grade students (unbeknown to me) were absorbing and mimicking the best of the South in what they were hearing each day. Phonics lessons, in particular those with short and long vowels, took on new meaning when a Southern drawl was blended with a Western twang.

On Mondays, I would prescribe a list of 20 words for the Friday spelling test. On Thursdays, I dictated the words for the practice test, and students self-assessed and promised to practice any words missed. Friday spelling tests usually produced a majority of students with 100% scores. This particular Thursday was no different—I gave the practice test, and students missed three or four words at most.

As it happened, that evening I became quite ill. I had to call for a substitute teacher for Friday. Of course, the lesson plans specified that the Friday spelling test be given, which the substitute diligently did.

After a weekend of recuperating, I returned to find neatly stacked and graded papers on my teacher's desk, along with a pleasant note from the substitute. She stated she had loved my class of students and had followed the lesson plans as best she could. As I reached for the pile of student spelling tests, I noticed that the substitute had left a separate little note on top. She had written: "Many of the students did not seem to know the words I was giving. Did I have the right list?" I checked her list and made a mental note, "Yes, she had given the correct words."

I quickly glanced through the stack of graded spelling test papers. To my surprise, not one student had scored 100%, and many had missed five or more words! After the students arrived, I passed out papers and asked what had gone wrong on their Friday spelling test. "Why did so many of you miss so many words?" The children chimed together: "We couldn't understand a word she said. Are you sure she had the right words?"

—Ms. Julie J. Conn
Exceptional Children
Sugarloaf Elementary

may not have considered. Teachers using constructivist and activity teaching strategies must be both well prepared and flexible. That is not a contradiction: It is just one of the phenomena of teaching from a constructivist perspective.

Never Just One

It would be nearly impossible to use only one teaching strategy in a single lesson. Even lectures usually include some questions. Discussions are loaded with questions. When students work together in groups, they share information with one another, ask questions, carry on discussions, and sometimes try to lecture other members of the group. Inquiry, whether done individually or in groups, depends on questioning and working through hypotheses, and sometimes acting out a problem. Role-playing, simulations, and drama draw on any number of teaching strategies to achieve desired results. When students are using resources, audiovisual equipment, computers, and the Internet, they are receiving lectures of sorts from books and videos, asking and answering questions, and sharing their information through discussions and presentations with their classmates.

Teachers who use a variety of strategies are likely to have a high degree of instructional success since students learn in so many different ways. Selecting the best teaching strategy to match students with subject matter is a teaching skill not easily mastered. But it can be accomplished when a teacher keeps in mind the needs and abilities of the learners, the content goals to be achieved, and the time and resources allowed by the context. Teachers must make hundreds of decisions a day regarding what they are going to teach and how they are going to teach it. Teacher knowledge of the best uses for a particular teaching strategy, how to most effectively implement the strategy, and the learner response to a particular approach are the key ingredients in any instruction.

"Watching a wide range of teaching styles is a great learning experience. I encourage all my teachers to visit other classrooms; and this year, I gave the teachers a list of periods that I would cover so that they could visit other teachers. Unless the culture of the school encourages and supports peer visitations and observations, it is difficult to implement. Peer visitations are a requirement of the inquiry program. Each class presents a unique challenge and a unique experience. Teachers should continually try to improve lessons and revise the curriculum. I try to implement technology into my classes when it proves useful. Technology can help engage students, allow for differentiated structure, and provide multiple opportunities" (Choi, 2012, pp. 401–402).

Technology for Teaching Strategies

Teachers have a wealth of entertaining resources at their fingertips through websites. Some are free. Some are not. Once you start to visit different sites, you will become a regular, looking for new interactive content and resources. Technology is all around us, and we use it for our personal pleasure and business without giving a moment's thought to how or why it works. In fact, the only time we really think about it is when it doesn't do what we want it to. Digital media in our homes comes at us constantly through music, voice, data, and video. The kids and young adults in the digital generation have no problem watching TV, listening to music, emailing friends, and surfing the Internet to see what's happening—all at the same time. *Multitasking* is a new vocabulary word, and for many, it has become habitual. It is not always safe, and it sometimes causes important pieces of information to be missed, but it is a part of our culture.

Switching perspectives from using technology for personal need or pleasure to using it in a classroom to augment student learning requires attention to what the technology does and what it can be used for. Integrating technology into teaching requires knowledge and skill—and time and work, as Mr. Martinez, the teacher interviewed at the beginning of this chapter, has pointed out. Perhaps more important, though, it requires that teachers who wish to integrate technology into teaching possess a curiosity about new ways of doing things and a willingness to learn how to do something they haven't done before. One of our colleagues teaches a graduate course for teachers titled Serious Games for Learning. It has to be fun. Teachers who grow with the changes in their profession will find joy in the amazing technology tools that become available to them. Following are some examples of ways teachers can use common technology tools and applications in instruction and managing a classroom.

SMART Boards, MP3 Players, and Tablets

Regardless of the product name—SMART Board, Promethean ActivBoard Touch, or just whiteboard—the technology behind the product provides an interactive display connected to a computer and projector. Users are able to control the display using a pen, a finger, or a stylus. Search YouTube for videos about SMART Boards to see teachers use interactive whiteboards for a variety of purposes.

iStock/franckreporter

A picture can be worth a thousand words. It allows us to see things as they are, and not as we imagine them to be.

From numerous cell phones and stereo systems, MP3 players can be found just about anywhere. MP4 players will play files that are audio or video, or a combination. iPads are MP4 players. They can deliver highly compressed digital files such as movies, games, books, and a wealth of applications.

Tablets provide easy access and freedom of use through their connectivity and light and robust casings. Teachers can keep track of student assignments, check the library for availability of specific texts, plan next month's field trip, develop a data chart for collection of artifacts during the field trip, and download a topographical map of the designated field trip site.

Digital Cameras

Will Weber, a professor in the College of Education at the University of Houston, would tell his college classroom management students to "catch students being good." He said that positive reinforcement is the most powerful management tool in a teacher's possession. Take pictures of your students being wonderful and load the pictures on a computer and project them to the SMART Board so everyone can see. Selfies are all the rage. Have students take snaps of themselves doing something great. When things get a little out of hand in the classroom, run the photos as a slide show. Soon all students will get the picture, and order will be restored without you having to say a word. A picture really is worth a thousand words.

In the process of helping your students see themselves in action, it is important to remember that such pictures or videos are not for viewing outside of the classroom or for the other-than-intended purpose. Teachers must always protect students' privacy and never share pictures of students without permission from parents or from the students themselves.

An opposite approach would be to take a series of pictures of a classroom out of control, put them on a computer monitor, and ask the students to explain what's happening and what can be done so it does not happen again. Students sometimes think they are invisible to the all-seeing eyes of a teacher. They're wrong, of course, but showing the students what the teacher sees, rather than just telling them, can be a mighty behavior management tool.

Digital pictures can be used to show student progress and what it looks like when students are learning and growing. Teachers take pictures of class accomplishments and create slide shows. With current technology, it is easy to share these slide shows with parents and other teachers. Each student can have a photo journal of his or her personal record of achievement.

Pictures can provide background for a story or lesson. If you are teaching a story set in Yosemite National Park, you can download pictures of Yosemite from the Internet and create a slide show so the students have visual images of the park during the reading of the story and afterward during questions about the story. Maybe no one in the class has actually been to Yosemite, but the addition of pictures provides a virtual trip for all students and adds an engaging dimension to the story.

Video Recording

In addition to the video-recording capacity of most digital cameras, nearly all cell phones have camera and video-recording applications. Gone are the days of having to tape an event with a cumbersome tape recorder. At any school performance, parents have their cell phones and small video recorders ready to capture images of their children. Teachers can also record students' performances in the classroom. Sometimes it is difficult to record students and teach them at the same time, but more than likely, even elementary students will have no difficulty assuming the role of photographer to assist the teacher. Filming lessons can make learning entertaining. Imagine the titles "Kate Learns to Add," "Shannon and Sean Build an Ant Farm," "Room 68 Crosses the Potomac," and "Terry Totally Rocks at Soccer." The possibilities are endless, and the learning potential through technology is exceptional. When capturing student learning in pictures or videos, teachers must remember to also respect students' privacy.

WHAT MAKES TEACHING STRATEGIES WORK?

Teacher knowledge, skill, dedication, disposition, enthusiasm for helping students learn, and ability to assess student learning are the catalysts that can bring any teaching strategy to its full potential. Teachers who can motivate students to learn by making the content engaging and meaningful, who can use the context in which the students must learn to their best advantage, and who understand the needs of the students use a variety of teaching strategies.

Knowing a variety of instructional strategies and having the flexibility to change them both within and among lessons are two of the greatest assets a teacher can have. Without variety and flexibility to capture the interest and attention of students, it is unlikely that any other key behavior, however well executed, will have the desired effect (Borich, 2011).

During your first attempts at teaching a small group of students or an entire class, it may be that you will feel more confident and competent with only one teaching strategy. The fear of losing control, that the students won't pay attention to you, or that they won't learn what you need to teach them may keep you locked within the parameters of this one teaching strategy. That's natural. We begin learning in small chunks, and we feel very comfortable when we know how to do something, so we practice it and get better at it and feel even more confident as we continue to practice that particular skill. However, the research base in education tells us that teachers who use a range of teaching strategies have a greater chance of meeting the learning needs of their students and of helping students develop academically. It becomes every teacher's responsibility to develop skill in using a variety of strategies to help students connect with the content. Over time, effective teachers learn to make any teaching strategy work for them.

The Importance of Planning

Planning is of the utmost importance in making a variety of teaching strategies work for you and the students. Some types of plans work better with some types of teaching strategies. You will hear and read about the importance of planning in nearly all of your teacher education course work. In your personal life, you have no doubt had much opportunity to plan, but as a student, you have been mainly concerned with enacting the plans of others. Your teachers have told you what they expect you to do, and in best-case scenarios have provided you with examples, directions, and a timeline for achieving the objective. In becoming a teacher, you will need to make the shift from enacting the plans of others to creating plans for others to follow.

Plans need to be detailed, thorough, and doable. Plans must be based on accurate content information, a comprehensive understanding of the context, and both theoretical and practical knowledge of learner capabilities and potential. Plans must include objectives that will meet established curricular goals. In other words, they must make sense across many dimensions. There are many lesson plan formats for teacher education candidates to follow. Often, individual teacher education programs and specific content-area instructors will provide a homegrown lesson plan format that they expect all of the candidates to use. The concept of what should be included in a lesson plan has a theoretical base, while variations on the concept are widespread among educators.

CHALLENGING ASSUMPTIONS
IS COOPERATIVE GROUP WORK BENEFICIAL TO HIGH-PERFORMING STUDENTS?

The Assumption

High-performing students do not benefit from working cooperatively on group projects with students who are achieving at lower levels. Students, and occasionally their parents, may complain that by being placed in groups with lower-achieving students, they simply end up doing the work for others and are not challenged to learn at the high levels that they are capable of.

The Research

The benefits of cooperative learning have been extolled through extensive research. It has been claimed that cooperative learning is one of the best researched of all teaching strategies. The research indicates that cooperative learning consistently improves achievement and that students who learn cooperatively have greater retention of the information learned. Working in cooperative learning groups has been shown to encourage positive relationships among all students, improved relations among different ethnic groups, and improved relationships between mainstreaming students with learning disabilities and others. Cooperative learning groups also promote positive feelings about learning and about one's own abilities. Higher-level thinking is promoted through cooperative group learning.

Implications

While the reasons to use cooperative learning groups in a classroom are clear, the potential for individual student success in any cooperative learning group often rests directly on a teacher's ability to plan tasks that require input from each student and address individual needs. In addition to planning appropriate tasks, a teacher must make certain that all students have the opportunity to stretch their learning and reach ever-increasing levels of achievement.

1. Have you ever worked in a cooperative group where one member did no work? What did you do?

2. What might a student of high ability learn from working in a group with a person who always received low scores?

3. What might be the result of having all top-scoring students work together in a group?

Sources: Johnson, D. W., & Johnson, R. (1999). *Learning together and alone: Cooperation, competition, and individualization* (5th ed.). Boston, MA: Allyn & Bacon; King, A. (2002). Structuring peer interactions to promote high-level cognitive processing. *Theory Into Practice, 41*, 31–39.

Instructional Theory Into Practice

Educator Madeline Hunter (1994) proposed that seven basic elements of an effective lesson—(1) anticipatory set, (2) instructional objective, (3) instructional input, (4) example of intended learning outcome, (5) check for understanding, (6) guided practice, and (7) independent practice—help form the foundation for any plan involving any teaching strategy. These elements might not be arranged in the same order, and some of the elements might not be shared with the students to encourage discovery or inquiry learning. Whether all of Hunter's seven basic elements of an effective lesson are shared with the student, they should be part of the instructional plan in one form or another.

Beginning teachers and teachers in training need to keep their plans close by for easy reference. How many of us have had the experience of driving to a new destination (map on the car seat next to us if we have no GPS navigator), checking reference points, and trying to read street signs? Cell phones can be used to get directions when we're on the road, but most school administrators would frown on teachers phoning out to get advice on exactly how to proceed with a lesson in progress. Plans help teachers reach benchmarks and goals and bring the students along. It is a complex and time-consuming task to write a lesson plan. One reason for developing the skill of writing effective lesson plans early in your career is so that once you do write a plan, use it, and judge it as top-notch, you won't have to write the whole plan over again and again, though you may have to modify it for different groups of students. The Internet is a rich resource of lesson plans to provide examples and get you started on planning your own lessons.

The Planning Cycle

Effective teachers are always planning. They think through the design and implementation of lessons long before it is time to actually teach them. They collect artifacts, talk to other teachers and friends about what they want to do, and maybe even try out a plan for a lesson on an unsuspecting family member. Freiberg and Driscoll (2004) explain teacher planning through four phases of a planning cycle (see Figure 12.2).

The first phase, preplanning, may find a teacher sitting quietly in a backyard swing looking at a sky full of clouds and listening to the sound of the wind in the trees. The teacher starts to think about ways to teach a unit on climate and weather to next year's third graders. What do the Common Core State Standards for science say that eight-year-olds need to know about weather? What would they find most interesting about weather? How would it be possible for them to experience weather conditions in other parts of the world? How many children's books does the school library have on weather?

FIGURE 12.2 ■ A Lesson Planning Cycle

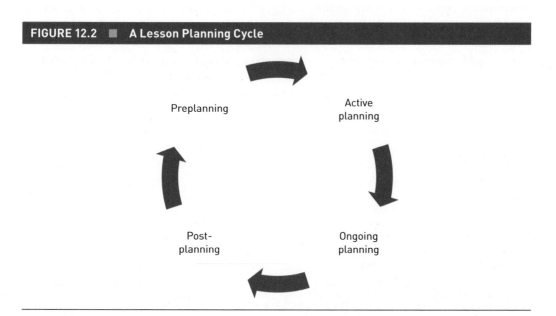

Source: Adapted from Freiberg, J. H., & Driscoll, A. (2004). *Universal teaching strategies.* Boston, MA: Allyn & Bacon.

Questions come together in ideas, and ideas spur teachers on to action. The teacher collects and organizes resources. Before you know it, it is fall, the school year has begun, and it is time to teach a lesson on weather.

The active planning phase of Freiberg's cycle is when teachers actually write the lesson plans they intend to teach. The teacher opens the mental box of weather lessons that has been created in the brain, or filing cabinet, or computer program where all the ideas collected during the preplanning stage have been stored, and begins to write the actual plan.

Ongoing planning takes place while the teacher is actually teaching the lesson. A student's question may prompt the teacher to include a bit of information that wasn't in the original plan, or to read an excellent book recommended by the school librarian, or to show the children an unusual and exciting weather pattern that develops outside the school. The world is full of reasons teachers need to be ready to include ongoing planning in their teaching strategies repertoire.

Postplanning is what teachers do when the lesson is over, the school is quiet, and most everyone has gone home for the day except the custodian, the principal, and a few dedicated teachers. In postplanning, the teacher asks if the goals of the lesson were achieved, if necessary standards were covered, if student learning met expectations, and if there are changes that should be made next time the lesson is taught. In postplanning, the teacher is engaging in reflection on practice. After this period of reflection, the planning cycle begins again as the teacher considers how this lesson might be taught in the future.

Experienced teachers will suggest that it's a good idea to plan more than you actually expect to teach. Teachers should also let the students know the plan. No one likes to be kept in the dark. In explaining or discussing the plan with the students, the teacher may become aware of an approach or idea that the students or a particular student may be interested in that the teacher had not included. Through interactions with students about plans, an opportunity to uncover the curriculum may present itself.

Whatever teaching strategy is used for the lesson, there must be planning. We remember once hearing a teacher say that she was going to "wing it" for an upcoming lesson. No doubt that teacher believed spontaneity was going to get the students where they needed to be. Teachers don't have wings, and they don't fly: They soar on well-thought-out plans. Every student deserves a teacher who knows what the students need to learn, has planned how best to engage them in the process of learning, and knows how to determine if the students have learned the lesson content. Anything short of that just doesn't work in a teacher's world of accountability.

Getting Students Ready to Learn

One of the most critical parts of any teaching strategy is how it is applied in the beginning of the lesson. How do your university instructors begin their lectures? With stories? With anecdotes? By directing your attention to a picture or a chart? Did math classes you attended begin with a "stumper" problem on the board for you to try to solve in the first few minutes of class? When you entered your psychology class, was there a sealed envelope on each desk with instructions not to open it until an exact moment? Such simple devices can capture our attention. They are often mysterious, and frequently so compelling that we don't need to be reminded to pay attention. Our own internal monitoring devices are turned on, and learning has us in its grasp.

Attention-getting activities may include a quick demonstration with an unexpected outcome or asking students to close their eyes and visualize an unlikely event. Attention getting does not need to be elaborate, but it should gain each student's attention.

Bracketing, or, Let's See, Where Was I?

Did you ever walk into a room in your own house and wonder why you were there? Have you ever forgotten something you went to the store to buy? Have you ever left your house and worried that maybe you forgot to turn off the stove? Of course you have. Some students come to school and can't remember what you talked about the day before. So much has happened to them in the interim that they may have misplaced the last bit of information they received at school before heading home, or to their part-time job, or to soccer practice. There's a lot going on in teachers' and students' lives. Part of a teacher's job is to help the students remember where they are in the process of learning in school.

Bracketing is a strategy that teachers can use at the beginning of a lesson or at the end of the lesson. Teachers talk the students through the process of bracketing what happened between yesterday's lesson and today's lesson and set it aside so that the ideas from content studied previously can be easily associated with the ones they are about to learn. For example, a teacher reminds students of the class discussion on magnets held the previous day. She acknowledges that after class the students were engaged in activities unrelated to the discussion and that particles of information from other experiences may have gotten mixed in with the information the students were carrying around about magnets. Then she tells the students it is time to organize the information and ideas surging around in their thinking. Find all the information about magnets, focus on it, and attempt to set aside unrelated information to access at a later time. Bracketing often becomes a habit of mind and can aid considerably in focusing attention on instruction.

The practice of bracketing information can help students focus their attention and thinking on the topic of instruction.

Sponges

Another simple yet effective technique used by teachers to gain student attention at the beginning of a lesson, or to keep student attention during the lesson, is the sponge. This term describes review or extension activities that help to keep learning on track. Sponges can also be used effectively to summarize a lesson through an enjoyable activity. For example, at the end of a lesson on parts of speech or sentence construction, have students in the classroom call out four letters as you write them on the board or overhead projector. Then ask the students to come up with a four-word sentence where each word in the sentence begins with the letters written on the board. It may take a few seconds for the first sentence to be formed, but once you have written two or three sentences on the board, the students' ideas will come at you like wildfire. Such an activity could be used to introduce a lesson or as a wrap-up. Visit the website "A to Z Teacher Stuff" (http://atozteacherstuff.com/) for additional ideas on sponge activities. This website has a wealth of ideas about everything you might want to do in the classroom.

Evaluating Learning

The purpose of assessment is to measure student learning. Since different teaching strategies tend to stimulate different types of learning, it is important for teachers to learn about and be able to use a wide variety of assessment strategies. It would be illogical to evaluate student learning following a role-playing situation with a multiple-choice test. And a test on the facts and rules of one content area would not work for a classroom of students who were researching different subjects. Assessment should become a part of every teacher's repertoire of teaching strategies so that teachers apply knowledge of assessment in planning, in decision making, and in communicating with students.

Knowledge about learners is gained through interactions with and observations of the students. Teachers need to observe students, to record their observations, and to seek information about students from outside the classroom. Teachers also need to be clear about the methods of assessment they are using and to what end they are using them. You will learn more about assessing student learning in Chapter 13 of this text; as you do, keep in mind the connection between the content, the context, the learner, and assessment and teaching strategies.

Teacher Work Sample or Analysis of Student Work

Teachers can also document student work and their own effectiveness as teachers by a process of work samples. Perhaps you have already been introduced to Teacher Work Samples (TWSs) or Analysis of Student Work (ASW) in your teacher education program. The process of developing a TWS or ASW offers evidence of your ability to design and implement standards-based instruction, assess student learning, and reflect on the teaching and learning process. These products also provide credible evidence of your ability to facilitate learning of all students. TWSs and ASWs are sources of evidence your instructors and supervisors use along with classroom observations and other measures to assess your performance as a teacher relative to national and state teaching standards.

Understanding the Connection Between Teaching Strategies and Curriculum

In Chapter 10 of this text, you were introduced to the role curriculum plays in instruction and learning. What we discover in learning about teaching strategies is that they share a symbiosis with curriculum. Teaching strategies cannot really exist without curriculum, and vice versa. They rely on one another for successful delivery; they are different sides of the same coin. Of what use would a teaching strategy be if there was no purpose for using it? Curriculum supplies the purpose. Curriculum is what we teach. Instruction is how we teach the curriculum, and the strategies we use should be relevant to both.

In many ways, the teacher is in control of the curriculum, though sometimes it may seem otherwise, given the heft of district curriculum guides and state and federal curriculum policies. Curriculum materials can be used in different ways. Teachers use curriculum materials according to their own personal practical knowledge. They consider how curriculum can be applied in the context and best meet the needs of the students. Teachers use different approaches to teaching to make the relevance and significance of curriculum apparent to the students. Teachers have to be able to visualize what written curriculum looks like in action. The talent it takes to make the transition from text to action is much greater than the talent it takes to recognize the curriculum action once it occurs, but a teacher must possess both talents.

HOW ARE DIFFERENT STRATEGIES USED FOR DIFFERENT PURPOSES?

We all remember clearly the teachers we had who were able to help us "see" and understand concepts that were new to us or difficult for us to grasp—teachers who used all manner of paraphernalia to help us connect what we already knew about the world in general to what we had to learn specifically. These were the teachers who carried schoolbags full of objects they had collected that we could hold and manipulate, while they talked us through ideas, lessons, and experiments.

Doing math is different from teaching math. Teaching math, as well as other subjects, is as much an art as it is a science. Teachers must train themselves to think like artists at times. They must constantly draw on creativity in their approach to teaching. If you approach teaching strictly from an empirical perspective, you're painting by the numbers. Art is a creative way of organizing reality. The logic of teaching is the logic of the well-organized artist whose palette is arranged methodically so that his or her creativity can have free rein.

Culturally Relevant Teaching Strategies

Culturally relevant teaching strategies refers to the ways generic strategies are modified or implemented to address the fact that students' orientations to learning may be influenced by their cultural backgrounds. The ways in which students interact with one another and with the teacher also may be influenced by their cultural background (Irvine & York, 2001). Students who live in an Italian or Jewish neighborhood in New York City, students from a fishing town in Florida, students who attend an inner-city school in Chicago or Los Angeles, and students from a small mining town in a remote area of northern Nevada will bring different backgrounds to school and have different orientations to learning. Teaching strategies that accommodate the ways student learning is influenced by cultural background have a greater chance of meeting students' needs for learning.

Some students require less structure and want to solve problems on their own with a minimum of teacher help. Planning lessons that provide opportunities for students to learn within differently structured contexts is part of what makes teaching such an interesting and engaging profession. In her book *Culturally Responsive Teaching: Theory, Research, and Practice* (2010), Geneva Gay describes the diverse roles and responsibilities teachers must assume in a culturally responsive classroom.

Strategies for English Language Learners (ELLs)

Many students in your future classrooms will have limited or no English-language capacity. You will be responsible for helping these students learn the content. Since the role of language has a strong influence on student learning and may place students who do not speak, read, or understand English at a disadvantage, you will be expected to implement strategies that diminish this disadvantage. Some schools may use a "pullout" approach, allowing limited English proficiency (LEP) students to spend part of the day in a special bilingual class. However, chances are that all teachers will need to possess some skill in using strategies to help LEP students learn. The first step in teaching LEP students should always be to show respect for students' cultural backgrounds. It doesn't take much energy for a teacher to learn how to pronounce a student's name correctly, but the effort will make a world of difference in the student's attitude toward the teacher and consequently toward learning.

Homework as a Teaching Strategy

One of the best pieces of advice we received from experienced teachers when we began our professional careers was to never have students do homework that they had not started in class or that they weren't sure how to complete. No teacher wants a student to go home and report, "I don't know why I'm doing this, and I don't understand it at all."

Homework is a form of interactive practice in which the learner is interacting with the content. When the teacher is not present to mediate this interaction, though, the student had better be absolutely clear about what needs to be done and why. Homework is an extension of classroom learning and, when planned carefully, can assist student achievement; but like every other strategy a teacher uses, homework should fit the content, the context, and the learner. If practice makes perfect, then it becomes a teacher's responsibility to somehow monitor the practice that occurs during homework so that it will not become imperfect practice. One educator suggests that no homework should be assigned until the teacher has completed the same work. A flipped classroom puts homework exercises in the classroom and makes the traditional teacher lecture or video something students can watch at home or on their own before engaging in activities related to the content under the supervision of a teacher.

CONNECTING TO THE CLASSROOM

This chapter introduced you to some of the teaching strategies that teachers employ in the classroom. There are many reasons teachers use a variety of teaching strategies to help students access information. As you visit classrooms for observation and practice, be alert to the rationale a teacher might have for using one strategy over another. Here are some ideas to help focus your observations.

1. Students do not all learn in the same manner.

2. Learning skills and facts is more easily facilitated by some strategies than others.

3. Space and time have major influences on the strategies teachers can use.

4. Materials and resources may influence the strategies teachers use.

5. Most effective lessons utilize more than one teaching strategy.

6. A teaching strategy should always match the method by which students will be assessed.

SUMMARY

Understanding that instruction is the systematic delivery of content to a unique set of individuals in a specified context is part of the specialized knowledge of a professional teacher.

- What are teaching strategies? A teaching strategy is the yeast in the lesson that makes it rise to meet students' interests and abilities. Teaching strategies provide the pedagogical framework for the professional teacher to deliver the content and to build instruction and activities around standards and the required curriculum.

- What makes teaching strategies work? Part of making teaching strategies work is being able to assess their impact on student learning, so teachers have to collect data and use those data to guide future practice. Teaching strategies used correctly have the power to transform a ripple on a pond to a wavelength and frequency in a student's mind.

- How are different strategies used for different purposes? We're not the same as people or as learners. Each of us sees the world from a single perspective born of a million different influences and effects. Not all students discover the same bit of information simultaneously, if at all. Teachers must always look through the eyes of their students to see where learning connects for each of them.

KEY TERMS

activity approach 368

cooperative learning groups 364

direct or explicit instruction 367

fishbowl 362

indirect or implicit instruction 367

learning cycle 355

metacognition 367

modeling 368

problem-based learning 368

scaffolding 368

strategy 355

taxonomies 360

wait-time I 362

wait-time II 362

CLASS DISCUSSION QUESTIONS

1. It would be unreasonable to expect a novice practitioner to enter the classroom highly knowledgeable of and skilled in the use of multiple approaches to teaching. Which teaching strategy would you like to learn first? What advice is of most worth in this process? How might you practice a teaching strategy even before you have a classroom of your own?

2. Resources are like advice: They fall into categories of useful and not so useful. What types of resources are most likely to help teacher education candidates increase their knowledge of teaching strategies? What are some ways to store and organize resources so they will be readily available when needed?

3. The diversity of student characteristics in a classroom can make some teachers lack confidence in their ability to meet the learning needs of all students. What examples have you seen when the strategy clearly matched the students' backgrounds?

4. Helping students identify and build on their strengths is an often underemphasized tenet of teaching. Recognizing one's own strengths can lead to confidence. Feeling confident when teaching a group of students leads to competence. Consider your strengths: How will these help you in teaching? Which strategies do you believe will benefit most from the strengths you possess?

SELF-ASSESSMENT

What Is Your Current Level of Understanding and Thinking About Teaching Strategies?

One of the indicators of understanding is to examine how complex your thinking is when asked questions that require you to use the concepts and facts introduced in this chapter. After you answer the following questions as fully as you can, rate your knowledge on the Assessing Your Learning rubric to self-assess the degree to which you understand and can apply a variety of instructional strategies.

1. In what ways would a teacher have to plan differently for a lecture and organizing cooperative group work?

2. What is the planning cycle that teachers use in lesson implementation?

3. What activities might teachers use to get their students ready for learning?

4. Should teachers be aware of the different approaches to learning that their students possess?

Assess your current level of understanding of how the teaching strategies can improve student learning.

Assessing Your Learning Rubric

	Parts & Pieces	Unidimensional	Organized	Integrated	Extensions
Indicators	Elements/concepts are talked about as isolated and independent entities. Some important names are provided in isolation.	One or a few concepts are addressed, while others are underdeveloped, or not mentioned.	Deliberate and structured consideration of all key concepts/elements.	All key concepts/elements are included in a view that addresses interconnections.	Integration of all elements and dimensions, with extrapolation to new situations.
Using teaching strategies to improve student learning	Able to name one or two phases of the planning cycle.	Can describe the planning necessary for use of one strategy but does not compare this process to another strategy.	Is articulate in describing ways teachers' knowledge of strategies can promote student learning.	Combines knowledge of strategies and students' learning styles.	Adjusts planning and teaching strategies to students' learning styles to prepare students for learning.

FIELD GUIDE
FOR LEARNING MORE ABOUT . . .

Teaching Strategies

Go back and read the introduction to the field guide in Chapter 1. Think about what you are learning about teaching and what you might include in your field guide related to the topics in this chapter.

Ask a Teacher	Ask a teacher what his or her favorite teaching strategy is and why he or she prefers it over others. Have the teacher tell you how he or she learned it and developed skill in using it. Also, ask the teacher if the strategy is most effective with any particular content area.
Make Your Own Observations	Plan a short lecture on a subject you feel will be of interest to students at a specific grade level. Be sure to follow the five guidelines discussed in the chapter (audience, focus, organization, clarity, and pacing). Make an outline of your lecture. Visit a classroom when the teacher is delivering a lecture. Compare your lecture structure to the one the teacher used. If the teacher used a lecture structure different from the one you outlined, ask why.
Reflect Through Journaling	Think of something you learned and who taught it to you. For example, how did you learn to tie your shoes, scramble an egg, play a musical instrument, dance, or wash a load of clothes so all the clothes didn't come out some shade of pink or dusty brown? Describe the process. How did the person who helped you learn teach you? What strategies did he or she use? Did the teacher use repetition, written instructions, or a demonstration? Did you have to practice on your own, or did the teacher work through the process with you? Write a brief description of the learning process you went through. What teaching strategies work best for you?
Build Your Portfolio	Teachers who continue to grow and learn access the resources available to them, work with other professionals, and collect data representing their teaching performance and the performance of their students. You have no doubt already begun a Professional Development portfolio. This is a perfect place to keep a record of your growth in understanding and using an array of teaching strategies. These would be good ideas to put on your mental rolodex. Make a list of the key components of one teaching strategy you have observed and understand. Describe how you might have used it in one of your practicum experiences. Select a content area (e.g., reading, math, science, social studies, art, or music) that you are interested in teaching. Write six questions you could ask to elicit differing levels of student thinking. Make certain the questions you write will help the students achieve the objective of a particular lesson. Write one question for each of the levels in Bloom's (1956) taxonomy.

(Continued)

(Continued)

Read a Book	Everyone who teaches should read *Enhancing Teaching* by Madeline Hunter (1994, Macmillan). It is easy to read, addresses many aspects of designing instruction to help students achieve success in school, and is written from the personal perspective of an educator who understands the teacher's role.
	Read *What Great Teachers Do Differently* by Todd Whitaker (2007, Taylor & Francis). This second edition of Whitaker's book focuses on the specific things that great teachers do that others do not, and lists 17 things that matter most in classroom teaching. The book describes the beliefs, behaviors, attitudes, and interactions that form the fabric of life in our best classrooms and schools.
	Read *Teach Like Your Hair's on Fire* by Rafe Esquith (2007, Penguin Random House) for some delightful insights into keeping students engaged in learning.
	Another recommended read is Nieto, S. (2009). *The light in their eyes: Creating multicultural learning communities* (10th ed.). New York, NY: Teachers College Press.
Search the Web	Visit **http://visibleclassroom.com/** for a look at ways to have your teaching evaluated through distant technologies. This program is out of the University of Melbourne in Australia. It is intended to help you see your use of teaching strategies. Seeing your own teaching and watching video demonstrations of effective teaching can help you improve your practice. And it is interesting to see ways teachers in other countries use teaching strategies to help students learn.
	Visit **www.teachingchannel.org/videos** for examples of teacher training, real-life applications, and discussions of teaching strategies in the planning stages and in action.
	Search for these ideas on the Internet: anchor charts, Aztec Learning System, MobyMax, Study Island, Everyday Math, Words in Action, and SLANT techniques.

STUDENT STUDY SITE

$SAGE edge™

Get the tools you need to sharpen your study skills. **SAGE edge** offers a robust online environment featuring an impressive array of free tools and resources.

Access practice quizzes, eFlashcards, video, and multimedia at **edge.sagepub.com/hall3e**.

13 ASSESSING STUDENT LEARNING AND USING THE RESULTS

© Elliott Asp

EDUCATOR INTERVIEW

Dr. Elliott Asp

Meet Dr. Elliott Asp. Currently, he is a consultant in relation to assessing learning. Recently, he was the interim superintendent of the Colorado Department of Education. Before this assignment, he was an assistant superintendent for performance improvement in the Cherry Creek (Denver, Colorado) School District, and before that director of assessment in the Douglas County (Colorado) School District. Throughout his career, Dr. Asp's endeavors have focused on helping teachers and principals learn about the new assessment approaches and facilitating their developing understanding of the critical relationships between assessments, instruction, and student learning.

"I was hired in Cherry Creek to change the system," Dr. Asp explains. "The mission there was continuous improvement. No matter how good you are, you can get better. Our job was to push the district in the direction of positive change. When at the Colorado Department of Education, I advised the state superintendent and school districts about assessment approaches and the uses of data."

Dr. Asp is a nationally recognized expert in assessment of student learning. He has published many papers and is regularly sought after to assist school districts engaged in improving the assessment of student performance.

Q: What do you see as being important for teachers to know about assessment?

A: The first thing teachers need is to have a firm understanding of the difference between formative and summative assessment. They need to understand how formative assessments can be used as a process to inform instruction and really improve student achievement. In the past, teachers would be more focused on testing and "How do I give grades?" rather than on "How do I give meaningful feedback?" In particular, they need to see assessment as being broader than just a test or quiz.

Q: What do you see as being the key differences between testing and assessing?

A: Testing is usually viewed as an event—for example, some sort of summative event that says we are going to see how you are at this point in time. I see formative assessment as much more of a process. The teacher is trying to get a handle on where kids are and where to go next with instruction. The teacher is seeing how much progress the students have made over time in terms of achieving a goal. Testing is more of an event: "I do something and I am done, rather than charting progress and growth and using the information to determine where I go next."

Q: Do you see that secondary teachers can apply these ideas?

A: They are learning more about assessment, too. In addition, they have to reeducate their students so that they understand and use formative assessments. Secondary students tend to come in thinking that all that is important is the grade, not what they learned. These students ask, "How come you are not grading this piece, just giving me feedback?" Secondary teachers not only have to learn the techniques of formative assessment; they have to change the mindset of the kids. We use a book called *Mindset: The New Psychology of Success*, by Carol Dweck (2007). It deals with changing the mindset of kids to a growth mindset. It is not that you are either smart or dumb. The reason you do well is because you work hard.

Q: What do you expect a first-year teacher to know and be able to do in relation to assessing student learning?

A: More than anything, I really want them to have at least some knowledge and skill in the area of a variety of ways of assessing, particularly in formative assessments. There are a variety of techniques, but they come down to two things: feedback and questioning. First, feedback can take the form of teachers giving feedback to students and thinking about how to do that in an effective and efficient way—thinking about what effective feedback looks like and how I manage that in a classroom. Second is the ability to ask questions that get at what kids are thinking. Feedback gets at it in a way that sets high expectations for all students. This is tricky since the way you ask questions and give feedback conveys high expectations.

Q: How do you see joy in teaching?

A: That is a great question! You can see joy in teaching in several ways. First is in the relationships with kids and families. If you don't find joy in kids and developing relationships with their families, you probably are not going to be very happy in teaching. Another is in watching students grow both academically and personally. Also I enjoy seeing teachers grow professionally—seeing their skills improve and seeing them get better at handling various situations, whether the situations involve academic growth of kids or how to motivate and get kids involved in more meaningful ways in classrooms— and teachers having support of colleagues and being part of Professional Learning Communities where there is excitement about improving their practice.

Q: We interviewed you for the last edition of this book. What have you learned since?

A: I have been giving a lot of thinking to how much time districts and the state spend on the annual testing. The tests are administered in the spring, and the schools get the results back about time for the beginning of the new school year. If they spend more than September on the results, it is a waste of time. In the end, the results don't tell you a whole lot. Another point is how important formative assessment is in defining high-quality instruction.

Questions to Consider

1. If you were being interviewed for a teaching position by Dr. Asp, what questions would you expect him to ask?

2. What do you think he means when he says he expects teachers to "understand how formative assessments can be used as a process to inform instruction and really improve student achievement"?

3. Dr. Asp talks a lot about the differences between formative and summative assessment. Do you know what he is talking about?

4. What are your current ideas about how to give meaningful feedback to students? Is there more to it than providing test scores and grades?

INTRODUCTION

Today's teachers cannot escape hearing, talking, and reading about testing and assessing. Teachers are told that assessing is a key component of all lesson plans. Curriculum and instruction experts constantly talk about assessing student learning. Teacher educators, as well as school district administrators like Dr. Asp, are constantly pointing out that good instruction involves high-quality teachers continually assessing their students and making adjustments in instruction. At the same time, school districts, state policy makers, and the federal government have mandated annual testing of students and licensing tests for teachers. Policy makers and the media focus intently on test results and use the scores to rank schools, school districts, and states. In recent years, some states have begun to use test scores to evaluate teachers and principals.

So, what's all the fuss about? Teachers continually observe their students, evaluate their homework, give tests, and assign grades. Why do some people talk about *testing* and others seem to prefer the term *assessing*? The answers to these questions are found inside three other questions. The first two important questions for aspiring teachers are "What are different methods for assessing student work?" and "How do I determine grades and prepare report cards?" As important as each of these questions is, a third question is even more to the point: "How do I use the information about students' current level of understanding to adjust my instruction?" Each of these questions is addressed in this chapter. Highly effective teachers have the knowledge, skills, and understanding to address all three of these questions in their teaching.

WHY IS ASSESSING SO IMPORTANT?

We find a lot of confusion when teachers are giving benchmark tests two or three times a year, which tend to be more summative. This is different from having an ongoing process. Yes, the benchmarks can be used in a formative way, but they tend to be only used to make final judgments.

—Dr. Asp

Most school years begin with district- and school-based staff meetings. One of the major topics will be how the district and each school did on the previous year's state-mandated tests. The talk will include terms like *CRTs*, *NRTs*, and *cut scores*. Principals and teachers will ask: "Will we be using the same CRTs as last year?" "What about the NRTs that the district had us doing in February?" "You know, that is the real problem: The CRTs are performance based, while the NRTs are multiple choice. No wonder our test scores are not improving." NRTs? CRTs? Performance based? Many beginning teachers will have no idea what they are talking about!

Teachers, administrators, policy makers, and parents talk a lot about testing and assessing, but it is not always clear that they are talking about the same things. There are very important differences to keep in mind. **Tests** are structured opportunities to measure how much the test taker knows and can do at a particular point in time. The test conditions should be consistent for all test takers, and there is an expectation that each individual will make a maximum effort. **Assessing** is the process that entails interpreting test results and developing a plan for what will be done next.

Good teachers are always checking for student understanding through observation and listening to student discourse.

iStock/XiXinXing

THE WHYS AND HOWS FOR ASSESSING

Teachers need to keep in mind why they are testing and/or assessing. Just because it is Friday does not necessarily mean that it is time for a test. There should be a clear understanding about the purpose of all assessment efforts. There are a number of reasons for assessing that will be of help to the teacher. Often forgotten is that there are a number of purposes for assessing that are of direct benefit to the students. Teachers need to think carefully about why they are assessing, and they need to pay particular attention to how the assessment activity will contribute to increasing further student learning.

A metaphor to illustrate these two important concepts is how property tax rates are determined. Every few years, the value of houses, stores, and other real estate is reexamined. The potential sale price is estimated by comparing its value to like properties that have been sold recently. That price is similar to a student's score on a test. The tax assessor examines the property and its likely sale price, as if it were for sale, and sets the amount of tax to be paid accordingly. Determining the final tax amount requires some interpretation and judgment. The tax bill is not a simple calculation; rather, the assessor takes into consideration a number of factors such as condition, trends in the neighborhood, and the amount of taxes paid for like properties.

A parallel process takes place in assessing student learning. The test score has little meaning until the assessor interprets it and compares the results to how the student has done earlier. The assessor will likely compare the student's score to those obtained by students in similar and different situations. The assessor also takes into consideration the special needs of each student. The assessor then develops recommendations and plans for next steps for instruction.

Two Ways of Thinking: Formative Versus Summative

There are two very different ways of thinking about assessing. An expert assessor understands both and keeps both in mind. When the purpose is purely to provide feedback on student progress and to guide preparation of tomorrow's lessons, it is called formative evaluation. When test results are used to make conclusions about how much a student has learned or to decide whether a student is ready to move to the next grade level, it is called summative evaluation.

Another way to describe these two ways of thinking is to consider why the testing is being done. Is it "testing *of* learning" or "testing *for* learning?" Testing of learning is to determine how much has been learned in order to draw a conclusion (e.g., assign a grade), which is summative. Testing for learning is to determine how much has been learned so far and to guide next steps in instruction in order to have further learning, which is formative. Some indicators of these two ways of thinking are presented in Table 13.1.

Effective teachers are doing formative evaluations about student learning continually. They build in spot-checks within lessons, review assignments, and monitor students at work throughout the day. When they assign report card grades and at the end of the school year recommend or don't recommend promotion, they are making summative decisions. In most states, the results of mandated testing are used to make summative judgments such as qualifying for high school graduation, ranking of schools, and eligibility for teacher licensure.

Purposes for Assessing

Within these two general ways of thinking about testing and assessing, there are a number of different purposes. For each purpose, the design of the assessment is different, but each must have an acceptable level of quality, given understanding of how the results will be used. Also, the type of learning being assessed is associated with certain kinds of assessments being more appropriate. An additional very important consideration is taking into account the characteristics of the students being

TABLE 13.1 ■ Two Ways of Thinking About Assessing	
Assessment *for* Learning	Assessment *of* Learning
Diagnostic	Concluding
Adjust for student differences	Treat all students the same
Less rigorous test construction	High test rigor
Use as baseline	End point
Checking on progress	Setting a grade
There may be collaboration	Each student works alone
Developmental	Competitive
Varied approaches to answer	Getting the right answer

assessed. For example, there is an obvious mismatch when English Language Learners (ELLs) are given a mathematics word-problem test in English and their scores are treated the same as those of students whose native language is English.

Table 13.2 provides a scale that moves from purely formative to purely summative. The Purpose and Examples columns list examples of the two ways to think about assessing student learning. In reviewing this table, you will see that there is a flow from top to bottom. The purpose of assessments at the top is formative, while for those at the bottom it is summative. As the examples illustrate, the quality of the test has to increase as the purpose becomes more summative. Regardless of the purpose, more-effective teachers are thinking and asking, "How can I use the results of this assessment to adjust my instruction and increase student learning?"

TABLE 13.2 ■ Different Purposes for Testing and Assessing

	Type	Purpose	Examples
FORMATIVE	Diagnosing readiness for learning	Finding out what students already know, and don't know, and whether they have the prerequisite knowledge and skills for an upcoming lesson Finding out if students have certain learning difficulties or skill deficiencies	A diagnosis indicating that students are not writing introductory sentences for paragraphs, or that when given a table of numbers, most students cannot construct bar graphs correctly
	Checking for understanding within lessons	Spot-checking to see if students are "getting it"	Asking for "thumbs up" or "thumbs down" Short teacher question–student answer strategy during a lesson Having students do a sample problem Having one or more students solve an example in front of the class Having students explain to each other how they solved a problem
	Checking for indicators of learning progress across lessons	Seeing what has been learned, retained, understood, and misunderstood from lesson to lesson	Reviews Pop quizzes Homework assignments Online discussions Submission of drafts
	Adjusting instruction	Monitoring to see the effects of adjustments in instruction within each lesson and across each day Determining if some strategies seem to result in more learning	Obtaining information about the current understanding of students Engaging in self-reflection Thinking about what can be done next to improve student learning
	Assessing gains in student learning	Determining the amount of growth in student learning at the end of lessons, units, and terms	Teacher-made tests Grading of student reports and major products Grade/department/district interim assessments
	Reporting progress	Providing grades to students and parents	Report cards Parent conferences
SUMMATIVE	Gatekeeping	Decisions about pass/fail, promotion/retention	End-of-term grades Scores on district and state standardized tests

Considering the Quality of Assessments

Careful and thorough assessment work is absolutely necessary when it is time to report progress or to make gatekeeping decisions. Even though talking about it makes us feel uncomfortable, a reality today is that much of the testing that is being done by school districts, states, schools, and teachers is for the purpose of sorting students. Students are not being allowed to advance to the next level of schooling (e.g., middle school to high school) unless they pass a test. No pass, no play policies, introduced in Chapter 8, prohibit students from participating in sports and band unless they maintain a certain Grade Point Average. And teacher education candidates cannot become licensed to teach unless they pass a state-mandated licensure exam. When tests are used to gate-keep, there is likely to be little room for interpretation or accommodation of special situations or unique individual differences. Instead, there is **high-stakes testing**, where a particular score, called a cut score (see Chapter 1), is established. Those who have a higher test score are eligible to move on to the next level. Depending on the purpose of the test, those who score lower cannot move on to the next level, graduate, or receive a license to teach.

One way to view the tensions between the purpose of the assessment and the quality of the test is presented in Figure 13.1. The left-hand side of the continuum signifies major teacher responsibility for the design of tests and the interpretation of the results. As your eyes move across the continuum from left to right, the role of the teacher as test maker decreases, while expectations for test quality increase. For example, a teacher-made test should not be used to make a high-stakes decision such as a grade promotion or graduation decision. Note also that for high-stakes decisions there should be more than a single assessment: There should be **multiple assessments**. As the decision to be made becomes more high stakes, more than one measure should be applied. This is one of the hotly debated issues in today's state and federal education policy environment, where most of the time the score on a single test is used to make a high-stakes decision.

Teachers need to think through how the amount of rigor in their assessments compares with the weight of the decision being made. Assessing learning at the end of a unit requires more rigor than daily checking for understanding. Assessing learning for a semester or a year is an even larger responsibility, requiring much more careful construction of the measure(s) and extensive consideration of how to interpret and report the results.

Teachers also need to make sure that the tests that they construct are closely based on the curriculum and benchmarks. Students' scores on a teacher-made test that has little correlation with the district and state standards will not be as helpful to the students or the teacher as will the measure that has a clear relationship to the standards and benchmarks.

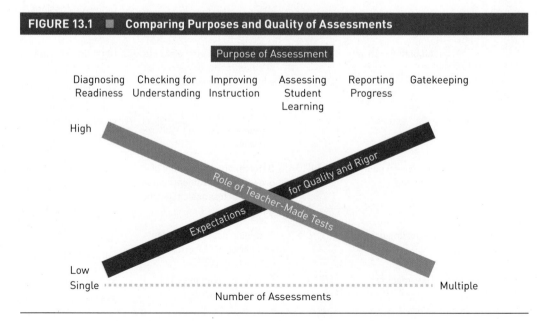

FIGURE 13.1 ■ Comparing Purposes and Quality of Assessments

A Caution

One important caution for teachers to keep in mind is that all of their assessments can face close scrutiny if someone challenges one of their decisions. Parents and often students will question a grade. There also is the possibility of legal action challenging a particular assessment and/or decision. For example, a suit could be filed on behalf of a student where there is an indication of discrimination, or where there is parent disagreement about promotion. Another possibility for legal action arises when there is a belief that a particular test was not scored correctly or that the test used was not an appropriate estimate of the amount of student learning. In summary, as is illustrated in Figure 13.1, it is very important for teachers to think carefully about the quality of each assessment activity and its purpose. They also should keep careful documentation about each assessment just in case someone has questions.

Two Very Different Kinds of Tests

Whenever testing is done, one of the most critical decisions relates to how the resulting test scores will be compared. A test score by itself has no meaning. A student could have a test score of 33, or 5, or 357. The score does not make any sense until it is compared with something. One of the interesting and important parts of testing is determining which comparison to make. In today's schools, two very different ways of comparing test scores are being used. One way to interpret a test score is to compare it with how other students did on the same test. The other way is to compare the score with a certain level of performance. Teachers need to understand these two very different ways of interpreting test results. Unfortunately, there is a great deal of confusion and misunderstanding about the two ways of thinking and their consequences.

Norm-Referenced Tests (NRTs)

The most widely used and well-understood approach to comparing test scores is when the test score of one student is compared with the scores of other students. This is called a **Norm-Referenced Test (NRT)**. The comparison group for teacher-made tests is typically the other students in the class. For standardized tests and high-stakes tests, the comparison group of test takers will be a large sample of similar students. The sample could be all other third graders in the state or a national sample of like students.

When all of these students take a well-designed test, the distribution of their scores will form a **normal curve**. If a perfect test score was 100, then the scores for all students would be distributed across the total possible range of test scores, as is illustrated in Figure 13.2. Very few students would have extremely low or extremely high scores, and the one test score received by the highest number of students would be 50. The average, or "mean," test score for all students would be 50. Keep in mind that this is a *theoretical* view of the distribution of test scores. Rarely would the test scores from a teacher-made test fit this profile, nor should they. Regardless of how the comparison group is assembled, in NRTs one student's test score is compared with the scores of other students.

Criterion-Referenced Tests (CRTs)

An important alternative way to compare test scores is to identify a level of performance, a *criterion*, and then check to see if a particular student's score is above or below that level. As the name implies, with **Criterion-Referenced Tests (CRTs)** each student's test score is compared with a defined level of performance, rather than with how other students have done. This approach is particularly useful when student learning is being defined in terms of standards and benchmarks.

Criterion-Referenced Tests (CRTs) compare each student's level of performance with a particular level of accomplishment. Clearing the bar is what counts, not how this student's performance compares with how other students do.

iStock/Colleen Butler

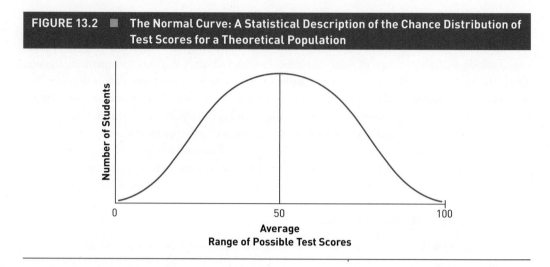

FIGURE 13.2 ■ The Normal Curve: A Statistical Description of the Chance Distribution of Test Scores for a Theoretical Population

With CRTs, the assessor asks, "Has the student attained the desired standard or benchmark?" Rather than comparing the student's level of learning with how well a comparison group of students has done, the test result is compared with the level of learning stated in the benchmark or standard.

Comparing Norm-Referenced Test (NRT) and Criterion-Referenced Test (CRT) Scores

Teachers, school leaders, and policy makers often confuse the two ways of thinking about test results. Some simple examples can be helpful in clarifying the differences between NRTs and CRTs. In high school track meets, one of the standard events is the high jump. Athletes run up to a horizontal bar and attempt to roll their body over the bar without knocking it off its brackets. In a norm-referenced view, the height that one athlete is able to clear would be compared with the heights reached by a sample of other students. If the average 10th-grade girl can clear 48 inches and Malinda cleared 60 inches, her performance is far above average. In the criterion-referenced view, a certain height would be set as the benchmark, and if the student cleared that height, that would be seen as success. Ralph cleared 50 inches, which was the minimum level of performance set for his age group. In both ways of thinking, students can be seen as "winners." The difference is the basis of comparison for the decision.

Characteristics of Effective Assessments

Test and assessment experts have identified several criteria that teachers should use when considering the selection and uses of assessments developed by others and in making their own. For example, one important question is "How hard should the assessment be?" If the test is too easy, then it will not discriminate between those students who understand a lot and those who have limited understanding. A test that is too difficult will lead to student frustration and the teacher having little information about how much students have learned. Another important characteristic of good assessments is that they are related clearly to the desired learning outcomes—that is, to the standard. Some of the important technical aspects of test construction are introduced next.

Level of Difficulty

One of the biggest challenges for expert test makers and teachers is developing test items that are not too easy and not too hard. A test can be too difficult for many reasons. If the assessment includes words that the students don't know, or if an activity or diagram is not clear, then students will do poorly. They may know the information, but they do not understand how to show it. Of course, there also are the tests that ask students about information that was not covered in class, projects, readings, or other

UNDERSTANDING AND USING DATA
LOOKING FOR AN ACHIEVEMENT GAP

The Problem

A very important task for teachers is to be able to use data to understand and illustrate achievement gaps. Unfortunately, achievement gaps are all too common in today's schools.

Examine the table of data for fifth-grade student achievement in mathematics in one school. What can you say based on these test score means? Is there any indication of an achievement gap? What are the trends across the school years? How else could these data be displayed in order to better "see" any patterns?

Achievement in Mathematics by Racial/Ethnic Categories: Fifth-Grade Means (One Elementary School)							
	2009–2010	2010–2011	2011–2012	2012–2013	2013–2014	2014–2015	Across Years
White and Asian	53.67	51.43	54.44	55.41	53.05	53.57	53.58
Nonwhite	32.56	31.06	33.22	35.08	36.29	39.71	36.87
Whole Group	47.32	44.30	47.18	45.24	44.67	46.64	45.89

Interpreting the Data

Rarely will trend data be a perfect straight line from low to high, or high to low. The data presented for the white and Asian fifth-grade mathematics scores are typical. From year to year, the means vary, but there is no clear direction other than each year being about the same. However, there is a clear pattern for the test score means with nonwhite fifth graders. The average test score increased each year after the 2010–2011 school year. But this trend by itself does not tell us if the achievement gap is shrinking. A comparison has to be made of the differences in means with the white and Asian test takers.

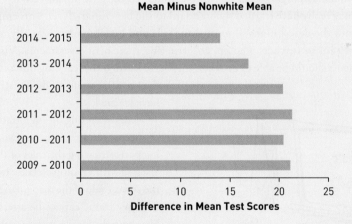

Achievement Gap = White and Asian Mean Minus Nonwhite Mean

One interesting way to illustrate the size of the achievement gap is to determine its size each year by subtracting the nonwhite mean from the white and Asian mean. When a bar graph is constructed using these differences, the decreasing achievement gap is more easily seen. The most significant drops took place in the most recent two years. Why do you suppose this pattern occurred?

assignments. Many beginning teachers are concerned that all of the students might get high grades on a test and therefore As. To prevent this from happening, they might make test items too complicated or difficult. In these situations, the teacher has not fully thought through the reason for the assessment. Is it to check for understanding (i.e., formative)? Or is it to determine the amount of learning, or to determine a final grade (i.e., summative)?

Validity

Another important characteristic of tests is that they measure what is intended—in other words, that they have **validity**. The first way to judge validity is to look at the items/tasks that students must do. Do these look as if they are related to the standards, benchmarks, and learning objectives? For example, if the learning outcome has to do with reading comprehension and the test does not ask students to read, there is a clear need to question the validity of the test. A test of students' ability to multiply and divide probably should not be done with a handheld calculator. Having students in marching band play the music without looking at the sheet would be a direct and valid test if the criterion was that the music be memorized. In constructing test items, take time to look them over and ask, "Is what I am asking the student to do in this test clearly representative of the learning objective?"

Reliability

Another important characteristic of tests has to do with whether or not the test scores for students who seem to be similar in their learning are similar—in other words, whether or not the test has **reliability**. Test reliability is important for teachers to consider when they plan to use the same test with different classes. The high school history teacher may want to use the same test item with different classes. Or the elementary teacher may use last year's test with this year's students. Or two teachers may use the same test. A highly reliable test should provide similar results from similar students. There is a problem when two groups of students have dramatically different scores on the same test! This can happen when teaching two different classes the same lesson. The question then confronting the teacher(s) is "Was the same material covered with each set of students, or is there something wrong with the test so that similar students score differently?"—that is, is this a question of test reliability?

Performance Tasks

Another characteristic of good assessments is asking for student **performance**—in other words, asking a student to do an activity rather than a mental exercise. When the assessment is based on students applying their learning through accomplishing an activity, there is greater certainty that they really have learned the standard to the benchmark level. This emphasis on performance is built into the descriptions of most standards and benchmarks. Actually, these descriptions can be very helpful to teachers who are constructing their own assessments. Visualizing the actions that students should be able to do when they have learned the learning outcome can lead to assessment tasks that require them to demonstrate through action what they have learned.

Understanding the importance of performance is why a driver's license test normally has two parts: a written part and a driving part. Knowing the rules of the road is important and can be assessed with a multiple-choice test. The ability to drive the car on the correct side of the road, to use turn signals, and to drive safely in heavy traffic cannot be assessed with a multiple-choice test. Having only a written test would not be valid. Aspiring license holders must demonstrate that they can perform by driving.

Authentic

The two-part driving test also is a good example of an **authentic task**. The assessments are based in learning the rules of the road and demonstrating performance by driving. Assessment tasks that are clearly related to the benchmarks and standards, as well as to real-world applications, are called authentic. Writing a poem, doing a science experiment instead of watching a video, and taking a side in a debate are authentic. Reading, writing, and watching a video about something are not authentic.

"Yes, I'm counting off for misspelling. We're having a spelling test."

It is much easier for students to demonstrate what they have learned when the tasks are related to their background and world experiences. Basing assessments on context with which the students are not familiar is likely to lead to misunderstandings about how much they have learned. There are many disturbing examples of assessments that are not responsive to students' backgrounds—that is, culturally responsive (see Chapter 2). For example, asking low-income students in the desert Southwest to write about how to build a snowman would not be responsive to their culture. Teachers, as well as commercial test makers, must be extremely careful in constructing assessment tasks to make sure that they are not assuming background and context that have not been a part of the knowledge and experience of the students being assessed.

Assessing for Different Types of Learning

Up to this point, our discussion of testing and assessing has addressed the different purposes, two ways of thinking (formative/summative), differences between NRTs and CRTs, and some of the characteristics of good assessments, including asking for performance and using authentic tasks. What hasn't been addressed is the type of learning being assessed. There are a number of useful models that teachers can use for organizing and sorting the level and extent of student learning. One of the most widely used is *Bloom's Taxonomy of Educational Objectives Handbook I: Cognitive Domain*, first published in 1956. This taxonomy was developed as a way to describe different levels of learning, or **Depths of Knowledge (DOK)**.

Bloom's taxonomy (see Table 13.3) has become an education classic and continues to provide a very useful set of categories for gauging the type of learning that is expected in assessment tasks. The taxonomy is equally useful for teachers and other test makers when they are constructing tests, as they think about the type of learning they want students to demonstrate.

Questions to ask each level were introduced in Chapter 12 (Table 12.2). For example, asking students to provide facts and figures (Level I, Remembering) they *remember* is very different from asking students *to apply* their knowledge of certain facts to solve a problem (Level III, Applying). An even higher level of learning is required to provide reasoned judgment to *evaluate* the strengths and weaknesses associated with certain phenomena (Level V, Evaluating). Of course, Bloom's taxonomy has to be adjusted for the grade level and subject area being assessed. What would represent Analysis for seventh-grade students would not be the same for high school seniors or second-grade students. Still, within each class, all levels of Bloom's taxonomy can be applied in the construction of assessments and in making clear the expectations in objectives.

Accommodating Different Types of Learners

The final assessment topic to be introduced has to do with accommodating different types of learners and students with special needs. An assessment that is perfect for middle-class suburban students may not be appropriate for poor urban students. The reverse may also be true: An assessment that worked well with an urban high school English class may not make sense with a rural high school English class. And exceptional learners (see Chapter 3) must be considered in all assessment work. Two particularly important student learner populations that all teachers must consider are ELLs and students with special needs.

iStock/Wavebreakmedia

Authentic performance tasks are based in the standards and benchmarks, as well as in real-world applications.

TABLE 13.3 ■ The Six Levels of Bloom's Taxonomy of the Cognitive Domain		
Cognitive Level	**Skill**	**Assessment Tasks**
Level VI: **Creating**	Using original thinking to develop a communication, make predictions, and solve problems for which there is not a single correct answer	How did you solve a particular problem, and what is your conclusion? How would you improve _____?
Level V: **Evaluating**	Making judgments about the quality of a solution or the solution to an issue or problem	What do you think will happen? What information would you want to have?
Level IV: **Analyzing**	Identifying causes, reasons, or motives; analyzing information to reach a generalization or conclusion; finding evidence to support a specific opinion, event, or situation	What factors/elements are part of the problem? Design a study, prepare a report, develop a presentation that draws a conclusion
Level III: **Applying**	Applying previously learned information to answer a problem; using a rule, a definition, a classification system, or directions to solve a specific problem that has a correct answer	What facts would you apply to a new problem or situation?
Level II: **Understanding**	Going beyond simple recall and demonstrating the ability to arrange and organize information mentally; putting previously learned information into one's own words	What is the main idea? Write a summary, draw a picture
Level I: **Remembering**	Using memory or senses to recall or reorganize information	Provide names, facts, and procedures. What/who is _____?

Source: Bloom, B. S. (Ed.). (1956). *Taxonomy of educational objectives handbook I: Cognitive domain.* New York, NY: David McKay Co; Anderson, L. W., & Krathwohl, D. R. (2001). *A taxonomy for learning, teaching and assessing: A revision of Bloom's taxonomy of educational objectives* (Complete ed.). New York, NY: Longman.

Accommodating Students With Special Needs

A particularly challenging problem for teachers as well as professional test makers is developing assessments that are appropriate for students with special needs. Each student will have unique needs and is likely to have a tendency to do better with certain types of test situations. However, there is a legal distinction for students who have been formally identified as having special needs. Students with *recognized* learning disabilities, physical handicaps, and other special needs will have an assigned school district team, including the parents, and an Individualized Education Program, or IEP (see Chapter 3).

A key component of each student's IEP will be information related to any accommodations that must be made in assessments. Introduced in Chapter 3, accommodations are those adjustments that are made in order to ensure that a student with special needs is not placed in an unfair or disadvantageous situation for instruction or testing. In developing tests and other assessments, the classroom teacher has a responsibility to be knowledgeable about any and all accommodations that have been specified in student IEPs.

In addition to whatever accommodation information is provided in a student's IEP, another readily accessible resource is each state's department of education website. A federal requirement is that each state will provide a list of acceptable accommodations. As an example, some of Pennsylvania's accommodations are presented in Table 13.4.

Always keep in mind that teacher initiative is a very important element in student success. Teacher initiative is important to student success in testing, too. For example, one high school teacher had a

TABLE 13.4 ■ Examples of Appropriate Testing Accommodations for Students With Special Needs and English Language Learners (Pennsylvania)

Test Preparation

- Read directions to the student (reread as necessary).

- Use sign language or the student's native language to give directions or to simplify the directions. This may include American Sign Language or spoken English with sign support.

- Provide audiotape directions verbatim.

Test Administration

- Prompt the student to remain on task.

- Read test items (for Mathematics or Writing items only). (Do not read Reading test items.)

- Check periodically to make sure the student is marking in correct spaces.

- Provide materials to the student to mask portions of the test to direct the student's attention to specific areas.

- Provide materials to the student to use colored stickers or highlighters for visual cues.

Test Response

- Allow the student to answer questions orally (Mathematics and Reading only).

- Use enlarged answer sheets.

- Allow the student to point to response.

- Allow the student to answer on a typewriter or computer. (Turn off Spelling, Grammar Checker, and Thesaurus.)

Timing/Scheduling

- Increase or decrease opportunity for movement.

- Permit additional breaks or extended rest breaks for the student during the testing session.

- Increase test time.

Setting

- Allow the student to use adaptive or special furniture, such as a study carrel.

- Test in a separate room or in a small group to reduce distractions.

- Test in a special education or bilingual classroom, if appropriate.

- Reduce stimuli (e.g., limit number of items on desk).

- Provide for reduced acoustical distraction.

Assistive Devices

- Allow augmentative communication systems or strategies, including letter boards, picture communication systems, and voice output systems. (No voice output for Writing.)

- Provide magnifier, large print, or Braille materials.

- Provide pencil grips.

Other Options

- Provide sign language interpreter, if necessary. (Mathematics and Reading only—no sign language output for Writing.)

Source: Adapted from Pennsylvania Department of Education Division of Evaluation and Assessment. (2003). *Testing accommodations for the Pennsylvania System of School Assessment, 2002–2003.*

student who did well with all assignments but failed every test. The teacher reflected on this discrepancy between consistent indications of achievement during instruction and the string of Fs on tests. The teacher called a parent to help in understanding what was happening. It seems that the student would freeze and so was not able to read the test questions during formal test-taking situations. The teacher then adjusted the test setting by presenting the test questions on audiotape and allowing the student extra time. From then on, the student passed the tests.

Accommodating English Language Learner (ELL) Students

The accommodation examples presented in Table 13.3 also can be appropriate for ELL students. With their continually increasing number, there is additional pressure on schools and school districts to do all that they can to ensure a fair opportunity for ELL students to demonstrate what they have learned. There continue to be federal mandates that students, including ELLs and those with special needs, take the annual state tests. This has led to states setting accommodations for ELL students. In many ways, these accommodations are applicable in the classroom as well. For example, the New Mexico Public Education Department's *Student Assessment Accommodations Manual (2017–2018)* provides extensive information that teachers can apply. The following are useful guidelines for making accommodations:

- Do not change the purpose of the test
- Do not change the content of the test
- Do not provide the student with an unfair advantage
- Continue to allow the testing contractor to be able to score the test
- Do not violate test security
- Do not change the focus of what is being assessed

Each of these points is important for teachers to keep in mind as they develop their own assessments. Teachers have the responsibility of providing all students with the opportunity to fairly demonstrate what they have learned, while at the same time not providing an unfair advantage for some or creating a disadvantage for others.

WHAT ARE SOME WAYS TO TEST STUDENT LEARNING?

I want to be looking at samples of student work and seeing how those are changing over time. I would look at whether students can apply what they are learning in different settings, including new and novel settings. I would be looking at how kids rate their own work and provide feedback to others about their work—how sophisticated their feedback is about writing or a project they are working on. These are indicators of the goals of the class and whether or not students' knowledge and understanding of these goals is increasing in meaningful ways.

—Dr. Asp

Testing has become a very important component of the work of teachers and students. Teachers must continually assess developing student understanding, and each year, school districts and the state are testing students' learning in several subjects. An important message for beginning teachers is that from the very first day in the classroom, they must have expertise in developing different types of tests. From the first day onward, each of the purposes for assessing must be addressed. Within each lesson and across the school day, teachers need to be engaged in informal assessing of each student. Across the weeks and semesters, teachers must develop summative tests and report student grades. All of these activities are done in order to make adjustments in instruction and increase student learning. They also are done within the context of anticipation of the testing that the school district and state will require toward the end of the school year.

Checking for Understanding Within Lessons

When the term *testing* is used, don't think only of paper-and-pencil exams. That is why in this chapter we have used the term *assessments*. There are a variety of ways to probe and examine students' understanding and the extent of their learning. Expert teachers continually assess by using informal ways before, during, and in follow-up to each lesson. For example, when teachers employ the all-too-familiar "Q&A" tactic during a lesson, their intent is to use short questions that require lower-level (Bloom's taxonomy Levels I and II) student responses as a way to spot-check understanding across a number of students.

Some of the ways to check for understanding are summarized in Table 13.5. Most certainly as a student, you have experienced all of these at one time or another. The reason for summarizing them here is to refresh your memory about the variety of ways that teachers can easily appraise how student learning is progressing. None is particularly difficult to use, but using a variety is important since some students will naturally do better with some strategies than with others.

Teacher Observation

Quite naturally, one of the most prevalent concerns for beginning teachers is classroom management. When teachers have these concerns, their observations of students focus on whether all students are attentive, they are not misbehaving, and they are not creating distractions. Observing student behavior in order to assess classroom management is a necessary first step. However, when observing for classroom management, keep in mind that one significant reason for student misbehavior is that the students do not understand what they are supposed to be doing.

A critical difference between novice teachers and expert teachers is found in the extent to which the purpose for a teacher's observations of students extends beyond a focus on classroom management.

TABLE 13.5 ■ Checking for Understanding Within Lessons		
Strategy	**Teacher Actions**	**What to Look For**
Teacher observation for classroom management	Looking around, listening for procedural questions/confusions, asking if students understand what they are to be doing	Portion of students who are engaged and not misbehaving or creating distractions; students asking procedural questions
Teacher observation for student understanding	Walking around, listening for student use of academic language, looking for student focus on tasks	Students using academic language, doing assigned activities, contributing to the assigned topic
Teacher questioning	Closed questions for short answers, open-ended questions to encourage higher levels of thinking	Short facts and yes/no answers; extended answers from several students
Use of "thumbs up" and clickers	At any point asking for current understanding by pointing thumb up or down, asking one or a few questions that all students must respond to	Percentage of correct answers
Pop quiz	Unannounced brief quiz or survey	Degree to which students provide correct answers
Homework	Assignments that can be accomplished outside of class time	Portion of correct submissions; points of confusion and misunderstandings
Drafts of assignments	Review of early outlines and drafts of major products	Gaps in understandings and areas of omission
Student self-reflection	Student talk, student journals	Students can describe what they know/don't know and what they need to learn next

Expert teachers go further by continually observing students in order to pick up clues about their extent of understanding and engagement with learning the material. For example, by looking around the classroom, teachers can immediately see if students are reading or writing or calculating. During group work, expert teachers are monitoring to see that all students are participating. In lab work, teachers check to see if each student has set up the equipment properly and if it is working safely. By walking around the classroom, teachers can look over shoulders at student work and listen in on student-to-student talk. Are they asking procedural ("How do I do this?") questions, or are they explaining their reasoning using academic language?

Some teachers walk around the classroom primarily to monitor for misbehavior. Expert teachers have a higher-level purpose; they are checking for student learning and understanding. (It is disappointing to be able to report that in some classrooms, teachers do not walk around the classroom and monitor closely what students are doing. They just sit at their desk, doing some other task, only occasionally looking up to see what students are doing. *Do not become this type of teacher.*)

Teacher Questioning

Of course, teacher questioning is a very useful way to check on student understanding. Teachers are always asking **closed questions**, those that ask for a yes/no reply or seek specific information about procedures and facts (lower-level DOK). With closed questions, student answers are brief so many students can be spot-checked in a few minutes. Another type of teacher questioning uses **open-ended questions**, which require students to provide an explanation, interpretation, or elaboration. Open-ended questions will require higher-level student thinking (Bloom's taxonomy Levels IV, Analysis; V, Synthesis; and VI, Evaluation).

Open-ended questions also require more time for the teacher to ask and for students to construct their responses. One way to save time and take advantage of open-ended questions is to pose a single, well-thought-out, open-ended question and then allow several students to present their responses. The teacher may ask closed questions for clarification purposes as each student responds. This way, more students are able to construct a thoughtful response. With both types of questions, the teacher is listening for the extent and depth of student understanding and learning.

Student Self-Reflection

Teacher questioning is used continually to check on student understanding and learning. In fact, it is overused in most classrooms. There are some other ways to check on student progress during lessons. One tactic that is underused is student self-reflection. Instead of the teacher assuming all of the responsibility for determining where students are, place some of the responsibility on the students. After all, it is the students who have to do the learning. Asking students to talk or write about what they know or don't know is an important activity.

This type of self-reflection should be tied to the learning objectives for the lesson, which should be based on the curriculum standards and benchmarks. In today's environment of high accountability, it is especially important for students to be assessing themselves in terms of the extent of their current understanding and learning in relation to how they will be tested. So ask them to describe their current level of understanding in relation to a specific benchmark and its standard.

Also ask them to identify what they need to work on and what to learn next. An interesting side note for you to consider here is the earliest grade level where it is reasonable to expect students to be able to self-reflect about their learning. Do you think children in the intermediate grades (four, five, and six) can do this, or is this skill something that only high school students can do? Actually, it is possible for kindergarten students to learn to be self-reflective about their learning.

Checking for Understanding After the Lesson

Once the lesson, unit, or series of assignments related to a major topic have been taught, assessing student learning has a different purpose. At these times, the purpose is most likely summative; grades will be determined. Therefore, the form and quality of the test take on more importance. Even though the test is probably teacher made, there is an expectation that it will be fair and without bias. Constructing such tests takes concerted effort.

TEACHERS' LOUNGE
DO I HAVE TO?

Antonio is a fifth grader attending a Title I school in a predominantly Hispanic section of a large city in the Southwest. He and his classmates realize he is one of the top three math students in the class of nearly 30 students. However, this knowledge has not diminished his willingness to help others understand their assignments. It is common to observe Antonio helping those who ask him for assistance.

Antonio's teacher has taught third grade and been the school's science specialist. Due to budget cuts that eliminated her position, she returned to a regular classroom assignment. She earned her teaching credentials through an alternative licensure program and has stayed in contact with her elementary mathematics methods instructor since the instructor had been involved in grant activities at the school for several years.

When she was assigned to a fifth-grade class, she asked me, as her former math methods instructor, to visit the class during math time a couple of days a week and assist in any way possible. Sometimes I work with small groups. I often participate in large-group instruction by asking probing questions the classroom teacher might not think to ask.

The mathematics program used at Antonio's school is *Investigations in Number, Data, and Space* (2007). This program is designed to help elementary students develop conceptual as well as procedural knowledge and skills. A common assessment procedure is to require students to explain how they solved a problem.

During a recent unit on volume, the students had been doing activities that help them understand the difference between area and volume, as well as "discovering" for themselves that volume can be found by multiplying length, width, and height. In order to determine how many of the students had developed the formula ($l \times w \times h$), the teacher presented the following assessment item:

> How many one-inch cubes will fit in a box that's 20 inches long, 12 inches wide, and 10 inches high? Explain how you solved the problem so you could convince your classmates your answer is right.

As soon as the teacher finished reading the item, Antonio turned to me and said, "I know the answer." I responded, "I'm sure you do, but we're really interested in how you'd convince your classmates."

Antonio's gaze passed over his classmates, and he rolled his eyes, looked up at me, and asked, "Do I have to convince *all* of them, or can I just convince *most* of them?"

—Dr. Virginia Usnick
Professor of Mathematics Education
University of Nevada, Las Vegas

Objective Tests

The more formal tests that teachers develop frequently use test items that are called objective. **Objective tests** get their name from the characteristic that the answers are either right or wrong. There is no gray area in scoring well-constructed objective test items. Everyone who scores the test items will agree on which of the possible student responses is correct. One advantage of using objective test items is that scoring the student responses can be done quite quickly. Another advantage is that a wide range of student knowledge can be assessed relatively quickly since answering objective test items takes less time than items that require students to construct an original response. A disadvantage is that constructing good objective test items is not as easy as it seems and takes considerable time.

There are different types of objective test items ranging from true–false to fill-in-the-blank to multiple choice. Each format is particularly good at testing a certain type of learning, and each has certain keys to construction that teachers need to keep in mind. Regardless of the item format, it is important to be sure that there is a clear relationship to the learning objective(s), benchmark(s), and standard(s). Several of the typical objective test item formats are presented in Table 13.5. This table also offers a few tips for constructing good objective test items.

Formal testing of student learning, especially for high-stakes decisions, must be done in secure and closely monitored settings.

Watch Out for Bias in Test Items

No matter the test item format, an important responsibility for teachers is to make sure that each item does not unwittingly include some form of bias. It is all too easy to accidentally write a test item that includes a sexual, racial, or cultural bias. There also is risk of including a socioeconomic status (SES) bias. SES refers to the level of wealth, education, and social class and the range of experiences that a teacher and students bring to the classroom. Check all test items for the following:

1. Overuse of *he* or *she*, or stereotyping of boys and girls

2. The use of terms that may be offensive to certain ethnic and cultural groups

3. The use of examples from middle-class experiences that poor children may not have had (e.g., travel to Disneyland)

4. Selection of content and examples that will have different meanings to students from different parts of the country (e.g., a *blizzard* for students from New England will likely mean a heavy snowstorm, while for students in the desert Southwest it is a special type of milkshake from Dairy Queen)

5. Built-in implicit expectations that *some* (boys, girls, ELLs, students with special needs, "the brightest") will do better or worse on the test item than others

Subjective Tests

Objective test items take time to write, provide students with a limited number of response options, and can be scored quickly. An alternative test item format is called a **subjective test**. Subjective test items pose a problem or task, and students must construct an original response, which must be scored individually. Subjective test items are easier to write and more challenging for students to answer, and they require judgment and interpretation by the teacher in scoring each response. A very important strength of subjective test items is that each student's response is the student's own work and usually requires higher-order thinking. The following are examples of different types of subjective test items along with a few tips for constructing effective ones.

Table 13.6 includes summary points to keep in mind when developing subjective test items.

Short-Answer Items

DIRECTIONS:

If you were writing objective test items for seventh-grade students in an inner-city school, what are three elements of good test items that you would want to be sure to attend to? Be sure to explain your reasoning.

_____

_____

_____

Short-answer test items are an effective way to test for students' use of vocabulary, their ability to think using key concepts, and their success at constructing a brief narrative response. Another advantage of short-answer items is that several of them can be presented within a typical class period. A challenge is that each student's response will be unique and open to interpretation. Variations in interpretation come when some students interpret the test item in different ways. There also can be variation in how the teacher interprets what students have written. This challenge of interpretation is a component of all subjective test items, thus the name.

There are a number of techniques that can be used to reduce the subjectivity, while still requiring originality in the student response. For example, in the test item presented above, the number of elements is specified (i.e., three). This removes any debate about whether a response that provides only one

TABLE 13.6 ■ Test Item Formats and Tips for Writing

Objective Test Item Format	Tips for Writing Good Items
True–False	• Write items that are clearly true or false. • Avoid using absolute terms such as *always*, *never*, and *only*. • Avoid double negatives. • Don't include two ideas/parts in a single item.
Matching Items	• Provide a title for the lists of items. • Place the longest list on the left. • Consider having one or two extra response options.
Fill-in-the-Blank	• Require one-word responses. • Include the label for an amount of something. • Write clear statements.

Subjective Test Item Formats	Tips for Writing Good Items
Short Answer	• Set a limit (number of pages) to the size of the response. • Specify the number of elements. • Delimit the range to specific areas that the students should have learned.
Essay	• Be careful to circumscribe the topic without being too prescriptive. • Decide in advance which items will be scored. • Decide if spelling and grammar will count.
Open-Ended	• Determine whether there will be group or only individual responses. • Establish in advance the criteria for evaluating group work. • Plan to monitor student work during the response construction process. • Consider ways for students to share/publish their works.

or two elements is sufficient. Without adding the request for the response to include three reasons, there could be debate about the need to provide more in the response than the number of elements. The challenge in writing subjective test items is to reduce the unnecessary ambiguity in what is expected while at the same time delimiting what the students are to demonstrate based on what they have learned. The following are two other types of subjective test items.

Essay Test Items

DIRECTIONS:

A very important skill for teachers to develop is writing good test items. In this chapter, you have been reading about different test item formats. Each format is particularly useful for testing certain levels of learning and understanding, and each has particular technical elements that must be addressed. Teachers must understand when to use each test item format. For a subject area that you will be teaching, describe the types of test items that you would use in writing an end-of-unit, one-class-period test. Use at least three test item formats, and include an example test item for each. Be sure to describe your reasoning. Use five to eight pages to write your answer. Organization, composition, and spelling will count.

One of the most useful ways to test higher-order student thinking is the essay. Essay writing requires students to organize complex ideas and to use what they have learned in new ways. Essay test items present a situation or problem and ask each student to construct his or her own response. Essay test responses are expected to be long and well organized, and to include detail as well as analysis, synthesis, and evaluation. The challenge in writing essay test items is to circumscribe the topic without making the item so prescriptive that students do not have to think long and hard in composing their essay. We all have experienced essay test items that were so open and vague that we had no clear idea of what a good response would include.

The major challenge for the teacher comes when it is time to score an essay test. First, the ease with which an essay test item can be constructed is out of balance with the time it takes to read each student's multipage response. It takes extended time to read each paper and to decipher student penmanship (if handwritten). Another challenge is deciding which components will be scored. How much weight will be given to the quantity of facts and terms that are used? Will there be a clear distinction between lower-level and higher-level thinking? Will grammar and spelling be counted? Will there be one composite score, or will each of these questions result in a separate score? An additional challenge with older students is judging whether a particular response really reflects understanding or is bluffing.

Open-Ended Formats

DIRECTIONS:

By the end of this semester, you should have in place the foundations for what will become your professional portfolio. This foundation should include (a) a summary of your education and work experience, (b) a description of your academic record, (c) documentation that you have passed all entry tests and requirements, (d) artifacts that indicate the type of product you produce, and (e) the first draft of your education philosophy statement.

There are a number of other formats that teachers can use to assess the extent of student learning and especially student higher-order thinking. These various formats are open-ended. They require students to organize and construct their response in creative and unique ways. Open-ended formats include portfolios, exhibits, group projects, investigations, creative works and performances, technology-based productions and presentations, panels, and juries. Student work in response to an open-ended format task will take extended time and should be based on a number of weeks of cumulative class work.

Teacher supervision during the time period when students are constructing their open-ended response can be tricky. Beyond monitoring student engagement and the effort of each student, there is the need to not provide too many suggestions and hints while at the same time facilitating student success with producing a final product.

Open-ended formats require extended time for students to produce the final product. One way to maximize student learning is to build in time for students to report, share, present, or exhibit their product. This can become a major celebration and a highly visible way for students and teachers from across the school to see what has been going on in your classroom. In one elementary school, as part of the writing program, all students made a book. Examples of their writing were displayed all around the school, and there was a book fair held so that everyone could see and read the works of other students.

Group Work

Don't forget that open-ended format items can be structured for students working in groups or as teams. Group projects add a challenge for the teacher when it comes to evaluating the contributions of each student individually. One way to accommodate this challenge is to assign each student an individual grade as well as a grade for the group. Another approach is to have each student grade the other members of the group in terms of the effort and/or the extent of their contributions to the group's product.

Which Format Is Best?

Deciding on which test item format to use, as with so much of teaching, comes back to consideration of the expected learner outcomes. What are the most important facts, concepts, and understanding that students should be acquiring? These are the elements that should be tested. Some of the test item formats can be fun for students to do, especially the open-ended ones. But teachers must always keep in mind that testing in the classroom must be grounded in state and district standards and benchmarks. Also continue to think about the level of thinking, learning, and understanding that is expected. Bloom's taxonomy (Table 13.2) has been used in this chapter to illustrate DOK (Depth of Knowledge) because it is such a useful way to think about the level of learning and depth of understanding that is being tested. Fill-in-the-blank test items work well for recall of vocabulary, but they are not useful for testing application of what has been learned.

Table 13.5 provides a number of tips for writing open-ended test items. For every test item that teachers develop, one final check should be made for any sort of bias or discrimination. It is surprisingly easy to accidentally build into a test item favoritism for certain students or an unfair disadvantage for certain students. Teachers must be very careful in constructing test items to ensure that all students have an equal opportunity to show what they have learned.

Rubrics Are an Important and Informative Assessment Tool

"I rewarded two of my students for passing notes in class. It's so refreshing to see any of them actually writing."

Another very useful tool for assessing student work is rubrics (see Chapter 1). Rather than summarizing performance on a test with a score, a number, or a letter, rubrics provide descriptions of different levels of accomplishment. Within a rubric, there will be brief descriptors or indicators of the different levels of accomplishment. An example of a rubric for assessing four-year high school student writing of research papers in the Edmond (Oklahoma) public schools is presented in Table 13.7. With rubrics of this type, a large part of the mystery is taken out of subjective evaluation. Each of the points in the rubric describes a level of performance that can be observed and that is distinguishable from the other levels.

The beginning point for developing a rubric is writing down observable descriptions of different levels of quality or completeness. For example, teachers (and their students) could note example elements for each letter grade and use these as the beginning steps for developing rubrics. Rubrics can be **holistic rubrics** for evaluating the total effort. Rubrics also can be used to evaluate subparts or components of the effort. For example, one rubric could be used to assess the overall level of thinking (Bloom's taxonomy again) that was used in a student report, while another rubric could be used to evaluate the correctness of grammar and spelling. Some useful tips to keep in mind when developing rubrics are presented in Table 13.8.

HOW DO TEACHERS AND STUDENTS USE FORMATIVE ASSESSMENTS TO ADJUST INSTRUCTION AND IMPROVE LEARNING?

Even with a summative test or a grade at the end, I would want to look at the progress the students have made, specific ways their work has improved, and how much better they are at understanding their own strengths and weaknesses. Those kinds of features would tell me a lot more about what a student knows.

—Dr. Asp

Developing tests and evaluating student assignments are important tasks. One way of thinking about these tasks is to aim everything toward making the end-of-term summative decision about the grade to

TABLE 13.7 ■ Rubric for Assessing High School Student Writing Proficiency				
Domain	**Score "One"**	**Score "Two"**	**Score "Three"**	**Score "Four"**
Development of Ideas	Simply repeats the topic with no development of the idea.	Some focus, with little development of a theme/idea.	Main idea is clear, and in general the idea is developed toward a theme or conclusion.	Main idea is fully developed with additional ideas introduced while not losing track of the overall theme.
Strength of Persuasion	Fails to take a position.	Position is vague/unclear.	States a position and defends/persuades with support and use of relevant evidence.	Presents a position clearly, presents evidence in support of the position, and frames the issues.
Writing Style	Shows almost no structure, organization, or coherence.	Has minimal organization; digresses, rambles.	Uses a variety of sentence structures and word choices.	Demonstrates involvement with the text; speaks purposefully to the audience.
Grammar/ Mechanics	Many and serious violations of standard grammar and mechanics.	Limited sentence structure and word choices; consistent errors in grammar.	Uses a variety of sentence structures and word choices; a few errors in grammar and mechanics.	Uses multiple sentence structures and word choices; few, if any, errors in grammar and mechanics.
Use of Sources	No, or only a single, source is cited; citation is partial or incorrect.	A few sources are cited, but not clearly tied to theme of paper; citations are partial or incorrect.	At least five appropriate sources are cited; citations are correct.	At least five sources are cited; several additional well-selected sources are cited; citations are correct.

TABLE 13.8 ■ Tips to Keep in Mind When Developing Rubrics
1. Both cognitive and performance rubrics can be developed.
2. Have the different levels cover a broad range of possible student performance.
3. Have students brainstorm examples and indicators for each level of performance.
4. Rubrics may have any number of levels, but they typically have three to five.
5. Describe each level of performance so that it can be easily observed and distinguished clearly from other levels.
6. The levels of performance may be associated with letter grades: A = exceeds expectations, B = meets expectations, C = almost meets expectations, D/F = does not meet expectations.
7. Have students use rubrics to evaluate their own and their peers' work.

be placed on the report card. There is an alternative way of thinking. Instead of focusing on the grade, more effective teachers focus on the learning. Each assessment provides information about how much each student knows now. Each assessment also becomes the baseline for measuring learning from here. This approach begins with analyzing each student's work and determining how instruction needs to be adjusted in order to move each student's learning forward. This is what formative assessment is about.

Using assessments as tools for facilitating learning is a very different way of thinking. In this approach, teachers (and students) are looking at the results of quizzes, tests, and other assignments as indicators of progress. They are seen as mile markers along the highway of learning. They are not focusing on determining a "final" grade. Each assessment is seen as a mile marker of how far learning has come. Each provides diagnostic information that can be used to guide deciding on the instruction that will best facilitate getting to the next mile marker. Each assessment also is reviewed in regard to what worked well, and not so well, to have learning come as far as it has.

Four Levels of Formative Assessment

One of the most influential scholars in regard to formative assessing is W. James Popham, a UCLA Emeritus Professor. Dr. Popham's career-long academic work has centered on ways to think about and apply evaluation methodologies in teaching. He has proposed four levels of formative assessments (Popham, 2008), introduced in Table 13.9. Review of this table may lead to one or more aha moments for you, especially if you have been thinking of teaching and testing in the traditional summative way. Popham's four levels clearly illustrate the importance of continually thinking in terms of how information about the current level of understanding can be used to further advance student learning.

Level 1: Teachers' Instructional Adjustments

Keep in mind that instruction and assessment are not the same thing. Instruction is what the teacher does to help students learn the curriculum and especially the standards. Assessments provide information about the current level of student learning. Formative assessment is the process a teacher and students use to make adjustments in instruction in order to further student learning. The teacher's task naturally begins with review of the desired learning outcomes. Then appropriate instructional activities are planned.

A key planning task is to plan for formal pre- and post-assessments. Key planning questions include "What do students know already?" And, following the lesson, "How has their understanding changed?" Don't forget to ask "At what key points within the lesson will I do spot-checks on students' understanding? What questions will I ask? What should be observed about student talk that will be indicators of increasing understanding?"

In a formative assessing approach, all of these sources of information are considered, and adjustments in instruction are made *within* the lesson as well as in *planning* the next lesson. Key subtasks are to consider each student's progress as well as progress of the whole class.

Level 2: Students' Learning Tactic Adjustments

This level of formative assessment may be a new idea for some teacher candidates. Even up to this point in this chapter, we have pretty much been describing the teacher's role in assessment, but it also is important to keep in mind the students' role. Students should be engaging their own formative assessment processes to aid in improving their learning. They need to be self-assessing, too. Student self-assessing questions include "What is the standard? What are the benchmarks I need to be learning now? How well am I doing against these? What do I know now, and what do I need to work on next? What should I do to adjust my learning strategies?" As Popham (2008) points out, "Level 2 formative assessment consists of *student-determined* adjustments in learning tactics, not *teacher-dictated* adjustments the students are then supposed to make" (p. 72; emphasis in original).

More than likely, most students will not automatically know how to do their own formative assessing. They will need instruction in how to consider the types of tactics that will help them learn. With

In standards-based education, it is important that students understand how their current work compares with key benchmarks. Here a student and his teacher discuss ways he can improve his writing.

© Gene Hall

TABLE 13.9 ■ Popham's Four Levels of Formative Assessment
Level 1: Teachers' Instructional Adjustments
Teachers collect evidence by which they decide whether to adjust their current or immediately upcoming instruction in order to improve the effectiveness of that instruction.
Level 2: Students' Learning Tactic Adjustments
Students use evidence of their current skills-and-knowledge status to decide whether to adjust the procedures they're using in an effort to learn something.
Level 3: Classroom Climate Shift
Teachers consistently apply formative assessment to the degree that its use transforms a traditional, comparison-dominated classroom, where the main purpose of assessment is to assign grades, into an atypical learning-dominated classroom, where the main purpose of assessment is to improve the quality of teaching and learning.
Level 4: School-wide Implementation
An entire school (or district) adopts one or more levels of formative assessment, chiefly through the use of Professional Development and teacher learning communities.

Source: Popham, W. J. (2008). *Transformative assessment* (p. 49). Alexandria, VA: Association for Supervision & Curriculum Development.

"I don't think it was a very productive year for Ms. Read. We learned to use all twenty six letters, and she only learned to use the 'C'."

the teacher's help, students need to come to understand the learning expectations for each lesson. They need to know what's coming next. They need to know how their learning progress will be judged. This latter point means that they also need to know the steps they need to take to progress in their learning.

Level 3: Classroom Climate Shift From Traditional to Formative Assessment

As important as the teacher's and the students' approaches to formative assessment are, in the end the feel of the whole classroom has to change. The climate or culture of a classroom is different when formative assessment is foundational. Popham (2008) identifies three key dimensions of the classroom: learning expectations, responsibility for learning, and the perceived role of classroom assessment. He also talks about a shift from traditional classroom climate to assessment-informed classroom climate (p. 94).

For example, there is a shift from an expectation that the most motivated students will progress to a view that substantial learning will occur with all students. Responsibility for learning shifts from the teacher as primarily responsible for learning to students assuming major responsibility for their own learning *and* that of their classmates. Instead of tests being seen as data for comparing students and assigning grades, assessments are used to inform adjustments in instruction *and* students adjusting their approaches to learning. Development of this type of classroom culture requires teacher leadership, trust, and social construction by the teacher and the students. By the way, this type of learning-centered classroom culture can be constructed in the primary grades and kindergarten. It is not something that can only exist with older students.

Level 4: School-wide Implementation of a Formative Assessment—Centered Culture

As you have read in the excerpts from the interview with Dr. Asp, it is possible not just for a few classrooms, or for one or two schools, but for an entire school district to make the shift to formative assessments as the shared way of teaching and learning. One key to a school or a district making this major change in thinking and action is leadership. Without the understanding, vision, and active support of the principals and district office leaders, teachers and students will be hard-pressed to make the change. Another important resource is access to related Professional Development that goes beyond teacher workshops. Modeling and coaching supports are other required strategies. When all of these elements come together, it is possible for teachers, administrators, and students to construct a Professional Learning Community that is centered on improving learning for all students, and for the adults.

Response to Intervention or Response to Instruction (RTI)

Our description of formative assessment began with what a teacher and his or her students can do in a classroom. We, as well as Drs. Asp and Popham, then suggested that a whole school or district could approach teaching and learning using the principles of formative assessment. A related approach that is used in many states and school districts is called Response to Intervention (see Chapter 3), also known as **Response to Instruction (RTI)**. RTI is a multilevel approach for addressing the needs of all students by differentiating between those who are keeping up and those who are struggling or seriously falling behind. The approach combines screening, progress monitoring, and a multilevel prevention strategy into a process for **data-based decision making** for all students (visit the Center on Response to Intervention at www.rti4success.org).

Student Improvement Team (SIT) and Response to Intervention (RTI)

Implementing RTI involves all of a school's staff, teachers (regular and special education), administrators, and instructional strategy specialists. One frequently observed mechanism for sustaining RTI is to establish a special committee with a name such as **Student Improvement Team (SIT)** or **data team (DT)**. The SIT/DT will have representatives for a grade level(s)/subject(s), a school administrator,

CHALLENGING ASSUMPTIONS
MOST STUDENTS, ESPECIALLY THOSE IN ELEMENTARY SCHOOL, CANNOT SELF-ASSESS OR SET THEIR OWN LEARNING GOALS.

The Assumption

A major theme in this chapter is that not only teachers but also their students should be assessing what they know now and what they need to learn next. The standards and related benchmarks provide the target. Students should be able to unwrap the standards and describe what they are learning. Through this process, students can be more purposeful in how they approach learning, and through the use of evaluation tools such as rubrics, they can map their progress and celebrate their accomplishments. Additionally, students need to understand which learning strategies work best for them.

Most parents and too many teachers either do not understand or do not accept this assumption. The following is a frequently heard comment: "Well, that might work with some students in high school, but it won't work in elementary schools."

The Research

In two randomized controlled trials, researchers found positive effects when students were given assessment data and provided with feedback about strategies that they could use. In one study (Phillips, Hamlett, Fuchs, & Fuchs, 1993), the teachers provided the feedback. In the other study (May & Robinson, 2007), the students had access to an interactive website that gave them their test scores and provided advice for improving their scores.

Contrary to the assumption that students can't self-assess, these study findings and other study findings say they can, and should. Also, the study findings are consistent with Popham's (2008) emphasis on teachers and students engaging in formative assessing. The findings are supportive of instructional strategies that lead to students understanding the learning targets of each lesson and the related standards and indicators of learning success. Although not directly addressed in these studies, students engaging in formative assessment is an expectation in many schools and school districts. In his interview, Dr. Asp described some of how this can work.

Implications for Teaching and Learning

The Institute of Education Sciences document cited below (L. Hamilton et al., 2009) provides a set of recommendations for improving student learning based in research. The document offers a direct recommendation in relation to the assumption challenged here: Teach students to examine their own data and set learning goals (L. Hamilton et al., 2009, p. 19). Teachers should (1) explain expectations and assessment criteria; (2) provide feedback to students that is timely, specific, well formatted, and constructive; (3) provide tools that help students learn from feedback; and (4) use students' data analyses to guide instructional changes.

The IES report (L. Hamilton et al., 2009) also identified potential roadblocks, including the possibility that students will view feedback as a reflection on themselves rather than seeing it as a focus for improvement, and that teachers may be concerned about taking the time to explain rubrics and to help students analyze feedback. Actually, if all teachers were to facilitate the development of self-assessment skills in their students, each of these roadblocks would vanish.

Sources: Hamilton, L., Halverson, R., Jackson, S. S., Mandinach, E., Supovitz, J., & Wayman, J. D. (2009, September). *Using student achievement data to support instructional decision making.* Washington, DC: U.S. Department of Education, Institute of Education Sciences, National Center for Education Evaluation and Regional Assistance. May, H., & Robinson, M. A. (2007). *A randomized evaluation of Ohio's Personalized Assessment Reporting System (PARS).* Philadelphia, PA: Consortium for Policy Research in Education. Phillips, N. B., Hamlett, C. L., Fuchs, L. S., & Fuchs, D. (1993). Combining classwide curriculum-based measurement and peer tutoring to help general educators provide adaptive education. *Learning Disabilities Research & Practice, 8*(3), 148–156. Popham, W. J. (2008). *Transformative assessment.* Alexandria, VA: Association for Supervision and Curriculum Development.

reading and mathematics specialists, one or more special education teachers, and at least one member who is skilled at organizing and displaying student data.

Typically, these teams will meet once a week for 30 to 60 minutes. At each meeting, the performance of individual students is reviewed. The heaviest attention will be given to those students who are struggling. Assessment information will be displayed. The team will discuss alternative instructional and/or behavioral interventions that might help. An agreement is reached about the exact steps that will be taken and how student progress will be monitored. The students' teacher(s) will then proceed to implement the interventions, assess student progress, and bring a report back to a subsequent meeting.

An important organizing framework for this teamwork, especially within RTI, is "the triangle" (shown in Figure 13.3). Within the triangle are different levels of intervention. Three levels, or "tiers," have been defined:

- For all students, RTI begins at the bottom of the triangle by monitoring their learning progress. Tier I entails the use of evidence-based instructional strategies and differentiated instruction for all students.

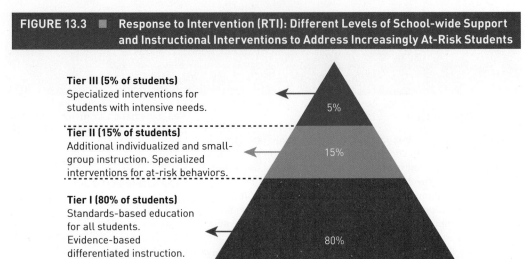

FIGURE 13.3 ■ Response to Intervention (RTI): Different Levels of School-wide Support and Instructional Interventions to Address Increasingly At-Risk Students

Tier III (5% of students)
Specialized interventions for students with intensive needs.

Tier II (15% of students)
Additional individualized and small-group instruction. Specialized interventions for at-risk behaviors.

Tier I (80% of students)
Standards-based education for all students. Evidence-based differentiated instruction. Universal screening and progress monitoring.

- Tier II focuses on students who are identified through assessments and teacher observations as being at risk of having lower learning outcomes. They are falling behind the others in their class. Through the SIT, there is discussion and development of a plan for these students to receive targeted supplemental instruction that usually takes place within the regular education classroom.

- Tier III is for those students who did not progress with the Tier II interventions. They need intensive supplemental instruction that needs to be delivered in small groups or individually.

In the RTI model, there is continuous monitoring of progress and regular review of how each student is doing. Following efforts at each of the RTI tiers, if students are not making progress in learning, they may be referred to screening for determination of a learning disability.

The RTI framework, along with the use of a school-based committee such as a SIT/DT, provides one very constructive approach to improving learning for all students. This approach represents a very

THINKING DIFFERENTLY
UNOBTRUSIVE MEASURES

The normal ways to measure student learning are through tests, homework, and grading reports and projects. Each of these measures is obtrusive. Students are fully aware that their work is being appraised. There is direct effort by the teacher to assess how students have learned. Sometimes in social science research, the measures will be unobtrusive. That is, the measures do not intrude on the subject. One classic example comes from marketing. Manufacturers, advertisers, and grocers all want to know the product preferences of customers. One unobtrusive measure to answer this question is to see which floor tiles are more worn and require replacement more often—those places are where the customers go to seek out certain products. Often architects and the builders of new buildings won't place the sidewalks until they see where people walk.

Teachers and administrators are under heavy pressure to be rigorous in their testing, which always is obtrusive. Unobtrusive measures could be applied in schools and classrooms. For example, which instructional supplies are used the most? Which books, computers, or apps do most students have and use? What about rummaging through the trash can and examining the work that students throw away? What mistakes are they making that have led them to start all over? Another unobtrusive measure lies within the content of student answers. When students are asked to provide examples, their responses will be related to the class content. The responses also provide clues about the students' background of experience and/or the richness of their vocabulary. Unobtrusive measures most certainly can enrichen teachers' understanding of what students bring to the lessons and how their learning is progressing.

effective way to incorporate all aspects of the formative assessment model. It provides a systematic approach to continuous assessment, time for careful reflection, use of evidence-based interventions, and review of the outcomes of making adjustments in instruction—all of which are designed to address the goal of learning for all students.

Uses of Technology in Assessing and Testing

As you might expect, technology applications are many, diverse, and in some examples very complicated. Some of the more important widespread ones are introduced here.

Learning Management System

Teachers, schools, school districts, and each state have established technology systems to record, compile, and analyze test information. Most school districts now provide teachers with computer-based systems for recording, analyzing, and reporting test scores and related assessment information. Parents can access the learning management system to find out about their child's test scores, as well as other items such as homework assignments. Look back at Table 8.1 to see an example of the variety of technology databases a school principal can access.

Computer-Based Testing

In the past, teachers wrote the test, administered the test, and scored the students' responses. Increasingly, all of these steps are being done with technology and online. The days of the test booklet and sharpened Number 2 pencils are rapidly coming to an end. In addition to the obvious advantages of security and automatic scoring, technology is increasingly making it possible to have more complex test items. Video segments and interactive elements are being developed. One important application that was first applied with special education students is **adaptive testing**. Instead of all students responding to all of the same test items, the difficulty of following items is adjusted based on a student's responses to earlier items. Another adaptation can be inserting breaks and adjusting the length of the test period.

Two Testing Consortia

Over the past decade, the U.S. Department of Education funded two major initiatives to develop tests based in the Common Core State Standards. There has been a great deal of controversy about whether this has been a move toward having a national curriculum. Both of the initiatives have been organized around the formation of state consortia. Over time, which states are in, and out, of each consortium has varied a great deal. Both consortia have developed new tests that are technology based:

> *Partnership for Assessment of Readiness for College and Careers (PARCC)* has developed tests (K–12) in mathematics and English language arts. An expressed purpose is to give teachers, schools, students, and parents information about the extent to which students are on track for success after high school. This consortium even releases current and past years' test items so that teachers can improve teaching and learning.

> *Smarter Balanced Assessment Consortium* also has developed computer-based tests in mathematics and English language arts that are aligned with the Common Core State Standards. The system has three components: formative assessments (during instruction), interim assessments (optional periodic tests), and summative assessments (end-of-year tests). A feature of these tests is adaptive testing.

Using Technology to Monitor Cheating

As sad as it is to write this, with the many forms of technology now available, students have expanded the ways of cheating. In response, technology applications to detect cheating are increasingly being used by schools and teachers. There are technology resources to scan text documents to check if they have been copied. Monitoring or blocking radio signals in test rooms reduces the prevalent use of cell phones and other transmitting devices. In at least one case, a major test publisher has monitored the social networking accounts of students by searching for key words such as *exam*.

ASSESSMENT ISSUES AND CHALLENGES

In this chapter, we have introduced basic concepts and practices related to teachers' use of assessments. The importance of teachers, and students, using assessment information to increase learning has been a theme. Another topic has been introducing information related to test item quality. With this information as a foundation, we can now explore some of the major issues and challenges. As with most other aspects of teaching and learning, there are a number of critical issues and challenges that future teachers need to be considering.

Balanced Assessment Systems

As you know from experience and have read in this chapter, there is an amazing array of assessments available. There are standardized tests for making high-stakes decisions. There are teacher-made tests, and there are the many interim assessments provided by teacher teams and school districts. The critical question is how to balance all of these different assessments. Shepard, Penuel, and Davidson (2017) offer two core principles. The first is that assessments should be coherent. That is, they should be related to and integrated with the curriculum, not isolated from it. Second, assessments should be grounded in a model of learning. In other words, assessments should be based in shared models of teaching and learning that take into account motivation, relevance, relationship to learning goals, and equitability. When these two principles are clearly addressed, the assessment system will be balanced.

Data-Based Decision Making

This phrase is being used a lot. Principals and superintendents talk about data-based decision making. Teachers are placed in "data teams." Schools, districts, and states post displays of data and encourage "deep" discussions that are based in "evidence." The intent is to encourage teachers, and principals, to study the available data and make instructional decisions based on the analyses. Unfortunately, in some settings, the phrase and the related activities have become a ritual that does not clearly examine individual student needs and/or lead to the implementation of instructional approaches that facilitate increased student learning.

Test Security

A very serious responsibility for school administrators and teachers is to preserve the security of high-stakes standardized tests. As you start spending time in schools, you will hear a lot about who has the responsibility for test security and the steps that are taken to prevent cheating. Test booklets are kept locked in a very secure location. Each test is numbered, counted, and recounted. Each teacher will be responsible for maintaining test security when tests are administered. If a single test is misplaced, or possibly seen/copied by a student, there will be serious consequences. The entire testing session may be abandoned, all students will have to retake a different form of the test, and it is possible an administrator or teacher will lose his or her job.

Test Cheating

Using a test score, especially from a single test, to make a high-stakes decision about graduation, licensing, pay, or keeping one's job is bound to have consequences. It is easy to think of a student test taker cheating. Frequently, students are caught using their cell phone to photograph and transmit test items. However, there are much larger cases that affect many more people. One of the recent examples unfolded in Atlanta, Georgia, where 35 educators were indicted. Under the intense pressure of the then-superintendent and administrators, teachers changed responses on test sheets, which inflated scores for whole schools. Eleven former teachers, principals, and administrators were convicted of racketeering, and most were sentenced to prison.

Opting Out

An initial purpose of the 2001 No Child Left Behind (NCLB) legislation was to hold states accountable for increasing student performance as measured through annual standardized testing. A number of threats and punishments in the act placed increasing pressure on schools. A natural response by teachers and administrators was to put more time into **test prep**. Kindergarten children would spend days on learning how to correctly bubble in their answers on test booklets. Older students would take many practice tests, and there would be school-wide pep rallies the days before testing began. There has been a gradually increasing questioning of all the time that is being invested in testing. This resistance has now taken the form of opting out. Parents in a number of schools, districts, and states ranging from Long Island, New York, to Boulder, Colorado, have boycotted their children sitting through more testing sessions. In the spring of 2015, the 600,000-member New York State United Teachers union called on parents to keep their children out. The way the NCLB system worked, the school was punished by having too low of a participation rate, and the absent students' scores were entered as zeros. More recently, with the Every Student Succeeds Act (ESSA), the punitive aspect has diminished, but the resistance has continued. For example, in 2017, in a rural Colorado district, only 15 of 500 students took the state test.

Connecting Student Test Scores to Educator Evaluation and Pay

In the past, there were occasional suggestions that in some way teachers' pay should be correlated with how well their students do. Under the Barack Obama administration, the U.S. Department of Education launched a major multistate program titled Race to the Top. A key component of that program was that teacher and principal evaluation and pay should be tied to test scores. Although this sounds simple, there are many complicating elements. For example, what level of technical quality should the test have? Will there be only one test, or multiple? How will pay be set with secondary school teachers who see 150 students a day, in schools where students have five or six different teachers each day? Also, some students are slower learners, which can mean less growth on test scores. Will the teachers of slow learners receive less pay?

Preserving Confidentiality Versus Appropriate Access

Take a moment to think about all of the assessment data that are being collected on each student: standardized tests each year, unit and interim tests, homework assignments, report card grades, and more. Most of these data are stored in teacher, school, district, and state computer databases. Each student's identification is associated with his or her data set. Depending on need, many different people have access to certain data elements. Determining who has access, and to which elements, is a major challenge. Having systems and procedures that preserve confidentiality, block unqualified access, and at the same time have ease of access for those with a need to know is not easy, or even likely possible.

Testing Individual Learning Versus Group Work

If you stop and think about it, all of the content of this chapter has been about assessing the learning of individuals. There has been no mention of group work, which is what adults normally do. In 2015, one of the major international studies, the Program for International Student Assessment (PISA), tested 15-year-olds in 50 countries and regions. The test was of collaborative problem solving. U.S. students ranked 39th in math but 13th in collaborative problem solving. In general, girls scored better than boys, and students who played video games scored lower than those who said they didn't (Barshay, 2017). Should teachers and the U.S. school system assess student group work?

Reducing the achievement gap requires that all students have the opportunity to learn.

In 2018, for the first time, PISA has assessed global competence. This concept entails individuals being able to examine issues of global and cultural significance, and to understand and appreciate different perspectives. Additionally, the assessment tests the extent to which students are able to engage appropriately and effectively across cultures. The first-time assessment asks students to examine news articles and to recognize outside influences on perspectives and worldviews. Teaching for global competence adds a whole new challenge for teachers and schools.

Don't Forget the Achievement Gap

Whether we are talking about NRTs versus CRTs, or testing versus assessing, or summative versus formative, or RTI, it is imperative that as a teacher you continually be thinking about all of your students having opportunities to learn. Examine your formative assessment notes, the results of tests, and your reports of summative grading to see if any categories of your students are not making satisfactory progress. Often, teachers are not aware that they are treating girls, or boys, or ELLs, or some other category of students differently. Disaggregating your assessment information by category of student will tell you a lot about how well you are matching instruction with the needs of all your students.

CONNECTING TO THE CLASSROOM

This chapter first introduced two very different ways of thinking about the purposes for assessment (see Table 13.1). Then different approaches to testing, including CRTs and NRTs, and the construction of different types of test items were described. The remainder of the chapter focused heavily on formative assessment. The importance of continually checking for understanding and being ready to adjust instruction cannot be overemphasized, and neither can the importance of students doing self-formative assessing at all grade levels and for all content areas. The following summary points should be kept in mind as you engage with assessing student learning:

1. The primary purpose for assessment should be to help students learn, which means that teachers must continually use a variety of methods to assess the extent to which each student's understanding is increasing.

2. Don't forget that students have a responsibility to self-assess and to use the results of tests and other assessments to reflect and identify steps they can take to improve their learning.

3. Norm-Referenced Tests (NRTs) compare one student's achievement with how other students have done.

4. Criterion-Referenced Tests (CRTs) compare one student's achievement with a particular level of proficiency or performance.

5. Bloom's taxonomy is a very useful tool for classifying test items and teacher questions. Low-level questions seek recall of facts and procedures. High-level questions ask students to analyze, synthesize, and evaluate using what they know and understand.

6. There are a number of serious issues related to assessing and testing. For example, the increasing amount of testing is leading to an opting-out movement.

SUMMARY

In this chapter, we have introduced basic concepts and procedures for assessing student learning. We also have focused on the importance of thinking about teaching and learning in terms of formative, instead of summative only. Key topics include the following:

- Norm-Referenced Tests (NRTs) compare the performance of one student with the performance of a comparison group of students.

- Criterion-Referenced Tests (CRTs) compare the performance of each student with a particular level of accomplishment.

- Teachers need to develop knowledge and skill in constructing different types of objective and subjective test items.

- Formative assessment is the foundational perspective for planning, delivering, and adjusting instruction in order to continuously improve learning.

- Response to Intervention (RTI) is an organized school- or district-wide three-tier approach to data-based decision making that entails assessing learning, making adjustments in instruction, and monitoring progress for all students.

KEY TERMS

adaptive testing 409

assessing 385

authentic task 392

closed questions 398

Criterion-Referenced Tests (CRTs) 389

data-based decision making 407

data teams 408

Depth of Knowledge (DOK) 393

formative evaluation 386

global competence 412

high-stakes testing 388

holistic rubric 403

multiple assessments 388

Norm-Referenced Tests (NRTs) 389

normal curve 389

objective tests 399

open-ended questions 398

performance 392

reliability 392

Response to Instruction (RTI) 407

Student Improvement Team (SIT) 408

subjective tests 400

summative evaluation 386

test prep 411

tests 385

validity 392

CLASS DISCUSSION QUESTIONS

1. A major emphasis in this chapter has been on having you think less about summative assessments for the purpose of grading, and think much more about the uses of formative assessments to improve student learning. The idea is to have teachers shift their thinking from preoccupation with "What am I teaching?" to continually thinking about "What evidence do I have that each of my students is learning?" What do you see as being the biggest challenges to making this transformational change in your thinking and that of your students?

2. One of the purposes for assessment that was introduced in this chapter is for students' self-reflection about their learning. What can teachers do to help students use assessments for self-reflection and to adjust their learning tactics? At what grade level are students ready to self-assess? In other words, do you think that it would be useful for primary-grade teachers to work with their students on self-assessment? Or, in elementary school, is this really only the teacher's job? What about changing the mindset of high school students who are interested only in their grade?

SELF-ASSESSMENT

What Is Your Current Level of Understanding and Thinking About Assessing Student Learning and Results?

Answer the following questions and then score your responses using the Assessing Your Learning rubric.

1. As a teacher, what do you see as the major differences between summative and formative assessment?

2. In your teaching, how will you engage students in assessing their own learning?

3. There are major differences between CRTs and NRTs; when and in what ways should teachers use each of these test designs?

4. As a teacher, what will you do to protect confidentiality of assessment information?

5. You will likely teach in a school that has some model of RTI. What do you see as being implications of RTI for you and your students?

Assessing Your Learning Rubric

	Parts & Pieces	Unidimensional	Organized	Integrated	Extensions
Indicators	Elements/concepts are talked about as isolated and independent entities. Some important names are provided in isolation.	One or a few concepts are addressed, while others are underdeveloped, or not mentioned.	Deliberate and structured consideration of all key concepts/elements.	All key concepts/elements are included in a view that addresses interconnections.	Integration of all elements and dimensions, with extrapolation to new situations.
Assessing student learning and results	Names one or two concepts, such as the types of test items, without placing them into a formative or summative context; or can name only one or two of the RTI tiers.	Only describes one model, such as summative evaluation and assigning grades; describes one tier of RTI in detail, but provides little information about other tiers.	Describes and compares NRTs and CRTs; or describes formative and summative assessment; or describes the three tiers of RTI; and includes a few examples/implications.	Describes key concepts (e.g., NRT/CRT, formative/summative assessments, or RTI) and interrelates the role of the teacher and students with clear examples.	Presents an integrated view of summative and formative assessment (or RTI), provides clear examples, identifies issues, and points out areas where she or he plans to develop more in-depth understanding.

FIELD GUIDE
FOR LEARNING MORE ABOUT . . .

Assessing Student Learning and Results

To further increase your understanding about testing, formative assessment, and RTI, do one or more of the following activities.

Ask a Teacher	1. For a particular lesson, ask a teacher about what he or she will do to check on understanding before, during, and after.
	2. Look over the various assessments that a teacher has used across a term to evaluate student work. Ask the teacher to explain the reasoning for the different forms of assessment that have been used. To what extent does she or he focus on thinking in terms of summative versus formative assessment? To what extent and in what ways are his or her students expected to engage in formative assessment?
	3. Ask a teacher or principal to describe for you how the RTI process works. Listen for how much his or her approach is formative versus summative.
Make Your Own Observations	1. Attend a meeting of the SIT or other committee, such as a data team, in a school that is organized to review student progress. This committee may be organized around RTI, or it may be a screening committee, to determine whether or not a student should be referred for screening for a possible disability. What data does this committee use? Have there been different adjustments to instruction for certain students? Does it appear that the committee is thinking more in terms of summative or formative assessment?
	2. Find a rubric for some component of student learning for a subject that you plan to teach. When you next visit a classroom where that subject is being taught, use the rubric to score examples of student work. Compare your scoring with that of the teacher. Did the teacher use a rubric or some other scoring system? If possible, check with some of the students about how they have assessed their learning. Do they use rubrics as well? Do the students benchmark their learning to the standards?
Reflect Through Journaling	The major theme throughout this chapter has been describing and distinguishing between the two major purposes of assessments. Making the major change in thinking from using test scores to assign grades (summative) to using evidence to improve learning (formative) is a challenge for teachers, students, principals, and parents. At this point, how clear are you about these two purposes? As you look over the grades you are receiving in your current teacher education courses, which way are you seeing them? As a teacher, what reminders about assessment will you want to be sure to keep in mind?

Build Your Portfolio	It is never too soon to start drafting ideas about the strategies you will use to check for understanding. For a subject that you plan to teach, select a unit, chapter, or week's worth of lessons and construct a set of questions you could use. Be sure to keep in mind a combination of objective and subjective probes. Use Bloom's taxonomy (Table 13.5) as a guide for developing checks that will assess different levels of DOK (Depth of Knowledge). One easy way to test your ideas can be done the next time you visit a classroom. Ask the students about what they are doing. How do they assess how much they know? Can they describe what they need to learn next?
Read a Book	In his interview, Dr. Elliott Asp talked about the challenges involved in helping students (and teachers) make a change in their thinking about the purposes of assessment. He has had teachers read a book about mindsets: *Mindset: The New Psychology of Success*, by Carol Dweck (2007, Random House/Ballantine Books). You will find this to be an interesting read.
	Assessing learning progress of students with special needs can be a challenge for teacher education candidates. *Assessing Learners With Special Needs: An Applied Approach* (7th ed.), by Terry Overton (2011, Pearson), is a comprehensive resource. The book begins with setting the legal and ethical context for assessing students with special needs. Chapter topics include assessing academics and behavior, as well as early childhood.
	Understanding by Design (2nd ed.), by Grant Wiggins and Jay McTighe (2005, Association for Supervision & Curriculum Development), has become a classic reference. The basic approach is to develop an understanding of the relationships between learning outcomes, assessment, and the design of curriculum. In this approach, development of assessment begins with being clear about the learning outcomes. Then one does "backward mapping" to design instruction and assessments. The authors walk the reader through each topic and then draw implications for the design of instruction, including examination of how the way teachers teach is linked to how and what students learn.
	Grading Smarter, Not Harder: Assessment Strategies That Motivate Kids and Help Them Learn, by Myron Dueck (2014, ASCD), presents a different way of thinking about grading. The author builds the case against traditional grading and offers many strategies and examples for assessing learning that lead to better grading practices.
Search the Web	**Testing Accommodations:** There are many governmental and professional association websites that provide information about appropriate accommodations for special education and ELL students. One that you might not automatically think of searching is the U.S. Department of Justice, Civil Rights Division. There is a useful report titled "ADA Requirements: Testing Accommodations."
	School District Assessment Office: Go to the website for a school or school district where you would like to become a teacher. Most districts will have an assessment office. Search within the site for information about the types of assessments and tools that are provided to teachers. Does the information provided on this website suggest that there is more interest in summative or in formative assessment? Does the site provide any information about how the school or district is doing RTI? Develop a list of questions you will want to ask in order to learn more details about what the school or district is doing.
	Comparing Schools/Districts: The web represents a powerful resource for obtaining information about any of the public schools in the country. However, there always has to be caution in assuming that all of the information is accurate. Still, exploring and comparing information about student performance in different schools and school districts can be informative. For example, use the search term "comparing schools side by side." You will find a number of sites where you can compare test scores of one school/district with another. You can compare where you attended school with another. Or examine schools/districts where you would like to teach. Keep in mind when doing this that you are using the same single high-stakes test scores to make comparisons that we have spent this chapter cautioning against.
	Criticisms of High-Stakes Testing: For a satirical critique of high-stakes testing, go to YouTube and search "John Oliver Standardized Testing."

STUDENT STUDY SITE

$SAGE edge™

Get the tools you need to sharpen your study skills. **SAGE edge** offers a robust online environment featuring an impressive array of free tools and resources.

Access practice quizzes, eFlashcards, video, and multimedia at **edge.sagepub.com/hall3e.**

BECOMING TOMORROW'S HIGHLY EFFECTIVE TEACHER

14 SUCCEEDING IN YOUR TEACHER EDUCATION PROGRAM, AND BEYOND

© Alethea Maldonado

TEACHER INTERVIEW

Ms. Alethea Maldonado

Ms. Alethea Maldonado is in her second year of teaching. Her full-time assignment is to teach English as a Second Language (ESL) at Cedar Creek High School in Cedar Creek, Texas. It is a 5A (the largest size) school that opened in 2010. It has 1,400+ students, 52% male and 48% female, with a large Hispanic enrollment. In total, 73% of the enrollment is minority. There are 101 full-time teachers. It is one of four high schools in the Bastrop Independent School District.

Ms. Maldonado received an associate's degree from Austin Community College. *At the beginning, I bounced around a lot. I couldn't figure out what I wanted to do.* She then worked as a counselor at a Mexican American cultural center in Austin. *I was there about two years working side by side with a classroom teacher. At that point, I realized that I could see myself becoming a teacher. From there, my next step was to go to Texas State University, where I got a bachelor's degree in English.* She then entered a graduate program for teacher certification and obtained a master's degree. *I loved it. I am glad I ended up there.*

LEARNING OUTCOMES

After reading this chapter, you should be able to do the following:

1. List important steps (activities and tasks) you want to accomplish during your teacher education program in order for you to become a high-quality beginning teacher.

2. Determine the key steps you will need to take to be hired for your first teaching position.

3. Describe ways you as a teacher education candidate and beginning teacher can be a leader.

4. Identify ways that experienced teachers have found joy in teaching, and identify ways that you, too, can have joy throughout your career.

Q: **What is your current teaching assignment?**

A: I teach five different ESL classes. I teach English Language Development, which is for my more advanced English speakers. I teach Newcomers, which are my "babies," who are new to the United States. I teach classes for students who are at a more intermediate level in their language proficiency. I see a lot of my kids more than once. I have five preps, which is definitely overwhelming.

I was hired, last year, thinking I would teach only one section of ESL, and that I would teach practical writing to ESL kids. Then our full-time ESL sub left, and I adopted her classes. In my second year of teaching, they gave me all the ESL classes. I really enjoy working with those kids.

Q: **Do you have other assignments?**

A: That is a funny story. I graduated with my master's in December 2015. In the spring of 2016, I worked as a long-term sub at a high school and started applying for jobs. As I was ending my interview at Cedar Creek High School, I saw someone I thought I recognized.

He said, "Oh, yeah, Maldonado, what are you doing here?" It ended up that he had been a coach at my high school. He had asked me to play volleyball when he was a coach and teacher at my high school, but I didn't want to play that year. He still remembered me. As soon as I left, he went straight to the principal and said, "I want her on my coaching staff." The principal asked what he knew about me.

That is how I got into coaching volleyball. At our school, you have to coach two sports. So right now, I am coaching softball.

Q: **Who are your students?**

A: I have students from Mexico, Honduras, El Salvador, and Colombia. They come to our school, and they have very different backgrounds. Some of them have come across the border and get placed in refugee camps until they are placed with families. They are here to learn English and to get a good education in our public schools. When they arrive at our school, they are evaluated by our ESL Department and the Language Proficiency Assessment Committee. They are placed in my classes if they need that extra language support, the sheltered instruction aspect in learning English.

Q: **Did you have a mentor assigned in your first year of teaching?**

A: What I appreciate about my school is that you are assigned a mentor for your first year. That mentor checks in with you. If you need any help, he or she is your go-to person. My mentor was the Spanish teacher. She helped a lot, for example, in making calls to homes. She was very fluent in Spanish and helped me explain to parents if their child was not getting homework done, was missing too many classes, or was at risk of failing. She was always open and there for me.

This year, I have support from the district ESL specialist who always is checking to see how I am doing. She provides professional development throughout the year, but she is always a phone call or email away from me.

Q: **How do you know that your students are learning?**

A: When they are engaged, and they are asking questions to better understand whatever I am teaching. They are present. It really is up to me to be looking at the dynamics of my classroom. If I can get them wanting to learn, if they are making jokes about what they are learning, then I know they are engaged.

Q: **What are you learning now?**

A: Oh, man! I am learning a lot. I am still trying to figure out the whole ESL program, and what materials and practices I should include in my classroom. Every day, I try to become a better teacher, and just reflect on the day. I am learning so much about being a better teacher and being a better content teacher. I continue to work on getting to know my kids as learners and human beings. I am taking what they share with me every day and using that to create better lessons and a supportive classroom environment.

You don't stop being a student when you become a teacher. The really cool thing about teaching is that the learning never stops.

Q: What advice do you have for those who are now studying to become teachers?

A: Reach out to your professors! They are always willing to help you, and I found that so refreshing. Any question or concern that I had, my professors were willing to sit down and talk to me in person and help me throughout the process and stresses of grad school. I have one particular professor who I consider to be my mentor. She helped me pass my second attempt at my graduate program's exam, and she even wrote letters of recommendation as I began applying for teaching positions. I still keep in touch with her to this day. I share with her the successes I have in my classroom.

To go from sitting in the classroom, creating scenarios of theories and strategies in my head, and how they would work out, to being in the classroom is a challenge. Dealing with students who maybe aren't going to react the way you want them to is a challenge. You can't be hard on yourself. Every day, reflect on how things went. What can I do differently to engage that one student? Always focus on the positive, those little successes. You are new to this profession, and mistakes are inevitable. What is so great about this job is that you get to wake up the next day and try again.

Q: How do you go about working with parents?

A: The parent support with ESL kids is different. There are some cultural differences and also that language barrier. Sometimes, it is hard to get ahold of the parent or guardian. Parents don't always pick up the phone. We leave messages and emails.

This makes me think about something that happened recently. I have a student who was failing the six-week period. She was skipping school. Her father called me with concern. We set up a meeting. My teaching assistant, who is fluent in Spanish, sat in on the meeting. The father was concerned. He shared with me that the daughter was having a hard time living in the United States. Her father brought her here to get a better education, but she didn't get along with her stepmother.

In those kinds of cases, I am open to parents or guardians telling me what is going on in their lives because I share their concern. I want them to know how much I care and that I am just as concerned as they are. I welcome parents checking on how their child is doing in school and making sure they do their homework. I am still working on relationships with students, parents, and guardians. That's something I am still learning. Our ESL Department is working toward an environment in which parents and students can be involved with each other in our community.

Q: What brings you joy?

A: For me, it is just being able to serve my students, my colleagues, my school campus, and my community. I always knew that I wanted to serve somehow and just be useful. Knowing that people depend on me, especially my students, and having a sense of responsibility to be there for them brings me joy. Everything happened for a reason in my life to get me to this point. All the people I have met. The connections I have made with my students and my colleagues. Being able to coach sports that I love, like softball. Being a part of a community like I am. Everything I am a part of at my school. The subject I teach. The kids I am able to teach. The campus itself. All of that brings me joy.

Some days are harder than others. I am happy at my job through all of it. I enjoy it. I enjoy the people that I am able to surround myself with.

Questions to Consider

1. How would you feel about having many ESL students in your classes and school?

2. Ms. Maldonado was supported in getting her current teaching job by one of her former teachers. What adult contacts and networks do you have to support your becoming a teacher?

3. Joy for Ms. Maldonado is based not only in teaching her students but also in her being a member of several communities beyond her classroom. How do you see yourself engaging with adults beyond your classroom?

INTRODUCTION

Teaching is one of the most important professions. Now, more than at any other time in history, students, parents, communities, and the nation need outstanding teachers. As has been described in Chapters 1 through 13, because the need is so great and teaching is so complex, the preparation to become a teacher is more rigorous than ever before. The expectations for beginning teachers are higher too. For all of these reasons, it is very important for you to take advantage of every opportunity presented throughout your teacher preparation program. Now is the time to begin anticipating what you will need to know, be able to do, and have on record as you seek and obtain your first full-time teaching position. Failure to be thinking ahead could result in not obtaining your most preferred teaching position.

Each of the previous chapters has opened with an interview with a practicing teacher or an administrator. Each interviewee was selected because he or she is a highly successful professional. In each interview, you have access to important insights and practical recommendations. In this chapter, there are excerpts of interviews with three exceptional educators. When interviewed, two were in their second year of teaching. They know firsthand what it is like to move from a teacher education program to being a beginning teacher. The third interview is with a full-time teacher leader. She is mid-career and is an example of an increasingly important career path that is opening up to exceptional teachers.

This chapter begins with recommendations for succeeding in your teacher education program. In this section, we offer concrete suggestions for what you need to do as you move through your teacher education program. One important activity for you to be doing now and on into the future is to take time and reflect on "how it's going." As you will see, the three interviewees continually reflect about what their students are learning and what they plan to do next. To help with your developing skill in reflecting, we introduce a research-based framework for understanding your evolving concerns and thoughts about becoming a teacher.

The chapter then addresses steps and tips for obtaining your first teaching position. How will you apply for a teaching position? What kinds of documentation will you need to have, and how can you prepare for the position interview? If you start anticipating and planning now, you will see how much of what you do in the remainder of your preparation program will be useful to you in seeking, applying for, and obtaining the perfect teaching position.

One other important topic that you need to have in mind is leadership. While in your teacher education program and as a teacher, there will be many opportunities for you to lead. Doing so is important to you now as a candidate and even more so when you become a teacher.

In summary, this chapter introduces topics, themes, and recommendations related to completing your teacher education program, obtaining a teaching job, and being successful in your early years of teaching.

WHAT ARE KEYS TO SUCCEEDING IN YOUR TEACHER EDUCATION PROGRAM?

I have a boyfriend who has a bachelor's degree and has not been sure about what to do. Recently, I really pushed him to get into a teacher education program. Right now, he is in his first semester of grad school in secondary education. I know how overwhelmed he feels. He is not sure which grade level, or subject, he wants to teach. I just tell him to be open to everything your professors are teaching you. Think about all the theories and strategies they are introducing and think about ways you can apply them to make a difference as a teacher. My best advice: Just be open throughout the entire process.

—*Ms. Maldonado*

As you continue with your preparations to become a teacher, you will take a number of professional education courses and have a variety of clinical and field experiences. As you will have heard already from your fellow candidates, some courses and experiences are perceived as being "better" than others. What you will discover is that regardless of the perceived quality of the course or experience, the really good candidates use it to their advantage. They use every assignment and activity as an opportunity to learn more about teaching, student learning, and what classrooms and schools are like. Regardless of the situation, the high-quality candidates learn and contribute to the learning of others. They are able to do this because they understand themselves, what teaching is about, and the importance of using every experience and opportunity to learn more. They also collect evidence to document their efforts and what they have learned, and artifacts that indicate the differences they make. They do all of this in spite of their feelings of not knowing it all and being very busy. The following frameworks can help you understand and use every situation as a learning experience.

Strive to Learn in Every Setting

In everything that you do in your teacher preparation program, *make it a learning experience.* If an instructor gives you an assignment that is confusing, ask for clarification. If you are not fully satisfied with a field placement, think through what you can do to still learn from the experience. Use every assignment and experience as an opportunity to learn more about teaching. In every situation, there is the potential to find an idea that can help you become a better teacher. Finding these ideas is your responsibility. Here are three particularly useful strategies:

1. Take advantage of every field experience to learn something.

2. Have in mind a generic teaching model that can be used to examine any teaching situation.

3. Whenever possible, collect samples of teacher and student work.

The Importance of Each and Every Field Experience

Striving to learn in field experiences is very important for aspiring teachers. Candidates consistently report that the most important part of their preparation program was student teaching. This is the capstone experience where everything that has been introduced, studied, and dissected throughout your professional education courses is brought together in the "real" world. This is the time when you get to teach. Naturally, your first concerns will be about preparing each lesson. However, do not lose sight of why you are there and presenting the lesson: to help each and every student learn. Be sure to incorporate formative assessment questions and tasks, and obtain evidence of the extent to which your students are learning.

As important and significant as student teaching is, do not underestimate the important learning opportunities that come with all of the earlier clinical activities and field experiences. Whether it is observing a lesson, or monitoring student behavior on the playground or in the cafeteria, there are opportunities to learn. Your learning will not always be about teaching; it might be about characteristics of students, or classroom or school procedures. Take advantage of every activity as an opportunity to learn something new. One way to do this is to set a personal objective: *In every experience, I will seek to learn at least one new thing.* When you engage each experience with the expressed intention of learning something new, you will!

Also, be sure to express your appreciation to the teacher(s) who permitted you to be there. They did not have to open the door. Teachers are under tremendous pressure to make every minute count. Many are self-conscious about letting anyone observe them. Without their openness, you would have to learn the basics of teaching OTJ (on the job). So be sure to say "thank you."

Emerson Elliott's General Model of Effective Instruction

Throughout this text, the authors have emphasized the importance of teachers focusing on student learning. We have described a broad array of contextual factors (e.g., student diversity, special needs, and English Language Learners, or ELLs) and introduced several instructional strategies (e.g., different ways of grouping students). The importance of assessing student learning and methods for doing so (e.g., standards and rubrics) has been emphasized. Given the large number of methods, strategies, and factors that have been introduced, it now should be helpful to offer a general model that can serve as an overall organizer, reminder, and guide. Such a model can help you keep in mind the critical components of instruction. You can use this model as a guide when preparing your lessons and in observing the teaching of others. When the components of this model are addressed, it is very likely that there will be high-quality teaching that results in all students learning.

One such model has been proposed by Emerson Elliott (2005) (see Table 14.1), who is a national expert on accreditation of teacher education and assessing high-quality teaching. His model "defines expectations for evidence that PreK–12 student learning has occurred, constructed around a core of activities in which the candidate takes responsibility for a significant unit of instruction" (p. 1). This model is generic; it can be applied to all levels of schooling, different kinds of students, and all subject areas. Each of the core activities is basic to effective and high-quality teaching. Each of the elements outlined in Table 14.1 has been introduced and emphasized throughout this textbook.

Collecting Examples, Notes, and Artifacts

Throughout your preparation program, you will have many opportunities to document your learning. You have heard about the archeologist collecting artifacts. You need to do this too. By now, you should have started a file drawer, a box, and a digital file of products related to what you have been doing and learning. If you haven't started by now, you likely will have already missed out on having some piece of evidence that you will wish you had kept at some point in the future. Saving examples of lesson plans, assessments, and student work will be useful as you take more professional education courses and as you plan lessons in future clinical and field experiences.

One of your major responsibilities as you complete your preparation program is to become knowledgeable and skilled at doing each of the elements outlined in the Generic Teaching Model (Table 14.1). They may be given different names. Whatever they are called, these are the essential components of high-quality instruction. By the end of your program, you will need to have artifacts in your portfolio that document your capabilities to do each of the components of this model. Be sure to collect specific examples and artifacts related to each component of the model. You will need to have a full understanding of and skill in doing each element of this model before you interview for that first teaching position. Having documents, exhibits, photos, and assessment results will be very useful to illustrate the quality

TABLE 14.1 ■ A General Teaching Model With Core Activities for a Significant Unit of Instruction That Leads to PreK–12 Student Learning	
Sets appropriate expectations for evidence that PreK–12 student learning has occurred, constructed around a core of activities in which the candidate **takes responsibility for a significant unit of instruction**, and	
JUDGES PRIOR LEARNING	Undertakes a systematic assessment (based in standards and benchmarks) to understand the prior PreK–12 student learning in the area he or she will teach;
PLANS INSTRUCTION	Plans an appropriate sequence of instruction to advance PreK–12 student learning, based on the prior assessment;
TEACHES	Teaches PreK–12 students to acquire and use content knowledge in meaningful ways, engaging those who bring differing background knowledge and learning needs, and providing students with opportunities to demonstrate the use of critical and creative thinking skills;
ASSESSES	Conducts a concluding objective test or alternative assessment(s);
ANALYZES	Analyzes the results of the concluding assessment(s), documenting the student learning that occurred at individual and group levels, including explanations of results from students who learned more or less than expected, and results from each subgroup of students; and
REFLECTS	Reflects on change in teaching that could improve results.

Source: Elliott, E. (2005). *Student learning in NCATE accreditation.* Washington, DC: National Council for the Accreditation of Teacher Education.

CHALLENGING ASSUMPTIONS

SHOULD STUDENT TEACHING BE DONE IN THE MOST DIFFICULT AND HARD-TO-STAFF SETTINGS?

Many suggest that student teaching assignments should be in the most challenging schools—schools with more low-performing students and more teacher turnover—the rationale being that these schools are the most likely settings for the first assignments of beginning teachers and that more can be learned from having intensive experiences in these settings. The counterrationale is that student teachers can learn more in schools that are easier to staff and offer desirable teaching conditions.

Most studies of learning outcomes focus on what the students learn. In the study reported by Matthew Ronfeldt (2012), the focus was on examining the outcomes of the school placements of student teachers. Two of the study questions were (1) Were teachers who student-taught in a difficult-to-staff school more or less likely to leave teaching in the first five years? and (2) Did teachers who student-taught in a difficult-to-staff school have higher or lower student gains when compared with teachers who student-taught in easier-to-staff schools?

Study Design and Method

Administrative and survey data from nearly 3,000 New York City teachers, their students, and their schools were analyzed. The teachers in the study sample were, on average, 30 years old, 65% white, and 75% female. Forty-seven percent of the sample came through an early entry teacher education program, either Teach For America or Teaching Fellows.

Study Findings

The study found that (1) teachers who student-taught in easier-to-staff schools had higher retention rates, (2) teachers who student-taught in easier-to-staff schools were more effective at raising test scores, and (3) teachers who did their student teaching in easier-to-staff schools had better retention and achievement gains even if they had their subsequent full-time teaching assignments in the hardest-to-staff schools with the most underserved student populations.

Implications

The findings from this study suggest that future teachers learn more about teaching when their student teaching placement is in schools that are functioning more effectively. In these settings, they can experience more effective instruction, be mentored by more effectively functioning teachers, and experience what it is like to be in a school that overall is doing well. The findings from the Ronfeldt (2012) study suggest that what student teachers learn in these settings is carried into their succeeding years as full-time teachers.

As your time for student teaching nears, you will want to think about the opposing beliefs about where to be placed for student teaching and to consider carefully the findings from this study.

Source: Ronfeldt, M. (2012, March). Where should student teachers learn to teach? Effects of field placement school characteristics on teacher retention and effectiveness. *Educational Evaluation and Policy Analysis, 34*(1), 3–26.

---

of your teaching. Make sure that along the way you collect many examples of student work, and be sure that you preserve confidentiality.

Understanding Your Concerns: A Research-Based Framework for Reflection

Something that is very important is reflection. I kept a journal my first year of student teaching and my first year as a teacher. I would write down things as they happened. Then I would look back at how I handled different situations. Sometimes I would tweak it and write what I would do the next time that happened. I still have that journal. I would recommend reflection, because you can learn so much.

—Ms. Amber Velasquez
Second-Year Teacher
Round Rock, Texas

Regularly jotting down concerns is an important strategy for reflection.

Marmaduke St. John/Alamy Stock Photo

Walking into the school as a teacher for the first time is exciting and a little scary.

There are three very important components to reflection. The first is to appreciate how important the process of reflecting can be to your learning and continually improving in your teaching. The second is to keep a journal: Keeping a journal provides a record of your efforts, what worked well, and what you will want to do differently next time. The third important aspect is that reflection is a personal experience. Your journaling and thinking about what you have done, what you are doing, and what you will do is all about your becoming an exceptional teacher. These same notes and insights also become important examples for you to draw from when you are applying for your first teaching position.

In order to understand their students, teachers must first understand themselves. This does not require a complex psychological analysis; however, each of us will have certain feelings and perceptions about every situation. In addition, each of us may perceive the same situation differently. Depending on our own perceptions, we construct our personal interpretations of what each situation means. Teachers do this all the time when talking with students and colleagues, and when thinking about what they and others are doing.

To help you in refining your reflection efforts, we offer a research-based framework and related tools. This framework is called the Concerns Model. It provides a structure for sorting and organizing your thoughts. The model also provides a method for reflecting on your developing perceptions and feelings about becoming a teacher. It is developmental. As you move through your preparation program, you will be able to chart the changes in your perceptions and feelings. This is a very useful and easy-to-use framework to help you in reflecting on your current thoughts about teaching.

What Are Your Concerns Right Now?

Understanding that all of us filter and ascribe personal meaning to events and actions is very important, especially for teachers. For example, teacher education candidates worry about getting good grades and wonder what it will feel like to be in front of a whole class of students. This is the personal side of teaching: identifying and understanding our **concerns**. At any time, you will have a mixture of feelings, perceptions, worries, and preoccupations about teaching. To illustrate this idea, take a minute to respond to the following task.

OPEN-ENDED CONCERNS STATEMENT

As you think about becoming a teacher, what are your concerns? Don't say what others are concerned about; instead, what are *your* concerns at this time? (Write/type a description of your concerns using complete sentences.)

Don't read any further until you have written your response.

Understanding Your Concerns

The activity of writing your concerns is easy. Developing an understanding of what you have written is guided by more than 50 years of research. Researchers have documented that the concerns of teacher education candidates can be placed in categories and used by candidates and the program faculty to improve learning. In the end, teachers who understand their own concerns are better able to understand the concerns of their students and colleagues.

It turns out that our concerns can be sorted into a set of easy-to-understand categories. The original research on teacher concerns was pioneered by Frances Fuller (1969), a professor at The University of

Comstock/Comstock/Thinkstock

Texas at Austin. Since then, the analysis of concerns has expanded beyond teachers and now includes understanding the concerns of people involved in change (Hall & Hord, 2015).

Major Areas of Teacher Concern

Teacher education candidates, teachers, and others will typically fall into one of four areas with regard to their concerns: Unrelated, Self, Task, and Impact. Since becoming a teacher represents a major change process, the Concerns Model certainly applies. The following are general descriptions of each of these areas of concern:

Unrelated Concerns. There is little or no concern about teaching. Instead, the concerns are about other topics such as work, a family problem, getting along with a roommate, or an upcoming event such as getting tickets for a concert.

Self Concerns. Having enough information and wanting to know more are of concern, as are one's adequacy and ability to be a successful teacher. Doubt might be about knowing enough content, controlling the class, knowing how to teach a particular lesson, or being uncomfortable when standing in front of the class. These concerns can pop up each time you enter a new classroom or are getting ready to teach a lesson for the first time.

Task Concerns. Finding the time to fit everything in, getting all the materials organized, preparing lesson plans, and grading papers are likely topics of concern. Learning the how-to-do-its of teaching and coordinating schedules are other indicators of Task concerns. Teachers have a lot to do, so being concerned about getting it all done should make sense to you.

Impact Concerns. Ideas about what could be done to further improve your effectiveness as a teacher and especially concerns about student learning are indicators of Impact concern. Thinking about ways to increase all students' learning, improve one's effectiveness as a teacher, and get the last two students to understand are clear indicators of Impact concern. Another concern could be about working with one or more fellow teachers so that *together* you can have a greater effect on student learning.

The four basic areas of concern can be more finely delineated into what are called the **Stages of Concern**. These are described in Table 14.2. In the full model, there are two parts to Self concerns and three parts to Impact concerns. Within Self concerns are the desire to know more (Stage 1, Informational) and worry about being successful (Stage 2, Personal). These are very reasonable feelings and perceptions to have, especially when doing something for the first time, such as teaching a whole class. The Impact concern area is divided into three stages. At Stage 4, Consequence, the focus is on student learning in the teacher's own classroom. When a teacher starts working with one or more colleagues in order to increase learning, he or she will likely have Stage 5, Collaboration, concerns.

There Is a Developmental Pattern to Teacher Concerns

It is very important to keep in mind that there are no "bad" areas of concern. All areas of concern are possible. In fact, there are some general patterns to how teacher concerns evolve. Teacher education candidates will have more Self and Task concerns, while experienced teachers have more Impact concerns. If you think about it, this difference in the distribution of concerns makes sense. Beginners are more likely to have doubts about their ability to do something (Self concerns) and to be more preoccupied with logistics and getting everything done (Task concerns). These areas of concern are also characteristic of first-year teachers.

Impact concerns are more likely to be present with those who are more experienced, comfortable, and confident with what they are doing. This is the time when teachers truly focus on improving student learning. Most teachers won't have a majority of their concerns being about Impact until after they have taught for several years.

Assessing Your Concerns

Assessing one's concerns is easy. Once there is an understanding of the four areas of concern and the more specific Stages of Concern, as outlined in Table 14.2, a person's concerns can be analyzed.

TABLE 14.2 ■ Stages of Concern

IMPACT	6	REFOCUSING	The focus is on the exploration of more universal benefits from the innovation, including the possibility of major changes or replacement with a more powerful alternative. The individual has definite ideas about alternatives to the proposed or existing form of the innovation.
	5	COLLABORATION	The focus is on coordination and cooperation with others regarding use of the innovation.
	4	CONSEQUENCE	Attention focuses on impact of the innovation on students in their immediate sphere of influence.
TASK	3	MANAGEMENT	Attention is focused on the processes and tasks of using the innovation and the best use of information and resources. Issues related to efficiency, organizing, managing, scheduling, and time demands are of utmost importance.
SELF	2	PERSONAL	Individual is uncertain about the demands of the innovation, his or her (in)adequacy to meet those demands, and his or her role with the innovation. This includes analysis of his or her role in relation to the reward structure of the organization, decision making, and consideration of potential conflicts with existing structures or personal commitment. Financial or status implications of the program for self and colleagues may also be reflected.
	1	INFORMATIONAL	A general awareness of the innovation and interest in learning more detail about it is indicated. The person seems to be unworried about him- or herself in relation to the innovation. He or she is interested in substantive aspects of the innovation in a selfless manner such as general characteristics, effects, and requirements for use.
	0	UNRELATED	Little concern about or involvement with the innovation is indicated.

Source: For more information, see Hall, G. E., & Hord, S. M. (2015). *Implementing change: Patterns, principles and potholes* (4th ed.). Upper Saddle River, NJ: Pearson.

Whether written or spoken, most concerns can be sorted into one of the four areas, and then the specific stage can be identified using the descriptions in Table 14.2.

As a first example of how to assess an Open-Ended Concerns Statement, read what you wrote in response to the Open-Ended Concerns Statement task that was presented earlier. Do the following:

1. **As you look at your whole statement:** Which area of concern (Unrelated, Self, Task, or Impact) is most present? Were your concerns mainly related to teaching or more about other things (i.e., Unrelated)? Were your concerns centered mainly on your ability to succeed in your college courses (i.e., Self)? Did they relate to preparing a lesson and organizing schedules (i.e., Task)? Did any part of your statement relate to student learning (i.e., Impact)? As you read what you wrote, what is the overall view—Unrelated, Self, Task, or Impact?

2. **For each of your sentences:** Which Stage(s) of Concern was most present? Use the definitions presented in Table 14.2 as the guide for assessing the Stage of Concern that each of your sentences represents. Sometimes what you have written will not be as easy to figure out, but with a little practice, sorting concern statements becomes easier.

3. **Reflecting:** What do you see as being most important about your Open-Ended Concerns Statement? Are you currently more focused on Self, Task, or Impact concerns? Keep this analysis in mind as you continue reading.

Implications of the Concerns Model for Teacher Education Candidates

Once a teacher's concerns have been analyzed, the very important follow-up question should be this: "What needs to be done to address the concerns and to facilitate my continuing to improve?" This question is what makes the Concerns Model so important for teacher education candidates and inservice teachers. When you understand your concerns, you can do something about them. Effective teacher education programs are designed with candidate concerns in mind. For example, most candidates have concerns about managing the classroom (Task concerns), so many preparation programs include a course on classroom management. Another important component of effective teacher education programs is how to assess student learning (Task and Impact concerns). So, more and more programs are including courses related to assessing.

Candidates who understand their concerns can do many things on their own to address them. For example, candidates with Self concerns will be more hesitant to ask questions of others: "What if they think my question is stupid?" Understanding this tendency can help you assert yourself more. This insight should also help you to be more understanding when your students have Self concerns. Students who are hesitant about trying something new most likely have some Self concerns. These are key times for teachers to be more supportive.

Monitoring Your Concerns About Teaching Over Time

As you continue in your teacher education program and as you become a first-year teacher, it will be important for you to document the evolution of your concerns. At regular intervals, respond again to the Open-Ended Concerns Statement. You will likely see a progression in your concerns. Ideally, by the end of student teaching, you will have fewer Self and Task concerns and some Impact concerns. However, as you become a first-year teacher, what do you think will happen to your concerns?

Most first-year teachers will return to having more Self and Task concerns. They have a lot to learn, many lessons to prepare, and meetings to attend, and they also have to get to know their colleagues and the principal. It makes sense that first-year teachers will have more Self and Task concerns. This is okay. It is what happens to all of us when we are experiencing something new (Hall & Hord, 2015).

Implications for You

We have introduced the idea of concerns with the hope that your understanding your concerns will help you in being reflective. Having a framework of categories for assessing your feelings and perceptions is an important place to start in being reflective. Understanding your concerns will help you take steps to resolve many of them. As we stated above, the more you understand about yourself, the more quickly you can come to understand the concerns of others.

The Concerns Model can help you in another way: What about your classmates? What do you hear about their concerns when they talk about a particular course, an assignment, or visiting a school? Which area of concern are they reflecting, Unrelated, Self, Task, or Impact?

The concerns idea also applies to your students. What concerns are they reflecting when they say, "I don't know if I can do this," "Ah, homework tonight. I already have two hours of it for two of my other classes!" or "I have compared my writing to the rubric on the wall. I need to work on topic sentences"?

What About Ms. Maldonado's Concerns?

Reread the opening interview for this chapter with Ms. Maldonado. Which areas of concern and which specific Stages of Concern did she talk about?

Clearly, her overall perspective is based in Impact concerns. She not only expressed concerns about her students' learning (Stage 4, Consequence), but she also

Teachers need to share their concerns about individual students as well as about how the whole school is doing.

iStock/Steve Debenport

UNDERSTANDING AND USING DATA
ANALYZING TEACHERS' CONCERNS ABOUT TEACHING

In most of the chapters in this text, the Understanding and Using Data feature has required you to work with quantitative data. The task required working with numbers or graphic representations and developing an interpretation. In addition, each of these activities was based in data about students or schools. The task for this chapter is different in two ways. First, the subject is teachers and aspiring teachers like you. Second, the data are qualitative instead of quantitative.

Open-Ended Concerns Statements From Three Student Teachers

The following three paragraphs were written by three student teachers.

JoAnne

Yesterday, right in the middle of my lesson, one of my students raised his hand and asked me who I went out with Saturday night! I did a mental "gulp!" Then, I said that we were in the midst of the lesson now. I just went on with the lesson. It really shook me. I don't really mind saying whatever I was doing, because they really did see me Saturday night. Should I have had him stay after school for asking? I felt like ignoring it—it was the only thing I could think to do at the time. But I'm not sure if I was losing control. Will they disrespect me for it? I don't know how to react to it.

Greg

Now, I am less concerned about their learning the facts and more interested in their seeing the general patterns and understanding the concepts. If there is a word or concept they don't understand, we stop and go over it. I realize more clearly now how little they know and how lacking their background is. When I can help them make the connections between their experiences and the lesson, they really get it.

Sue

My father wants me to get a teaching certificate. Right now, I am most concerned about getting married. We have booked the hotel and have the photographer too. But there is so much to do in the next two months!

Your Task

Analyze each of these Open-Ended Concerns Statements. Use the descriptions of the four areas of concern presented in Table 14.2. What areas and Stages of Concern are represented in each statement? First, reread each Concerns Statement and determine its overall flavor. Does it sound most like Unrelated, Self, Task, or Impact? Then read each sentence and assign a specific Stage of Concern to it. Sketch out a summary of your analysis before reading further.

Analyzing and Summarizing Teacher Concerns Statements

The three Open-Ended Concerns Statements reflect very different Stages of Concern. One way to summarize each teacher's concerns would be to construct a table that identifies the major area of concern and the specific Stage of Concern.

Student Teacher	Overall Area of Concern	Stage(s) of Concern
JoAnne	Self	Stage 2, Personal
Greg	Impact	Stage 4, Consequence
Sue	Unrelated (about teaching)	Stage 0, Unrelated

Given how different each student teacher's concerns are, each person should probably be supported individually. Before reading further, think about what you would do to address each person's concerns.

Addressing Their Concerns

JoAnne's concerns could be addressed through a talk with her cooperating teacher or student teacher supervisor. There will definitely be times when students ask inappropriate questions or ask them at the wrong time. JoAnne's choice to not let the question disrupt the flow of the lesson certainly made sense. In this particular case, JoAnne might also consider not going to the certain places on the weekend where her students will see her.

Greg clearly has Impact concerns at Stage 4, Consequence. He is focused on how well his students are learning. He also is discovering how important it is to be knowledgeable about the learning background and experiences each student brings to his classes. Now his challenge is in helping students build a bridge/scaffold from where they are to understanding the concepts that he is teaching. He might want to read more about informal ways to assess student understanding, and learn more about his students' background of out-of-school experiences that could be used to help them understand in-class content.

Sue doesn't seem to have teaching-related concerns. Although each of us will have personal things going on in our lives, when it comes to being a successful teacher, the non-teaching concerns need to be set aside. Someone needs to help Sue focus on her responsibilities as a teacher. She also should seriously consider this question: "Do I *really* want to be a teacher?"

offered suggestions for your learning as a teacher education candidate (Stage 4, Consequence). Ms. Maldonado also expressed Impact concerns about the importance of working with colleagues and the community (Stage 5, Collaboration). Given that at the time of the interview she was nearing the end of her second year of teaching, in terms of the Concerns Model she is clearly well along to becoming a student-learning-oriented high-quality teacher.

WHAT ARE THE KEYS TO BEING HIRED AS A BEGINNING TEACHER?

I am Round Rock bred and have made the full circle. I went to school here, I graduated from here, I did my student teaching here, and now I teach here. Also, I always have been a mentor to children, even in high school. It is something I enjoy doing. I feel so strongly about doing something in my own community. I want to help the upcoming generation. This is my way of staying in tune with what I like to do.

—Ms. Velasquez

Back in Chapter 1, we introduced you to the big picture of what is entailed in becoming a teacher. In each of the succeeding chapters, we introduced major aspects of teaching. It is not too early for you to now begin thinking about what will be needed and what it will be like to seek and get your first teaching position. There will be a number of applicants competing for most positions. This is especially true for low-need areas such as elementary, social studies, and physical education. As discussed in Chapter 1, there are a number of steps and requirements that you must complete to become a fully qualified teacher. Now is the time to begin anticipating and preparing what you will need to have accomplished and be able to demonstrate so that you are the one who will be hired for the teaching position you would most like to have.

Requirements for Obtaining a Teacher License

The licensing requirements for public school teachers are set by each state. In addition, federal legislation, such as what happened under the No Child Left Behind Act of 2001, can mandate that each state establish certain requirements for teachers. For example, over the past several decades, each state has had to develop a teacher evaluation model that is at least in part based on student test scores.

The following are typical basic requirements for obtaining a teaching license:

- Successful completion of a state-approved preparation program. Programs may be offered by a higher education institution, a school district, or another agency.

- **Criminal background check**, including fingerprinting. No one with a criminal record may teach.

- Passing state-required tests, typically of content and pedagogical knowledge. In some states, examples of teaching performance, such as a portfolio or teacher work sample, may be required.

- Having a major and perhaps advanced study in the subject(s) you plan to teach.

In addition to state requirements, each school district may have specific requirements. If you have not done so, check both your state and your preferred school district websites for the specific requirements you must meet in order to be eligible to apply for a teaching position.

Getting Your First Teaching Position

All of the effort that you are putting into becoming a teacher will be for naught if you are not successful in obtaining a teaching position. The demand for teachers varies from community to community and state to state. In general, there are more openings in the Southwest. The following are a few suggestions for being successful in your search.

Specialty-Specific State-wide Teacher Shortages

As was just mentioned above, there are many teaching specialties where there are many more qualified applicants than job openings. In general, there will be many applicants for regular elementary school teaching jobs. In general, there will be shortages of teacher applicants for special education, math, and ESL. Figure 14.1 is a summary of where there are more shortages. If you become qualified in one of these specialties, obtaining a position will be easier. If you plan to teach in a low-need specialty, you should think now about what additional qualifications you can represent. For example, speaking Spanish is a high need in all content areas and grade levels. Being qualified to coach, such as Ms. Maldonado is doing with volleyball and softball, will be a benefit. Either way, keeping in mind now the specialty-specific areas of teacher shortages will help you compete for the opening you would like to fill.

Where to Look for Teaching Positions

All public school openings will be published and open to all qualified applicants. The place to begin, if there is a particular school district where you would like to teach, is by checking its website. The district home page will include a link to the Human Resources Department or even directly to positions that are currently open. Even if you will not be teaching for several years, now would be a good time to check a district's website and to study the position requirements. Take careful notes about the required qualifications to be an applicant, and what is entailed in making an application.

Education Week is the national newspaper for the K–12 education profession. It is published weekly during the school year and reports on national, state, and local education topics. At the back will be many pages of classified advertisements, where school districts publish their position openings. You can also check the *Education Week* website.

FIGURE 14.1 ■ **Number of States Reporting Specialty-Specific Teacher Shortages**

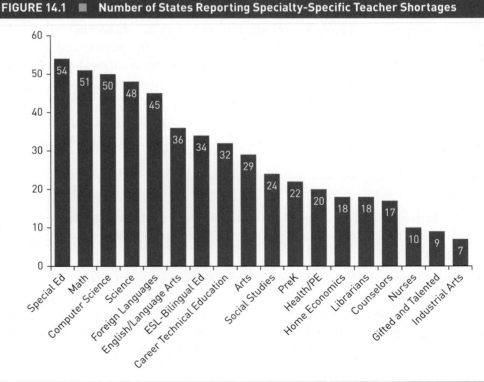

Source: Data are from the U.S. Department of Education Office of Postsecondary Education.

Note: Data include all 50 states, the District of Columbia, American Samoa, Guam, the Northern Mariana Islands, Palau, Puerto Rico, and the U.S. Virgin Islands.

Don't forget to check out state education department websites, many of which list job openings. If you are interested in teaching overseas, check the following:

U.S. Department of Defense Education Activity (DoDEA). To serve the families of U.S. military personnel stationed overseas, the U.S. Department of Defense operates schools and districts in many locations in Europe, Japan, Korea, and the Middle East. DoDEA also operates schools on some military bases in the United States.

Overseas Schools. The U.S. Department of State and many other government agencies have personnel working in other countries. Many of these families support the operation of independent local schools. These schools are not funded directly by the U.S. government, but they are supported by them through teacher professional development and website links. Although each school does its own hiring, school administrators and teacher recruiters regularly visit association meetings in the United States.

Private Schools. There are many private schools in other countries that employ American teachers. For example, children of oil company employees based in the Middle East can attend company-supported schools, which use American curriculum and teachers (e.g., Aramco in Saudi Arabia). Various church groups support schools in other countries too. Probably the best approach to finding out about openings for teachers is to make direct contact with a particular school's office.

Teaching English Abroad. Another strategy for gaining a teaching position overseas is to teach English to students of the host country. A number of countries such as Japan, South Korea, and China are very active in recruiting teachers of English. A potential downside to this strategy is that many of the positions provide little, if any, salary. Many of the opportunities are in rural or very isolated areas, which means one needs to be more adventuresome and ready to live, and teach, with fewer of the accustomed amenities.

Ideas for Your Professional Résumé

An important document, which you should begin preparing now, is a professional résumé (see Table 14.3). This is a one- (or no more than two-) page summary of your qualifications and related experiences. Although most of the categories seem obvious, preparing a strong résumé will take some time and thought. Your portfolio tasks, reflection pieces, and artifacts will be useful resources.

Keep in mind that employers are looking not only for teachers who have good grades but also for those who can document that they can make a major difference in student learning. They also will be looking for teachers who will be a resource to the school and contribute to the community. They will be interested in your past work experiences, even if they were not in education. One good experience to be able to list is having been a substitute teacher. Your résumé provides the opportunity to document not only that you meet the basic requirements for the position but also that you bring additional related expertise and valuable experience.

Another important task with developing your résumé is to customize it for each position you seek. Drafting a more generic résumé now is a good starting point. At the time that you apply to a particular school district and for a particular position, refine your résumé to better match the position description. Select, organize, and present your qualifications in a format that matches the position requirements. Have references who know you and, if possible, something about the position you are applying for. Did you happen to note how a past association helped Ms. Maldonado get her teaching job?

As you have heard many times, be careful about what you have on social media. Once posted, it doesn't come down, for sure. Increasingly, employers are searching all of social media as part of their standard background checking. Also, be sure that for any postings where other people are identifiable, or you are presenting the works of others, you have their permission. This is doubly essential for images of children.

Teacher Dispositions Are Very Important

As necessary as meeting the official licensure requirements and completing program requirements are, an unstated, but very important, criterion for becoming a teacher is disposition (see Chapter 1). The attitudes,

TABLE 14.3 ■ Professional Résumé: Suggestions for Topics and Elements
Select, organize, and present these items in a format that matches your qualifications to the position requirements.
Name
Address
Phone Number
Email (*Don't use a silly email address*)
Social Media (*Make sure there is nothing embarrassing on any of your postings*)
Philosophy/Bio Paragraph: In one paragraph, describe who you are and why you want to be a teacher. What do you believe about teaching and students? Why are schools important?
Qualifications (*Each of the following is important*)
Education: List college degrees and any specialized certificates. Don't forget to name the institution(s), and probably the dates for each. You might want to include GPA or other indicators of strength and quality.
Licensure: Name the (state) license and areas of certification.
Special Certifications: Name any endorsements, such as special education or ELL.
Recognitions: List honors, awards, and other forms of recognition.
Special Skills: Do you have areas of expertise or special skills, such as speaking a second language? Have you lived in different places, or abroad? Have you had leadership experiences in work, your community, or your church?
Examples of Your Teaching: Have available artifacts of the work and evidence of the learning that has taken place when you have been teaching. Be able to provide photos of students and their work (don't forget to have parent permissions) and/or videos of your teaching.
Work Experience: List past work experiences. These may include nonschool work. List those that demonstrate that you are reliable, that you can hold a job over time, and that you will bring a range of experiences to the classroom. Experience as a substitute teacher can be a bonus.
Community Service: Describe ways that you have been, or are, involved in giving back through volunteer activities, or in other ways providing service to one or more parts of your community.
Outside Interests: Perhaps you will want to list hobbies or other activities that are an important part of your life. These can be especially useful for high school teachers who are expected to work with cocurricular activities and to coach sports.
References: List two to three references with their contact information. Be sure to have their permission to be listed as a reference.

"The principal has sat in on so many of my classes, I'm thinking of giving him the exam."

© Conan de Vries

beliefs, and values that teachers hold about students, the subjects they teach, their colleagues, their students' parents, and the school are critical. Teachers who are not excited about the subjects they teach cannot develop enthusiasm for the subject in their students. Teachers who believe that certain students (e.g., male, female, brown, white, special needs, or ELL) cannot learn will not be able to help those students learn. Teachers who do not see value in their colleagues, parents, and the school cannot help the school be successful.

Reflect back on the interview with Ms. Maldonado. There is nothing negative or undercutting about anything that she says. She is enthusiastic, and she reflects a belief that all students can learn and that she can be a positive influence on students, colleagues, and her community. Everything that she said had to do with opportunities and possibilities, not barriers. High-quality teachers always think, teach, and lead with a view that the glass is half full, not half empty.

In case you have not already made the connection, the whole presentation about the Concerns Model is one easy way to understand teacher dispositions. School district administrators want to hire teachers with Impact concerns, not those with never-ending Self and Task concerns.

Electronic Job Application

Most school districts require you to submit your application online. The application steps will be clearly explained on the district's Human Resources website. It will be best to study the site and determine information and documentation you will need before going very far into the application. More than likely, the first step in the process will be the need for you to register, which will entail setting your username and password. Somewhere on the site will be a listing of the various teaching position descriptions. Typically, one will be for elementary schools and others for each of the secondary school subject areas. You will want to study these descriptions closely. Note that in some districts, individual schools may list additional requirements.

In a job interview, it is likely that teacher applicants will be asked to provide evidence of how they have affected student learning.

iStock/Alexander Raths

The organization of the website will likely be unique for each district. Still, the information you will need to submit will include some combination of (a) your letter of application (which should address each element in the position description), (b) your teacher license and other credentials, (c) your education and training, (d) related professional experiences and accomplishments, (e) a statement of your philosophy, (f) your résumé, and (g) letters of reference. Be sure that each of your submissions looks professional and has no typos or spelling errors.

What Are Career Path Possibilities for Teachers?

Although at this point you are thinking mostly about completing your initial teacher education program, becoming licensed to teach, and obtaining your first full-time teaching position, it is not too early to learn about the various career options that are open to teachers. In the past, most teachers stayed in the classroom as teachers for 20 or 30 years. (One of your authors once interviewed a teacher who had taught kindergarten in the same school and in the same classroom for 26 years!) Today, the career options for teachers are many, beginning with changing grade levels and schools within the same district. Some teachers move on to ever-expanding roles within the education profession. Later in this chapter, you will meet Mrs. Erinn Green, who was a classroom teacher and now works with district leadership to plan system change and coaches principals in implementing those plans. She also stays in touch with students since coaching individual teachers in their classrooms is a part of her current job.

Graduate Study

Pursuing one or more graduate degrees is a regular way that teachers keep learning and become qualified to advance in their careers. In most school districts, obtaining a certain number of hours of advanced study or a graduate degree will be reflected in increases in salary. There are many possibilities in terms of degree options and areas of concentration. The first step for most teachers is to take graduate course work and obtain a master's degree. This degree could be in curriculum and instruction; educational technology; or a subject area such as literacy, history, mathematics, or science education. Other teachers will want to receive advanced preparation in special education, educational psychology, or assessment. Most colleges offer master's degrees in each of these areas.

Another direction for graduate study is educational leadership. Earning a graduate degree in educational leadership will be important if you wish to become a school administrator. Most of these

TEACHERS' LOUNGE
"OUTDOOR SCIENCE: WHAT CAN GO WRONG?"

© Melinda Maile

It was my first review as a brand-new first-grade teacher. I remember the butterflies and chills as I prepared my students for an outdoor science experiment. The stage was set. The students were properly prepped, and we headed out to the school playground to complete our experiment with prisms. The principal was a retired Marine Corps officer and seemed to keep his composure in the most challenging situations. Little did I know my lesson was going to be more than he could bear.

As my 18 first-grade students gathered in a circle and I began the review portion of the lesson, Mr. Marks stood quietly and wrote notes. I could feel his serious stare as I asked the students the prompted questions. Suddenly, I noticed the circle was two students short. My chills turned to sweats as I began to look around for Steven and Luke. I felt fear as I said to myself, "This is not happening!"

I felt relief when I frantically turned around to see the two boys standing at the monkey bars arguing. I quickly gave the students instructions on a game to play to keep them occupied while I ran over to the monkey bars to collect my missing students. Mr. Marks followed me to the monkey bars to observe my handling of the situation. The situation was not what I was expecting.

Steven had handcuffed Luke to the monkey bars. Now that Mr. Marks and I were on the scene, the two boys were crying hysterically. Luke kept pulling his wrists with force in an effort to free himself. This was my chance to prove that I could discipline my students. I leaned down to be eye to eye with Steven. In my stern teacher voice, I said, "Steven, unlock Luke immediately!" Steven looked at me, barely able to speak through his tears, and said, "I don't have the key." I sternly replied, "Where did you get the handcuffs?" He slurped a few tears away and said, "Out of my mommy's underwear drawer."

I wasn't sure whether to laugh or cry. I looked at Mr. Marks, who never smiles, and saw his cheeks bulging and his lips tighten as he attempted to control his laughter. This was my chance to keep my composure, so I looked at my worthy supervisor and said, "Would you like to call Steven's mother and ask for the key, or should I?" Mr. Marks couldn't hold the laughter in anymore. He burst out laughing. Then he took a deep breath and pulled himself together. He directed me to stay with my class as he returned to his office to make the emergency phone call to Steven's mother.

I surrounded Luke and Steven with my students, and we completed the science experiment. As our lesson was finishing, Mr. Marks walked across the playground with the key in his hand. As he freed Luke from the handcuffs, he turned to me and said, "I do not think you will see much of Steven's mother the rest of the year. I have never seen a face as red as hers when she delivered the key."

My class returned to our room and moved on to our next lesson. Thank goodness first graders have such a short attention span. Within five minutes, the excitement was forgotten. As for my review, the comments written were "Mrs. Maile has the ability to control her students and handle herself professionally in unexpected and stressful situations."

—Mrs. Melinda Maile
First-Grade Teacher

programs will include meeting the state qualifications for school administrator certification. Some of these programs focus less on license preparation and more on leadership development per se. Most master's degrees will entail around 36 semester hours of course work.

Once a master's degree has been completed, there is the possibility of pursuing the doctoral degree. Depending on the institution of higher education, one of two doctoral degrees will be available. The EdD is a doctoral degree specifically designed for educators. In most institutions, this will be a practitioner-oriented course of study. The PhD may be practitioner oriented, but more often it is more research focused. In either case, the program will include advanced course work, and the final degree completion component will be the dissertation study. This will be an original research study addressing teaching, learning, curriculum, leadership, or some other aspect of schooling. Most doctoral programs will include 30 to 40 hours of course work beyond the master's, and approximately 12 hours of credit for the dissertation. Teachers who wish to become faculty members in colleges or universities will need a doctoral degree.

Although furthering your professional education is a number of years away, beginning to understand now what the steps and qualifications entail can help in thinking about your ideal professional future. Having this basic information may be of help in talking with your peers about what they want to do in the future. This information will also be important from time to time as you advise students about what is entailed in getting a college education.

Becoming a School Administrator

The most obvious career progression is to "move up" the administration ladder. Becoming a Department Chair, a dean, an assistant/vice principal, and then principal is the career path chosen by some teachers. Nearly all school and district administrators were teachers earlier in their careers; this includes nearly all superintendents. Normally, an aspiring administrator will spend several years at each level. Developing deeper knowledge about the work and the issues comes with firsthand experience in doing each position. For example, assistant principals are developing a school-wide understanding and will be implementing policies and procedures related to student conduct. They will be part of the decision making in regard to school budgets, teacher and student schedules, and hiring. They will be observers in personnel matters. However, they will not be responsible for the final decision. The principal has the ultimate decision-making authority. So, being a Department Chair, dean, and assistant/vice principal are important opportunities to learn. An additional benefit of time in these positions is that your principal will be a readily available coach and mentor.

School and District Office Staff Roles

There also are many school and district office staff assignments open to teachers. Personnel in staff positions do not have line authority over others. They do not supervise others; instead, they work with others. Within schools, there are a number of specialist positions such as for literacy or technology, as well as community liaisons and special education resource teachers. Most of these positions will be filled by certified teachers. They work with a large segment of students or across the whole school. Many other staff positions are available in the district office including curriculum coordinators; staff developers; technology directors; and the professionals who work with federal funds such as Title I, bilingual, compensatory education, and special education. The whole area of testing and assessment has become another major area of employment. In brief, there are many career options within schools and the district office for teachers who wish to expand their horizons and move into leadership positions.

IN WHAT WAYS CAN CANDIDATES AND TEACHERS BE LEADERS?

I have colleagues, specialists, the principal, and many parents coming into my classroom. Also, I am on the District Advisory Council. A teacher from every school is on this council. We meet with the superintendent once a month to discuss issues going on within the district. He bounces ideas off the teachers to see which way he wants to go. I will continue to work on my teaching craft during the summer months, by teaching enrichment courses to students for the district and by attending professional development trainings focused on my personal learning goals.

As a leader, I go back to the idea that it is business, not personal. If anything needs to be addressed, it is because it is going to affect the overall wellness of my kids. So, I just lay out expectations. If I have a problem with parents, I address it with them.

As a leader, you are responsible for maintaining professionalism at all times. Problems that threaten your goal of the academic achievement of your students need to be addressed immediately. Laying out expectations and norms with the colleagues you work with not only promotes collaboration but also guarantees respect for all professionals. Concerns with parents need to be handled confidentially and immediately. Establish rapport with parents at the start of the year. Concerns can easily be resolved if you are aware that each parent is working toward the academic achievement of his or her child!

—Ms. Velasquez

Contrary to what you may have thought, leadership is not reserved to the principal or the superintendent. All members of an organization have leadership responsibilities. This is true for schools, businesses, church groups, and families. Unfortunately, too many teacher education candidates and teachers assume that they have no leadership responsibilities. In fact, the opposite is true—every member of the school staff, including those who refuse to participate, affects potential progress and success. Leadership skills and functions can be learned, and participating in different ways can be informative, influential, interesting, and even fun. Now is the time for you to become aware of your leadership skills and the roles you can play. There are many unofficial and informal ways to contribute to leadership, and there are formal leader positions and career paths for those who are motivated to make a difference in what the whole school or district accomplishes. Taking on leadership roles now, inside and outside your teacher education course work, is important.

Different Ways Teachers Can Lead

Teachers tend to first think about leadership as something that administrators do. In this way of thinking, the only people who are leaders are those who have official titles and responsibilities such as the principal, Department Chair, vice principal, and superintendent. However, scholars make a careful distinction between **leaders** and **leadership**. Leaders are those with formal, and informal, roles and responsibilities related to a group or the whole school accomplishing its objectives. Leadership encompasses the actions of leading. All members of the school staff have a leadership responsibility. You cannot escape this responsibility; you either help or hinder the attainment of the desired ends. Teacher leadership is accomplished in a number of ways.

Formal Teacher Leadership

There are many opportunities for teacher education candidates and beginning teachers to have formal leader responsibilities. For example, teachers provide leadership for grade-level teams. There are other ways that a beginning teacher can lead, including serving on school committees, coordinating a cocurriculum such as pep squad or yearbook, or being an assistant coach.

During the remainder of your teacher education program, there will be a number of opportunities for you to be a formal leader. These include serving as the representative to organize candidates for an accreditation visit, chairing the student education association or honor society, and serving on the student advisory board. During student teaching, there may be opportunities to assume some responsibility within the school. The basic message here is that rather than avoiding leader assignments, take them on. This is the best way to learn more about being a leader—by doing it!

Informal Teacher Leadership

As important as formal leader roles can be, the informal roles are important also. One of the least understood is that of **followership**. As good as the formal leader may be, he or she will accomplish little unless the members of the group/team/committee/staff do their parts. Being a constructive member of the group; offering to help; contributing positively to the discussions; and being sure to complete assigned tasks, with high quality and on time, are important skills for all followers. Each of us has experienced the colleague who sits in meetings with folded arms, and the one who grades papers rather than contributing to the discussion. We also have experienced the team member who promises to do a task and then doesn't deliver. Effective followership entails participating, volunteering help, and completing assigned tasks.

A related concept is **distributed leadership**. The primary assumption in this model of leadership is that rather than leadership being the sole responsibility of the formal leader at the top of the organization, a.k.a. the principal, leadership should be distributed to many people and be seen as a shared responsibility. Distributed leadership is particularly useful in schools where teachers are seen as professionals whose work is not to be closely supervised. As professionals, teachers are expected to assume and share responsibilities for leadership.

Leading Adults Is a Big Challenge for Beginning Teachers

As good as being a teacher leader may sound, there will be challenges—especially for first-year teachers. Based on her experience, Ms. Velasquez offered the following insights:

I do find it challenging. Last year, I found it more challenging, because not only did I have the first-year teacher stigma; I had my age. What parent wants to be talked to about any problem with his or her child by a 22-year-old? It was difficult. I found that I not only had to have inner confidence, but I also had to have outer confidence. The more confidence that I showed, the better I was received.

As much of a cliché as it sounds, dressing professionally helped a lot. Through my actions, I showed them that I know what I am talking about. Their coming into my classroom, seeing how I run my classroom, how my classroom management skills are, and how I interact with their child really calmed down my parents who knew I was a first-year teacher. At the beginning of the year, I had really a lot of parent involvement. Then, around December, it all went away. So it was kind of like they were testing me out; then, once I built a relationship with them, and they knew what I was about, all my parents kind of eased up.

Working With Colleagues

Teachers have to communicate with each other all the time. In secondary schools, a teacher of content, such as math, science, or English, will have contact with 120 or more students. These teachers should be sharing information with colleagues about how each student is doing. In most elementary schools, students will have contact with more than one teacher. These other adults will have insights about each student that can be important. The bus driver and the school secretaries, as well as physical education and music teachers, are major factors in each student's learning.

Most certainly, beginning teachers will have to focus first on what is going on in their classroom. As a junior member of staff, it is important to do more listening than talking. With time, first- and second-year teachers find ways to share with their colleagues and often take the lead. One example is described in the "Informal Teacher Leadership" feature on the following page. Ms. Maldonado describes how taking advantage of an opportunity to display student work evolved into a major responsibility for teacher leadership.

Working With Parents

There is a big difference between **engaging parents** and **involving parents**. It is relatively simple to engage parents by having occasional notes for students to take home, or leaving a voice mail message. A much higher level of investment is needed to fully involve parents in the school and teachers' classrooms (see Table 14.4). Involving parents means making them a necessary part of what goes on. Parents want to be of help to the teacher, and they most certainly want to know how to help at home with their child's learning. The more parents understand about what is going on, the more supportive they can be. The children of involved parents are likely to have better school attendance and better grades. They also are more likely to complete homework assignments. Look back at the anecdote from Ms. Maldonado in the opening interview for this chapter. There was a case of a concerned parent contacting the teacher.

In some schools, parents will be a direct support to individual teachers. For example, in Ms. Velasquez's school, there is a designated room for parents. There are three to six parents there every day!

Our parents are very involved. They will be on campus every day. If teachers have something they need done, such as a bulletin board, copies, or something cut out, a parent will volunteer to do that. There is a room called the Pro Center. That is where the parents are, and they take on jobs that a teacher might not have time for. They are there all the time. Also, they organize events and fund-raisers.

At a minimum, teachers must communicate with the parents of the students in their classroom. This is another form of leadership. In some schools, parents will be available to help in the classroom. In those situations, teachers must develop skill in organizing and guiding what parents do. In Ms. Velasquez's school, there is more:

In my case, lots of the parents have college degrees. Two of my parents are former second-grade teachers. So they conduct small reading groups. We also have a program called "Watch D.O.G.S." (Dads of Great Students). It is pretty much a dads' organization. The dads take off from work and come to our school for the whole day. They come to their child's classroom and go to other classrooms, or they help the teacher with whatever he or she needs.

INFORMAL TEACHER LEADERSHIP

HOW A STUDENT WRITING PROJECT BECAME A RESOURCE FOR COLLEAGUES

In her interview, Ms. Maldonado described a neat example of how informal teacher leadership can develop. She begins by describing a writing project she introduced to her students. As her story unfolds, you can see how an important project for student learning led to a second-year teacher becoming a resource for colleagues.

Q: What kind of leadership roles do you have?

A: It's funny that you would ask right now. I am part of the Heart of Texas Writing Project. My school district paid for all the English teachers for this school year to be trained. As the ESL teacher, I was included. I went through a week of training. Everything they were teaching about writing, and kids taking ownership in their writing, was all the things I believe in as a writer.

It inspired me to go back to my classroom. The Writing Project was about building the kids up, having them write pieces, and publishing them where there is a big audience, besides the teacher who is reading your work. So, I had this idea.

Every year, the Mexican American Cultural Center, where I had worked, has the *Día de los Muertos* ("Day of the Dead") Festival. I decided to have my students publish a piece at this event. My kids wrote children's books and memoirs to build an alter-ego connected to their writings. Hundreds of people came to this event, and my students' work was on display in the cultural center's art gallery space for a month. After seeing the display, the Heart of Texas Writing Project asked me to speak at a workshop about my experience in having my kids publish. That is one leadership experience I can think of right now.

There will be opportunities throughout the school year for beginning teachers to share with and learn from colleagues.

At my school now, I am kind of that go-to person for doing the Writing Project if other teachers have any questions, and I have all sorts of lesson plans to share with them. As a new teacher, I am slowly now starting to see myself as a leader and to push myself to take on those leadership roles.

Outside of school, I volunteer for the Neighborhood Conference Committee (NCC), which addresses truancy within the Round Rock School District. It deals with first-time truancy offenders. Once they have been visited by a truancy officer, their last step before they are referred to the courts is to come before NCC. NCC makes a positive action plan to help each of these kiddos see the light, so to speak.

TABLE 14.4 ■ Suggestions for Increasing Parent Involvement

1. Give your students "talking points" to tell parents about what they are learning.

2. Make home visits a regular practice.

3. Help parents develop a home environment that supports their children's learning (e.g., "no-TV nights").

4. Provide parents with a way to guide and check on their child's homework (e.g., a rubric, a description of the learning objective, or an assignment that parents can do with their child).

5. Establish a way to have two-way communication—teacher to parents *and* parents to teacher—*in the parents' language.*

6. Encourage parents to volunteer in your classroom (e.g., putting up bulletin boards and/or guiding small-group work).

7. Attend events and activities in the community.

8. Survey parents about what their children like about your classroom and about any concerns they might have.

9. Place your lesson plans and assignments online. (This is a requirement in many districts.)

10. Keep in mind that parents are likely to have Self concerns about meeting you, so be calm, supportive, and informed.

11. Keep your school administrators informed about the ways you are planning to involve parents in your classroom.

One indicator of the increasing importance of parent involvement is that in many districts and schools, there will be staff positions for community/parent coordinators. The emphasis in this position is to develop plans and to do activities that link teachers and parents for improving student learning. A new indicator of the increasing importance of parent involvement is that some states—for example, Massachusetts and Connecticut—have built aspects of parent/family engagement into the teacher evaluation systems.

Teacher Leaders as Full-Time Specialists

As has been described in several ways already in this chapter, career opportunities in education are many optioned. Teachers can continue in the classroom, or they can engage one of the many options. Some take the administrator career path, while others move into district office staff positions. Increasingly, another role is opening for expert teachers, that of full-time instructional coach. This role is for teachers with an established record of excellence as a teacher. They will be identified as expert teachers and persons who can help other teachers improve. The role has become increasingly important as schools have been placed under intense pressure to improve the learning outcomes for all students.

Developing Full-Time Teacher Leaders Is Widespread

This new role is also being implemented in other countries. For example, in Australia, these professionals are called "leading teachers." In the United Kingdom, they are called "middle leaders" or "specialist leaders of education (SLEs)." In general, here in the United States, they are called teacher leaders (see Chapter 8) or **instructional coaches**. Some districts and states have moved further by formalizing the role in policy. For example, beginning in the fall of 2016, an Iowa state statute (Senate 2284) required school districts to have in place a teacher leadership and compensation system. The goals for this initiative are outlined in Table 14.5. Note that the Iowa plan is state-wide, specifying responsibilities such as supporting new teachers, and has the intention of encouraging teachers to continue teaching. The legislation also addresses compensation.

Instructional coaches can be assigned full-time to facilitate improvement within one school. In other settings, they will work with several schools. Within the school, they will work with individual teachers, introduce new practices, guide grade-level teams and departments, and lead school-wide professional development sessions. They will teach model lessons, lead discussions of data related to student learning, and be a mentor to new teachers. However, instructional coaches have no responsibility for teacher evaluation. They do work with the school administrators in relation to planning school improvement and facilitating whole-school initiatives. The following interview is an example of what one full-time teacher leader does.

TABLE 14.5 ■ Goals of the Iowa Teacher Leadership and Compensation System

1. **Attract able and promising new teachers** by offering a more competitive starting salary and a variety of enhanced career opportunities.

2. **Retain the most effective teachers in teaching** (as opposed to administration or to leaving the field altogether) by providing enhanced career opportunities.

3. **Encourage professional growth in teaching** practice by recognizing and rewarding teachers who seek out learning opportunities aligned with local goals.

4. **Promote collaboration** by developing and supporting opportunities for teachers in schools, in districts, and state-wide to learn from each other.

5. **Reward initiative and competence** by creating pathways for career opportunities that come with increased leadership and compensation.

6. **Improve student performance** by strengthening instruction.

Source: Adapted from Task Force on Teacher Leadership and Compensation Final Report, Iowa Department of Education, Grimes State Office Building, Des Moines, IA 50319-0146 10/15/2012.

TEACHER INTERVIEW

INTERVIEW WITH A TEACHER LEADER WHO COACHES DISTRICTS, SCHOOLS, AND TEACHERS

© Erinn J. Green

Meet Mrs. Erinn J. Green, a full-time teacher leader.

Q: **What is your job title?**

A: I am a Secondary Program Specialist at the Virginia Department of Education's Training and Technical Assistance Center (TTAC) based at Virginia Commonwealth University in Richmond.

Q: **What do you do?**

A: My role is instructional and systems change coach. I focus on assisting schools and districts with the development of action plans to make sustainable change. I provide technical assistance to support them as they work to accomplish their school improvement goals.

Q: **How long have you had this job?**

A: I have been working at TTAC for three and a half years.

Q: **Do you work with teachers, principals, or district offices?**

A: A little bit of everything. In the larger districts, we work at the district level as well as the building level. I partner with central office personnel, school administrators, and teacher leaders to develop long-term action plans to improve outcomes of students with disabilities.

I then go into schools to provide professional development linked to the change plans. My favorite part of the job is getting to know teachers as I support them with integrating new practices into their classrooms. I miss the classroom. I miss my students. I miss being a part of a school community, so building relationships with teachers helps me stay connected to students and the day-to-day classroom successes and challenges.

Q: **What were you doing before this?**

A: Prior to working at TTAC, I was a special education teacher in a high school for three years. During my first year, I taught collaborative science courses and was moved into algebra 1 and geometry for my second and third years. Teaching math was fantastic because I had amazing co-teaching partners. The school was in its second year of turnaround and had an external partner who was working with the administration and faculty to improve progress toward meeting their annual measurable objectives. There were a lot of people in and out of our classrooms and opportunities for additional support. Throughout the three years, I took advantage of TTAC support and received coaching to improve my instructional, behavioral, and collaborative practices. I had wonderful students; a passionate, dedicated TTAC coach; and phenomenal colleagues.

Q: **Were you the special education teacher or the content teacher?**

A: Special education teacher. I co-taught the majority of the time while teaching at the secondary level.

Q: **Did you know all those math areas?**

A: I've always enjoyed math, but I learned a tremendous amount from my co-teaching partners. There were a lot of behavior challenges and factors outside our locus of control, but within our classrooms, the three of us worked exceptionally well together. I did not realize it at the time, but I attribute our success to collective teacher efficacy. We were invested in our students, established common goals, knew our instruction made a difference in students' lives, and took pride in our work. We all learned from each other and shared responsibilities. It was my teaching utopia.

Q: **Was this the beginning of your teaching career, or was there something before that?**

A: After graduating from college, I worked in a private therapeutic wilderness school for three years as a counselor and social worker. I started coaching volleyball at one of the local school districts, and the athletic director took an interest in me and encouraged me to consider applying to teach. I took the courses to get my provisional teaching license and was hired as a fifth-grade special education teacher. Throughout my first three years of teaching, I took classes to earn my teacher certification and master's degree in K–12 special education curriculum.

Q: **All right, now, how does all of this past experience roll into what you are currently doing?**

A: I think about this a lot in my current position. As a program specialist, I am asked by the Virginia Department of Education to support schools that are not meeting their annual measurable objectives or students with disabilities who are not making sufficient progress. The environments of unaccredited schools are often stressful for teachers due to pressure to increase standardized test scores, challenging student behaviors, and unclear expectations from building or central office leadership. Fortunately, all of my past experiences developed a strong knowledge base, even though I didn't know it was happening. My experience working with a diverse group of students in a variety of settings provides me with perspective that improves my ability to coach teachers in schools with diverse needs.

Q: **What have you learned about being a full-time teacher leader?**

A: As a teacher leader, you have to become more selective about the things you say and how you handle your day-to-day frustrations. If you are viewed as a teacher leader, those around you are listening all the time to how you react to changes in the school, student behavior, or a challenging colleague. You have to have a level of self-awareness,

© Erinn J. Green

self-control, and self-reflection to guide what you say. It is important to assume best intentions and to stay optimistic.

Q: We have talked about your career, and we have talked about your current position. Let's move to the readers of this textbook, aspiring teacher candidates. What advice do you have for them?

A: If you can keep the mindset that every experience is a learning opportunity, you can reframe the crazy and maintain perspective. Find a trusted colleague—not a colleague who is going to complain all day, but a colleague you can vent about frustrations with—and work together to come up with a solution. Give yourself permission to be upset and process difficult situations, but find a productive way to deal with the stress and push forward. If you try something and it doesn't quite work out, take the time to self-reflect, figure out what did work, and modify your approach next time.

Every step along the way, I have had an unofficial mentor (meaning he or she was not assigned by the school, but took a special interest in me) who has had my best interests in mind. Having a person you can go to for support to help you get back on track is critical to your sanity and your students' success.

Also, be willing to take risks in teaching and your relationships. Try new instructional approaches that push you out of your comfort zone. Have courageous conversations with students and colleagues. Taking risks allows you to grow as an educator.

Focus on what's in your locus of control from day to day. There are things you can't do anything about, but you can control what goes on in your classroom.

It is easy to get frustrated with your students or when things around you don't go the way you planned. Rather than blaming things on others, you need to take a look at yourself first. Ask yourself, "How did I contribute to this situation? What could I have done differently? Was my instruction engaging? Did I meet students' instructional needs?" Before you start to pick apart students' responsibilities in tough situations, take a look at yourself.

Q: What are you learning now?

A: What I am trying to figure out is how to support people with integrating research-based practices into practical, everyday use—taking the research and translating it into user-friendly instructional strategies that will have a positive impact on student performance. I know good teaching when I see it and I can feel it when I walk into a classroom, but I am trying to figure out how to support teachers who are not naturally self-reflective and eager to learn. I am focused on improving my coaching to increase self-awareness and shift mindsets in educators I support to increase student achievement.

Q: One last question: What brings you joy?

A: I love hearing about teacher and student success. When I was in the classroom, I had the opportunity to see my students grow every single day. Finding things to celebrate was easy. Now, as an external support, progress seems slow. Celebrating with teachers about something new they tried that worked for their students is rewarding. I also enjoy being a listening ear for teachers as they process the daily challenges they face so they can be their best for their students.

As my network of educators expands across the state, I have enjoyed connecting people working to find the best fit for their career in education.

Reflection Questions

1. What do you see being the key benchmarks across Mrs. Green's career that prepared her for her current job?

2. Go back to the Concerns Model (Table 14.2). Which Stages of Concern do you see in Mrs. Green?

3. As you think ahead in your career, would you like to have a job as a full-time teacher leader/coach? Why or why not?

WHERE ARE PLACES TO FIND THE JOY OF TEACHING?

One of the major themes embedded within each chapter of this text is *the joy of teaching*. The authors see this theme being critical, since having joy in what you do as a teacher is so important to you and to the students and adults you work with. A key question asked in each educator interview was about joy. Joy is about emotions. It is seeing success in each student, in each one taking delight in his or her learning, and in how the class is growing. Joy includes the great pleasure that comes from making a difference in each and every student. It comes in the satisfaction of having a lesson go well. It also comes in grappling with the major challenges in teaching and schooling, and knowing that being a teacher is important.

© David Quintanar

iStock/Christopher Futcher

There is much joy to be found in teaching and learning—for students and their teachers.

When asked what brings her joy, Ms. Velasquez observed,

> *Knowing I am giving back to my community. That's a huge part of it. I get a chance to teach in my own community. Seeing the children grow. There are very quantitative data. You can see a child grow in reading. You can see a child grow in writing. And you also can see children grow socially through their interactions every day.*

People in business gain a great deal of their satisfaction from the amount of money they make and through their efforts to grow a business. Teachers most certainly are not joyful when they see the size of their paychecks. For teachers, the joy comes from the difference they make in the lives of their students. There is joy in seeing the light bulb come on for a student who has been struggling to understand a concept. There is joy in seeing the whole class work together to share strategies for solving a puzzling problem. Teachers have enormous responsibilities. Almost completely by themselves, elementary teachers are responsible for the care and learning of 30 students for an entire school year. Secondary teachers will be responsible for 150 students or more each day! There is satisfaction and purpose in this level of responsibility and in making a positive difference.

Joy and Satisfaction in Teaching Can Be Career Long

Teaching is a very significant and special profession that most people do not get the opportunity to do. Most adults never have the opportunity to teach. Yet most adults can readily name one, two, or even three teachers who made all the difference to them and what they have become. This is another of the many ways that teachers experience joy in teaching. When former students return and describe the difference the teacher made in their lives and how successful they are now, the teacher will be delighted.

Your authors have inserted elements of joy into each chapter. Seeing the joy in teaching is in large part the responsibility of the observer. Some teachers can list everything that is wrong with teaching

THINKING DIFFERENTLY
EXTRA STEPS FOR GETTING THE PERFECT TEACHING JOB

You may be thinking that once you have submitted the formal application for a teaching position, there is nothing further you can do. Actually, there is more that can be done, including learning more about the school and district. If you read closely the interviews with Ms. Maldonado and Mrs. Green, you will see another step that can be taken. Networking was important to both. They knew people who were connected to the school. These networks were based on past activities that just happened to come together to support their job application.

and have to think hard to remember the good parts. Other teachers only see the joy in their students, themselves, and their school. This difference in teachers is not simply a matter of how old they are or how long they have been teaching: It also is a part of one's spirit. There are really old (we should say "experienced") teachers who are still enthusiastic and looking for opportunities to learn new things. Some teacher education candidates already are grumps, while others are laughing at themselves and overflowing with excitement about learning to teach. In many ways, experiencing the joy in teaching is your responsibility.

CONNECTING TO THE CLASSROOM

Key themes in this chapter have been related to your being successful in your teacher education program and being successful in your first year of teaching. Two important additional themes addressed the importance of teacher leadership and beginning to imagine what your career might be like in the years ahead. The following suggestions will help you apply these themes as you advance through your teacher education program and anticipate your first year as a teacher.

1. Understanding your concerns is as important as understanding the concerns of your students. No one has Impact concerns all of the time. For example, teacher education candidates have many Self and Task concerns, which is understandable given all that they have to learn and be able to do.

2. Elliott's Generic Teaching Model outlines the basic tasks and steps that should be a part of planning, presenting, and evaluating each lesson. Keep these components in mind when observing other teachers and in reflecting on your teaching. The model can also be a guide for reflecting on a whole day or week of instruction.

3. As you move through your teacher preparation program, check carefully and make sure that each course you take will count in two ways: (1) toward program completion, and (2) toward obtaining a teaching license from the state. All too often, candidates get to what they think is the end of their program and then discover that a course did not count or they have not taken one that is required.

4. Approach every field and clinical experience as an opportunity to learn. Make it a personal challenge to identify one lesson you can take away from every assignment.

5. Make a personal commitment not just to participate but also to lead some type of activity or effort each term.

6. Schedule a 15-minute period each week where you stop doing and reflect on this question: "What was joyful about the things I did this week?"

SUMMARY

This chapter addressed achieving success in your teacher education program and in your first year of teaching. These key topics were discussed:

- Take advantage of every experience to be successful in your teacher education program.

- Understanding your concerns and the concerns of others is a useful guide for your own professional learning.

- A general teaching model can be a guide for all grade levels and subject areas.

- Continue developing your leadership experiences and skills.

- Much can be learned from experienced teachers.

KEY TERMS

concerns 426

criminal background check 431

distributed leadership 438

engaging parents 439

followership 438

instructional coach 441

involving parents 439

leaders 438

leadership 438

Stages of Concern 427

CLASS DISCUSSION QUESTIONS

1. How do you think the different areas of concern (Unrelated, Self, Task, and Impact) relate to whether a teacher experiences joy in teaching? Do you have to have Impact concerns to experience the joy?

2. A major theme in this chapter is teacher leadership. What opportunities do you have now to practice leadership? Followership?

3. What did you learn from the interview with Mrs. Green? Can you imagine your career evolving in similar ways?

4. What tips have you picked up about steps you should take in the remainder of your teacher education program that will help you obtain your desired teaching job?

SELF-ASSESSMENT

What Is Your Current Level of Understanding and Thinking About Succeeding in Your Teacher Education Program, and Beyond?

One of the indicators of understanding is to examine your current depth of understanding when asked questions that require you to use the concepts and facts introduced in this chapter. After you answer the following questions as fully as you can, rate your knowledge on the Assessing Your Learning rubric. Use your rubric ratings to self-assess the degree to which you understand and can apply the information presented in this chapter. Also, use your rubric ratings as a formative assessment and guide to plan the next steps you will take to learn more.

1. Where do you see yourself at this time in terms of the different areas of teacher concerns? What do you plan to do next to address these concerns?

2. What are the different elements of Elliott's teaching model? Which of these elements can you now do well? What will you do to learn more about those elements where you feel less proficient?

3. What items are important to include in a résumé? For the items you have already, what does each represent about your potential to be a high-quality teacher?

4. What aspects of leadership/followership do you need to work on? When and where will you be engaging these?

5. What areas of knowledge and skill do you need to target in order to be well qualified for your first teaching position? Explain why you see these as being so important.

Assessing Your Learning Rubric

	Parts & Pieces	Unidimensional	Organized	Integrated	Extensions
Indicators	Elements/concepts are talked about as isolated and independent entities. Some important names are provided in isolation.	One or a few concepts are addressed, while others are underdeveloped, or not mentioned.	Deliberate and structured consideration of all key concepts/ elements.	All key concepts/ elements are included in a view that addresses interconnections.	Integration of all elements and dimensions, with extrapolation to new situations.
Succeeding in your teacher education program and beyond	Offers only general or vague items to be needed for licensure; does not name different areas of concern, or elements of a generic model of instruction.	Identifies only one area for growth, such as classroom management; provides no elaboration of why this is important.	Names major categories such as parts of a résumé, areas within the Concerns Model, and/or aspects of leadership and describes why these are priority areas for growth.	Goes beyond naming major areas and identifies specific knowledge and skill areas, and explains how each will help increase teaching expertise.	Describes major areas for growth, identifies knowledge/ skills that need to be developed, and charts actions to be taken in the short term and longer term to learn more.

FIELD GUIDE
FOR LEARNING MORE ABOUT . . .

Succeeding in Your Teacher Education Program, and Beyond

In Chapter 1, you were introduced to the concept of a field guide for learning more about your surroundings. The artifacts and information you have collected for each of the earlier chapters provide a rich array for you to consider as you move ahead with your teacher preparation program.

For this chapter, the field guide tasks and activities need to be viewed as a combination that is a summary of the whole and a foundation for charting your professional growth from here. Remember to keep taking field notes as you complete the activities suggested here. These notes should include facts and descriptions of your observations. Your field notes should also include date, time of day, the grade or group you are observing, and your reflections and aha moments. All three teachers interviewed for this chapter emphasized the importance of reflection.

Be sure to regularly write a paragraph of your current concerns. You will be able to look back at these notes at various times in the future to see how your concerns have changed. Your notes also can help you review how you handled particular teaching situations. All of this is a form of journaling that will help you understand the steps you are taking in becoming a teacher. Remember, also, to collect pictures and samples. A picture can be worth a thousand words.

Ask a Teacher	Ask one or more first- or second-year teachers what knowledge or skill they wish they had learned more about during their preparation program.
	Ask a principal what she or he looks for in hiring a beginning teacher. Compare what the principal says with what you now have on your résumé.
Make Your Own Observations	There are many indicators of joy in teaching. Walk around your college classrooms and building, or a school's classrooms and building. Take field notes on the activities and indicators of joy. Which students and which teachers seem to be enjoying what they are doing? Which seem not to be joyful? What are indicators of the differences?
	Use the topics presented in the interview with Mrs. Green to interview a full-time teacher leader. Develop a chart that outlines her career path. What do you see as themes for how her career has developed? For example, did she come directly out of high school to teaching? Use Table 14.2 to assess her concerns. Keep in mind that for teacher leaders, Impact concerns will be about how they are facilitating adults improving.
Reflect Through Journaling	The Concerns Model provides a useful framework for you to chart your continuing development as a teacher. Review your journal notes for each of the preceding chapters. How have your concerns changed? What new areas have popped up? Do you see any type of pattern in terms of how the amount of concerns at each level (Unrelated, Self, Task, Impact) has evolved? How do you think your concerns will change over the next year?
	In this chapter, there have been excerpts from interviews with two second-year teachers and a full-time teacher leader. As you read these interviews and now as you think about yourself as a future teacher, what are your thoughts, feelings, and concerns? What are your priority topics and areas where you know you must learn more? In what areas have you already experienced joy? Jot down your current thoughts and reflections about how you are developing as a teacher and what your learning priorities are for the next parts of your teacher education program.
Build Your Portfolio	Start a folder for storing each of the Open-Ended Concerns Statements that you write. By the end of your program, you should have 6 to 10 of these. Develop a table or graph to illustrate how your concerns have changed over time. As part of your reflections, write a short analysis of how your concerns have evolved.
	Review the list of suggested items for a professional résumé outlined in Table 14.3. Start now collecting documents, artifacts, and the records that you will need to have to prepare your résumé. When the time comes to apply for your first full-time teaching position, you will find it very helpful to have collected materials and examples along the way. Also, be sure to note those item areas where you currently have very little or nothing.
	At various times as you have been reading this text, you have probably thought about one or more of your teachers who made a significant difference in your life, and perhaps in your decision to become a teacher. Now is the time to write a letter to that teacher. Tell him or her what you are doing now and describe the way(s) that teacher impacted you. The following letter, "Email From a First-Year Teacher," is what a first-year teacher wrote to one of her teachers. In your teaching career, we hope some of your students will take the time to write similar letters to you.
Read a Book	As the title of Alan M. Blankstein's book, *Failure Is Not an Option: 6 Principles for Making Student Success the Only Option* (2010, Sage), makes clear, the mission of every teacher and school needs to be having all students learning. This award-winning book provides a positive and proactive stance about what to do and what not to do. Leadership by teachers is essential to a school having trust, a shared vision, a focus on student success, and engaged parents.

(Continued)

(Continued)

	Building and sustaining partnerships between schools, parents, and communities requires ongoing involvement of teachers. *Educational Partnerships: Connecting Schools, Families, and the Community*, by Amy Cox-Peterson (2011, Sage), goes beyond presenting the need and provides steps for developing and sustaining connections with families and the broader community. There are many components, elements, and possibilities in teacher leadership. One in-depth analysis is a book by Nathan Bond and Andy Hargreaves: *The Power of Teacher Leaders: Their Roles, Influence and Impact* (2015, Routledge). The first part addresses learning to lead, and the second part describes a number of teacher leader roles. Finally, the third part examines impacts and the importance of inquiry.
Search the Web	Check out the website for the school district where you want to teach. Go to the Human Resources section and review the teacher position description. Make notes about what you will need to have in order to qualify for a position. Also, list the things you need to accomplish between now and then to make you extra well qualified to be hired to teach in that district. Surf the web using the term *teacher leadership*. You may be surprised at the number of resources and efforts to support teacher leaders, their professional development, and ways to network. For example, the National Education Association has established Teacher Leader Model Standards that distinguish between teacher and principal leadership. AIR/SEDL has publications related to teacher change leadership, and ASCD has material that explores the wide range of ways that teachers can be leaders. As another activity, carefully think about the characteristics of teacher leaders that are being identified on some of the websites. Develop a checklist of different knowledge and skills that teachers as leaders should possess. Add a column to assess your current level of leadership expertise. Add another column where you can name leadership activities you have done, and another column where you include times when you have been especially effective as a follower.
Email From a First-Year Teacher (to One of Her Teacher Education Faculty)	In my previous life as an Air Force airman, we were taught three core values: (1) Integrity First, (2) Service Before Self, and (3) Excellence in All We Do. It usually takes a few years of working as part of a team to truly internalize how those values translate into consistent mission accomplishment. But since the moment I got it, I've found that those three guidelines can apply to almost any endeavor in life. As a first-year teacher, I've felt all the normal pressures. Pressure every week to produce an organized lesson plan. Pressure every hour to keep the students' attention. Pressure every minute to avoid making mistakes that the kids can use against me later. Pressure to stay consistent with the rest of the department. And, of course, pressure to prepare my students for the proficiency exams. After a while, I realized that I wanted to spend more time actually teaching and less time analyzing all the various pressures of the job. I learned that, in the crucible of the classroom, the only thing I really cared about were the kids. The other worries only came later. They were like irritating, but meaningful, afterthoughts. It eventually got on my nerves that I was even spending time thinking about it. And slowly, as I became a better teacher, I started to understand why I was becoming more irritated and less worried: I realized my heart was in the right place, and I was doing my best. I believe we should all stop worrying about the "tensions" of teaching and simply use the Air Force core values to guide us. Integrity: Have a philosophy about what you want *your* students to learn in *your* class. Make sure it includes overarching themes and specific learning goals. Stick to your philosophy—always. Service Before Self: When you sign up to teach America's youth, you are in the service of our collective future. Yeah, that's a little soap-boxy, but it's true. Understand that educating is reason No. 1 why you go to work—above your paycheck, your benefits, or your summer vacation. Excellence in All We Do: The word is *excellence*, not *perfection*. Do your best, and don't let mistakes get in the way of your performance. Keep your eyes open. Don't just learn from your own mistakes and successes: Learn from others', too. Be involved enough with other teachers that you can accrue second- and third-degree experience, which will make you as excellent as possible. I believe teachers who can adopt those three concepts will be happier and more effective. And they'll realize that the other "tension" is just noise that can get in the way of the mission. *Elissa Richmond*

STUDENT STUDY SITE

⑤SAGE edge™

Get the tools you need to sharpen your study skills. **SAGE edge** offers a robust online environment featuring an impressive array of free tools and resources.

Access practice quizzes, eFlashcards, video, and multimedia at **edge.sagepub.com/hall3e**.

Ability: Capacity to achieve as a result of physical or mental aptitude and training.

Accommodations: Purposeful additional supports or adjustments in instruction that give students with disabilities access to the content being taught and ensure that a student with special needs is not placed in an unfair or disadvantageous situation for instruction or testing.

Accountability: Teachers, administrators, and other school officials taking responsibility and being held responsible for student learning and the effective and efficient use of public resources.

Accreditation: Recognition by a professional organization such as AdvancED or the Council for the Accreditation of Educator Preparation (CAEP) that an educational institution meets standards.

Achievement gap: The differences among groups of students in their performance on assessments, especially standardized tests.

Active listening: Intentionally focusing on the speaker and showing respect for his or her needs, interests, and abilities.

Activity approach: A strategy that helps students develop an understanding of the link between the conscious world and the objective world by engaging in projects and other activities.

Adaptive testing: A computer-based test that adapts to the test taker's ability level.

Adequacy: The degree to which there are sufficient funds to accomplish the objectives.

Adequate Yearly Progress (AYP): A specified level of increase in a school's yearly test scores.

Administrative law: The regulations, rules, and procedures, based on legislation, that specify what states, schools, teachers, and others must do.

Affirmations: Positive comments and supports.

Agency fees: A requirement that public employees pay union fees regardless of whether or not they are members.

Assertive discipline: An approach of classroom management in which teachers manage the class in a firm but positive manner and insist on responsible behavior from students.

Assessing: The process of evaluating the work and performance of students to determine what has been learned and develop a plan for next steps to help students learn.

Assimilation: The process by which groups adopt or change the dominant culture.

At risk: Students who may fall behind in learning and may drop out of school.

Authentic task: An assessment task that is clearly related to the benchmarks and standards, as well as to real-world applications.

Authoritarian: A form of management that requires submission to the strict rule of a teacher or another person.

Authorize: Legislative action that establishes authority for a certain activity to take place.

Autism: A disability that appears in early childhood and is characterized by difficulty with social skills, repetitive behaviors, communication skills, and interactions with others. Autism is also referred to as an *autism spectrum disorder* to reflect the wide variation in symptoms, skills, and challenges faced by each person with autism.

Axiology: The branch of philosophy that deals with questions concerning the nature of values.

Back-to-basics: A return to a less complex time when the focus of schooling was simply on learning the basic subjects of reading, arithmetic, grammar, and history in a traditional way.

Benchmarks: A description of performances required to meet a standard at an expected level.

Bilingual education: The use of English and the native language of students in instruction to ensure that students are able to understand the concepts being taught.

Board of trustees: A governing body that has responsibility for developing the official policies and guidelines for the educational system.

Born again: Individuals who have had a religious experience that led them to recommit themselves to God and Jesus Christ as an evangelic.

Brain architecture: How the brain is "wired" through genetics and interactions with the environment and personal experiences.

Budget: The predetermined amount of money available for an authorized activity.

Bullying: An act that occurs when a student or group of students intimidate or harass another student.

Canon: The books, values, and principles that are widely accepted for the education of children and youth.

Case law: Law that is established as a result of judicial decisions.

Catechism: A series of questions and answers, usually on religious doctrine.

Chain of command: A frequently used phrase to refer to the up/down line relationships in an organization chart that determine who reports to whom.

Charity schools: Schools established for poor children in urban areas prior to the common school.

Charter schools: Publicly funded schools that are allowed to be innovative and operate somewhat independently of the public school system in which they are located.

Chief Academic Officer (CAO): A position that provides district-wide leadership in relation to instruction, assessment, curriculum, and improvement of the overall quality of educational services.

Chief State School Officer (CSSO): A state superintendent of public instruction or commissioner of education who may be elected or appointed by the state board of education or governor.

Choice: Providing parents the option to decide which school their child will attend.

Choice theory: William Glasser's (1997) model that calls for teachers to help students satisfy their five psychological needs (the need for survival, the need to belong, the need for power, the need for freedom, and the need for fun) so that students can choose appropriate behavior individually and as a group.

Civil rights: The rights of personal liberty guaranteed by the Thirteenth and Fourteenth Amendments to the U.S. Constitution and by acts of Congress.

Closed questions: Questions that require one word, facts, or short answers.

Coalition: Multiple interest groups that have joined forces to influence how a school board or legislator votes.

Cognitive framework: A set of intellectual abilities expressed through thought and action.

Color blind: All students are treated the same without regard for or attention to their race and ethnicity.

Common Core State Standards (CCSS): Standards in mathematics and English language arts for each grade level that were written jointly by the National Governors Association and the Council of Chief State School Officers and have been adopted in whole or in part by most states.

Common schools: Eighteenth-century schools that mixed students from different socioeconomic levels in the same classes using the same curricula.

Compulsory attendance: Required attendance at school from an age and to an age set by state legislatures.

Concerns: Thoughts, preoccupations, and worries in relation to becoming a teacher and/or teaching.

Conduct management: Maintaining conduct through the establishment of rules and guidelines of behavior.

Consensus oriented: Decision making through open dialogue, rather than by way of ultimatums and refusals to negotiate.

Content management: Planning the physical environment, deciding on the procedures that will be applied during the school day, and instruction of lessons.

Continuing resolution: Deciding to keep the budget the same as it was in the last year.

Cooperative learning groups: A heterogeneous group of students working together to solve problems or help one another learn.

Corporal punishment: A teacher paddling or spanking a student.

Corporate income tax: Taxes paid by corporations to federal and state governments.

Couch surfing: Moving from house to house for temporary sleeping arrangements.

Covenant management: Managing relationships, having highly developed communication skills, and knowing ways the combined effects of content management and conduct management will influence interactions in the classroom.

Criminal background check: A school district's process for determining whether teachers have a criminal record, which would prevent them from teaching. This process usually requires teachers to be fingerprinted.

Criterion-Referenced Tests (CRTs): Assessments in which each student's test score is compared with a defined level of performance rather than with how other students have done.

Cultural borders: A social construct based on cultural membership that is political based on differences in power.

Cultural capital: Endowments such as academic competence, language competence, and wealth that provide an advantage to an individual, family, or group.

Cultural relativism: Judging other cultural groups through the lens of members of that culture rather than applying the standards of one's own culture.

Culturally responsive teaching: An educational strategy that affirms the cultures of students, views the cultures and experiences of students as strengths, and reflects the students' cultures in curricula.

Culture: Socially transmitted ways of thinking, believing, feeling, and acting within a group that are transmitted from one generation to the next.

Current expenditures: Funds spent during a specific school year.

Curriculum: The lessons and academic content taught by teachers to help students meet standards and objectives. The curriculum generally includes books, videos, readings, presentations by teachers, and related assessments.

Cut score: The score determined by the state that must be achieved to pass a test such as the teacher licensure test; the test score that determines whether one passes or fails.

Cyberbullying: Harassment of children, young people, and adults through posts on social media such as texting and Facebook.

Data-based decision making: Using test scores and information from other assessments as the basis for planning instruction.

Data teams: A special committee that reviews the performance of individual students. The team includes representatives from all grade levels/subjects, a school administrator, reading and mathematics specialists, one or more special education teachers, and at least one member who is skilled at organizing and displaying student data. Some schools call this group a Student Improvement Team.

De facto segregation: The voluntary separation or isolation of racial, ethnic, or socioeconomic groups in a community, leading to neighborhood schools attended by students from one group.

De jure segregation: Segregation of residential areas that is brought about through laws and the actions of state and local officials.

Deculturalizing: The educational process that destroys a student's culture and replaces it with a new culture.

Deficit ideology: Blaming oppressed people for their own economic disparities and/or considering them intellectually and culturally inferior to the dominant group.

Democratic classroom: Engagement of students in shared decision making and in taking responsibility for building a democratic learning environment.

Depth of Knowledge (DOK): A taxonomy for describing different levels of learning.

Developmental model: A model of how children grow and how they learn in which there are predictable phases and stages to child development.

Developmentally appropriate practices: An approach to teaching and curriculum development that is grounded in the research about how students learn and develop at different ages.

Differentiate: To adjust instruction so that it matches the learning needs, learning preferences, interests, and readiness of each student.

Differentiated instruction: Teaching in ways that provide multiple options for learning based on the learning needs, learning preferences, interests, and readiness of each student.

Dilemma: A complex problem with two or more solutions.

Direct or explicit instruction: Teaching of information or a skill through a lecture or demonstration.

Disability: A long-standing physical, mental, or emotional condition that can make it difficult for a person to do activities such as walking, climbing stairs, dressing, bathing, communicating, learning, or remembering.

Dispositions: The attitudes, beliefs, and values that teachers hold about students, the subjects they teach, their colleagues, the parents, and the school.

Distributed leadership: Sharing of leadership across teachers and administrators as a joint responsibility.

Dominant social group: A social group that holds cultural prominence and power in terms of the values, images, and norms perpetuated by a society (e.g., heterosexuals, Christians, millionaires, and whites would be considered dominant social groups in U.S. culture).

Dual language education programs: A bilingual education program in which students who are native English speakers and students who are English language learners become proficient in both English and the native language of the ELL as the two languages are used in the classroom for academic instruction.

Education Management Organization (EMO): A private company that receives payment to operate a school.

Elementary and Secondary Education Act (ESEA): Federal legislation first passed in 1965 that established national priorities and programs for improving schools and education.

Empowering policies: Statements or guidelines that identify a goal or vision but leave open the means for achieving the desired end.

Enculturation: The process of learning one's cultural expectations for behavior, communications, and ways of knowing.

Engaging parents: Providing general information to parents without seeking their active participation.

English as a Second Language (ESL): An educational program for teaching English language learners in which instruction is delivered in English.

English for Speakers of Other Languages (ESOL): An educational program for children and adults whose native language is not English to develop their English skills and proficiency in processing academic English language.

English Language Learners (ELLs): Students and adults who are not native English speakers.

Epistemology: Examines questions about how and what we know, and how knowing takes place.

Equity: The state of fairness and justice across individuals and groups. It does not mean the same educational strategies across groups, but does expect somewhat equal results.

Essentialism: A school of philosophy based on the belief in a fundamental core of knowledge that any functioning member of society must possess.

Ethnicity: Membership based on one's national origin or the national origin of one's ancestors when they immigrated to the United States.

Evangelicals: Christians who believe in the literal authority of the Bible, the importance of being "born again," and a commitment to sharing the Christian message.

Existentialism: A school of philosophy that sees a world in which individuals determine for themselves what is true or false.

Extrinsic rewards: Those rewards that are given to students by others. Such rewards are external to a student's self-motivation.

Fair use: The conditions under which a teacher and others may use certain materials without the permission of the copyright holder.

Federalism: Involvement of the federal government in making decisions about education for the whole nation.

Field-based supervisors: The teachers or other school professionals who provide support for teacher candidates when they observe and work in schools.

Fishbowl: A form of dialog that can be used when discussing topics within large groups. The advantage of fishbowl is that it allows the entire group to participate in a conversation.

Followership: Being a constructive member of the group, offering to help, contributing positively to the discussions, and being sure to complete assigned tasks, with quality and on time. Entails participating and volunteering help.

Formative evaluation: Assessment of student work that provides feedback on student progress and guides preparation of future lessons.

Fourteenth Amendment: The amendment ratified during the Reconstruction era on July 9, 1868, to provide citizenship to all persons born or naturalized in the United States other than American Indians and Asians. It also reaffirmed and extended the Civil Rights Act passed in 1866 and served as the foundation for *Brown v. Board of Education of Topeka* and other civil rights cases in the 20th and 21st centuries.

Free and universal education: Public education for all children and youth.

Full-Time Equivalent (FTE): A budgeting calculation that combines the number of part-time students to be equal to one full-time student.

Gender: The behavioral, cultural, and psychological traits typically associated with one's sex or sexual identity.

General intelligence: A person's ability to perform cognitive tasks.

Global competence: Being able to examine global and intercultural issues from multiple perspectives.

Governance: The processes and administration of managing an organization for the purpose of making decisions and implementing actions.

Heterosexism: An irrational fear or hatred of people whose sexual orientation is other than heterosexual that can lead to prejudice, discrimination, and violence against Lesbian, Gay, Bisexual, Transgender, and Queer or Questioning (LGBTQ) individuals.

High-needs students: Students at risk of educational failure or otherwise in need of special assistance and support.

High-poverty schools: Schools in which more than three-fourths of students are from low-income families.

High-stakes testing: Tests that are used for gatekeeping, such as passing to the next grade or being qualified for a job.

Highly qualified teacher (HQT): Specifications in the federal No Child Left Behind legislation to ensure that all classrooms are staffed by teachers who hold a bachelor's degree, have been fully licensed by the state, and have proven they know each subject they teach by passing a standardized test.

Holistic rubrics: Assignment of levels of performance across multiple criteria rather than a specific level for each criterion.

Home school: Children are taught at home by a parent or tutor.

Horizontal communication: Communications across the various levels in the organization chart.

Human Resources (HR): The department with responsibility for hiring employees and ensuring that they are paid and have benefits such as health care and retirement.

I-messages: Messages in communication that avoid placing blame and allow speakers to express their feelings directly and specifically.

Immersion: A program in which a language other than English is used for instruction that helps students develop their skills in a second language.

Inclusion: The integration of students with disabilities into the regular classroom. The term has been expanded to include the integration of all students from different social and cultural groups into all classrooms.

Indigenous: The population that is native to a country or region. In the United States, American Indians, Hawaiians, and Alaska Natives are indigenous populations.

Indirect or implicit instruction: Involvement of students in inquiry activities in which they investigate the content and attend to context. The teacher becomes a facilitator of learning content rather than the deliverer of the content.

Individualized Education Program (IEP): A program that indicates the accommodations and special services that must be provided to a student with disabilities. The IEP must be developed by parents, teachers, special educators, and other specialists such as a school psychologist or occupational therapist.

Instruction: The act of teaching based in assessments, the learning outcomes, and the curriculum.

Instructional coach: A school-based master teacher who is assigned full-time to plan and deliver professional development and coach teachers.

Integration: Students from different ethnic, racial, and socioeconomic groups attend the same schools and participate in the same classes and activities within the school.

Intelligence Quotient (IQ) test: A measure of intelligence reached by comparing a student's score on the Stanford–Binet Intelligence Scales to that of his or her age group.

Interest group: A formal or informal group whose members are advocates for a common interest.

Intermediate teachers: Teachers of Grades 4–6.

Intermediate units: Educational organizations that pool resources and share costs to provide educational services such as special education to multiple school districts. They may be called a Board of Cooperative Educational Services, Regional Educational Service Agency, Service Center, or County Office of Education, depending on the state or region of the country.

Intrinsic rewards: Internal satisfaction with one's performance on tasks such as helping a child learn rather than external incentives such as salary or prestige.

Intrinsically active: A child's interactions with the environment that become more dynamic and change thinking as children grow.

Involving parents: Making parents a necessary part of what goes on at school.

Jim Crow laws: Laws and practices that segregated whites from blacks in the use of facilities such as water fountains, restrooms, hotels, buses, restaurants, movie theaters, and schools.

Journals: Documents in which teacher candidates record their thoughts about a topic or their reflections on the teaching of a lesson, student behavior, and other classroom events.

Judicious discipline: A philosophy that creates an environment respectful of the citizenship rights of students.

Knowledge: Awareness of or familiarity with information, facts, concepts, and ideas about someone or a topic that has been learned through education or lived experience.

Leaders: People with formal and sometimes informal responsibility for accomplishing a task or activity.

Leadership: A responsibility to help a group or whole school accomplish its objectives.

Learning cycle: Kolb and Fry's (1974) four-stage cycle of learning in which "immediate or concrete experiences" provide a basis for "observations and reflections." These "observations and reflections" are assimilated and distilled into "abstract concepts," producing new implications for action that can be "actively tested," in turn creating new experiences.

Least Restrictive Environment (LRE): Education of students with disabilities in regular classrooms with their classmates without disabilities to the maximum extent appropriate.

Lesson plans: A teacher's detailed guide for delivering classroom instruction and facilitating learning.

LGBTQ: An acronym for Lesbian, Gay, Bisexual, Transgender, and Queer or Questioning individuals.

Line relationships: One position has direct supervisory authority over another.

Local control: Authority for decision making regarding schools that is in the hands of those nearest the site, whether it is the district or a school.

Local Education Agencies (LEAs): School districts that include a cluster of schools in the same geographic area.

Locus of control: The extent to which teachers believe they can control events in the classroom. Teachers with a strong locus of control generally create a well-managed classroom as compared to teachers who believe everything that happens is beyond their control.

Looping: An educational practice in which teachers remain with the same students for two or more grades.

Low-poverty schools: Schools in which fewer than 25% of the students are eligible for free or reduced-price lunch.

Magnet schools: Public schools that are organized around a theme or themes such as Science, Technology, Engineering, and Mathematics (STEM) or fine and performing arts. Magnet schools draw students from across the school boundaries in a school district.

Mainstreaming: Placing students with special needs in the general education classroom as their readiness and skills permit.

Manifest destiny: A future event that is believed to be inevitable or cannot be avoided.

Maturation: The emergence of personal and behavioral characteristics, including ways of thinking, as one grows older.

McKinney-Vento Homeless Assistance Act: The federal legislation that outlines the education rights and protections for homeless children and youth.

Mentors: Experienced teachers who coach and guide new teachers through their first years of practice.

Metacognition: Thinking about one's own thinking, which includes deciding on a specific choice or solution and acting on one's decisions.

Metaphysics: A school of philosophy that is concerned with questions about the nature of reality and humans' attempts to find coherence in the realm of thought and experience.

Micromanaging: The tendency to become overly involved in the day-to-day operations of a school or school district.

Mindfulness: A mental state in which we pay attention to our thoughts, feelings, and body sensations in a given moment without judging them.

Model minority: A group that is stereotypically characterized as academically and economically successful because of the group's norms or culture.

Modeling: A way of learning in which students or teachers learn how to act or behave by observing others.

Modifications: Adjustments to instruction or assessments to assist students with disabilities and English language learners in accessing the content and being assessed appropriately to determine their level of learning.

Morals: Generally accepted personal or cultural values and codes of conduct for behavior.

Multicultural curriculum: A curriculum that incorporates the history, culture, contributions, and experiences of multiple ethnic, socioeconomic, language, and religious groups as well as females, males, and students with exceptionalities. A multicultural curriculum also addresses issues of power, discrimination, and inequality.

Multiple assessments: More than one type of evaluation instrument used to determine student learning and needed support for improving learning.

Multiple Intelligences (MI) theory: Howard Gardner's theory that classifies intelligence into seven (later nine) abilities. Gardner holds that everyone has strengths with some abilities and weaknesses with others.

Multiple perspectives: Views from people or groups of people whose histories and experiences provide different ways of looking at current or past events, policies, research, and practices in the world.

National Assessment of Educational Progress (NAEP): A congressionally mandated project that uses a common assessment across states to assess fourth, eighth, and twelfth graders in selected schools that are representative of the U.S. student population. NAEP reports the results of its assessments in the Nation's Report Card on the academic performance of students in reading, mathematics, and eight other subjects.

National Board for Professional Teaching Standards (NBPTS): The organization that has developed standards for accomplished teachers and a process for determining whether practicing teachers meet those standards.

National STEM Standards: Standards for the teaching of science, mathematics, engineering, and technology at the college level that were developed by the Committee on Undergraduate Science Education in collaboration with the Center for Science, Mathematics, and Engineering Education and the National Research Council.

Naturalized citizenship: Citizenship for an immigrant with all the rights of a native-born citizen except for being eligible to be the president or vice president of the United States.

Nihilism: A philosophical position that argues the world, and especially human existence, is without objective meaning, purpose, comprehensible truth, or essential value.

No pass, no play: Policies that prohibit students from participating in sports and band unless they maintain a certain Grade Point Average (GPA).

Normal curve: The distribution of test scores in which the largest number of scores are in the middle with few test takers achieving the highest and lowest scores.

Norm-Referenced Tests (NRTs): The test score of one student is compared with the scores of other students who have taken the same test.

Objective tests: Test items that can be scored as right or wrong without the influence of a scorer's bias.

Onsite staff developer: Master teachers who serve as mentor, model teacher, peer coach, and teacher trainer within a school.

Open-ended questions: Questions that require elaboration, higher-level thinking, and longer responses.

Opportunity gap: The disparity in access to quality schools, effective teachers, and educational resources that provides obstacles to a student's ability to perform academically at high levels.

Organization chart: A graphic representation of line and staff relationships and levels of authority within an organization, school, or school district.

Out-of-field teachers: Educators assigned to teach a subject in which they did not major in college and for which they have not been licensed to teach.

Outsourcing: Contracting with outside companies to provide services such as cleaning buildings, driving school buses, or accounting.

Pan-ethnic: Ethnic membership based on national origin from a large geographic region that includes numerous countries. Examples are African Americans and Asian Americans.

Parent–Teacher Organizations (PTOs): Groups of teachers and parents who have organized to support student learning in a school.

Pedagogy: Theory and practice of education and teaching effectively to help students learn.

Perennialism: A school of philosophy that offers a conservative and traditional view of human nature. In this school of thought, humans do not change much, but they are capable of analytical thinking, reasoning, and imagination, and should be encouraged along these lines.

Performance: Tasks that ask students to do an activity rather than a mental exercise.

Performance assessment: An assessment that is based on students applying their learning through accomplishing an activity, which shows that they really have learned the benchmark and standard.

Per-pupil expenditure: The total number of dollars spent divided by the number of students. It is used as an indicator of a community's commitment to and support of public education.

Personal income taxes: Taxes paid by individuals to federal and state governments based on their level of income.

Personalized learning: An approach to learning that uses technology and other resources to place students at the center of learning and tailor instruction to the individual needs of students.

Pessimism: A general belief that things are bad and tend to become worse.

Policies: The official stated overarching parameters for what can and cannot be done and how it can be done within an organization.

Portfolio: A compilation of works, records, and accomplishments that a student prepares for a specific purpose in order to demonstrate his or her learning, performances, and contributions.

Positive Behavioral Interventions and Supports (PBIS): An approach to school discipline that focuses on defining and modeling positive behaviors by students and school personnel.

Pragmatism: A school of philosophy that is concerned about practice and the practical, which is viewed as dynamic and evolving.

Prescriptive policies: Policies or guidelines that set limits and specify the procedures that are to be used.

Primary teachers: Teachers of Grades K–3.

Private schools: Schools that operate with little, or no, public funding.

Privatizing: Contracting with outside for-profit companies to provide services such as cleaning buildings, driving school buses, or accounting.

Probationary teachers: Teachers who are not yet tenured. Probationary teachers are generally not eligible for due process if their contract is not renewed.

Problem: A matter that needs fixing for which one or more solutions can be devised.

Problem-based learning: When instruction is focused on a relevant problem and data are provided to students to help them reach solutions.

Procedural due process: A procedure to ensure that a person has been treated fairly and that proper procedures have been followed.

Profession: A career that requires specialized knowledge and advanced college preparation, often beyond the baccalaureate.

Professional Learning Communities (PLCs): An approach to organizing the adults in a school to meet regularly or a school-wide effort focused on developing a collaborative culture around student and adult learning.

Proficiencies: Knowledge, skills, or dispositions that students are expected to acquire to meet a set of standards.

Progressive income tax: Income tax that is graduated with those having a higher level of income paying a larger percentage.

Progressivism: A school of philosophy marked by progress, reform, or continuing improvement. The tenets of progressivism demonstrate respect for individuality, a high regard for science, and receptivity to change.

Prohibitions: Rebukes and telling a child not to do something.

Proselytize: Recruit new members to one's own faith.

Race: A sociohistorical concept based on society's perception that differences among people based on the color of their skin exist and that these differences are important.

Racism: The belief that one race is superior to all others and thereby has the right to dominance.

Reduction in Force (RIF): Eliminating jobs due to budget cuts.

Reflections: Thinking about one's actions and the result of such actions.

Refugees: Persons recognized by the U.S. government as being persecuted or legitimately bearing persecution in their home country because of race, religion, nationality, or membership in a specific social or political group.

Regressive income tax: A form of taxation in which those with less ability to pay pay proportionately more.

Reliability: The degree to which a test consistently measures what it is designed to measure.

Resegregation: The de facto segregation of students as a result of the return to neighborhood schools after de jure segregation has been dismantled for the most part.

Response to Instruction (RTI): See Response to Intervention (RTI).

Response to Intervention (RTI): A multilevel approach for identifying struggling students and intervening to meet their academic or behavioral needs before they are classified as eligible for an Individualized Education Program (IEP).

Restorative justice: An approach to student discipline that focuses on repairing the harm caused by the offender through building cooperative relationships with victims and the community as a whole.

Rubrics: A scoring instrument that indicates criteria for meeting a standard or expectation and the levels of performance such as inadequate, proficient, and beyond expectations.

Rule of law: Expectations and requirements that are enforced equally for all.

Scaffolding: Beginning instruction with small tasks the learner already knows and building on that knowledge to move students progressively toward more in-depth understanding.

School board: The school district governing body that has responsibility for developing the official policies and guidelines for the educational system.

School Resource Officer (SRO): A trained police officer placed in a school for safety and security reasons.

School-to-prison pipeline: Policies and practices in schools that lead to students being arrested for minor and more serious offenses in schools that place them in the juvenile justice system.

School vouchers: State-funded scholarships that help parents pay for their children to attend private rather than public school.

Schools in Need of Improvement (SINOI): Schools that fail to make adequate yearly progress in any one disaggregated category, leading to the school being placed on a list of SINOI.

Schools of philosophy: Different perspectives on answering the broad philosophical questions posed through metaphysics, epistemology, and axiology from differing perspectives. The schools of philosophy most often mentioned in terms of the implications they have for education are idealism, realism, perennialism, pragmatism, progressivism, essentialism, and existentialism.

Secondary teachers: Teachers of Grades 7–12.

Secular: Not religious in nature. Sometimes identified as based on science rather than religion.

Secular humanism: A dogma stressing the ethical consequences of human decisions that are based on science and philosophy rather than religion and belief.

Self-contained classroom: One teacher is assigned responsibility for teaching students in the same grade all subjects in the same classroom.

Self-fulfilling prophecy: A phenomenon in which a teacher's expectations for a student's achievement are established early in the school year and match the student's achievement at the end of the school year.

Sensitive periods: Times in which the environment has a greater impact on the development of specific areas of the brain.

Sex: The identification of a person as male or female based on biological differences.

Sexting: The act of using a cell phone or other technology to send or receive sexually explicit pictures, video, and/or text.

Sexual orientation: One's sexual attraction to persons of the same or opposite sex or both.

Sin taxes: Taxes on products and services such as cigarettes and alcohol whose value has been questioned on religious grounds.

Social justice: Caring for and supporting people who are less advantaged than you.

Socialization: The process of learning the social norms and expectations of society.

Socioeconomic status (SES): Composite of the economic status of families or persons on the basis of occupation, educational attainment, and income.

Socratic method: A questioning strategy that guides students toward independent thinking.

Specific abilities: Particular tasks such as language development, memory, and auditory perception.

Staff relationships: Interactions with other members of the faculty and staff whom one does not supervise with the expectation that they will communicate, coordinate, and work together.

Stages of Concern: Levels that people may move through as they experience any type of change.

Standard: A statement about overarching values in education that the majority of people agree on. A standard is an acknowledged measure of comparison for quantitative or qualitative value, a criterion, a norm, or a degree or level of excellence that is achieved.

Standards-based curriculum: A course of study designed to help students meet the proficiencies identified in standards adopted by a school or state.

State Education Agency (SEA): The state agency responsible for public education in the state.

Statute: A law by a legislative body that sets the general boundaries and some of the limits, but not the specific details, of the legislation, which is the administrative law.

Stereotype threat: A phenomenon in which the common stereotypes about a group influence how people in that group see themselves.

Stereotypes: Exaggerated, and usually biased, views about a group based on prior, and often wrong, assumptions.

Strategy: An instructional method or technique teachers use to deliver instruction.

Student-centered learning: Learning directed by students in which they participate actively in their learning rather than being a passive receptacle and develop autonomy and independence as they are involved in what and how content will be taught as the teacher moves to a facilitator and learner role in the process.

Student Improvement Team (SIT): A special committee that reviews the performance of individual students. The team includes representatives from all grade levels/subjects, a school administrator, reading and mathematics specialists, one or more special education teachers, and at least one member who is skilled at organizing and displaying student data.

Subjective test: An assessment that poses a question, problem, or task for which students must construct an original response for which there is no right or wrong answer. The scoring of the responses could vary across reviewers based on their own biases and opinions.

Substantive due process: Protection against the loss of the rights granted in the Constitution, such as freedom of expression.

Summative evaluation: The use of assessment results to make conclusions about what a student has learned or to decide whether a student is ready to move to the next grade level.

Superintendent: The chief executive officer of a school district.

Taxonomies: Classification systems of the learning hierarchy that progress from simple to complex.

Teacher leader: A part-time or full-time assignment for a master teacher to guide the professional learning of teachers.

Team teaching: A staffing plan in which two or more teachers work together to plan and teach a common group of students.

Test: A set of questions or problems to be answered by students for the purpose of assessing how much a student knows and can do at a particular point in time.

Test prep: Instruction that is devoted to teaching students how to prepare for and take tests, especially standardized tests.

Tort law: Wrongs related to failure to act properly or acting improperly.

Tracking: The practice of separating students based on their academic abilities or other factors to receive instruction that is supposed to be most appropriate for their abilities.

Transition: The move from one level of schooling to another such as from elementary school to junior high/middle school. It also refers to movement from one activity to another in a classroom.

Trauma-sensitive schools: Schools that use their understanding of the impact of traumatic events on a student's learning and social and emotional behavior to provide safe and supportive educational environments for all students.

Twice exceptional (2e): Students who are academically able and who have an identified disability.

Unconditional positive regard: Expressing basic acceptance and support of a person regardless of what the person says or does. This term is attributed to Carl Rogers.

Unfunded mandate: Legislation that is not funded at the level required to meet the goal of the legislation.

Universal design: Creation of buildings, environments, and products that are accessible to students with a wide range of abilities and other characteristics.

Universal Design for Learning (UDL): Making learning accessible to both students with disabilities and students without disabilities by creating learning environments, instructional goals, instructional strategies, resources, and assessments that accommodate individual learning differences.

Unpaid furlough days: The requirement that employees, especially teachers and other public employees, take one or two days a month off without pay.

Validity: The extent to which a test accurately measures what it is intended to assess.

Value added: Assessment that provides evidence of a teacher's performance in improving student achievement as measured by standardized tests.

Values: The behaviors, principles, ideals, or morals that reflect what we view as important.

Vertical communication: Communication that moves down, and up, the organization chart of personnel in schools.

Virtual school: Instruction is delivered online.

Vocabulary gap: The difference in the number of words children know at different stages of their development that are influenced by factors such as poverty and the education of their parents.

Voucher: A certificate for a certain amount of public funds provided to support students attending a school of choice.

Wait-time I: The time a teacher waits after asking a question that gives students the opportunity to think about a response.

Wait-time II: The time a teacher waits after a student has responded to a question, providing other students the opportunity to add an additional response or ask for clarification.

Waivers: Exemptions to a required regulation.

Walkout: A widespread action of public employees to step out of their daily work and protest conditions and too limited support, especially financial.

Whole child approach: An approach to education that emphasizes the need to address a child's physical, social, and emotional well-being, as well as cognitive development.

Zero tolerance policies: School policies that call for punishing any infraction of a rule.

Adair, J. K., Colegrove, K. S., & McManus, M. E. (2017, Fall). How the word gap argument negatively impacts young children of Latinx immigrants' conceptualizations of learning. *Harvard Educational Review, 87*(3), 309–334.

Aguilar, E. (2016, August 9). When we listen to students. *Edutopia* Retrieved from www.edutopia.org/blog/when-we-listen-students-elena-aguilar.

Alexander, K., & Alexander, M. D. (2001). *American public school law* (5th ed.). Belmont, CA: Wadsworth/Thomas Learning.

Alexander v. Holmes County Board of Education, 396 U.S. 19 (1969).

Almarode, J. T., & Daniel, D. B. (2018). Educational neuroscience: Are we there yet? In G. E. Hall, L. F. Quinn, & D. M. Gollnick (Eds.), *The Wiley handbook of teaching and learning* (pp. 175–198). Hoboken, NJ: Wiley Blackwell.

Alston v. School Board of City of Norfolk, 112 F.2d 992 (1940).

Amarao, C. (2013). Factsheet: How bad is the school-to-prison pipeline? Infographic from SuspensionStory.com. Accompaniment to *Tavis Smiley Reports: Education Under Arrest* Episode 6, aired on PBS, March 16, 2013. Retrieved from http://www.pbs.org/

American Association of Colleges for Teacher Education. (2010, March). *The clinical preparation of teachers: A policy brief.* Washington, DC: Author. Retrieved from https://coe.uni.edu/sites/default/files/wysiwyg/AACTE_-_Clinical_Prep_Paper.pdf

American College Health Association, National College Health Assessment. (2013). *Spring 2013 reference group executive summary.* Retrieved from https://www.acha.org/documents/ncha/ACHA-NCHA-II_ReferenceGroup_ExecutiveSummary_Spring2013.pdf

American Heart Association. (2013, March 22). *The American Heart Association's recommendations for physical activity in children.* Dallas, TX: Author. Retrieved from https://www.heart.org/en/healthy-living/fitness/fitness-basics/american-heart-associations-recommendations-for-physical-activity-in-children

American Library Association. (n.d.). *Number of challenges by reasons, initiator, & institution (1990–99).* Chicago, IL: Author. Retrieved from http://www.ala.org/advocacy/bbooks/frequentlychallengedbooks/statistics/1990-99

American Library Association. (2017, April). *The state of America's libraries 2017: A report from the American Library Association* (Kathy S. Rosa, ed.). Retrieved from www.ala.org/news/state-americas-libraries-report-2017

American Psychological Association. (2013). *Stress in America: Are teens adopting adults' stress habits?* Retrieved from http://www.apa.org/news/press/releases/stress/2013/stress-report.pdf

American Psychological Association. (2018). *Sexual orientation & homosexuality.* Washington, DC: Author. Retrieved from www.apa.org/topics/sorientation.pdf

Anderson, J. (1988). *The education of blacks in the South, 1860–1935.* Chapel Hill, NC: The University of North Carolina Press.

Anderson, L. W., & Krathwohl, D. R. (2001). *A taxonomy for learning, teaching and assessing: A revision of Bloom's taxonomy of educational objectives* (Complete ed.). New York, NY: Longman.

ASCD. (2018). *Whole child.* Retrieved from http://www.ascd.org/whole-child.aspx

Atwell, N. (2013). *Systems to transform your classroom and school.* Portsmouth, NH: Heinemann.

Atwell, N. (2015). *In the middle: A lifetime of learning about writing, reading, and adolescents.* Portsmouth, NH: Heinemann.

Au, W., Brown, A. L., & Calderón, D. (2016). *Reclaiming the multicultural roots of U.S. curriculum: Communities of color and official knowledge in education.* New York: Teachers College Press.

Ausubel, D. (1963). *The psychology of meaningful verbal learning.* New York, NY: Grune & Stratton.

Ausubel, D. (1967). *Learning theory and classroom practice.* Toronto, Canada: The Ontario Institute for Studies in Education.

Ayan, D., & Seferoglu, G. (2011). Using electronic portfolios to promote reflective thinking in language teacher education. *Educational Studies, 37*(5), 513–521.

Bagley, W. C. (1907). *Classroom management: Its principles and techniques.* New York, NY: Macmillan.

Banich, M. T., & Compton, R. J. (2018). *Cognitive neuroscience* (4th ed.). New York, NY: Cambridge University Press.

Barrett v. Walker County School District (N.D. Ga, 2016). No. 16-11952. Decided: October 02, 2017.

Barrows, S., Peterson, P. E., & West, M. R. (2017, Spring). What do parents think of their children's schools? *EducationNext, 17*(2). Retrieved from http://educationnext.org/what-do-parents-think-of-childrens-schools-ednext-private-district-charter/

Barshay, J. (2017, November). U.S. ranks No. 13 in new collaborative problem-solving test. *The Hechinger Report.*

Basile, K. C., DeGue, S., Jones, K., Freire, K., Dills, J., Smith, S. G., & Raiford, J. L. (2016). *STOP SV: A technical package to prevent sexual violence.* Atlanta, GA: National Center for Injury Prevention and Control, Centers for Disease Control and Prevention. Retrieved from https://www.cdc.gov/violenceprevention/pdf/sv-prevention-technical-package.pdf

Beane, J. A. (2001). Introduction: Reform and reinvention. In T. S. Dickinson (Ed.), *Reinventing the middle school* (pp. xiii–xxii). New York, NY: RoutledgeFalmer.

Benson, J. (2014). *Hanging in: Strategies for teaching the students who challenge us most.* Alexandria, VA: ASCD.

Berg, E. L. (2003). Kindergarten. In P. S. Fass (Ed.), *Encyclopedia of children and childhood: In history and society.* Farmington Hills, MI: Gale. Retrieved from http://www.faqs.org/childhood/Ke-Me/Kindergarten.html

Berwick, C. (2015, March 17). Zeroing out zero tolerance. *The Atlantic.* Retrieved http://www.theatlantic.com/education/archive/2015/03/zeroing-out-zero-tolerance/388003/

Bethel School District No. 403 v. Fraser, 478 U.S. 675 (1986).

Bloom, B. S. (Ed.). (1956). *Taxonomy of educational objectives handbook I: Cognitive domain.* New York, NY: David McKay Co.

Bloomfield, L. (2007). *How everything works.* New York, NY: Wiley.

Board of Education of Oklahoma City v. Dowell, 498 U.S. 237 (1991).

Board of Education v. Pico, 457 U.S. 853, 102 S.Ct. 2799, 73 L.Ed.2d 435 (1982).

Board of Education of the Westside Community Schools v. Mergens, 496 U.S. 226 (1990).

Board of Regents of State Colleges v. Roth, 408 U.S. 564 (1972).

Bob Jones University v. U.S. and Goldsboro Christian Schools v. U.S., 461 U.S. 574 (1983).

Boger, J. C., & Orfield, G. (Eds.). (2005). *School resegregation: Must the South turn back?* Chapel Hill: University of North Carolina Press.

Bolling v. Sharpe, 347 U.S. 497 (1954).

Borich, G. D. (2011). *Effective teaching methods* (5th ed.). Upper Saddle River, NJ: Pearson/Prentice Hall.

Borich, G. D., & Tombari, M. L. (2003). *Educational assessment for the elementary and middle school classroom* (2nd ed.). Upper Saddle River, NJ: Merrill/Prentice Hall.

Boyer, C. (2015). *Why? 1,111 answers to everything.* Washington, DC: National Geographic Kids.

Boykin, A. W., & Noguera, P. (2011). *Creating the opportunity to learn: Moving from research to practice to close the achievement gap.* Alexandria, VA: ASCD.

Boyle, A., August, D., Tabaku, L., Cole, S., & Simpson-Baird, A. (2015). *Dual language education programs: Current state policies and practices.* Washington, DC: U.S. Department of Education, Office of English Language Acquisition.

Brenan, M. (2017, December 26). Nurses keep healthy lead as most honest, ethical profession. *Gallup.* Retrieved from http://news.gallup.com/poll/224639/nurses-keep-healthy-lead-honest-ethical-profession.aspx

Bridges, B. K., Awokoya, J. T., & Messano, F. (2012). *Done to us, not with us: African American parent perceptions of K–12 education.* Washington, DC: Frederick D. Patterson Research Institute, UNCF.

Bright, N. (2013). *Those who can: Why master teachers do what they do.* Lanham, MD: Rowman & Littlefield.

Bright, N. (2015). *Rethinking everything: Personal growth through transactional analysis.* Lanham, MD: Rowman & Littlefield.

Brown, S. E. (2015, October 21). *Philosophies of education comparison.* Retrieved from https://sarahellenbrown.com/2015/10/22/philosophies-of-education-comparison

Brown v. Board of Education of Topeka (Kansas), 347 U.S. 483 (1954).

Bruner, J. S. (1957). *Going beyond the information given.* New York, NY: Norton.

Bruner, J. (1962). *On knowing: Essays for the left hand.* Cambridge, MA: Harvard University Press.

Bruner, J. (1966). *Studies in cognitive growth.* San Francisco, CA: Wiley.

Budge, K. M., & Parrett, W. H. (2018). *Disrupting poverty: Five powerful classroom practices.* Alexandria, VA: ASCD.

Burant, T., Christensen, L., Salas, K. D., & Walters, S. (2010). Creating classrooms for equity and social justice. In T. Burant, L. Christensen, K. D. Salas, & S. Walters (Eds.), *The new teacher book* (pp. 157–162). Milwaukee, WI: Rethinking Schools.

Bureau of Indian Affairs. (n.d.). *About us.* Retrieved from https://www.bia.gov/about-us

Cambron-McCabe, N. H., McCarthy, M. M., & Thomas, S. B. (2004). *Public school law: Teachers' and students' rights* (5th ed.). Boston, MA: Pearson.

Canter, L., & Canter, M. (1992). *Assertive discipline: Positive behavior management for today's classrooms.* Santa Monica, CA: Lee Canter & Associates.

Carnine, D. W., Silbert, J., Kame'enui, E. J., Tarver, S. G., & Archer, A. L. (2012). *Direct instruction reading.* Upper Saddle River, NJ: Prentice Hall.

Cavanagh, T. (2018). Restorative justice: An alternative approach to school discipline. In G. E. Hall, L. F. Quinn, & D. M. Gollnick (Eds.), *The handbook of teaching and learning* (pp. 529–548). Hoboken, NJ: Wiley.

Center for Research on Education, Diversity & Excellence. (n.d.). *Five standards for effective pedagogy and learning.* Retrieved from http://manoa.hawaii.edu/coe/credenational/the-crede-five-standards-for-effective-pedagogy-and-learning/

Center for Research on Education Outcomes. (2013). *National charter school study: 2013.* Stanford, CA: Author, Stanford University. Retrieved from http://credo.stanford.edu/documents/NCSS%202013%20Final%20Draft.pdf

Center on Teaching and Learning, University of Oregon. (n.d.). *Big ideas in beginning reading.* Eugene: Author. Retrieved from http://reading.uoregon.edu/big_ideas/voc/voc_what.php

Center on the Developing Child at Harvard University. (2016). *From best practices to breakthrough impacts: A science-based approach to building a more promising future for young children and families.* Retrieved from https://developingchild.harvard.edu/resources/from-best-practices-to-breakthrough-impacts/

Centers for Disease Control and Prevention. (2015). *Suicide: Facts at a glance 2015.* Retrieved from https://www.cdc.gov/violenceprevention/pdf/suicide-datasheet-a.pdf

Centers for Disease Control and Prevention. (n.d.). *The obesity epidemic and United States students.* Retrieved from https://www.cdc.gov/healthyyouth/data/yrbs/pdf/us_obesity_combo.pdf

Cheang, J. (2018, May 7). *Asian American mental health and the "model minority" myth.* Alexandria, VA: Mental Health America. Retrieved from http://www.mentalhealthamerica.net/blog/asian-american-mental-health-and-%E2%80%98model-minority%E2%80%99-myth

Child Trends. (2016, December 1). *It matters—Parental involvement in school.* Retrieved from https://www.childtrends.org/multimedia/matters-parental-involvement-school/

Child Trends. (2018, February). *Making the grade: Integrated student supports.* Retrieved from https://www.childtrends.org/videos/making-grade-integrated-student-supports/

Children's Defense Fund. (2015). *Ending child poverty now.* Washington, DC: Author. Retrieved from http://www.childrensdefense.org/library/PovertyReport/EndingChildPovertyNow.html

Choi, J. (2012). Teaching strategies. In G. E. Hall, L. F. Quinn, & D. M. Gollnick (Eds.), *Introduction to teaching: Making a difference in student learning* (pp. 383–413). Thousand Oaks, CA: Sage.

Churchill, W. S. (1943, October 28). *Speech to the House of Commons.* Meeting in the House of Lords. Retrieved from https://api.parliament.uk/historic-hansard/commons/1943/oct/28/house-of-commons-rebuilding

Clark, C. M., & Peterson, P. L. (1986). Teachers' thought processes. In M. C. Wittrock (Ed.), *Handbook of research on teaching* (pp. 255–314). New York, NY: Macmillan.

Cleveland Board of Education v. LeFleur, 414 U.S. 632 (1974).

Cohen, P. N. (2017, September). Families are changing—And staying the same. *Educational Leadership, 75*(1), 46–50.

Collins, E., & Scott, P. (1978). Everyone who makes it has a mentor. *Harvard Business Review, 56*(4), 89–101.

¡Colorin colorado! (n.d.). *How to create a welcoming classroom environment.* Washington, DC: Author. Retrieved from http://www.colorincolorado.org/educators/reachingout/welcoming/

Comfort v. Lynn School Committee, 126 S.Ct. 798 (2005).

Common Core State Standards Initiative. (n.d.). *Standards-setting criteria.* Retrieved from http://www.corestandards.org/assets/Criteria.pdf

Cooper v. Aaron, 358 U.S. 1 (1958).

Council of Chief State School Officers. (2013, April). *InTASC Model Core Teaching Standards and Learning Progressions for Teachers 1.0*. Washington, DC: Author.

Cox, J. W., & Rich, S. (2018, March 25). Scarred by school shootings. *The Washington Post*. Retrieved from https://www.washington post.com/graphics/2018/local/us-school-shootings-history/?noredirect =on&utm_term=.27e30b0dd9b1

Craig, S. E. (2017). *Trauma-sensitive schools for the adolescent years: Promoting resiliency and healing, Grades 6–12*. New York, NY: Teachers College Press.

Cremin, L. A. (1951). *The American common school: An historical conception*. New York, NY: Teachers College Press, Columbia University.

Cuban, L. (2004). Why has frequent high school reform since World War II produced disappointing results again, and again, and again? In *Using rigorous evidence to improve policy and practice: Colloquium report*. New York: MDRC. Retrieved from https://www.mdrc.org/publications/391/conf_agenda.html

Danielson, C. (1996). *Enhancing professional practice: A framework for teaching*. Alexandria, VA: Association for Supervision and Curriculum Development.

Darling-Hammond, L. (1999). *Teacher quality and student achievement: A review of state policy evidence*. Seattle: Center for the Study of Teaching and Policy, University of Washington.

Darling-Hammond, L. (2013). Inequality and school resources: What it will take to close the opportunity gap. In P. L. Carter & K. G. Welner (Eds.), *Closing the opportunity gap: What America must do to give every child an even chance* (pp. 77–97). New York, NY: Oxford University Press.

Darling-Hammond, L., Hammerness, K., Grossman, P., Rust, F., & Shulman, L. (2005). The design of teacher education programs. In L. Darling-Hammond & J. Bransford (Eds.), *Preparing teachers for a changing world: What teachers should learn and be able to do* (pp. 390–441). San Francisco, CA: Jossey-Bass.

Davis, L. C. (2015, August 31). When mindfulness meets the classroom. *The Atlantic*. Retrieved from https://www.theatlantic.com/education/archive/2015/08/mindfulness-education-schools-meditation/402469/

Davis, M. R., & Loewus, L. (2017, November 7). Students share lessons learned about personalized learning. *Education Week, 37*(12), 25–28.

Degner, J. (2016, November 15). How universal design for learning creates culturally accessible classrooms. *Education Week*. Retrieved from https://www.edweek.org/tm/articles/2016/11/14/udl-creates-cultural-competency-in-classroom.html

deLara, E. W. (2016). *Bullying scars: The impact on adult life and relationships*. New York, NY: Oxford University Press.

DePaoli, J. L., Balfanz, R., Bridgeland, J., Atwell, M., & Ingram, E. S. (2017). *Building a grad nation: Progress and challenge in raising high school graduation rates* (2017 Annual Update). Retrieved from http://new.every1graduates.org/wp-content/uploads/2017/05/2017-BGN-Report-vFINAL.pdf

Dewey, J. (1933). *How we think: A restatement of the relation of reflective thinking to the educative process* (2nd ed.). Boston, MA: Houghton Mifflin.

Dewey, J. (1943). *The school and society*. Chicago, IL: University of Chicago Press.

Dewey, J. (1963). *Experience in education*. New York, NY: Collier Books.

Dewey, J. (1997). *Democracy and education*. Detroit, MI: Free Press.

Downey, L. W. (1988). *Policy analysis in education*. Calgary, Alberta, Canada: Detselig Enterprises.

Doyle, W. (1986). Classroom organization and management. In M. Wittrock (Ed.), *Handbook of research on teaching* (3rd ed., pp. 392–431). New York, NY: Macmillan.

Duckworth, E. (1996). *The having of wonderful ideas and other essays on teaching and learning* (2nd ed.). New York, NY: Teachers College Press.

Duke, J. H. (1982). Foreword. In R. Valdez (Ed.), *The wild sheep of the world*. Mesilla, NM: Wild Sheep and Goat International.

Dweck, C. (2007). *Mindset: The new psychology of success*. New York, NY: Random House/Ballantine Books.

East Hartford Education Association v. Board of Education of Town of East Hartford, 562 F.2d 838 (1977).

ED*Facts* Data Groups 695 and 696. (2017, October 25). *Table 1. Public high school 4-year adjusted cohort graduation rate (ACGR), by race/ethnicity and selected demographic characteristics for the United States, the 50 states, and the District of Columbia: School year 2015–16*. Washington, DC: National Center for Education Statistics, U.S. Department of Education. Retrieved from https://nces.ed.gov/ccd/tables/ACGR_RE_and_character istics_2015-16.asp

Edwards, P. A. (2016). *New ways to engage parents: Strategies and tools for teachers and leaders, K–12*. New York, NY: Teachers College Press.

Eliot, L. (2012). *Pink brain, blue brain: How small differences grow into troublesome gaps—and what we can do about it*. London, United Kingdom: Oneworld.

Elliott, E. (2003). *Assessing education candidate performance: A look at changing practices*. Washington, DC: National Council for Accreditation of Teacher Education.

Elliott, E. (2005). *Student learning in NCATE accreditation*. Washington, DC: National Council for the Accreditation of Teacher Education.

Englander, E. K. (2013). *Bullying and cyberbullying: What every educator needs to know*. Cambridge, MA: Harvard University Press.

Epstein, J. L. (2018). *School, family and community partnerships: Your handbook for action* (4th ed.). Thousand Oaks, CA: Corwin.

Everson v. Board of Education, 330 U.S. 1 (1947).

Evertson, C., & Emmer, E. T. (2013). *Classroom management for elementary teachers* (9th ed.). Upper Saddle River, NJ: Pearson.

Every Student Succeeds Act of 2015, Pub. L. No. 114–95 § 114 Stat. 1177 (2015).

Everyone Graduates Center. (2018). *Early warning and response systems*. Baltimore, MD: The Johns Hopkins University School of Education. Retrieved from http://new.every1graduates.org/tools-and-models/early-warning-and-response-systems/

Faria, A., Sorensen, N., Heppen, J., Bowdon, J., Taylor, S., Eisner, R., & Foster, S. (2017, April). *Getting students on track for graduation: Impacts of the early warning intervention and monitoring system after one year*. Washington, DC: Institute of Education Sciences, U.S. Department of Education & Regional Educational Laboratory at American Institutes for Research. Retrieved from https://ies.ed.gov/ncee/edlabs/projects/project.asp?projectID=388

Farkas, S., Johnson, J., & Duffett, A. (1999). *Playing their parts: What parents and teachers really mean by parental involvement*. New York, NY: Public Agenda.

Federal Interagency Forum on Child and Family Statistics. (2017). *America's children: Key national indicators of well-being, 2017*. Retrieved from https://www.childstats.gov/pdf/ac2017/ac_17.pdf

Federal Register. (2018, May 8). *Child nutrition programs: Income eligibility guidelines*. Retrieved from https://www.federalregister.gov/documents/2018/05/08/2018-09679/child-nutrition-programs-income-eligibility-guidelines

Feldman, D. L., Smith, A. T., & Waxman, B. L. (2017). *"Why we drop out": Understanding and disrupting student pathways to leaving school*. New York, NY: Teachers College Press.

Fine, C. (2011). *Delusions of gender: How our minds, society, and neurosexism create difference.* New York, NY: Norton.

Fish, D. W. (Ed.). (1867). *The American educational series: A full course of practical and progressive text-books; and almanac.* New York, NY: Ivison, Phinney, Blakeman & Co.

Fisher v. University of Texas at Austin, 136 S.Ct. 2198 (2016).

Flesch, R. (1955). *Why Johnny can't read.* New York, NY: Harper & Row.

Flesch, R. (1983). *Why Johnny still can't read.* New York, NY: Harper & Row.

Florey v. Sioux Falls School District, 619 F.2d 1311 (1980).

The 49th annual PDK poll of the public's attitudes toward the public schools. (2017, September). *Phi Delta Kappan, 99*(1), K1–K32. https://doi.org/10.1177/0031721717728274

The 50th annual PDK poll of the public's attitudes toward the public schools. (2018, September). *Teaching: Respect but dwindling appeal.* Retrieved from http://pdkpoll.org/assets/downloads/pdkpoll50_2018.pdf

Freiberg, J. H., & Driscoll, A. (2004). *Universal teaching strategies.* Boston, MA: Allyn & Bacon.

Freire, P. (1967). *Education as the practice of freedom.* London: Writers and Readers Publishing Cooperative.

Freire, P. (1970). *Pedagogy of the oppressed.* New York, NY: Continnum.

Froyen, L. A., & Iverson, A. M. (1999). *Schoolwide and classroom management: The reflective educator-leader* (3rd ed.). Upper Saddle River, NJ: Prentice Hall.

Fruth, J., & Woods, M. (2015). Academic performance of students without disabilities in the inclusive environment. *Education, 135*(3), 351–361.

Fuller, F. (1969). Concerns of teachers: A developmental conceptualization. *American Educational Research Journal, 6*(2), 207–226.

Gagné, R. M. (1985). *The conditions of learning and theory of instruction.* New York, NY: CBS College.

Gándara, P. (2013). Meeting the needs of language minorities. In P. L. Carter & K. G. Welner (Eds.), *Closing the opportunity gap: What America must do to give every child an even chance* (pp. 156–168). New York, NY: Oxford University Press.

Garcetti v. Ceballos, 547 U.S. 410 (2006).

Gardner, H. (2011). *Frames of mind: The theory of multiple intelligences.* New York, NY: Basic Books.

Gathercoal, F. (1997). *Judicious discipline* (4th ed.). San Francisco, CA: Caddo Gap Press.

Gay, G. (2010). *Culturally responsive teaching: Theory, research and practice* (2nd ed.). New York, NY: Teachers College Press.

Gay, G. (2018). *Culturally responsive teaching: Theory, research, and practice* (3rd ed.). New York, NY: Teachers College Press.

Gershenson, S., & Papageorge, N. (2018, Winter). The power of teacher expectations: How racial bias hinders student attainment. *EducationNext, 18*(1). Retrieved from http://educationnext.org/power-of-teacher-expectations-racial-bias-hinders-student-attainment/

Giroux, H. A. (2010). Rethinking education as the practice of freedom: Paulo Freire and the promise of critical pedagogy. *Policy Futures in Education, 8*(6). Retrieved from http://journals.sagepub.com/doi/pdf/10.2304/pfie.2010.8.6.715

Gladwell, M. (2009). *What the dog saw: And other adventures.* New York, NY: Little, Brown.

Glasser, W. (1997). A new look at school failure and school success. *Phi Delta Kappan, 78*(8), 597–602.

Glenn, C. L. (2011). *American Indian/First Nations schooling.* New York, NY: Palgrave Macmillan.

Goldhaber, D. D., & Anthony, E. (2004). Can teacher quality be effectively assessed? *Urban Institute.* Retrieved from http://www.urban.org/url.cfm?ID=410958

Gonzaga University v. Doe, 536 U.S. 273 (2002).

Gonzalez, T., & Mulligan, E. (2014). Creating classrooms for all learners. In E. B. Kozleski & K. K. Thorius (Eds.), *Ability, equity, & culture: Sustaining inclusive urban education reform* (pp. 107–133). New York, NY: Teachers College Press.

Gordon, T. (1989). *Teaching children self-discipline: Promoting self-discipline in children.* New York, NY: Penguin.

Gorski, P. (2013). *Reaching and teaching students in poverty: Strategies for erasing the opportunity gap.* New York, NY: Teachers College Press.

Goss v. Lopez, 419 U.S. 565 (1975).

Graff, C. S., & Vazquez, S. L. (2014). Family resistance as a tool in urban school reform. In E. B. Kozleski & K. K. Thorius (Eds.), *Ability, equity, & culture: Sustaining inclusive urban education reform* (pp. 80–104). New York, NY: Teachers College Press.

Grant, L. (2004). Everyday schooling and the elaboration of race-gender stratification. In J. H. Ballantine & J. Z. Spade (Eds.), *Schools and society: A sociological approach to education* (2nd ed., pp. 296–307). Belmont, CA: Wadsworth/Thomson.

Gratz v. Bollinger, 539 U.S. 244 (2003).

Green v. County School Board of New Kent County, 391 U.S. 430 (1968).

Greene, M. (1988). *The dialectic of freedom.* New York, NY: Teachers College Press.

Gruenert, S., & Whitaker, T. (2015). *School culture rewired: How to define, assess, and transform it.* Alexandria, VA: ASCD.

Grumet, M. R. (1988). *Bitter milk: Women and teaching.* Amherst: University of Massachusetts Press.

Grutter v. Bollinger, 539 U.S. 306 (2003).

Guasco, M. (2017, September 4). The fallacy of 1619: Rethinking the history of Africans in early America. *Black Perspectives.* Retrieved from https://www.aaihs.org/the-fallacy-of-1619-rethinking-the-history-of-africans-in-early-america/

Gutek, G. L. (1986). *Education in the United States: An historical perspective.* Englewood Cliffs, NJ: Prentice Hall.

Gutek, G. L. (2002). History of elementary education. In G. L. Gutek, J. McCarthy, L. F. Quinn, K. R. Howey, & L. M. Post (Eds.), *Encyclopedia of education.* Retrieved from http://www.encyclopedia.com/doc/1G2-3403200209.html

Gutek, G. L. (2012). *Friedrich Froebel (1782–1852)—Biography, Froebel's kindergarten philosophy, the kindergarten curriculum, diffusion of the kindergarten.* Retrieved from http://education.stateuniversity.com/pages/1999/Froebel-Friedrich-1782-1852.html

Guttmacher Institute. (2017, September). *Adolescent sexual and reproductive health in the United States.* Retrieved from https://www.guttmacher.org/fact-sheet/american-teens-sexual-and-reproductive-health

Hakuta, K., Butler, Y. G., & Witt, D. (2000). *How long does it take English learners to attain proficiency?* Berkeley: The University of California Linguistic Minority Research Institute. Retrieved from https://web.stanford.edu/~hakuta/Publications/%282000%29%20-%20HOW%20LONG%20DOES%20IT%20TAKE%20ENGLISH%20LEARNERS%20TO%20ATTAIN%20PR.pdf

Hall, G. E., & Hord, S. M. (2015). *Implementing change: Patterns, principles and potholes* (4th ed.). Upper Saddle River, NJ: Pearson.

Hamilton, L., Halverson, R., Jackson, S. S., Mandinach, E., Supovitz, J., & Wayman, J. D. (2009, September). *Using student achievement data to support instructional decision making.* Washington, DC: U.S. Department of Education, Institute of Education Sciences, National Center for Education Evaluation and Regional Assistance.

Harold, B. (2016, October). Personalized learning: What does the research say? *Education Week, 36*(9), 14–15.

Harold, B. (2017, November 7). 6 key insights: RAND Corp. *Education Week, 37*(12), 10–11.

Hattie, J. (2009). *Visible learning: A synthesis of over 800 meta-analyses relating to achievement.* New York, NY: Routledge.

Heddens, J. W., Speer, W. R., & Brahier, D. J. (2009). *Today's mathematics: Concepts, methods, and classroom activities* (12th ed.). New York, NY: Wiley.

Henderson, A., & Mapp, K. (2002). *A new wave of evidence: The impact of school, family, and community connections on student achievement.* National Center for Family and Community Connections with Schools. Austin: Southwest Educational Development Laboratory. Retrieved from http://www.sedl.org/connections/resources/evidence.pdf

Hendrie, C. (2000). In black and white. In *Education Week, Lessons of a century: A nation's schools come of age.* Bethesda, MD: Editorial Projects in Education.

Henry, G. T., Bastian, K. C., & Fortner, C. K. (2011). Stayers and leavers: Early-career teacher effectiveness and attrition. *Educational Researcher, 40*(6), 271–280.

Henry J. Kaiser Family Foundation. (2014, August). *Sexual health of adolescents and young adults in the United States.* Retrieved from https://kaiserfamilyfoundation.files.wordpress.com/2014/08/3040-08-sexual-health-of-adolescents-and-young-adults-in-the-united-states.pdf

Heppen, J. B., & Therriault, S. B. (2009). *Developing early warning systems to identify potential high school dropouts.* Washington, DC: National High School Center, American Institutes for Research.

Hernandez, D. J. (2011). *Double jeopardy: How third-grade reading skills and poverty influence high school graduation.* Baltimore, MD: The Annie E. Casey Foundation.

Hill, C., & Kearl, H. (2011). *Crossing the line: Sexual harassment at school.* Washington, DC: American Association of University Women.

Hirsch, E. D., Jr. (1987). *Cultural literacy: What every American needs to know.* New York, NY: Knopf Doubleday.

Hixson, L., Hepler, B. B., & Kim, M. O. (2012, May). The Native Hawaiian and other Pacific Islander population 2010. In *2010 1 Briefs* (C2010BR-12). Retrieved from http://www.census.gov/library/publications/2012/dec/c2010br-12.html

Hobson v. Hansen, 269 F. Supp. 401 (1967).

Hoerr, T. R. (2014, April). Tips for better parent-teacher conferences. *Educational Leadership, 71*(7), 86–87.

Hollins, E. R. (2011). The meaning of culture in learning to teach: The power of socialization and identity formation. In A. F. Ball & C. A. Tyson (Eds.), *Studying diversity in teacher education* (pp. 105–130). Washington, DC: American Educational Research Association.

Hong, S. (2011). *A cord of three strands: A new approach to parent engagement in schools.* Cambridge, MA: Harvard Education Press.

Hopwood v. Texas, 78 F.3d 932 (5th Cir. 1996).

Hord, S. M. (2004). Professional learning communities: An overview. In S. M. Hord (Ed.), *Learning together, leading together: Changing schools through professional learning communities* (Chapter 2). New York, NY: Teachers College Press.

Howard, T. C. (2014). *Why race and culture matter in schools: Closing the achievement gap in America's classrooms.* New York, NY: Teachers College Press.

Howton, R. (2017, August 7). Turn your classroom into a personalized learning environment. *ISTE.* Retrieved from https://www.iste.org/explore/articleDetail?articleid=416

Hudson, P. (2017). Five reasons why listening is important for teachers. *International Teacher Magazine.* Retrieved from https://consiliumeducation.com/itm/2016/09/28/five-reasons-why-listening-is-important-for-teachers/

Hunter, M. (1994). *Enhancing teaching.* New York, NY: Macmillan College Publishing.

Hussar, W. J., & Bailey, T. M. (2014, February). *Projections of education statistics to 2022* (41st ed.). Washington, DC: Institute of Education Sciences, National Center for Education Statistics, U.S. Department of Education. Retrieved from https://nces.ed.gov/pubs2014/2014051.pdf

Ingersoll, R. M. (2003). *Is there really a teacher shortage?* Seattle: Center for the Study of Teaching and Policy, University of Washington.

Ingersoll, R., Merrill, L., & May, H. (2014). *What are the effects of teacher education and preparation on beginning teacher attrition?* CPRE Research Report (#RR-82). Philadelphia: Consortium for Policy Research in Education, University of Pennsylvania.

Ingersoll, R., Merrill, L., & Stuckey, D. (2014, April). *Seven trends: The transformation of the teaching force.* CPRE Research Report (#RR-80). Philadelphia: Consortium for Policy Research in Education, University of Pennsylvania.

Ingraham v. Wright, 430 U.S. 651 (1977).

Institute for Educational Leadership & Coalition for Community Schools. (2017). *Community schools: A whole-child framework for school improvement.* Washington, DC: Institute for Educational Leadership.

Investigations in number, data, and space: Grade 5. (2007). Upper Saddle River, NJ: Pearson/Prentice Hall.

Irvine, J., & York, D. (2001). Learning styles and culturally diverse students: A literature review. In J. Banks & C. Banks (Eds.), *Handbook of research on multicultural education* (pp. 484–497). San Francisco, CA: Jossey-Bass.

Iverson, A. M. (2003). *Building competence in classroom management and discipline* (4th ed.). Columbus, OH: Merrill Prentice Hall.

Jacobson, R., & Blank, M. J. (2015). *A framework for more and better learning through community school partnerships.* Washington, DC: Coalition for Community Schools and Institute for Educational Leadership.

Jacobson, R., Villarreal, L., Muñoz, J., & Mahaffey, R. (2018, February). It takes a community. *Educational Leadership, 99*(5), 8–14.

Jamentz, K. (2002). *Isolation is the enemy of improvement: Instructional leadership to support standards-based practice.* San Francisco, CA: WestEd.

James, W. (1975). *Pragmatism.* Cambridge, MA: Harvard University Press.

Janus v. American Federation of State, County, and Municipal Employees, Council 31, No. 16-1466, 585 U.S. ___ (2018).

John Dewey (1859–1952): Experience and reflective thinking, learning, school and life, democracy and education. (n.d.). *StateUniversity.com.* Retrieved from http://education.stateuniversity.com/pages/1914/Dewey-John-1859-1952.html

Johnson, D. W., & Johnson, R. T. (1990). Social skills for successful group work. *Educational Leadership, 47*(4), 30–32.

Johnson, D. W., & Johnson, R. T. (1999a). *Learning together and alone: Cooperative, competitive and individualistic learning* (5th ed.). Boston, MA: Allyn & Bacon.

Johnson, D. W., & Johnson, R. T. (1999b). The three Cs of school and classroom management. In H. J. Freiberg & J. E. Brophy (Eds.), *Beyond behaviorism: Changing the classroom management paradigm* (pp. 119–144). Boston, MA: Allyn & Bacon.

Johnson, L. B. (1965, January 12). *The educational message to Congress.* Retrieved from http://www.lbjlibrary.net/collections/on-this-day-in-history/january.html

Jones, F. (2003). More time on task, less goofing off. *Tools for Teaching: Discipline, Instruction, Motivation.* Santa Cruz, CA: Fredric H. Jones & Associates.

Jordan-Young, R. M. (2011). *Brainstorm: The flaws in the science of sex differences*. Cambridge, MA: Harvard University Press.

Joyce, B. R., & Weil, M. (2000). *Models of teaching* (6th ed.). Boston, MA: Allyn & Bacon.

Joyce, B., & Weil, M. (2008). *Models of teaching* (8th ed.). Englewood Cliffs, NJ: Prentice Hall.

J. S. v. Blue Mountain School District, 593 F.3d 286 (2010).

Kaestle, C. F. (1983). *Pillars of the republic: Common schools and American society, 1780–1860*. New York, NY: Hill & Wang.

Kaestle, C. F., & Radway, J. A. (2009). *A history of the book in America: Print in motion: The expansion of publishing and reading in the United States, 1880–1940*. Chapel Hill: University of North Carolina Press.

Kagan, J. (1998). *Three seductive ideas*. Cambridge, MA: Harvard University Press.

Kalambouka, A., Farrell, P., Dyson, A., & Kaplan, I. (2007). The impact of placing pupils with special educational needs in mainstream schools on the achievement of their peers. *Educational Research, 49*(4), 365–382.

Kamenetz, A. (2014, November 8). 5 great teachers on what makes a great teacher. *NPREd*. Retrieved from http://www.npr.org/sections/ed/2014/11/08/360426108/five-great-teachers-on-what-makes-a-great-teacher

Kang-Brown, J., Trone, J., Fratello, J., & Daftary-Kapur, T. (2013). *A generation later: What we've learned about zero tolerance in schools*. Washington, DC: Vera Institute of Justice, Center on Youth Justice.

Kauchak, D., & Eggen, P. (2005). *Introduction to teaching: Becoming a professional* (2nd ed.). Upper Saddle River, NJ: Merrill Prentice Hall.

Kessler, R. C., Amminger, G. P., Aguilar-Gaxiola, S., Alonso, J., Lee, S., & Ustim, T. B. (2007, July). Age of onset of mental disorders: A review of recent literature. *Current Opinion in Psychiatry, 20*(4), 359–364. doi:10.1097/YCO.0b013e32816ebc8c

Kiang, D. (2018, June 19). Strategies for supporting girls in computer science. *Education Week* blogs. Retrieved from http://blogs.edweek.org/edweek/edtechresearcher/2018/06/when_i_started_teaching_computer.html?M=58524517&U=1712656&cmp=eml-enl-dd-news3-rm&print=1

Kimmel, M. (2009). *Guyland: The perilous world where boys become men*. New York, NY: Harper.

Kinsey Institute. (2017). *Historical report: Diversity of sexual orientation*. Retrieved from https://kinseyinstitute.org/research/publications/historical-report-diversity-of-sexual-orientation.php

Klein, A. (2016, March 31). The Every Student Succeeds Act: An ESSA overview. *Education Week*. Retrieved from http://www.edweek.org/ew/issues/every-student-succeeds-act/

Kliebard, H. M. (2004). *The struggle for the American curriculum, 1893–1958*. New York, NY: Routledge.

Knox County Education Association v. Knox County Board of Education, 158 F.3d 361 (1998).

Koball, H., & Jiang, Y. (2018, January). *Basic facts about low-income children*. New York, NY: National Center for Children in Poverty. Retrieved from http://www.nccp.org/publications/pdf/text_1194.pdf

Kohn, A. (2006). *Beyond discipline: From compliance to community* (2nd ed.). Alexandria, VA: Association of Supervision and Curriculum Development.

Kolb, D. A., & Fry, R. E. (1974). *Toward an applied theory of experiential learning*. Cambridge, MA: MIT Alfred P. Sloan School of Management.

Kosciw, J. G., Greytak, E. A., Giga, N. M., Villenas, C., & Danischewski, D. J. (2016). *The 2015 National School Climate Survey: The experiences of lesbian, gay, bisexual, transgender, and queer youth in our nation's schools*. New York, NY: Gay, Lesbian & Straight Education Network. Retrieved from https://www.glsen.org/sites/default/files/2015%20National%20GLSEN%202015%20National%20School%20Climate%20Survey%20%28NSCS%29%20-%20Full%20Report_0.pdf

Kosslyn, S. M., & Miller, G. W. (2013, November 29). There is no left brain/right brain divide. *Time*. Retrieved from http://ideas.time.com/2013/11/29/there-is-no-left-brainright-brain-divide/

Kottler, J. A., Zehm, S. J., & Kottler, E. (2005). *On being a teacher* (3rd ed.). Thousand Oaks, CA: Corwin.

Kozol, J. (2007, September). Letters to a young teacher. *Phi Delta Kappan: The Journal for Education*, 8–20.

Krebs, C. P., Lindquist, C. H., Warner, T. D., Fisher, B. S., & Martin, S. L. (2009). College women's experiences with physically forced, alcohol- or other drug-enabled, and drug-facilitated sexual assault before and since entering college. *Journal of American College Health, 57*(6), 639–647.

Krogstad, J. M., & Gonzalez-Barrera, A. G. (2018, February 26). Key facts about U.S. immigration policies and proposed changes. *Pew Research Center*. Retrieved from http://www.pewresearch.org/fact-tank/2018/02/26/key-facts-about-u-s-immigration-policies-and-proposed-changes/

Krogstad, J. M., Passel, J. S., & Cohn, D. (2017, April 27). 5 facts about illegal immigration in the U.S. *Pew Research Center*. Retrieved from http://www.pewresearch.org/fact-tank/2017/04/27/5-facts-about-illegal-immigration-in-the-u-s/

Kubota, R., & Lin, A. (2009). Race, culture, and identities in second language education: Introduction to research and practice. In R. Kubota & A. Lin (Eds.), *Race, culture, and identities in second language education: Exploring critically engaged practice* (pp. 1–23). New York, NY: Routledge.

Landis, R., & Reschly, A. (2013). Reexamining gifted underachievement and dropout through the lens of student engagement. *Journal for the Education of the Gifted, 36*(2), 220–249.

Lau v. Nichols, 414 U.S. 563 (1974).

Lawrence, D. H. (1915). *The rainbow*. New York, NY: Random House.

Lawson, A. E. (1995). *Science teaching and the development of thinking*. Belmont, CA: Wadsworth.

Layshock v. Hermitage School District, 593 F.3d 249 (2010).

Lemon v. Kurtzman, 403 U.S. 602 (1971).

Lemov, D. (2010). *Teach like a champion*. San Francisco, CA: Jossey-Bass.

Lieberman, A., & Miller, L. (1984). *Teachers, their world, and their work: Implications for school improvement*. Alexandria, VA: Association for Supervision and Curriculum Development.

Linder, D. (2002). *The Scopes trial: An introduction*. Kansas City: University of Missouri–Kansas City School of Law.

López, G., & Bialik, K. (2017, May 3). Key findings about U.S. immigrants. *Pew Research Center*. Retrieved from http://www.pewresearch.org/fact-tank/2017/05/03/key-findings-about-u-s-immigrants/

Lopez, M. H., Krogstad, J. M., & Flores, A. (2018, April 2). Most Hispanic parents speak Spanish to their children, but this is less the case in later immigrant generations. *Pew Research Center*. Retrieved from http://www.pewresearch.org/fact-tank/2018/04/02/most-hispanic-parents-speak-spanish-to-their-children-but-this-is-less-the-case-in-later-immigrant-generations/

Lopez, S. J., & Sidhu, P. (2013). U.S. teachers love their lives, but struggle in the workplace. *Gallup*. Retrieved from http://www.gallup.com/poll/161516/teachers-love-lives-struggle-workplace.aspx

Lortie, D. C. (1975). *Schoolteacher: A sociological study*. Chicago, IL: University of Chicago Press.

Lortie, D. C. (1977). *Schoolteacher: A sociological study* (2nd ed.). Chicago, IL: University of Chicago Press.

Losen, D. J. (2011). *Discipline policies, successful schools, and racial justice*. Boulder: National Education Policy Center, University of Colorado.

Lotkina, V. (2016, September 15). What communication apps got wrong about parental engagement. In *Education Week's Education futures: Emerging trends in K–12*. Retrieved from http://blogs.edweek.org/edweek/education_futures/2016/09/what_communication_apps_got_wrong_about_parent_engagement.html

Lu, A. (2014, June). Common Core sparks flood of legislation. *Las Vegas Sun*, p. 1. Retrieved from stateline.org

Lucas, J. L., Blazek, M. A., Raley, A. B., & Washington, C. (2005). The lack of representation of educational psychology and school psychology in introductory psychology textbooks. *Educational Psychology, 25*, 347–351.

Martin, J. (2002). *The education of John Dewey: A biography*. New York, NY: Columbia University Press.

Martin, J. A., Hamilton, B. E., Osterman, M. J. K., Curtin, S. C., & Matthews, T. J. (2013, December 30). Births: Final data for 2012. *National Vital Statistics Reports, 62*(9). Retrieved from http://www.cdc.gov/nchs/data/nvsr/nvsr62/nvsr62_09.pdf

Martin, J. A., Hamilton, B. E., Osterman, M. J. K., Curtin, S. C., & Matthews, T. J. (2015, January 15). Births: Final data for 2013. *National Vital Statistics Reports, 64*(1).

Martin, S. E. (2014, April 7). Troops to Teachers program offers post-Army careers. *Army Flier*. Retrieved from https://www.army.mil/article/123290/troops_to_teachers_program_offers_post_army_careers

Marzano, R. J., Pickering, D. J., & Pollack, J. E. (2001). *Classroom instruction that works: Research-based strategies for increasing student achievement*. Alexandria, VA: Association for Supervision and Curriculum Development.

Masci, D., Brown, A., & Kiley, J. (2017, June 20). 5 facts about same-sex marriage. *Pew Research Center*. Retrieved from http://www.pewresearch.org/fact-tank/2017/06/26/same-sex-marriage/

May, H., & Robinson, M. A. (2007). *A randomized evaluation of Ohio's Personalized Assessment Reporting System (PARS)*. Philadelphia, PA: Consortium for Policy Research in Education.

McCarthy, N. (2016, March 31). America's most prestigious professions in 2016 [Infographic]. *Forbes*. Retrieved from https://www.forbes.com/sites/niallmccarthy/2016/03/31/americas-most-prestigious-professions-in-2016-infographic/#7bfb026a1926

McEwin, C. K., Dickinson, T. S., & Jenkins, D. M. (2003). *America's middle schools in the new century: Status and progress*. Westerville, OH: National Middle School Association.

McFarland, J., Hussar, B., de Brey, C., Snyder, T., Wang, X., Wilkinson-Flicker, S., . . . Hinz, S. (2017). *The condition of education 2017* (NCES 2017–144). Washington, DC: National Center for Education Statistics, U.S. Department of Education. Retrieved from https://nces.ed.gov/pubsearch/pubsinfo.asp?pubid=2017144

McGrail, E., Sachs, G. T., Many, J., Myrick, C., & Sackor, S. (2011). Technology use in middle-grades teacher preparation programs. *Action in Teacher Education, 33*(1), 63–80.

McNeil, J. D. (2003). *Curriculum: The teacher's initiative* (3rd ed.). Upper Saddle River, NJ: Pearson Education.

Méndez v. Westminster School District, 64 F.Supp. 544 (S.D. Cal. 1946), aff'd, 161 F.2d 774 (9th Cir. 1947) (en banc).

Mendler, A. (2014, January 23). Why do we need to learn this? *Edutopia*. Retrieved from https://www.edutopia.org/blog/why-do-we-need-to-learn-this-allen-mendler

Meredith v. Jefferson County (Kentucky) Board of Education, 551 U.S. 701 (2007).

Meriam, L. (1928). *The problem of Indian administration*. Baltimore, MD: Johns Hopkins Press. Retrieved from https://tm112.community.uaf.edu/files/2010/09/MeriamEducation.pdf

Merikangas, K. R., He, J. P., Burstein, M., Swanson, S. A., Avenevoli, S., Cu, L., . . . Swendsen, J. (2010, October). Lifetime prevalence of mental disorders in U.S. adolescents: Results for the National Comorbidity Survey Replication—Adolescent Supplement (NCS-A). *Journal of American Academy of Child and Adolescent Psychiatry, 49*(10), 980–989.

MetLife. (2012). *MetLife survey of the American teacher: Teachers, parents, and the economy*. Retrieved from https://www.metlife.com/about/corporate-responsibility/metlife-foundation/reports-and-research/survey-american-teacher.html

MetLife. (2013). *Survey of the American teacher: Challenges for school leadership*. Retrieved from https://www.metlife.com/about/corporate-responsibility/metlife-foundation/reports-and-research/survey-american-teacher.html

Meyer, P. (2011, Winter). The middle school mess. *Education Next, 11*(1). Retrieved from http://educationnext.org/the-middle-school-mess/

Miech, R. A., Johnston, L. D., O'Malley, P. M., Bachman, J. G., Schulenberg, J. E., & Patrick, M. E. (2017). *Monitoring the Future national survey results on drug use, 1975–2016: Volume I, Secondary school students*. Ann Arbor, MI: Institute for Social Research. Retrieved from http://www.monitoringthefuture.org/pubs/monographs/mtf-vol1_2016.pdf

Miel, A. (1946). *Changing the curriculum: A social process*. New York, NY: D. Appleton-Century.

Miller v. Mitchell, 598 F.3d 139 (2010).

Miller v. Skumanick, 605 F.Supp.2d 634 (2009).

Milliken v. Bradley, 418 U.S. 717 (1974).

Milner, H. R. (2010). *Start where you are, but don't stay there: Understanding diversity, opportunity gaps, and teaching in today's classrooms*. Cambridge, MA: Harvard University Press.

Milner, H. R., IV. (2015). *Rac(e)ing to class: Confronting poverty and race in schools and classrooms*. Cambridge, MA: Harvard Education Press.

Minahan, J., & Rappaport, N. (2013). *The behavior code: A practical guide to understanding and teaching the most challenging students*. Cambridge, MA: Harvard University Press.

Mitchell, D., Hinueber, J., & Edwards, B. (2017, February). Looking race in the face. *Phi Delta Kappan, 98*(5), 24–29.

Mitchell, D. E., & Mitchell, R. E. (2003). The political economy of education policy: The case of class size reduction. *Peabody Journal of Education, 78*(4), 120–152.

Moore, S. (1998). Proposition 13 then, now and forever. *Cato Institute*. Retrieved from http://www.cato.org/publications/commentary/proposition-13-then-now-forever

Morris, M. W. (2016). *Pushout: The criminalization of black girls in schools*. New York, NY: New Press.

Morton, M. H., Dworsky, A., & Samuels, G. M. (2017). *Missed opportunities: Youth homelessness in America: National estimates*. Chicago, IL: Chapin Hall at the University of Chicago. Retrieved from http://voicesofyouthcount.org/wp-content/uploads/2017/11/ChapinHall_VoYC_NationalReport_Final.pdf

Mt. Healthy City School District Board of Education v. Doyle, 429 U.S. 274 (1977).

Musu-Gillette, L., Robinson, J., McFarland, J., KewalRamani, A., Zhang, A., & Wilkinson-Flicker, S. (2016). *Status and trends in the education of racial and ethnic groups 2016* (NCES 2016–007). Washington, DC: U.S. Department of Education, National Center for Education Statistics. Retrieved from https://nces.ed.gov/pubs2016/2016007.pdf

National Alliance to End Homelessness. (2018). *How many children and families experience homelessness?* Retrieved from https://endhomelessness.org/homelessness-in-america/who-experiences-homelessness/children-and-families/

National Alliance for Nutrition & Activity. (2010). *Factsheet: Healthy, hunger free kids act*. Retrieved from https://cspinet.org/sites/default/files/attachment/hhfka-summary-factsheet.pdf

National Alliance for Public Charter Schools. (2018). *Charter school FAQ*. Retrieved from https://www.publiccharters.org/about-charter-schools/charter-school-faq#different

National Assessment of Educational Progress. (2015a). *Mathematics & reading at Grade 12*. Retrieved from https://www.nationsreportcard.gov/reading_math_g12_2015/#

National Assessment of Educational Progress. (2015b). *The nation's report card*. Retrieved from https://www.nationsreportcard.gov/

National Assessment of Educational Progress. (2017). *The nation's report card: NAEP data explorer*. Washington, DC: U.S. Department of Education. Retrieved from https://www.nationsreportcard.gov/ndecore/xplore/NDE

National Association for Gifted Children. (n.d.). *What is giftedness?* Retrieved from https://www.nagc.org/resources-publications/resources/what-giftedness

National Association for Gifted Children & Council of State Directors of Programs for the Gifted. (2015, November). *2014–2015 state of the states in gifted education*. Retrieved from http://www.nagc.org/sites/default/files/key%20reports/2014-2015%20State%20of%20the%20States%20%28final%29.pdf

National Association of School Psychologists. (2015). *Creating trauma-sensitive schools: Supportive policies and practices for learning*. Bethesda, MD: Author.

National Board for Professional Teaching Standards. (2002). *What teachers should know and be able to do*. Retrieved from http://www.nbpts.org/sites/default/files/what_teachers_should_know.pdf

National Center for Education Statistics. (2016). Table 205.30. *Digest of Education Statistics*. Retrieved from https://nces.ed.gov/programs/digest/d16/tables/dt16_205.30.asp

National Center for Education Statistics. (2017, May). *Indicators of school crime and safety*. Retrieved from https://nces.ed.gov/programs/crimeindicators/ind_08.asp

National Center for Education Statistics. (2018, April). *Children and youth with disabilities*. Retrieved from https://nces.ed.gov/programs/coe/indicator_cgg.asp

National Center for Families Learning. (2014). *Annual survey reveals more parents admit they struggle helping their kids with homework*. Retrieved from http://www.familieslearning.org/public/uploads/press_releases/1411005306.PGuQ.Homework-Survey.pdf

National Center for Health Statistics. (2016). *Health, United States, 2016: With chartbook on long-term trends in health*. Retrieved from https://www.ncbi.nlm.nih.gov/pubmed/28910066

National Clearinghouse for English Language Acquisition. (2017). *Tools and resources for providing English learners with a language assistance program*. Retrieved from https://ncela.ed.gov/files/english_learner_toolkit/2-OELA_2017_language_assist_508C.pdf

National Commission on Excellence in Education. (1983). *A nation at risk: The imperative for educational reform*. Washington, DC: U.S. Department of Education.

National Commission on Teaching and America's Future. (2003). *No dream denied: A pledge to America's children*. Washington, DC: Author.

National Conference of State Legislatures. (2013, June 17). *Postcard: Teen pregnancy affects graduation rates*. Retrieved from http://www.ncsl.org/research/health/teen-pregnancy-affects-graduation-rates-postcard.aspx

National Conference of State Legislatures. (2018). *School vouchers*. Retrieved from http://www.ncsl.org/research/education/school-choice-vouchers.aspx

National Education Association. (2011). School-family engagement: Staff preparation and support are vital. *Policy Brief*. Retrieved from http://199.223.128.55/assets/docs/PB35schoolfamilycommunity2011.pdf

National Education Association. (2013, May). *Wraparound services: An NEA policy brief*. Retrieved from https://www.nea.org/assets/docs/Wraparound-Services-05142013.pdf

National Education Association. (2015, March). *Education support professionals: Meeting the needs of the whole student*. Retrieved from https://www.nea.org/assets/docs/150306-ESP_DIGIBOOK.pdf

National Governors Association & Council of Chief State School Officers. (2015). *Common Core State Standards Initiative frequently asked questions*. Retrieved from http://www.cgcs.org/domain/106

National Institute on Drug Abuse, National Institutes of Health, U.S. Department of Health and Human Services. (2017, December). *Monitoring the future survey: High school and youth trends*. Retrieved from https://www.drugabuse.gov/publications/drugfacts/monitoring-future-survey-high-school-youth-trends

National Physical Activity Plan Alliance, Centers for Disease Control and Prevention. (2016). *Secular changes in physical education attendance among U.S. high school students, YRBS 1991–2013*. Retrieved from https://www.cdc.gov/healthyschools/physicalactivity/pdf/Secular_Trends_PE_508.pdf

National PTA. (n.d.). *History*. Retrieved from https://www.pta.org/home/About-National-Parent-Teacher-Association/Mission-Values/National-PTA-History

National Public Radio, Robert Wood Johnson Foundation, & Harvard T. H. Chan School of Public Health. (2017). *Discrimination in America*. Retrieved from https://www.hsph.harvard.edu/horp/discrimination-in-america/

National Scientific Council on the Developing Child. (2014). *Excessive stress disrupts the architecture of the developing brain: Working paper 3* (Updated ed.). Retrieved from http://www.developingchild.harvard.edu

National Vital Statistics System, National Center for Health Statistics, Centers for Disease Control and Prevention. (2014). *10 leading causes of death by age group, United States—2014*. Retrieved from https://www.cdc.gov/injury/images/lc-charts/leading_causes_of_death_age_group_2014_1050w760h.gif

New Jersey v. T.L.O., 469 U.S. 325 (1985).

New Mexico Public Education Department. (2017–2018). *Student assessment accommodations manual*. Retrieved from https://webnew.ped.state.nm.us/wp-content/uploads/2018/03/Accommodations-Manual-2017-2018_biogrid-changes_final.pdf

NIDA Blog Team. (2016, September 26). *Should schools be ready for opioid overdoses?* Rockville, MD: National Institute on Drug Abuse for Teens. Retrieved from https://teens.drugabuse.gov/blog/post/should-schools-be-ready-opioid-overdoses

Nieto, S. (2018). *Language, culture, and teaching: Critical perspectives* (3rd ed.). New York, NY: Routledge.

Norris, T., Vines, P. L., & Hoeffel, E. M. (2012, January). The American Indian and Alaska Native population: 2010. In *2010 Census Briefs* (C2010BR-10). Retrieved from http://www.census.gov/library/publications/2012/dec/c2010br-10.html

Norton, P., & Wiburg, K. M. (1998). *Teaching with technology*. Orlando, FL: Harcourt Brace.

Nye, B., Konstantopoulos, S., & Hedges, L. V. (2004). How large are teacher effects? *Educational Evaluation and Policy Analysis, 26*(3), 237–257.

Oakes, J. (1985). *Keeping track: How schools structure inequality*. New Haven, CT: Yale University Press.

Oakes, J., Maier, A., & Daniel, J. (2017). *An evidence-based strategy for equitable school improvement*. Boulder, CO: National Education Policy Center and the Learning Policy Institute. Retrieved from https://learningpolicyinstitute.org/product/community-schools-equitable-improvement-brief

OK2BME. (2018). *What does LGBTQ+ mean?* Retrieved from https://ok2bme.ca/resources/kids-teens/what-does-lgbtq-mean/

Oliva, P. (2005). *Developing the curriculum.* Boston, MA: Pearson/Allyn and Bacon.

Oliva, P., & Gordon, W. R., II. (2012). *Developing the curriculum* (8th ed.). Boston, MA: Pearson Education.

Olson, L. (2000). The common good. In *Education Week, Lessons of a century: A nation's schools come of age.* Bethesda, MD: Editorial Projects in Education.

Olson, L. S. (2014, July). *Why September matters: Improving student attendance.* Baltimore, MD: Baltimore Education Research Consortium.

Oner, D., & Adadan, E. (2011). Use of web-based portfolios as tools for reflection in preservice teacher education. *Journal of Teacher Education, 62*(5), 477–492.

Oregon Department of Education. (n.d.). *Essential skills: Definitions and graduation requirements.* Retrieved from https://www.oregon.gov/ode/educator-resources/essentialskills/Documents/es_definitions_grad-requirements.pdf

Orfield, G., & Frankenberg, E. (2014, May 15). *Brown at 60: Great progress, a long retreat and an uncertain future.* Los Angeles, CA: The Civil Rights Project/Proyecto Derechos Civiles. Retrieved from https://www.civilrightsproject.ucla.edu/research/k-12-education/integration-and-diversity/brown-at-60-great-progress-a-long-retreat-and-an-uncertain-future/

Owasso Independent School District v. Falvo, 534 U.S. 426 (2002).

Parents Involved in Community Schools Inc. v. Seattle School District, 551 U.S. 701 (2007).

Passel, J. S., & Cohn, D. (2016, November 17). Children of unauthorized immigrants represent rising share of K–12 students. *Pew Research Center.* Retrieved from http://www.pewresearch.org/fact-tank/2016/11/17/children-of-unauthorized-immigrants-represent-rising-share-of-k-12-students/

Passel, J. S., & Cohn, D. (2017, February 9). 20 metro areas are home to six-in-ten unauthorized immigrants in U.S. *Pew Research Center.* Retrieved from http://www.pewresearch.org/fact-tank/2017/02/09/us-metro-areas-unauthorized-immigrants/

Paulson, A. (2014, September 23). Record number of homeless children enrolled in U.S. public schools. *The Christian Science Monitor.* Retrieved from http://www.csmonitor.com/USA/Education/2014/0923/Record-number-of-homeless-children-enrolled-in-US-public-schools-video

Pennsylvania Department of Education Division of Evaluation and Assessment. (2003). *Testing accommodations for the Pennsylvania System of School Assessment, 2002–2003.* Retrieved from http://www.beitberl.ac.il/centers/hadraha/documents/accomodation.pdf

Perda, D. (2013). *Transitions into and out of teaching: A longitudinal analysis of early career teacher turnover* (Unpublished doctoral dissertation). University of Pennsylvania, Philadelphia.

Perma-Bound School Library. (n.d.). *Texas state standards for science: Grade 4.* Retrieved from www.perma-bound.com/state-standards.do?state=TX&subject=science&gradeLevel=4

Pesce v. J. Sterling Morton High School District 201, Cook County, Illinois, 830 F.2d 789 (1987).

Pew Research Center. (2015, December). *Parenting in education: Outlook, worries, aspirations are strongly linked to financial situation.* Retrieved from http://assets.pewresearch.org/wp-content/uploads/sites/3/2015/12/2015-12-17_parenting-in-america_FINAL.pdf

Pew Research Center. (2018). *Religious landscape study.* Retrieved from http://www.pewforum.org/religious-landscape-study/

Phillips, N. B., Hamlett, C. L., Fuchs, L. S., & Fuchs, D. (1993). Combining classwide curriculum-based measurement and peer tutoring to help general educators provide adaptive education. *Learning Disabilities Research & Practice, 8*(3), 148–156.

Piaget, J. (1985). *The equilibrium of cognitive structures: The central problem of intellectual development* (T. Brown & K. L. Thampy, trans.). Chicago, IL: University of Chicago Press. (Original work published 1932)

Pickering v. Board of Education Township High School District 205, 391 U.S. 563 (1968).

Pierce v. Society of Sisters, 268 U.S. 510 (1925).

Plessy v. Ferguson, 163 U.S. 537 (1896).

Plumb, J. L., Bush, K. A., & Kersevich, S. E. (2016, Spring). Trauma-sensitive schools: An evidence-based approach. *School Social Work Journal, 40*(2), 37–60. Retrieved from http://www.communityschools.org/assets/1/AssetManager/TSS.pdf

Plyler v. Doe, 457 U.S. 202 (1982).

Popham, W. J. (2008). *Transformative assessment.* Alexandria, VA: Association for Supervision and Curriculum Development.

Popham, W. J. (2011). Assessment literacy overlooked: A teacher educator's confession. *The Teacher Educator, 46*(4), 265–273. doi:10.1080/08878730.2011.605048

Prochner, L., Cleghorn, A., & Drefs, J. (2015, May). Our proud heritage: The 200-year legacy of infant schools. *Young Children, 70*(2). Retrieved from https://www.naeyc.org/resources/pubs/yc/may2015/infant-schools

Quay, S. E., & Quaglia, R. J. (2004). Creating a classroom culture that inspires student learning. *The Teaching Professor, 18*(2), 1.

Ray, B. (2016). Research facts on homeschooling. *National Home Education Research Institute.* Retrieved from http://www.nheri.org/research/research-facts-on-homeschooling.html

Redford, K. (2018, January 24). When it comes to universal design for learning, don't wait to be an expert. *Education Week.* https://www.edweek.org/tm/articles/2018/01/24/when-it-comes-to-universal-design-for.html

Regents of the University of California v. Bakke, 438 U.S. 265 (1978).

Reilly, K. (2016, August 30). Is homework good for kids? Here's what the research says. *Time.* Retrieved from http://time.com/4466390/homework-debate-research/

Reutter, E. E., Jr. (1975). The courts and student conduct. *National Organization on Legal Problems of Education.* Retrieved from http://openlibrary.org/works/OL3478740W/The_courts_and_student_conduct

Reynolds, D. (2017, January 12). Gallup Poll: A record number of Americans identify as LGBT. *Advocate.* Retrieved from https://www.advocate.com/people/2017/1/12/gallup-poll-record-number-americans-identify-lgbt

Rich, M. (2013, March 28). Beleaguered? Not teachers, a poll on "well-being" finds. *The New York Times,* Education.

Rich, M. (2014, June 18). Gates Foundation urges moratorium on decisions tied to Common Core. *Las Vegas Sun.* Reprint from *The New York Times* News Service.

Riddick v. School Board of the City of Norfolk, Virginia, 784 F.2d 521, 543 (4th Cir. 1986).

Rivkin, S. G., Hanushek, E. A., & Kain, J. F. (2005). Teachers, schools, and academic achievement. *Econometrica, 73*(2), 417–458.

Robelen, E. W. (2010, June 9). Some lawmakers seeking to rein in Texas board. *Education Week, 29*(33), 1, 20.

Robertson, C. (2004). *Understanding comprehensive reform: Component four: Measurable goals and benchmarks.* SERVE: University of North Carolina, Greensboro. Retrieved from http://.www.serve.org/UCR/UCRCompFour.html

Robinson, S. (2011, February 16). Education master's programs: Add value or shut down. *Education Week*. Corrected June 26, 2015. Retrieved from http://www.edweek.org/ew/articles/2011/02/16/21robinson.h30.html

Rodriguez v. San Antonio Independent School, 337 F. Supp. 280 (1971).

Rogers, C. (1969). *The freedom to learn*. Columbus, OH: Merrill.

Rogers, C., & Freiberg, H. J. (1994). *Freedom to learn*. Upper Saddle River, NJ: Prentice Hall.

Ronfeldt, M. (2012, March). Where should student teachers learn to teach? Effects of field placement school characteristics on teacher retention and effectiveness. *Educational Evaluation and Policy Analysis*, 34(1), 3–26.

Rose v. Council for Better Education, 790 S.W.2d 186 (1989).

Rosenshine, B., & Stevens, R. (1986). Teaching functions. In M. C. Wittrock (Ed.), *Handbook of research on teaching* (3rd ed., pp. 376–391). Upper Saddle River, NJ: Merrill/Prentice Hall.

Rothstein, R. (2013). Why children from lower socioeconomic classes, on average, have lower academic achievement than middle-class children. In P. L. Carter & K. G. Welner (Eds.), *Closing the opportunity gap: What America must do to give every child an even chance* (pp. 61–74). New York, NY: Oxford University Press.

Rousseau, J.-J. (1762). *Émile, ou de l'éducation*. Paris, France: A la Haye.

Rubinkam, M. (2014, May 18). Grade-school math has parents flummoxed. Associated Press. Reprinted in the *Las Vegas Review-Journal*.

Rumberger, R. W. (2011). *Dropping out: Why students drop out of high school and what can be done about it*. Cambridge, MA: Harvard University Press.

Sadaker, M. P., & Sadaker, D. M. (2000). *Teachers, schools, and society*. New York, NY: McGraw-Hill.

San Antonio Independent School District v. Rodriguez, 411 U.S. 1 (1973).

Sanders, W. L., & Rivers, J. C. (1996). *Cumulative and residual effects of teachers on future student academic achievement*. Research Progress Report. Knoxville: University of Tennessee Value-Added Research and Assessment Center.

Santa Fe Independent School District v. Doe, 530 U.S. 290 (2000).

Saylor, J. G., & Alexander W. M. (1974). *Planning curriculum for schools*. Boston, MA: Holt McDougal.

Schuette v. Coalition to Defend Affirmative Action, 133 S.Ct. 1633 (2013).

Schug, M. C., Tarver, S. G., & Western, R. D. (2001). Direct instruction and the teaching of early reading: Wisconsin's teacher-led insurgency. *Wisconsin Policy Research Institute Report*, 14(2).

Senate Committee on Labor and Public Welfare. (1969). *Indian education: A national tragedy—A national challenge*, 91st Cong., 1st sess. Washington, DC: U.S. Government Printing Office.

Shepard, L. A., Penuel, W. R., & Davidson, K. L. (2017, March). Design principles for new systems of assessment. *Phi Delta Kappan*, 98(6).

Shepherd University. (2016). *Teacher shortage documentation*. Retrieved from http://www.shepherd.edu/wordpress-1/wp-content/uploads/2017/03/1__Teacher_Shortage_Documentation.pdf

Shields, C. M. (2002, Spring). A comparison study of student attitudes and perceptions in homogeneous and heterogeneous classrooms. *Roeper Review*, 24(3), 115–120.

Short, D. J., & Boyson, B. A. (2012). *Helping newcomer students succeed in secondary schools and beyond*. Washington, DC: Center for Applied Linguistics.

Shulman, L. (1986). Those who understand: Knowledge growth in teaching. *Educational Researcher*, 15(2), 4–14.

Simms, M. (2017, May 3). *"Model minority" myth hides the economic realities of many Asian Americans*. Washington, DC: Urban Institute. Retrieved from https://www.urban.org/urban-wire/model-minority-myth-hides-economic-realities-many-asian-americans

Simpson, D., Bruckheimer, J., Robins, S., & Foster, L. (Producers), & Smith, J. (Director). (1995). *Dangerous minds* [Motion picture]. U.S.: Hollywood Pictures, Via Rose Productions, Simpson-Bruckheimer Productions.

Slavin, R. E. (1987). Ability grouping and student achievement in elementary schools: A best-evidence synthesis. *Review of Educational Research, 57*, 347–370.

Slavin, R. (1993). *Student team learning: An overview and practical guide*. Washington, DC: National Education Association.

Smith, J. (2014, November 13). The 10 most prestigious jobs in America. *Business Insider*. Retrieved from http://www.businessinsider.com/most-prestigious-jobs-in-america-2014–11

Snyder, T. D., de Brey, C., & Dillow, S. A. (2016, December). *Digest of education statistics 2015* (NCES 2016–014). Washington, DC: National Center for Education Statistics, Institute of Education Sciences, U.S. Department of Education.

Snyder, T. D., de Brey, C., & Dillow, S. A. (2018). *Digest of education statistics 2016* (NCES 2017–094). Washington, DC: National Center for Education Statistics, Institute of Education Sciences, U.S. Department of Education.

Snyder v. Millersville University, 2008 WL 5093140 (E.D. Pa. 2008).

Spanierman v. Hughes, Druzolowski, & Hylwa, 576 F.Supp.2d 292 (D. Conn. 2008).

Spencer, H. (1860). What knowledge is of most worth? In H. Spencer (Ed.), *Education: Intellectual, moral, and physical* (pp. 21–96). New York, NY: Appleton. Retrieved from http://psycnet.apa.org/books/12158/001

Spring, J. (2001). *The American school: 1642–2004* (6th ed.). Boston, MA: McGraw-Hill.

Spring, J. (2011). *The American school: A global context from the Puritans to the Obama era* (8th ed.). New York, NY: McGraw Hill.

Spring, J. (2016). *Deculturalization and the struggle for equality: A brief history of the education of dominated cultures in the United States* (8th ed.). New York, NY: Routledge.

Spring, J. (2018). *The American school: From the Puritans to the Trump era* (10th ed.). New York, NY: Routledge.

Staessens, K. (1993). Identification and description of professional culture in innovating schools. *Qualitative Studies in Education*, 6(2), 111–128.

Stallings, J. A. (1990). *Effective use of time program*. Houston, TX: University of Houston.

State v. Scopes, Tenn. 105, 289 S.W. 363 (1927).

Steele, C. M. (2010). *Whistling Vivaldi and other clues to how stereotypes affect us*. New York, NY: Norton.

Stewart, A. (2015). *First class: The legacy of Dunbar, America's first black public high school*. Chicago, IL: Chicago Review Press.

Stoker, G., Liu, F., & Arellano, B. (2017, December). *Understanding the role of noncognitive skills and school environments in students' transitions to high school*. Washington, DC: Institute of Education Sciences, U.S. Department of Education & Regional Educational Laboratory at SEDL. Retrieved from https://ies.ed.gov/ncee/edlabs/projects/project.asp?projectID=4476

Strauss, V. (2014, June 10). Gates Foundation backs two-year delay in linking Common Core test scores to teacher evaluation, student promotion. *The Washington Post*. Retrieved from http://www.washingtonpost.com/blogs/answer-sheet/wp/2014/06/10/gates-foundation-backs-two-year-delay-in-linking-common-core-test-scores-to-teacher-evaluation-student-promotion/

Stuart v. School District No. 1 of Village of Kalamazoo, 30 Mich. 69 (1874).

Sullo, B. (2011, July 23). Choice theory. *Funderstanding*. Retrieved from https://www.funderstanding.com/educators/choice-theory/

Suzuki, B. H. (2002). Revisiting the model minority stereotype: Implications for student affairs practice and higher education. *New Directions for Student Services, 97,* 21–23.

Swann v. Charlotte-Mecklenburg Board of Education, 402 U.S. 1 (1971).

Sylwester, R. (2003). *A biological brain in a cultural classroom: Applying biological research to classroom management.* Thousand Oaks, CA: Corwin.

Taba, H. (1962). *Curriculum development: Theory and practice.* New York, NY: Harcourt Brace Jovanovich.

Taie, S., & Goldring, R. (2017). *Characteristics of public elementary and secondary school teachers in the United States: Results from the 2015–16 National Teacher and Principal Survey First Look* (NCES 2017–072). Retrieved from https://nces.ed.gov/pubsearch/pubsinfo.asp?pubid=2017072

Tatum, B. D. (2017). *Why are all the black kids sitting together in the cafeteria? And other conversations about race.* New York, NY: Basic Books.

Teaching for Change. (2016). *Between families and schools: Creating meaningful relationships.* Washington, DC: Author.

Templeton, B. (2008, October). *10 big myths about copyright explained.* Retrieved from https://www.templetons.com/brad/copymyths.html (Original work published 1994)

Teranishi, R. T. (2010). *Asians in the ivory tower: Dilemmas of racial inequality in American higher education.* New York, NY: Teachers College Press.

Thiers, N. (2017, September). Unlocking families' potential: A conversation with Karen L. Mapp. *Educational Leadership, 75*(1), 40–44.

Thomas, W. P., & Collier, V. P. (2001). *A national study of school effectiveness for language minority students' long-term academic achievement.* Santa Cruz, CA: Center for Research on Education, Diversity & Excellence.

Tinker v. Des Moines Independent Community School District, 393 U.S. 503 (1969).

Tomlinson, C. A. (2014). *The differentiated classroom: Responding to the needs of all learners* (2nd ed.). Alexandria, VA: ASCD.

Tomlinson, C. A. (2017). *How to differentiate instruction in academically diverse classrooms* (3rd ed.). Alexandria, VA: ASCD.

Tyler, R. W. (1949). *Basic principles of curriculum and instruction.* Chicago, IL: University of Chicago Press.

Tyson, K. (2013). Tracking, segregation, and the opportunity gap: What we know and why it matters. In P. L. Carter & K. G. Welner (Eds.), *Closing the opportunity gap: What America must do to give every child an even chance* (pp. 169–180). New York, NY: Oxford University Press.

Urban, W. J., & Wagoner, Jr., J. L. (2009). *American education: A history.* New York, NY: Routledge.

U.S. Census Bureau. (1880). Total population of school age, according to state laws, with the enrollment, attendance, teachers, income, expenditure, and school-fund for the public schools of the states and territories of the United States, for each school year, from 1871 to 1879, inclusive. *Statistical Abstract of the United States: 1880* (No. 149). Retrieved from https://www2.census.gov/library/publications/1881/compendia/1880statab.pdf

U.S. Census Bureau. (2001, October 3). Population by age, sex, race, and Hispanic or Latino origin for the United States: 2000 (Census 2000 PHC-T-9). *Census 2000 Summary File 1.* Retrieved from https://www.census.gov/population/www/cen2000/briefs/phc-t9/tables/tab01.pdf

U.S. Census Bureau. (2012). *Census of governments: Finance—survey of school system finances.* Washington, DC: Author.

U.S. Census Bureau. (2015, October 28). Detailed languages spoken at home and ability to speak English for the population 5 years and over for United States: 2009–2013. *American Community Survey.* Retrieved from https://www.census.gov/data/tables/2013/demo/2009-2013-lang-tables.html

U.S. Census Bureau. (2016a). Language spoken at home. *2012–2016 American Community Survey 5-year estimates.* Retrieved from https://factfinder.census.gov/faces/tableservices/jsf/pages/productview.xhtml?pid=ACS_16_5YR_S1601&prodType=table

U.S. Census Bureau. (2016b). Historical poverty tables: People and families—1959–2016. *Current population survey: Annual social and economic supplement.* Retrieved from https://www.census.gov/data/tables/time-series/demo/income-poverty/historical-poverty-people.html

U.S. Census Bureau. (2016c). Language spoken at home by ability to speak English for the population 5 years and over. *2012–2016 American Community Survey 5-year estimates.* Retrieved from https://factfinder.census.gov/faces/tableservices/jsf/pages/productview.xhtml?pid=ACS_16_5YR_B16001&prodType=table

U.S. Census Bureau. (2016d). Selected characteristics of the native and foreign-born populations. *2012–2016 American Community Survey 5-year estimates.* Retrieved from https://factfinder.census.gov/faces/tableservices/jsf/pages/productview.xhtml?pid=ACS_16_5YR_S0501&prodType=table

U.S. Census Bureau. (2016e, July 1). *Quick facts: United States.* Retrieved from https://www.census.gov/quickfacts/fact/table/US/PST045216

U.S. Census Bureau. (2017a). America's families and living arrangements: 2017 (C tables). *Current population survey, 2017 annual social and economic supplement.* Retrieved from https://census.gov/data/tables/2017/demo/families/cps-2017.html

U.S. Census Bureau, Population Division. (2017b, June). *Annual estimates of the resident population by sex, age, race alone or in combination, and Hispanic origin for the United States and states: April 1, 2010 to July 1, 2016.* Retrieved from https://factfinder.census.gov/faces/tableservices/jsf/pages/productview.xhtml?src=bkmk

U.S. Census Bureau. (2017c, October 5). *Facts for features: American Indian and Alaska Native heritage month: November 2015.* Last revised: October 5, 2017. Retrieved from https://www.census.gov/newsroom/facts-for-features/2015/cb15-ff22.html

U.S. Census Bureau. (2017d). Family households by type, age of own children, age of family members, and age of householder: 2017 (Table F1). *Current Population Survey: 2017 annual social and economic supplement.* Retrieved from https://www.census.gov/search-results.html?page=1&stateGeo=none&searchtype=web&cssp=SERP&q=Table+F1+Family+households%2C+by+Type%2C+Age+of+Own+Children&search.x=0&search.y=0

U.S. Census Bureau. (2017e). *QuickFacts.* Retrieved from https://www.census.gov/quickfacts/fact/table/US/PST045217

U.S. Census Bureau. (2017f). Table P-20. Educational attainment—workers 25 years old and over by median earnings and sex: 1991 to 2016. *Current Population Survey: Annual social and economic supplements.* Retrieved from https://www.census.gov/data/tables/time-series/demo/income-poverty/historical-income-people.html

U.S. Census Bureau. (2018a). *Asian-American and Pacific Islander heritage month: May 2018.* Retrieved from https://census.gov/content/dam/Census/newsroom/facts-for-features/2018/cb18-ff05-asian.pdf

U.S. Census Bureau. (2018b, March 13). *Older people projected to outnumber children for first time in U.S. history* (Press release number: CB18–41). Retrieved from https://www.census.gov/newsroom/press-releases/2018/cb18-41-population-projections.html

U.S. Department of Education. (2014, January). *Guiding principles: A resource guide for improving school climate and discipline.* Washington, DC: Author.

U.S. Department of Education. (2016, March 25). *$3.2 million grant competition to support teaching, studying of Native American languages funds to aid preservation, revitalization of native languages.* Retrieved from https://www.ed.gov/news/press-releases/32-million-grant-competition-support-teaching-studying-native-american-languages-funds-aid-preservation-revitalization-native-languages

U.S. Department of Education. (n.d.). Definitions. *Race to the Top district competition draft.* Washington, DC: Author. Retrieved from http://www.ed.gov/race-top/district-competition/definition

U.S. Department of Education, Institute of Education Sciences, National Center for Education Statistics, National Assessment of Educational Progress. (2014a). *2013 mathematics and reading: Grade 12 assessments.* Retrieved from http://www.nationsreportcard.gov/reading_math_g12_2013/#/

U.S. Department of Education, Institute of Education Sciences, National Center for Education Statistics, National Assessment of Educational Progress. (2014b). *The nation's report card.* Retrieved from http://nces.ed.gov/nationsreportcard/naepdata/

U.S. Department of Health and Human Services. (2015). *2015 poverty guidelines.* Retrieved from aspe.hhs.gov/poverty/15poverty.cfm

U.S. Department of Health and Human Services, Administration for Children and Families, Administration on Children, Youth and Families, Children's Bureau. (2017). *Child maltreatment 2015.* Retrieved from http://www.acf.hhs.gov/programs/cb/research-data-technology/statistics-research/child-maltreatment

U.S. Department of Health and Human Services, Centers for Disease Control and Prevention. (2016, June 10). *Youth risk behavior surveillance—United States, 2015.* Retrieved from https://www.cdc.gov/healthyyouth/data/yrbs/pdf/2015/ss6506_updated.pdf

U.S. Department of Homeland Security, Office of Immigration Statistics. (2017). *Yearbook of immigration statistics: 2016.* Retrieved from https://www.dhs.gov/sites/default/files/publications/2016%20Yearbook%20of%20Immigration%20Statistics.pdf

U.S. Department of Labor, Bureau of Labor Statistics. (2015). *Employment projections.* Retrieved from http://data.bls.gov/projections/occupationProj

U.S. Library of Congress. (n.d.). *Copyright and primary sources.* Retrieved from http://www.loc.gov/teachers/usingprimarysources/copyright.html

Vespa, J., Armstrong, D. M., & Medina, L. M. (2018, March). Demographic turning points for the United States: Population projections for 2020 to 2060. *Current Population Reports* (P25–1144). Washington, DC: U.S. Census Bureau. Retrieved from https://www.census.gov/content/dam/Census/library/publications/2018/demo/P25_1144.pdf

Vygotsky, L. (1978). *Mind in society: The development of higher psychological processes.* Cambridge, MA: Harvard University Press.

Waitoller, F. R., & Thorius, K. A. K. (2016, Fall). Cross-pollinating culturally sustaining pedagogy and universal design for learning: Toward an inclusive pedagogy that accounts for dis/ability. *Harvard Education Review, 86*(3), 366–389.

Wallace v. Jaffree, 472 U.S. 38 (1985).

Wattenberg, W. (1967). *All men are created equal.* Detroit, MI: Wayne State University Press.

Webb's depth of knowledge guide. (2009). Retrieved from http://www.aps.edu/sapr/documents/resources/Webbs_DOK_Guide.pdf

Weber, W. A. (1994). Classroom management. In J. M. Cooper (Ed.), *Classroom teaching skills* (5th ed., pp. 234–279). Lexington, KY: D. C. Heath.

Weir, K. (2016, March). Is homework a necessary evil? *Monitor on Psychology, 47*(3). Retrieved from http://www.apa.org/monitor/2016/03/homework.aspx

Wertheim, B. (2017, November 15). 4 simple ways to teach mindfulness in schools. *The Blog, HUFFPOST.* Retrieved from https://www.huffingtonpost.com/becca-wertheim/4-simple-ways-to-teach-mi_b_12916594.html

White House. (2011). *State of the Union address.* Retrieved from https://obamawhitehouse.archives.gov/the-press-office/2011/01/25/remarks-president-state-union-address

Wiggins, G., & McTighe, J. (2005). *Understanding by design: Expanded 2nd edition.* Alexandria, VA: Association for Supervision and Curriculum Development.

Wiles, J. W., & Bondi, J. C. (2015). *Curriculum development: A guide to practice* (9th ed.). Boston, MA: Pearson.

Windschitl, M. (1999). The challenges of sustaining a constructivist classroom culture. *Phi Delta Kappan, 80,* 751–755.

Wong, H. K., & Wong, R. T. (1998). *The first day of school: How to be an effective teacher.* Mountain View, CA: Harry K. Wong Publications.

Woodlock v. Orange Ulster B.O.C.S., 281 Fed. Appx. 66–2008 (2006/2008).

Woodward, C. V. (1971). *Origins of the New South, 1877–1913.* Baton Rouge: Louisiana State University Press.

Woolfolk, A. (2004). *Educational psychology* (9th ed.). Needham Heights, MA: Allyn & Bacon.

Wright, E. (1999). *Why I teach: Inspirational true stories from teachers who make a difference.* Rocklin, CA: Pima.

Zalaznick, M. (2017, October 18). K12 leaders see flexibility in alternative credentialing. *District Administration.* Retrieved from https://www.districtadministration.com/article/k12-leaders-see-flexibility-alternative-credentialing

Zelman v. Simmons-Harris, 536 U.S. 639 (2002).

Zirkel, P. A., & Clark, J. H. (2008). School negligence case law trends. *Southern Illinois University Law Journal, 32,* 345–363.

InTASC Standards Correlation Guide